Marketing Management:

A Planning Approach

Marketing Management:
A Planning Approach

G. David Hughes
University of North Carolina

Addison-Wesley Publishing Company
Reading, Massachusetts • Menlo Park, California
London • Amsterdam • Don Mills, Ontario • Sydney

This book is in the
Addison-Wesley series in Marketing
Consulting Editor: Yoram J. Wind

ISBN 0-201-03057-8
BCDEFGHIJK-DO-79

To my wife, Elizabeth B.,
and our children,
David Barrett and Scott Andrew

Foreword

Marketing Management: A Planning Approach is the first fully integrated planning-oriented marketing text because it provides an integrated framework for the application of marketing concepts, theories, and findings. Much of the integration is provided by planning worksheets that provide the student with a system for learning and applying marketing concepts to marketing cases.

Professor Hughes brings to the introductory marketing-management area the perspective of a marketing scholar, an innovative researcher, and a marketing consultant. This combination of the theoretical with the practical—the novel methodological development with the realities of management application—characterizes this cohesive and comprehensive marketing text.

It is with true pleasure that we introduce this new path-breaking book as the first text in the Addison-Wesley Marketing Series. We hope that teachers and students will find the book as exciting and valuable as we and the numerous faculty members who class-tested the book found it to be.

Yoram J. Wind

Preface

This text is designed for the MBA first course in marketing and the second course at the junior and senior level where there is a desire for an analytical approach, but not a heavily quantitative one. The focus is one of strategic planning. It is an action-oriented textbook that requires student participation because marketing management is a process for thinking through a problem, not a body of knowledge to be passively absorbed. Examples, problems, caselettes, and complete cases are designed to help the reader develop this process. After studying this text and experiencing the process of solving cases, the reader should have the confidence that he or she can develop a marketing plan or can evaluate those that have been developed by others.

What are the elements of the strategic-planning process? A careful analysis of many corporate planning documents, discussions with executives, and review of the literature on planning identified four elements—analysis, synthesis, creation, and communication. *Analysis* begins by asking critical questions and then moves to the gathering of key facts to answer these questions. Analysis also requires making appropriate assumptions and commissioning relevant research when the available facts are inadequate and assumptions are not acceptable. Analysis also includes the use of theories and models from the behavioral and managerial sciences to reach logical conclusions. *Synthesis* takes these conclusions and translates them into market opportunities and problems, the most important of which are then rank-ordered. This ranking serves as the basis for creating marketing goals and alternative strategies. Alternative strategies are the *creative* step in the planning process. These strategies must be *communicated* effectively to superiors for approval and to line personnel for implementation.

Very few individuals excel in all four of these areas. I have found that it is possible to grade case solutions for each of these elements and to give feedback to students that will help them correct deficiencies. It has been my experience that business students tend to be strong in analysis. Synthesis is a difficult concept to convey at first, but students do learn the process quickly. Creation of alternatives comes easily to students who have a varied background. Some students think that they will never be creative. It is unlikely that we can teach creativity in a marketing management course, but we can identify the individuals who have this talent and reinforce it. The communication skills of today's students are generally weak. The instructor is able to identify all of these weaknesses and can work with the student on specific needs. It is very rewarding to see how rapidly students improve when they understand the roots of their problems.

Two worksheets were developed to make it possible to teach the basics of marketing management in a strategic-planning framework. The Environmental Analysis Worksheet asks the critical analytical questions; organizes facts, assumptions, and the additional research needed; and facilitates the ranking of opportunities and problems. This process, known as the *situation analysis,* requires the ability to analyze information and synthesize the resulting conclusions into a list of problems and opportunities.

The Strategy Worksheet requires the ranking of opportunities and problems and the development of profitable strategies. Identifying alternative strategies requires creativity, and the marketing plan requires the ability to communicate. Thus these two worksheets provide the means by which the instructor may identify the student's weaknesses in the four important areas of analysis, synthesis, creation, and communication. Furthermore, the student may diagnose his or her weaknesses before submitting a case solution.

These worksheets provide structure, but they are not rigid. They are an open system, so that they may be adapted to different approaches or a variety of case situations. They have been applied to many cases from the Intercollegiate Case Clearing House. Suggested cases may be found in the Instructor's Manual. The worksheets have been used for consulting assignments and in corporate training programs. In fact, they were originally developed for a corporate training program where the task was to develop a working knowledge of marketing management in a short time. The worksheets are not a checklist, but a means for handling details without losing sight of the broad process for strategic marketing planning. Classroom testing has revealed that the student learns the material at twice the speed when the worksheet approach is used.

The content of the text is traditional. Concepts such as market segmentation, the product life cycle, and the marketing mix are discussed and illustrated. The most radical change is in the organization of the chapters. The discussion of marketing research appears early in the text (Chapter 3) rather than at the end. This positioning reflects the real world of marketing management. The manager must have information to answer the critical questions that are raised at the beginning of the planning process. Marketing research generates this information. The marketing manager is not expected to be a marketing researcher, but must be able to communicate with researchers and know the applications and limitations of research methods.

Another break with tradition is the placement of the chapters on organization early in the text (Chapters 4 and 5). Whether this placement is appropriate depends on one's view of marketing management. If the view is that of a brand manager, then discussions of organizational missions, goals, and design may not be relevant, so they may be treated at the end of the text. If the viewpoint is that of the chief marketing executive, then the missions, objectives, and goals of the organization must be understood before a strategy can be developed. An understanding of organizational designs is important because the implementation of the marketing plan requires people. Organizing the marketing effort can be the difference between a successful and unsuccessful implementation of a plan.

The text is divided into five parts. Part I introduces the reader to the processes of marketing management and planning. This section stresses the need to ask the critical questions and to find information to answer these questions. The worksheet approach is introduced and illustrated with a complete case.

Part II examines the missions, objectives, goals, and designs of marketing organizations. The need to identify success factors is stressed and illustrated.

Part III examines the position of the company or brand in its environment (situation analysis). The situation analysis includes an understanding of the generic demand for the product, the brand's market position, competition, and public policy. A chapter on industrial marketing analysis illustrates how the concepts from consumer marketing are adapted to industrial market analysis, as well as those techniques which are unique to industrial marketing.

The development of a marketing strategy, a creative process requiring examples, is discussed in Part IV. Many case examples are presented of successful and unsuccessful strategies. The chapters in this part are traditional to the extent that they cover the marketing mix—product, price, channels, advertising, and personal selling. Part IV breaks with tradition in Chapter 17, however, by presenting marketing strategy from the viewpoint of the retailer. This chapter is included for two reasons. First, it helps the marketing manager within the firm to understand the retailing viewpoint as he or she develops a channel strategy. Second, the chapter illustrates career opportunities for business students in retailing. The chapter on advertising presents career opportunities in advertising. A chapter on international marketing strategy is also included in Part IV. Another break with tradition is the placement of the chapter on evaluation and control in the section on marketing strategy. The reasoning is straightforward: Evaluation and control are part of the strategic process because measurable goals must be established for each element of the marketing mix.

Cases are used in the text as examples, with some cases appearing several times throughout the book. (The relevance of specific cases to the text material is shown in Table 1.) Small cases, or caselettes, appear at the ends of chapters to emphasize specific points. Part V contains five contemporary cases in marketing planning. The first is concerned with the purchase of an extensive information system for sales management. The second is a venture into a methane generator to help conserve scarce energy resources. The third case illustrates how the process of marketing planning may be applied to a nonprofit health-care organization. The fourth case requires a decision on the selection of a channel of distribution during a period of shortages and inflation. The final case requires the development of a marketing plan that will coordinate the marketing effort of newly acquired companies. These cases may be used to supplement the cases that the instructor presently uses. Professors who classroom tested the worksheet approach continued to use many of their usual cases.

Because they require a complete marketing plan, the last four cases in Part V may be used throughout the book. They have been designed to meet the students' objections of not covering a case in depth or "not finishing a case." Using short cases does not solve this problem because they lack data for an adequate analysis.

TABLE 1. Relevance of cases to text material

Chapters	Caselettes								Cases				
	RJR and Celanese outlines (2)	A shopping center (6)	An apartment complex (6)	Positioning soft drinks (7)	International Minerals and Chemicals (8)	Scoop Ice Cream, 1972 (9)	The Mutual Insurance Co. (16)	Dean & Wilson, Inc. (16)	Burroughs Wellcome Co. (20)	Methane generator (21)	Wake Health Services, Inc. (22)	April Showers (23)	S&L (24)
Introduction													
1. Introduction to Marketing Management													
2. The Planning Process	1				1	1			2	2	1	1	1
3. Marketing Information for Management Decisions	2		2	1	2	1	1		1	2	1	2	2
Organizing the Marketing Effort													
4. The Corporate Environment for Marketing Planning	2				2				2		1	1	1
5. Organizational Strategies of Marketing									2		2	2	1
Situation Analysis													
6. Analyzing Consumers' Generic Needs and Behavior	1	1	1						1		1	1	1
7. Analyzing the Brand's Market Position	2	2	1		1				1		1	1	1
8. Industrial Market Analysis					1				1				
9. Analyzing Competition	2	2	1		1				1		1	1	1
10. Analyzing the Public Policy Environment									1	2	2		
Marketing Strategies													
11. Creating Marketing Mix-Strategies	2		1		1				2	1	1	1	
12. Product Strategies	2	2	1		1				2	1	2	2	
13. Pricing Strategies	2	2			1				2		1	2	
14. Channel and Logistics Strategies					1				2		1	2	
15. Advertising and Promotional Strategies	2		1		1				2	1	2	2	
16. Sales Management Strategies						1	1	1	1			2	2
17. Marketing Strategies of an Intermediary—Retailers							2					1	1
18. International Marketing Strategies											2		
19. Evaluation and Control						2			1	2	2	1	2

1 = Primary subject matter of the case.
2 = Secondary subject matter of the case.
The chapter in which the case appears is noted
in parentheses.

By using one case several times throughout the book, the student does not have to continue to make a large investment in "learning the cast of characters."

Developing a new approach to the teaching of marketing management requires considerable assistance from individuals, most of whom are acknowledged in the following section. I must also acknowledge the input from students who recommended changes and enthusiastically supported the worksheet approach. I look forward to additional input from students, professors, and practicing marketers on ways that this approach may be improved.

Chapel Hill, North Carolina
March 1978

G.D.H.

Acknowledgments

Writing a textbook on marketing management requires input from academic and industry sources. I have been fortunate in having a high level of such input and would like to acknowledge the support that made this book possible.

Reviews of the complete manuscript and detailed comments were provided by the following academic reviewers: Professor Richard N. Cardozo, College of Business Administration, University of Minnesota; Associate Professor John F. Monoky, Jr., College of Business Administration, University of Toledo; Professor John G. Myers, School of Business Administration, University of California, Berkeley; Assistant Professor Robert A. Westbrook, School of Business Administration, Duke University; Professor Jerry Wind, Wharton School, University of Pennsylvania; and several anonymous reviewers.

Selected chapter reviews were provided by the following: Professor Jack N. Behrman, School of Business Administration, University of North Carolina, former Assistant Secretary of Commerce for Foreign Affairs, for reading and making many suggestions for Chapter 18; Professor William S. Stewart, Professor of Business Law, School of Business Administration, and Professor Paul Verkuil, Professor of Law, both of the University of North Carolina, for reviewing portions of Chapter 10; Professor Arch G. Woodside, Jr., College of Business Administration, University of South Carolina, for reading and providing comments on Chapter 14.

Detailed comments of the manuscript from the students' viewpoint were provided by Neil M. Wagner, MBA student; and Metin Gurol and E. Cameron Williams, Ph.D. students, School of Business Administration, University of North Carolina.

Many revisions in the worksheet approach were the result of classroom testing by: Assistant Professor Phillip E. Downs, School of Business Administration, College of William and Mary; Professor C. William Emory, Graduate School of Business Administration, Washington University; Professors James E. Littlefield and Rollie Tillman, School of Business Administration, University of North Carolina; and Assistant Professor Robert A. Westbrook, Graduate School of Business Administration, Duke University.

Marketing practitioners provided reviews of selected chapters. I am indebted to the following: Richard H. Behrman, Director of Marketing Research, Liggett & Meyers Incorporated, for reading Chapter 3 and suggesting changes; Richard A.

Druckman, Director of Product Planning & Research, E. R. Squibb & Sons, Inc., for reading Chapter 3; Peter S. Howsam, Vice President, Marketing, Burroughs Wellcome Company, for material and critical reviews of Chapters 1, 4 and 5; Dr. Kenneth A. Longman, President, Benson & Benson, Inc., former Vice President, J. Walter Thompson, for reading and commenting on Chapter 15; Ian MacFarlane, President, MacFarlane & Co., Inc., and Past Vice President, Industrial Division, American Marketing Association, for reading and commenting on Chapter 8; Stanley Nitzberg, Loan Representative, Retailing Division, First National Bank of Chicago, for research assistance and a critical review of Chapter 17; and Charles H. Singler, General Sales Manager, Burroughs Wellcome Company, for reading, supplying material, and making many suggestions for Chapter 16 and for permitting the writing of Chapter 20.

Extensive effort was made to provide examples from the real-world of marketing. I am indebted to the following marketing executives for these examples: Herbert Ahlgren, Vice President, Association of National Advertisers, Inc., for permission to abstract parts of the Scoop Ice Cream case; F. Lehman Beardsley, Vice President, Public Affairs, Miles Laboratories, Inc., for the current job description of the product manager in the Consumer Products Division of Miles Laboratories; P. W. Beck, Director of Planning, Shell International Chemical Company, for permission to use its directional policy matrix; William L. Etter, Manager, Quantitative Analysis, Consumer Research Services, General Mills, Inc., for permission to reproduce an example of General Mills' concept screening program; Teresa Gannon, Sales Service Executive, Axiom Market Research Bureau, Inc., for permission to use Target Group Index (TGI) data; Malcolm D. Gray, Director of Marketing Services, Scott Paper Co., for permission to reproduce a diagram of the sphere of activities of a product manager; Walter M. Haimann, Executive Vice President, Joseph E. Seagram & Sons, Inc., for permission to reproduce an advertisement; James F. Hind, Vice President, Planning, R. J. Reynolds Tobacco Co., for permission to publish the RJR outline for a brand marketing plan; Robert J. Lavidge, President, Elrich & Lavidge Inc., for materials describing his laboratory technique for testing advertisements; Robert D. Martin, Financial Analyst, Hanes Corporation, formerly a mortgage banker, for developing the caselettes on the demand analysis for real estate investments; W. A. McMinn, Vice-President, Industrial Chemical Group, FMC Corporation, for permission to reproduce its marketing organizational chart; Joseph L. Narr, Director, Public Information, The Conference Board, for permission to reproduce materials which appeared in its publications; P. Skuy, President, Ortho Pharmaceutical (Canada) Ltd., for permission to publish findings of Ortho's research on the similarities among the functions of general managers and product managers; Bill Tower, President, Maxwell House Division, and John Whiteman, Manager, Public Communications, General Foods Corporation, for the marketing organizational chart of the Maxwell House Division; Ira B. Wheeler, Vice President, Marketing, Celanese Corp., for permission to reproduce the Celanese general outline for developing a marketing plan; H. R. Young, Marketing Manager, Worthington Pump Corp. USA, for permission to reproduce a diagram of Worthington's marketing process; and Richard F. Zenko, Sales Promotion Manager, Canada Dry Corporation, for permission to reproduce an illustration of premiums for Canada

Dry Ginger Ale. I am also indebted to the companies that provided their marketing planning outlines for analysis, but asked to remain anonymous.

Publishers were kind in their permissions to reproduce material, as will be noted throughout the text. A special note of thanks is due the American Marketing Associaton and the *Harvard Business Review* for extensive permissions.

Keith O. Nave, Editor, and the staff of Addison-Wesley exercised great tolerance and patience during this undertaking.

Miss Linda Wilson handled the typing of the manuscript and related details with great calm and care.

My wife, Elizabeth, provided understanding throughout the task and edited the entire manuscript.

I am indebted to all of these contributors, but accept the responsibilities for errors. With so much qualified assistance, it has not been easy to introduce errors, but I have managed. I would like to hear from those careful readers who have discovered them.

Contents

PART II   ORGANIZING THE MARKETING EFFORT

PART III SITUATION ANALYSIS

PART V STRATEGIC DECISION CASES

Marketing Management:

A Planning Approach

Part I. Introduction to Marketing Management

An understanding of marketing management requires an understanding of the role of marketing in society, the economy, and the firm. Chapter 1 provides an overview of these complex roles. It also examines in some detail the skills that are required of a marketing manager. The primary task in marketing management is planning.

The marketing-planning function requires skills in analysis, synthesis, creation, and communication. Analysis of existing facts, assumptions, and research data is required to reach logical conclusions about the product's environment. These conclusions must be synthesized into statements of opportunities and problems. Strategies must be created to tap opportunities and solve problems. These strategies must be communicated to top management for approval and to those individuals who will be responsible for implementing the plan. The Environmental Analysis Worksheet and the Strategy Worksheet help the planner to perform all of these tasks without becoming lost in details. Chapter 2 explains how these worksheets are used.

The experienced marketing planner knows what critical questions to ask and where to find information to answer them. Chapters 2 and 3 give examples of critical questions that must be asked at each stage in the planning process. Chapter 3 illustrates how the information is gathered to answer these questions. This chapter includes a discussion of frequently used marketing-research techniques.

CHAPTER 1

An Overview of Marketing and Marketing Management

LEARNING OBJECTIVES   After studying this chapter you should:

1. Understand why it is important for administrators to understand the activities of a marketing manager.
2. Understand the role of marketing in society.
3. Understand the position of marketing in different business philosophies.
4. Know in broad terms the functions of a marketing manager.
5. Identify the personal skills required of a marketing manager.
6. Understand the planning process in broad terms.
7. Be able to define and use the following concepts:

Marketing	Market-oriented firm
Marketing activities	Integrated firm
Marketing concept	Basic functions of a firm
Production-oriented firm	Planning
Technology-oriented firm	Social marketing

THOUGHT STARTERS

1. What are critical questions? What are some critical questions that must be answered in the planning process?
2. Can marketing be eliminated in a planned economy?
3. Does marketing cost too much?
4. Where does one "plug in" to the planning process?

WHY STUDY MARKETING MANAGEMENT?   The need for an understanding of marketing management varies. Someone who is considering a career in marketing needs to have a knowledge of the tools and a hands-on experience in marketing management. The individual who plans a career in business, but not in marketing, needs to understand the role of marketing management among the other functions in a business organization. The individual with broad interests just wants to know what the marketing manager does in a complex, modern economy. This text meets these three needs by conveying the complexity and excitement of marketing as seen through the activities of marketing management. Meeting these three needs without bogging down in details requires a structure. That structure is provided by two planning worksheets—the Environmental Analysis Worksheet and the Strategy Worksheet. These worksheets permit one to handle the details of a marketing problem without losing sight of the overall marketing process.

There are no spectators in marketing. As buyers of goods and services, we are all familiar with marketing in supermarkets, gas stations, restaurants, television commercials, personal selling, and newspaper and magazine advertisements. But this familiarity blinds us to the complexity of the marketing activities in an affluent, mass-production economy. The roles played by marketing managers are complex also. The purpose of this book is to illustrate the roles played by marketing executives and to teach the process of marketing management.

WHAT IS MARKETING? Marketing may be defined briefly as those *activities* that relate an *organization successfully* to its *environment*.[1] The main *activities* are the identification of unmet needs, the development of products and services to meet these needs, pricing, the distribution of goods to the marketplace, and the communication of the ability of the products and services to meet these needs.

Organizations that use marketing are not limited to commercial firms. Marketing techniques are also used by governments, fund-raising organizations, health-care institutions, political groups, and philanthropic organizations.[2] Commercial organizations include manufacturers, wholesalers, retailers, advertising agencies, and the advertising media such as television, newspapers, magazines, and direct mail.

"Successful" will be defined differently by different organizations. Politicians using marketing methods measure success in terms of the number of votes. Fund raisers relate success to the amount of funds raised per dollar of expense. Health-care organizations use measures of persons served, reductions in rates of mortality, or days lost from work. Commercial organizations measure success in terms of return on investment, profits, sales, and market share. A firm may use several measures, varying them at different points in a product's life cycle. Early in the life of a product the goal may be to gain market share. After the product has reached the growth stage, the criterion for success may be profit. The criterion for success over the entire product life cycle may be return on investment.

Ultimate control of the marketing activities is provided by the billions of decisions that are made by buyers. When we stop to think about our daily decisions, we see that we exercise influence over hundreds of companies through our decisions of what to buy and not to buy. For example, if we chose to eat breakfast, did we have eggs, toast, jelly, cereal, milk, coffee, a breakfast bun, cold cereal, hot creal, or did we choose to skip breakfast entirely? To what extent did we use electricity through lighting, heating, air conditioning, and using the radio and television? Did we get a haircut, go to the cleaners, or visit the laundry? How many magazines, newspapers, radio stations, TV stations, direct-mail advertising, and other media influenced us today? If we used our automobile today, we influenced not only the auto industry, but also the entire automobile transportation industry, which includes highways, gasoline, tires, equipment used to build and maintain highways, cement manufacturers and manufacturers of related equipment, and unions in the auto industry. Many of these decisions must be made every day; others are made automatically once we choose a certain life-style. The fact remains that whether these decisions are made overtly daily or less frequently, the sum total of all the decisions is what guides marketing activities.

MARKETING'S ROLES IN SOCIETY   Marketing plays many important roles in a complex, affluent economy. It provides feedback loops to guide production. It provides mass-marketing techniques to permit the utilization of mass-production techniques. These two roles enable marketing to reconcile the dynamics of supply and demand. By promoting new products and new styles broadly through the mass media, marketing stimulates social change and raises standards of living. All of these roles must be measured against the cost of marketing. Does marketing cost too much? These points require expansion.

Guides Production   The influence of marketing systems on an economy or in a firm depends on the relationship between supply and demand. Production systems dominate during periods of shortages, whereas marketing systems dominate when there is a surplus. Figure 1.1 illustrates this point by contrasting the sequence of events for firms which are oriented toward production, technology, or marketing with the sequence of events for an integrated firm.

Production is the starting event for a production-oriented firm. A concern for the market acceptability occurs after the product is produced. A firm must be technologically oriented when research and development make new products obsolete in a few years. As noted in Fig. 1.1, the events in such a firm begin with the output of product research and development. In contrast, a market-oriented firm starts its sequence of events with market research, which feeds into research and development, which in turn will guide production.

Focusing on the market led to the development of the *marketing concept* as an organizational philosophy for many companies. This concept states that all major product and promotional decisions should begin with an understanding of the needs of the consumers. Business activities are organized into profit centers so that all activities

Fig. 1.1   Four possible business philosophies for the firm.

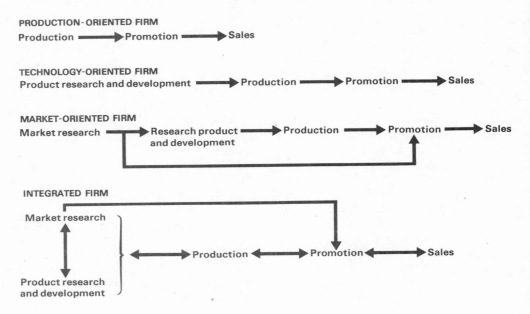

are focused toward the marketplace and so that the impact of the market on profit can be measured directly.

The ideal approach would be an integrated one, in which the sequence of events of a firm begins with market research and product research *working together* on the need for the product and the feasibility and capacity for producing it. The integrated approach illustrated in Fig. 1.1 is superior to the other approaches and represents the direction that many advanced marketing firms are taking. The production-oriented firm suffers from producing products that are not really needed by the market, thereby increasing the cost of promotion and selling. When the technological orientation is carried to extremes, the products can be an engineer's dream and a marketer's nightmare. An overriding market orientation creates problems in the opposite direction. This could easily result in the proliferation of products, none of which is profitable. By contrast, the integrated system is an open system in that there is two-way communication among all its elements (illustrated in Fig. 1.1 by two-headed arrows).

Marketing systems can help to stimulate productivity. A classic example occurred during the early part of the twentieth century when coal mine operators introduced mechanical equipment in the mine to make the miners more productive. To the operator's surprise, production did not increase; instead, the miners reduced the number of hours worked to the level required to maintain their previous standard of living. The operators countered by stocking the company store with new products, such as refrigerators, which were desired by the miners' wives. New life-styles provided the motivation. The mining families raised their standards of living, and productivity in the mines increased.

More complex examples have been noted in developing countries after the introduction of new fertilizers, seeds, and farming techniques. In India, for example, new methods greatly increased agricultural production, but there was no marketing system through which the farmer benefited from increased production and improved quality. Instead, all rice was treated as one grade, and one price was paid to all farmers, regardless of the quality of their crops. Furthermore, storage and transportation systems were inadequate, so that the surpluses were not distributed to neighboring provinces. Lacking any positive stimulation from the marketing system, the farmers soon reduced the quantity and quality of their output.

The mission of marketing in the firm and in the economy varies according to the relationship between supply and demand. When demand exceeds supply, the marketing systems emphasize the logistics of bridging the gaps in time and space between the producer and the consumer. At the other extreme, an economy with the capacity to supply more than is demanded requires marketing systems that attempt to understand consumers' needs and modify their demand patterns. These systems emphasize market research and promotion. This type of economic situation leads to the *marketing concept*, which emphasizes identification of consumer needs *before* production of the product.

An affluent economy that moves into a period of scarcity lies between these two extremes and would probably take features from the marketing systems of both. Marketing during scarcity should attempt to both identify consumers' needs before products are made *and* develop efficient systems of logistics and information exchange. Marketing methods may be used to *reduce* the demand for scarce resources, a process that has been called demarketing.[3]

Mass Production Requires Mass Marketing Advertising, shopping centers, discount houses, and consumerism are extensions of the Industrial Revolution. Technology increased productivity and reduced the cost of production, but it also increased the void between the producer and the buyer. Before the Industrial Revolution, the silversmith, the cobbler, and the baker all communicated directly with their buyers. Mass production has separated these producers in time and space, creating the need for institutions to perform this communication process. Modern, affluent societies have become dependent on mass-communication systems for information leading to individual and social choices.

Reconciles the Dynamics of Supply and Demand   The reconciliation of supply and demand is made difficult by the forces that make supply and demand very dynamic in an affluent economy. On the supply side, competition is made dynamic by the creation of new products through research and development and by excess industry capacities that occur when a firm expands its capacity without considering the plans of other firms. Demand is made dynamic by a hierarchy of needs, diminishing marginal satisfaction, and a desire for freedom of choice. Maslow observed that an individual has a hierarchy of needs, beginning with physiological ones that support life and moving through the needs for safety, belonging and love, esteem, and self-actualization.[4] Maslow noted that as one of these needs is filled, the next one emerges, so that a fully developed individual has a complex pattern of needs.

Diminishing marginal satisfaction means that a consumer gets fewer increments of satisfaction from consuming more of the same product. This means that the consumer prefers an assortment of goods rather than greater quantities of a single good. Consumers' freedom to choose the quality and quantity of goods introduces great uncertainty in the demand for goods and services. Marketing could be made more efficient by removing this freedom of choice, but such efficiency violates our concept of democracy.

Stimulates Social Change   The mass media, mass distribution, and credit make innovations available to everyone. No longer is it necessary for the diffusion of an innovation to begin with the upper social class. Television, newspapers, and magazines communicate new products and new fashions to everyone simultaneously. Shopping centers, discount houses, and credit systems bring the new products and services within the physical and fiscal reach of most of the members of society.

Marketing communication, especially television commercials and the programs they support, can create social change by giving segments of society new personal goals. "Revolutions are brought about not because people are poor but because they discover that they can alleviate their poverty."[5] The high-speed, visual communication of television no doubt makes the disadvantaged segments of the population aware of the fact that they *can* alleviate tleir poverty.

Does Marketing Cost Too Much?   The answer to this question depends on one's evaluation of the alternatives. It may be possible to reduce the cost of marketing by reducing the variety of products and the freedom of choice. Critics of advertising are rarely critical of personal selling, but it is certainly a more expensive method of communicating information about some products. Thus in an affluent economy, we may be critical of advertising, but we cannot eliminate it until a better means of communication is developed.[6]

There is an old saying: "You can eliminate a middleman, but you cannot eliminate his functions." People who form neighborhood food-buying cooperatives to eliminate middlemen's expenses and profits still must perform the functions of buying, financing, breaking bulk, and storing, as well as managing the entire operation—just as they must be performed by middlemen such as supermarkets.

The Russians learned a similar lesson during the 1930s, when they eliminated the wholesale link between producers and retailers.[7] Retailers did not know which producers could supply their needs. The functions formerly performed by the warehouse were shifted to the transportation services. The breaking of bulk lot into smaller orders for retailers and the temporary storage of inventories were shifted to railroad warehouses. Bookkeeping costs and transportation costs increased and the quality of service declined. Thus the middleman was eliminated, but not his functions.

Does marketing cost too much? The answer depends on the value that a person places on his or her freedom of choice, time, and the alternatives available for performing the marketing activities.

THE MARKETING MANAGER   The title of the marketing executive in a company will vary among industries, companies, and levels within a company, but the functions these individuals perform are identical. Lower-level executives in the grocery-products industry (soaps, soups, cereal, etc.) are known as *product or brand managers*. Their counterparts in an advertising agency are the *account executives*. In a department store the basic marketing-executive title is that of a *buyer*. At the next higher level, the marketing executive in these three industries is known as a group product manager, an account supervisor, and a merchandise manager, respectively. The generic term *marketing manager* will be used in this text.

Regardless of titles, marketing executives have the common task of identifying marketing opportunities and problems in the marketplace and developing marketing strategies to exploit the opportunities and solve the problems. The strategic tools of the marketing manager are the product, its price, its channels of distribution, and its promotion (advertising and personal selling). These four tools are known as the marketing mix. The marketing manager combines them into strategies that will produce profitable sales.

The successful marketing manager, therefore, must have superior skills in analyzing opportunities and problems and in developing strategies. The goal of this book is to help you develop these skills.

The Marketing-Management Process   The activities of a marketing manager can be described as a process that begins with an analysis of the market, continues to the development of strategies, and ends with a profit plan. This whole process is known as marketing planning. A flow chart of the marketing-planning process appears in Fig. 1.2.

The identification of market opportunities and problems begins with an analysis of the social, economic, political, and technical environments in which the firm operates. Then an analysis of the generic demand for the product category (e.g., soup, automobiles, or steam turbines) will lead to the selection of target market segments. Analyses of brand demand and competition lead to decisions of where to position the brand in the marketplace. Public-policy considerations must be analyzed to determine the social and legal dimensions of marketing opportunities and problems. The outcome of this analysis is a rank-ordering of the opportunities and problems within the environment in which the firm operates. The Environmental Analysis Worksheet helps the marketing manager through this process.

The development of a marketing strategy begins with a linkage between the opportunities, problems, and the marketing goals of the firm. The variables in the

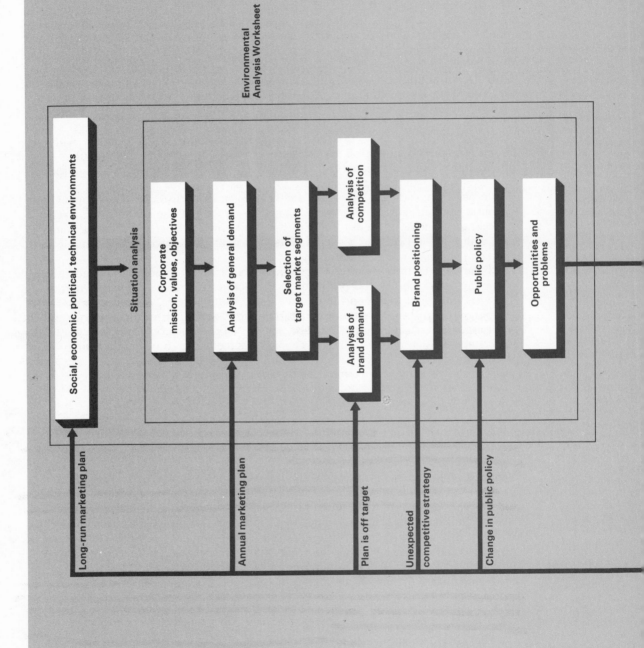

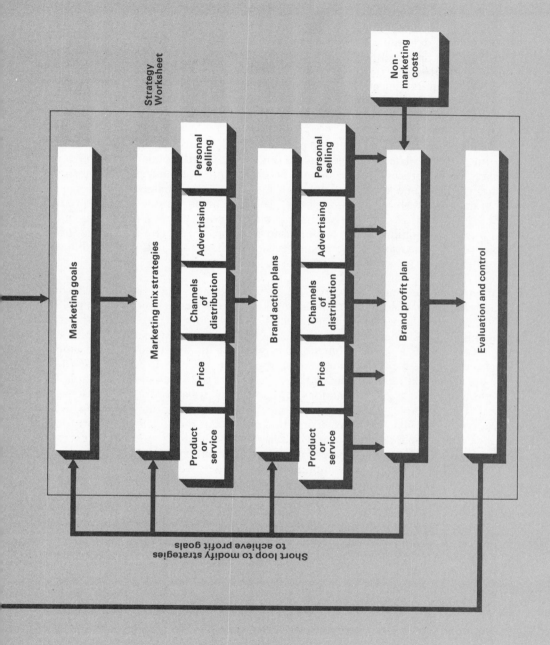

Fig. 1.2   Marketing–planning process.

marketing mix are the tools for developing a strategy that will enable the firm to achieve its goals. These strategies must be translated into tactics (which are also known as brand action plans). The cost of the action plan is carried into the profit plan. Non-marketing costs, such as the cost of the product and administrative costs, enter into the profit plan to determine the profit (or contribution) of the brand profit plan. If the plan does not produce the target profit, it will be necessary to cycle through the strategy process (the short loop in Fig. 1.2), altering the tactics, the strategies, and perhaps even the marketing goals until an acceptable profit plan emerges. The Strategy Worksheet helps the marketing executive to develop a profitable strategy. (The Environmental Analysis and Strategy Worksheets will be illustrated in the following chapter.)

Where does the marketing-planning process begin? It depends on who is planning and the time horizon. The most senior marketing executive will be concerned with long-range plans, so the process will begin with an examination of the trends in the social, economic, political, and technical environments. The brand manager will begin an annual brand plan with an analysis of the generic demand for the brand's product category. An unexpected competitive strategy may require a revision of the plan at the point of brand positioning; a new law or court decision will require a reevaluation of the public-policy dimensions of the plan. Revision of the plan would begin at different points in the process, as shown in Fig. 1.2.

The Functions of Marketing Management A survey of 360 marketing executives revealed some important changes in the functions of the marketing manager between the years 1971 and 1976.[8] By 1976 the marketing manager had become more involved in new-product planning, pricing, customer service, and packaging. Corporate strategic planning had become recognized as a separate function and was "for the first time included among the functions responsible to the chief marketing executive."[9]

The functions that report to the marketing executive are summarized in Table 1.1. Note that the percentage of the functions so reporting varies according to industry size and type. For example, marketing planning is the most important function in all classifications except financial firms. Corporate planning is most likely to report to the marketing executive in industrial firms with sales under $200 million (60.2 percent) and least likely to do so in utilities (14.3 percent). (This information will be useful to anyone who is planning a career in marketing and wants to be involved in planning at the corporate level. The small industrial firm would be a better choice than a utility.)

Reading down the column of functions reporting to the chief marketing executive reveals the diversity of functions for which a marketing executive is responsible. This diversity creates the excitement and challenge that attract people to careers in marketing management.

During the past five years, firms have become more oriented toward the market, which has made the role of the chief marketing executive more responsive to external influences. Increased government regulation, vocal consumer groups, dramatic shifts in consumer buying habits, shortages of raw materials and capital, and rising marketing costs have made the job of the chief marketing executive especially challenging during the first half of the 1970s.

The chief marketing executive has become a strong staff member requiring financial, legal, economic and social forecasting skills, in addition to the expertise in traditional marketing functions. The increased competitive risk in erroneous

TABLE 1.1   The functions reporting to the chief marketing executive

Functions reporting to chief marketing executive	All companies	All industrials	Industrials by sales		
			Under $200MM	$200MM–$499MM	$500MM or more
Marketing planning	87.0%	85.2%	88.2%	86.8%	79.7%
Market research	79.0	78.3	83.9	77.9	71.0
General marketing	75.1	71.7	73.1	77.9	63.8
Sales promotion	72.2	66.5	65.6	75.0	59.4
Product advertising	63.2	63.5	61.3	73.5	56.5
Corporate advertising	60.9	61.3	66.7	61.8	53.6
New product planning	57.2	58.3	65.6	58.8	47.8
Sales training	55.0	52.2	57.0	55.9	42.0
Product publicity	51.0	51.7	50.5	57.4	47.8
Pricing	51.3	56.5	65.5	50.0	50.7
Sales research	50.7	47.8	57.0	38.2	44.9
Field sales management	47.0	47.8	53.8	48.5	39.1
Merchandising	45.3	43.5	47.3	44.1	37.7
Customer service	43.3	44.3	46.2	47.1	39.1
Corporate planning	38.2	45.7	60.2	41.2	30.4
Public relations	37.4	38.7	48.4	39.7	24.6
Dealer relations	29.2	32.6	38.7	29.4	27.5
Packaging	26.9	28.3	33.3	25.0	24.6
Product service	26.6	30.9	37.6	29.4	23.2
Inventory control	15.6	20.0	17.2	20.6	23.2

	Nonindustrials by category				
	Banking	Financial	Insurance	Transportation	Utility
Marketing planning	93.5%	68.8%	87.5%	95.5%	100.0%
Market research	90.3	81.3	75.0	81.8	85.7
General marketing	83.9	56.3	87.5	86.4	85.7
Sales promotion	93.5	75.0	91.7	86.4	66.7
Product advertising	87.1	62.5	58.3	72.7	23.8
Corporate advertising	90.3	68.8	41.7	68.2	14.3
New product planning	77.4	50.0	87.5	50.0	4.8
Sales training	41.9	50.0	91.7	63.6	66.7
Product publicity	61.3	56.3	70.8	45.5	14.3
Pricing	45.2	31.3	20.8	77.3	28.6
Sales research	51.6	31.3	75.0	72.7	57.1
Field sales management	3.2	37.5	91.7	59.1	47.6
Merchandising	51.6	31.3	58.3	63.6	33.3
Customer service	38.7	18.8	29.2	63.6	66.7
Corporate planning	19.4	18.8	29.2	36.4	14.3
Public relations	51.6	43.8	41.7	22.7	14.3
Dealer relations	—	12.5	33.3	50.0	28.6
Packaging	45.2	18.8	16.7	18.2	—
Product service	22.6	6.3	20.8	27.3	14.3
Inventory control	3.2	—	—	18.2	9.5

Results do not add to 100 percent due to multiple responses.

Heidrick and Struggles, Inc., "Profile of a Chief Marketing Executive," 1976. This survey included 360 executives in leading United States companies. Used with permission.

judgments of markets, the advent and acceptance of sophisticated and practical computer modeling techniques, and the accelerating rate of change in our society have made the chief marketing executive's role more scientific than intuitive, more strategic than tactical.[10]

The marketing executive of the future will continue to need skills and techniques for the identification of consumer needs and the filling of these needs. The marketing executive of the late 1970s must be a true Renaissance person who will draw on the diversity of his or her educational background to meet the corporate objectives while balancing the requirements of stockholders, government agencies, consumers, and society. "Market segmentation will become a more common means to profitability in a no-growth or slow-growth environment."[11] Rising marketing costs will require improved marketing productivity, which will require the marketing executive to develop skills in motivating and training his or her staff. Shorter product life cycles will demand more sophisticated environmental forecasting and greater flexibility.

The demands on the chief marketing executive are high, but so are the rewards. The average 1976 salary and bonus of the chief marketing executive in industrial firms was $84,000. The lowest salary and bonus for a chief marketing executive was in banking, $49,300. Additional perquisites included stock options, an automobile, a town club membership, and a country club membership.[12]

The Education and Experience of the Marketing Manager The undergraduate education of the chief marketing executive tends to vary across industry types. The survey of chief marketing executives found that when all companies were considered, 37 percent of these executives had a liberal arts undergraduate degree, 35 percent majored in engineering and science, and 28 percent majored in business.[13] Forty-two percent had advanced degrees. The chief marketing executives' prior career experiences were as follows: direct sales, 74 percent; staff marketing, 52 percent; advertising/promotion, 35 percent; production, 24 percent, engineering/product research, 22 percent; distribution, 22 percent; and finance, 16 percent.[14]

The Attributes of Marketing Managers The survey asked the chief marketing executives which of their attributes contributed to their success. The attributes cited most frequently were ability to contribute to top-management decisions, skill in motivating employees, planning ability, and expertise in judging markets.[15]

One very successful company in the packaged-groceries industry seeks the following qualities in its brand managers. It wants individuals who set high goals and have a record of achieving them. It wants individuals who are results-oriented rather than process-oriented. Candidates should have demonstrated leadership qualities for changing organizations, not merely maintaining them.[16]

The president of Ortho Pharmaceutical Company of Canada concluded that "other than the general manager of a company, the product manager is the only other individual in the organization who is obliged to show concern for every single aspect of the product under his responsibilities. He has to do it, however, without the authority which goes with the general manager's function, but in concept, their interests need to be the same."[17] This is an indirect way of stating that product management is good training for top management.

In 1971 Ortho had a consultant identify the skills necessary for a division manager and a product manager. The study revealed that these two positions required the same skills, but that three additional skills were required of the product manager. Of the eleven skills that were held in common, six were classified as critical and five were considered desirable but not critical. These eleven skills were as follows.

Critical skills

1. Identifies those factors with the greatest influence on results and gives these factors priority attention. Recognizes when the priority of a factor needs to be changed.
2. Innovates within the bounds of corporate policy. Open to suggestions and encourages others to innovate.
3. Sets high standards for selection, training, and evaluation; gives balanced appraisals of subordinates, not just criticism. Builds on strengths.
4. Departs from traditional practices when they are no longer adequate.
5. Reacts selectively on specific problems without overreacting; avoids creating a new problem in the process of solving the existing one.
6. Lets individuals know what is expected of them by establishing goals and measures of performance.

Desirable but not critical skills

7. Increases competence through favorable responses to training, supervision, and self-development programs.
8. Demonstrates leadership qualities that inspire others; assumes leadership roles, sets a good example, supports management, and is effective in oral and written communication.
9. Shows willingness to make personal sacrifices to get the job done.
10. Sets high standards for self and others.
11. Shows willingness to face unpleasant situations.

Skills required for product management

1. Coordinates and negotiates with other functions, without authority over other functions.
2. Opens up two-way communication with other functions.
3. Has a knowledge or understanding of the technical skills of marketing.

After using these skills as criteria for selection, Ortho concluded that they were exceptionally helpful in selecting people who made positive contributions to the firm.

In summary, the attributes for positions in marketing management are basically the same as those for general management. Therefore, marketing management is a good training ground for top management.

WHAT IS PLANNING? Planning is the key activity of marketing management. It provides a common structure for all of the marketing manager's activities. Therefore, we must understand planning as a management process.

An understanding of corporate planning begins with an understanding of the basic function of the firm. The firm generates a return on its investment by converting its resources into goods or services and by then selling them to customers. The resources are physical (plant, machinery, and inventory), financial (capital and credit), human (technical and managerial skills), and goodwill. Each of these resources is exhausted during the conversion process. *Survival* of the firm depends on planning for the *replenishment* of resources. Growth of the firm requires planning for a *balanced expansion* of these resources.

Corporate strategic planning for most firms is a phenomenon of the last five years. Each planner tends to have his or her own definition of the planning process. One of the clearest definitions has been provided by Ackoff.

> Wisdom is the ability to see the long-run consequences of current actions, the willingness to sacrifice short-run gains for larger long-run benefits, and the ability to control what is controllable and not to fret over what is not. Therefore the essence of wisdom is concern with the future. It is not the type of concern with the future that the fortune teller has; he only tries to predict it. The wise man tries to *control* it....
>
> Planning is the design of a desired future and of effective ways of bringing it about. It is an instrument that is used by the wise, but not by the wise alone. When conducted by lesser men it often becomes an irrelevant ritual that produces short-run peace of mind, but not the future that is longed for....
>
> Thus there are three attitudes toward the future, which, ordered from the most to the least prevalent are (a) wait and see, (b) predict and prepare, and (c) make it happen.
>
> Those who benefit most from the future are those who have helped create it....
>
> ... planning is a process that involves making and evaluating each of a set of interrelated decisions before action is required, in a situation in which it is believed that unless action is taken a desired future state is not likely to occur, and that, if appropriate action is taken the likelihood of a favorable outcome can be increased.[18]

Several points in Ackoff's discussion need to be emphasized. First, forecasting is not planning, but it is generally a part of a plan. Forecasting is a state of "predict and prepare." Planning is making the future happen. Second, marketing plans must distinguish between controllable and uncontrollable variables. Controllable variables include the marketing mix—product, price, channels, promotion. Market research and the marketing organization are controllable variables that help to implement these four strategic variables. Uncontrollable variables include consumer demand, competition, nonmarketing costs, and public policy (e.g., antitrust laws, the Federal Trade Commission, and the consumer-protection movement). These uncontrollable variables represent the environment to which the marketer must adapt. Identifying target market segments where a product has a competitive advantage is one form of adaption.

A third point made by Ackoff is that the planning process involves interrelated decisions. This is especially true in marketing, where so many controllable and uncontrollable variables must be considered and where there are no general theories or models that will predict the effect of different combinations of these variables. These interrelated decisions and the uncertainty of the outcomes make marketing planning more of an art than a science. *Strategic* marketing planning is a very creative process. Because of this interrelatedness, uncertainty, creativity, and the uniqueness of each industry and company, it is impossible to prescribe a general procedure for creating a marketing plan.

Ackoff's definition emphasizes the point that the planning process is appropriate only when the likelihood of a favorable outcome is increased. Planning is a wasteful exercise if it cannot alter events to make the outcome more favorable to the planner. Also, planning would be an unnecessary and expensive ritual if the cost of planning were to exceed the expected gains from planning. Thus planners must weigh the costs and benefits of planning.

Tilles provides a more operational definition by noting that "a long-range plan is a statement of strategy, sequenced over time, expressed in terms of resource requirements and funds flows, and representing a consensus of the top-management team."[19] This definition emphasizes the basic function of a company—the conversion of resources into a flow of funds. It also notes that a plan is a dynamic document in that strategy must be sequenced over time. And finally, it acknowledges that a plan must be supported by the power structure before it can be implemented.

SOCIAL MARKETING The period of the mid- to late-1960s was one of great social concern on college campuses. The response of many marketing educators was social marketing.

The term *social marketing* has several meanings. It can mean identifying segments of the market that have a high concern and therefore will be responsive to products or services that reflect this concern. For instance, a market segment that is concerned about ecology will be responsive to a product that is nonpolluting. Social marketing may also mean the application of marketing techniques to improve society.[20] Most frequently, however, the term is used to describe the application of marketing techniques to nonprofit organizations, such as those dealing with fund raising,[21] health services,[22] population problems,[23] recycling solid wastes,[24] food costs to minorities,[25] and incorporating the ecology into the marketing strategy.[26] This broader application of marketing concepts began in the late 1960s.[27] These social applications may have been marketing professors' response to student demands for socially relevant courses[28] or a guilt feeling about the profit motive.[29]

The application of marketing techniques to nonprofit organizations is based on the observation that these organizations perform functions very similar to those of profit-oriented organizations. Both types of organizations provide a product or service in return for financial or political responses. They perform the same tasks of resource attraction, resource allocation, and persuasion.[30] It follows, therefore, that techniques developed in profit organizations will improve operations in nonprofit organizations.[31] This conclusion may not always be valid, however. For example, the revised Postal Service has used many marketing techniques, but improvements in its operations have been difficult to identify.

Interest in the application of marketing techniques to social problems remained largely with marketing educators until the end of the 1970s, when energy shortages began to affect companies' profits. When energy costs increased, business executives rapidly gained social concern about such a small thing as a throwaway beer can. The can requires three ounces of bauxite, which must be shipped 1500 miles from Jamaica and converted into aluminum with electricity that would burn a 100-watt bulb for five hours.[32]

Federal energy policies will drastically alter the container industry. Recycling programs will become more active. Reusable containers will be reintroduced, reversing the trend toward disposable ones. Disposable plastic bottles will replace some disposable glass and aluminum containers, because plastic containers require less energy to produce. Products will be developed that reduce the need for a rigid container by having the user add water at the point of use. Such a carbonated soft drink is already in development (see Chapter 19). Big cars and labor-saving household appliances may be taxed to discourage buyers. Thus the impact of energy shortages will have an impact on marketing strategies of many companies, thereby taking social marketing out of the classroom.

THE PLAN OF THE BOOK   The purpose of this book is to help you develop analytical skills and skills in developing strategies. The building of analytical skills begins with the ability to ask the critical questions. Answers to these questions generate data that must be analyzed and synthesized into logical conclusions. These conclusions form the basis for identifying marketing opportunities. The Environmental Analysis Worksheet helps the marketing manager to ask the critical questions, analyze the data, and translate the conclusions into opportunities and problems. This worksheet is flexible, so that data analysis may include advanced multivariate statistical techniques, simple tabulations and ratios, or whatever is appropriate for the data and the preferences of the manager.

Developing strategies is a creative process that cannot be reduced to models; therefore, we cannot present generalized strategies that can be applied to generalized opportunities and problems. It is unlikely that creativity can be taught, but it can be encouraged through the use of examples. Therefore, the chapters on strategy are replete with examples of the marketing strategies of familiar brands—e.g., McDonald's, Pampers, Tylenol, Lysol, and Kodak.

The Strategy Worksheet helps the marketing manager to make the links between the opportunities, problems, marketing goals, and strategies. It facilitates a comparison between the present strategy and a proposed strategy. It forces the manager to think through the effect of the proposed strategy on sales, marketing-mix costs, and non-marketing costs. Furthermore, the Strategy Worksheet requires the translation of recommendations into a profit plan.

In the following chapter a short case will be presented to illustrate the application of the worksheet approach to planning. A discussion in that chapter will show you how to use the worksheets to critique your marketing plan prior to its evaluation by others (the teacher in the classroom or a superior in industry).

The worksheets provide the organization for the book. Chapters focus on major sections of the worksheet, thereby guiding you through the processes of analysis and strategy development. The learning objective is to make you confident in developing a marketing plan of your own and in evaluating the plans of others.

SUMMARY   Skills in analysis and strategy development are required of successful marketing managers (and chief corporate executives). This text is designed to help you develop these skills. The Environmental Analysis Worksheet will be used to help the manager ask the critical questions when analyzing the market and organize data so that the important opportunities and problems may be identified. The Strategy Worksheet provides a means for relating the opportunities, problems, marketing goals, and strategies. The strategies are then translated into their effects on the profit plan.

The role of the marketing executive is broadening to include corporate strategic planning and greater involvement in new-product planning, pricing, customer service, and packaging. This expanded role requires more sensitivity to external influences, such as increased government regulation, consumer groups, highly dynamic demand, shortages, and rising costs. Studies have shown that in addition to the skills required of a division manager, the product manager needs the skills of coordinating without authority, communicating with all functions, and knowing marketing techniques.

Planning may be defined as *making the future happen.* The marketing manager controls the future by identifying market segments where he or she has competitive advantages and by then developing a marketing-mix strategy to exploit these advantages.

The interest in social marketing was largely in the classroom in the late 1960s. Shortages of raw materials and energy moved social marketing into the business world.

DISCUSSION QUESTIONS

1. What is marketing? What are the main marketing activities? Illustrate these marketing activities for organizations involved in: (a) producing consumer package goods (e.g., toothpaste, cake mixes); (b) producing consumer durable goods (e.g., radar ovens, color TV's, cars); (c) producing consumer fad goods (e.g., yo-yos, frisbees, pet rocks); and (d) producing industrial goods (e.g., integrated circuits for minicomputer/calculator firms).

2. Describe the strengths and weaknesses of each of the four possible business philosophies for the firm with reference to: (a) resource allocation or misallocation; (b) ability to react to competition; (c) ability to react to changes in consumers' desires or needs; and (d) ability to conform (comply) with changes in consumer-protection legislation.

3. For each of the four situations described in question 1, discuss the need and extent for planning by the organizations. Include in your discussion the uncertainties of: (a) changing consumer desires (perceived needs); (b) changing consumer-safety legislation; and (c) new competition entering the industry.

4. Would the marketing executive of a nonprofit organization be concerned with competition? Why or why not?

5. "Socialist governments have not eliminated marketing as an economic activity; marketing is in fact necessary to the efficient operation of socialist economies." Do you agree or disagree with this statement? Discuss.

6. Try to imagine a society in which there is no marketing activity (that is, none of the marketing functions is fulfilled). Try to describe such a society.

7. It is generally agreed that marketing is more "art" than "science" today. What changes will make it more "science"?

8. What is the relevance of the marketing concept when an affluent economy moves into a state of scarcity?

9. In measuring the efficiency of marketing systems, should the marketing manager express marketing costs in absolute terms (e.g., dollars) or relative terms (e.g., share of sales)? How will these different measures affect the answer to the question: "Does marketing cost too much?"

10. Why should marketing managers learn to ask the critical questions?

NOTES

1. For a discussion of definitions of marketing, *see* S. D. Hunt, "The Nature and Scope of Marketing," *Journal of Marketing* **40** (July 1976): 17–28.

2. P. Kotler, *Marketing for Non-Profit Organizations* (Englewood Cliffs, N.J.: Prentice-Hall, 1975); and G. Zaltman and R. Duncan, *Strategies for Planned Change* (New York: Wiley/Interscience, 1976).

3. P. Kotler and S. Levy, "Demarketing, Yes, Demarketing," *Harvard Business Review* (November–December 1971): 74–80.

4. A. H. Maslow, *Motivation and Personality*, 2d ed. (New York: Harper & Row, 1970).

5. J. S. Chipman, "The Nature and Meaning of Equilibrium in Economic Theory," in *Functionalism in the Social Sciences*, ed. D. Martindale, Monograph 5 (Philadelphia: American Academy of Political and Social Science, 1965), pp. 35–64.

6. F. M. Nicosia, *Advertising Management, and Society* (New York: McGraw-Hill, 1974).

7. M. I. Goldman, *Soviet Marketing* (New York: Free Press, 1963).

8. "Profile of a Chief Marketing Executive" (New York: Heidrick and Struggles, Management Consulting–Executive Selection, 1976).

9. *Ibid.*, p. 5.

10. *Ibid.*, p. 11.

11. *Ibid.*

12. *Ibid.*, p. 6.

13. *Ibid.*, p. 8.

14. *Ibid.*, p. 10.

15. *Ibid.*

16. Private communication.

17. P. Skuy, "Pharmaceutical Product Management Today and Tomorrow." (Talk delivered at the Pharmaceutical Product Management Seminar, Pharmaceutical Advertising Club of Canada and the Pharmaceutical Marketing Club of Ontario, February 15, 1977.)

18. R. L. Ackoff, *A Concept of Corporate Planning* (New York: Wiley/Interscience, 1970), pp. 1, 56, 4.

19. S. Tilles, "Business Definition and Levels of Generalization," in *Business Strategy*, ed. H. Igor Ansoff (Baltimore: Penguin, 1969), pp. 180–209.

20. P. Kotler and G. Zaltman, "Social Marketing: An Approach to Planned Social Change," *Journal of Marketing* 35 (July 1971): 3–12.

21. W. A. Mindak and H. M. Bybee, "Marketing's Application to Fund Raising," *Journal of Marketing* 35 (July 1971): 13–18.

22. G. Zaltman and I. Vertinsky, "Health Service Marketing: A Suggested Model," *Journal of Marketing* 35 (July 1971): 19–27.

23. J. U. Farley and H. J. Leavitt, "Marketing and Population Problems," *Journal of Marketing* 35 (July 1971): 28–33.

24. W. G. Zikmund and W. J. Stanton, "Recycling Solid Wastes: A Channels-of-distribution Problem," *Journal of Marketing* 35 (July 1971): 34–39.

25. D. E. Sexton, Jr., "Comparing the Cost of Food to Blacks and to Whites," *Journal of Marketing* 35 (July 1971): 40–46.

26. H. H. Kassarjian, "Incorporating Ecology into Marketing Strategy: The Case of Air Pollution," *Journal of Marketing* 35 (July 1971): 61–66.

27. P. Kotler and S. J. Levy, "Broadening the Concept of Marketing," *Journal of Marketing* 33 (January 1969): 10–15.

28. R. D. Buzzell, "How Can Research Contribute to Improved 'Marketing' in Non-Business Organizations?" Working paper, Marketing Science Institute, October 1970.

29. D. Luck, "Broadening the Concept of Marketing—Too Far," *Journal of Marketing* **33** (July 1969): 53–55.

30. B. P. Shapiro, "Marketing for Nonprofit Organizations," *Harvard Business Review* (September–October 1973): 123–132.

31. J. N. Sheth and P. L. Wright, *Marketing Analysis for Societal Problems* (Urbana, Ill.: Bureau of Economic and Business Research, 1976).

32. A. Takas, "Societal Marketing: A Businessman's Perspective," *Journal of Marketing* **38** (October 1974): 2–7.

SUGGESTED READINGS

Allen, L. A. *Professional Management: New Concepts and Proven Practices* (New York: McGraw-Hill, 1973).

Ewing, D. W., *The Human Side of Planning* (New York: Macmillan, 1969).

Gaedeke, R. M., ed., *Marketing in Private and Public Nonprofit Organizations* (Santa Monica, Calif.: Goodyear, 1977).

Levitt, T., "Marketing Myopia," *Harvard Business Review* (July–August 1960): 45–56.

Miller, E. C., *Marketing Planning*, AMA Research Study 81 (New York: American Management Association, 1967), p. 89.

Mockler, R. J., "Theory and Practice of Planning," *Harvard Business Review* (March–April 1970): 148–154.

Stern, M. E., *Marketing Planning: A Systems Approach* (New York: McGraw-Hill, 1966).

ENVIRONMENTAL ANALYSIS WORKSHEET

Environmental elements	Facts	Assumptions or research needed	Conclusions
Organizational values, objectives, and policies (4)			
Organizational design (5)			
Situation			
Generic demand (6)			
Brand demand (7)			
Competition (9)			
Public policy (10)			
Opportunities (2)			
Problems			

MARKETING PLAN (CONSUMER PRODUCT)

Current performance
Recommendations
Effect of recommendations on income
Situation analysis
Opportunities and problems
Strategies
Tests and research
Supporting documents
   Comparative budgets
   Media allocation schedule
   Promotion control sheet

STRATEGY WORKSHEET

Opportunities and problems in rank order to importance

    1.
    2.
     .
    n.

	Current strategy	Alternatives and recommended strategy	Estimated Effect
Demand strategy			
Generic			
Brand			
Strategic goals			
Financial			
Marketing			
Marketing-mix strategies			
Product (12)			
Pricing (13)			
Channel and logistics (14)			
Advertising and promotional (15)			
Sales management (16)			
Research (3)			
Profit plan			
Evaluation and control (19)			

CHAPTER 2

The Planning Process

LEARNING OBJECTIVES   After studying this chapter you should:

1. Understand in broad terms the worksheet approach to marketing planning.
2. Know the elements that are required in an Environmental Analysis Worksheet, a Strategy Worksheet, and a marketing plan.
3. Know how the worksheets may be used to detect faulty analysis.
4. Appreciate the importance of identifying the problem (or opportunity).
5. Begin to develop the ability to identify subproblems (or success factors).
6. Understand how to rank-order subproblems (or success factors) according to their importance.
7. Begin to develop the ability to ask the critical question.
8. Know the process for solving a case with the worksheet approach.
9. Relate your skills to those required for marketing planning.
10. Be able to define and use the following concepts:

Situation analysis	Opportunities	Priority index
Generic demand	Success factors	Profit plan
Brand demand	Problems	Break-even analysis
Public policy	Subproblems	

THOUGHT STARTERS

1. What are some common errors in an environmental analysis?
2. Is a complete analysis always necessary?
3. Why has there been a sudden interest in strategic planning?

In the previous chapter we saw that environmental analysis and strategy development are central to the marketing-planning process. In this chapter we will analyze a small case, using the worksheet approach so that you will have a complete example to refer to as we pursue the details of marketing management in later chapters.

THE WORKSHEET APPROACH   Figure 1.2 introduced the worksheet concept in broad terms. Figure 2.1 shows more details of the worksheets and how they feed information into the marketing plan. The components of each of these worksheets will now be briefly described.

The Environmental Analysis Worksheet The left-hand column of the Environmental Analysis Worksheet (Fig. 2.1) shows the major topics that should be considered in a marketing plan. In Fig. 1.2 we saw that the brand manager enters the process with an examination of the generic demand. The analyses of generic demand, brand demand, competition, and public policy are known as the *situation analysis*. The situation analysis provides the basis for the development of a brand marketing plan.

The "Facts" column of the worksheet summarizes the data presently known to the manager. These data are the answers to the critical questions. The experienced manager is adept at knowing which questions to ask and limits questions to those dimensions of the problem that are *relevant* and *controllable*. An inexperienced manager or a student who is new to the case method has a tendency to collect irrelevant data, "just to be on the safe side." Excess data can lead to an elaborate analysis of the wrong problem. If the critical question is understood, only relevant data will be gathered.

Rarely are all the facts available to solve a problem. The analysis may require additional research to gather missing information. The analyst must assess the benefits of the additional data to the planning process before investing in research. Assumptions are frequently used when facts are missing. Key assumptions need to be made explicit, so that others reading the plan may challenge them. The marketing manager may challenge an assumption by a brand manager and request an investment in the necessary research to generate the facts. Some managers review key assumptions throughout the year as a means for tracking the planning process for a brand. Column three of the analysis worksheet should be used to record research needed and assumptions that were made during the analysis.

The extreme right-hand column of the analysis worksheet is the "Conclusions" column. Beginning with the facts and using assumptions and research findings, the marketing manager reaches a logical conclusion. Thus a "hole" in this column signals that the individual is new to planning and does not know the critical questions to ask. Conclusions that do not follow from the facts and assumptions are known as *non sequiturs*. Non sequiturs reveal illogical thinking, which occurs when the manager has reached a conclusion prior to the analysis, but has "gone through the exercise" of gathering data. The analysis worksheet, therefore, provides the novice planner with a means for evaluating his or her plan before showing it to others.

Evaluating the analysis. A marketing manager (or a professor) may detect faulty analysis by reading down the columns. Reading down the "Facts" column will reveal errors in facts; reading down the second column will reveal many common weaknesses in planning. For example, inexperienced planners tend to request research when a proper analysis of existing data would be adequate. Research is frequently requested without considering its cost relative to its benefit. Some planners forget to show the cost of research in the brand profit plan.

Making *reasonable* assumptions is a subjective, personal matter. Both the assumption and what is reasonable will vary according to each individual's perception of the facts. Thus the young brand manager should be prepared for challenges to his or her assumptions and to make assumptions only after careful, reasoned consideration.

By reading down the "Conclusions" column, one can detect errors in the statement of problems and opportunities. The arrows in the right-hand column of the analysis worksheet (see Fig. 2.1) show that the conclusions should lead to logical statements of problems and opportunities. A problem that does not follow from the conclusions

ENVIRONMENTAL ANALYSIS WORKSHEET

Environmental elements	Facts	Assumptions or research needed	Conclusions
Organizational values, objectives, and policies (4)			
Organizational design (5)			

Situation
  Generic demand (6)
  Brand demand (7)
  Competition (9)
  Public policy (10)			

Opportunities (2)			
Problems			

MARKETING PLAN (CONSUMER PRODUCT)

Current performance
Recommendations
Effect of recommendations on income
Situation analysis
Opportunities and problems
Strategies
Tests and research
Supporting documents
  Comparative budgets
  Media allocation schedule
  Promotion control sheet

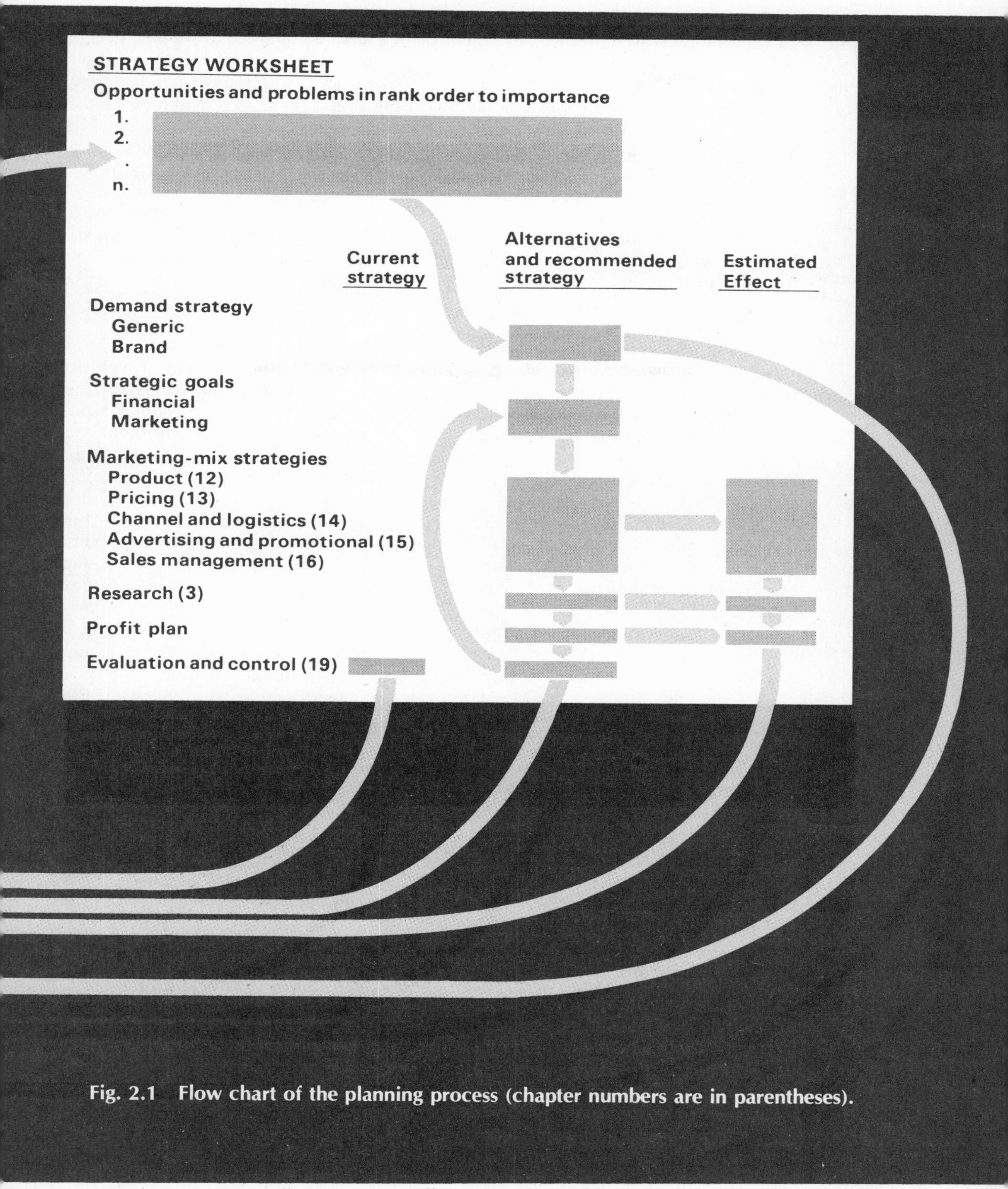

STRATEGY WORKSHEET

Opportunities and problems in rank order to importance

1.
2.
.
n.

Current
strategy

Alternatives
and recommended
strategy

Estimated
Effect

Demand strategy
   Generic
   Brand

Strategic goals
   Financial
   Marketing

Marketing-mix strategies
   Product (12)
   Pricing (13)
   Channel and logistics (14)
   Advertising and promotional (15)
   Sales management (16)

Research (3)

Profit plan

Evaluation and control (19)

Fig. 2.1   Flow chart of the planning process (chapter numbers are in parentheses).

may be the result of illogical thinking, but most frequently it reveals that the planner has leapt on a favorite problem and then tried to build an analysis to support it.

Is all of this analysis necessary? If the problem is clear and correct, the manager may proceed to the identification of the subproblems and on to the development of a strategy. Administrative conflict occurs when the brand manager's definition of the problem does not agree with the superior's. Should the brand manager engage in an analysis, at some cost in time and money, to define the problem or instead develop a strategy for the problem that is given and face the blame for developing a bad strategy? There is no correct answer for this dilemma.

A complete analysis may not always be necessary or possible when a case is used in the classroom. Cases may be focused on specific problems, such as sales management, for which the learning experience does not require a complete situation analysis. The point of entry in such an instance may be the development of a strategy. In this case only the Strategy Worksheet would be necessary.

Determining the problem to be solved. A thorough analysis should reveal a central problem and many subproblems which *cause* the central problem. The central problem can be solved only after determining the *contribution* that each subproblem makes to the central problem and the *control* that the marketing manager has over the subproblem. Both of these factors must be considered when determining which problem should be attacked first. Clearly, the manager will not want to focus on a trivial subproblem. Furthermore, it would be futile to focus on a subproblem over which the manager has no control.

Effectively identifying and weighting subproblems is a management skill. In the previous chapter we saw that Ortho Chemical Co. regarded as a basic skill the ability to identify the important dimensions of a problem and the willingness to change the weights of these dimensions as conditions change. Failure to change weights as conditions change would result in solving a trivial problem. The example that follows will illustrate one approach for ranking subproblems. We will consider the case of a marketing manager who was concerned about a decline in sales in the industrial pump division and therefore asked the sales manager to investigate the situation.

After riding with the salespeople, the sales manager identified the following five subproblems: (1) the product was adequate but not unusual; (2) there was a decline in the chemical industry, a major user of pumps; (3) the salespeople were on straight salary to encourage them to service the accounts; (4) top management had not clearly stated the role of the sales force in the total communication effort; and (5) salespeople received inadequate supervision from their district sales managers.

After identifying the subproblems, the second task for the general sales manager was to estimate how much each subproblem contributed to the problem of declining sales. The third task was to estimate what proportion of each causal factor was controlled by the sales manager.

The sales manager held a meeting with the district managers to determine the weights. It should be noted that these weights are the *present* weights, thereby emphasizing that they will change as conditions change. The weights of the relative *contribution* column should total 1.00 if the subproblems listed exhaust all of the causes for the main problem. Totaling the relative *control* weights would be meaningless. The results of this analysis appear in Table 2.1.

The sales manager weighted the first two factors low, concluding that these were largely excuses given by the salespeople, since pumps were basically an unexciting product and other companies had increasing sales of pumps. Compensation was

TABLE 2.1   Sample weighting of subproblems

Subproblems (i.e., factors causing the main problem)	Present relative contribution to the problem		Present relative control over subproblem		Priority index	Rank
	(1)		(2)		(1) × (2) = (3)	
1. Unexciting product	.15	×	.20	=	.03	5
2. Decline in chemical industry	.10	×	.50	=	.05	3
3. Straight salary compensation	.25	×	.75	=	.19	1
4. Lack of clear goals from top management	.20	×	.20	=	.04	4
5. Inadequate supervision from district managers	.30	×	.33	=	.10	2
	1.00					

weighted heavily because of its effect on how sales representatives allocate their time. Straight salary is frequently used when the salespeople are required to service accounts extensively, but the sales manager concluded that the sales representatives were giving more service than the product required. The failure of top management to set clear goals affects all levels of the organization, including the sales force. Supervision of salespeople must be increased when sales are declining.

The relative control that a sales manager has over these factors is a subject for debate. One may question the .50 weight given to the factor of declining sales in the chemical industry. Although there is little that one can do about improving the economic plight of the chemical industry, the sales manager can identify other industries with better potential and initiate programs that will redirect salespeople's efforts. The sales manager has considerable control over the sales representatives' compensation plan. The sales manager shares with the regional and district sales managers the responsibility for the amount of supervision given to the sales force. Thus this factor is weighted .33.

The priority index is calculated by multiplying columns one and two. This index reveals that the top-priority item is a new compensation plan, perhaps one that includes salary and commission. The second most important factor is the need to improve supervision.

The Strategy Worksheet   The subproblems that were selected for immediate attention are rank-ordered at the top of the Strategy Worksheet, so that the brand manager will keep the strategy focused on the problems at hand. In Chapter 11 we will examine methods for relating these subproblems to alternative strategies.

The Strategy Worksheet outlines the major decision areas of marketing. There must be a strategy for generic and brand demand, for example. Strategies must be consistent with the financial and marketing strategic goals, so the latter are also stated on the worksheet. The marketing-mix strategy represents the creative part of strategy development, and a major section of this text will be devoted to this topic. The proper use of information can give a brand a comparative advantage, so research is included on the Strategy Worksheet. The profit plan summarizes historical data and the estimate of the new strategy's effect on profit.

The columns in the Strategy Worksheet permit one to compare the present strategy and the recommended strategy. (In Chapter 11 the recommended strategy will be expanded to include alternatives and contingency plans.) For those elements that affect profit, the estimated effect of the recommended strategy is reported in the right-hand column. This column provides the basis for much of the profit plan.

The worksheets are summary documents. In some cases the cell entry will include a reference to an appendix that gives a supporting analysis. One advantage of a worksheet is that it gives the analyst an opportunity to see the data in any order, not just sequentially, as would occur with a checklist. Random visualization will reveal new relationships and new creative alternatives. The consulting firm of Arthur D. Little, for example, developed a 17- by 22-inch "Strategy Center Profile" so that clients could see all of the relevant data when they were developing a corporate strategic plan.[1]

A worksheet should not be confused with a planning checklist. A checklist simply suggests points to consider. The worksheet goes beyond this function to help in the assembly of key facts into a logical order. These facts are then translated into conclusions, problems, opportunities, and strategies. The worksheets provide the inputs for the brand profit plan, as is illustrated in Fig. 2.1. Completion of the worksheets constitutes a *marketing audit* of a brand.

The Marketing Plan   The final form used to present the marketing plan will vary greatly among firms. The format shown in Fig. 2.1 is used by several firms in the consumer-products field.[2] The first three headings—"Current performance," "Recommendations," and "Effect of recommendations on income"—are for busy executives. These three key components of a plan can be presented in one page. The remainder of the plan provides the support for this first page. The arrows in Fig. 2.1 show where the data come from when the plan is put in its final form for management approval.

The worksheets are presented here in very brief form so that you can see the entire planning system and the relationships among its parts. In later chapters each of the major elements will be expanded for a deeper understanding.[3]

ASKING THE CRITICAL QUESTION   An experienced planner intuitively asks the critical questions when analyzing a marketing problem. He or she knows what data are relevant and what to do with them after they are collected. One of the goals of the worksheet approach is to teach the new planner to ask the critical questions. It is not possible to list all of the questions that would be relevant to all industries, products, and brands, but illustrative questions for the major sections of the worksheets are possible. The young brand manager will want to seek the advice of his or her superiors, peers, and staff persons in identifying the critical questions for a plan.

Environmental Analysis Critical Questions   Some of the most common critical questions that are asked during an analysis of the planning environment are as follows.

Organizational values, objectives, and policies.   What are the personal values of those persons in control? How are these values translated into organizational objectives? How do policies constrain alternative means for meeting goals? These questions may be beyond the scope of the brand manager, but they should certainly be considered by the marketing manager in developing a long-range (three- to five-year) plan.

Organizational design.   How are resources, responsibility, and authority organized to achieve objectives within policy constraints? Who is the chief marketing executive, and what are his or her functions? Is a brand manager system used?

Situation analysis. What are the unmet needs in the marketplace? Who will sell how much of what to whom, when, where, and how? These questions must be refined to include questions of generic demand, brand demand, competition, and public policy.

Generic Demand. How do general economic conditions affect the sales of this industry? What are the income and price elasticities of this product category? Are industry sales growing or declining? Are there time-series patterns, such as a trend, cycle, seasonal, or fad? Is the product in the introductory, growth, stable, or declining stage of its product life cycle? What are the characteristics of the buyers that will permit us to form market segments of heavy, medium, and light users? (Characteristics commonly used to segment the market include age, education, marital status, income, geographic location, life-style, and attitudes.)

Brand Demand. What are the strengths and weaknesses of our brand? Is our market share growing, static, or declining? What percentage of the potential buyers are aware of the benefits of our brand? What percentage of the market has tried our brand? What is the repurchase rate? What is our distribution rate? (That is, what percentage of the desired stores stocks our product?) How do consumers perceive the benefits of our product relative to those of a competitive brand?

Competition. What does it take to be a success in this industry? Is the market structure competitive or oligopolistic? Is there a surplus of productive capacity in the industry? Is entry easy? What are competitors' marketing strategies? How will competitors react to changes in our strategies?

Public Policy. How do antitrust regulations, regulatory agencies, the consumer-protection movement, and environmental concerns influence our opportunities and constrain our alternative strategies?

Opportunities and problems. What opportunities and problems does the situation analysis reveal? What are the subproblems that create the problem? How much control does the planner have over these factors?

Strategic Critical Questions Strategic critical questions focus on an *evaluation* of the past strategy and new alternative strategies. Are we meeting the financial and marketing goals? Are the generic and brand demand strategies still the best? Are we missing opportunities because our present problems (or successes) are preventing us from searching for new opportunities? Some of these questions need to be asked in more detail.

Goals. Are the financial goals profit, return on investment, payback period, or some other financial criterion? Is marketing performance judged by sales, market share, or profits?

Marketing-mix strategies. What is the best positioning of our brand among competitive brands? What price should we use to attain our goals? What is the role of the sales force in the overall communication strategy? What is the role of advertising? What is the message? How do we express it? Where do we say it? What roles will the channel of distribution (wholesalers, retailers, etc.) perform, and how will they be compensated?

Brand action plan (tactics).   How do we implement the strategies? How do we recruit, train, and motivate the sales force? How do we create effective copy and artwork that will communicate the strategic message? What media do we use—television, radio, magazines, newspapers, direct mail, or what? How do we motivate the channel of distribution?

Profit plan.   What are the current brand sales, cost of goods sold, marketing expenses, and contribution to profit? How will the proposed strategies affect these costs and profits? What is the break-even volume (price) under the proposal?

Evaluation and control.   How will we measure the effectiveness of the marketing strategies and their execution? Will the new plan require the development of new systems for evaluation and control?

These questions do not exhaust the questions that a planner may ask. We will see additional questions in later chapters.

AN APPLICATION OF THE WORKSHEET APPROACH   Figure 2.1 provides an overview of the marketing planning process. To illustrate the process, we will examine a brief marketing case. A marketing case is a brief synopsis of a marketing situation. The case situation below is simplified by the fact that because the product is new, there are no historical brand data.

To help you identify the facts, take notes on a case by underlining key facts, noting in the left-hand margin the appropriate classification for the Environmental Analysis Worksheet and in the right-hand margin for the Strategy Worksheet. These facts can be transferred easily to the appropriate worksheet.

The 1971 Marketing Plan for the Introduction of Scoop Ice Cream Mix[4]

ENVIRONMENTAL ANALYSIS WORKSHEET		STRATEGY WORKSHEET
	Consolidated Groceries planned to introduce *Scoop Ice Cream Mix* nationally. This was its first entry into the dairy category. The mix is composed of milk, sugar, butterfats, salt, stabilizing gums, and fresh eggs, all of which are mixed and freeze dried into nuggets. These nuggets are encased in an egg-shaped gelatin capsule with a thin candy shell for protection and stability. A pint of ice cream is prepared by beating a capsule in a bowl with four ounces of cream, milk, or water, depending on the desired richness. In 30 minutes it freezes into an ice cream, or it can be chilled and served as a *pudding*. The mix comes in chocolate and vanilla, but the consumer can add flavors when mixing, especially if a flavored *milk shake* is desired.	Product
Generic demand: Sales trend		Other product uses and potential competitors
Total market	Ice cream is an old product, with only *1.5 percent increase per year* in gallons consumed. In 1970 *approximately 0.778 billion gallons* were consumed, 60 percent of which was con-	
Seasonal	sumed from *May to September*. Housewives are the prime	

Age profile of heavy consumers	purchasers, but children from *7 to 12 years old consume 50 percent*, and those from *13 to 18 consume 30 percent* of the annual gallonage. Per capita consumption has remained

Age profile of heavy consumers

Trend
Geographic segments

Price segments

Price trends

purchasers, but children from *7 to 12 years old consume 50 percent*, and those from *13 to 18 consume 30 percent* of the annual gallonage. Per capita consumption has remained approximately *constant for a decade at 15 quarts.* Research data showed that the highest proportion of users was in the *North Central region (80 percent in 1970)*; the lowest, in the *Southeast (58 percent)*. Ice cream is consumed in all socioeconomic groups. In 1970, *20 percent of the gallonage was premium priced ($2.03/gallon), 54 percent was medium priced ($1.56), and 26 percent was low priced ($1.12)*. In recent years the *premium-priced ice creams have lost share, and low-priced ones have gained share.*

Supermarkets sold 63 percent of all ice cream, *ice cream stores sold 18 percent*, and *drug stores sold 8 percent*. Supermarkets may carry *three to five ice cream brands*. Ice cream is not generally part of the dairy department, but is frequently sold in a separate ice cream department.

Traditional ice cream channels

Scoop comes in a *plastic half-gallon container* that can be used to freeze the ice cream. Eight capsules are packaged in each container. A case of 12 containers sells to the *retailer for $10.00*. The suggested *retail price is $1.00 per container.*

Product package

Trade price
Suggested retail price

For 1971, costs as a percentage of factory sales were estimated as follows: fixed costs, 38 percent; variable costs, 12 percent; media/production costs, 15 percent; sampling/couponing, 4 percent; trade allowances, 4 percent; other promotion, 2 percent; sales force, 6 percent; distribution costs, 4 percent; and administration and market research, 2 percent. Sales are forecasted at *2.4 million cases.*

Profit plan:
Costs

Brand unit sales estimate

Unit sales

Competition:
Oligopolistic market structure

The ice cream industry tends to be regional, because of the cost of shipping refrigerated products. Of the 750 small regional companies, *15 account for 65 percent of the total ice cream production.*

Organizational design

The Scoop *product manager* is required to present an annual marketing plan to the *group product manager*. Consolidated Groceries uses a standardized format containing the following items: (1) brand's current performance, (2) recommendations, (3) effect of the recommendation on income, (4) situation analysis, (5) opportunities and problems, (6) strategies, and (7) tests and research.

The Scoop 1971 Environmental Analysis Worksheet. The environment in which Scoop is being considered appears in Table 2.2. The "Facts" column is completed by transferring the notes in the left-hand margin of the case description. The assumptions are reasonable ones and are made where needed to continue the analysis. These assumptions could be replaced easily in the real world by making a few phone calls.

The "Conclusions" column summarizes appropriate calculations and the logical thoughts that follow from the facts and assumptions. By reading down this column, the planner can easily summarize the marketing opportunities and problems that require *changes* in the marketing strategy. (In the Scoop case there is no present strategy, so a completely new strategy must be developed.)

TABLE 2.2 1971 Scoop Ice Cream Mix Environmental Analysis Worksheet

Environmental elements	1970 Current facts	Assumptions/ research needed	Conclusions
Consolidated Groceries' values, objectives, and policies	Little is known	Assumed that the goal is profit; the policy, quality food.	The strategies must generate profits, and quality cannot be compromised.
Organizational design	Product-manager system		The marketing plan is the authority for the allocation of all marketing effort.
Situation analysis *Generic demand*	0.778 billion gallons		Average price = 0.20($2.03) + 0.54($1.56) + 0.26($1.12) = $1.54. Market in dollars = $1.54 × 0.778 = $1198 million
Time patterns	1.5% growth/year	Assumed that this trend will continue.	
	60% of season from May to September Trend toward low-priced ice creams Consumption rate constant at 15 qts/person/year		Scoop must take sales from existing products. Summer promotion must be heavy. This trend will help Scoop's introduction and growth. It is unlikely that Scoop can alter this rate.
Consumer profiles	Heavy users ages 7 to 18, all incomes, North Central (80%). Light users in the Southeast (58%).	Research is needed to determine why low usage in Southeast.	Introduce Scoop to the youth market in the North Central states. Perhaps Scoop can increase usage in this segment.
Brand demand Scoop (millions)	2.4 cases, $24.0 forecasted for 1971	Assume 12 gallons of ice cream/case	Sales at retail = Scoop sales × markup = $24 × 1.20 = $28.8.
Scoop market Share in dollars in cases			$28.8/$1198 = 2.4% share of dollars. 2.4/(0.79/12) = 3.6% share of cases
Determinants of share Brand position Awareness Trial rate Repurchase rate	Low-cost ice cream Unknown Zero, new product Zero, new product		Good positioning given price trends. Heavy advertising will be required. Promotion required to stimulate trial. Perceived product benefits determine repurchase rate.

Category	Assessment	Implication
Distribution rate	None at present, but Consolidated knows the industry.	Promotion to the trade will be necessary, however, due to limited shelf space.
Competitive national advertising		Little competition at the national level.
Competition		
Market structure	Assumed low because competitors are regional. 15 of 750 regional firms sell 65% of ice cream.	2% of firms have 65% of market, an oligopoly. This is important when competitive reaction is important, e.g., price wars.
Industry success factors	Quality product that tastes good and channel support.	Product and channel development are vital to Scoop's success.
Industry capacity	Capacity adequate given slow growth. Entry is easy.	No price wars due to excess capacities.
Public policy		
Antitrust		Scoop will add to competition; therefore, antitrust laws are not violated.
Regulatory agencies	Scoop must comply with standards of the Food and Drug Administration (FDA) Federal Trade Commission (FTC) requires proof of advertising claims.	No problem, because of our high standards for quality.
Consumerism		Make certain that copy claims can be proved.
Environment	Energy saved because mix does not require refrigeration, and container is reusable.	Use these themes in copy to wholesalers, retailers, and youth market.

Opportunities

(1) There is an opportunity for a quality ice cream at a low price. (2) The do-it-yourself trend should support the concept of an ice cream mix. (3) Scoop is positioned well as an ice cream because of the trend toward lower-priced ice creams. (4) Its positioning as a pudding or a milk shake mix is unknown, but gives us added uses. (5) Given the market structure and the lack of a national competitor, the market shares needed seem attainable. (6) The channel will be pleased by the compactness of the product and the fact that it does not require refrigeration, but it may decrease the sales of ice creams on which the channel makes a higher profit because of the higher price. (7) The product and Consolidated policies are consistent with public policies, especially the environmental features of the product.

Problems

(1) Successful introduction of Scoop will require sufficient advertising to create awareness and overcome the resistance to the work required in preparing Scoop. (2) A high distribution rate is required, because this is a convenience product. (3) Promotion to the trade must convince retailers that the addition of Scoop will increase their profits, not just shift them from the three to five brands of ice cream that they are presently carrying. (4) Consumer trial rate must increase rapidly to establish brand loyalty before competition enters. (5) We must balance the need for heavy advertising and promotion (e.g., sampling) against the corporate goal of attaining a profit. (6) Scoop must take most of its sales from competition, because per capita consumption is constant and generic demand has increased at a low 1.5% per year. (7) To achieve the goal of 2.4 million cases, Scoop must attain a market share of 2.4% in dollars and 3.6% in cases. (Scoop must sell more cases because of its lower price.)

Success-Factor Weights.   The planner's next task is to list the problems in the order of their importance to the success of the Scoop introduction. The term "problems" seems inappropriate, because this is a new product and problems have not yet developed. Therefore, instead of "problems" we will use the phrase "factors for successful introduction." One possible weighting of these success factors is shown in Table 2.3. The priority index indicates that the 1971 strategy should focus on creating awareness of Scoop's benefits and achieving a high level of distribution rates.

The success-factor weights may vary at different stages in a product's life cycle. Thus later marketing plans must reflect changes in the importance of these success variables. The weights shown in the table reflect the planner's opinion that successful introduction depends on a high distribution rate in stores. Creating awareness of benefits was given the lowest weight because the analyst considered price the major benefit, which could be communicated very easily. Awareness is the most fully controlled variable because Scoop may advertise directly to the consumer through mass media. Distribution rates, in contrast, require the cooperation of the retailers. Scoop must convince them to use their scarce shelf space for the new product. This may mean removing an existing product from the shelf. In Chapter 11 we will see how the rankings of the success factors help to determine the selection of alternative strategies.

TABLE 2.3   **A possible weighting of success factors**

Success factors	Present relative contribution to success	Present relative control over factor	Priority index	Rank
	(1)	(2)	(1) × (2) = (3)	
1. Create buyer awareness of Scoop's benefits	.20	.90	.18	1
2. Increase trial rate	.25	.40	.10	3
3. Increase repeat-purchase rate	.25	.30	.08	4
4. Achieve high distribution rates	.30	.50	.15	2

The Scoop 1971 Strategy Worksheet.   The Scoop Strategy Worksheet for 1971 appears in Table 2.4. Because Scoop is a new product, there is no column for current strategy. The problems that the strategy should solve are ranked at the top of the worksheet. The ranking of these problems is reflected in the profit plan. Awareness is ranked first. Media expenditures, designed primarily to create awareness, are budgeted at 15 percent of sales, the largest single item. Distribution is ranked second. The budget for developing channels of distribution totals 14 percent of sales (trade allowance, 4 percent; sales force costs, 6 percent; and distribution costs, 4 percent). Sampling and couponing, costing 4 percent of sales, will get buyers to try Scoop and, we hope, hasten the time when they will repurchase it. Thus after estimating the costs for the 1971 strategy, it appears that they are consistent with the ranking of the problems for 1971.

Note that there are few facts from the case in the Strategy Worksheet. Once the analysis has established the priority of problems, the planner must then use his or her experience and creativity to develop a strategy. Opportunities for you to practice this inductive process will occur in later chapters.

TABLE 2.4   Scoop 1971 Strategy Worksheet

Rank order of problems:
1. Create buyer awareness of Scoop's benefits.
3. Increase trial rate.

2. Achieve high distribution rates.
4. Increase repeat purchase rate.

Decision areas	Recommended strategy	Estimated effect on profit plan
Demand strategy		
Generic	Accept the static state of the market. Do not attempt to increase per capita consumption or switch nonusers.	Generic demand will increase at the present rate of 1.5%/year, and per capita consumption will remain at 15 qts/person.
Brand	Position Scoop as an economical, quality ice cream that uses a new process—freeze dry—to avoid refrigerated storage.	This positioning should achieve the goal of 2.4 million cases, with the minimum of reaction from traditional ice cream brands.
Strategic goals		
Financial	Be profitable the first year because of the expected high cost of capital in 1971.	The profit plan will show a profit for 1971.
Marketing	Attain a 2.4% unit share (in $) of the standard ice cream market.	This goal is reasonable, given the market structure and a good strategy.
Marketing-mix strategies		
Product	The product consists of freeze-dry nuggets that can be mixed easily into an ice cream. Available flavors are vanilla and chocolate. The mix will also produce a pudding or a milk shake.	An ice cream mix could be promoted successfully. The concept becomes too complicated by the pudding and milk shake uses. Save these concepts for later promotions.
Package	A plastic half-gallon container can be used to freeze the ice cream and later as a refrigerator container.	This container will appeal to the price-conscious and the environmentalists.
Price	Retail at $1.00/gallon, sell to the retail trade at $0.8333. Be prepared to drop if necessary to protect share.	The retail price should be attractive to the buyers presently spending $1.12. Retailers will get $16\frac{2}{3}\%$ margin on the retail price.
Channels	Distribute primarily through supermarkets, where we have experience. Offer deals of 60¢/case for display allowances in May–June and July–August.	Our reputation will help gain distribution, but we must compete for shelf space. This will increase the retailer's margin and improve our distribution rate.
Advertising Promotion	Use sampling and coupons to get trial and repeat use.	In 1971 we should attain a trial rate of 30% of those aware and a 20% repeat rate.

TABLE 2.4. (cont.)

Rank order of problems:
1. Create buyer awareness of Scoop's benefits.
2. Achieve high distribution rates.
3. Increase trial rate.
4. Increase repeat purchase rate.

Decision areas	Recommended strategy	Estimated effect on profit plan
Advertising copy	"Make it at home and save money."	Attain a 60% recall of Scoop's quality and price.
Advertising media		
Target audience	Mothers and children ages 7–18 living in the North Central region.	Attain a 60% recall of Scoop's quality and price.
Media and weight	Heavy in TV for coverage, frequency and visualization of ease of preparation. Use some print during summer.	Attain a 60% recall of Scoop's quality and price.
Continuity	Network daytime TV yearround, with early nighttime spots in May to September.	Attain a 60% recall of Scoop's quality and price.
Personal selling	Convince retailers to give Scoop good shelf positioning. Check stock levels.	Our experienced sales force can accomplish this.
Research	Do focus-group interviews in the Southeast to determine why ice cream usage is low.	This should reveal the major reasons at a cost of approximately $12,000.

Profit plan
Industry sales (millions)

	1971	
$ value	$1,217	
Cases	65.8	
% increase over last year	1.5%	

Brand sales, at mfg. prices (millions)

$ Value	$ 24.0	100.0%
Cases	2.4	
% Increase (units)	100%	

Cost of goods

Fixed Costs	$ 9.12	38%
Variable Costs	2.88	12%
Total costs of goods	12.00	50%

Gross margin	$12.00	50%

Marketing expenses
Advertising

Media/production	$ 3.60	15%
Sampling/couponing	0.96	4%
Trade allowance	0.96	4%
Other promotions	0.48	2%
Total advertising expenses	$ 6.00	25%

TABLE 2.4. **(cont.)**

Rank order of problems:
1. Create buyer awareness of Scoop's benefits.
2. Achieve high distribution rates.
3. Increase trial rate.
4. Increase repeat purchase rate.

Decision areas	Recommended strategy		Estimated effect on profit plan
Sales force	$ 1.44	6%	
Distribution	0.96	4%	
Administration	0.48	2%	
Total expenses	$ 8.88	37%	
Contribution to profit and overhead	$ 3.12	13%	

Break-even points

Fixed cost coverage	1.55 million cases	[$9.12 million/$10 − $4.10*) = 1.55M]
To make a profit of 10% of sales	1.95 million cases	[$9.12M + 0.1 ($24M)/($10 − $4.10*) = 1.95M]

Evaluation and control

Product tests	In 1972 do blind product tests to see if 1971 users of Scoop evaluate its benefits favorably.	
Price studies	During 1971 monitor Nielsen Retail Index or SAMI† for competitors' price changes.	Estimated cost, $25,000
Channel	During 1971 monitor Nielsen Retail Index or SAMI to determine distribution rate.	
Advertising	During 1971 measure recall of Scoop's quality and price among target audience.	Estimated cost, $15,000

* Variable costs included all marketing costs except sales force (6%) and administration (2%), which are part of overhead in this case.
† The Nielsen Retail Index provides data on products sold through retail outlets. SAMI (Selling Areas-Marketing, Inc.) reports warehouse withdrawals to food stores.

Once the marketing-mix strategies have been established, they must be translated into plans of action (i.e., tactical plans). Advertising and personal selling provide an example. Specific advertising media must be selected. If we are using television, should we use network TV or spots? Which networks should we use? Which newspapers and magazines should we use? Many of these decisions will be made by Scoop's advertising agency.

The details of the sales management action plan would include an estimate of the capacity of the sales force to handle the assigned strategy. If the sales force is inadequate, expansion of the sales force will require expenditures for recruiting and training salespeople.

Break-Even Analysis. Most of the details of the Strategy Worksheet are self-explanatory, with the exception of the break-even calculations. Break-even, in units, represents the number of units that must be sold to make a zero profit, that is, to break even. This figure is calculated by dividing the fixed costs by the profit margin per unit. The profit margin is the selling price minus the variable costs.

Fixed costs are those that do not vary in *total* as additional units of the product are sold. The president's salary and the cost of the selling space are costs that are fixed in total, for example. As more units are sold, the cost *per unit* declines, but the total remains the same. Variable costs, by contrast, fluctuate in total according to the number of units sold, but they will be *constant per unit*. As more units are sold, the total costs will increase. Because these costs *vary* with the volume sold, they are known as *variable costs*. Salespersons' commissions and the cost of receiving merchandise are variable costs.

The break-even model, therefore, is as follows:

$$\text{Break-even quantity in units} = \frac{\text{Fixed costs}}{\text{Selling price} - \text{variable costs}} \quad (2.1)$$

To compute the break-even point for a desired profit, the amount of profit is treated as a fixed cost and added to the numerator of the equation. This break-even calculation is a quick and easy way to estimate the number of units that must be sold to cover the fixed costs, i.e., to "break even." Its simplicity, however, is deceptive. There are difficulties in forecasting price and costs, and the formula does not consider economies of scale.

Returning to Fig. 2.1, we see that the two worksheets can be translated easily into any planning format required by management. To illustrate the Scoop marketing plan for 1971, we will follow the requirements of Consolidated Groceries, which is very similar to the outline in Fig. 2.1.

The 1971 Scoop marketing plan. The key point in the 1971 Scoop marketing plan, which appears in Table 2.5, is that it *communicates* very efficiently. All of the key information is summarized in sections I–III. The remaining sections support the first three, presenting data in a logical order, going from the situation analysis to the strategies, and ending with specifying the research needed. By using a uniform format, Consolidated can easily compare the performance of Scoop with the other brands it sells.

You may be surprised to have learned that a short case, such as the Scoop case, requires extensive work to generate a good marketing plan.

MARKETING-PLANNING SKILLS Planning in marketing requires four distinctly different skills—analysis, synthesis, creation, and communication. *Analysis* is required to examine the brand's environment. This step in the planning process involves working with numbers and translating them into logical conclusions. *Synthesis* is the ability to see interrelationships among these conclusions. The output of synthesis is a clear definition of the main problem and the subproblems. In the case of an untapped opportunity, the synthesis will yield a clear statement of the opportunity (e.g., a new product) and the factors required to make it a success. The Environmental Analysis Worksheet requires skills in analysis and synthesis.

The development of alternative strategies is a very *creative* process and, like all creative processes, is a skill that must be developed. Problems and cases in later chapters are designed to encourage the development of creative skills.

Once the brand marketing plan is developed, the brand manager must "sell" it to

TABLE 2.5   Scoop Ice Cream Mix[5] 1971 marketing plan

I. BRAND'S CURRENT PERFORMANCE

Scoop Ice Cream Mix is expected to achieve its initial target objectives this year of 2.4 million cases, representing $24.0 million in sales and $3.12 million in net profits.

II. RECOMMENDATIONS

The 1971 objective of Scoop Ice Cream Mix is to obtain a 2.4% share of the retail ice cream market in dollars and a 3.6% share in cases. This represents shipments of 2.4 million cases and factory sales of $24.0 million. To achieve this objective, the brand will spend $3.6 million in advertising and $2.4 million in promotion.

III. EFFECT OF THE RECOMMENDATION ON INCOME

Proposed 1971 (millions)

Volume	
value	$24.0
cases	2.4
Share (in $)	2.4%
Cost of goods	$12.0 (50%)
Advertising/promotion	6.0 (25%)
Other costs	2.88 (12%)
Pretax profits	3.12 (13%)

IV. SITUATION ANALYSIS

A. The market

1. *Size.* The total retail value of the ice cream market is approximately $1.2 billion, representing an estimated consumption rate this year of 0.79 billion gallons. The market traditionally increases at an annual rate of about 1.5%.

    Competition consists of about 750 small regional companies, of which 15 account for about 65% of total ice cream production. No one has a dominant position in the market nationally.

2. *Consumer.* Though the housewife is the prime purchaser of ice cream, the prime consumer is the 7–12-year-old (accounting for 50% of consumption) and the 13–18-year-old (accounting for 30% of consumption). Consumption is universal among all socioeconomic groups, with consumption among large households greater than among small households. The appeal of this product category is strongest in the North Central region of the United States and weakest in the South.

3. *Pricing.* The price for a gallon of ice cream can vary significantly, depending on its quality. Average prices are as follows:

	1970 Retail price/gallon
Premium-price brands (20%)	$2.03
Medium-price brands (54%)	1.56
Low-price brands (26%)	1.12
Scoop	1.00

4. *Seasonality.* Ice cream is consumed throughout the year, with the May–September period alone accounting for 60% of all consumption.

B. Scoop Ice Cream Mix

1. *The product.* Scoop is a freeze-dried mix, made up in chocolate and vanilla flavors, which requires no refrigeration until it is prepared for serving.

2. *Manufacturing.* Production confirms that plant capacity is adequate to meet next year's sales objectives.

TABLE 2.5 (cont.)

V. OPPORTUNITIES AND PROBLEMS

A. Opportunities—Success is anticipated for the following major reasons:
1. A trend toward lower-priced ice creams
2. A trend toward do-it-yourself activities
3. A superior-tasting product
4. The brand's dominant advertising expenditures in the market
5. Trade preference for smaller shelf space and no refrigeration

B. Problems, in rank order, include:
1. Creating awareness of Scoop's benefits
2. Achieving high distribution rates
3. Increasing trial rates
4. Increasing repurchase rates

VI. STRATEGIES

A. Marketing

The objective of the Scoop strategy is to achieve a 2.4% share of the regular ice cream market in dollars and 3.6% in cases. To achieve this objective, the brand's basic marketing strategy is to:

1. Position Scoop as a high-quality ice cream that children prefer, but that costs less than regular ice cream.
2. Continue spending in advertising and promotion at an A to S ratio of 25% to build distribution and trial and to preempt consumer awareness of the product category in terms of Scoop's superior quality.
3. Spend more heavily during the warmer months of the year to capture new users during this period.
4. Maintain a generally higher trade margin and lower retail price than competition in order to capitalize on Scoop's low-cost production process, which refrigerated products cannot match without sacrificing quality.

B. Copy

The objective of Scoop's advertising is to convince mothers of children (ages 7–18) that their families will prefer the taste of Scoop over ready-made ice creams and that it costs less. To achieve this, advertising will:

1. Employ the copy theme, "Make it at home and save money."
2. Emphasize the superior, "home-made" taste of Scoop due to its exclusive freeze-drying process.
3. Attain the high recall demonstration of Scoop's lower retail price versus store-bought ice cream.

C. Media

Scoop's media objective is to reach mothers of young children as often as practical and to provide added frequency during the summer season.
Television will continue to be the brand's medium because it:
1. Delivers efficient messages with broad coverage and good frequency.
2. Provides the best cumulative line frequency against the primary market, i.e., women with children under 18.
3. Permits a high degree of appetite appeal and visualization of the enjoyment of good eating, combined with Scoop's unique demonstrations on product preparation and price relationships.

TABLE 2.5 (cont.)

Network daytime television will be used to deliver year-round reach and frequency at maximum efficiency. Early nighttime TV spots will be used in the summer months to reach a family audience during the high-consumption season. Print media will also be used during the summer months to support the brand's two national consumer promotions scheduled for that period.

D. Promotion

Scoop's promotion objective is to obtain the leader's share of trade merchandising, i.e., in-store displays and advertising features, especially during the high-consumption season. To achieve this, the brand's strategy is to:
1. Maintain trade margins generally above that of regular ice cream brands by responding instantly with case allowances to match that of competition.
2. Offer two display allowances averaging 60¢/case during the periods of May–June and July–August.

VII. TESTS/RESEARCH

	Estimated costs
Focus-group interviews to identify the causes of low consumption in the Southeast.	$12,000
Nielsen retail index to monitor competitive prices and our distribution rates.	25,000
Two consumer telephone surveys to measure recall of Scoop's quality and price and trial rate.	15,000
Total research	$52,000

those superiors who must approve it and those peers and subordinates who will implement it. This selling requires oral and written *communication* skills. These are particularly important skills for the brand manager, who has no line authority over production, advertising, selling, and other departments which will implement the plan. The brand manager has only his or her ability to communicate persuasively. This need to be able to communicate effectively was already noted in the discussion of the skills required of brand managers in the pharmaceutical industry (Chapter 1). This point will be expanded in Chapter 5 when we discuss the brand-management system.

Creative and communication skills are required to complete the Strategy Worksheet and to write the marketing plan. Few individuals excel in all four skills. Cognitive styles and previous training tend to make an individual favor either analysis and synthesis or creation and communication. The individual who has all of these skills is rewarded well.

THE SURGING INTEREST IN STRATEGIC PLANNING During the mid-1970s many companies, such as General Electric, duPont, IBM, Shell, and N. V. Philips Electronics, started or increased their efforts in corporate strategic planning.[6] This sudden interest in corporate strategic planning can be traced to the great increase in the uncertainty and complexity of the social, political, economic, technical, and competitive environments which these firms found themselves in during this period.[7] Longer lead times in implementing plans were required by this uncertainty and by shortages in resources and capital. "Planning is a watchdog of lead time."[8] A firm must pay for failing to take sufficient lead time by the increased cost for expediting a project or it must miss an opportunity altogether.[9] While the required lead times increased, the increased competition from domestic and foreign sources decreased the product life cycle of new products, which made timing even more important.

This surge of interest in planning can blind us to some shortcomings in the planning process. Planning takes considerable resources, especially the time of leading executives. It can become an end in itself and an excuse for not taking action. In 1977, for example, Wall Street analysts concluded that Heublein paid too much attention to marketing and strategic long-range planning "and not enough time to running the store" of its subsidiary, Kentucky Fried Chicken.[10] The result was reduced store traffic and lower profits. The long-range planner, therefore, must not forget that a plan is useless if the firm goes bankrupt in the short run.

SUMMARY The Environmental Analysis Worksheet helps the marketing manager to ask the critical questions, collect relevant data, draw logical conclusions, and then identify problems, subproblems, opportunities, and success factors. A ranking of the subproblems (or success factors in the case of a new opportunity) is the starting point for developing a marketing strategy. A brand manager may critique his or her own analysis by reading down the columns and across the rows, looking for common errors in analysis.

The ranking of subproblems or success factors is facilitated by the computation of a priority index. This index requires estimates of the relative contribution and control of each subproblem or success factor.

The Strategy Worksheet displays on one page marketing goals, present strategies, the proposed strategy, and the effect of the proposal on the profit plan. This full display on one page permits random visualization that will reveal new relationships and new creative alternatives.

Marketing planning requires skills in the analysis and synthesis of facts and in creating and communicating strategies. Individuals who have all of these skills are rare, so they are rewarded well.

DISCUSSION QUESTIONS

1. Why is it important to ask critical questions? What are some additional critical questions that you think should be asked during the analysis of generic demand, brand demand, competition, and public policy?

2. What are some advantages and disadvantages in calculating the priority index for subproblems and success factors?

3. Criticize the worksheets and marketing plan for Scoop Ice Cream. Are the assumptions reasonable? Are there implicit assumptions that need to be made explicit? What *alternative* strategies would you consider?

4. The worksheet approach was applied to a consumer good in this chapter. Do you think it could be applied to an industrial product? Could it be applied to an industrial service organization, such as a consulting firm? If no, why not? If yes, would any changes be necessary?

5. What is the difference between subproblems and success factors?

6. The planning outlines for R. J. Reynolds and Celanese Corporation are shown in Tables 2.6 and 2.7. The R. J. Reynolds Co. uses its outline for its tobacco products. Celanese manufactures chemicals. Compare and contrast the two outlines. What are the differences in the industries of the two firms that require a difference in the emphasis in the plan?

TABLE 2.6 Outline of an annual brand marketing plan for RJR (formerly the R. J. Reynolds Tobacco Company)*

I. STATEMENT OF BUSINESS
  A. Brief summary of brand's performance during current year
  B. Share trend of brand
  C. Volume trend of brand

II. FINANCIAL SUMMARY
  A. Brief summary of brand's current financial picture—current year versus next year
  B. Brand's P&L for current year and next year
  C. Brand's P&L for latest five-year period

III. MARKETING PLAN
  A. Statement of brand's marketing objective
  B. Statement of brand's marketing strategy—how the marketing objective will be achieved
  C. Marketing rationale—supporting points for marketing strategy

IV. ADVERTISING PLAN
  A. Statement of brand's advertising copy objective
  B. Statement of brand's advertising copy strategy
  C. Advertising rationale—support for strategy

V. MEDIA PLAN
  A. Objective
  B. Strategy
  C. Rationale
  D. Request for funds and itemized budget

VI. SALES PROMOTION PLAN
  A. Objectives
  B. Strategy
  C. Rationale
  D. Request for funds and itemized budget

VII. BACK-UP MATERIAL

(Supporting data for foregoing section)

* D. S. Hopkins, *The Short-Term Marketing Plan*, Conference Board Report No. 565 (New York: Conference Board, 1972), Reynolds, p. 26. Used with permission.

TABLE 2.7 Celanese general outline for developing the marketing plan*

I. INFORMATION BASE
  A. Economic indicators (e.g., GNP, FRB)—five- to ten-year trends and projections
    1. Significance to this industry
  B. Major industry, market, and competitive trends and characteristics, including:
    1. Total industry potential (domestic, government, export)—five-year historical record
      a) Identification of major end-use markets and their individual characteristics (growing, static, or declining; seasonal or cyclical)—five-year history of volume for each major end use
      b) Consuming locations

TABLE 2.7 **(cont.)**

    2. Characteristics of current and expected producers
       a) Comparison of captive or integrated versus noncaptive markets
       b) Past and expected future performance (i.e., capacity versus utilization)
       c) Share of market for each competitor
       d) Producing locations
       e) Magnitude and importance of foreign competition
    3. Special requirements of the market (e.g., quality, package, service)
    4. Trends in marketing practices for the product
       a) Direct versus distributor sales
       b) Commodity versus brand or trade name
       c) Use of advertising and merchandising
    5. Pricing and price stability—five-year history
    6. Competition from unlike materials (e.g., metal versus plastic)
    7. Trends in cost, sales, and margin relationships
  C. Company's current and relative marketing position for this or similar products
    1. Past performance versus plan
    2. Past share of market
    3. Capacity versus past sales
    4. Sales by end use
    5. Sales by profit classification; comparison to other segments of the product line
  D. What it takes to succeed in this industry with this product
  E. Company marketing strengths and weaknesses—product line, distribution, operational, support functions (i.e., technical service, merchandising)

II. BASIC ASSUMPTIONS

  A. Five-year industry forecast—estimated growth of total market, segments, major end uses or product types
  B. Five-year price predictions—anticipated changes in price levels and probable impact on product sales
  C. Expected changes in the composition of the competitive structure of the market
  D. Probability of significant technical innovations
  E. Conclusions—an analysis of how these external assumptions will affect the product line

III. STATEMENT OF STRATEGY (long and short term)

  A. Distribution techniques
  B. Pricing
  C. Profitability
  D. End-use emphasis
  E. Share of market

IV. MARKETING OBJECTIVES

  A. Basic objectives—volume, price, profit, share of market—for five following years (including the planning year, by month)
  B. Subgoals—those goals which, when attained, are a step toward achieving the marketing objective

V. PROGRAMS

  A. Programs (the specific action steps necessary to accomplish the marketing objective) may include sales, advertising, merchandising, product development, or support by other departments, such as manufacturing or technical
  B. Each part of a program needs approximate completion dates, the assignment of definite responsibility, and an indication of costs

TABLE 2.7 (cont.)

VI. FINANCIAL SUMMARY

A. The total costs of marketing, administration, support, and improvement programs to achieve subgoals and objectives

VII. MEASUREMENT OF PERFORMANCE

A. A method to evaluate progress toward objectives, with a time schedule, is required

The Development of Marketing Objectives and Plans, A Symposium, Experiences in Marketing Management, No. 3 (New York: Conference Board, 1963), p. 22. Reprinted by permission.

NOTES

1. C. E. Smith, "The Content and Process of Strategy." Paper delivered at a conference on corporate strategic planning, sponsored jointly by the Institute of Management Science and the Operations Research Society of America, New Orleans, February 28 to March 2, 1977.

2. D. S. Hopkins, *The Short-Term Marketing Plan,* Conference Board Report No. 565 (New York: Conference Board, 1972).

3. These worksheets are similar to the balance sheets and income statements in accounting. These basic documents give an overview of the accounting process, and parts are expanded to illustrate accounting concepts.

4. This case is abstracted from the "Scoop Ice Cream Mix" case, which was developed for the Association of National Advertisers (ANA) by Booz, Allen and Hamilton, Inc., for use in ANA Seminars on Creative Advertising. The case material is copyrighted by the ANA and appears in its publication, *Effective Marketing Management,* by F. Beaven Ennis, copyrighted 1973. Permission to abstract the case and use parts of the marketing plan in the above text has been granted by Mr. Herbert A. Ahlgren, Vice President of ANA. This permission is gratefully acknowledged. Some data have been modified to emphasize particular points of marketing. Therefore, the solutions discussed later in this text will differ from those in the ANA text.

5. *Ibid.*

6. Statements made by the corporate strategic planners of these companies at the Corporate Strategic Planning Conference cited in note 1.

7. M. van Beusekom, Director of Corporate Strategic Planning, N. V. Philips Electronics, "Strategic Planning at Philips." (Paper delivered at the conference cited in note 1.)

8. *Ibid.*

9. *Ibid.*

10. J. J. O'Connor, "Kentucky Fried Chicken Bone in Heublein's Throat?" *Advertising Age,* March 7, 1977, p. 3.

SUGGESTED READINGS

Lorange, P., and R. F. Vancil, *Strategic Planning Systems* (Englewood Cliffs, N.J.: Prentice-Hall, 1977).

Steiner, G. A., "Rise of the Corporate Planner," *Harvard Business Review* (September-October 1970): 133–139.

Winer, L., "Are You Really Planning Your Marketing?" *Journal of Marketing* 29 (January 1965): 1–8.

ENVIRONMENTAL ANALYSIS WORKSHEET

Environmental elements	Facts	Assumptions or research needed	Conclusions
Organizational values, objectives, and policies (4)			
Organizational design (5)			
Situation			
Generic demand (6)			
Brand demand (7)			
Competition (9)			
Public policy (10)			
Opportunities (2)			
Problems			

MARKETING PLAN (CONSUMER PRODUCT)

Current performance
Recommendations
Effect of recommendations on income
Situation analysis
Opportunities and problems
Strategies
Tests and research
Supporting documents
   Comparative budgets
   Media allocation schedule
   Promotion control sheet

Opportunities and problems in rank order to importance
1.
2.
.
n.

	Current strategy	Alternatives and recommended strategy	Estimated Effect
Demand strategy			
Generic			
Brand			
Strategic goals			
Financial			
Marketing			
Marketing-mix strategies			
Product (12)			
Pricing (13)			
Channel and logistics (14)			
Advertising and promotional (15)			
Sales management (16)			
Research (3)			
Profit plan			
Evaluation and control (19)			

CHAPTER 3

CHAPTER 3

Marketing Information for Management Decisions

LEARNING OBJECTIVES   After studying this chapter you should:

1. Know how the marketing manager uses information to answer critical questions.
2. Know how frequently information must be gathered for the various steps in marketing planning and some of the usual sources of information. (If you know statistical techniques, you should know the various methods needed at each planning stage.)
3. Be aware of the large amount of information that is needed to develop a new product.
4. Appreciate why a survey is among the last of the data sources.
5. Understand the importance of forecasting and some methods which are frequently used.
6. Begin to develop the ability to create alternatives and use decision trees to organize information for choosing among alternatives.
7. Be aware of the process for determining if research is worth the cost.
8. Know how to reduce the cost of research.
9. Be able to define and use the following concepts:

Marketing information systems	Current dollars	Product life cycles
Secondary, subscription, and primary sources of data	Constant dollars	Alternatives
	Triangulation	Decision trees
	Interactive computer models	Personal risk functions
		Expected value

SOME ANALYTICAL QUESTIONS FOR OPENERS

1. What information will the marketing planner need?
2. How frequently will this information be required?
3. What are the sources of this information?
4. How will the data be analyzed?

THE NEED FOR A MARKETING INFORMATION SYSTEM   A sophisticated marketing planner must be able to ask the right questions *and* must know where to get valid and reliable information to help answer those questions. In this chapter we will relate the planning questions from the previous chapter to the problem of building a marketing information system. An information system is based on the answers to five questions: (1) What information is required? (2) How frequently will we need the information? (3) What are the sources of information? (4) How are the resulting data analyzed? (5) Is the information worth the cost?

This chapter takes the marketing planner's viewpoint toward marketing research, not that of the marketing researcher. The goal is to make the planner a sophisticated *user* and *contractor* of research. The planner will know his or her needs and the limitations of research. An understanding of the roles and limitations of research will enable a marketing manager to work more effectively with researchers.

Table 3.1 summarizes some of the questions that must be asked at each stage of planning. The second column of the table suggests the frequency for reviewing these

TABLE 3.1   Informational needs for the planning process

Planning questions[1]	Frequency of review	Illustrative sources of information[2]	Methods of analysis[3]
Environmental Analysis Worksheet[4] *Organizational values, objectives, and policies* (4)			
What are the values and objectives of those persons who are in control?	Infrequently; during reorganization	Outside consultants who use individual and group depth interviewing, tests of values, and specification of objectives	Subjective methods, using organizational theories; statistical tests of significance
Marketing organizations (5)			
How are resources, responsibility, and authority organized?	During an occasional organizational audit	Analysis of communication networks, workloads, and productivity by inside or outside consultants	Flow charts; subjective analysis of quality and quantity of work
Situation analysis Generic demand: (6 and 8)			
What are the unmet needs? What are the profiles of users and nonusers? What are the trend, cycle, seasonal, and fashion time patterns? What are the segments for the product type?	At least annually; continuous monitoring is ideal	Secondary sources; unstructured depth individual or group interviews; surveys	Forecasting methods, including regression and econometrics; subjective analysis; segmentation analyses including discriminant analysis, cluster analysis, factor analysis, and AID
Brand demand: (7 and 8)			
What are the trends in our brand? In competitors? What are our brand benefits? What are the levels of awareness and preferences for our brand? What is our distribution rate? What are the segments for the brand?	At least annually; continuous monitoring during early stages of product life cycle and in highly competitive markets	Internal data; syndicated sources; proprietary market research	From simple tabulations to models of brand switching; segmentation analysis, including the methods noted above, plus multidimensional scaling
Competition: (9)			
What are the industry success factors, capacities, and competitive structures? How is our brand positioned in benefit space? What are our strengths and weaknesses?	At least annually, more frequently in highly competitive industries	Trade journals; industry studies; consultants; proprietary research	Economic market analysis; brand mapping; historical analysis; experience curves

TABLE 3.1 **(cont.)**

Planning questions[1]	Frequency of review	Illustrative sources of information[2]	Methods of analysis[3]
Public policy: (10) How do the antitrust laws, regulatory agencies, the consumer movement, and environmental concerns affect our strategies?	At least annually; the sensitivity of strategies to public policies varies among companies; monitoring should be continuous in some cases	Recent court decisions; recent decisions by regulatory agencies, such as the Federal Trade Commission, speeches by key regulators; agency program planning budgets	Content analysis for early warning of a change in policy doctrine or interpretation
Strategy Worksheet *Marketing-mix strategies* (11) **Product: (12)** Does the product need to be repositioned? Should it be dropped? Can costs be reduced? Does it meet needs adequately?	Information is needed continually during the early stages of a product's life cycle; at maturity, annual reviews will be sufficient; rapid changes in technology will increase the frequency of reviews	Blind product tests in the laboratory or home; packaging tests; concept testing	From subjective analysis to preference models to predict brand share; relevant multivariate statistical methods include analysis of variance, conjoint measurement, and multidimensional scaling
Price: (13) What is the price elasticity? What price must we charge to break even? For a given ROI? What are competitors' costs and prices?	At least annually, with more frequent reviews at the late stages of the product life cycle	Historical data for the firm and industry; pricing experiments in the laboratory or store	Regression; analysis of variance; conjoint measurement
Channel: (14) Which channels are the most productive? Is a new channel strategy needed? Should we drop outlets?	At least annually	Company historical cost and sales data; productivity experiments by product, channel, and customer type	Regression; analysis of variance
Advertising: (15) What copy theme should we use? When does a theme wear out? Should we use print or electronic media? Which ones? How frequently?	Annually or when market conditions require a more frequent change	Historical data; experiments	Regression; analysis of variance
Personal selling: (16) How should we recruit, train, motivate, and compensate the sales force? How should territories be determined?	At least annually	Sales statistics, including sales, calls, costs, and percent of sales closed/sales presentations; call reports	Tabulations; averages; ratios; computer simulations; models to optimize sales calls
Research: (3) Are the data worth the cost of research?	Annual for syndicated sources; require of all ad hoc research projects	Historical data, including opinions; small projects to estimate cost and benefits	Cost/benefit analysis; Bayesian analysis of the worth of additional information

TABLE 3.1 (cont.)

Planning questions[1]	Frequency of review	Illustrative sources of information[2]	Methods of analysis[3]
Profit plan			
What are our sales and costs? What are the trends in costs? Do learning and experience curves apply? (9) Should data be adjusted for inflation? What is the payback period?	At least annually	Historical internal and industry data; engineering estimates; trade journals; trade associations	Accounting and financial methods
Evaluation			
Are we achieving our corporate strategic objectives?	At least annually	Sales, costs, share of market internal data	Tabulation
Are we achieving our marketing tactical goals?	Depends on the product and industry; in competitive industries review should be weekly	Internal data for sales, costs, share of market, awareness, brand preferences; distribution rates	Tabulation; tracking graphs
Control			
How do we implement and control the performance of the marketing plan?	At least quarterly reviews; continuous in competitive industries, new-product introductions, or after major changes in strategies	The human element is crucial, which defies full quantification; data for evaluation will be used for control	Budgeting procedures; PERT; Gantt charts; employee evaluation procedures

1. This list of questions only illustrates those that must be asked by planners. The specific questions will vary according to industry and products.
2. For an annotated bibliography of more than 150 sources, *see* G. D. Hughes, *Demand Analysis for Marketing Decisions* (Homewood, Ill.: Richard D. Irwin, 1973), Appendix A.
3. For a nontechnical discussion of these methods, *see* the appendix to this chapter.
4. The number in parentheses is the chapter in which this topic will be discussed in detail.

planning questions, which in turn indicates how frequently the marketing information system must supply data at each stage of planning. The third and fourth columns illustrate the sources of information and the methods of analysis that are used. The informational needs of planners and the sources of data vary so widely across products, services, and industries that generalizations are impossible. Thus the entries in Table 3.1 should be viewed as a brief overview. Additional sources of data will be illustrated in later chapters.

THE FREQUENCY OF INFORMATION NEEDS

Conditions that Increase the Frequency   Reading down the second column of Table 3.1 reveals the wide range of frequency for gathering marketing information. Reviews of *organizational* values, objectives, and policies are infrequent, so their measurement occurs only during those infrequent reviews of a company's mission or organization. In contrast, information for *brand demand* analysis or *product* strategies may be required weekly, especially when a product is in the early stages of its life cycle or when it is in a competitive market situation.

An increase in the activities of the Justice Department, the Federal Trade Commission, consumer movements, and environmental concerns will increase the frequency with which the *public policy* dimensions of the marketing plan must be reviewed. Rapid changes in technology can make a product obsolete. Thus in industries where rapid changes take place, it will be necessary to increase the frequency with which *product* information is gathered.

Information Needed for New Products Information is vital for new-product development, introduction, forecasting, and monitoring. To illustrate its role in these stages we will examine the ten marketing research steps that are used by E. R. Squibb & Sons, Inc., a pharmaceutical firm.[1]

1. **Identifying attractive opportunity areas.** Identification of opportunities requires the identification of present and future needs and means for meeting these needs. Because the development and introduction of a new drug may take ten years of effort, the pharmaceutical researcher must estimate future needs and future technology that could make a drug obsolete before it is introduced. The research techniques available include *Delphic* studies and *futuristic* forecasting. Delphic studies have experts estimate the probability of future events, such as a successful drug for cancer. Futuristic forecasting involves an expected-value approach to forecasting. (An expected value is the probability that an event will occur times the value of the event occurring.)

2. **Designing the ideal product.** Surveys are generally used to identify those product attributes or benefits that should be in a product. Multidimensional scaling is used to create a map of respondents' perceptions of brands. Competitive brands appear close to each other on the map. (We will see examples and applications of this technique in Chapters 7 and 9.)

3. **Testing the product concept.** The salient attributes of the "ideal product" are described to small groups of respondents in *focus-group sessions*. Their reactions give direction to future research.

4. **Identifying the most attractive promotional targets.** This phase is known as *market segmentation*. The task is to identify the profiles (age, speciality, location, etc.) of physicians who prescribe in the product category being considered (e.g., flu shots). Profiles of heavy, medium, and light prescribers give direction to the promotional strategies for each of these segments.

5. **Developing the trademark.** A good trademark is an important part of a communication strategy. Squibb uses *creative sessions* that stimulate the members of the creative committee to generate trademark ideas that will be submitted to search and registration procedures.

6. **Preparing the economic evaluation.** The Marketing Research Department provides data and recommendations for five-year projections of market trends, market shares, and competitive activity. This information is used to estimate the financial contribution that the new product will generate.

7. **Testing the communications program.** Package designs and medical-journal advertising are pretested, using a variety of techniques, including the *eye camera* method. This method traces respondents' eye movements as they examine a package or advertisement to identify areas of major interest.

8. **Test marketing.** When appropriate, test markets are used. (Test marketing is discussed more fully in Chapter 12.)

9. **Sales forecasting.** Forecasting begins in step 6 and is refined with updated information throughout the entire product life cycle. (See Appendix 3.2 for a discussion of several approaches for forecasting.)

10. **Development of a monitoring system.** The final step in the process for developing new products is the design of a monitoring system to provide appropriate feedback on the progress of new products.

SOURCES OF INFORMATION In building an information system, the marketing planner will need to consider a variety of sources of information. These sources may be divided into three classifications—*secondary*, *subscription*, and *primary*. We will discuss them here in general terms. It would be impossible to review all of them for all industries, because of space limitations and because they change so rapidly. There are more than 150 secondary and subscription sources that are relevant to the marketing planner.[2]

Secondary Sources Secondary sources include data that have been collected for some purpose other than the problem at hand. For example, the United States Department of Commerce, Bureau of the Census, collects data on population, housing, retailing, wholesaling, and manufacturing. These data rarely answer the marketing question fully, but they do provide an inexpensive rough cut that gives direction to more refined methods. In Chapters 6, 7, and 8 we will see how these and other secondary data are used to conduct a demand analysis. *Internal* secondary data include a company's accounting and sales records. *External* secondary data are frequently available in business libraries, which make them very low-cost in comparison with subscription and primary data.

Subscription Sources Subscription sources include a wide variety of data that are collected by research firms for special purposes and are made available to marketers for a fee. In some cases the term "subscription" is very appropriate, because the data are collected by trade publications. The "Survey of Buying Power," which appears annually in a July issue of *Sales and Marketing Management*, is an example. This survey provides data on state, county, and city retail sales, population, income, and buying-power indexes. It can be very helpful in estimating market potentials, selecting channels of distribution, and allocating promotional expenditures.

Extensive surveys conducted by W. R. Simmons and Axion Research measure product usage, brand preference, and media usage by consumer profiles (age, sex, income, education, and in some cases social-psychological dimensions) that are relevant to brand preference. The data from *Target Group Index* data, the publication of Axion Research, will be used in Chapter 6 to illustrate a demand analysis for soft drinks.

Audits of products as they move through retail stores provide the planner with measures of the success of his or her strategy and plan. The food store and drug store audits by the A. C. Nielsen Company are well known to planners in the food and drug industries. Computerized warehouse inventories in food stores have made it possible to audit movements out of the warehouses. Selling Areas–Marketing, Inc., provides its SAMI Reports in selected markets which account for more than 70 percent of the food store sales in the United States. Pharmaceutical firms use audits of prescriptions filled by pharmacists to track the success of a drug's marketing plan. Store audits provide information about competitive product movement and competitive promotional efforts. These audits do not provide insight into the profiles of consumers by usage rate or their brand preferences.

Panel data require the cooperating respondent to record all purchases for a specified period of time. The Market Research Corporation of America (MRCA) panel requires 7500 housewives to record their purchases in a weekly diary. These data include the profiles of consumers, which can be very useful when studying their brand-switching behavior. Cooperating physicians record all of their activities with their patients for a period of 48 hours.

Daniel Starch and Staff provides data on readership of magazines; A. C. Nielsen provides data on readership and television viewing.

The field of marketing research has reached a state of maturity that provides the planner with a wide variety of research sources to consider. But these sources will not always meet the planner's needs, and she or he will have to do primary research. One disadvantage of subscription sources is that they are also available to competitors. Some marketers buy this type of research so that they will know as much about their competitors as their competitors know about them.

Primary Sources Primary data are collected to answer specific marketing questions. A survey is frequently used as a primary source of information. Focus-group interviews, a qualitative approach, are used to identify subproblems. A structured questionnaire is then given to a random sample of respondents to find solutions to these problems.

The focus-group interview process allows members of the group to provide some of the stimuli for discussion. It gives unstructured, rich data in the language of the consumers. It can be inexpensive and fast. Subjects for these interviews are not selected randomly, and there is no structured measuring instrument, such as a questionnaire. The interviewer must be an expert in group interviewing *and* thoroughly familiar with the client's marketing situation in order to summarize the data into a meaningful report.

After the problem has been identified, it is necessary to identify the variables that are relevant to its solution. Additional qualitative research, case studies, and behavioral science theories are used at this step in the research process. Ackoff notes that "*one cannot specify what information is needed for decision making until an explanatory model of the decision process and the system involved in it has been constructed and tested.*"[3] To illustrate this point, Ackoff provides an example of an oil company that built a model to estimate the sales volume of future service stations. It considered 70 variables and built a multiple-regression model that had 35 statistically significant variables. A later research project built a model using the variable "perceived lost time of the customer," which replaced 33 of the 35 variables. Thus a better model of the consumers' decision processes greatly reduced the need for data.

To test hypotheses, such as the effectiveness of a price change, it will be necessary to design a study that will have experimental and control groups. The price will be changed in the experimental group but not in the control group. A comparison of sales to those two groups will reveal the effect of a price change. A statistical test known as *analysis of variance* is frequently used to determine if there is a statistically significant difference between the experimental and control groups. Experiments may be done in laboratory situations or in stores. In the case of grocery products, the laboratory situations include a simulated supermarket. This arrangement has the advantage of being faster and cheaper than conducting tests in the stores. It also has the advantage of not revealing your strategy to your competitors.

Personal interviews, mail questionnaires, and telephone interviews are used to gather survey information. The complexity of the problem and the cooperativeness of respondents play an important part in deciding which method should be used. Recently there has been a shift from personal interviews to telephone interviews in consumer research because of the increasing costs and the decreasing response rates of personal interviews.

Primary research may be conducted totally by the firm or with outside assistance. The research may be supervised by qualified researchers within the firm, but outside research organizations may be used to provide expertise and capacity. Or, the research may be supervised and executed totally by an outside organization. In the last two instances the client and researcher must work closely together. Some key steps in which the client should be included in the design and execution of a study are the definition of the problem, the development of the measuring instrument (e.g., the questionnaire), the determination of the types of analysis that will be used, and the way in which the findings will be presented. By cooperating at these key points, the client and the researcher will strive toward a common goal—a better marketing strategy.

Steps in a Mail Survey You can always spot the naive marketing manager. He or she is the first person to recommend doing a survey. The experienced manager, by contrast, will attempt to use existing data before specifying the expensive and time-consuming process of survey research. Existing data include those within the firm and in published sources that may be found in library and government sources.

To illustrate the steps of a survey and their interrelationships, we will examine the details of a survey of nurses. This case has been chosen to illustrate how marketers are able to assist nonprofit institutions, such as hospitals.

The problem was stated by a staff physician as follows: "Can marketing research help us with our nursing problem?" Further investigation led to the following refinement: "How can we recruit nurses and then retain them after they are on the staff?" A literature search revealed that this problem was common to many hospitals, but there was no common solution. Thus a survey was necessary for the client.

The flow chart in Fig. 3.1 illustrates the steps required in the nurse survey. These steps and their interrelationships are typical of a survey. Each box describes the step, and the number in parentheses indicates the number of weeks required to complete the step. Note that many of the steps may be completed concurrently, thereby shortening the overall time required.

The research project begins with a definition of the problem. The client and researcher must agree on the definition. The client should share all available information with the researcher. An inexperienced client may be tempted to withhold information "to test the validity of the findings." But such withholding will only increase the cost of gathering information, because existing information will reduce the sample size and therefore the cost of the survey.

After the client and the researcher agree on the ranking of the subproblems, the research proceeds down three tracks simultaneously—field work, questionnaire design, and data analysis. These tracks interrelate along the way and finally converge when the first computer runs are made. These runs are the first attempt to use the newly generated data to solve the subproblems. The plan of tabulation and analysis will suggest new questions and new analysis that could not be anticipated during the original design of the analysis. After a second analysis of the data, the questions are answered and the data are reduced to tables and figures. The final report is in written and oral

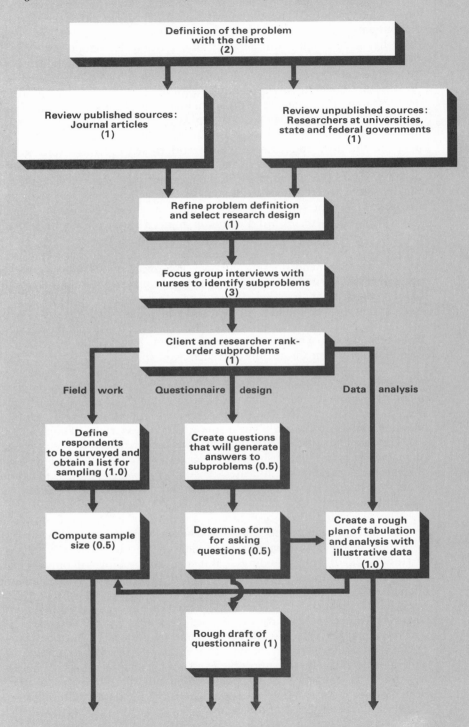

Fig. 3.1 Flow chart for a mail survey (weeks for completion appear in parentheses).

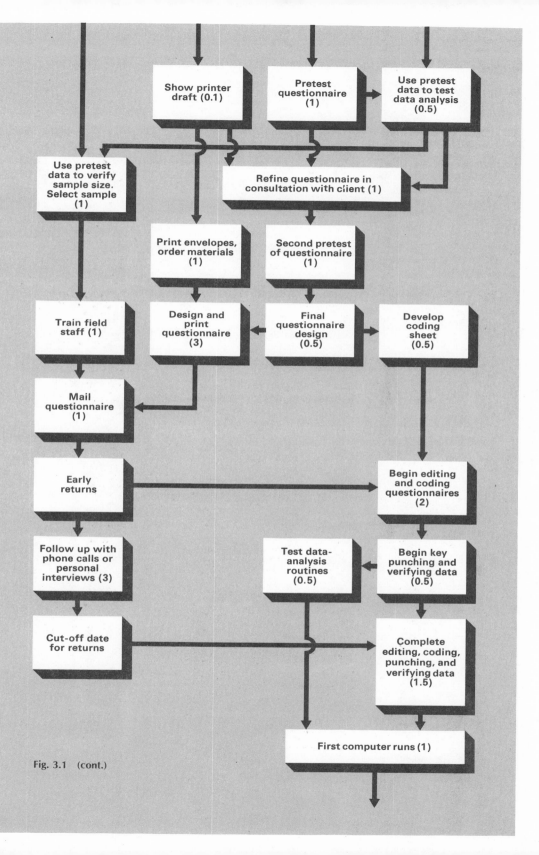

Fig. 3.1 (cont.)

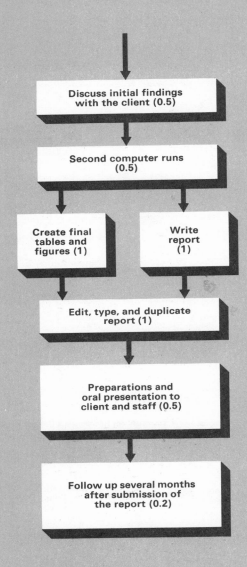

Fig. 3.1 (cont.)

forms. Several months after the final report, the researcher contacts the client to see if any additional assistance is necessary to implement the findings and to learn of applications of the findings.

When contracting for research, a marketing manager may use a flow chart like that in Fig. 3.1 as a control device to see if the survey is on schedule and within budget estimates. By adding the completion dates for each event, the budget estimate, and the person in charge of the event to Fig. 3.1, it is possible to monitor the progress of the survey.

This study took about 25 weeks to complete. For some problems a telephone survey with short questions may be used. Some research firms stand ready to do overnight phone surveys so that their clients may have the answers the next day. Thus the duration of the survey depends on the complexity of the problem being studied.

FORECASTING

Administrative Uses for Forecasts   Forecasts play a key role in all administrative functions of a firm. Top management requires forecasts for overall planning. The *finance* department needs them to estimate cash flows and control expenses and budgets; the *marketing* manager, to formulate goals and strategies. Forecasts are necessary to measure performance, compensate salespeople, and control the marketing system. *Production* uses forecasts to schedule production and maintain optimal inventories. Forecasts enable the *purchasing* department to make purchases on favorable terms. *Personnel* departments use forecasts to hire and train personnel. *Engineering* departments may use forecasts to schedule maintenance and repair of production equipment. Thus the development of a brand sales forecast should be regarded as an important undertaking.

Forecasting Methods   A study of forecasting methods by the National Industrial Conference Board identified five methods.[4] The jury of *executive opinion* combines the subjective estimates of top executives. The *sales force composite method* draws on the knowledge that the sales force has of local conditions. *Users' expectations* require users to make subjective estimates of their needs for the coming year. (This method is more appropriate for industrial goods than for consumer goods.) Because these three methods are subjective, they share the common limitation of personal bias. *Time-series analysis* uses historical data to identify trend, cycle, seasonal, and random effects, on the assumption that history will repeat itself. Critics of time-series analysis say that this is like speeding down the highway while looking only in the rearview mirror—all is fine so long as the road does not turn. *Mathematical and correlation techniques* relate sales to other measurable variables where the other variables either *lead* sales or can be forecasted reliably. The main assumption in the mathematical technique is that the functional relationships among the variables will remain the same over time, thereby giving reliable forecasts.

In practice, the planner should not rely on a single method. A good forecaster uses several methods and reconciles the results, in the same way that a navigator takes bearings on several landmarks to establish his or her position. Figure 3.2 illustrates the concept of *triangulation* as it applies to a navigator sailing down the coast. The radio tower represents historical data and gives only one reference point. The hotel gives a second reference point—current data. The bearing on the lighthouse is future data and therefore should receive more weight than the other two bearings. These three bearings form a triangle, because there is a lack of precision in navigating, as there is in forecasting. The navigator, assuming that he or she is in the center of triangle and given the fact that the peninsula is dead ahead, will want to repeat the measures, perhaps

Fig. 3.2   Navigation by triangulation.

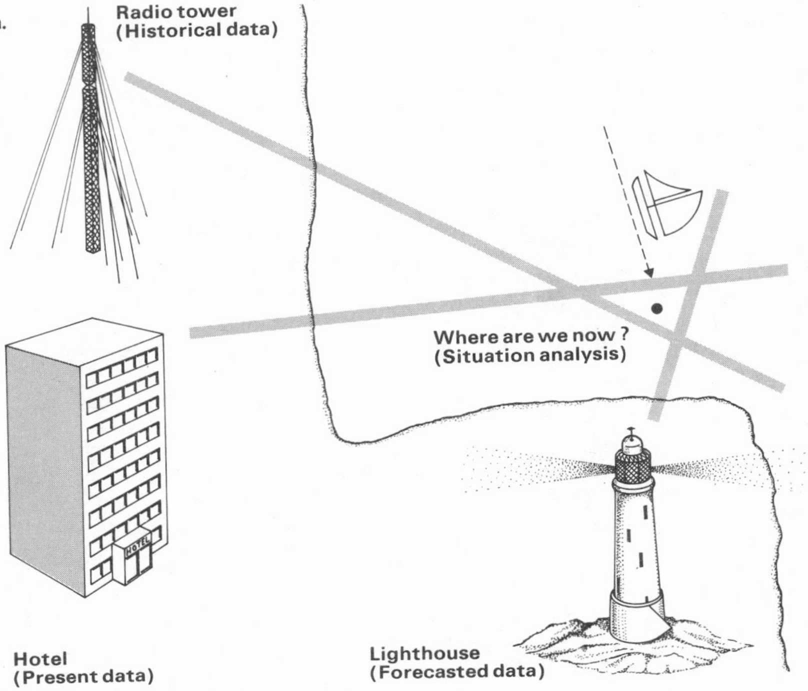

Radio tower
(Historical data)

Where are we now ?
(Situation analysis)

Hotel
(Present data)

Lighthouse
(Forecasted data)

adding new bearings, in order to take appropriate action. The similarities between this example and sales forecasting are obvious.

The Conference Board identified nine steps used in forecasting sales:

1. Determine the purpose of the forecast;
2. Divide the company product line into homogeneous groups;
3. Determine the factors affecting sales of each product group and their relative importance;
4. Choose the forecasting methods best suited for the job;
5. Gather and analyze all available data;
6. Check and cross-check analysis and deductions;
7. Make assumptions about factors that cannot be measured or forecasted;
8. Convert deductions and assumptions into specific product and territorial forecasts;
9. Review and revise.

"The selection of a method depends on many factors—the context of the forecast, the relevance and availability of historical data, the degree of accuracy desirable, the time period to be forecast, the cost/benefit (or *value*) of the forecast to the company, and the time available for making the analysis."[5]

The concept of a *product life cycle* has many applications in marketing management. The S-shaped curve in Fig. 3.3 illustrates three stages in this cycle—product introduction, rapid growth, and steady state. The sales forecaster must identify that point in time when the product "takes off" and the percentage of the market that is using the product when the curve levels to form the steady state. The forecaster must also determine the

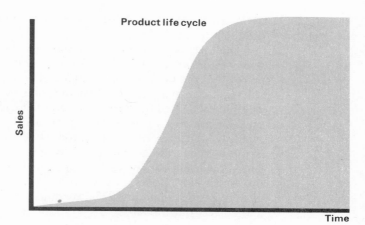

Fig. 3.3 Marketing decisions and forecasting techniques that are determined by the product life cycle. (J. C. Chambers, S. K. Mullick, and D. D. Smith, "How to Choose the Right Forecasting Technique," *Harvard Business Review* (July–August 1971): 45–74. Reprinted by permission. Copyright © 1971 by the President and Fellows of Harvard College; all rights reserved.)

Stages in the life cycle	Product development	Introduction	Rapid growth	Steady state
Typical decisions	Amount of development effort Product design Business strategies	Optimum facility size Marketing strategies, including distribution and pricing	Facilities expansion Marketing strategies Production planning	Promotions Specials Pricing Production planning Inventories
Forecasting techniques	Delphi Method Historical analysis of comparable products Priority pattern analysis Input - output analysis Panel consensus	Consumer surveys Tracking and warning systems Market tests Experimental designs	Statistical techniques for identifying turning points Tracking and warning systems Market surveys Intention-to-buy surveys	Time series analysis and projection Causal and econometric models Market surveys for tracking and warning Life-cycle analysis

rate of growth, or slope of the curve, during the rapid growth stage of the cycle. These three bits of information give the curve its S shape.

The position of a product in its life cycle determines the kinds of decision the manager must make. Figure 3.3 illustrates the typical decisions that must be made during the stages of product development, introduction, rapid growth, and steady state. Each of these decisions in turn requires a different forecasting technique. Techniques that are appropriate at each stage in the life cycle are illustrated in the lower part of this figure.

When choosing a forecasting technique, the planner should consider the accuracy of the technique, its ability to identify turning points, the data required, its cost, and the time required to implement the method. Chambers, Mullick, and Smith have provided an excellent comparison of techniques according to these characteristics. Nine of the methods used frequently in sales forecasting are summarized in Appendix 3.2, which will help the planner to evaluate the costs and benefits of forecasting techniques.[6]

FORECASTING MODELS

A Simple Linear Regression Linear regression is a simple method for forecasting that is used by many firms to estimate linear time trends. A linear time trend assumes that there are no influences such as business cycles or seasonal effects. To illustrate this method, as well as the need to use it with caution, we will examine how it could be used to forecast the production of petroleum.

The first task is to identify an independent variable that may be closely associated with petroleum production. Gross national product (GNP) was selected, because petroleum is so important to so many of our industries. Therefore, an increase in GNP will require an increase in petroleum production. A line was fitted to the data in Fig. 3.4. The equation fitted by the least-squares method of regression is shown at the bottom of the figure. It was a good fit, as is indicated by $R^2 = 0.956$; in other words, 95.6 percent of the variance in petroleum production is associated with the variance in GNP. Before we congratulate ourselves, however, we must examine a scatter diagram of the actual data and the forecasting line. In Fig. 3.4 we see that between 1972 and 1975 our forecasting model greatly overestimated petroleum production. There was a 35 percent overestimate in 1975. We must find an explanation for this overestimation and correct our model.

An examination of Fig. 3.4 suggests several changes in our model. Instead of fitting a straight line, we could fit a curve. Fitting a curve may improve the results, but we must have a reason for using a curve. For instance, was there a change in automobiles or driving habits that would have drastically reduced the demand for petroleum products? Because there was no evidence to support such a drastic change between 1972 and 1975, there must be another explanation.

Perhaps inflation is an explanation. This was a period of double-digit inflation, and

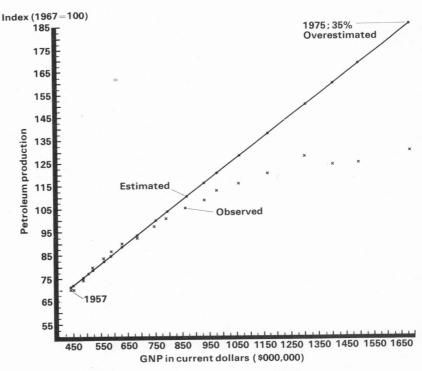

Fig. 3.4   Actual and estimated petroleum production index (1967 = 100) with gross national product (GNP) in current dollars.

Petroleum production index $=30.4+0.092$ GNP (current \$); $r^2=0.956$
Technical note: The high r^2 is due to time series autocorrelation.

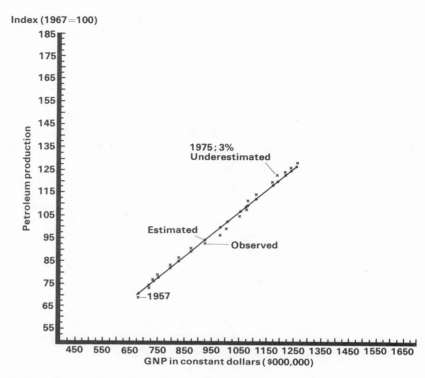

Index (1967=100)

1975; 3% Underestimated

Estimated

Observed

x—1957

GNP in constant dollars ($000,000)

Fig. 3.5   Actual and estimated petroleum production index with gross national product (GNP) in constant dollars.

Petroleum production index=3.6+0.099 GNP (1972 dollars); r^2=0.981.
Technical note: The high r^2 is due to time series autocorrelation.

GNP is expressed in current dollars. Thus more dollars would be required for the same amount of petroleum, which would place the observed data points to the right of the estimating line. To test this explanation and to improve our ability to forecast, we must deflate the current GNP data to constant dollars. Figure 3.5 uses constant—1958—dollars for GNP. The curve fits slightly better—from 95.6 percent to 98.1 percent of the variance. The dramatic difference is in the plot of the observed data in relation to the estimating line. The worst estimate for both models was 1975, but using *constant* dollars yielded only a 3 percent underestimate, whereas *current* dollars resulted in a 35 percent overestimate.

This example emphasizes several important points in using linear regression to forecast. First, failure to consider the effects of inflation will produce misleading forecasts. Second, the old dictum of "correlation does not mean causation" has been demonstrated. The high correlation, as expressed in terms of R^2, did not ensure a good prediction. In testing a forecasting model, one must compare the observed events with the predicted ones.

More Complex Models   Inflation is not the only cause for adjustment. Special promotions to retailers or a new advertising campaign must be reflected in the forecasting model. Researchers at Corning Glass Works thought that one product line was insensitive to the business cycle, until adjustments were made to account for the effect of heavy promotions during these periods.[7] To account for many influences, such as the effects of promotion, inventories in the channels of distribution, and external economic effects, it is necessary to use more than a single equation. Econometric modeling is a multiple-equation approach, and this type of model has been found to be more effective for medium-term (several years) forecasting.[8]

Corporate forecasters are predicting a range instead of a forecast because of the increasing uncertainty in economic and competitive conditions.[9] Although a range forecast is more realistic, it does complicate planning, because either strategies must be developed along the range or the marketing manager must make value judgments about the future.[10] If plans are developed along the range of the forecast, the plans not selected for immediate implementation become contingency plans.

ORGANIZING THE MARKETING INFORMATION SYSTEM

The Roles and Participants in an Information System The marketing information system consists of a network of departments, external firms, software, and hardware that gathers, interprets, and presents information to marketing decision makers. Within the firm, the departments that collect marketing information include marketing research, economics, cost accounting, engineering, public relations, and those departments that maintain relations with wholesalers and retailers. External firms include consultants and marketing research firms.

Planners should use caution in applying sales forecasts, even when the methods are sophisticated. The years 1974 and 1975 were particularly hard on forecasters. Three prominent *econometric services* predicted an economic *growth* of one percent or less for 1974 and an inflation rate of about six percent. During 1974 there was a 4.4 percent *decline* in output and an inflation of 11.4 percent. The unpredicted events were the quadrupling of oil prices by the Organization of Petroleum Exporting Countries, bad crop years in Russia and China, and a devaluation of the dollar. The Federal Reserve Bank of Boston concluded that "forecasts not based on formal econometric models appeared to be generally as accurate or more accurate."[11]

Corporate sales forecasters have had their problems, too. A survey showed that the average error in forecasts was 6.9 percent. Past sales were the major variable for predicting future sales.[12] Another survey revealed that even the large companies relied on simple forecasting techniques, such as growth rates, linear time trends, moving averages, and exponential smoothing.[13]

Marketing research includes the collection of data on market potential, competition, products, pricing, channels, advertising, and personal selling. The variety of marketing research is summarized in Table 3.2. This table shows types of research that is done by the marketing research department, by other departments within the firm, and by outside firms. The variety of demands on the market research department illustrates that marketing research is much more than a survey of consumers.

Marketing research is frequently described as "listening to the consumer." It is disturbing to note how small the budget for listening is. Firms with sales of $500 million or more spent 0.07 percent of sales on marketing research; firms in the $25 to $50 million range spent 0.30 percent of sales.[14] Clearly marketing firms are spending much more to talk to the consumer through advertising and personal selling than they are to listen.

The 1973 survey of marketing research revealed two important trends. In 1963 only 23 percent of the marketing research directors reported to the president or a vice-president. In 1973 this figure had increased to 45 percent.[15] This shift not only reflects the importance of the marketplace to top decisions, but also forces the researcher to do research that is relevant to important decisions.

TABLE 3.2   The marketing research activities of 1322 companies*

	Market research department	Percent of firms where the research is done by:		Total
		Another department	Outside firm	
Advertising research	19%	8%	19%	46%
Business economics and corporate research	33	23	2	58
Corporate responsibility research	9	16	4	29
Product research	40	14	8	62
Sales and market research	36	15	5	56

* Consumer and industrial marketers, advertising agencies, wholesalers, publishers, and broadcasters.
Abstracted from D. W. Twedt, ed., *1973 Survey of Marketing Research* (Chicago: American Marketing Association, 1973), p. 41.

The second trend has been an increase in the use of outside suppliers of research. In 1963, 37 percent of the research was sent outside. By 1973 this had increased to 49 percent. This shift reflects the desire for flexibility, objectivity, additional capacity, and expertise in special techniques. It also reflects the fact that marketing firms are less willing to absorb the cost of training market researchers; therefore, the outside suppliers are becoming training grounds.

Computerized Information Systems   The growth of computers and remote terminals that can be placed in an executive's office led enthusiastic information-system designers to make many promises in the 1960s that have not materialized in the 1970s. Thus many executives are not impressed with the term *marketing information system*. Montgomery concluded that this disillusionment is the result of oversell and underuse.[16] He notes that much of the problem can be traced to *decision theorists' preference to work on data systems rather than on the decision process and its environment.*

Another reason for disillusionment is the failure of the information-systems developers and the decision makers to work together. The result of this lack of cooperation can be disastrous. On the one hand, decision makers may place too much trust in data simply because the data came from a computer. But on the other hand, decision makers may reject all data from the computer because they do not agree with simplifying assumptions. Marketing-information designers should bear in mind the fact that the only reason for a marketing information system is the development of better marketing strategies. *Thus to build a marketing information system, one must begin with an understanding of the process of making strategic decisions.*

Whirlpool Corporation solved its problem of computerized *information inundation* by concentrating on improved *usage* of data for product planning, forecasting, pricing, promotion planning, field sales management, and financial planning.[17] The company built a reference room where data display was simplified and made fun. The results were twofold: data were now eagerly sought and used, and computer-printing costs were down 50 percent.

Interactive Computer Models   "In many respects, the biggest bottleneck in the managerial use of models is not their development but getting them used."[18] Computerized data banks were not being accepted. Marketing models were not being accepted. One would think that a combination of these models would be completely rejected. Such is not the case if the system is designed properly. Managers will accept an interactive model if it is "simple, robust, easy to control, adaptive, as complete as possible, and easy to communicate with."[19] By making the model interactive, the manager may be able to sit at a terminal and communicate with the data bank and with the models for processing the data and to interject personal judgment into the decision process. Little used the term "decision calculus" to describe an interactive model-based procedure for processing data and judgment. He developed BRANDAID, which is an interactive model, to help in the development of a marketing plan.[20] In later chapters we will see that models have been developed to deal with the decision of advertising strategies, the media mix, and the allocation of the sales effort.

Computerized *simulation* models for marketing planning were not used by many firms, according to a survey that was reported in 1976.[21] Rather, the most common application was cash-flow analysis. Marketing planning ranked eleventh of 12 applications reported. Only 33 percent of the firms used planning models for marketing. Over half of the 346 respondents represented companies with sales in excess of $500 million. We must conclude, therefore, that most marketing planners are processing information for planning without the aid of a computer. We hope that the worksheet approach described in Chapter 2 will help them to gather and transform the relevant data into useful information for decision making.

Decision Trees   Decision trees can help the manager to organize the necessary data data for choosing among alternatives. Figure 3.6 illustrates how the alternatives, their expected values, and their costs may be organized to choose a strategy for achieving a 40 percent trial rate for a new ice cream mix. (The trial rate is the percentage of persons who have tried the product at least once.)

The decision tree begins with a precise statement of the subproblem—"to achieve a 40 percent trial rate in six months." Three alternatives are considered—television advertising, magazine advertising, and sampling. A 40 percent trial rate will generate $1.5 million in revenue, but each alternative has a different probability of attaining this rate within six months. It was estimated that television had a 0.5 probability, magazines a 0.25 probability, and sampling a 0.8 probability. The expected value for each of these alternatives is computed by multiplying $1.5 million times the probability of achieving the goal. The expected values in this example are $0.75 million,

Fig. 3.6   Organizing alternatives with a decision tree.

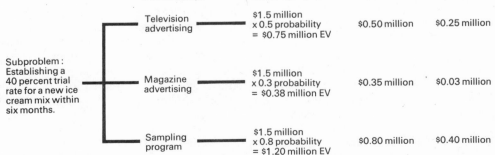

	Alternatives	Expected value (EV)	Cost	Net expected contribution
Subproblem: Establishing a 40 percent trial rate for a new ice cream mix within six months.	Television advertising	$1.5 million x 0.5 probability = $0.75 million EV	$0.50 million	$0.25 million
	Magazine advertising	$1.5 million x 0.3 probability = $0.38 million EV	$0.35 million	$0.03 million
	Sampling program	$1.5 million x 0.8 probability = $1.20 million EV	$0.80 million	$0.40 million

$0.38 million, and $1.20 million, respectively. Sampling, therefore, has the highest expected value. The costs of these alternatives must be deducted from these expected values to yield the net expected contribution from each alternative. In this example, sampling has the largest contribution to overhead and profits. Thus the manager would recommend a sampling program.

IS THE INFORMATION WORTH THE COST?   In designing an information system, we must always weigh the benefits of the information. Cost/benefit analyses should be used to evaluate the worth of data that are gathered continuously, as well as special one-time projects. If the additional information does not reduce the uncertainty of the decision, there has been no benefit from the research.

Decisions must always be made in a state of uncertainty. Full information is impossible to attain. The late Professor Wroe Alderson stated that "attempts to gain full information can bankrupt the firm." The planner, therefore, must be able to estimate the *expected value of research.*

The expected value of information may be computed by comparing the expected payoff under *uncertainty* with the expected payout under *certainty.* To illustrate the concept, we will use an example that is unrealistic because it assumes perfect information.[22]

Assume that a marketing manager is considering introducing a new product. His or her market forecast indicates that there is a 0.80 probability of success.[23] If the manager builds a plant to manufacture the product and it is a success, profits will be $400,000. If the product fails, the loss will be $600,000. The *expected value* for this situation is $200,000 [($400,000 × .80) − ($600,000 × .20) = $200,000]. These alternative outcomes are summarized on the top branch of the decision tree in Fig. 3.7. The manager may decide to consider another alternative—subcontracting with another firm to manufacture the product. The profit and loss associated with this alternative are $200,000 and $100,000, respectively. The expected value for this alternative is $140,000, which is summarized on the middle branch of the figure. A third alternative is to do nothing, which has an expected value of zero. The double-slashed lines on the middle and lower branches of this diagram show that these are not the best alternatives to take.

Fig. 3.7   A decision tree without information.

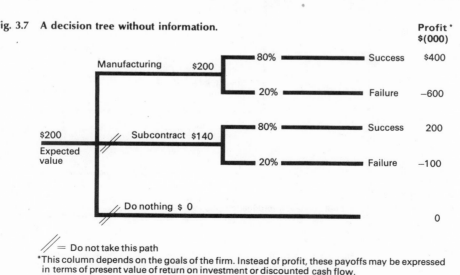

// = Do not take this path
*This column depends on the goals of the firm. Instead of profit, these payoffs may be expressed in terms of present value of return on investment or discounted cash flow.

The marketing manager may decide to buy some market information to determine which path to take. For simplicity we will assume that the manager can buy perfect information, which is offered for $150,000. Should the information be bought? The decision tree in Fig. 3.8 will help the marketing manager make the decision. If the perfect information shows that the product will be a success, a profit of $400,000 can be made by manufacturing the product. What is the probability that the perfect market information will indicate a success? Our best estimate now is still 0.80. Therefore, the expected profit for this alternative is $320,000. From this profit we must subtract the $150,000 cost of the market information. The net expected value after buying the perfect market information is $170,000, which is less than the $200,000 we could expect without the perfect information. Therefore, the manager should not buy the information.

How much is perfect information worth? The expected value of perfect information is the difference between the expected profit with perfect information and the expected profit without it. In this case it is $320,000 less $200,000, or $120,000. Thus the marketing manager should not pay more than $120,000 for perfect information and should pay less for imperfect information.

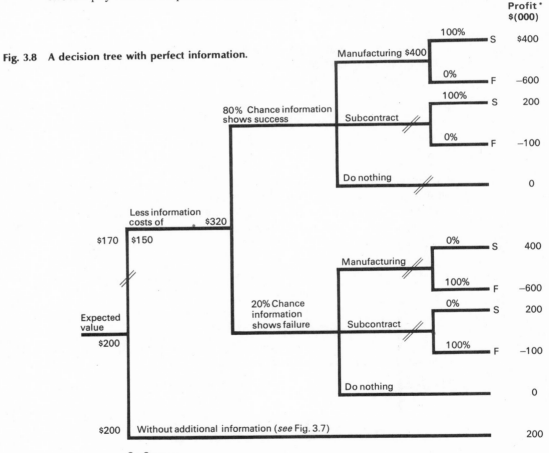

Fig. 3.8 A decision tree with perfect information.

S = Success
F = Failure
// = Do not take this path
*This column depends on the goals of the firm. Instead of profit, these payoffs may be expressed in terms of present value of return on investment or discounted cash flow.

INCLUDING PERSONAL RISK FUNCTIONS IN THE DECISION ANALYSIS Decision makers have a greater aversion to a loss than to a profit. This difference is explained by a concept known as personal risk function, or utility theory. A personal risk function is the result of a decision maker's personal experiences and the reward systems of the company. The decision maker may have internalized the fact that the company will penalize a person who makes a loss more than it will reward him or her for making a profit of the same size. This asymmetry of reward systems is due in part to the fact that there is no limit on the up side, but the limit on the down side is bankruptcy and the loss of an opportunity to try again.

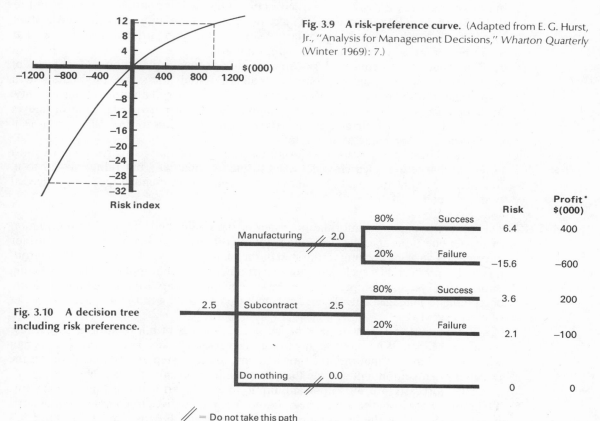

Fig. 3.9 A risk-preference curve. (Adapted from E. G. Hurst, Jr., "Analysis for Management Decisions," *Wharton Quarterly* (Winter 1969): 7.)

Fig. 3.10   A decision tree including risk preference.

// = Do not take this path

*This column depends on the goals of the firm. Instead of profit, these payoffs may be expressed in terms of present value of return on investment or discounted cash flow.

Figure 3.9 illustrates a risk-preference curve. The lower, left-hand quadrant of this curve is the loss area. Note that the curve is steeper in this quadrant than in the upper, right-hand quadrant, which is the profit area. This steepness signifies that there is a greater risk associated with a loss than with a profit. For instance, the risk preference associated with a $1.0 million profit is 10, but a loss of this same amount has a risk preference of -30. These risk-preference curves are unique to each individual. They require the manager to participate in an experiment in which she or he makes numerous simple decisions. These decisions form the risk-preference curve.

Figure 3.10 is like Fig. 3.7 except that risk indices have been added for each of the profits and losses. The expected values are now an expected risk index instead of an expected profit. For instance, 2.0 is computed as follows: $(.80 \times 6.4) - (.20 \times 15.6) = 2.0$. Introduction of risk preference has changed the decision. Given the risk-preference curve shown in Fig. 3.9, the manager will choose to subcontract the manufacturing of the product.

THE MOUNTING COSTS OF RESEARCH   The mounting costs of market research require the planner to be a sharp buyer and to search for more efficient ways to generate the same quality of information for less money. Some of the opportunities for cutting costs include substituting telephone interviews for personal ones, eliminating open-end questions that are expensive to code, collecting only the information that is relevant to the decision, avoiding oversampling "just to be safe," tabulating only the information that is really needed, doing sequential research,[24] and standardizing research so that it can be compared across divisions within the firm.

The concept of sequential research requires some explanation. One form of sequential research is simply doing a small-scale study first and proceeding to a large-scale study only if the decisions require a further reduction of uncertainty. Another form of sequential research requires the supplier to present a proposal in stages, with reports at the end of each stage, with the option to turn off the project if the decision can be made at any point.

In concluding a discussion of information systems and marketing research, we must note that marketing research is not a substitute for creativity, but rather an aid to it. Research may indicate *what* to say about a product, but the creative specialist is needed to determine *how* to say it.[25]

SUMMARY   The role of the marketing information system is to provide valid and reliable information to answer questions at each step in the planning process. The frequency of the need for information varies according to the step in the planning cycle, the competitive environment, the product life cycle, and the environment of public policy. The marketing information system attempts to bring the state of uncertainty within the limits that are acceptable to management. These limits will vary according to the management styles of chief executives.

The planner will want to use the secondary sources of information first, because these are cheaper. When contracting for primary research, such as a survey, the planner will want to have estimates of the time and cost for each step and to know who in the research organization will assume the operational responsibility for each step.

Sales forecasts are an important input to all departments within a company. Techniques vary from the subjective opinions of top executives to complex econometric models. Because of the importance of the forecast and because no one method has proved to be the most valid, the planner will want to use several methods.

Marketing research is only a part of the marketing information system. *Market* research tends to mean research that is concerned primarily with demand and competition. Market*ing* research includes market research and research on the elements in the marketing mix. The *marketing information system* brings together data from non-marketing departments, such as economics, cost accounting, engineering, wholesalers, retailers, and outside research suppliers.

Translating the vast amount of marketing information into a form that can be used by chief marketing executives remains a challenge. Interactive computing systems which store and process data have shown some promise when they permit the executive to interject personal judgment.

Executives must use their judgment to determine if the information is worth the cost of gathering and processing. They must resist the temptation to collect data simply because "it would be interesting to know if...."

APPENDIX 3.1: A NONTECHNICAL DISCUSSION OF MULTIVARIATE STATISTICS

The right-hand column of Table 3.1 summarizes the methods of analysis frequently used at each stage in the planning process. The unstructured methods, such as depth interviews, require the subjective analysis of the interviewer. When the data can be measured with more precision, mathematical analyses may be used. Being concerned with the total strategy and plan rather than with the mechanics of an analytical technique, the marketing planner should resist the temptation to learn the mathematical structure behind the latest analytical technique if this new knowledge detracts from his or her basic planning role. A planner with a new technique can be like a small child with a new hammer: Both search for places to apply their new tool, sometimes with disastrous results.

This discussion of analytical methods will be limited to a description of what the techniques can do for the marketing planner.[26] We begin with the *chi square test*, which measures the probability that a set of data could have occurred as a result of chance. For example, we would use the chi square test to determine whether women or men are more likely to purchase an orange-flavored soft drink. We could conduct a survey, or we could *observe* buyers at a vending machine. We would count the number of women who bought an orange soda or a cola and the number of men who made these purchases. These data would be summarized into a 2×2 table. The chi square test would test the hypothesis that women buy orange drinks, whereas men buy colas. The results of these tests could help the vendor of soft drinks decide what product mix to put in the machines at the men's and the women's dormitories.

Regression analysis attempts to predict the magnitude of a dependent variable (e.g., sales), given a measure of the magnitude of an independent variable. For example, regression analysis may establish a mathematical relationship between the number of bottles of soft drinks consumed in a family and the number of children in the family. A bottler could estimate the demand for soft drinks in each county by using a regression model and the census data that report the number of children in each county. These predictions would help the bottler to decide whether to expand into new counties.

Multiple regression could be used when more than one variable is needed to predict sales. For instance, soft drink sales may be predicted by the number of children in the family *and* the family's disposable personal income. In such a case, the bottler would need measures of both of these predictor variables.

Discriminant analysis is used when the dependent variable is not continuous. Sales of soft drinks are continuous data, but perhaps the best data available are only dichotomous, such as *user/nonuser*. If we knew the age, income, family size, geographic location, and other characteristics of the population and whether they use soft drinks, discriminant analysis would give us the profiles of users and nonusers.

Cluster analysis is a scheme that classifies consumers or products into groups. As with any classification method, the goal of cluster analysis is to *maximize the similarities within* the groups and to *maximize the differences between* groups. Such classification schemes are at the heart of the concept of *market segmentation*. By dealing with smaller homogeneous groups, the marketer is able to focus the product and promotion with greater precision, thereby making it more efficient. The marketer can also build brand loyalty, thereby insulating the brand from competitive attacks. (See Fig. 9.1 for an example.)

Another technique that can be used to cluster products or people is known as *factor analysis*. A second application of factor analysis is the reduction of a large number of variables to a smaller number of factors without losing much of the information in the process. The market researcher will want to use as few variables as possible when attempting to *explain* or *predict* buying behavior. The reduction of variables reduces the costs of gathering and analyzing the data. It also makes it possible to develop more precise marketing strategies, because a few key variables are identified. Returning to the service station location problem noted earlier in this chapter, it was easier to develop a location strategy when it was known that the key variable was "perceived lost time of the customer" than when there were 33 variables.[27]

When a researcher needs to compare the arithmetic means of an experimental and a control group, the *student's t test* is appropriate. When there are several experimental groups, the most efficient analytical method is *analysis of variance* (also known as the F test).

The *Automatic Interaction Detection (AID)* method of analysis is a form of analysis of variance.[28] This technique is used to identify the characteristics of those market segments with the highest probability of buying a brand or product. Given a set of profile variables about users and nonusers, AID splits the sample, searching for the characteristics of the highest users. For instance, heavy buyers of a brand of a grocery product were found to be women who lived in the North Central region of the United States, who were heavy product users, and whose family income was less than $12,500.[29]

Conjoint measurement is similar to analysis of variance in that it can deal with experimental designs that will examine several *levels of variables*, several *different variables*, and their *interaction* effects. For instance, conjoint measurement could handle a test of two variations of a product's taste, three different package designs, and two levels of price. Conjoint measurement differs from analysis of variance in that conjoint measurement can use rank-order data. Thus respondents may be able to rank-order their preferences for all of the combinations of product taste, package, and price, but they cannot tell us how much one combination is preferred over another. Conjoint measurement enables the researcher to derive the respondents' utilities for all of these product, package, and price attributes. Furthermore, it estimates utilities for their interactions. Interaction utilities help the planner to decide which price to charge for each product-package combination.[30]

Multidimensional scaling techniques place respondents' *perceptions* of products and brands into psychological space. This technique derives the attributes that buyers use when selecting brands *and* places these brands in the space that is formed by these attributes. Although the technique can produce *n*-dimensional analysis, buyers rarely use more than three or four attributes when they choose a brand. These projections of brands into perceived psychological space are generally reduced to two-dimensional brand maps. These maps help product planners look for "holes" that will help them to develop new brands. They also help planners to anticipate competition.[31] (See Figs. 7.2 and 9.2 for examples.)

APPENDIX 3.2: FORECASTING METHODS

	Delphi method	Exponential smoothing	Box-Jenkins	X-11	Trend projections
Description	A panel of experts is interrogated by a sequence of questionnaires in which the responses to one questionnaire are used to produce the next questionnaire. Any set of information available to some experts and not others is thus passed on to the others, enabling all the experts to have access to all the information for forecasting. This technique eliminates the bandwagon effect of majority opinion.	This technique is similar to the moving average, except that more recent data points are given more weight. Descriptively, the new forecast is equal to the old one plus some proportion of the past forecasting error. Adaptive forecasting is somewhat the same except that seasonals are also computed. There are many variations of exponential smoothing: some are more versatile than others, some are computationally more complex, some require more computer time.	Exponential smoothing is a special case of the Box-Jenkins technique. The time series is fitted with a mathematical model that is optimal in the sense that it assigns smaller errors to history than any other model. The type of model must be identified and the parameters then estimated. This is apparently the most accurate statistical routine presently available but also one of the most costly and time-consuming ones.	Developed by Julius Shiskin of the Census Bureau, this technique decomposes a time series into seasonals, trend cycles, and irregular elements. Primarily used for detailed time series analysis (including estimating seasonals); but we have extended its uses to forecasting and tracking and warning by incorporating other analytical methods. Used with special knowledge, it is perhaps the most effective technique for medium-range forecasting—three months to one year—allowing one to predict turning points and to time special events.	This technique fits a trend line to a mathematical equation and then projects it into the future by means of this equation. There are several variations: the slope-characteristic method, polynomials, logarithms, and so on.
Accuracy					
1. Short term (0–3 months)	Fair to very good	Fair to very good	Very good to excellent	Very good to excellent	Very good
2. Medium term (3 months–2 years)	Fair to very good	Poor to good	Poor to good	Good	Good
3. Long term (2 years and up)	Fair to very good	Very poor	Very poor	Very poor	Good

	Delphi method	Exponential smoothing	Box-Jenkins	X-11	Trend projections
Identification of turning points	Fair to good	Poor	Fair	Very good	Poor
Typical applications	Forecasts of long-range and new-product sales, forecasts of margins.	Production and inventory control, forecasts of margins and other financial data.	Production and inventory control for large-volume items, forecasts of cash balances.	Tracking and warning, forecasts of company, division, or department sales.	New-product forecasts (particularly intermediate- and long-term).
Data required	A coordinator issues the sequence of questionnaires, editing and consolidating the responses.	The same as for a moving average.	The same as for a moving average. However, in this case more history is very advantageous in model identification.	A minimum of three years' history to start. Thereafter, the complete history.	Varies with the technique used. However, a good rule of thumb is to use a minimum of five years' annual data to start. Thereafter, the complete history.
Cost of forecasting 1. With a computer	$2000 +	$.005	$10.00	$10.00	Varies with application
2. Is calculation possible without a computer?	Yes	Yes	Yes	No	Yes
Time required to develop an application and make a forecast	2 months +	1 day –	1–2 days	1 day	1 day –
References	North & Pyke, "'Probes' of the Technological Future," HBR May-June 1969, p. 68.	Brown, "Less Risk in Inventory Estimates," HBR July-August 1959, p. 104.	Box-Jenkins, Time Series Analysis, Forecasting & Control (San Francisco, Holden-Day, Inc., 1970).	McLaughlin & Boyle, "Short-term Forecasting," AMA Association Booklet, 1968.	Hadley, Introduction to Business Statistics (San Francisco, Holden-Day, Inc., 1968); Oliver & Boyd, "Techniques of Production Control," Imperial Chemical Industries Ltd.

	Regression	Econometric model	Input-output model	Life-cycle analysis
Description	This functionally relates sales to other economic, competitive, or internal variables and estimates an equation using the least-squares technique. Relationships are primarily analyzed statistically, although any relationship should be selected for testing on a rational ground.	An econometric model is a system of interdependent regression equations that describes some sector of economic sales or profit activity. The parameters of the regression equations are usually estimated simultaneously. As a rule, these models are relatively expensive to develop and can easily cost between $5000 and $10,000, depending on detail. However, due to the system of equations inherent in such models, they will better express the causalities involved than an ordinary regression equation and hence will predict turning points more accurately.	A method of analysis concerned with the inter-industry or interdepartmental flow of goods or services in the economy or a company and its markets. It shows what flows of inputs must occur to obtain certain outputs. Considerable effort must be expended to use these models properly, and additional detail, not normally available, must be obtained if they are to be applied to specific businesses. Corporations using input-output models have expended as much as $100,000 and more annually to develop useful applications.	This is an analysis and forecasting of new-product growth rates based on S-curves. The phases of product acceptance by the various groups such as innovators, early adapters, early majority, late majority, and laggards are central to the analysis.
Accuracy				
1. Short term (0–3 months)	Good to very good	Good to very good	Not applicable	Poor
2. Medium term (3 months–2 years)	Good to very good	Very good to excellent	Good to very good	Poor to good
3. Long term (2 years and up)	Poor	Good	Good to very good	Poor to good
Identification of turning points	Very good	Excellent	Fair	Poor to good
Typical applications	Forecasts of sales by product classes, forecasts of margins.	Forecasts of sales by product classes, forecasts of margins.	Forecasts of company sales and division sales for industrial sectors and subsectors.	Forecasts of new-product sales.

	Regression	Econometric model	Input-output model	Life-cycle analysis
Data required	Several years' quarterly history to obtain good, meaningful relationships. Mathematically necessary to have two more observations than there are independent variables.	The same as for regression.	Ten or fifteen years' history. Considerable amounts of information on product and service flows within a corporation (or economy) for each year for which an input-output analysis is desired.	As a minimum, the annual sales of the product being considered or of a similar product. It is often necessary to do market surveys.
Cost of forecasting 1. With a computer	$100	$5000 +	$50,000 +	$1500
2. Is calculation possible without a computer?	Yes	Yes	No	Yes
Time required to develop an application and make a forecast	Depends on ability to identify relationships.	2 months +	6 months +	1 month +
References	Clelland, de Cani, Brown, Bush & Murray, *Basic Statistics with Business Applications* (New York, John Wiley & Sons, 1966).	Evans, *Macro-economic Activity: Theory, Forecasting & Control* (New York, Harper & Row Publishers, Inc., 1969).	Leontief, *Input-Output Economics* (New York, Oxford University Press, 1966).	Bass, "A New Product Growth Model for Consumer Durables," *Management Science,* January 1969.

DISCUSSION QUESTIONS

1. Why should a brand manager be familiar with marketing research techniques?
2. Discuss information that you would need if you faced the following situations:
   a) The annual review of a marketing plan for a well-established brand.
   b) A competitor is introducing a new powdered drink as a product-line extension to its canned fruit juices. You sell only soft drinks.
   c) Your sales force is spending too much time with small customers.
   d) One of your most profitable products is in the mature, stable part of its life cycle.
3. Draw a flow chart for a telephone survey to determine if your product warranty is understood by recent purchasers of your electric golf carts.
4. Describe the forecasting procedure you would use to forecast the demand for electric golf carts for next year. How would your methods change for a three-year forecast? (The forecast will be used to develop the annual marketing plan.)
5. What criteria would you use to evaluate a proposed computerized marketing information system?
6. Return to the strategy worksheet for Scoop Ice Cream in Chapter 2. Select one strategy and identify at least two alternative strategies which you think would accomplish the same end. Then develop a decision tree like that in Fig. 3.6.
7. You are contracting with an outside supplier for a mail survey. How might you lower the costs of the survey? How would you maintain control of the project?

NOTES

1. R. A. Druckman, "Coordinating New Product Development," 1976 Abstracts of papers presented before the American Pharmaceutical Association, Academy of Pharmaceutical Sciences, Orlando, Florida, November 14–17, 1976, pp. 19–20.
2. G. D. Hughes, *Demand Analysis for Marketing Decisions* (Homewood, Ill.: Richard D. Irwin, 1973), Appendix A.
3. R. L. Ackoff, *A Concept of Corporate Planning* (New York: Wiley/Interscience, 1970), p. 116.
4. *Forecasting Sales*, Studies in Business Policy, No. 106 (New York: National Industrial Conference Board, 1964).
5. J. C. Chambers, S. K. Mullick, and D. D. Smith, "How to Choose the Right Forecasting Technique," *Harvard Business Review* 49 (July-August 1971): 45.
6. See also J. C. Chambers, S. K. Mullick, and D. D. Smith, *An Executive's Guide to Forecasting* (New York: Wiley, 1974).
7. J. C. Chambers and S. K. Mullick, "Forecasting for Planning: Causal Techniques," *Planning Review* 4 (January 1976): 17–19.
8. R. L. McLaughlin, "A New Five-Phase Economic Forecasting System," *Business Economics Journal* (September 1975): 49–60.
9. Chambers and Mullick, *op. cit.*
10. *Ibid.*
11. Quoted in "Daddy, What's an Econometrician?" *Forbes*, July 15, 1976, p. 71.
12. D. J. Dalrymple, "Sales Forecasting Methods and Accuracy," *Business Horizons*, December 1975, pp. 69–73. It is interesting to note that the survey also revealed that consultants were used infrequently and that the computer was used only 50 percent of the time.
13. T. H. Naylor and H. Schauland, "A Survey of Users of Corporate Planning Models," *Management Science* (May 1976): 927–937.

14. D. W. Twedt, ed., *1973 Survey of Marketing Research* (Chicago: American Marketing Association, 1973), p. 32.

15. *Ibid.*, p. 25.

16. D. B. Montgomery, "The Outlook for MIS." *Journal of Advertising Research* **13** (June 1973): 5–11.

17. J. D. Sparks, "Taming the 'Paper Elephant' in Marketing Information Systems," *Journal of Marketing* **40** (July 1976): 83–91.

18. J. D. C. Little, "Models and Managers: The Concept of a Decision Calculus," *Management Science* **16,** 4 (April 1970): B483.

19. *Ibid.*

20. J. D. C. Little, "BRANDAID: An On-Line Marketing Mix Model," Working Paper 586-72 (Cambridge, Mass.: M.I.T., Sloan School of Management, February 1972).

21. Naylor and Schauland, *op. cit.*

22. For a more complete discussion, *see* F. M. Bass, "Marketing Research Expenditures: A Decision Model," *Journal of Business* (January 1963): 77–90; P. E. Green and D. S. Tull, *Research for Marketing Decisions* (Englewood Cliffs, N.J.: Prentice-Hall, 1966). For a criticism of the technique, *see* G. Assmus, "Bayesian Analysis for the Evaluation of Marketing Research Expenditures: A Reassessment," *Journal of Marketing Research* (November 1977): 562–568.

23. This example is adapted from E. G. Hurst, Jr., "Analysis for Management Decisions," *Wharton Quarterly* (Winter 1969): 2–7, 36.

24. J. L. Pope, "12 Ways to Cut Marketing Research Costs," *Marketing News*, June 6, 1975, p. 6.

25. C. E. Eldridge, "How Marketing Research Works," Part 7, *Marketing Insights*, April 17, 1967, pp. 16–18.

26. For a more detailed discussion, *see* K. K. Cox and B. M. Enis, *The Marketing Research Process* (Pacific Palisades, Calif.: Goodyear, 1972); P. E. Green and D. S. Tull, *Research for Marketing Decisions*, 3rd ed. (Englewood Cliffs, N.J.: Prentice-Hall, 1975); B. Schoner and K. P. Uhl, *Marketing Research: Information Systems and Decision Making*, 2d ed. (New York: Wiley, 1975).

27. For a further discussion of factor analysis, *see* W. D. Wells and J. N. Sheth, "Factor Analysis," in *Handbook of Marketing Research*, ed. R. Ferber (New York: McGraw-Hill, 1974), pp. 2–458 to 2–471.

28. *See* Green and Tull, *op. cit.*, pp. 332–336.

29. H. Assael, "Segmenting Markets by Group Purchasing Behavior: An Application of the AID Technique," *Journal of Marketing Research* **7** (1970): 153–158.

30. For an additional discussion and citations, *see* Green and Tull, *op. cit.*, pp. 634–647.

31. For a complete discussion of multidimensional scaling, *see* Green and Tull, *op. cit.*, Chapter 16; and P. E. Green and V. R. Rao, *Applied Multidimensional Scaling* (New York: Holt, Rinehart and Winston, 1972).

SUGGESTED READINGS

Aaker, D. A., ed., *Multivariate Analysis in Marketing: Theory and Application* (Belmont, Calif.: Wadsworth, 1971).

Ackoff, R. L., "Management Misinformation System," *Management Science* **14** (December 1967): B147–B156.

Argyris, C., "Management Information Systems: The Challenge to Rationality and Emotionality," *Management Science* **17** (February 1971): B257–B292.

Basu, S., and R. Schroder, "Incorporating Judgments in Sales Forecasts: Application of the Delphi Method at American Hoist & Derrick," *Interfaces* **7,** 3 (May 1977): 18–27.

Brown, R., A. S. Kahr, and C. Peterson, *Decision Analysis for the Manager: An Overview* (New York: Holt, Rinehart and Winston, 1974).

Brown, R. V., "Do Managers Find Decision Theory Useful?" *Harvard Business Review* (May-June 1970): 78–89.

Butler, W. F., and R. A. Kavesh, *How Business Economists Forecast* (Englewood Cliffs, N.J.: Prentice-Hall, 1966).

Chambers, J. C., S. K. Mullick, and D. A. Goodman, "Catalytic Agent for Effective Planning," *Harvard Business Review* (January-February 1971): 110–119.

Chambers, J. C., S. K. Mullick, and D. C. Smith, *An Executive's Guide to Forecasting* (New York: Wiley, 1974).

Churchman, C. W., and A. H. Shainblatt, "The Researcher and the Manager: A Dialectic of Implementation," *Management Science* **11** (February 1965): B69–B87.

Cox, D. F., and R. E. Good, "How to Build a Marketing Information System," *Harvard Business Review* (May-June 1967): 145–154.

Dearden, J., "MIS Is a Mirage," *Harvard Business Review* (January-February 1972): 90–99.

Enis, B. M., and C. L. Broome, *Marketing Decisions: A Bayesian Approach* (Scranton, Pa: Intext, 1971).

Frank, R. E., and P. E. Green, *Quantitative Methods in Marketing* (Englewood Cliffs, N.J.: Prentice-Hall, 1967).

Gatty, R., "Multivariate Analysis for Marketing Research: An Evaluation," *Applied Statistics* **15** (November 1966): 146–158.

Green, P. L., *Analyzing Multivariate Data* (New York: Dryden Press, 1978).

Green, P. E., and Y. Wind, *Multiattribute Decisions in Marketing: A Measurement Approach* (New York: Holt, Rinehart and Winston, 1973).

Hammond, J. S., III, "Do's and Don'ts of Computer Models for Planning," *Harvard Business Review* (March-April 1974): 110–123.

Honomichl, J. J., "Research Top 20: Companies Posted 16% Gain Last Year," *Advertising Age*, April 11, 1977, pp. 3, 82–88.

Lipstein, B., "An Evaluation of Response Errors in Market Surveys." (Paper delivered at AMA Conference, Portland, Oregon, August 13, 1974.)

Makridakis, S., and S. C. Wheelwright, "Forecasting: Issues and Challenges for Marketing Management," *Journal of Marketing* (October 1977): 24–38.

Pessemier, E. A., "Forecasting Brand Performance Through Simulation Experiments," *Journal of Marketing* **28**, 2 (April 1964): 41–46.

Pokempner, S. J., *Information Systems for Sales and Marketing Management*, Conference Board Report No. 591 (New York: Conference Board, 1973).

Shakun, M., "Management Science and Management: Implementing Management Science via Situational Normativism," *Management Science* **18** (April 1972): 367–377.

Sheth, J. N., "Multivariate Revolution in Marketing Research," *Journal of Marketing* **35** (January 1971): 13–19.

———, "Multivariate Analysis in Marketing," *Journal of Advertising Research* **10** (February 1970): 29–39.

Vancil, R. F., "The Accuracy of Long-Range Planning," *Harvard Business Review* (September-October 1970): 98–101.

Waldo, C., and D. Fuller, "Just How Good Is the 'Survey of Buying Power?'" *Journal of Marketing* (October 1977): 64–66.

Wheelwright, S. C., and C. G. Clarke, "Corporate Forecasting: Promise and Reality," *Harvard Business Review* (November-December 1976): 40–42ff.

Wheelwright, S. C., and S. Makridakis, *Forecasting Methods for Management*, 2d ed. (New York: Wiley, 1977).

Part II. Organizing the Marketing Effort

The corporate environment for planning includes the statement of corporate missions, objectives, goals, and policies. Planners must understand how the personal values of executives determine corporate policies which place constraints on strategic alternatives. Strategic planning requires identification of the success factors in the industry and a definition of the business. A *business* is the matching of a market segment and a product (or service) through a marketing strategy. Chapter 4 discusses these points.

The implementation of a plan requires resources that include capital, equipment, information, and people. How can these be organized to achieve the corporate goals most effectively? There is no one answer to this question because there is no perfect organizational design for all situations. The position of a product in its life cycle will determine some of the organizational needs. Changing technology will alter the requirements of the organization. Thus marketing organizations must adapt to changes in the market and product. Chapter 5 discusses various marketing organizational designs, especially the continuously evolving brand-management system.

ENVIRONMENTAL ANALYSIS WORKSHEET

Environmental elements	Facts	Assumptions or research needed	Conclusions

Organizational values, objectives, and policies (4)

Organizational design (5)

Situation
   Generic demand (6)
   Brand demand (7)
   Competition (9)
   Public policy (10)

Opportunities (2)

Problems

MARKETING PLAN (CONSUMER PRODUCT)

Current performance
Recommendations
Effect of recommendations on income
Situation analysis
Opportunities and problems
Strategies
Tests and research
Supporting documents
   Comparative budgets
   Media allocation schedule
   Promotion control sheet

<u>STRATEGY WORKSHEET</u>

Opportunities and problems in rank order to importance
1.
2.
.
n.

	Current strategy	Alternatives and recommended strategy	Estimated Effect

Demand strategy
  Generic
  Brand

Strategic goals
  Financial
  Marketing

Marketing-mix strategies
  Product (12)
  Pricing (13)
  Channel and logistics (14)
  Advertising and promotional (15)
  Sales management (16)

Research (3)

Profit plan

Evaluation and control (19)

CHAPTER **4**

The Corporate Environment for Marketing Planning

LEARNING OBJECTIVES After studying this chapter you should:

1. Understand the need to consider the environment within a corporation prior to developing a marketing plan.
2. Appreciate the role of personal values in the planning process.
3. Understand why it is not possible to maximize sales and profits at the same time.
4. Understand how corporate policies constrain the number of alternatives that a planner may consider.
5. Know the elements of a goal.
6. Be aware of some frequently used marketing strategies.
7. Be able to define and use the following concepts:

Mission	Success factors
Objectives	Defining the business
Policies	Marketing myopia
Goals	Personal values
Strategies	Portfolio approach
Action plan (tactics)	

SOME ANALYTICAL QUESTIONS FOR OPENERS

1. How will the personal values of chief executives influence strategic marketing planning?
2. What is the business?
3. What are the success factors?
4. How should the goals be expressed?

THE NEED TO UNDERSTAND THE CORPORATE ENVIRONMENT A strategy cannot be developed in isolation. It must support the corporate missions, objectives, policies, and goals, as well as the strategies and action plans for other products. The marketing manager, therefore, must be well informed about each of these elements, which will be collectively known as the corporate environment for marketing planning.

Figure 1.2 showed that the *product* manager begins the annual product plan with an evaluation of the generic demand for the product as the *marketing concept* requires. The *marketing* manager, in contrast, has a broader view of the planning process. He or she must plan beyond a year and plan for all of the company's products. This broader view requires consideration of the social, economic, political, and technical environments of the firm. In the long run, corporate missions, objectives, policies, and goals may be changed. In the annual plan the product manager must regard them as fixed and adapt to them. Thus the product manager is not a free-wheeling entrepreneur, but part of an ongoing organization.

UNDERSTANDING THE TERMS   The terms *mission, objectives, policies, goals, strategies,* and *action plans* (tactics) are frequently used interchangeably in everyday conversation. But to the planner they carry specific meanings. The distinctions among these terms may be illustrated in the context of a football game.

The *mission* of a football team may be to develop school spirit. (Mission tends to be a very general and sometimes vague concept.) This school spirit may be part of the educational mission of the school, which includes developing leadership through athletic programs.

The *objective* of the team is quite clear—to win the game. The coaches' *policies* will reflect the values of the school and constrain team activities. Thus fair play and using the whole squad may be policies that limit the alternatives that may be used to achieve the objective. Whereas the overall *objective* is to win by having the highest score, more immediate goals include scoring points through touchdowns and field goals. Thus a *short-term goal* may be to place the football in a good position for a field goal. *Strategies* are alternative means for reaching a goal. In football a strategy may be to retain possession of the ball, which limits the use of passes to short, well-controlled situations. If a ground play is called, the *tactic* deals with the specifics of who touches the ball and where he will run. The tactics are the *execution* of a strategy. The success of this final player determines the success of the team. There are many parallels between a football team and marketing organizations.

As we move from missions to tactics, we move from broad concepts to specific courses of action, and the distinctions between adjacent terms are frequently vague. The confusion between adjacent terms may result from the differences in the positions of the persons in an organization. To top management, a concept may appear to be very specific, so it will be described as a *tactic*. To the final actor, such as the person who writes the advertising copy, the concept is not precise, so he or she describes it as a *strategy*. Thus the terms "strategy" and "tactic" are defined according to the perspective and organizational locus of a particular planner.

THE CORPORATE MISSION   To develop marketing strategies, the planner must be able to answer the question: "What is our business?" Corporations frequently have clever slogans to define their business. For example, a research-oriented firm may have a slogan such as "Translating discovery into use" or "Progress is our most important product." A bank may have as its slogan "Let's build tomorrow together." These slogans make us feel warmly toward the company and convey that it regards itself as a change agent, but a marketing planner needs a more precise definition of a business.

Identifying the Success Factors Each industry has three to six factors that are necessary for success. In the pharmaceutical industry, for example, these factors are research, an effective sales force, and effective promotion. The grocery products industry requires new-product development, high levels of distribution in retail food stores, and effective advertising.

Economic conditions can alter the success factors within an industry, so long-range planning requires that these be reevaluated. For example, in the automobile industry styling, efficient dealer organizations, and control on costs are the prime factors. However, the oil shortage and the tendency for automobiles to look alike may be reducing the importance of styling and increasing the factor of efficiency.

Success variables change as the social, political, and technological environments change. The success factors during the 1950s were related to product technology and market opportunities. During the 1960s success factors were defined in terms of efficiency. In the 1970s the success factors became the unmeasurable variables—political and environmental.[1]

This change in the broad planning environment produced new success factors and required changes in a firm's goals, policies, and strategies. A company may choose a strategy of not adapting, but improving the business environment by taking an active role in influencing legislation. It may restructure the thrust of the corporation by viewing the total company as a portfolio of investments and upgrade its investment to a higher return. This strategy will require that the company divest itself of poorer businesses and acquire higher-yield ones through acquisition or research and development. The company will need to develop new schemes to motivate executives so that their efforts are directed toward future benefits, not just current financial results. Finally, the importance of personal leadership must be acknowledged during these periods of changing environments. The planning process should yield a net saving of the time of leaders, not consume more time. The loneliness of the long-distance planner should be acknowledged. The farther one looks into the future, the more likely one is going to be wrong. The reward structure for long-range planners should not discourage forward thinking by penalizing long-range errors.[2]

We may conclude, therefore, that holding to an old success factor may be a fatal strategy. Although some scientists would like to return to the old days of high research productivity, many firms are switching to a strategy of dominance in *marketing research and development, not technology.*[3]

Defining the Business Alfred P. Sloan, former chairman of General Motors, emphasized the importance of defining the automobile business in developing the successful strategy for General Motors.[4] In 1921 the Ford strategy was a single Model-T aimed at the lowest-price market, the market it had dominated for more than a decade. General Motors had no clear definition of its business. It was not competitive with Ford in the low-price field, which was the market with greatest volume and the greatest growth potential. Instead, GM was operating in the middle market with brands that competed and took volume from each other. Ford had 50 percent of the total car and truck market, whereas Chevrolet had 4 percent. Sloan concluded that a strategy of meeting Ford head-on in this market would be suicidal. The Chevrolet strategy, therefore, became one of taking a bite from the upper end of this low-price market, conceived as a price class, to build Chevrolet volume on a profitable basis.

A *business* may be defined as a given product group, a given market, and a connection between the two.[5] The same product sold to two different markets represents two different businesses. For example, an automobile sold to a consumer is one business; an automobile sold as part of a taxi cab fleet is a different business. Each of these businesses requires a different strategy.

Where do we begin to define our business? The *marketing concept* states that we should begin with an understanding of the needs of the market and work back to design a product that will fit these needs. But the resources and capacities of the firm are limited. Therefore, to be realistic, our capacities and resources limit the kinds of products and services we may provide. The latter approach has been called "inner-directed" planning.[6]

A clear definition of a business gives direction to the planning process. This definition emphasizes the importance of identifying the size of the present market and its growth rate. In defining the business, we must identify the "success factors" in its industry. Present and potential competition must be identified. The resources of the business must be clearly established—personnel, materials, facilities, services, and equipment. The buyers' decision process must be understood in order to design and sell the product. Distribution and promotional connections must be made between the market and the product. The definition of the business must take into consideration the dynamics of the economic, social, political, and technological environments in which the firm operates. Separate definitions and marketing plans must be made for each of a company's businesses. A large, diversified company, such as General Electric or General Foods, requires a uniform planning procedure so that top management can see clearly the best alternative uses of the corporate resources. The worksheet approach helps the marketing manager coordinate all of these activities.

How broadly should a business be defined? Some years ago Professor Theodore Levitt, in a famous article entitled "Marketing Myopia," pointed out the dangers in defining one's business too narrowly.[7] According to Professor Levitt, the railroads lost to the trucking business because they failed to recognize that they were in the business of transportation, not railroading. Similarly, the movie industry failed to define its business as entertainment and therefore lost to the television industry. But there are dangers in a definition that is overgeneralized.

A critical issue in defining a business is to do so at the most meaningful level of generalization. Unfortunately, there is a prevalent notion that if one merely defines one's business in increasingly general terms—such as transportation rather than railroading—the path to successful competitive strategy will be clear. Actually, this is hardly ever the case, and more often, the opposite is true. In the case of the railroads, passengers and freight represent very different problems, and short haul versus longer haul are completely different strategic issues. Indeed, as the unit train demonstrates, coal handling alone can be isolated as a meaningful strategic issue.[8]

CORPORATE OBJECTIVES

Personal Values   Corporate objectives are an extension of the personal values of those in power. For example, product design will be the dominant theme of a corporation in which the power structure is composed largely of scientists. An engineering-oriented firm will emphasize efficiency, a marketing firm will emphasize creativity and sales, accountants will probably emphasize cost, and a finance domination will stress profits.

Executives' personal values do more than influence corporate objectives; they also influence strategies, which are the alternative means for achieving objectives. The influence of executives' values on objectives and strategies is illustrated in two cases summarized in Table 4.1. In the first case the president of a small manufacturer of duplicating equipment ranked high in social and aesthetic values. His corporate objective was a slow to moderate growth. His marketing strategy was an emphasis on a single product, an independent-agent form of sales organization, a high-quality product with aesthetic appeal, and refusal to compete on a price basis. The top management team of Acoustic Research, Inc., a manufacturer of high-fidelity sound systems, ranked high on theoretical and social values. These values led to the marketing strategy of scientific truth and integrity in advertising; honest dealings with suppliers, dealers, and employees; and high quality at the lowest price to consumers. The objective of the firm was a "vaguely defined concept of a minimum acceptable level of profitability."[9]

Since strategies represent alternative means for achieving goals, a corporate policy represents the elimination of some alternative courses of action. For example, a pharmaceutical firm may decide to distribute its products through "ethical channels of distribution," which means that it will distribute through drug wholesalers and not directly to chain stores. The planner, therefore, cannot develop a channel strategy that would distribute directly to chain warehouses.

Executive values frequently have a dominant influence on the product policy of a

---

TABLE 4.1   **The influence of values on objectives and strategies**

Case 1

Values: The president of a small manufacturer of office duplicating equipment ranked high on social value, security, welfare of employees, and aesthetic value.

Objectives and strategies:

1. Slow to moderate growth
2. A single product
3. Independent-agent form of sales organization
4. Quality product with aesthetic appeal
5. Refusal to compete on price

Case 2

Values: The top management team of Acoustic Research, Inc., a manufacturer of high-fidelity loudspeaker systems, ranked high on theoretical and social values.

Objectives and strategies:

1. Scientific truth and integrity in advertising
2. Lower margins to dealers
3. Truth and honesty in relations with suppliers, dealers, and employees
4. High quality at the lowest possible price to the consumer
5. A vaguely defined concept of a minimum 'acceptable level of profit

W. D. Guth and R. Tagiuri, "Personal Values and Corporate Strategy," *Harvard Business Review* (September-October 1965): 123–132. Reprinted by permission. Copyright © 1965 by the President and Fellows of Harvard College; all rights reserved.

firm. For instance, managers of a hand-tool manufacturing company rejected diversification proposals that involved extending the present line of tools, because they were bored with that product line. Instead, they diversified into valves and couplings, which presented a technological challenge. A durable-goods company rejected diversification into packaged consumables as not being in the company's "style."[10]

Objectives are increasingly "inner-directed" rather than "other-directed."[11] "Inner-directed" refers to a perspective that emphasizes the values and capacities of the firm. "Other-directed" goal-setting procedures consider only the opportunities in the marketplace. The inner-directed approach includes an assessment of executive values, strengths, talents, abilities, as well as their limitations. The ideal planning process balances these internal capacities with external opportunities.

Burroughs Wellcome Company, a pharmaceutical firm, expresses its objectives and strategies as follows:

(Objectives)   The key objective of the company is to promote its growth, profitability, and prestige by:

(Strategies)
1. operating with excellence in discovering, manufacturing, and marketing within the United States products that contribute to good health through the prevention, detection, or treatment of disease in humans and animals;

2. providing stable employment, with opportunity, for Wellcome people; and

3. making the appropriate contributions to the social climate of the communities in which the company operates.

The dominant values in this objective are growth, profitability, and prestige. The strategies are stated in positive terms rather than in terms of policy contraints, but they do limit the alternatives for achieving growth, profitability, and prestige to the discovering, manufacturing, and marketing of health-related products. Thus the restraining policies are implicit in this statement of strategy. Stable employment, employee opportunities, and social contributions to the community serve to constrain the alternatives available to Burroughs Wellcome planners as they attempt to achieve the dominant values of the firm.

Financial Values   The social-psychological objectives of a firm are translated into economic objectives, such as profit, sales, internal investment, turnover of investment, market share, rate of growth, inventory turnover, cumulative cash flow, backlog of orders, or earnings per share of common stock. Although all of these objectives are laudable, it is impossible to achieve all of them. Many corporations establish an impressive list of multiple objectives. For example, in talking with security analysts, the chief executive of an international petroleum company expressed the objectives of his corporation as follows:

1. Emphasize the search for gas and oil in North America.

2. Build up the oil and gas business outside the United States.

3. Become a factor in the chemical business.

4. Achieve a growth in earnings of eight percent to ten percent a year.

5. Reach a return of ten percent on investment as soon as possible.

6. Compare favorably with other companies in the business according to a whole host of traditional industry measures.[12]

These objectives sound reasonable enough, but a closer examination reveals that they are conflicting. The first three are growth objectives—search for gas and oil, build up oil and gas business, and enter the chemical business. The next two objectives are profit-oriented goals—achieve a growth in earnings and reach ten percent on investment. All of these objectives cannot be achieved simultaneously.

Figure 4.1 illustrates how growth objectives and profit objectives conflict. Here we see the familiar cost curves from the microeconomic analysis of the firm. To maximize the total revenue of the firm, it should operate at output level OQ_4, but to maximize revenue in this case is to operate at a loss. If the goal is to maximize profit, the firm should operate at the output level represented by OQ_2.[13] If the firm operates at a point below OQ_1 or above OQ_3, it will be operating at a loss.

Once objectives have been defined, it becomes necessary to make trade-offs in choosing among conflicting objectives. Figure 4.1 illustrates the need to compromise between long-run growth and short-run profitability.

Degree of risk is frequently a dominating criterion for choosing a set of objectives.

The determination of the company's objectives should represent a careful weighing of the balance between the performance desired and the probability of its being accomplished. This balance is critical. Strategic objectives which are too ambitious result in the dissipation of assets, the destruction of morale, and create the risk of losing past gains as well as future opportunities. Strategic objectives which are not ambitious enough represent lost opportunity, and open a door to complacency.[14]

Fig. 4.1   Conflicting objectives.

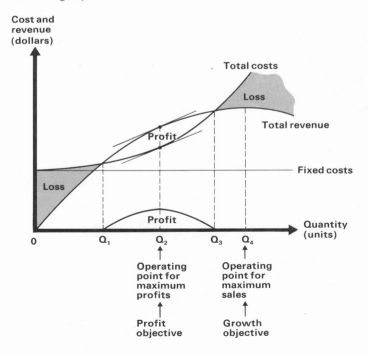

A Portfolio Approach   Many companies are beginning to view their product mixes as an investment portfolio. A variety of matrices have been developed to help companies classify the investment worth of each product and develop an appropriate strategy. The matrix in Table 4.2 was developed by the Shell International Chemical Company. In Chapter 9 we will see a matrix developed by the Boston Consulting Group.

The Shell International Chemical Company uses a three-by-three matrix to classify its products. The horizontal dimension places the products into three profitability classifications—unattractive, average, and attractive. The vertical dimension evaluates the company's competitive capabilities as weak, average, and strong. The strategy that Shell uses in each of the nine cells appears in Table 4.2.[15]

TABLE 4.2   The Shell Chemical directional policy matrix

Company's competitive capabilities	Outlook for profitability		
	Unattractive	*Average*	*Attractive*
Weak	Disinvest	Phased withdrawal	Double investment or quit
Average	Phased withdrawal	Custodial strategies less clear	Try harder
Strong	Use to generate cash	Growth sufficient for internal financing of expansion	Use all investment necessary to retain the preeminent market position

P. W. Beck, "The Directional Policy Matrix—A New Aid to Corporate Planning," Chemical Economics and Planning, Shell International Chemical Co., Ltd., London, November 1975.

CORPORATE POLICIES   Strategies are the alternative means for achieving objectives. *Policies* limit the alternative means that may be used. Policies, like objectives, reflect the values of the power structure in the organization. The planner must know these policies so as to avoid recommending strategies that are outside the acceptable set of alternatives. To make such a recommendation is to ensure that the plan will be rejected. To illustrate this point we can refer to the Burroughs Wellcome statement of objectives, which limited the company to achieving growth, profitability, and prestige within the industry of health-related products. A plan that recommended the introduction of a new cosmetic would automatically be rejected, because such a strategy is outside the policy of the firm.

Policies build a "fence" around acceptable strategies within the marketing mix, as shown in Fig. 4.2. In the center of the figure we see the objectives of a firm, such as growth, profit, and prestige. The spokes in this figure represent the marketing-mix variables. Alternative strategies are constrained by corporate policies. Product quality may range from low to high. Channel distribution may be intensive or exclusive, the latter being used for prestige reasons. Advertising and personal selling may be extensive or limited. Price strategies range from high prices (a skimming strategy) to low prices (a penetration strategy). The bounds set by the corporate policies are shown by the dotted lines. The area within the dotted lines includes those strategies which are acceptable to top management. The greater this area, the greater the flexibility in creating strategies.

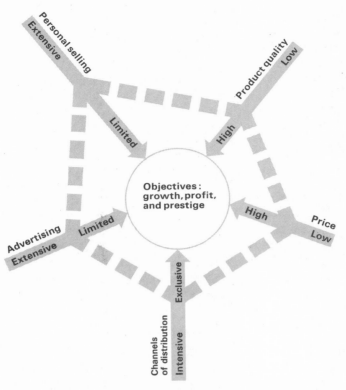

Note : The dotted lines represent corporate policy constraints.

Fig. 4.2   How corporate policies limit strategies.

CORPORATE GOALS   Although there is no general agreement in the planning literature on the definitions of *objectives* and goals,[16] there is an important distinction, and this distinction must be understood for corporate planning. The term *objectives*, as developed above, is a desired end-state, constrained by acceptable policies. In contrast, "*goals* are objectives whose attainment is desired by a specific time within the period covered by the plan; for example, 'to acquire our own distribution system by 1975' or 'increase our market share by ten percent by 1975' are goals."[17] A goal, therefore, is an objective that has been expressed in terms of the *magnitude* to be achieved and the *time* period for achievement. "Increase the market share by ten percent by 1975" or "change brand awareness from 40 to 60 percent next year" are good goal definitions because they are expressed in both magnitude and the date for accomplishment.

Control systems require this precise definition of goals. If the marketing system falls short of the desired target, early-warning feedback can provide the stimulus for appropriate action. Corrective action may be a reevaluation of the strategy, a reevaluation of the goals, or a reallocation of the resources. If the performance of a brand is less than the target market share, for example, it may be necessary to spend more resources on advertising and promotion. On the other hand, if the target market share was exceeded, it may be possible to reallocate promotional effort to other brands. Thus control systems, budgets, and profit planning depend on a clear definition of an objective in measurable terms, which is a goal. The problems of joint cost and joint revenues for multiple-product firms make measurement extremely difficult. It is the measurement of appropriate variables, not the lack of models of marketing systems, that makes it difficult to determine if goals have been accomplished.

There are three steps in the objective- and goal-formulation phase of planning:

1. Specification of corporate objectives and their translation into goals. Such a translation constitutes a *schedule* for the attainment of goals.
2. Provision of an operational definition of each goal and specification of the measures to be used in evaluating progress with respect to each.
3. Elimination of (or provision of means for resolving) conflicts between goals; that is, for deciding what to do when progress toward one goal requires sacrificing progress toward another.[18]

Marketing organizations with sophisticated planning systems are able to make a refinement on our definition of a goal. They express goals dynamically, such as "six percent growth per year" rather than "$X by the end of the next planning cycle." The use of a growth rate rather than a fixed volume of sales has two advantages in marketing planning. First, it makes it possible to track the results of the plan and determine quickly when it is going out of control. Second, it enables us to reflect nonlinear responses in the marketing strategy. A sales goal of X dollars per year implies that sales are a straight line throughout the year. There are many situations in marketing in which the relationship of sales to time is nonlinear, however. As we saw in the previous chapter, the life cycle of a product tends to be an S-shaped curve. As a market becomes saturated, the curve flattens. Pricing strategies of skimming versus penetration produce nonlinear relationships. Similarly, an advertising strategy of *blitz* versus *building* will yield nonlinear relationships between sales output and time.

Just as there is a hierarchy of strategies, there is a hierarchy of goals. There are top-level corporate goals (e.g., "operate with excellence ..."), and there are more specific marketing goals (e.g., "achieve a specific level of awareness"). Each of these goals is specified by a different level of management. The corporate goal would be determined by the chief executive officer; the marketing goal, by the chief marketing officer; and the level of awareness, by the product manager.

CORPORATE STRATEGIES Strategies are alternative means for achieving corporate goals. So far our definition of strategy is incomplete, because it fails to consider the costs of the alternative means for achieving goals. To overcome this deficiency, we may define *corporate strategies as alternative ways of employing corporate resources to achieve corporate goals.* This definition acknowledges three components of strategies—identification of corporate goals, the development of new and better alternatives for achieving these goals, and the determination of the resources required for each of these alternatives.

The development of a corporate strategy does not begin with the definition of a goal and end with the selection of one alternative; rather, it requires much interaction among goals, alternatives, and the resources required for various alternatives. Limited resources may require a lowering of the goals or the development of new alternatives. Thus the final strategies may not emerge until after many rotations around the short loop in Fig. 1.2, which illustrated the planning process.

The Creative Process of Identifying Alternatives   The most creative step in marketing planning is the identification of alternative uses of resources to achieve corporate goals. There is no theory or model to aid in this phase of the plan. Generating a new alternative can be just as creative as painting a picture or composing music.

Developing effective strategies must be an inductive process; there are just too many alternatives to proceed deductively. To illustrate the astronomical number of alternatives available to the marketing planner, reflect on the plight of the planner who is considering five alternatives within each of the following five elements of the marketing mix: product development, price, channels of distribution, advertising, and personal selling. If all possible combinations were to be evaluated, the planner would have to consider 3125 separate alternatives. When these elements of the marketing mix are discussed in detail in later chapters, you will realize that to limit each element of the marketing mix to only five alternatives represents a gross oversimplification. We must conclude, therefore, that the creation of successful strategies is an art, not a deductive science.

Examples of Marketing Strategies   Although we cannot identify all of the strategies available to each element in the marketing mix, we can present the ranges that are commonly used. For instance, product development may be based on an *undifferentiated product strategy*; one product is produced, and promotion is varied to make it attractive to all markets. Or, product development may be based on a *strategy of market segmentation*; each segment has a product developed to meet its unique needs. The undifferentiated strategy could lead to excessive promotional costs, whereas the high-segmentation strategy could lead to excessive product development, inventory, and distribution costs. The optimal strategy would be one between these two extremes, but the problem is identifying that point. Pricing strategies may range from those of penetration to those of skimming. A *penetration strategy* consists of introducing the new product with a low price in order to penetrate the market, thereby precluding competitive entry. A *skimming pricing strategy* starts with a high price and is then lowered to tap additional market segments, with the hope that the lower price is reached quickly enough to prevent a competitor from entering the market.

Advertisers must frequently choose between a push or a pull strategy. The *pull strategy* consists of promoting directly to the customer and pulling the product through the channel; the *push strategy* promotes to the channel, with the intent of having the channel promote the product to the ultimate buyer. Distribution strategies may range from a few *exclusive* outlets for specialty goods to intensive distribution for convenience products. A new channel strategy may completely revolutionize the industry. The introduction of L'eggs panty hose to supermarkets instead of department stores completely changed the buying patterns for quality women's hosiery and altered the channels of distribution in the hosiery industry. New-product development can also change channels of distribution. For instance, potato chips have a short shelf life, which limits their manufacture and distribution to regional suppliers. The development of Pringle's Potato Chips by Procter and Gamble altered the potato chip competitive scene. The long shelf life of this new product makes it possible for Procter and Gamble

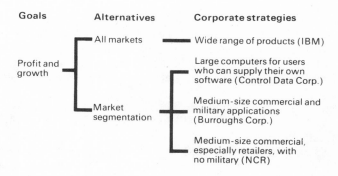

Fig. 4.3 Computer manufacturers' strategies in the 1960s.

to distribute its products through the same channels of distribution as its soaps, which also have a long shelf life.

Figure 4.3 illustrates how several companies may have the same goals but develop different corporate strategies because they choose different alternatives. In this figure we see the strategies that were followed by several computer companies during the early 1960s. Growth was clearly the goal of each of these companies, but IBM chose to serve all markets, whereas Control Data Corporation, Burroughs Corporation, and NCR chose to concentrate on specific market segments. The three companies using the segmentation approach identified three different segments as appropriate to their resources. Control Data Corporation developed large computers for such users as universities, which had the capability of developing their own software. Burroughs Corporation concentrated on medium-sized commercial and military computing needs. NCR concentrated on medium-sized commercial applications, especially those in retailing, but chose to avoid the military market. Thus we see that four companies with the same goal and in the same industry used four different marketing strategies.

Choosing Among Alternative Strategies Once the alternative strategies have been identified, the marketing executive must choose one or a few of the strategies for implementation. The process used to make this choice includes three steps: (1) identifying the criteria, (2) measuring the benefits and costs of each alternative, and (3) applying decision rules.

The criteria for choosing a strategy are based on the corporate objectives and marketing goals that have been discussed. Measuring the benefits and costs of each alternative strategy is made extremely difficult in marketing because of (1) the interactions in the marketing mix and (2) uncertainties. Interactions include joint revenues and joint costs that cannot be separated easily in multiproduct firms. There are also interactions among all of the elements of the marketing mix. For instance, the combination of a reduced price and advertising will be more effective than the sum of the individual effects of these strategies. It is difficult to measure the *synergistic* effects of these interactions.

Measuring the benefits and costs of a strategy can never be accomplished with certainty; thus there must be some provision for expressing the uncertainty. There are several ways to express uncertainty. We may attach a probability of occurrence to the event, in the same way that the weatherman estimates "a 90 percent chance of rain today." The marketing counterpart of such an estimate may be: "There is a .90 probability that the new product will achieve a sales level of $10 million the first year." Uncertainty could also be expressed as a range, e.g., "New-product sales will be somewhere between $8 million and $12 million." We could also make estimates of probabilities at each level along the range, yielding a probability distribution along the range of sales.

Once these measures have been made, the executives must process the information and make a choice. Decision-theory analysis has been used successfully by General Electric, duPont, and Pillsbury.[19]

The final decision rules that are used to select an alternative strategy may be a combination of goals that vary over the life cycle of a product. For example, the decision rule for selecting a strategy in the early stages of a product introduction may be: "Maximize sales to gain a viable share of the market in order to establish our product before competition enters." The next decision rule could be one that uses a combination of criteria: "Maximize sales with a minimum profit level of 10 percent of sales." The rule during later stages may be: "Maximize return on investment." Each of these rules will screen out strategies that are not appropriate. For instance, the first rule would encourage advertising expenditures; the last rule would reduce advertising to keep marketing investments in the product low as it reaches maturity.

PIMS Strategic Planning In 1972 the Marketing Science Institute initiated a PIMS (*Profit Impact of Marketing Strategies*)study. This study pooled data from 50 companies on more than 600 business units to identify those factors that influence the profitability of a business and to determine how return on investment (ROI) changes in response to changes in both marketing strategy and marketing condition.[20] The major findings were:

1. Market share is strongly linked to profits;
2. Product quality is positively related to return on investment;
3. High marketing expenditures are not justified when product quality is low;
4. High research and development expenditures are profitable when market share is high;
5. A high ratio of total investment to sales and a low market share is a return on investment "disaster";
6. The larger, more diversified companies tend to have larger returns on investment.[21]

Analytical procedures such as those used in the PIMS project are used in industry. Reginald H. Jones, chairman of General Electric, stated that the GE system of strategic planning provides the basis for allocating resources to areas of the greatest earnings growth while minimizing investments in the lower, more static growth areas.[22]

ACTION PLANS The demanding process of developing a corporate strategy is not an end in itself, but rather a prelude to action that should attain superior competitive performance.[23] The translation of a strategy into action requires a comprehensive program that specifies who will do what with which corporate resources, where, when, and how. In military parlance these specifications are known as *tactics*; in marketing planning these detailed programs are known as *action plans*, *brand plans*, or implementation of a strategy. The term *action plans* will be used in this text. The action plan specifies in detail how resources will be used on behalf of a brand to achieve its goal.

"The need for an explicit strategy stems from two key attributes of the business organization: first, that success depends on people working together so that their efforts are mutually reinforcing; and second, that this must be accomplished in the context of rapidly changing conditions."[24] The next chapter focuses on the first attribute—the need for people to work together in mutually reinforcing ways.

SUMMARY Having to work within the context of the organization, the marketing manager must fully understand the values that give it direction. These values, ranging from the most general to the most specific, are the organization's mission, objectives, policies, and goals. The activities that lead to the achievement of these values are strategies and action plans (or tactics).

DISCUSSION QUESTIONS

1. Define corporate missions, objectives, policies, strategies, and tactics.
2. What is the difference between the marketing concept and the inner-directed planning concept?
3. Explain why revenue maximization and profit maximization are incompatible objectives.
4. Define and give an example of penetration pricing, skimming pricing, push promotion, and pull promotion strategies.
5. In economics, the goal of the firm is assumed to be "profit maximization." Criticize the theoretical and practical implications of this assumption. In the real business world, what other goals could a company have?
6. This chapter indicated that "corporate objectives are an extension of the personal values of those in power." Try to name various groups that might be in power in a corporation and what kinds of friction they will cause with other groups while emphasizing their own objectives.
7. For an industry you are familiar with, try to explain the marketing strategies of the companies in that industry in terms of their target markets and the marketing mixes they use to achieve their goals.
8. What might be some success factors for:
   a) a high-volume discount retail chain
   b) a small food processor specializing in canned items with regional appeal in the southeastern United States
   c) a shipbuilding firm.
9. Evaluate the following set of (hypothetical) corporate objectives:
   a) Increase market share annually, by 5 percent or more, to achieve an ultimate share of 25 percent of the market;
   b) Increase earnings by at least 7 percent per year;
   c) Achieve and maintain a return on investment of 9 percent;
   d) Build and maintain an image of quality and service to the consumer;
   e) Keep the price of firm's stock high.

NOTES

1. P. W. Beck, Deputy Head of Strategic Analysis, Shell International Chemical Company. (Paper delivered at the Institute of Management Science and Operations Research Society of America Conference on Corporate Strategic Planning, New Orleans, March 1, 1977.)

2. This paragraph is based on a paper by M. G. Allen, Vice President, Corporate Strategy and Planning, General Electric Co., delivered at a conference on corporate strategic planning, sponsored jointly by the Institute of Management Science and the Operations Research Society of America, New Orleans, February 28–March 2, 1977.

3. *Ibid.*

4. A. P. Sloan, Jr., "Product Policy and Its Origins," *My Years with General Motors* (New York: Doubleday, 1964), pp. 82–94.

5. S. Tilles, "Making Strategy Explicit," excerpted in H. I. Ansoff, ed., *Business Strategy* (Baltimore: Penguin, 1969), pp. 180–209.

6. D. W. Ewing, *The Human Side of Planning* (London: Macmillan, 1969) pp. 80–81.

7. T. Levitt, "Marketing Myopia," *Harvard Business Review* (July-August 1960): 45–46. This article was republished in the *Harvard Business Review* (September-October 1975: 26ff), with comments by Levitt on some of the "bizarre" things that happened as a result of the article (pp. 180–181). Marketers tended to respond to every consumer whim, which led to unprofitable product proliferation.

8. Tilles, *op. cit.*, p. 186.

9. W. Guth and R. Tagiuri, "Personal Values and Corporate Strategy," *Harvard Business Review* (September-October 1965): 123–132.

10. R. L. Ackoff, *A Concept of Corporate Planning* (New York: Wiley/Interscience, 1970), p. 25.

11. Ewing, *op. cit.*, pp. 80–81.

12. H. C. Egerton and J. K. Brown, *Planning and the Chief Executive* (New York: Conference Board, 1972), p. 10.

13. Students familiar with calculus will recognize that this profit maximization point represents that point in output where the slopes of the total cost and total revenue curves are equal, i.e., where marginal revenue equals marginal cost.

14. Tilles, *op. cit.*, p. 201.

15. P. W. Beck, "The Directional Policy Matrix—A New Aid to Corporate Planning," Chemical Economics and Planning, Shell International Chemical Co., Ltd., London, November 1975.

16. Egerton and Brown, *op. cit.*, p. 8.

17. Ackoff, *op. cit.*, pp. 23–24.

18. *Ibid.*, p. 24.

19. R. V. Brown, "Do Managers Find Decision Theory Useful?" *Harvard Business Review* (May-June 1970): 78–89.

20. S. Schoeffler, R. D. Buzzell, and D. F. Heany, "Impact of Strategic Planning on Profit Performance," *Harvard Business Review* (March-April 1974): 137–145.

21. Because these findings were derived through regression analysis, they must be interpreted with caution. It should also be noted that the cooperating companies were large firms, and the relationships have yet to be replicated for medium- and small-size firms.

22. R. H. Jones, in the General Electric 1973 annual report, p. 5.

23. Tilles, *op. cit.*, p. 207.

24. *Ibid.*, p. 181.

SUGGESTED READINGS

Christopher, W. F., "Marketing Planning that Gets Things Done," *Harvard Business Review* (September-October 1970): 56–64.

Lorange, P., and R. F. Vancil, *Strategic Planning Systems* (Englewood Cliffs, N.J.: Prentice-Hall, 1977).

ENVIRONMENTAL ANALYSIS WORKSHEET

Environmental elements	Facts	Assumptions or research needed	Conclusions

Organizational values, objectives, and policies (4)

Organizational design (5)

Situation
    Generic demand (6)
    Brand demand (7)
    Competition (9)
    Public policy (10)

Opportunities (2)

Problems

MARKETING PLAN (CONSUMER PRODUCT)

Current performance
Recommendations
Effect of recommendations on income
Situation analysis
Opportunities and problems
Strategies
Tests and research
Supporting documents
    Comparative budgets
    Media allocation schedule
    Promotion control sheet

STRATEGY WORKSHEET

Opportunities and problems in rank order to importance

   1.
   2.
     .
   n.

	Current strategy	Alternatives and recommended strategy	Estimated Effect

Demand strategy
  Generic
  Brand			

Strategic goals
  Financial
  Marketing			

Marketing-mix strategies
  Product (12)
  Pricing (13)
  Channel and logistics (14)
  Advertising and promotional (15)
  Sales management (16)			

Research (3)			
Profit plan			
Evaluation and control (19)			

CHAPTER 5

Organizational Strategies of Marketing Management

LEARNING OBJECTIVES   After studying this chapter you should:

1. Be aware of the trends in organizational strategies in marketing.
2. Understand the brand-management system—its activities, strengths, and weaknesses.
3. Understand how the responsibility of a brand manager changes over the life cycle of a product.
4. Know what it takes for a product-management system to be successful.
5. Be sensitive to the influence of new values on organizational strategies.
6. Know why new college graduates seek positions in brand management.
7. Be able to define and use the following concepts:

Functional designs	Group product manager
Market-oriented designs	Brand coordinator
Team designs	Brand champion
Product manager	Product life cycle
Brand manager	Postindustrialism

SOME ANALYTICAL QUESTIONS FOR OPENERS

1. How are resources, responsibility, and authority organized?
2. Who is the chief marketing executive and what are his or her functions?
3. Where are the strategic decisions made?
4. Does the organizational design reflect the success factors?
5. Is there a brand-management system? Are the conditions such that this system will work?

Many marketing plans fail because the planner did not consider the fact that the organization was not capable of implementing the plan. Short-range plans will require adaptation to the existing organization, whereas long-range plans may require re-designing the organization. Therefore, understanding and working with people is vital to planning and implementing plans. The young planner needs to consider the human element of planning early in the planning processes, not after it is too late. The long-range planner must recognize that the organizational strategies may be the most critical part of the plan. This chapter examines some of the long- and short-range organizational marketing strategies. Throughout this discussion it is important to note that marketing organizations are in a continual state of change, reflecting the firm's ongoing need to adapt its marketing activities to its ever-changing environment.

TRENDS IN ORGANIZATIONAL STRATEGIES IN MARKETING Marketing organizations have gone through three stages of development. The most common organizational design prior to the 1950s was a functional one. In this design the specialized activities of packaging, advertising, personal selling, etc., were organized into homogeneous units. The period from the 1950s to the 1970s saw a shift to a team approach, headed by a brand manager. All of the functions were represented on the team and focused on the success of a single brand of a product. During the 1970s many firms shifted to a market-oriented organizational strategy. Marketing functions were organized according to industry classifications, end users, and channels of distribution. This shift was probably due to the rapid changes in the marketplace in terms of new-product development and competition. This type of marketing organization makes the firm more responsive to the changing needs of the consumer and to competitive changes. A market-oriented organization is clearly an application of the *marketing concept*. During the discussion of sales-management strategies (Chapter 16), we will see how many firms organize their sales forces according to the market. This type of organization has been common in industrial marketing (Chapter 8), but it is new to many consumer goods firms.

THE BRAND-MANAGEMENT SYSTEM The brand-management system is used extensively as an organizational marketing strategy, especially for packaged groceries, drugs, and personal-care items. This system has many strengths, but it also has its weaknesses. It is the first level of management for a person seeking a career in marketing, occurring three to five years after the person enters the firm. Thus it is important to know what a brand manager is and is not.

First, we must clarify the distinction between the terms *brand manager* and *product manager*. Although they are frequently used interchangeably, the two terms refer to different things. The term *brand manager* is used when a company has several brands within a product category. For instance, General Foods' Maxwell House Division has several brands of coffee, each with its own brand manager. A company with only one brand of coffee, on the other hand, may use the term *product* manager. Regardless of the function, the tasks will be the same, and the terms will be used interchangeably in this text.

Comparing the Functional and Brand Manager Designs The organizational chart for a functional organization appears in the upper part of Fig. 5.1. The functional design groups similar activities. Thus, for example, all persons who perform advertising roles are grouped together.

The brand-management design groups together all persons who are concerned with a particular product. The *product* is the focus in this design rather than the activity that is to be done on behalf of the product. A *brand manager* heads the product *team*, which will include representatives from advertising, selling, promotion, market research, etc.

The functional system is adequate for the firm with one or two products. But as the number of products increases, the vice-president for marketing cannot handle

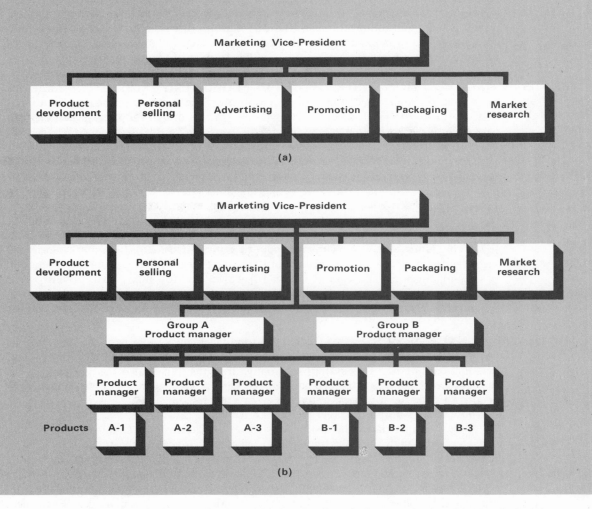

Fig. 5.1 Two common marketing organizations: (a) a functional marketing organization; (b) a product management (team) organization.

all of the details associated with planning. Brand-manager systems were developed to make one person responsible for a brand's development and profitable promotion. The origins of this system are generally traced to the grocery packaged-goods industry, with considerable credit given to Procter & Gamble and General Foods. This design is also used extensively in industrial-marketing organizations and to some extent in service industries.

The product-management design shown in Fig. 5.1 reveals a common weakness of this design. Although responsible for the profitable development and promotion of a product, the product manager has neither a staff *nor any authority* over the functional persons who must perform the work. This is the classic organizational problem of *responsibility without authority.* A product manager's only authority over the functional members of the team is through their assignments in the marketing plan. This plan is approved by the top marketing manager, a vice-president in this case, who also has authority over the functional managers. *Instead of authority*, the product manager must *depend on persuasion* to gain the cooperation of functional members of his or her product team. Thus product-management designs emphasize persuasion rather than coercion.

The activities of a product manager may be seen in the job description of a Miles Laboratories product manager (Table 5.1). The basic activities are those common to top managers—planning, setting objectives, developing copy and media strategies, scheduling, control, evaluating results, and cooperating with other departments.

TABLE 5.1   **Job description of a product manager, Miles Laboratories, Inc.**

Department	Marketing—U.S.
Division:	Consumer Products Division
Location:	Elkhart, IN
Reports to:	Group Product Manager

JOB FUNCTION

Maximize product sales growth and profitability through comprehensive business management, including the development and execution of the total marketing effort required for the brand.

PRINCIPAL ACTIVITIES/OBJECTIVES

1. Develop and recommend short- and long-range strategy for the marketing of the assigned products. This includes the identification of brand-extension opportunities.
2. Develop and recommend short- and long-range sales and profit objectives for assigned products. Working with sales management, monitor and forecast progress against plans.
3. Develop and recommend marketing plans that by design ensure achievement of sales and profit objectives for the planned year and that are consistent with the brand's short- and longer-term objectives and strategies.
4. Introduce new products (brand extensions) on regional or national basis.
5. Provide effective direction to advertising agencies assigned the responsibility for developing creative advertising for the assigned brands. Working with medical and legal departments, isolate product claims that optimize.
6. Develop and recommend media strategy for use by the media department and the advertising agency in developing media plans. Evaluate media plans against strategy and delivery against the target audiences.
7. Develop and recommend objectives and strategies for consumer and trade promotions. Working with the sales promotion department, field sales management, and the advertising agency, develop programs that meet both the objectives and strategy.
8. Constantly monitor and control marketing expenditures to ensure that they are within approved budget limits.
9. Develop and recommend pricing policy and strategies for the assigned brands. Working with manufacturing and financial departments, isolate opportunities for implementation of cost savings programs.
10. As appropriate review product packaging design and recommend modifications that will improve on-shelf impact and that are consistent with trade regulations.

TABLE 5.1 (cont.)

11. Working with the market research department, identify research programs that provide actionable information about the market and market conditions which when applied will build the business.

NATURE AND SCOPE

The product manager reports to the group product manager and has reporting assistant product manager(s) and a secretary. The product manager's primary task is to ensure that the product meets or exceeds sales and profit objectives. The product manager is generally involved in the development and execution of marketing plans for his or her brands. The product manager must work with the field sales force, manufacturing, financial planning, medical, and marketing services departments. It is the incumbent's responsibility to ensure that all necessary coordination takes place with various division and corporate staff departments. The incumbent must be able to work effectively with varying departments within an advertising agency. The incumbent must present concise, meaningful, and decision-oriented presentations to senior management of the corporation.

KNOW-HOW

Normally, a bachelor's degree is necessary, with an MBA desirable. Minimum experience should be three to five years of progressively responsible marketing experience in a consumer packaged goods environment. Field sales training and experience would be a definite plus in helping to carry out the duties of the position. The incumbent should be well seasoned in the areas of consumer advertising, sales promotion, trade relations, and marketing research. To be effective in the job, the incumbent must qualify as follows—(1) possess sound business judgment and be able to relate both his or her and the staff's activities to maximize profit and build new business; (2) show the ability to lead as well as manage people and be concerned for their growth; (3) be firm as well as diplomatic and tactful; (4) should excel in both oral and written communication with all levels of corporate management.

PROBLEM SOLVING

The most important challenge is to see that both the incumbent and his or her people identify the marketing opportunities for the brands under their control and sort out and implement those programs which offer the greatest return on investment. The incumbent must identify brand-extension opportunities and successfully implement their launch into the marketplace. In the area of communication, he or she must determine the optimum marketing strategy, basic selling proposition, and creative strategy and see that they are executed properly. The incumbent must identify the most economical means of testing business-building ideas. In the area of people management, he or she must provide the environment necessary for maximum performance of staff. In the financial area, he or she must strive to consistently meet and/or exceed the profit commitment to the division. The incumbent must work effectively within a highly regulated environment.

ACCOUNTABILITY

The incumbent is free to operate in the area of creative marketing management. Most initial decisions are made by the incumbent and his or her staff. During frequent reviews, the incumbent must ultimately defend or sell his or her program to divisional management or members of corporate management. The incumbent is responsible for staying within previously approved budgets, meeting profit plans, and adhering to company policy.

Provided by Miles Laboratories, Inc.

Product managers have top-management impact without the rank or compensation of top managers.[1] But there are important differences between product managers and top managers. Product managers are not risk-taking, decision-making entrepreneurs.[2] It is these functions that make executives highly paid. Product managers must operate within the limitations of corporate policies and procedures.

Product management is frequently a training ground for higher marketing positions. Figure 5.2 dramatically illustrates the broad marketing experience available to the product managers at Scott Paper Company. Clearly, *the product manager must be a marketing generalist.*

The organizational design of the marketing activities of the Maxwell House Division of General Foods Corporation (Fig. 5.3) illustrates the use of the brand-management system in the grocery products field. The division is organized around products. At the top of the product organization are managers for regular coffees, modified coffees, and new product/business development. Group product managers are the next lower-level product management, followed by product managers and associate product managers. The emphasis on promotion in this industry is reflected in the presence of managers for promotion within the marketing services department.

Fig. 5.2 Sphere of activities and working relationships of Scott Paper Company's product managers. (*The Product Manager System,* New York: The Conference Board, Experiences in Marketing Management, No. 8, 1965, pp. 75–76. Reprinted by permission of the publisher and Scott Paper Co.)

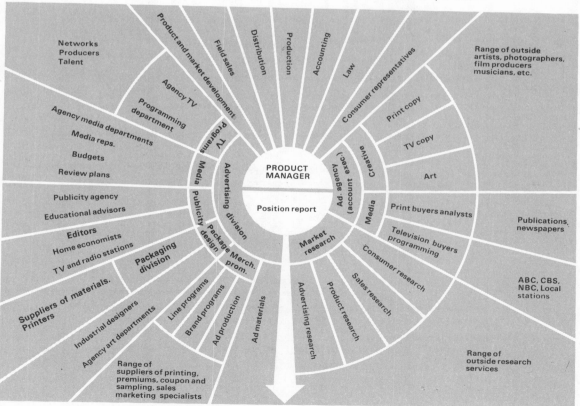

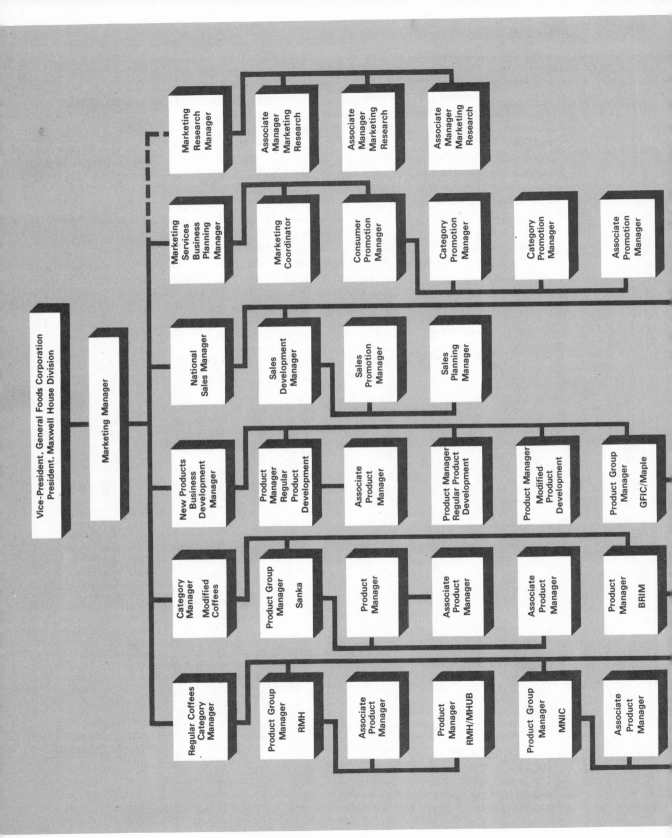

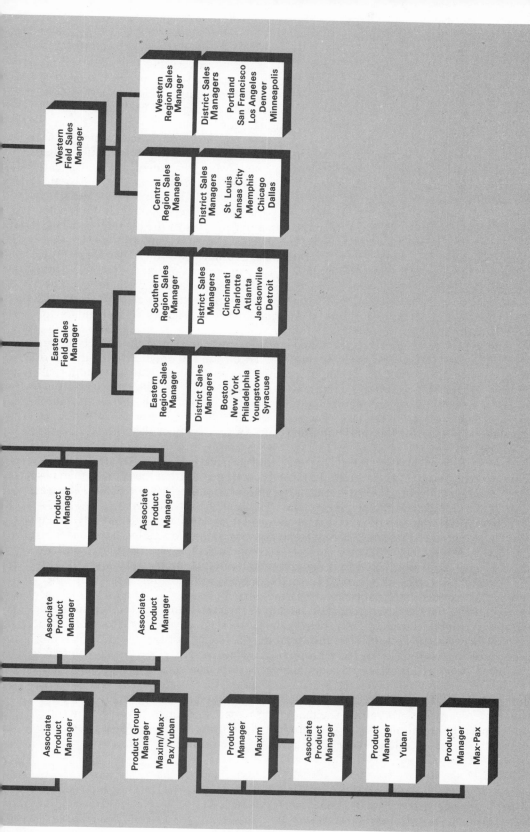

Fig. 5.3 Organization of the marketing department of the Maxwell House Division of General Foods Corporation. (Reprinted by permission.)

Marketing research plays a key role in this industry, so there is a marketing research manager and three associate managers. There are no advertising managers in this organization because the advertising function is a major part of the product manager's role. It has been observed that the spread of the brand-management system has been accompanied by a decline in the status of advertising managers in companies.[3]

Burroughs Wellcome Company, a pharmaceutical company, takes a different approach to the relationship between functional activities and brand management. Persons with full-time functional activities also are product planners. This design provides a combination of experiences for persons who are part of a management-training program. The individual gains in-depth experience in a functional area and the broad experience required for marketing planning. These planners have generally returned to the home office after a successful period as drug representatives in the sales force. Therefore, they bring reality and competitive insights to the planning process.

Because Burroughs Wellcome planners have primary responsibility to their functional jobs, they must be given adequate assistance for their planning. This assistance takes several forms. First, there is a group product planner in the marketing services department who assists three to five planners. Second, there is an extensive marketing information system, most of which is computerized for easy access by the planner. Finally, there is a training program for new planners and seminars for experienced ones.

In the previous chapter we saw that a company must recognize the success factors for its industry. These success factors must be reflected in the organizational design of the company. Product development, promotion, and marketing research are important success factors in the grocery products, as was illustrated by the Maxwell House organization. Industrial marketing requires success factors in areas such as technical services and engineering services. These services are reflected in Fig. 5.4, which is the organization chart for the marketing and sales organization of the FMC Industrial Chemical Group.

A comparison of Figs. 5.3 and 5.4 provides insights into the differences between consumer and industrial marketing. In Fig. 5.4 it will be noted that the product manager plays a less prominent role. The reporting relationship suggests that technical services are as important as product management. There is an advertising manager in Fig. 5.4, which suggests that the product managers do not perform much of an advertising function. The fact that there are two sales managers and one advertising manager (who is under the sales director) reflects a common fact in industrial marketing—personal selling is more important than advertising in industrial marketing.

How do the roles of persons in a marketing organization relate to each other? Figure 5.5 answers this question for a pharmaceutical company. The product manager is responsible for the development of individual product plans; for implementing the approved plans in coordination with the managers of sales, advertising, and promotion; and for reviewing the results. The group product manager assists in product planning, implementing, and reviewing for a group of products in such a way as to maintain a balanced marketing effort. The sales manager is responsible for developing field sales programs, establishing quotas and budgets, recruiting, training, and motivating the sales force. The advertising manager counsels in the development, implementation, and evaluation of advertising programs. The marketing research manager develops, interprets, and reports information necessary for product planning and control. All of these managers' efforts are coordinated by the marketing vice-president, who approves plans,

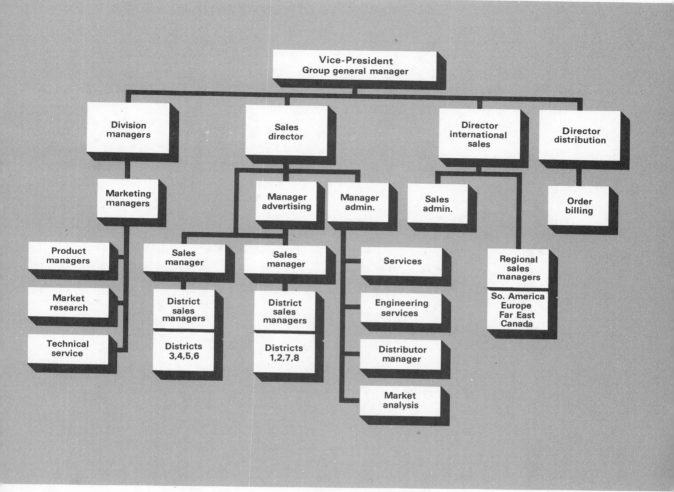

Fig. 5.4 Marketing and sales organization, Industrial Chemical Group, FMC Corporation. (Reprinted by permission.)

maintains a system of controls, and develops strategies and procedures. The direct line of responsibility continues through the division manager, who establishes objectives, undertakes the development of new products, and performs the activities of planning, implementation, and control at the division level. Thus the product manager's plan becomes part of the total corporate planning effort. The activities of planning, implementation, and control take place at each level of management. The development of broad strategies and procedures, however, is reserved for the higher levels of management.

Company President

Division Manager

- Establish objectives and operating procedures for the division
- Approve operating plans for the division
  - — Marketing
  - — Manufacturing
  - — Research and medical
  - — New-product development
- Develop long-term plans for the division
  - — Markets
  - — Products
  - — Organization
  - — Plant and equipment
- Control results against plans and initiate action to effect improvement
- Identify the division's public relations requirements and participate in the implementation of an effective public relations program
- Ensure implementation of overall company research and medical affairs, resolve any questions which arise
- Undertake the development of new products as a prime responsibility and coordinate the marketing, research and medical, production, and finance activities involved in translating a new product idea into a commercially feasible product

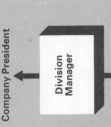

Administrator New Products Marketing

- Develop and recommend test marketing practices for new products
- Develop and direct an effective test marketing program
- Prepare test marketing presentations for management
- Determine scope of test markets
- Coordinate test marketing functions with appropriate division executives
- Formulate and recommend product objectives and goals
- Evaluate product market performance and if appropriate recommend national distribution

Vice-President Marketing

- Recommend division marketing procedures
- Develop basic marketing strategy
- Direct the development of product marketing plans and programs
- Review recommended plans, modify as appropriate, consolidate, and recommend approval of the consolidated programs
  - — Field sales
  - — Advertising and promotion
  - — Test marketing
- Direct implementation of the approved marketing program
- Control marketing results against plans

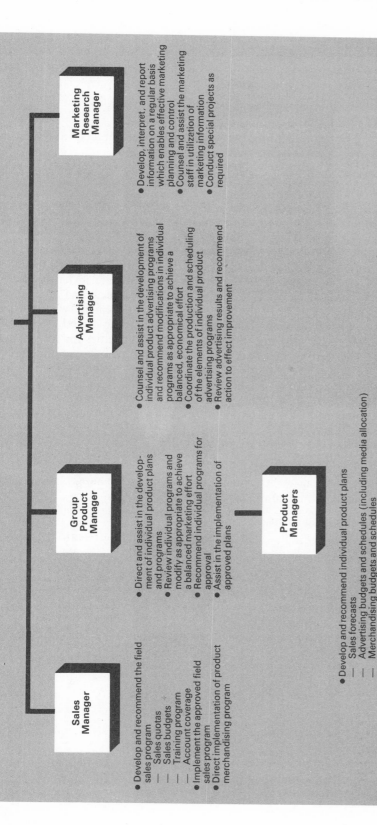

Sales Manager

- Develop and recommend the field sales program
  - Sales quotas
  - Sales budgets
  - Training program
  - Account coverage
- Implement the approved field sales program
- Direct implementation of product merchandising program

Group Product Manager

- Direct and assist in the development of individual product plans and programs
- Review individual programs and modify as appropriate to achieve a balanced marketing effort
- Recommend individual programs for approval
- Assist in the implementation of approved plans

Advertising Manager

- Counsel and assist in the development of individual product advertising programs and recommend modifications in individual programs as appropriate to achieve a balanced, economical effort
- Coordinate the production and scheduling of the elements of individual product advertising programs
- Review advertising results and recommend action to effect improvement

Marketing Research Manager

- Develop, interpret, and report information on a regular basis which enables effective marketing planning and control
- Counsel and assist the marketing staff in utilization of marketing information
- Conduct special projects as required

Product Managers

- Develop and recommend individual product plans
  - Sales forecasts
  - Advertising budgets and schedules (including media allocation)
  - Merchandising budgets and schedules
  - Pricing
  - Product improvement
- Implement approval plans through coordination with the sales manager and the advertising and sales promotion manager
- Review results against plan and recommend action to effect improvement

Fig. 5.5   Marketing department in a product division of a pharmaceutical company. (The Product Manager System, New York: The Conference Board, Experiences in Marketing Management, No. 8, 1965, p. 113. Reprinted by permission.)

Levels of Product Manager Responsibility   The amount of responsibility given to a product manager varies with such factors as the importance of the product, its position in the product life cycle, the amount of staff support available, and, of course, the depth of his or her experience. There are three gradations of responsibility:

1. the *brand coordinator* position, which has bureaucratic responsibility but no entrepreneurial responsibility;
2. the *brand champion* position, which has bureaucratic responsibility, as well as responsibility for making entrepreneurial recommendations;
3. the *brand director* position, which has bureaucratic responsibility along with responsibility for entrepreneurial action and profits.[4]

The brand coordinator and brand champion are most common, with the brand directorship reserved for a rare situation, such as new-product introduction in a firm that introduces new products infrequently.

The brand coordinator uses his or her extensive experience with the brand and organization to cut through red tape and get action for the brand. This person tends to be at the level of responsibility necessary for a product that is late in its life cycle. The brand champion is a protagonist, not the "president of his or her brand company." The latter posture creates an adversary problem with top management, whereas top management should be an ally. Brand champions rarely graduate directly to senior management within the same corporate entity, because their capacities for risk taking and innovation have not been tested.[5] Top management will move candidates for management positions out of the brand-champion system to other divisions for additional training and testing.

A brand director differs from a product manager in authority. The product manager has none; the brand director, higher in the organization, has authority. The brand-director form of product management is rarely seen.

Requirements for a Successful Product-Management System   For a product-management system to succeed, the following conditions must be met:

1. Strong support from top management;
2. Competent staff specialists, especially in advertising and marketing research;
3. A training program for product managers that will
   a) develop creative insight into the marketplace through
      1) an understanding of consumer behavior
      2) an understanding of advertising
      3) an understanding of research and its limitations, and
      4) a sense of industry and competitive trends;
   b) clarify the expectations of the product-management role;
   c) establish working relationships with functional areas;
4. Top-management control through the use of marketing plans;
5. Brand managers who are manageable, not free-swinging entrepreneurs;
6. Brand managers who, because of their lack of authority, are persuasive communicators with staff and line personnel;

7. The inclusion of procedures for resolving differences; and

8. Realistic measures of brand-management performance.

Some Limitations of the Brand-Management System   The limitations of the brand-management system stem from the conflict that is designed into the system. It is an advocacy role, so there is bound to be conflict between the brand manager and line personnel. It is a decentralized function, which prevents optimization in an organization that may be guided by such principles. The greatest limitation has been noted previously—the problem of responsibility for the success of the product without line authority. Staff-line competitive conflict may bring out the best in all parties, or it may create a destructive environment.

Many companies have been moving away from the usual form of the brand-management organization. PepsiCo, for example, has moved the major brand decisions to top management and is changing toward a more specialized, functional design.[6] Eastman Kodak reorganized in 1965 according to markets and channels of distribution. There are now "Kodak marketing divisions for business systems, consumer products, international operations, motion pictures and education, professional customers, commercial and industrial markets, and radiography. Each is a self-contained profit center."[7] Purex and Levi Strauss too have moved away from the brand-management system.[8]

The brand-management system is not dead, but it is becoming obvious that it is not appropriate for all marketing organizations. What are some of the limitations? The organizational limitations have been noted above. The second major limitation is the greatly expanded knowledge required of product managers. The new dynamics of the marketplace—new marketing technology, new forms of competition, consumerism, the legal implications of brand decisions, public policies, new channels of distribution, highly fragmented market segments, shorter product life cycles, capital shortages that require faster paybacks and greatly expanded information systems—have placed unreasonable demands on the knowledge that the brand manager must have. Many firms have concluded that a product manager cannot reach the level of expertise in all areas that is necessary to make the crucial strategic decisions. These companies either return to a functional design or provide the product manager with extensive staff support.

Other companies are lengthening the period that a product manager is on the job.[9] This tends to reduce the emphasis on short-range strategies, and it gives the product manager more time to learn the job. Some companies are considering making product management a final career position, so that individuals may become experts in the newly expanded roles. Another solution to the problem of the expanding roles is to create more brand managers. The H. J. Heinz Company has taken this approach by combining *product* management and *market* management.[10] It is creating product managers who are responsible for specific markets. Thus one ketchup product manager is responsible to the retail grocery market, and another ketchup product manager is concerned with restaurant chains. This design reflects the fact that each market has a different set of needs.

THE DYNAMICS OF ORGANIZATIONAL DESIGNS   When planning is decentralized to the level of the individuals who will be implementing the plan, the design of the marketing organization must reflect the dynamics of the marketplace. Two approaches for evaluating these dynamics are the product life-cycle approach and the investment-portfolio approach.

The Influence of the Product Life Cycle on an Organization Table 5.2 illustrates how the goals, strategies, and organizational design of a marketing firm vary over the life cycle of a product. Market penetration during product introduction focuses on the maximization of sales to gain market position, but at the end of the product's life cycle contraction may be necessary to maximize profits. (In Chapter 4 we noted that the objectives of maximization of sales and maximization of profits are in conflict at any given time.)

The organizational requirements of a new product are demanding. The leader must have risk-taking and entrepreneurial qualities. In the final stages of product development an efficient bureaucrat is needed. Staff requirements in the early stages include a heavy emphasis on marketing and promotion, but finance and logistics are emphasized at the last stage. Table 5.2 illustrates the dynamics of a marketing organizational design that are not reflected in the lines and boxes on an organizational chart.

An example of the product life-cycle influence The hospital-supplies industry provides an example of how the product life cycle influences the activities of a product manager.[11] During the late 1950s the role of the product manager was to support the missionary selling that was required to sell a new product line—disposable supplies. During the 1960s, economic expansion and tremendous growth in the industry required the

TABLE 5.2 **Relating goals, strategies, and organizational design to the product life cycle**

	Product life cycle			
	New or recycled	*Growth*	*Maturity*	*Decline*
Goals and strategies:				
Market penetration	Introduction	Expansion	Maintenance	Contraction
Risk/uncertainty	High	Moderate	Low	Low
Profit strategy	Investment	Growth	Maintenance	Milking
Organizational design:				
Brand management	Director	Champion	Champion	Coordinator
Information needs	Demand	Demand Competition Distribution	Demand, competition, distribution, costs	Costs, financial
Staff support	R & D, market research, venture groups, advertising	Market research, advertising	Marketing research, advertising, financial	Financial, distribution

Adapted from Stephen Dietz, "Get More Out of Your Brand Management," *Harvard Business Review* (July-August 1973): 135.

product manager to shift to the problems of forecasting the proper product, introducing product-line extensions, and coordinating sales and production. The entry of many competitors during the late 1960s and early 1970s shifted the product manager's role to concerns for market share, brand preference, and complex pricing strategies. In the 1970s, as the market stabilized, the emphasis shifted to long-range strategic business planning that would use available capacity and provide an acceptable return on investment.

The Investment-Portfolio Approach Many firms are viewing their product mix as an investment portfolio (Chapters 4 and 9). This approach requires that they consider the organizational needs of products in each investment category. General Electric considers the management strengths that are required for products (or businesses) in each category. Then it determines what criteria must be used to evaluate these managers.[12] The General Electric approach will be considered briefly.

A product or new business in the *investment/growth* category must have a manager who is enterprising and a strong leader. This manager must be evaluated according to his or her *future* performance. Developing such an evaluation scheme is difficult.

The investment category of *selectivity/earnings* requires a sophisticated and critical manager. This is a period of product maturation, so cost cutting is important. The manager will be evaluated according to current financial results.

The *harvest/divest* category requires a solid, experienced manager who is also a diplomat. He or she must close plants and deal with community problems related to closures. Evaluating this manager is also difficult, because the outcomes are subjective. Top management must be careful in placing this type of individual in an organization, because it signals to the division that it is about to be axed. The individual may not like the image of being *manager of dead products*, but it is a specialization that more companies will be considering.

THE NEED FOR NEW ORGANIZATIONAL DESIGNS The well-known and well-tested functional and decentralized organizational designs do not meet all of the individual and group needs in today's organizations. Post–Industrial Revolution values, organizational democracy, and new management technology have created new needs that require new structures.

New organizational designs must reflect the postindustrial values. The designs should include full and free communication, regardless of rank; power consensus rather than coercion or compromise; and influence based on technical competence and knowledge rather than whims or prerogative of power.[13] One should observe the limitations of such open and flexible organizations. They require a much stronger and better-qualified individual than does the highly structured organization. The organizational designer should not attempt to impose an open design on weak and timid individuals any more than she or he should attempt structure on strong individuals.

New Values and Emerging Organizational Structures The values of the Industrial Revolution are quite different from those of the post–Industrial Revolution. Table 5.3 compares the values of these two periods in economic development according to their influence on cultural values, organizational philosophies, and ecological strategies. In comparing these industrial and postindustrial values, note that the shift is from individual to group values. The organizational philosophies are moving from a mechanical approach to one in which organizations treat humans as humans. Competition is giving way to collaboration. Ecological strategies reveal a shift from defensive response patterns toward anticipating crises and taking the initiative with innovative administrations that create change.

TABLE 5.3   Changes in emphasis in the transition to postindustrialism

Type of change	From	Toward
Cultural values	Achievement	Self-actualization
	Self-control	Self-expression
	Independence	Interdependence
	Endurance of distress	Capacity for joy
Organizational philosophies	Mechanistic forms	Organic forms
	Competitive relations	Collaborative relations
	Separate objectives	Linked objectives
	Own resources regarded as owned absolutely	Own resources regarded also as society's
Ecological strategies	Responsive to crisis	Anticipative of crisis
	Specific measures	Comprehensive measures
	Requiring consent	Requiring participation
	Short planning horizon	Long planning horizon
	Damping conflict	Confronting conflict
	Detailed central control	Generalized central control
	Small local government units	Enlarged local government units
	Standardized administration	Innovative administration
	Separate services	Coordinated services

Charlton R. Price, "Between Cultures: The Current Crisis of Transition," in Warren H. Schmidt, ed., *Organization Frontiers and Human Values* (Belmont, Calif.: Wadsworth, 1970), p. 32. Reprinted by permission of the publisher.

These differences in values help explain why some organizations are in an ongoing state of turmoil. In simple terms, it is a matter of a generation gap: each generation is attempting to optimize a different set of values. Failure to recognize this value conflict results in a complete breakdown in communications within the organization. It is ironic that "while communication has become more sophisticated, understanding between generations and races and nations has declined. We are divided and alienated at the very time that we see most clearly our need for interdependence with one another and with nature."[14]

An organization that is *not* foresightful, innovative, and rational needs extensive planning effort, and in the extreme, planning may become an end in itself. Thus an organization that prides itself for extensive planning may be admitting that it lacks foresight, innovation, and rational decisions.

SUMMARY An effective marketing organization is needed to implement a marketing plan. There is no perfect marketing organizational design. Furthermore, the design must change over the life cycle of the product, and it must be responsive to the dynamics of the marketplace. Organizational designs have shifted from functional approaches to team approaches headed by a brand manager and recently to a more market-oriented organizational strategy.

The brand/product management system gives staff responsibility for the success of a brand or product without providing line authority. The brand manager must negotiate with advertising and sales managers for his or her brand's share of advertising and selling effort. Although this system has been successful in many firms, the dynamics of the marketplace have expanded the knowledge required of the brand manager so much that new designs are required. Some companies have added new staff functions to provide expertise, lengthened the term of service in product management, or further divided the product-management job into product/market managers.

Post–Industrial Revolution values, organizational democracy, and new management technology require the development of new organizational designs. Because the marketing department deals with the environment of the firm, it must be the first to experiment with these new designs.

APPENDIX 5.1: EVALUATING ORGANIZATIONAL DESIGNS

Whereas product managers must adapt to existing organizational designs, the marketing vice-president must consider changing the organizational design and establishing criteria for evaluating this design. This appendix will help in these related tasks.[15]

In evaluating organizational strategies, we should remember Drucker's warning that even an ideal structure will not guarantee performance, but the wrong structure will guarantee nonperformance.[16] This warning should remind us that the implementation of a plan and an organizational strategy requires recruiting, training, and motivating people.

CRITERIA FOR EVALUATING ORGANIZATIONS The organizational strategy is an extension of the process for developing a corporate strategy. Drucker identifies seven criteria for evaluating organizational strategies.[17] After brief definitions of these criteria, we will evaluate four organizational structures according to them. These criteria are as follows:

1. *Clarity* reflects the individual's need to understand his or her tasks, the group task, personal relationships with others in the group, and the availability of information.

2. *Economy* in the effort to control, supervise, and motivate people will minimize the allocation of resources to management activities. Where possible, self-control and self-motivation should be used.

3. The *direction of vision* of the organization should be toward the goals of the entire enterprise, not toward the goals of functional areas.

4. *Understanding one's task in relationship to the common task* requires communications that will help the individual relate his or her efforts to the common goal.

5. *Decision making* should be facilitated by the organizational design. For example, an organizational design that forces decisions to the highest level, when they could be made at a lower level, is an impediment to the decision-making process.

6. *Stability and adaptability* must be balanced, so that the individual does not feel like a transient in the organization. The structure should adapt to changes in its environment.

7. *Perpetuation and self-renewal* refer to the organization's need to develop future leadership. The organization should prepare and test persons for high management. Training at lower levels gives motivation to the younger members of an organization and minimizes the cost of their errors. To train well, an organization should not have too many levels before managerial ability can be tested. Self-renewal requires an organization that is accessible to new ideas.

FOUR ORGANIZATIONAL DESIGNS In designing an organizational strategy, a marketing planner is likely to choose from among four designs—functional, team, federalization, and systems. Each of these designs will be described briefly and compared according to the seven criteria given above. This comparison is summarized in Table 5.4. This table permits the designer of an organization to weight the importance of these criteria in the design plan and choose that organizational design or combination of designs that meets the needs of the organization.

Functional The functional and team designs focus on the work and the tasks that must be accomplished. The functional design groups similar talents into homogeneous units, and the work moves to these units to receive their specialized skills. The production line in a factory is a clear example of functional design. A university is designed functionally, with students moving to take courses in specialized functional departments. A functional design in marketing will include specialists in product development, advertising, promotion, packaging, and personal selling. Each function contributes to the movement of goods and services toward the ultimate consumer. A simple functional marketing organizational chart appears in the upper section of Fig. 5.1.

Referring to Table 5.4, we see that a functional marketing organization has the advantages of clarity, economy, and stability. Its disadvantages include the creation of parochial vision, the lack of a clear understanding of the enterprise goals, poor decision-making qualities, a resistance to change, and a failure to train top management. The functional design leaves much to be desired in marketing organizations.

Team A team is a small group of persons who focus on a specified task. Each individual is an expert in her or his field, so there is no superior/subordinate relationship. The team brings the expert to the work, whereas the work moves to the expert in the functional design.

Marketing teams tend to have a leader who is assigned permanently to that role. The product manager is a team leader for a specific product, with team members representing product development, packaging, promotion, and advertising. The common task is the profitable sales of the brand. The product manager is always

TABLE 5.4 An evaluation of four common organizational designs

Criteria	Work- and task-focused designs		Results-focused design: federalization	Relations-focused design: systems
	Functional	Team		
Clarity	Everyone understands his or her task	Low clarity unless leader creates it	Great clarity	Lacks clarity
Economy	Economical when organization is simple, but confusion sets in for complex organization	Low, continuing attention to management, deliberation, and communications	Considerable economy	Violates principles of internal economy, especially those in communications
Vision	Creates parochial vision	Everyone sees the common goal	Vision directed toward enterprise performance	Objectives clearly seen
Task relationships	Difficult to understand the common goal	Everyone sees common task but not his or her own task	Easy to understand own enterprise tasks	Difficult to understand own task and enterprise task
Decision making	Poor, because decisions made only at highest levels	If no self-discipline, group loses sight of organizational decision and makes subdecisions	The most satisfactory design for decisions and communication	Decision responsibility not clear
Stability/adaptability	Stable but resists adaptation	Great adaptability, but low stability	High stability, yet adaptable	Lacks stability, great adaptability
Perpetuation/renewal	Does not test and train leaders	Open to new ideas	Best design for management development	Tends not to test and develop managers; new-idea receptivity almost too great

Based on P. F. Drucker, *Management: Tasks, Responsibilities, Practices* (New York: Harper & Row, 1974), pp. 553–557.

concerned with this brand, which provides continuity to product planning. The functional members of the team serve on other corporate brands as well. The lower portion of Fig. 5.1 includes an organizational chart for the product-management system. Note that there is no direct link between the planner and the functional areas. *Control and decision making* in this system occur at higher levels and are delegated to the product manager and the functional representatives *through top management's approval of the marketing plan.*

Team designs may also be found in advertising agencies and department stores. A planning board in an advertising agency will represent the advertising functions of copy, art, media, and research. A merchandise manager in a department store will head teams that represent the functions of buying, promotion, and selling. Industrial marketers frequently use venture teams to develop a new product. Such a team typically has members from research and development, engineering, production, marketing, and finance. If successful, this team forms the nucleus of a new division in the corporation.

Returning to Table 5.4, we see that the advantages of the team design are its openness to new ideas, its adaptability, and an understanding of the common tasks and goals. The team approach requires strong leadership to attain clarity and maintain the proper relationships between individual and common tasks. There is the danger of a team member's becoming too fascinated by the common task or someone else's task to perform his or her own task inadequately. If the team is brought together for a single task or if it operates only infrequently, it lacks stability and has high costs of deliberation, communications, and management.

Federalization   A federalization design is an organization of autonomous businesses, with each unit responsible for its performance and contribution to the total company.[18] General Motors, Ford Motor Company, Chrysler Corporation, General Foods, and duPont use this design. Each company is made up of autonomous divisions that are responsible for contributions to the corporate goals. Control is maintained through centralized policies, planning, and measures of effectiveness. The divisions are kept small enough so that they can be organized along functional lines. This combination of federalization and functionalism takes advantage of both designs, while minimizing their weaknesses.

"Of all design principles available so far, federal decentralization comes closest to satisfying all design specifications."[19] It has clarity, economy, high stability with adaptability, and clear understanding of task relationships. Managers focus on the enterprise goals. This design is the only satisfactory one for communications, decisions, and management development.[20] "Federalization, if properly applied, makes top management capable of doing its own job precisely because it does not have to worry about operations, but can concentrate on direction, strategy, objectives, and key decisions for the future."[21]

Systems   The systems organization is a team composed of a wide variety of organizations instead of individual members. The National Aeronautics and Space Administration (NASA) is one of the most famous systems designs and, according to Drucker, one of the few successful ones. He notes further that the systems approach has worked only when there were almost unlimited budgets. "The attempt to use systems management to tackle major social problems—the much-touted promise of the sixties—is almost certain to be a total failure."[22]

It is not difficult to see why the systems approach is a poor organizational design. As we see in Table 5.4, it does not perform well on organizational criteria. It lacks clarity and stability. Task relationships are difficult to understand. Responsibility for decisions is vague. The effort required to maintain communications is unrealistic. (NASA executives spent two-thirds of their time in meetings.)[23] It does not test and develop managers. On the positive side, the system has good vision and is very adaptable and receptive to new ideas. Drucker concludes that "in no other organization structure is the ratio between output and effort needed for internal cohesion as unfavorable as in the systems structure."[24]

An understanding of the strengths and weaknesses of organizational designs helps the administrator to anticipate problems as well as to develop new designs for the implementation of plans. These organizational criteria should be applied to the analysis of cases, and organizational strategies should be included in case solutions.

DISCUSSION QUESTIONS

1. How are the success factors of a firm reflected in its organizational design?

2. With respect to the levels of product-management responsibilities, differentiate brand coordinator, brand champion, and brand director. What are the major weaknesses of the product-management design?

3. For each of the four stages in a product's life cycle—new or recycled, growth, maturity, and decline—describe the appropriate risk category, profit strategy, product-management responsibility level (see question 2), information needs, and staff support.

4. If you were in charge of recruiting and training product managers for a company, what kinds of qualities would you look for in the applicants? Design a training program for the potential product managers you have recruited.

5. What kinds of conflicts can you anticipate between product managers and (a) functional specialists, (b) functional line management? Make recommendations as to how you would go about preventing and/or resolving these conflicts.

6. How should a product manager be evaluated? Does your method create frustrations for the product manager? Discuss.

7. Would you like to be a product manager? Give reasons.

8. Drucker states that "of all design principles available so far, federal decentralization comes closest to satisfying all design specifications." Would it be a good idea to use "federalization" for small companies? Discuss.

9. What are the major functional areas in an enterprise? What would be the goals of each area? Will these conflict with the goals of other areas and/or of the goals of the enterprise as a whole? Discuss.

10. Discuss how the post–Industrial Revolution values will change the organization of marketing departments.

NOTES

1. P. F. Drucker, *Management: Tasks, Responsibilities, Practices* (New York: Harper & Row, 1974), pp. 449–450.

2. S. Dietz, "Brand Managers Are Not Entrepreneurs, But Should Interpret Market Creatively," *Marketing News*, April 1, 1974, p. 1.

3. S. Dietz, "Get More Out of Your Brand Management," *Harvard Business Review* (July–August 1973): 130.

4. *Ibid.*, p. 129.

5. *Ibid.*, p. 131.

6. "The Brand Manager: No Longer King," *Business Week*, June 9, 1973, p. 58.

7. *Ibid.*, pp. 61–62.

8. *Ibid.*, p. 58.

9. R. Donovan, "You'll Work within a Revised Product Management System in the Future," *Product Management* (November 1976): 28–29.

10. "The Brand Manager: No Longer King," *op. cit.*, p. 61.

11. This paragraph is based on D. Phadnis, "Training a New Product Manager," *Product Marketing* (April 1977): 35.

12. M. G. Allen, Vice President, Corporate Strategy and Planning, General Electric Co. (Paper delivered at a conference on corporate strategic planning, jointly sponsored by the Institute of Management Science and the Operations Research Society of America, New Orleans, February 28 to March 2, 1977.)

13. M. May, "Tomorrow's Management: A More Adventurous Life in a Free-Form Corporation," *Fortune* **74** (July 1966): 84–87, 148–150, in H. I. Ansoff, *Business Strategy* (Baltimore: Penguin, 1969), p. 137.

14. W. H. Schmidt, *Organizational Frontiers and Human Values* (Belmont, Calif.: Wadsworth, 1970), p. 173.

15. Drucker, *op. cit.*, Chapters 41–48.

16. *Ibid.*, p. 519.

17. *Ibid.*, pp. 553–557.

18. Drucker uses "federal decentralization" to distinguish this design from "decentralization." The latter term does not always mean that the units have autonomy and responsibility. Decentralization can lead to chaotic fragmentation. For simplicity's sake, the term "federalization" will be used instead of "federal decentralization." The phrase "profit-center decentralization" is also used to convey this concept.

19. *Ibid.*, p. 574.

20. *Ibid.*, pp. 574–575.

21. *Ibid.*, p. 575.

22. *Ibid.*, p. 597.

23. *Ibid.*, p. 595.

24. *Ibid.*, p. 596.

SUGGESTED READINGS

Clewett, R. M., and S. F. Stasch, "Shifting Role of the Product Manager," *Harvard Business Review* (January–February 1975): 65–73.

Dominguez, G. S., *Product Management* (New York: American Management Association, 1971).

Luck, D. J., and R. Nowak, II, "Product Management—Vision Unfilled," *Harvard Business Review* (May–June 1977): 143–157.

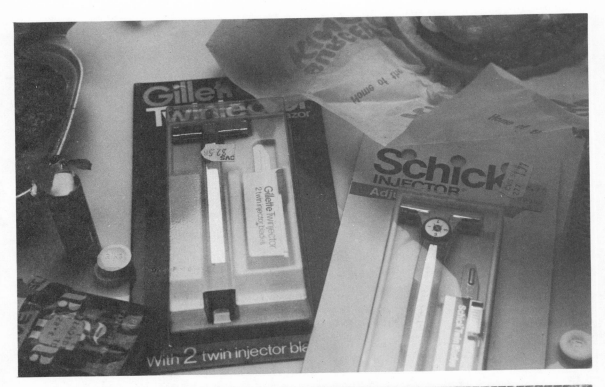

Part III. Situation Analysis

A situation analysis is an audit of all of the environments that impinge on a brand at a specific time. This analysis identifies marketing opportunities as well as problems faced by a brand. The analysis includes a detailed examination of generic demand, brand demand, competition, and public policy. Chapters 6, 7, 9, and 10 examine each of these components of a situation analysis. Chapter 8 examines those techniques that are unique to a situation analysis in industrial marketing.

Generic demand is the total needs of a population, whether or not the needs are being met by existing products. Thus generic demand may be more than total industry sales, because existing products may not be meeting all existing needs. A generic-demand analysis should reveal the market potential represented by these unmet needs. This analysis will identify benefits that are sought by the population. These benefits are translated into the product attributes of a new product. Chapter 6 examines generic-demand analysis.

Brand demand is frequently expressed in terms of market share. Market share is determined by the brand's marketing effort and that of competitors. Chapters 7 and 9 present methods for analyzing brand demand and competitive behavior.

Public policy, as related to marketing, may provide opportunities as well as problems and constraints on strategies. Chapter 10 examines the marketing implications of public policies that are designed to preserve competition, protect the consumer and the environment, and conserve natural resources.

ENVIRONMENTAL ANALYSIS WORKSHEET

Environmental elements	Facts	Assumptions or research needed	Conclusions

Organizational values, objectives, and policies (4)

Organizational design (5)

Situation
 Generic demand (6)
 Brand demand (7)
 Competition (9)
 Public policy (10)

Opportunities (2)

Problems

MARKETING PLAN (CONSUMER PRODUCT)

Current performance
Recommendations
Effect of recommendations on income
Situation analysis
Opportunities and problems
Strategies
Tests and research
Supporting documents
 Comparative budgets
 Media allocation schedule
 Promotion control sheet

<u>STRATEGY WORKSHEET</u>

Opportunities and problems in rank order to importance

    1.

    2.

     .

    n.

	Current strategy	Alternatives and recommended strategy	Estimated Effect

Demand strategy
    Generic
    Brand			

Strategic goals
    Financial
    Marketing			

Marketing-mix strategies
    Product (12)
    Pricing (13)
    Channel and logistics (14)
    Advertising and promotional (15)
    Sales management (16)			

Research (3)			
Profit plan			
Evaluation and control (19)			

CHAPTER **6**

CHAPTER **6**

Analyzing Consumers' Generic Needs and Behavior

LEARNING OBJECTIVES   After studying this chapter you should:

1. Know the most frequently used variables in consumer-behavior models of generic demand and brand demand.
2. Be able to ask the critical questions for an analysis of generic demand that will identify problems and opportunities in the market.
3. Be able to use tabulated data to identify market segments with high potential.
4. Be aware of the gains and losses in a segmentation strategy.
5. Know how to use a simple model to calculate the generic demand for each segment.
6. Understand how a generic-demand analysis is used to develop a product strategy.
7. Know how the behavioral sciences are used to analyze generic demand.
8. Be able to define and use the following concepts:

Generic demand	Implicit assumptions	New-product adoption
Market segmentation	Demographics	and diffusion
Uses	Family life cycle	Psychographics
Usage rate	Birth rates	Elasticities
Differentiated and	Life-styles	Utility
undifferentiated strategies	Husband-wife	Consumer expectations
Projecting key variables	decisions	and intentions
Potential demand	Social values	

SOME ANALYTICAL QUESTIONS FOR OPENERS

1. How do general economic conditions, i.e., inflation, recession, and gross national product (GNP), affect the sales and use of the product?
2. Are there time-series patterns of trend, cycle, season, or fad?
3. At what rate are industry sales growing or declining?
4. Where is the product in its life cycle?
5. What are the profiles of the heavy, medium, light, and nonusers?

The difference between marketing and promotion is that marketing begins with the identification of unmet needs and then develops a product or service to meet these needs. Promotion, in contrast, communicates the attributes of a product that is already in existence (see Fig. 1.1). Identifying consumer needs before the product is produced is at the heart of the marketing concept. The situation analysis, therefore, begins with an understanding of consumer needs and people's behavior in meeting these needs. This chapter begins the discussion of consumer behavior by examining how consumers decide to buy within a broad product category (e.g., cars, boats, soaps, shampoos, or soft drinks). The demand for a product category is called *generic demand*. Total sales for an industry are used as a measure of past generic demand for a product category.

Our discussion begins with a simple flow chart of a consumer's decision process.[1] Then we will see how a marketing manager would analyze data in search of an unmet need that could provide a marketing opportunity. Building on this example, we will see how the behavioral sciences have contributed to an understanding of consumer behavior. This example will lead to a simple algebraic expression for the market segmentation of generic demand.

A CONSUMER-BEHAVIOR MODEL   Figure 6.1 models a consumer's behavior leading to the purchase of a soft drink. This model tracks the decision process leading to the selection of a product category, which explains the process leading to *generic* demand. The last part of the model is concerned with *brand* demand, i.e., how the consumer chooses a single brand from among the many in the product category. Brand demand will be the subject of Chapter 7.

Needs (Benefits Sought)   All humans have five basic needs—physical, safety, belonging and love, esteem, and self-actualization.[2] The manner in which they meet these needs varies greatly according to differences among the consumers and their environments. Culture, religion, education, age, personal values, and life-styles—all influence how an individual meets these needs. The environment too will have considerable influence. For instance, the time of the day may determine how a person quenches his or her thirst. Coffee may be used at breakfast, iced tea at lunch, a soft drink in the afternoon, and a beer or a cocktail in the evening. To understand the consumer's decision process, therefore, we must know the environment in which he or she experienced the need. The personal experiences and the environment of the individual translate needs into benefits sought in a product. The producer attempts to design product attributes that provide the benefits sought.

Goals (Product Attributes Sought)   Consumers do not buy products; they buy bundles of attributes that will meet their needs. Although people may all buy the same generic product, such as a toothpaste, segments of the consumers will buy different brands, because they weight their needs differently. Thus parents may decide to buy the toothpaste brand that has an attribute to prevent decay. Young people may instead buy the brand that has a whitening ingredient or a mouthwash built in, to enhance their social acceptability.[3] Market segments emerge when individuals weight these product attributes differently.

The identification of needs by an individual and the realization that there are means for meeting these needs are the bases for consumer motivation. The consumer

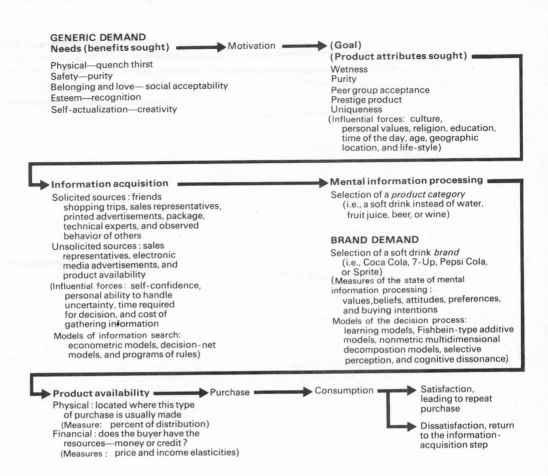

GENERIC DEMAND
Needs (benefits sought) ⟶ Motivation ⟶ **(Goal)**
(Product attributes sought)

Physical—quench thirst
Safety—purity
Belonging and love— social acceptability
Esteem—recognition
Self-actualization—creativity

Wetness
Purity
Peer group acceptance
Prestige product
Uniqueness
(Influential forces: culture,
personal values, religion, education,
time of the day, age, geographic
location, and life-style)

Information acquisition ⟶ **Mental information processing**

Solicited sources : friends
shopping trips, sales representatives,
printed advertisements, package,
technical experts, and observed
behavior of others
Unsolicited sources : sales
representatives, electronic
media advertisements, and
product availability
(Influential forces: self-confidence,
personal ability to handle
uncertainty, time required
for decision, and cost of
gathering information
Models of information search:
econometric models, decision-net
models, and programs of rules)

Selection of a *product category*
(i.e., a soft drink instead of water,
fruit juice, beer, or wine)

BRAND DEMAND

Selection of a soft drink *brand*
(i.e., Coca Cola, 7-Up, Pepsi Cola,
or Sprite)
(Measures of the state of mental
information processing :
values, beliefs, attitudes, preferences,
and buying intentions
Models of the decision process:
learning models, Fishbein-type additive
models, nonmetric multidimensional
decompostion models, selective
perception, and cognitive dissonance)

Product availability ⟶ Purchase ⟶ Consumption ⟶ Satisfaction,
leading to repeat
purchase

Physical : located where this type
of purchase is usually made
(Measure: percent of distribution)
Financial : does the buyer have the
resources—money or credit ?
(Measures :   price and income elasticities)

Dissatisfaction, return
to the information-
acquisition step

Fig. 6.1   A simplified model of consumer behavior—soft drink purchase.

must search for the attributes that will meet these needs and then search for products with these attributes. This dual search requires information.

Information Acquisition and Processing   The search for the product requires a search for information about products. As Fig. 6.1 shows, some of the information must be solicited, such as by asking friends or making a shopping trip, whereas other information is unsolicited, such as a television commercial or a sales representative's call. An individual's cognitive decision style will determine how much information is gathered. Someone who has not purchased the product before may lack confidence, so the information search may be extensive. A decision that must be made quickly may not permit an extensive information search. The cost of gathering information for a minor purchase may exceed the costs of making a wrong decision. Thus the need for information will vary greatly among consumers.

Models of consumers' acquisition of information have used three approaches. Econometric models have been used, but their utility has been questioned.[4] Decision nets have been used to describe the decision process that took place prior to a purchase. These nets, or decision trees, have been created from purchase protocols that were developed by having a buyer verbalize all thoughts while on a shopping trip.[5] These models are rich in description, but are of little use in predicting consumer behavior.

A third approach is to examine the rules consumers use at different levels of analysis. The purchase of an automobile, for example, may be analyzed at three levels. The first level is concerned with "value," which is dissected at the second level into "performance" and "cost." "Performance" is analyzed at the third level by considering "payload, acceleration, and mileage," while "cost" is divided into "mileage and price."

Decision rules will be used at each of these three levels to evaluate the product alternatives. The sophistication of the rules will depend on the sophistication of the buyer. Thus someone who buys a car every five years will not have the sophistication of someone who buys taxi fleets.[6]

The individual mentally processes the newly acquired information, along with past experiences and the present environment, to select one of the products in the product category that will meet his or her need. For the present example we will assume that the decision was to buy a soft drink. The thought process that leads to the purchase of a specific brand will be discussed in the next chapter.

ASKING THE CRITICAL QUESTIONS   The critical questions that must be answered in order to understand consumer behavior may be reduced to six simple questions—who, what, where, when, how, and why. We will now see how these questions help to analyze our example of the soft drink market.

Who, What, Where, When, How, and Why?   There are many existing sources of data that will help us to understand the soft drink market. To simplify our example we will use one source of data—the Target Group Index (TGI). The 1974 TGI data that we will use are the result of an annual survey of 10,000 men and 10,000 women, all of whom were 18 years and older. The questionnaire asked basic demographic, sociological, social-psychological, and economic questions. It asked the respondents to report the brands they buy when purchasing over 1000 goods and services. They also reported their media habits for television, radio, and magazines. Examples of the TGI data for soft drinks appear in Table 6.1.[7]

How many persons buy soft drinks? The data in Table 6.1 reveal that 119 million adult Americans buy soft drinks. What benefits are they buying? Continuing in Table 6.1, we see that 59 million adults use them as a mixer. We will assume that the other 60 million persons use them as a beverage.

Where are they bought and consumed? The South contains the largest percentage of users (32 percent); the mixer market tends to be in the Northeast (28 percent) and the suburbs (42 percent).

Who buys soft drinks? The demographic profile of users indicates that women buy more than men, the age group of 35–49 is the heaviest buyer segment, buyers are not employed, they are married, and they have children between the ages of 2 and 17. This demographic profile suggests that housewives are the largest purchaser of soft drinks and that they probably buy them as part of their weekly shopping. We will want to investigate this point further, because it has important implications for our advertising and channel strategies. This profile reveals a point that is frequently overlooked: the person who makes the buying decision and the one who consumes the product are not always the

TABLE 6.1 Profiles of soft drink market segments—1974

	Needs met					
	All uses		Mixer uses			
Profile variable	Users (1)	Nonusers (2)	Users (3)	Nonusers (4)	7-Up (5)	Orange juice (6)
Number of adults (millions)	119	18	59	78	26	23
Men	48%	45%	53%	44%	53%	51%
Women	52	55	47	56	47	49
Adults 18–24	20	6	21	15	23	28
25–34	22	8	24	17	26	23
35–49	27	19	28	25	26	24
50–64	21	31	19	25	18	16
65 or over	11	36	9	19	7	9
Northeast	24	25	28	22	21	27
North Central	26	26	26	26	32	25
South	32	38	26	36	24	26
West	17	20	20	16	23	22
SMSA central city	34	29	37	31	36	37
SMSA suburban	37	38	42	34	42	42
Non-SMSA	29	33	21	35	22	21
Graduated college	16	13	20	13	18	17
Attended college	21	16	24	17	25	25
Graduated high school	36	28	35	35	37	35
Did not graduate high school	27	43	21	36	20	23
Professional/managerial	17	12	20	13	20	17
Chemical/sales	15	11	17	13	17	17
Craftsmen/foremen	8	6	9	8	10	7
Other employed	19	14	17	19	18	20
Not employed	41	57	37	47	36	39
Household disposable income:						
$25,000 or more	8	6	10	7	9	8
$15,000–24,999	23	15	27	18	26	25
$10,000–14,999	30	22	30	28	32	29
$8000–9999	10	7	9	10	11	10
$5000–7999	16	19	14	19	14	16
Less than $5,000	14	30	10	20	9	12
White	88	87	87	89	90	84
Black	9	10	10	9	8	12
Other	3	3	3	2	3	3
Single	12	7	13	10	13	17
Married	78	72	79	77	80	74
Widowed/divorced/separated	9	21	8	13	7	8
No children in household	45	69	43	52	41	43
Children under 2	10	3	11	8	13	11
2 to 5	20	10	22	17	23	21
6 to 11	26	13	27	23	27	26
12 to 17	28	19	28	26	28	29

TABLE 6.1 (cont.)

Profile variable	All uses Users (1)	All uses Nonusers (2)	Needs met Mixer uses Users (3)	Mixer uses Nonusers (4)	Mixer uses 7-Up (5)	Orange juice (6)
Psychographic variables*						
Affectionate	32%	24%	35%	28%	35%	37%
Amicable	22	18	24	19	23	22
Awkward	27	20	28	25	27	29
Brave	47	36	50	43	52	52
Broadminded	38	31	40	35	41	40
Creative	23	19	25	21	25	26
Dominating	34	23	38	29	38	39
Efficient	27	24	27	26	27	28
Egocentric	15	11	16	13	16	18
Frank	31	27	32	29	31	31
Funny	20	17	21	19	21	22
Intelligent	25	24	27	23	24	27
Kind	46	41	47	44	47	47
Refined	44	38	46	41	46	46
Reserved	21	21	20	21	20	19
Self-assured	24	21	24	23	23	24
Sociable	38	32	41	35	40	41
Stubborn	41	27	42	36	44	42
Tense	38	28	38	35	39	39
Trustworthy	60	53	62	57	63	59
Buying styles*						
Brand-loyal	32	31	33	31	32	32
Cautious	38	35	37	37	38	36
Conformist	16	16	16	16	16	16
Ecologist	28	30	27	30	26	27
Economy-minded	36	34	33	38	33	34
Experimenters	26	22	27	25	26	28
Impulsive	22	15	23	20	23	23
Persuasible	31	26	31	30	31	32
Planners	45	36	45	43	46	42
Style-conscious	29	21	32	26	31	32

* Psychographics and buying styles are self-concept variables reported by the 20,000 respondents. Percents may not equal 100, due to rounding.
Target Group Index, 1974, Volume P-8. Used by permission of Axiom Market Research Bureau, Inc.

same individual. Therefore, it may be necessary to have a promotional strategy directed toward both persons.

Why do people buy soft drinks? This is a hard question to answer from existing data. Table 6.1 contains 20 *psychographic* variables on which respondents reported their self-concepts of their personalities. Comparing the percentages for users and nonusers, we see that users tend to regard themselves as affectionate, brave, dominating, stubborn, and tense. It is difficult to explain their motivation for buying from these psychographic dimensions, but nonetheless they can be very useful in developing advertising messages.

Buying style variables tell *how* people buy. A comparison of users and nonusers of soft drinks reveals that users tend to be more impulsive, persuasible, and style-conscious and that they are planners. The inconsistency in these findings must be explored further. If the impulsive dimension is important, this fact would stress the importance of in-store displays for our product.

Soft drinks are not an expensive product, so economic profiles do not seem important. It is interesting to note, however, that 61 percent of the users have a household disposable income of $10,000 or more.

Are There Market Segments?

By uses? Rather than develop one product for all users, we may want to consider developing a product for specific *segments* of the market, such as the mixer market. A comparison of the profiles of *all users* with those of the *mixer users* reveals a few differences. The mixer users tend to be men, live in the Northeast and the suburbs, be professionals, and have higher education and higher income. Psychographic and buying-style profiles are similar. At first we may want to conclude that one product could be developed and promoted in the same manner to the beverage and the mixer markets. Examination of the data reveals that a further tabulation is needed, however. The fact that the *mixer market* is included in the *all-uses market* may confound the profiles. Thus the marketing manager should request a tabulation of the data that will provide separate profiles for these two markets.

By usage rate? Many marketers have noted that 80 percent of their business comes from 20 percent of their customers. Therefore, it becomes important to examine the profiles of the heavy users of soft drinks. These data appear in Table 6.2.

By studying the *heavy-user segments*, we see sharper distinctions between the *all-uses segment* and the *mixer segment*. The data in Table 6.2 reveal that 60 percent of the all-user segment is under 35 years old, whereas only 37 percent of the mixer market is in this age classification. Without segmentation, the markets were similar—42 percent and 45 percent, respectively (see Table 6.1).

Continuing our comparison of heavy users for all uses with the mixer market, we see that the *all-uses* market is concentrated in the South, whereas the *mixer* market is in the Northeast. The mixer market has more college graduates, more professionals, higher incomes, more blacks, and fewer children in the household. There are no striking differences in psychographics or buying styles.

These comparisons of heavy users suggest that we could make one soft drink that would appeal to both the beverage and the mixer market segments, but it would have to be promoted differently to each market. Thus our *product* strategy would be *undifferentiated*, but our *promotional* strategy would be *differentiated* to reflect the fact that the mixer market is older, lives in the North, is more affluent, and is better educated than the beverage market.

This comparison of the total market with the heavy-user market segment illustrates an important point in demand analysis. The initial examination of the total market included a market of 119 million users of soft drinks for all purposes and 59 million for mixing cocktails. When we focused on the heavy-user segment, our market potentials

TABLE 6.2   **Profiles of soft drink market segments—heavy and light users**

Profile variable	All users Heavy users (1)	All users Light users (2)	Soft drinks as a mixer Heavy users (3)	Soft drinks as a mixer Light users (4)
Number of adults (millions)	25	36	16	22
Men	53%	45%	59%	48%
Women	47	55	41	52
Adults 18–24	34	11	18	21
25–34	26	16	19	25
35–49	23	29	28	28
50–64	12	26	23	18
65 or over	6	18	12	8
Northeast	23	25	30	27
North Central	24	27	25	27
South	38	26	27	26
West	15	22	19	19
SMSA central city	37	30	39	34
SMSA suburban	34	40	39	43
Non-SMSA	29	30	22	23
Graduated college	12	17	21	18
Attended college	24	20	21	24
Graduated high school	37	33	33	37
Did not graduate high school	27	30	25	22
Professional/managerial	15	18	20	17
Clerical/sales	17	13	14	18
Craftsmen/foremen	10	8	9	9
Other employed	22	17	17	17
Not employed	36	46	39	39
Household disposable income:				
$25,000 or more	7	8	12	9
$15,000–24,999	22	22	27	25
$10,000–14,999	29	30	25	33
$8000–9999	11	9	9	10
$5000–7999	19	15	15	14
Less than $5000	12	17	13	9
White	86	91	83	89
Black	11	7	14	8
Other	3	2	3	3
Single	20	8	15	10
Married	73	80	76	82
Widowed/divorced/separated	7	12	10	8
No children in household	38	51	47	39
Children under 2	13	8	8	12
2 to 5	25	16	18	24
6 to 11	29	25	25	28
12 to 17	28	28	29	28

TABLE 6.2 (cont.)

Profile variable	All users Heavy users (1)	All users Light users (2)	Soft drinks as a mixer Heavy users (3)	Soft drinks as a mixer Light users (4)
Psychographic variables:*				
Affectionate	36%	29%	33%	35%
Amicable	21	23	23	24
Awkward	29	26	25	29
Brave	50	45	50	50
Broadminded	40	36	38	38
Creative	26	21	24	23
Dominating	38	31	38	39
Efficient	27	25	26	27
Egocentric	19	13	18	15
Frank	34	29	33	30
Funny	25	18	22	20
Intelligent	27	23	28	24
Kind	47	45	45	46
Refined	43	45	48	44
Reserved	18	22	19	20
Self-assured	24	22	25	23
Sociable	41	37	42	40
Stubborn	45	37	41	42
Tense	42	36	39	37
Trustworthy	60	60	58	63
Buying styles:*				
Brand-loyal	29	33	33	33
Cautious	36	38	38	36
Conformist	16	16	16	14
Ecologist	29	29	26	27
Economy minded	35	36	33	33
Experimenters	29	23	27	25
Impulsive	29	19	23	21
Persuasible	31	30	31	30
Planners	44	46	44	44
Style-conscious	32	26	33	29
Rate used	More than once per day	Once per week or less	2 or 3 times per week or more	Once per month or less

* Psychographics and buying styles are self-concept variables reported by the 20,000 respondents. Percents may not equal 100, due to rounding.
Target Group Index, 1974, Volume P-8. Used by permission of Axiom Market Research Bureau, Inc.

dropped to 25 and 16 million persons, respectively. Thus there are losses as well as gains to market segmentation. Focusing on segments sharpens the differences among the profiles of users, which makes it possible to develop more efficient marketing strategies. *This gain in efficiency, however, has been accomplished at the cost of reducing the size of the market.*

The strategy of market segmentation may be "a rational and more precise adjustment of product and marketing effort to consumer or user requirements," but the gains from this precision must be weighed in terms of the loss in market potential.[8] The limitations of a strategy of market segmentation may be stated differently by noting that a product that is highly attractive to one segment may alienate other segments. For example, a soft drink that was promoted to young teenagers as a "youth beverage" was rejected by older teenagers as a drink for "kids."

The efficiencies of market segmentation must also be evaluated in terms of the effect on the total business system. When the strategy is carried to an extreme, there can be diseconomies of scale. Long production runs are reduced to short, inefficient ones. A production line becomes a job shop.

So far we have considered a strategy only for heavy users. Perhaps the *light-user* market represents an opportunity. At first it would appear that the light-user market has a greater potential because there are 36 million light users and only 25 million heavy users. But we must remember that the *potential demand is the number of users times their usage rate*. The last line in Table 6.2 reveals that the heavy users drink more than one soft drink per day, whereas the light users drink one once per week or less. Thus one heavy user is worth more than seven light users. To state it differently, the number of light users must be more than seven times the number of heavy users before the light-user segment becomes the segment with the greater potential.

An examination of the profile of the light user (Table 6.2) suggests that it would be difficult to develop an efficient marketing strategy for this segment. It is an older segment that may be set in its ways. People in this segment have lower incomes, so soft drinks may be a luxury. They have fewer children at home, so there is less pressure to buy soft drinks. They rate themselves lower on the psychographic variables of affectionate, brave, creative, dominating, egocentric, frank, funny, stubborn, and tense. Their buying styles tend to be more brand-loyal, less that of an experimenter, less impulsive, and less style-conscious. It would be difficult to develop a *copy strategy* that would cause these users to switch to our new product.

Another possible strategy for developing our new product would be to focus on the market that is *not* presently using soft drinks. In Table 6.1 we see that there are 18 million *nonusers*. Comparing their profiles with those of the users, we learn that the nonusers are older, have less education, tend to be unemployed, have lower incomes, and have no children in the household. After analyzing the nonuser, light-user, and heavy-user segments, we conclude that we should concentrate our initial efforts on the heavy-user segment.

What Will the Future Demand Be?   The data in Tables 6.1 and 6.2 are *static* in that they are for one point in time; they were collected in 1973 and published in 1974. A demand analysis requires that we *project key variables* over time to see what effect they would have on the potential market.

Age seems to be the *key variable* in the profile of *heavy users of soft drinks*. Teenagers influence family soft drink purchases, whereas older persons use them as mixers. Thus we must project the number of persons in important age classifications.

In Table 6.2 we see that 60 percent of the heavy users of soft drinks are under 34, whereas 63 percent of the heavy-mixer market are 35 or older. Before we decide whether to make a soft drink for the general market or the mixer market, we must examine the projections for these age brackets. Such projections are available from the

United States Bureau of the Census and the National Planning Association. Projections are shown in Table 6.3.

The projections for 1975 and 1990 are summarized in the upper part of Table 6.4. The percent-change column dramatically reveals that the baby boom of the '50s and '60s will mean a great increase in persons age 30 to 44. Recalling that young people drink soft drinks as a beverage and older persons use them as a mixer suggests that our new product should be a mixer. Between 1975 and 1990 the younger market will increase only 6.8 percent, whereas the older market will increase 23.7 percent. But wait. Fifteen years is a long time. If we calculate the *trend*, we find that to produce 23.7 percent in 15 years requires a growth rate of only 1.4 percent per year. Thus even the mixer market cannot be considered a high-growth industry.

To compute the heavy users' potential demand for soft drinks, we must estimate the number of times that soft drinks are used for all uses—as a mixer and as a beverage—for a time period, such as a year. These estimates appear in Table 6.4.

The generic demand for soft drinks consists of three variables—the number of persons in the segment (N), the proportion of this segment that uses soft drinks (P),

TABLE 6.3   **United States population by age group: 1960–1990 (000 omitted)**

	1960	1975	1975 + (−) 1960	1990	1990 + (−) 1975
0–5	20,337	16,216		17,752	
5–9	18,812	17,318		18,201	
10–14	16,923	20,062		17,154	
Subtotal	56,072	53,596	(2,476)	53,107	(489)
15–19	13,455	20,943		16,719	
20–24	11,124	19,404		17,823	
25–29	10,930	17,312		20,501	
Subtotal	35,509	57,659	22,150	55,043	(2,616)
30–34	11,979	13,802		21,290	
35–39	12,542	11,604		19,615	
40–44	11,680	11,117		17,287	
Subtotal	36,201	36,523	(322)	58,192	21,669
45–54	20,573	23,563		24,617	
55–65	15,627	19,867		20,357	
Subtotal	36,200	43,430	7,230	44,974	1,544
65–74	(b. 1895) 11,065	13,549 (b. 1900)		16,769 (b. 1925)	
75 & over	5,624	8,621		10,999	
Subtotal	16,689	22,170	5,472	27,768	5,607
Grand total	180,671	213,378		239,084	
Memo: total black	18,872	22,580	3,708	n.a.	

Projections based on series F—United States Bureau of the Census, quoted in *Advertising Age*, July 14, 1975, p. 21.

TABLE 6.4 **Computing generic demand for "heavy" users of soft drinks—all uses and as mixers**

	Age classifications	Number of persons* (in millions) 1975	Number of persons* (in millions) 1990	Percent change
All uses	15–19	20.9	16.7	−21.1%
	20–24	10.4	17.8	− 8.3
	25–29	17.3	20.5	+18.5
	30–34	13.8	21.3	+54.3
	Total	71.4	76.3	+ 6.8%
As a mixer	35–39	11.6	19.6	+69.0%
	40–44	11.1	17.3	+55.9
	45–54	23.6	24.6	+ 4.2
	55–65	19.9	20.4	+ 2.5
	Total	66.2	81.9	+23.7%

		Estimated times consumed		
All uses	Number of persons (N) (millions)	71.4	76.3	+ 6.8%
	Proportion of heavy users (P)	× $\quad$ 0.3†	0.3	0
	Estimated heavy users (millions)	21.42	22.89	
	Estimated annual frequency rate per capita (F)	× $\quad$ 700‡	700	0
	Estimated times used (millions) ($G = N \times P \times F$)	14,994	16,023	+ 6.8%
As a mixer	Number of persons (N_m) (millions)	66.2	81.9	+23.7%
	Proportion of heavy users (P_m) ×	0.144§	0.144	0
	Estimated heavy users (millions)	9.533	11.794	+23.7%
	Estimated annual frequency rate per capita × (F_m)	150	150	0
	Estimated times used (millions) ($G_m = N_m \times P_m \times F_m$)	1,430	1,769	+23.7%
As a beverage	Estimated times used as a beverage (subtract mixer uses from all uses) $G_b = G - G_m$	13,564	14,254	+ 5.1%

* Data from Table 6.3

† Proportion of heavy users $= \dfrac{\text{Number of heavy users}}{\text{Number of all users}} = \dfrac{.60 \times 25}{.42 \times 119} = 0.3$

‡ Estimated times user per year per capita (Table 6.2)
All uses: Approximately twice a day equals approximately 700 uses per year
As a mixer: Approximately three times a week equals approximately 150 times per year

§ Proportion of heavy users $= \dfrac{.63 \times 16}{.59 \times 119} = 0.144$

G = Generic demand, all uses; G_m = Generic demand, mixer; G_b = Generic demand, beverage and their frequency rate (F). Multiplying these variables yields the generic demand; thus the generic demand for soft drinks (G) in 1975 would be as follows:

$$G_{1975} = N_{1975} \times P_{1975} \times F_{1975}. \qquad (6.1)$$

To estimate the generic demand for soft drinks for 1985, we would have to estimate the values of N, P, and F for 1985. To generalize the equation, we will simply use the subscript "t" to indicate that a variable is unique to a time period. This should remind us that all variables should be based on the same time period.

Equation (6.1) may be expanded to summarize algebraically the concept of market segmentation. Assume that we are examining the mixer market. The entire market of light, medium, and heavy users may be expressed as follows:

$$G_t = (N_{t,l} \times P_{t,l} \times F_{t,l}) + (N_{t,m} \times P_{t,m} \times F_{t,m}) + (N_{t,h} \times P_{t,h} \times F_{t,h}) \qquad (6.2)$$

where the subscripts t, l, m, and h represent time, light users, medium users, and heavy users, respectively. Equation (6.2) may be generalized further, with the aid of the Greek symbol $\sum$ (meaning summation), as follows:

$$G_t = \sum_{i=1}^{3} N_{t,i} \times P_{t,i} \times F_{t,i}, \qquad (6.3)$$

where i represents the number of segments in the market. Equation (6.1) is a simple generalized model that summarizes the variables that are important in measuring the generic demand for soft drinks. Another product would include different variables. The form, not the variables, is generalized. Generic-demand analysis, therefore, requires the identification of the components of generic demand.

The computation of the generic demand in Table 6.4 illustrates several very important points to remember when conducting a demand analysis. First, although the growth rate for the mixer market is four times that of the beverage market, the beverage market will have eight times the potential of the mixer market in 1990 because of the higher usage rate among beverage users. This example illustrates the importance of estimating the *number* of persons in a segment *and* their consumption *rate*.

A second extremely important point is illustrated in Table 6.4. A clear organization of our calculations reveals *implicit assumptions*. The calculations here make two rather dangerous assumptions—that the proportion of heavy users and the consumption rates in 1990 will be the same as in 1973. The proportion of heavy users could easily change as a result of shifts in tastes, however. For instance, youth may decide to shift from soft drinks to tea. Similarly, the usage rate may drop because of basic changes in eating and drinking habits. One of the research recommendations should be to examine both of these estimates to determine if they are increasing or decreasing. These assumptions and the need for research should be noted in the "Assumptions/research needed" column of the analysis worksheet.

A limitation of this time-series analysis is that the population projection is made on only two points—1975 and 1990. Drawing a straight line with only two points is quite dangerous; a slight error in one estimate can lead to a wrong projection. Additional data are needed for a more reliable projection of this trend. This need should be noted in the "Research needed" column of the analysis worksheet.

Our time-series analysis considered only *trend*. Time-series economic data also contain elements of *cycles* around the trend, *seasonal* elements, and *random* elements, such as a sudden crop failure. Computerized techniques for decomposing time-series data are available. Several of these were noted in Chapter 3 and the appendix to that chapter. These other time-series effects should be studied.

These calculations of the generic demand for the beverage and mixer markets reinforce the earlier conclusion that we should develop a product that will appeal to the beverage and the mixer markets. This conclusion, it will be recalled, requires an *undifferentiated product strategy* but a *differentiated promotional strategy*.

DEVELOPING A PRODUCT STRATEGY Our analysis of generic demand led us to an undifferentiated product strategy. Our next task is to develop a product that will appeal to the beverage and the mixer markets. Several research techniques are available for identifying the unmet needs of these markets—e.g., focus-group interviews, cluster analysis, and nonmetric multidimensional scaling. Some of these methods were discussed in Chapter 3, and some will be discussed in Chapters 7 and 12. The present discussion will be limited to the analysis of secondary data—the TGI data in this case. The mixer market will serve as an illustration of how secondary data may be used to identify unmet needs.

To develop a successful new product, we must identify a need that is not being met well by present products. An examination of the data in Table 6.5 suggests such a need. The largest single *product type* consists of tart-flavored fruit drinks for mixing. If we add the *share of users* for lemon and lime, 7-Up, grapefruit, and orange juice, we see that these mixers account for 48 percent of the users. Given this strong preference for tart flavors, there may be an opportunity for an orange juice soft drink mixer. The other citrus fruits have a soft drink. Perhaps we could develop an orange-flavored soft drink for the mixer market that would be high-quality, have some orange juice in it, and would mix better than noncarbonated orange juice. Such a product would be easier to use than orange juice, because it would not require refrigeration after it was opened.

Our orange-flavored mixer would have a competitive advantage in that it would take market share from the orange juice industry, which generally does not promote to the mixer market. Thus we may expect fewer competitive reactions.

An orange juice soft drink mixer would compete directly with the two leaders in the mixer market—7-Up and orange juice. Returning to the right-hand columns of Table 6.1, we see that the profiles of these segments are very similar. This similarity should make it easier to promote our new product, because a single *media strategy* would be appropriate for both market segments. It would be necessary, however, to differentiate the message when competing directly with 7-Up or with orange juice.

The marketing manager has available a variety of statistical techniques to help in identifying marketing segments and analyzing the profiles of the persons in these segments. To simplify the discussion we have used only simple tabulations of data. Some of the multivariate statistical techniques were described briefly in Chapter 3 and its appendix. Examples of applications will be seen in Chapters 7, 9, and 12. Technical discussions of these techniques are available in other sources.[9]

At this point we have a good feel for the generic demand for soft drinks. We have examined the all-user and the mixer segments and have identified a possible unmet need in the mixer market. We decided to focus on heavy users. The nature of competitive

TABLE 6.5   Soft drinks and juices used as cocktail mixes, United States market

		All persons over 18 ,000	%	Primary users .000	%	Estimated % share of users
Do you drink them?						
Yes		59,122	43.1			
No		78,096	56.9			
If you do, how often do you drink them?						
More than once/day	H	2,840	2.1			
Once a day	H	4,312	3.1			
Two or three times/week	H	9,251	6.7			
Once a week	M	7,293	5.3			
Two or three times/month	M	13,569	9.9			
Once a month	L	6,312	4.6			
Less than once/month	L	11,131	8.1			
Which *kinds* do you drink?						
Colas		15,299	11.0	8,833	6	12
Club soda		10,673	8.0	5,988	4	9
Ginger ale		17,172	13.0	8,880	7	14
Quinine or tonic water		9,272	7.0	4,852	4	7
Lemon and lime sodas		7,378	5.0	3,423	3	6
7-Up		25,865	19.0	13,026	10	21
Grapefruit soda		3,721	3.0	1,732	1	3
Tomato juice		10,604	8.0	5,071	4	9
Orange juice		22,745	17.0	11,092	8	18
Other kinds		2,528	2.0	1,224	1	2

H, M, and L mean Heavy user, Medium user, and Light user, respectively.
Target Group Index, 1974, P-8, p. 259.

reaction has been examined. In the next chapter we will examine competition more carefully when we analyze *brand demand*. All of these conclusions would appear in the generic demand and the competitive-analysis sections of the marketing analysis worksheet. In the remainder of this chapter, we will summarize some of the marketing concepts that were used in this generic-demand analysis, plus some that are useful, but were not relevant to this analysis of generic demand in the soft drink market.

BEHAVIORAL SCIENCE DIMENSIONS OF CONSUMER BEHAVIOR   The profiles of soft drink users and nonusers reveal many of the contributions of the behavioral sciences to an understanding of consumer behavior. In this section we will briefly examine the major contributions from demography, sociology, social psychology, and economics. The first three behavioral sciences enable us to understand the *physical, social,* and *psychological needs* of consumers. Economic theory helps us to understand consumers' *economic capacity* to buy and their *willingness to buy at various price levels.*

Demographic Dimensions

Basic demographics. The profiles in Tables 6.1 and 6.2 illustrate many important demographic determinants of generic demand. These include sex, age, geographic location, city size, education, occupation, race, marital status, and the number of children in the household. Each of these variables reflects different consumer needs. For example, the clothing needs of a New Englander will be different from those of a Southerner. A person living in the country has a greater need for an automobile than does someone living in New York City. We have already seen that the number of teenagers in the family will influence soft drink consumption. Studies show that teenagers also influence automobile purchases, clothing purchases, travel, and home improvement. This influence is part of the family life cycle.

Family life cycle. Age classifications are not always a good predictor of the demand for products that are related to the stages in the life cycle of a family, because of differences in the age at which people marry. The several stages in the family life cycle and examples of the types of products bought at each stage are as follows:

1. Young singles not living at home—basic kitchen equipment, furniture, cars, stereos, equipment for the mating game, and vacations;
2. Newly married couples with no children—cars, refrigerators, stoves, sensible and durable furniture, and vacations;
3. Youngest child under six—washers, dryers, television, baby food, chest rubs and cough medicine, vitamins, dolls, wagons, sleds, and skates;
4. Youngest child six or older—foods, cleaning materials, bicycles, music lessons, and pianos;
5. Dependent children in teens or older—new and more tasteful furniture, auto travel, nonnecessary appliances, boats, dental services, and magazines;
6. No dependent children—vacations, luxuries, and home improvements;
7. No dependent children, head of household retired—medical appliances, medical care, products that aid health, sleep, and digestion.[10]

A generic-demand analysis for one of these family-related products or services must analyze the number of families that will be passing through each stage.

Although family life cycle is a good predicting variable for a large number of products and services, age is the best predictor for others, e.g., age-related health care, luxuries, slenderizing treatments, contractor's repairs, and coin-operated washing machines.

Birth rates. For long-range planning, the most important demographic variable is the birth rate. In 1963 the marketing research department of the Ford Motor Company observed that more than one million persons would reach driving age in 1963 and that most of these new drivers would buy second-hand cars, because at that time, there was no car designed for the youth market. The result of this analysis was the development of the Mustang. Today there are many automobiles designed for the youth market. This crest of teenagers in the mid-1960s was the result of the baby boom in the early '50s. As this crest moved across age classifications, it created demand for baby products, elementary schools, college facilities, and new homes. As this crest moved out of age-specific classifications, it left many industries with excess capacity. The "baby industry" illustrates the point. Faced with a declining market, Gerber, whose slogan was "Babies are our business, our only business," explored expansion into the nonbaby markets of peanut butter, ketchup, day-care centers, insurance, and "singles" dinners.[11] In Table 6.4 we saw that in 1990 this crest will create a bulge in the 30- to 45-year-old classification. Long-range planners are already considering the needs of this age classification.

Many analysts thought that there would be a second baby boom in the 1970s as the products of the first boom married and formed families. This boom has not materialized, because of important changes in life-styles. Marriages are being delayed, children are being postponed, the length of time between children has been increased, and the perception of the ideal family size has been reduced. All of these changes have reduced the birth rate from 3.1 to 2.1 children per American woman, with a profound effect on marketing planning for firms in the baby market.[12]

Sociological Dimensions Individuals have similar needs for food, shelter, clothing, and transportation, but their means for meeting these needs will be influenced greatly by their society, education, and life-styles. In order to understand the demand for specific products, therefore, we must understand the sociological dimensions of demand.

Life-styles. Market research has shown that the beer market presents an interesting example of the need to move from demographic to sociological data. The heavy beer drinker can be identified demographically as younger, with a middle income, a high school education, and in the craftsman occupational classification. But this demographic profile does not produce exciting advertising copy. The creative director of an advertising agency did his own basic research by putting on his "man on the street" clothes and taking a tavern tour of Chicago. He concluded that "the man who belongs to that 20 percent of the population that drinks 80 percent of the beer ... is a dreamer, a wisher, a limited edition of Walter Mitty. He is a sports nut because he is a hero worshipper."[13] Life-style research confirmed the research director's insights. The heavy beer drinker agreed with such statements as: "I like to take chances. If I had my way, I would own a convertible, I smoke too much, *Playboy* is my favorite magazine, I like danger, and I sometimes bet money at the races." He disagreed with such statements as: "I would rather spend a quiet evening at home than go out to a party, and I am careful what I eat to keep my weight under control."[14]

Husband-wife decisions. The purchase of durable household products is frequently the result of a joint husband-wife decision. Thus joint decisions are common for the purchase of dishwashers, air conditioners, TV sets, freezers, refrigerators, furniture, stoves, laundry equipment, automobiles, and floor coverings. An analysis of the decisions for automatic dishwashers revealed that 69 percent of the decisions were joint, 13 percent were made by men, and 18 percent were made by women.[15] It is interesting to note that the proportion of joint decisions increased with an increase in education, with 76 percent of the college graduates making joint decisions.[16]

Changing social values. "It's an ability to sniff out these social trends and to capitalize on them that enables some companies to beat the economic tides."[17] General Electric is focusing on the new interest in cooking. It has shifted resources from the "market-saturated personal care products, like hair dryers and blowers, and is spending more on food preparation appliances."[18]

Broad social changes were discussed in Chapter 4, where we noted the shift to the values of a post–Industrial Revolution. A shift in values on college campuses was detected between the late 1960s and the early 1970s.[19] By the early 1970s rebellion was gone, radical politics and new life-styles were separated, conventional careers were acceptable again, women's liberation had penetrated the campus, education was valued again, noncollege values caught up with college student values, and there was a return to the work ethic. According to Yankelovich, some of this shift in values was related to a downturn in the economy, which left students without jobs.

New-product adoption and diffusion. Networks of social communication play an important role in the *adoption* of new products by *innovative* consumers and the resultant diffusion of new products to the less adventuresome members of society. These communication networks provide the basis for social change.

Social communications play an important part in our purchase behavior. We all know someone who is proud of being an expert on the latest stereo equipment, new automobiles, the latest fashion, and the best movies. When we plan to make a purchase in these areas, we usually consult with such an individual, thereby saving the time that would be required to search out relevant information. Our needs are twofold: We must know what *product attributes* to consider and how each *brand rates along the product attributes.*

Studies of adoption and diffusion deal with the initial use of generic products, frequently before individual brands have been developed. One of the most famous diffusion studies examined the adoption of hybrid seed corn among Iowa farmers. There have been more than 1800 studies of diffusion in the fields of rural sociology, education, anthropology, medical sociology, industrial economics, geography, and marketing.[20] Most of the marketing studies have been conducted since the mid-1960s.

The "classical model" of the diffusion of a new idea, service, or product contains the following four elements: (1) the *innovation*, defined as an idea, practice, or object perceived as new by an individual or other relevant unit of adoption, (2) which is *communicated* through certain *channels*, (3) over *time*, (4) among the members of a *social system.*[21] The diffusion model should stimulate four important questions for the planner of a new-product introduction. What are the *profiles* of the *innovators*, who will be the first to adopt? What are the *sources of information* used by the *innovators*, the *early adopters*, the *early majority*, the *late majority*, and the *laggards?* What *sources of information* does an innovator use at the following stages of adoption: *awareness, evaluation, trial,* and *adoption?* What is the *rate of diffusion* from the innovator to the laggard?

Diffusion research has provided some generalized answers to these questions. Innovators tend to be highly educated, motivated to achieve, risk takers, change-oriented, cosmopolitan, exposed to mass media, exposed to interpersonal communication, deviates from social norms, and participators in group activities.[22]

Innovators use contact with change agencies as a primary source of information about new ideas. For the farmer this means contact with the agricultural agency. In other professions the innovator relies on technical journals. The laggard will rely on word-of-mouth communications from present users. The early and late majorities rely on the mass media for information about innovations.

The information sources change at various stages in the adoption process. The *awareness* of agricultural innovations is traced to the *mass media; evaluation* and *trial* depend on information from *friends* and *neighbors*; and *adoption* of the innovation depends on personal experience.[23] The marketing planner must consider the changing role of information sources as she or he develops a media strategy.

The *rate of adoption* of an innovation through a market segment depends on how highly integrated the group is. Because interpersonal communications play an important part in adoption, once a few persons have adopted an innovation, the rate of adoption accelerates. Models that examine the spread of epidemics have been applied to this diffusion process.[24] The concept of the rate of adoption has been linked to the product life cycle by Bass.[25] Thus the marketing concept of the product life cycle has a theoretical base in the concept of social-communication networks.

Social-Psychological Dimensions

Early applications. In their attempts to determine *why people buy products*, marketing researchers have borrowed extensively from social psychologists. *Attitude research* was utilized in marketing in 1935. *Motivation research* in the 1950s meant extensive depth interviews, using techniques borrowed from clinical psychologists. Measures of *social class* were also popular during this period. During the late 1950s and the 1960s, attempts were made to relate *personalities* to buying behavior.

All of these techniques contributed to our understanding of buying motivations, but each had severe limitations. Depth interviews were with small groups that did not represent the market for a product. These interviews generated extensive protocols that were difficult to analyze and report. Social-class measures suffered from a lack of standardization, and the results were no better than could be accomplished with demographic and economic variables.[26] Personality measures, using instruments such as the California Psychological Inventory and the Edwards Personality tests, gave disappointing results.[27] Personality measures seem to be too broad to explain anything as specific as buying a product or a brand. Life-style and psychographic variables were developed by marketing researchers to overcome this deficiency of overgeneralization. Psychographic variables are *situation-specific personality variables*, where the situation is the purchase and/or use of a product or a brand.

Recent developments—psychographics. Psychographics came into prominence in the late 1960s.[28] Two forces are responsible for the development of psychographic variables. First, marketers were aware of the limitations of demographic and economic variables.[29] Because they were disappointed with the results of personality and social-class variables, they were searching for new variables to explain buying motivation. Second, the development of the computer facilitated the use of multivariate statistical techniques to help the planner to determine the profiles of market segments that were heavy users, light users, and nonusers of a product or brand.

The rapid development of life-style and psychographic research has produced a diversity of definitions for these two concepts.[30] In addition, the terms are used interchangeably, which has created confusion. *Life-style* variables tend to include *behavioral*, mode-of-living variables that are determined by *social* forces. Life-style variables include *activities* (work, hobbies, sports, etc.), *buying styles* (conformist, style-conscious, ecologist, etc.), *cultural influences* (values, customs, taboos, etc.), and *interests* (family, job, community, media, etc.). Life-styles are measured by giving respondents a series of statements and asking them to scale how strongly they agree or disagree with the statement. Wells and Tigert, for example, used 300 statements, which included the following: "I shop a lot for specials"; "I usually keep my house very neat and clean"; and "I like ballet."[31]

Psychographic variables generally refer to those concepts that are *mental* and *individual*. These concepts include *attitudes, beliefs, opinions, perceived benefits of product attributes, self-concept* (affectionate, creative, self-assured, etc.), and *subjective probabilities*.

Applications of life-style and psychographic research. We have already seen how life-style research helped to develop a successful strategy for a beer. Demby reports the successful repositioning of a car-care product through the use of life-style research that identified three segments of motorists—the average motorist, who has a limited interest in car care; the preventive-care motorist, who wants to prevent problems; and the curative-care motorist, who attends to problems only as they occur.[32] The product became successful after it was directed toward the preventive-care market. Demby also reports that psychographic research was used to develop the successful American Motors' "Buyer Protection Plan."[33] The research identified the market segment that might buy an American Motors car if the plan were offered. But the most common use of life-style and psychographic variables is for the development of marketing strategies for brands, a topic that will be discussed in the next chapter.

Psychographic variables are self-rated personality measures. In the Target Group Index data, the respondent is asked to indicate level of agreement or disagreement with 20 personality adjectives. These adjectives, their definitions, and the rating scales are shown in Table 6.6.

Buying-style variables ask the respondent to report how he or she behaves when buying a product or a brand. The styles include brand-loyal, impulsive, and conformist. The ten buying styles measured in the Target Group Index are summarized in Table 6.6.

Tabulations of these data are useful when developing product and promotional strategies. A manufacturer who plans to develop a product or promotion that would be bought by new mothers will find the data in Table 6.7 relevant. The advertising copy directed toward pregnant women should try to reduce their tension, reinforce their feelings of creativity, and provide them with the factual information needed by cautious buyers who are new to a product class.

Psychographic profiles vary across market segments for the same generic product. The data in Table 6.8 illustrate this point for camera purchasers. A comparison of Nikon camera buyers with all camera buyers suggests that owning an expensive camera is an ego trip. Nikon buyers rate themselves as intelligent, nonconforming individualists. This information could be very useful when developing an advertising campaign for an expensive camera.

Economic Dimensions Consumer demand for goods and services plays a central role in the gross national product (GNP) of the United States. Over 60 percent of the GNP is for the personal consumption of durable goods, nondurable goods, and services. Thus economists are concerned with the prediction of consumer demand. This concern has led to the development of several theories and models that are useful to the marketing planner.

First, the planner must be concerned with the general economic outlook and how it relates to the demand for products. An automobile manufacturer may expect a decline

TABLE 6.6   Psychographic and buying-style variables

Psychographic variables:

Affectionate: passionate, loving, romantic
Amicable: amiable, affable, benevolent
Awkward: absentminded, forgetful, careless
Brave: courageous, daring, adventuresome
Broad-minded: open-minded, liberal, tolerant
Creative: inventive, imaginative, artistic
Dominating: authoritarian, demanding, aggressive
Efficient: organized, diligent, thorough
Egocentric: vain, self-centered, narcissistic
Frank: straightforward, outspoken, candid
Funny: humorous, amusing, witty
Intelligent: smart, bright, well informed
Kind: good-hearted, warm-hearted, sincere
Refined: gracious, sophisticated, dignified
Reserved: conservative, quiet, conventional
Self-assured: confident, self-sufficient, secure
Sociable: friendly, cheerful, likeable
Stubborn: hardheaded, headstrong, obstinate
Tense: nervous, high-strung, excitable
Trustworthy: competent, reliable, responsible

Buying-style variables:

Brand-loyal: "I always look for the name of the manufacturer on the package."
Cautious: "I do not buy unknown brands merely to save money."
Conformists: "I prefer to buy things that my friends or neighbors would approve of."
Ecologists: "All products that pollute the environment should be banned."
Economy-minded: "I shop around a lot to take advantage of specials or bargains."
Experimenters: "I like to change brands often for the sake of variety and novelty."
Impulsive: "When in the store, I often buy an item on the spur of the moment."
Persuasible: "In general, advertising presents a true picture of the products of well-known companies."
Planners: "I generally plan far ahead to buy expensive items such as automobiles."
Style-conscious: "I try to keep abreast of changes in styles and fashions."

Classifications of *Psychographics* and *Buying style* are based on self-ratings with respect to groups of adjectives on a five-point scale:

1. Agree a lot   2. Agree a little   3. Neither agree nor disagree   4. Disagree a little
5. Disagree a lot

Target Group Index, 1973, p. xi.

in sales if the economy faces a depression. The seller of automobile replacement parts, however, may anticipate an increase in sales, because consumers postpone the purchase of new cars and repair their present ones in a depression. When projecting industry sales, the planner will need to know how his or her industry reacted to previous economic trends, cycles, and seasonalities. Second, the planner will want to know how strategic changes in price will affect sales, and perhaps, those of a competitor.

TABLE 6.7   Psychographic traits of pregnant women

Psychographic traits	Pregnant women	All married women
Tense	141	121
Awkward	129	112
Amicable	77	107
Self-assured	77	87
Creative	130	101
Stubborn	154	100
Dominating	110	90
Broadminded	79	99
Impulsive buyers	137	106
Cautious buyers	80	107

Target Group Index, Research Bulletin **1**, 3, 1974, p. 2.

TABLE 6.8   Psychographic and buying styles of camera purchasers

Psychographics	Index (all adults = 100)		
	All camera purchasers	Cameras over $100	Nikon cameras
Awkward	106	79	77
Broadminded	112	123	150
Creative	119	141	158
Dominating	120	137	154
Efficient	114	130	150
Intelligent	117	156	206
Refined	110	127	136
Reserved	100	103	71
Stubborn	114	107	93
Tense	103	100	84
Conformists	88	93	59
Economy-minded	100	96	77
Experimenter	96	91	74
Persuasible	104	93	47
Style-conscious	114	92	67

Target Group Index, Volume P-38, 1973.

Elasticities.   The economic concept of *elasticity* provides insights for questions about the economy and the market strategies. *Elasticity*, in its most basic terms, is a ratio of the percent change in sales divided by a percent change in an economic variable, generally *price* or *disposable personal income*. To illustrate, assume that it has been observed that sales will increase 20 percent if price is lowered 10 percent. The *price elasticity* for this product is 2.0, which is calculated by dividing 20 percent by 10 percent. Similarly, we may compute an *income elasticity*. If sales increase 7 percent when *disposable personal income* increases 10 percent, we may say that income elasticity is 0.7 (7%/10%). When sales increase at a rate greater than the percent change in the economic variable, the elasticity ratio will be greater than 1.0, and we say that there is *elasticity*. We use the term *inelastic* demand when the ratio is less than 1.0. In the example above, we may say that the product is price-elastic, but income-inelastic. The automobile industry has tended to be the other way around. Automobile demand has been shown to be *price-inelastic* (0.8) and *income-elastic* (4.0).[34]

Utility. Economists have long used the concept of *utility* to explain consumers' behavior. Only recently have economists come to the conclusion that marketers have held for years; namely, that the demand is not for the product itself but for the attributes of the product. Thus economists have shifted to the notion that an understanding of consumer behavior requires an understanding of the utility derived from the product attributes.[35]

Consumer expectations and intentions. Because consumer expenditures are the largest component in the GNP, some researchers have combined psychological and economic concepts and measure consumers' *expectations* toward their *future income* and their *buying intentions* for specific goods, such as furniture, automobiles, a home, etc. Most of this work can be traced to the Survey Research Center, University of Michigan.[36] Attitudes have been found to be a useful variable in models of consumer durable-goods expenditures.

The behavioral sciences help the marketing manager to ask the critical questions during the analysis of generic demand. Those sciences also provide the measuring instruments and models that are necessary for this analysis, as was noted in Fig. 6.1.

THE DYNAMIC ENVIRONMENT FOR DEMAND ANALYSIS Marketing managers are facing new social, political, and technical environments that make analysis of consumers' needs and behavior a complex and dynamic process. Scarce resources require that products be redesigned to conserve materials and energy. An important attribute in household appliances is their energy requirements. Capital shortages lead to the need for shorter payback periods for new products. Changing values and life-styles emphasize basics—such as blue jeans, cosmetics made with natural ingredients, and use of public transportation. High divorce rates create single-parent families and single-person households, which change the type of living accommodations that are needed, along with the related furnishings. The concern for the environment creates a demand for products such as antipollution devices on automobiles, lead-free gas, and low-phosphate detergents.

To be sensitive to these opportunities, the alert marketer will need information systems that are faster, broader, more valid, and more reliable. The new breed of marketing manager will need to use resources more efficiently and be sensitive to the relationships between marketing decisions and public policy. Inflation, competition, raw-material shortages, and energy crises will require more contingency planning. In short, the role of the marketing manager is broadening and becoming much more complicated. Experience as a marketing manager is becoming good training for top management.

SUMMARY An analysis of a consumer market begins with the analysis of generic demand, or the demand for goods and services that will meet basic needs, such as food, shelter, clothing, and transportation. We measure generic demand by multiplying the number of people having the need times their usage rate. The generic demand for soft drinks, for example, was measured by multiplying the number of people who use soft drinks for a beverage or a mixer times the usage rate per year.

Market segmentation is the process for dividing markets into more homogeneous submarkets. It is easier to develop an efficient marketing strategy for these smaller market segments, because the buyers have similar needs. When marketing-segmentation strategies are carried too far, however, diseconomies in marketing and production occur.

A generic-demand analysis leads to a product strategy by identifying needs that are not being met. The marketing planner must draw on the behavioral sciences for an understanding of consumer behavior. The theories, models, and variables from demography, sociology, social psychology, and economics help the planner to ask the right questions when he or she is conducting a demand analysis.

DISCUSSION CASELETTES

THE GENERIC DEMAND FOR A SHOPPING CENTER

The case writer is Robert D. Martin, a mortgage banker.

The Real Estate Investment Trust (REIT) you work for has just consummated a foreclosure on a medium-size (150,000 square feet) shopping center in a small, affluent town near Boston, Massachusetts. The three-level shopping center is modern, enclosed, California type in structure and design, and can accommodate only specialty-type tenants as opposed to department and grocery stores. (Examples of specialty tenants are an imported-gift shop, a women's fashion shop, a unique type of restaurant, etc.)

The developer of the shopping center completed construction, but ran out of money to pay your interest and establish a leasing effort. Your foreclosure action triggered a bankruptcy, and the project has been tied up in the courts for about a year. The lack of attention the property received during this time naturally has created a credibility problem for the facility with the local community.

Your company now owns the shopping center, of which only 15 percent is leased. It is obvious that an aggressive leasing campaign will have a significant cost, yet to try to sell the facility without existing leases will definitely cause a substantial write-off of your loan. The questions posed to you are as follows:

1. Will the surrounding market support this facility?
2. If so, what are the key strategies in a marketing plan to lease space?

Questions for Discussion

1. How can the market for this retail facility be evaluated? What variables should one include in an analysis of generic demand? What sources of information are available?
2. What strategies would you use to attract occupants to this shopping center?

THE DEMAND FOR A PROPOSED APARTMENT COMPLEX

The case writer is Robert D. Martin, a mortgage banker.

As a mortgage loan analyst for a large insurance company, your boss gives you the attached information about a proposed apartment complex in a medium-size Southern city and asks you to make a recommendation about the project's potential. A local bank will finance the construction of the apartments, and your loan will fund when the facility is complete.

Questions for Discussion

1. What variables and sources of information would you utilize to evaluate the apartment market?

2. How can a generic-demand analysis be used to critique the following Pro Forma?

PRO FORMA OPERATING STATEMENT—MEADOW BROOK APARTMENTS

1975

GROSS INCOME ESTIMATE:

No. of units	Type	Rent/month		
25	Efficiencies	@ $120	=	$ 3,000
35	1 bedroom, 1-bath flats	@ $170	=	5,950
70	2 bedrooms, 1-bath flats	@ $190	=	13,300
55	2 bedrooms, 1 1/2-bath town house	@ $205	=	11,275
30	3 bedrooms, 2-bath town house	@ $245	=	7,350
215	*Totals*			$ 40,875
	Annualized			490,500
	Less: 5% for vacancy and rent loss			($24,525)

EFFECTIVE GROSS INCOME: $465,975

Annual expenses:

Management fee	$22,500	
Management salaries	18,000	
Maintenance salaries	25,000	
Maintenance and repairs	20,000	
Electricity	10,000	
Water and sewer	18,000	
Garbage pick-up	8,000	
Advertising and promotion	6,000	
Real estate taxes	35,000	
Insurance	10,000	
Miscellaneous	2,500	$175,000
Net income:		$280,975

PROPOSED LOAN: $2,000,000 at 10 percent interest rate and 30-year term. (For debt service to cover interest and principal, use a rate of 10.54 percent)
COMMENTS: Landlord will pay for tenants' water only; each apartment will have a separate electric meter. Amenities to include swimming pool, clubhouse, central laundry, and two tennis courts.

DISCUSSION QUESTIONS

1. Develop a rough marketing analysis worksheet to summarize the facts, the assumptions/research needed, and the conclusions that appear in the analysis of the soft drink market as analyzed in this chapter.

2. How far do you think market segmentation can be carried? What would be the smallest possible segment? Can you think of industries that have this kind of segment? Is there a chance for making profit in this kind of marketing? Do you think that consumer marketing and industrial marketing differ with respect to the sizes of their market segments?

3. If you were asked to develop a product strategy for a new product—a TV with the capability of recording programs for later viewing—how would you use your knowledge of the "new-product adoption and diffusion process"? Explain.

4. People do not demand the product itself, but rather the attributes of the product. Is this statement true? Try to remember the last time you (or your family) bought a car. Did you buy the car or its various attributes? Try to analyze your decision process and explain.

5. What is generic demand? What are the two components that determine generic demand?

6. What is market segmentation? What are two ways to segment a market? Give several examples of products on the market that are directed toward specific segments of the population. Is the segmentation achieved because these products themselves are differentiated or because their promotional strategies are differentiated?

7. What are some advantages and disadvantages of market segmentation?

8. List the important demographic determinants of generic demand.

9. What are some drawbacks of using social-class and personality measures to predict buying behavior? How do psychographic and life-style variables differ, and what advantage do they have for understanding buying behavior?

10. Define income elasticity and price elasticity.

NOTES

1. For more complex models, see J. A. Howard and J. N. Sheth, *The Theory of Buyer Behavior* (New York: Wiley, 1969); F. M. Nicosia, *Consumer Decision Processes* (Englewood Cliffs, N.J.: Prentice-Hall, 1966); and J. F. Engel, D. T. Kollat, and R. D. Blackwell, *Consumer Behavior*, 2d ed. (New York: Holt, Rinehart and Winston, 1973).

2. A. H. Maslow, *Motivation and Personality*, 2d ed. (New York: Harper & Row, 1970).

3. R. I. Haley, "Benefit Segmentation: A Decision-Oriented Research Tool," *Journal of Marketing* **32** (July 1968): 30–35.

4. L. V. Dominguez, "Econometric Analysis of Consumer Information Processing," in *Buyer/Consumer Information Processing*, ed. G. D. Hughes and M. L. Ray (Chapel Hill: University of North Carolina Press, 1974), pp. 24–50.

5. For a discussion and citations, *see* J. R. Bettman, "Decision-Net Models of Buyer Information Processing and Choice: Findings, Problems, and Prospects," in Hughes and Ray, *op. cit.*, pp. 59–74.

6. For a discussion of the model, the literature, and an experiment testing the model in an industrial setting, *see* G. W. Stiles, "Determinants of the Industrial Buyer's Level of Information Processing: Organizations, Situations, and Individual Differences," in Hughes and Ray, *op. cit.*, pp. 116–135.

7. The author acknowledges the kind permission of Axiom Market Research Bureau, Inc., for permission to publish these data.

8. W. R. Smith, "Product Differentiation and Market Segmentation as Alternative Marketing Strategies," *Journal of Marketing* (July 1956): 3–8.

9. D. A. Aaker, ed., *Multivariate Analysis in Marketing: Theory and Application* (Belmont, Calif.: Wadsworth, 1971); R. E. Frank, W. F. Massy, and Y. Wind, *Market Segmentation* (Englewood Cliffs, N.J.: Prentice-Hall, 1972); and P. E. Green and D. S. Tull, *Research for Marketing Decisions*, 3rd ed. (Englewood Cliffs, N.J.: Prentice-Hall, 1975).

10. W. D. Wells and G. Gubar, "Life Cycle Concept in Marketing Research," *Journal of Marketing Research* (November 1966): 360.

11. Joseph A. Morein, "Shift from Brand to Product Line Marketing," *Harvard Business Review* (September–October 1975): 56–64.

12. G. D. Hughes, *Demand Analysis for Marketing Decisions* (Homewood, Ill.: Richard D. Irwin, 1973), pp. 127–143; and L. A. Mayer, "It's a Bear Market for Babies, Too," *Fortune* (December 1974): 134–137 ff.

13. J. T. Plummer, "Applications of Life Style Research to the Creation of Advertising Campaigns," in *Life Style and Psychographics*, ed. W. E. Wells (Chicago: American Marketing Association, 1974), pp. 159–169.

14. J. T. Plummer, "The Concept and Application of Life Style Segmentation," *Journal of Marketing* **38** (January 1974): 33–37.

15. Target Group Index, *Client Research Bulletin* **1**, 3 (1973): 3.

16. H. L. Davis, "Decision Making Within the Household," *Journal of Consumer Research* (March 1976): 241–260; and R. Ferber and L. C. Lee, "Husband-Wife Influence in Family Purchasing Behavior," *Journal of Consumer Research* **1** (June 1974): 43–50.

17. "Food for Thought," *Forbes*, March 15, 1976, pp. 4, 29.

18. *Ibid.*, p. 28.

19. D. Yankelovich, *Changing Youth Values in the 70's* (New York: JDR 3rd Fund. Inc., 1974).

20. E. M. Rogers, "New Product Adoption and Diffusion," *Journal of Consumer Research* (March 1976): 290–301.

21. *Ibid.*, p. 292.

22. E. M. Rogers and J. D. Stanfield, "Adoption and Diffusion of New Products: Emerging Generalizations and Hypotheses," in *Applications of the Sciences in Marketing Management*, ed. F. M. Bass, C. W. King, and E. A. Pessemier (New York: Wiley, 1968), pp. 228–229.

23. H. F. Lionberger, *Adoption of New Ideas and Practices* (Ames: Iowa State University Press, 1960).

24. J. S. Coleman, E. Katz, and H. Menzel, *Medical Innovation, A Diffusion Study* (Indianapolis: Bobbs–Merrill, 1966).

25. F. M. Bass, "A New Product Growth Model for Consumer Durables," *Management Science* **15** (January 1969): pp. 215–227.

26. For a discussion of the limitations of social-class variables, *see* Hughes, *op. cit.*, Chapter 7; and J. H. Myers, R. R. Stanton, and A. F. Haug, "Correlates of Buying Behavior: Social Class vs. Income," *Journal of Marketing* **35** (October 1971): 8–15.

27. H. H. Kassarjian, "Personality and Consumer Behavior: A Review," in *Abstracts*, ed. D. L. Sparks (Chicago: American Marketing Association, Fall Conference, 1970), p. 19.

28. E. Demby, "Psychographics and From Whence It Came," in Wells, *op. cit.*, pp. 11–30.

29. R. E. Frank, "Market Segmentation Research: Findings and Implications," in Bass, King, and Pessemier, *op. cit.*

30. Excellent summaries of the development of the concepts are provided by Demby, *op. cit.*; Wells, *op. cit.*; and T. P. Hustad and E. A. Pessemier, *Segmenting Consumer Markets with Activity and Attitude Measures* (Lafayette, Ind.: Institute for Research in the Behavioral, Economic, and Management Sciences, Purdue University), Working Paper No. 298, March 1971.

31. W. D. Wells and D. J. Tigert, "Activities, Interests and Opinions," *Journal of Advertising Research* (April 1971): 27–35.

32. Demby, *op. cit.*

33. *Ibid.*

34. T. R. Dyckman, "An Aggregate-Demand Model for Automobiles," *Journal of Business* **38** (July 1965): 252–266; for a discussion of the various methods of computing elasticity, *see* Hughes, *op. cit.*, pp. 86–96.

35. K. Lancaster, *Consumer Demand: A New Approach* (New York: Columbia University Press, 1971) and "A New Approach to Consumer Theory," *Journal of Political Economy* **74** (April 1966): 132–157; and B. T. Tatchford, "The New Economic Theory of Consumer Behavior: An Interpretive Essay," *Journal of Consumer Research* (September 1975): 65–75.

36. For a review, *see* G. Katona, *Aspiration and Affluence* (New York: McGraw-Hill, 1971).

SUGGESTED READINGS

Assael, H., and A. M. Roscoe, Jr., "Approaches to Market Segmentation Analysis," *Journal of Marketing* (October 1976): 67–76.

Bennett, P. D., and H. H. Kassarjian, *Consumer Behavior* (Englewood Cliffs, N.J.: Prentice-Hall, 1972).

Bettman, J. R., "Relationship of Information-Processing Attitude Structures to Private Brand Purchasing Behavior," *Journal of Applied Psychology* **59**, 1 (1974): 79–83.

Cohen, J. B., ed., *Behavioral Science Foundations of Consumer Behavior* (New York: Free Press, 1972).

Day, G. S., *Buyer Attitudes and Brand Choice Behavior* (New York: Free Press, 1970).

Dhalla, N. K., and W. H. Mahatoo, "Expanding the Scope of Segmentation Research," *Journal of Marketing* **40** (April 1976): 34–41.

Engel, J. R., H. F. Fiorillo, and M. A. Cayley, *Market Segmentation—Concept and Applications* (New York: Holt, Rinehart and Winston, 1972).

Gatty, R., "Multivariate Analysis for Marketing Research: An Evaluation," *Applied Statistics* **15** (1966): 157–172.

Haines, G. H., Jr., *Consumer Behavior: Learning Models of Purchasing* (New York: Free Press, 1969).

Hong, A., "How Family Spending Patterns Adjust for Inflationary Spiral," *Advertising Age*, November 28, 1977, p. 3.

Kassarjian, H. H., and T. S. Robertson, eds., *Perspectives in Consumer Behavior*, rev. ed. (Glenview, Ill.: Scott, Foresman, 1973).

Myers, J. H., "Benefit Structure Analysis: A New Tool for Product Planning," *Journal of Marketing* (October 1976): 23–32.

Nicosia, F., and Y. Wind, eds., *Behavioral Models for Market Analysis: Foundations for Marketing Action* (New York: Dryden Press, 1977).

Reynolds, F., and W. Darden, "Construing Life Style and Psychographics," in *Life Style and Psychographics*, ed. W. D. Wells (New York: American Marketing Association, 1974), pp. 73–95.

Ward, S., and T. S. Robertson, eds., *Consumer Behavior: Theoretical Sources* (Englewood Cliffs, N.J.: Prentice-Hall, 1973).

Weber, J. A., *Growth Opportunity Analysis* (Reston, Va: Reston Publishing Company, 1976).

Ziff, R., "Psychographics for Market Segmentation," *Journal of Advertising Research* **11** (April 1971): 3–9.

ENVIRONMENTAL ANALYSIS WORKSHEET

Environmental elements	Facts	Assumptions or research needed	Conclusions
Organizational values, objectives, and policies (4)			
Organizational design (5)			
Situation			
Generic demand (6)			
Brand demand (7)			
Competition (9)			
Public policy (10)			
Opportunities (2)			
Problems			

MARKETING PLAN (CONSUMER PRODUCT)

Current performance
Recommendations
Effect of recommendations on income
Situation analysis
Opportunities and problems
Strategies
Tests and research
Supporting documents
   Comparative budgets
   Media allocation schedule
   Promotion control sheet

STRATEGY WORKSHEET

Opportunities and problems in rank order to importance

1.
2.
.
n.

	Current strategy	Alternatives and recommended strategy	Estimated Effect

Demand strategy
   Generic
   Brand

Strategic goals
   Financial
   Marketing

Marketing-mix strategies
   Product (12)
   Pricing (13)
   Channel and logistics (14)
   Advertising and promotional (15)
   Sales management (16)

Research (3)

Profit plan

Evaluation and control (19)

CHAPTER 7

Analyzing the Brand's Market Position

LEARNING OBJECTIVES   After studying this chapter you should:

1. Be able to analyze a brand's market position.
2. Be able to develop product and promotional strategies using brand maps.
3. Be familiar with some of the most frequently used models of the brand decision process and their limitations.
4. Know common strategies for positioning new brands and repositioning old brands.
5. Be able to diagnose a brand's current situation and develop a strategy based on this diagnosis.
6. Have a working knowledge of three basic strategies for expanding demand.
7. Be able to define and use the following concepts:

Market position	Promotional strategies
Brand maps	Beliefs, values, and attitudes
Perceptual brand positioning	Brand positioning and repositioning
Ideal brands	Brand cannibalism
Squatting between market segments	Problem tracking
Product attributes	Market share
Benefit segmentation	Strategic goals
Product strategies	Speciality, convenience, and shopping goods
Product-line extensions	Contingency planning

SOME ANALYTICAL QUESTIONS FOR OPENERS

1. What are the strengths and weaknesses of our brand?
2. Is the brand's market share growing, static, or declining?
3. What percentage of the potential buyers are aware of the benefits of the brand?
4. What percentage of the market tried the brand?
5. What is the repurchase rate?
6. What is the brand's distribution rate?
7. How do consumers perceive the benefits of our brand relative to competitive brands?

In the previous chapter we saw that the buyer mentally processes information to make two choices—the selection of a product category and the selection of a brand (or brands) within that category. In choosing a brand, the consumer evaluates the attributes of available brands in terms of his or her needs. The consumer's perception of the position of brands relative to his or her needs will determine brand preferences and in turn the market share of the brand. Therefore, it is crucial for the marketing manager to know the position of the brand. This chapter will examine methods for analyzing a brand's market position. Examples of familiar brands will illustrate brand strategies for positioning new brands and repositioning old ones.

BRAND MAPS   Brand maps help the marketing manager visualize vital information needed to develop a brand strategy. These maps also graphically illustrate the important marketing concepts of market segmentation, product attributes, brand strategies, and promotional strategies. Each of these concepts will be explained and illustrated with the aid of the hypothetical brand map in Fig. 7.1.

Fig. 7.1   A brand map for soft drinks market: beverage for teenagers.

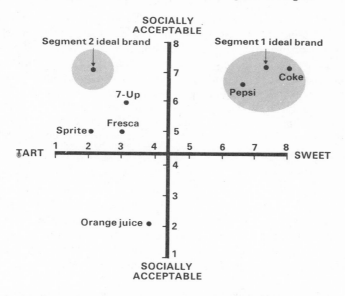

Note: Data are hypothetical and for illustrative purposes only.

Market Segmentation   The first thing to note in the brand map in Fig. 7.1 is that there are two segments within this market. These segments are identified as teenagers' perceptions of the *ideal soft drink*. Segment 1, the larger segment, prefers a drink that is sweet and socially acceptable. Segment 2 prefers a drink that is tart and socially acceptable. (Teenager peer pressure requires that a soft drink be highly acceptable in social situations.)

These two market segments illustrate an extremely important point in product strategy—*the danger of squatting between the stools.* Plotting respondents' preferences on a map clearly reveals that there are two distinct market preferences with regard to taste. If instead of plotting the preferences we had computed the *average* preference, we would have concluded that the ideal brand would have a socially acceptable scale value of 7.0 and a sweetness of approximately 4.7. Examining the map, however, we see that the socially acceptable scale value would be correct, but that the tart/sweet scale value of 4.7 lies between the two market segments. A product with a very slightly sweet flavor would be rejected by both markets. Thus the product would *squat between two segments* and be a failure.[1]

Product Attributes   The two dimensions in Fig. 7.1 represent two of the *product attributes* that are considered when choosing a soft drink—flavor and social acceptability. Other attributes are carbonation level, flavor strength, and number of calories. The importance of these product attributes varies according to the user's needs. For instance, most buyers prefer as a mixer a soft drink with a light flavor. Low-calorie soft drinks are preferred by middle-aged women. In developing our product strategy, we must remember that people do not buy a product, but rather a bundle of attributes. Furthermore, buyers weight these attributes differently. The differential weighting of needs produces market segments. To have a successful product, therefore, we must understand the needs of these market segments.

The consumer is interested in product attributes only to the extent that they are able to meet his or her needs. Those needs are often measured in terms of consumers' perceived benefits. For example, the toothpaste market has been segmented into four distinct markets, each with a different perceived benefit.[2] The *sensory* market is a children's market that chooses a toothpaste for its flavor and appearance. Teenagers are the *sociable* segment. They want a toothpaste that has a brightener. The *worrisome* segment has a large family, so it wants a toothpaste that prevents decay. The *independent* segment thinks that all toothpastes are the same, so it buys on the basis of price. Benefit segmentation requires a clear understanding of consumers' problems.

Product Strategies   Given a product map such as Fig. 7.1, a marketing strategist will attempt to develop a new product that will be closer to one of the ideal segments. The product may be a product-line extension strategy which modifies a present product. For instance, Pepsi Cola introduced Pepsi Light, which was a reduced-calorie cola with a taste of lemon. This product would appeal to persons concerned about weight but who did not want a sweet soft drink. Pepsi advertising compared Pepsi Light to Coca-Cola. Television commercials showed taste tests in which respondents preferred Pepsi Light to Coke.

The Coca-Cola Company used its sugar-free citrus soft drink, Fresca, to counter the Pepsi Light introduction. It showed television advertisements in which respondents preferred Fresca over Pepsi Light. The copy theme for Coke was changed to "Coke adds life to ..." in an effort to stop the Pepsi Cola inroad into the Coke market share.

The product strategy in brand positioning attempts to position a brand closer to an ideal segment, but not too close to a competitive brand. A brand that is too close to competition will confuse the consumer, so that its advertising may actually help the competition.

Promotional Strategies   Instead of moving the product toward the perceived ideal brand, the strategist may attempt to move the perception of the ideal brand closer to that of his or her brand. This would require a promotional strategy. Using Fig. 7.1 as an example, Sprite could advertise that it is for the person who thinks independently. Another promotional strategy might be to give the soft drink a more sociable image, as was done by 7-Up.

Promotional strategies are also required to correct misperceptions. For example, a very effective prescription drug did not have side effects. Physicians thought that any drug so effective was very likely to have side effects. Therefore, the pharmaceutical company advertised to physicians the results of clinical tests documenting the lack of side effects.

Brand maps make it possible to state precise goals for an advertising campaign. Using 7-Up and Fig. 7.1 as an example, the 7-Up strategist may want to move the brand image closer to the center of the ideal segment, segment 2. One alternative would be to promote the drink's tart flavor, thereby moving it from tartness level 3 to 2. This strategy may result in confusing 7-Up with Sprite and Fresca. The other strategy would be to try to promote the social acceptability of 7-Up. If this alternative is chosen, the strategist may define the promotional goal as: "Changing the perception of 7-Up from a 6 to a 7 in social acceptability in the next 18 months."

There may be several reasons for promoting one product benefit over another. First, consumers may weight the importance of benefits differently. The strategist may therefore decide to promote the most important benefit. Second, some benefits may be more difficult to communicate than others. For example, in the Scoop Ice Cream case it was necessary to use television to demonstrate that children could make the ice cream.

The decision to introduce an orange soft drink (Chapter 6) must be tested in the light of information on brand positioning. Orange juice as a beverage for teenagers squats between the two segments on the tart/sweet dimension and is socially unacceptable. The strategist must determine which benefit is more important to the consumer. The strategist must consider the costs of creating a socially acceptable image and then decide whether to abandon this market and focus on the adult-beverage and mixer markets.

MODELS OF THE BRAND DECISION PROCESS

Models of the process by which buyers choose a brand may be classified broadly as communication models and brand-choice models. Brand-choice models may be divided further into those using attitude variables and those using past buying behavior.

Communication Models

Communication models examine the influence of the message and the medium on an individual's beliefs. When these beliefs are combined with a person's values, attitudes are formed, and these attitudes in turn will influence one's behavior. Thus a change in a belief could lead to brand switching.

Balance models are used to predict how an individual will change his or her attitude under various communication situations. The basic balance model was presented by Heider as follows:[3]

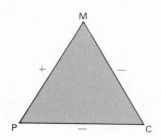

where the person (P) has a favorable attitude ($+$) toward the medium (M) and an unfavorable one ($-$) toward the concept (C). The individual's mental state will be in balance if the medium makes an unfavorable statement about the concept. This state would be unbalanced if the medium said something favorable about the concept. To restore his or her mental balance (i.e., cognitive consonance), the person must undergo a change in attitude toward either the medium or the concept.

Communication models use terms that have been borrowed from radio communication, e.g., transmitters, receivers, and filters. Thus an opinion leader in a community may act as a filter of information about new styles; the purchasing manager may act as a filter in industrial marketing.

The goal of the marketing communication effort is generally to get the individual to change beliefs about some component of the buying process, such as his or her needs, the relative importance of those needs, the attributes of the product, and the availability of the product. These beliefs may be combined with one's values to form an overall attitude toward an object. The Fishbein belief-value model expresses these concepts as follows:[4]

$$A_o = \sum_{i=1}^{n} B_i a_i, \tag{7.1}$$

where A_o is the attitude toward object o; B_i is the belief that attribute i is associated with o, measured in terms of probability; a_i is the person's evaluation of attribute i; and there are n attributes being evaluated. This model will be illustrated first with a verbal example and then with a numerical one.

Assume that we are selling a toothpaste that has only one attribute—it whitens teeth better than any other product does. We advertise this product to parents, teenagers, and South Sea islanders so extensively that they all believe that the product has this attribute. Will their attitude toward the product be the same? No, because each group holds a different value toward white teeth. Parents are more concerned with cavity prevention. Teenagers are highly concerned with whiteness because of the social implications. South Sea islanders chew on betel nut for social status. Since these nuts turn their teeth black, thereby giving them social status, they would have an unfavorable attitude toward our toothpaste. This example stresses the importance of knowing the values *and* beliefs of persons in our market segments. Generally, it is easier to change beliefs than values, because values are so basic to an individual. Beliefs—the probability that something exists—can frequently be altered through advertising.

To illustrate the Fishbein model numerically, consider the following example. Respondents are asked to divide ten points among four product attributes to reflect the value (or importance) of each attribute. Then they are asked to express their belief that brands A, B, and C possess these attributes. They express their beliefs in terms of probabilities, which sum is 1.0. The data may be summarized as in Table 7.1. In this example the first choice of this market segment is brand C, followed by brands A and B.

Cast in terms of probabilities and, values, an attitude is an expected value. Thus an attitude is the psychological counterpart of the decision-theory concept of expected value. It appears, therefore, that economists and psychologists have come to the same conclusion in their independent studies of the human decision process. The only difference is the measurement of value. Economic decision theory measures value in

TABLE 7.1   Expressing beliefs as probabilities

Attributes	Evaluation attribute (a)	Beliefs (B) that the following objects contain each attribute (expressed as a probability)			Attitude toward attributes (Ba)		
		A	B	C	A	B	C
Price	1	.2	.6	.4	.2	.6	.4
Whitener	2	.3	.2	.1	.6	.4	.2
Taste	2	.4	.1	.3	.8	.2	.6
Decay prevention	5	.1	.1	.2	.5	.5	1.0
Totals	10	1.0	1.0	1.0	2.1	1.7	2.2

terms of money or utility, whereas the psychological model measures it in terms of physical, cultural, and social factors.

Another communication model is concerned with the probability of individuals being at different levels in a hierarchy of communication effects. McGuire expressed the model as follows:[5]

$$\text{Probability of buying a brand} = P(p) \times P(a) \times P(c) \times P(y) \times P(r), \tag{7.2}$$

where P is a probability and p, a, c, y, and r refer to the presentation of a message, attention to the message, comprehension of the message, yielding to the argument, and retention of the favorable attitude, respectively. If any one of these levels has a probability of zero, the probability of someone's buying the brand is zero. This model can be used to diagnose communication problems and develop communication strategies to correct the problems.

Two additional communication concepts can be important to brand-advertising strategies. *Selective perception* occurs when an individual misperceives a message because of a prior bias toward the object. If the object is his or her first-choice brand, the selective perception may be in favor of the brand. Selective perception will also screen out information that is not needed. Thus an individual may not be aware of automobile advertisements until his or her present automobile needs to be replaced.

Cognitive dissonance occurs when an individual must choose between two attractive alternatives, such as two similar brands. *After* the choice is made, the individual will tend to seek information from friends and advertisements in support of the first-choice decision and lower his or her attitudes toward the second choice. In this case a change in behavior leads to a change in attitudes, which is counter to the usual sequence of events.

Brand-Choice Models   Brand-choice models use measures of attitudes or past brand-buying behavior to predict brand choice. We will examine examples of both of these models. Bear in mind that the attitude models are better at *explaining* brand choice and that the behavioral models are better at *predicting* brand choice. We will return to this distinction after examining the two types of models.

Attitude models. The measurement of an attitude amounts to asking respondents to place the brand along each of the attributes. Thus the positions of the soft drink brands along the attributes in the brand map in Fig. 7.1 are the respondents' attitudes toward these brands. The closer the brand is to a respondent's perception of an ideal brand, the more she or he prefers that brand. This perceptual preference may be expressed mathematically, using Fig. 7.1 as an example. We will compute a preference index number (P) that is inversely ($1/P$) related to the distance of 7-Up and Fresca from the ideal segment 2. We will let P_7 be the index number for 7-Up and P_F the preference index for Fresca. The calculations are given in Table 7.2.

TABLE 7.2   **Computation of preference index numbers**

Inverse of the preference index $(1/P)$		Benefit dimension		
		Tart/sweet		*Social acceptability*
$1/P_7$	$=$	$|3 - 2|$	$+$	$|6 - 7|$	(7.3)
$1/P_7$	$=$ 2			
$P_7 = 0.5$				
$1/P_F$	$=$	$|3 - 2|$	$+$	$|5 - 7|$	(7.4)
$1/P_F$	$=$ 3			
$P_F = 0.33$				

Note: The vertical bars mean the absolute value (without regard to sign) after the subtraction is made.

The index numbers in Table 7.2 mean that teenagers prefer 7-Up to Fresca. This is a rank-order preference, not a probability of buying a brand. To compute a probability, we would have to compute an index number for all brands, then normalize them so that they sum 1.0. Also, we should recognize that this model *does not measure share of market.* At most it can measure only the share of *persons who prefer a brand.* Intervening variables, such as price or distribution, prevent preference from being translated into action. We know also, from Chapter 6, that market share requires measures of the share of the number of users and their consumption rates.

These calculations are easier to remember if letters are used to represent the scale values for the attitudes toward both the brand and the ideal. We will therefore let B_{1j} represent the respondents' attitude toward brand j along the tart/sweet dimension. B_{2j} will represent brand j's position along the sociability dimension. Similarly, I_1 and I_2 will represent the position of the ideal segment along these two dimensions. Equations (7.1) and (7.2) may now be stated in more general form as follows:

$$1/P_j = |B_{1j} - 1_1| + |B_{2j} - I_2|. \qquad (7.5)$$

This model limits buyers to only two product-benefit dimensions. We may extend the model to as many dimensions as are necessary by using a little algebraic shorthand. Instead of numbering the dimensions, we will use i, and we will use the Greek letter sigma, $\sum$, to mean "sum," or "plus." Equation (7.5) may now be written in the more general form:

$$1/P_j = \sum_{i=1}^{n} (|B_{ij} - I_i|), \tag{7.6}$$

where the buyer uses n benefit dimensions when choosing a brand.

Equation (7.6) is sometimes referred to as a "city block" model because it does not take the shortest distance between the brand and the ideal. Taking the more direct route, using Euclidean space, the preference model is as follows:

$$1/P_j = \sqrt{\sum_{i=1}^{n} (B_{ij} - I_i)^2}. \tag{7.7}$$

The city block and the Euclidean models are illustrated in Fig. 7.2. The city block model uses two sides of the triangle; the Euclidean model uses the hypotenuse. Equations (7.6) and (7.7) assume that the product benefits are of equal importance to the buyer. This is not always the case, however. Teenagers, for example, are subject to peer pressure and so may regard the social acceptability of a soft drink as more important than its flavor. This weighting of the dimensions will alter the preferences.

Fig. 7.2   A comparison of the city block and Euclidean models.

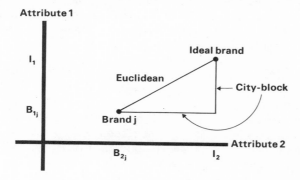

The city block model in weighted form is as follows:

$$1/P_j = \sum_{i=1}^{n} (W_i |B_{ij} - I_i|), \tag{7.8}$$

where W_i is the importance weight for the ith product attribute. British market researchers refer to this model as the St. James model.

TABLE 7.3 A weighted (compensatory) attitude model

Attributes (not ranked)	Attribute weights (W)	Attitudes toward brands (scaled 1 to 6; 6 = favorable)			Weighted attitudes		
		A	B	C	WA	WB	WC
1.	1	1	6	1	1	6	1
2.	2	6	1	1	12	2	2
3.	2	3	3	$1i$	6	6	2
4.	5	2	2	6	10	10	30
Totals	10	12	12	9	29	24	35

Decision: Buy C

Note:
1. Even though brand C is inferior on attributes 1, 2, and 3, the model selects C because it excels in attribute 4, which is weighted heavily by the decision maker, thereby *compensating* for deficiences on attributes 1, 2, and 3.
2. This model may be expressed in algebraic form as:

$$\text{Rank preference brand}_i = \sum_{i=1}^{n} W_i A_{ij},$$

where W_i = the weight or importance of attribute i
$\qquad A_{ij}$ = the attitude toward brand j along attribute i.

Because of intervening variables, the percentage of buyers preferring a brand will not necessarily equal the percentage of buyers. The most likely intervening variables are price and availability. Thus a buyer may prefer a brand but be unable to afford it. Or, a buyer's preferred brand may not be available in his or her favorite store. *A brand map, therefore, is a model of the mentally processed brand information, but it is not a complete model of consumer behavior.*

Limitations of Weighted Attitude Models. The Fishbein model is part of a class of attitude models known as weighted, or compensatory, models. Weighted attitude models have caused both practical and theoretical problems.

Table 7.3 illustrates a weighted attitude model for a four-attribute brand. The importance of the attributes is weighted by the respondent by dividing ten points among them. The respondent is then asked to rate each of the three brands on a scale of 1 to 6, with 6 the most favorable. Summing the weighted attitudes leads to the decision to choose brand C, even though it was inferior on three of the four attributes. The reason for this selection is that brand C excelled on attribute 4, which was weighted the heaviest of the four attributes. Thus this fourth attribute *compensated* for the deficiencies of the other three; hence the weighted-attitude model is called a compensatory model.

This deficiency in the weighted-attitude model may be overcome by stating the minimum acceptable levels for each attribute. In industrial selling the buyer will request bids that will conform to specifications establishing minimum levels of performance. Table 7.4 illustrates how the addition of a minimum acceptable level of performance will reduce the compensatory problem. Brand C fails to meet the test of a minimum

TABLE 7.4   Lower threshold (lexicographic-compensatory) weighted attitude model

Attributes (not ranked)	Minimum acceptable attitude	Attitudes toward brands (scaled 1 to 6; 6 = favorable)			Wts.	Weighted attitudes	
		A	B	C		W A	W B
1.	1	1	6	1	1	1	6
2.	1	6	1	1	2	12	2
3.	3	3	3	1	2	6	6
4.	2	2	2	6	5	10	10
				Totals	10	29	24

Decisions: 1. Reject brand C because it does not meet the minimum level of attribute 3.
2. Buy brand A.

Note: Without the threshold feature, the decision would have been to buy brand C, which would have a weighted attitude of 35.

acceptable level of 3, so it is eliminated from further consideration. This model may be called a lower-threshold model. It may also be called a lexicographic-compensatory model, because it combines the decision processes of the lexicographic and compensatory models.

Some decisions seem to begin with the decision maker rank-ordering the criteria which will be used to choose a brand. All brands are then considered according to the most important criteria. Brands not meeting this test are rejected from further consideration. The brands are not scaled along each attribute, but are either accepted or rejected; hence the term binary-choice model. (The term *lexicographic* is used because the decision process is the same as that used by lexicographers when they produce dictionaries.) Brands that meet the first criterion are evaluated along the second criterion, and so on.

Table 7.5 illustrates the binary, or lexicographic, model in graphic and matrix forms. This model is like a series of four sieves, one for each attribute. Brands passing through the first sieve continue to be candidates for selection. The process continues until a brand is selected. In matrix form the model amounts to giving a brand a zero or a plus according to whether it fails or passes the test of each criterion.

The theoretical problem with the weighted-attitude model is that weighting attitudes is like double counting. We noted in the Fishbein model that the evaluations assigned to attributes were weights reflecting an individual's personal values. The Fishbein model, therefore, states that weights are part of an attitude, so a weighted-attitude model amounts to counting the weights (or needs) twice.[6] Many marketing researchers continue to use the weighted-attitude model, however.

Past-behavior models. Brand-choice models based on past behavior recognize that humans are creatures of habit. Therefore, the best way to predict future brand behavior is to study past behavior. The basic model is in the form of:

$$B_t = kB_{t-1}, \tag{7.9}$$

where B_t is the probability of buying brand B in time t, k is an empirically derived

TABLE 7.5   A binary (lexicographic) choice model

Viewed as a series of sieves:

Criteria (rank-ordered)	Brands			
1.	A	B	C	D
		B	C	D
2.		B	C	D
			C	D
3.			C	D
				D
4.				D
				D

Decision: Buy D

Viewed in matrix form:

Criteria (rank-ordered)	Brands			
	A	B	C	D
1.	0	+	+	+
2.		0	+	+
3.			0	+
4.				+

Decision: Buy D

constant, and B_{t-1} is the probability of buying the brand during the previous time period.

Past-behavior models are useful in studying brand switching and learning.[7] Brand share, measured as a percent of the market, is generally used as the measure of probability of buying a brand. Because these probabilities are based on past behavior, they tend to be better predictors of behavior than attitude models are. Conversely, since probability models do not *explain* behavior, they are poor for diagnosing why a person did not buy. To develop a complete marketing strategy, one must use both behavioral and attitude models.

EXAMPLES OF BRAND-POSITIONING STRATEGIES   Now that we have seen the theory, models, and measures used to analyze a brand's position, we will examine the brand-positioning strategies of some well-known brands. Examples will include the positioning of new brands and the repositioning of old ones. The repositioning of old brands may be finding new uses for the old product or changing its image, which means changing the public's attitude toward the brand.

Positioning New Brands   To illustrate the excitement of brand strategies, we will examine four recent ones: Aim toothpaste, Schick Super II razor blades, Burger King, and Alka-2 chewable antacid tablets.

Aim toothpaste.   In 1971, 65 percent of the $380 million toothpaste market was based on the benefits of cavity prevention. Procter & Gamble's Crest had 36 percent of the market, its Gleem II had 8 percent, and Colgate-Palmolive's Colgate had 21 percent. Lever Brothers did not have a therapeutic brand. The cosmetic segment of the market focused on claims of whiteness and freshness. Lever Brothers dominated this market with Close-up, which had a 16 percent share, and Pepsodent, with a 6 percent share. Ultra Brite, a Colgate-Palmolive product, had 8 percent of the market.[8]

To be successful in the overall toothpaste market, Lever Brothers knew that its products had to be significantly different from existing brands. There were many well-known product failures among toothpastes, including Lever's Stripe. The company decided to combine two product attributes that were successful: stannous fluoride, the successful anticavity ingredient in other therapeutic toothpastes, and its patented clear-gel process, which had proved to be successful in Close-Up. In 1973 this combination yielded Lever's new product, Aim.[9]

In 1974 Colgate-Palmolive introduced Peak toothpaste. Its benefit claim was a *natural* (baking soda) cleaning formulation, as opposed to cavity prevention, whitening, or breath-freshening.[10]   The 1975 toothpaste scorecard tells an interesting story. Aim had 10 percent of the toothpaste market, which had now grown to over $450 million.[11] Therapeutics accounted for 73 percent of the market. Peak's share was 3 percent.

From which brands did Aim take its market share? In 1974 Aim had 7 percent; Crest, 38 percent. By 1975 Aim had 10 percent and Crest had dropped to 36 percent. During this same period Colgate dropped from 21 to 20 percent. Thus Aim's gain in share seemed to have come from Crest and Colgate.

Was Aim a total success for Lever Brothers? In 1971 the company had 22 percent of the market with two products. In 1975 it had 24 percent of the market with three products. During the period 1971 to 1975, Close-Up lost 6 percent and Pepsodent lost 2 percent. There are at least three explanations for this loss. First, the market wanted therapeutics, and Close-Up and Pepsodent were stressing whiteness. Second, competition may have gained share in the whiteness segment. (This explanation does not seem possible, because Ultra Brite lost 2 percent of the market.) A third possible explanation is *brand cannibalism*, which occurs when a company's new brand takes market share from its present brand. Thus clear-gel Aim may have cannibalized clear-gel Close-Up. Given the trend toward therapeutics, Lever probably had no alternative to a rapid move into this segment.

Schick Super II razor blades.   "At the time Gillette launched its Trac II shaving system, Schick had practically the identical product on its drawing boards. They faced a dilemma: how could they successfully introduce Super II at a time when single-edge users were switching to Trac II in droves?"[12] The Gillette loyalty was from the double-edge user. The Schick market franchise had been the single-edge shaver.

The Schick strategist concluded that Gillette either took its double-edge franchise for granted or was afraid to promote the Trac II to this market segment because it could cannibalize its own brand. Schick directed its advertising to the double-edge market. Gillette had always emphasized the benefit of closeness; Schick stressed safety and comfort. Research supported Schick's decision to stress safety in its Super II campaign. The television advertising copy said: "Schick puts both edges on your side." It showed a double-edge blade being broken so that both blades were on the same side. In short, this case illustrates the point that a brand strategy that is viable for one company may not be feasible for another company, because of *brand cannibalism*.

Burger King versus McDonalds. Batten, Barton, Durstine & Osborn (BBDO), the advertising agency for Burger King, asserts that good advertising requires *knowledge* of the *prime prospect*, his or her *problem*, and *knowledge of your product*—in that order. "If you become immersed in the product and all the things that go into it *before* you find out about your prospect and your prospect's problems—you may never discover the benefits in the product which can solve those consumer problems."[13] The fourth step in the BBDO process is creating imaginative, attention-getting advertising that holds people's interest.

The Burger King market segment was defined as people between the ages of 18 and 49 with children 12 and under. BBDO used a *problem-tracking* procedure to determine the prospects' problems. This procedure uses focus-group interviews to identify the problems and then measures the *problem frequency* and *intensity*. The procedure also measures *preemptability*, the degree to which current brands solve the problem. Marketing opportunities are found by comparing the scale values of each problem along the dimensions of frequency, intensity, and preemptability. A problem that is intense, frequent, and not preempted by present brands provides a brand opportunity.

Problem tracking indicated that one of the most frequently occurring problems for McDonalds' customers was having to wait for special orders.[14] The research revealed that this problem could be preempted by Burger King. The creative, attention-getting advertising that emerged from this finding was the successful copy theme: "Have it your way." The television commercial had a catchy jingle and included a soul version. This theme was carried into the stores with point-of-purchase (POP) materials.

The "Have it your way" campaign was a clear success. After nine months, Burger King had an awareness level comparable to that of McDonalds', which spent four times as much on advertising. Burger King's sales increased 38 percent.[15] The success of this campaign can be traced to *knowing the consumer's problem* and *creative communication*.

Alka-2. In 1975 the $435 million stomach-remedy market was led by Miles Laboratories' Alka-Seltzer, a powder that dissolves in water.[16] The $160 million chewable antacid segment was led by Warner-Lambert's Rolaids, with a 40 percent share of the tablet market. Of the 25 million persons who used chewable tablets primarily, most were middle-class, blue-collar workers, about 50 years old, and with annual incomes slightly less than $10,000.[17]

Miles Laboratories developed Alka-2 to enter the chewable-tablet market. The product benefits were described as "the antacid tablet that's built to fall apart. Chews easy. Chews fast. And it works fast, too. Cool and creamy, not as chalky, not as gritty."[18] The Miles goal was to convert 15 percent of the chewable-tablet users to Alka-2 during the first six months. The $10 million budget for *introductory promotion* used network television, direct-mail sampling, couponing, newspapers, and radio. The *maintenance budget* for the postintroduction year was set at $5 million, 10 percent more than the Rolaids budget. Alka-2 became the number-two brand in two test markets within four months.

Repositioning Old Brands

Lysol. Old products frequently can be revitalized by positioning them in expanding markets. Lysol disinfectant was a century-old product. "Scare" copy themes about germs did not stop the erosion of market share; in fact, experiments showed that this approach was actually hurting sales. The advertisements were stopped, and the product was *repositioned* from the small health-aid section of the supermarkets to the fast-turnover household cleaning-aids section.[19] Market-share erosion was reversed, and Lysol reached 50 percent of the disinfectant product category. Instead of scare copy, the new copy theme promised "to kill household germs and odors as you clean."

Vaseline. Vaseline petroleum jelly was also a 100-year-old brand. Sales were slipping because the product was perceived as largely for diaper rash and hair care. The birth rate declined and plastered-down hair styles were replaced by the soft, natural look. To survive, Vaseline would have to be repositioned in the market.[20]

Market research revealed that there was a need for a multiuse skin-care product for both sexes and all ages. Vaseline's brand slogan was changed to: "The skin survival kit." Television "slice-of-life" commercials dramatized skin-care problems, such as a father's chapped lips after a fishing trip. Brand awareness, sales, and consumption rates increased significantly.[21]

Arm & Hammer baking soda. The use of cake mixes replaced the baking of cakes from scratch, and this shift accounted for a decline in sales of baking soda. Arm & Hammer turned its sales around by finding new uses for its product. The company promoted baking soda as a refrigerator deodorant and for use in a box of cat litter. Sales increased dramatically. Instead of using a few teaspoons, as required in baking, consumers were now using a few boxes. It took only one commercial to persuade more than 30 million buyers to put a box of baking soda in the refrigerator.[22]

A BRAND DIAGNOSTIC AND PLANNING MODEL

In combining the concepts from Chapters 6 and 7 to build a brand diagnostic and planning model, we will use the soft drink case as an example. In Chapter 6 we defined the generic demand for soft drinks as the number of people in the market segment (N_k), times the percent of market segment k who used the product (P_k), times their frequency of use (F). The generic demand (G) for soft drinks in market segment k in time period t may be expressed algebraically as follows:

$$G_{kt} = N_{kt} \times P_{kt} \times F_{kt}. \tag{7.10}$$

In this chapter we discussed many of the determinants of brand demand, not all of which are relevant to the brand demand for soft drinks. The planner must develop a model that is *parsimonious*; it should have as few variables as are necessary to do the job. The variables will differ among products and according to the marketing task at hand. For instance, a new-product introduction requires the careful monitoring of the number of people who *try* the brand and the number who *repurchase* the brand. The repurchase rate indicates whether the product will be a long-term success.

For illustrative purposes we will build a diagnostic and planning model for a soft drink brand that is already established. We will assume that the planner wants to increase unit sales. In this case three key variables are important in the brand-demand model: (1) the *percentage* of people in the market segment who are *aware of the brand* (Pa_j); (2) the *percentage of those in the aware group who make brand j their first choice* (Pf_j); and (3) the *percentage distribution* (Pd_j) for the brand. This variable measures the probability that a person will find the brand in his or her usual store for purchasing soft drinks. If the distribution is in half of the stores, for example, the probability would be 0.50, and Pd_j would be 0.50. The market share for brand j in market segment k in time period t may be summarized algebraically as:

$$M_{jkt} = Pa_{jkt} \times Pf_{jkt} \times Pd_{jkt}. \tag{7.11}$$

We may combine Eqs. (7.10) and (7.11) to calculate the sales (S) of brand j, in units, as follows:

$$S_{jkt} = M_{jkt} \times G_{kt}. \tag{7.12}$$

The algebraic expression of this model may seem complicated to those who are not fond of mathematics, but the example in Table 7.6 illustrates that the model is quite simple. The variables in Eqs. (7.10) and (7.11) appear in the left-hand column of the table. The product is a brand of a tart-flavored soft drink, in 10-ounce bottles. The market segment is teenagers living in the South Atlantic states. The first column of figures summarizes the situation analysis on January 1, 1970. Columns 2–5 show the effect of each strategy. The *dates* at the top of the column show when each of these *strategic goals* should be accomplished.

The strategies appear at the bottom of Table 7.6. Given the situation in column 1, which strategy does the planner choose first? This is a difficult question to answer. Expected value, expected costs, creativity, experience, competitive reaction, and public policy all enter into the decision.

For illustrative purposes, we can start with the problem of the distribution rate (Pd_j) being only 0.60. The planner could take two courses of action. The most obvious one is to increase the number of stores in which brand j is sold. This strategy would take considerable time because of the need to promote to the stores and work out the logistics of stocking shelves. Another strategy, which has the effect of increasing distribution, is to convince the buyers that the brand is worth the effort of going to a store that stocks it. When buyers are willing to search for their preferred brand, the product is known as a *specialty good*. (A *convenience good* is a frequently used product for which the buyer is unwilling to spend much effort in searching for a specific brand. He or she will switch brands rather than search. When consumers spend considerable effort in comparing the benefits of various brands, a product is called a *shopping good*, e.g., an automobile.)

To keep the illustration simple, we will make the rather substantial assumption that all of the buyers will seek out the brand, which makes Pd_j equal to 1.00. The effect

TABLE 7.6 Brand situation analysis and strategy development (Product Class: tart-flavored soft drink; segment: k, e.g., teenagers in the South Atlantic States)

Demand components	Initial situation (Jan. 1970)	Strategy for each time period			
		13 weeks (March 31, 1970)	26 weeks (June 30, 1970)	52 weeks (Dec. 31, 1970)	78 weeks (June 30, 1971)
	(1)	(2)	(3)	(4)	(5)
GENERIC DEMAND					
Number of teenagers (N) (in millions)	4.0	4.0	4.0	4.1	4.2
Percentage of segment using the generic product (Pg)	0.20	0.20	0.30[2]	0.30	0.30
Frequency of use (10-oz. bottles) per week (F)	2.0	2.0	2.0	2.0	3.0[4]
Generic demand (millions of 10-oz bottles per week) in segment K (G_{kt}) = $N_{kt}\,Pg_{kt}\,F_{kt}$	1.6	1.6	2.4	2.5	3.8
MARKET SHARE OF BRAND USERS					
Percentage of persons aware of brand j (Pa_j)	0.30	0.30	0.30	0.50[3]	0.50
Percentage of aware group making brand j first-choice brand (Pb_j)	0.40	0.40	0.40	0.40	0.40
Percent distribution of brand j (Pd_j)	0.60	1.00[1]	1.00	1.00	1.00
Share of users for brand j (M_{jkt}) = $Pa_{jkt}\,Pb_{jkt}\,Pd_{jkt}$	0.072	0.12	0.12	0.20	0.20
Sales of brand j (S_{jkt}) (millions of 10-oz bottles per week) = $M_{jkt}\,G_{kt}$	0.12	0.19	0.29	0.50	0.76

Strategic goals:

[1] March 31, 1970 — Make the brand a specialty good among present users so that they seek out the brand. Alternative strategy: Improve distribution.

[2] June 30, 1970 — Increase the percentage of the segment using the product to 30 percent.

[3] December 31, 1970 — Make 50 percent of the segment aware of Brand j and convince this new 20 percent aware group that our brand should be their first choice.

[4] June 30, 1971 — Increase the frequency of use from 2.0 to 3.0 per time period by finding new uses for the product.

of this strategy is to increase the sales of our brand from 0.12 to 0.19 million bottles per week. We see in Table 7.6 that the planner hopes to accomplish this goal by March 31, 1970.

The planning goal for June 30, 1970, is to increase the percentage of teenagers who drink tart-flavored soft drinks from 20 percent to 30 percent. This will increase the generic demand to 2.4 million 10-ounce bottles per week. Our brand share of 12 percent will yield a brand demand of 0.29 million bottles per week.

By December 31, 1970, the planner wants 50 percent of the market segment to be aware of the brand. If all other numbers in the model remain the same, this increase in awareness will yield brand sales of 0.50 million bottles. This strategy makes an assumption that may not be realistic: It is unlikely that the 20 percent of the segment who become aware of the brand will immediately make it their first choice. Thus Pf_j in our model may actually drop below 0.40 percent because of the *dilution effect of the newly aware*. The planner may attempt a program that makes this group aware and convinced of the superiority of the product in one step. For instance, the planner may initiate a sampling program to have people try the product or use television commercials to show how the brand was selected over competition in blind product tests.

The final goal in this plan, for June 30, 1971, illustrates the point that plans are not necessarily for one year. By this date the planner hopes to have increased the consumption of tart-flavored soft drinks from two to three bottles per person per week. This will increase the generic demand to 3.8 million bottles per week and the brand sales to 0.76 million bottles per week.

At this point you may want to challenge some of the strategies used by the planner. For instance, there was no attempt to increase the percentage of the aware group which makes the brand its first choice (Pf_j). Instead of the June 30, 1971, goal of increasing the consumption to three bottles per week, what would be the effect on sales of increasing Pf_j to 0.60 percent? Using the data in column 4, we see that this would increase the market share to 0.30 percent and the brand sales to 0.75 million bottles per week. The advantage of this strategy over the one shown in column 5 is that it benefits only our brand. The strategy in column 5 benefits our competitors. This is a questionable strategy, since we have only 20 percent of the market.

The other strategies may be challenged similarly. This planning model helps us to ask many "what if" questions and trace through the effect of alternative strategies on sales, which was the goal in this case. This testing of alternative strategies is a form of *sensitivity analysis*. It enables the planner to evaluate the costs and benefits of alternative strategies.

For the sake of simplicity it was assumed that each goal was met. In reality, there should be *contingency plans* to deal with the *under-* and *overachievement of goals*. In each of these cases there may be a need to reallocate resources and reexamine goals. (Contingency planning will be discussed in Chapter 11.)

THREE BASIC DEMAND STRATEGIES   The marketing planner has three basic strategies available for exploring means for increasing sales. Each of these can be illustrated with the aid of the "pie chart" in Fig. 7.3. The first strategy is to *increase generic demand*, which is represented as an increase in the size of the pie. This strategy would focus on switching nonusers to users of the generic product, thereby increasing the proportion of users, P. It would also include strategies that would stimulate present users to use more of the product, thereby increasing F. For instance, dairy associations advertise: "Drink more milk." Such a strategy would be fine for company A, which dominates the market.

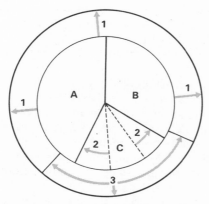

Note: Dotted lines represent the present situation; solid
lines represent the state that the three strategies would
provide.
Strategies:
1. Increase generic demand, by increasing P and/or F.
2. Increase market share (i.e., brand demand) by increasing M_j.
3. Increase generic demand and increase the share of
this increased generic demand, by a combination
strategy that expands the market for brand j.

Fig. 7.3 Three demand strategies.

Company C, however, would benefit only slightly from the "increase in the pie" because its present share is so small. If it were to try to increase generic demand, it would be doing its competitors a favor.

The second demand strategy is to *increase market share* by increasing the brand's "share of the pie," or M in Eq. (7.11). Brand C, for example, may attempt to cut into the market share of brands A and B. This may be a good strategy in the short run, but eventually C must anticipate a reaction from A and B as they attempt to regain their market share.

The third strategy is to *expand only the generic demand that can be attracted to your brand*. This amounts to increasing the generic demand and the share. In this case the strategist must identify nonusers who are attracted to the brand. For instance, a bank in Boston wanted to increase its savings deposits. It therefore developed a marketing strategy that appealed to young scientists and executives who were moving to the Boston area. Because this was an affluent group, this strategy greatly increased the bank's share of the savings deposits in Boston. After several years of using this strategy, the bank had the largest share of the savings deposits.[23]

SUMMARY Consumers' perceptions of how well a brand meets their needs play an important role in their choice of brands. The marketing manager, therefore, must analyze his or her brand's market position so as to develop product and promotional strategies that will improve its market share. Brand maps help the manager visualize the brand's position, set goals, and develop strategies.

Models of brand decision processes include communication models and brand-choice models. Communication models examine the influence of the message and the medium on an individual's beliefs. These beliefs combine with an individual's personal needs (i.e., values) to form an attitude toward a brand. Clusters of attitudes toward a brand in relationship to clusters of attitudes toward an ideal brand determine an individual's brand-preference ranks. The Fishbein belief-value model is used frequently by marketing researchers.

Brand-choice models use either measures of attitudes or past brand-buying behavior to predict brand preferences. Attitude models are based on the concept that preferred brands will be perceived as closer in attitude space to an ideal brand than less-preferred brands. The weighted-attitude models have practical and theoretical limitations that require care when used in studies of brand demand.

Brand-choice models based on past brand-buying behavior tend to be better predictors than attitude models, because they are more closely related to the phenomenon they are trying to predict, namely, behavior. Brand-choice models recognize that consumers are creatures of habit and will not switch brands without some good reason. Although these models are good at prediction, they are poor at explaining behavior; therefore, they should be used in combination with attitude models to develop complete marketing strategies.

The introduction of a new brand requires careful positioning in a market segment that is not dominated by a competitor. Old products may be positioned by finding new uses for them or by repositioning them in attitude space.

A diagnostic and planning model can be helpful in testing the effect of strategies designed to change generic and brand demands. Such models are unique to each product as it exists in its competitive environment and its life cycle. Once developed, the model can be used as a planning and control device.

BRAND POSITIONING RESEARCH ASSIGNMENT

The generic-demand analysis in Chapter 6 suggested that there may be a market for a new orange juice soft drink. You have been asked to create a brand map like the one in Fig. 7.1 for Coca-Cola, Pepsi Cola, 7-Up, and an ideal brand as part of the demand analysis for an orange juice soft drink. The market segment is the *young adult market*, which has been defined as persons 18 to 25 years old.

ASSIGNMENTS

1. Identify the product attributes that people use in selecting soft drinks. You may want to interview small groups of about eight persons in a focus-group interview situation. You could also interview them as they purchase soft drinks. Select the two most important attributes for further analysis.

2. Using the questionnaire in Table 7.7, interview 30 young adults, ages 18 to 25. (A team of five members will lighten the workload.) Tabulate the replies in the form shown in Table 7.8. Compute the average attitude for each brand along both dimensions.

3. Using the average attitudes for each brand, make a brand map.

4. Use the "city block" model, Eq. (7.5), to compute the preference index for Coca-Cola, Pepsi Cola, and 7-Up. Validate the model by comparing these ranks with the rank-order preferences reported by the respondents.

5. Recompute the preference indexes, using the weighted (or St. James) model, Eq. (7.8). Did the weights improve your results? Explain why they did or did not.

6. Given the results of your brand map, what do you recommend with regard to introducing an orange juice soft drink to the young-adult segment? Would such a drink require a product or a promotional strategy? What would be the product or promotional goals?

7. Create a "brand contour map" by plotting all of the coordinates for each respondent. Connect the points of equal frequency. The result will be a map that shows mountain peaks, slopes, and cliffs that represent the number of people at various points on the map. Does this contour map alter your conclusions in question 6?

TABLE 7.7   **Questionnaire of soft drink preferences**

Instructions to interviewer

1. Select a person 18 through 25 years old who is not in the class and who has not previously completed this questionnaire. (Normally a random sample would be used.)
2. Explain the reason for the study.
3. Let the respondent complete the questionnaire and ask if there are any questions.
4. Check the questionnaire for completeness before leaving.

We need your help to develop a new soft drink that will be used primarily as a beverage (not as a mixer).

How frequently do you drink soft drinks as a beverage? Please check one.

_____more than once per day   _____two to three times per month

_____once per day   _____once per month

_____two to three times per week   _____less than once per month

_____once per week

Please rank your brand preferences by placing a "1" beside your first choice, a "2" beside your second choice, etc.

_____Coca-Cola

_____Pepsi Cola

_____7-Up

_____Other (Please indicate) _____

We would like to know your evaluation of three soft drink brands—Coca-Cola (C), Pepsi Cola (P), 7-Up (S)—and your thoughts on an ideal (I) brand. To report your evaluation, please place C, P, S, and I over the number that reflects your evaluation. For example, if you were examining the design of the bottle, your answer could look like the following:

								No opinion
Old-fashioned bottle design	1	2	3	4	5	6	Modern bottle design	0

These answers would indicate that you think that Coca-Cola has an old-fashioned bottle design, that your perception of an ideal design is moderately modern, and that you do not care to express an opinion about the Pepsi Cola bottle design.

TABLE 7.7 (cont.)

Please repeat this technique for the three brands and your ideal, using attributes

_____ and _____ .

     C = Coca Cola   S = 7-Up
     P = Pepsi Cola   I = ideal

_____*   1   2   3   4   5   6   _____*

_____*   1   2   3   4   5   6   _____*

Please indicate the importance of these two attributes of soft drinks by dividing ten points, as follows:

_____* __

_____* __

           Total   10

(Does it add to 10?)

What is your age?_____   _____male?   _____female?

Thank you for your assistance.

(*Researcher to add the attributes at these points.)

TABLE 7.8   **Tabulation of soft drink responses along three attributes**

Respondent number	Coca-Cola (C)		Pepsi Cola (P)		7-Up (S)		Ideal (I)	
	1	2	1	2	1	2	1	2
1								
2								
3								
⋮								
Totals								
Averages								

(1 and 2 are the attributes identified by the researcher.)

DISCUSSION QUESTIONS

1. What are the objectives of the three basic strategies for increasing brand demand? Explain how each strategy affects (a) the number of people using a generic product, (b) the number of people using a brand, (c) the usage rate, and (d) competitors' market shares. From your knowledge of products on the market today, think of an example for each of the strategies above. What are the advantages and disadvantages of implementing each of the strategies above if your brand has a small market share?

2. Explain what is meant by "squatting between two stools." How can brand mapping prevent adopting this dangerous strategy?

3. What is the optimal product strategy to adopt in brand positioning with reference to consumers' brand preference and to competitive brands? What makes this strategy good? (Remember that intervening variables prevent preference from being translated into buying action.)

4. Define beliefs and attitudes. Why is it important for a brand manager to disaggregate attitudes into its two components? How can this information affect advertising strategy?

5. What are the advantages and disadvantages of the brand-choice models that were discussed in this chapter?

NOTES

1. In statistical terms this is the error of calculating an arithmetic mean when the distribution is bimodal. For a further discussion of the strategy of product quality, *see* A. A. Kuehn and R. L. Day, "Strategy of Product Quality," *Harvard Business Review* (November-December 1962): 100–110.

2. R. I. Haley, "Benefit Segmentation: A Decision Oriented Research Tool," *Journal of Marketing* **32** (July 1968): 30–35.

3. F. Heider, "Attitudes and Cognitive Organization," *Journal of Psychology* **21** (January 1946): 107–112. For a discussion of other balance models, *see* G. D. Hughes, *Attitude Measurement for Marketing Strategies* (Glenview, Ill.: Scott, Foresman, 1971), pp. 50–56.

4. M. Fishbein, ed., *Readings in Attitude Theory and Measurement* (New York: Wiley, 1967); and "The Search for Attitudinal-Behavioral Consistency," in *Behavioral Science Foundations of Consumer Behavior*, ed. J. Cohen (New York: Free Press, 1971), pp. 245–252.

5. W. J. McGuire, "An Information-Processing Model of Advertising Effectiveness." (Paper read at the *Symposium on Behavior and Management Science in Marketing*, Center for Continuing Education, University of Chicago, June 11, 1969.)

6. Many researchers—e.g., F. M. Bass and W. W. Talarzyk, "An Attitude Model for the Study of Brand Preference," *Journal of Marketing Research* **9** (February 1972): 93–96—have concluded from experiments that the weights did not improve the predictive power of attitude models. For a discussion of normalized ratings, *see* F. M. Bass and W. L. Wilkie, "A Comparative Analysis of Attitudinal Predictions of Brand Preference," *Journal of Marketing Research* **10** (August 1973): 262–269. It has been shown by Hughes, *op. cit.*, pp. 96–97, that using the semantic differential as a measuring instrument confounds the measures of weights and attitudes, so this conclusion may be unwarranted.

7. For a discussion of brand switching and the Hendry model, *see* M. U. Kalwani and D. G. Morrison, "A Parsimonious Description of the Hendry System," *Management Science* **23** (January 1977): 467–477.

8. E. B. Miller, "Aim Helps Lever Boost Its Toothpaste Share in 1975 ...", *Advertising Age* (October 20, 1975), p. 64.

9. C. Fredericks, "Aim Toothpaste vs. Crest and Colgate." (Paper delivered at the 1974 Regional Convention of the American Association of Advertising Agencies, New York, November 19, 1974.)

10. Miller, *op. cit.*

11. *Ibid.*

12. D. G. Pojednic, "Schick Super II Razor vs. Gillette Trac II." (Paper delivered at the 1974 Regional Convention of the American Association of Advertising Agencies, New York, November 19, 1974.)

13. R. Mercer, "Burger King vs. McDonalds." (Paper delivered at the 1974 Regional Convention of the American Association of Advertising Agencies, New York, November 19, 1974.)

14. *Ibid.*

15. *Ibid.*

16. "Alka-2 Plans to Roll Out with Heavy Ad Support," *Advertising Age* (August 4, 1975): 1, 40.

17. *Ibid.*

18. *Ibid.*

19. N. Giges, "100 Years Young, Lysol Revitalized as Marketing Success," *Advertising Age* (August 11, 1975): 3, 48.

20. T. V. Byor, "Revitalize That Old, Respected Brand with New Ads, Markets," *Advertising Age* (August 11, 1975): 22–24.

21. *Ibid.*

22. H. W. McMahan, "Alltime Ad Triumphs Reveal Key Success Factors Behind Choice of '100 Best'," *Advertising Age* (April 12, 1976): 78.

23. *See* "The Boston Five Cents Savings Bank," Intercollegiate Case Clearing House, 9M54.

SUGGESTED READINGS

Belk, R. W., "Situational Variables and Consumer Behavior," *Journal of Consumer Research* **2** (December 1975): 157–164.

Bettman, J. R., "A Threshold Model of Attribute Satisfaction Decisions," *Journal of Consumer Research* (September 1974): 30–35.

Calder, B. J., and M. Ross, *Attitudes and Behavior* (Morristown, N.J.: General Learning Press, 1973).

Cartwright, D., and F. Harary, "Structural Balance: A Generalization of Heider's Theory," *Psychological Review* **63** (1956): 277–293.

Cliff, N., "Scaling," in *Annual Review of Psychology*, ed. P. H. Mussen and M. R. Rosenzweig (Palo Alto, Calif.: Annual Reviews, 1973).

Coombs, C. H., R. M. Dawes, and M. Tversky, *Mathematical Psychology* (Englewood Cliffs, N.J.: Prentice-Hall, 1970), pp. 307–350.

Ehrenberg, A. S. C., *Repeat Buying—Theory and Applications* (New York: Elsevier, 1972).

Frank, R. E., W. F. Massy, and Y. Wind, *Marketing Segmentation* (Englewood Cliffs, N.J.: Prentice-Hall, 1972).

Green, P. E., and V. R. Rao, "Conjoint Measurement for Quantifying Judgmental Data," *Journal of Marketing Research* **8** (August 1971): 355–363.

———, and Y. Wind, *Multiattribute Decisions in Marketing: A Measurement Approach* (Hindsdale, Ill.: Dryden Press, 1973).

Hughes, G. D., *Demand Analysis for Marketing Decisions* (Homewood, Ill.: Richard D. Irwin, 1973).

———, "New Developments in Attitude Theory: Déjà Vu?" in *Moving Ahead with Attitude Research*, ed. Y. Wind and M. G. Greenberg (Chicago: American Marketing Association, 1977, pp. 3–8).

———, and M. L. Ray, *Buyer/Consumer Information Processing* (Chapel Hill: University of North Carolina Press, 1974.)

Jacoby, J., Jr., "Consumer Psychology: An Octennium," *Annual Review of Psychology* **27** (1976): 331–358.

Johnson, R. M., "Trade-Off Analysis of Consumer Values," *Journal of Marketing Research* **11** (May 1974): 121–127.

Lavidge, R. J., and G. A. Steiner, "A Model for Predictive Measurements of Advertising Effectiveness," *Journal of Marketing* **25** (October 1961): 59–62.

Massy, W. F., D. B. Montgomery, and D. G. Morrison, *Stochastic Models of Buyer Behavior* (Cambridge, Mass.: M.I.T. Press, 1970).

Ryan, M. J., and E. H. Bonfield, "The Fishbein Extended Model and Consumer Behavior," *Journal of Consumer Research* **2** (September 1975): 118–136.

Schoeffler, S., R. D. Buzzell, and D. F. Heany, "Impact of Strategic Planning on Profit Performance," *Harvard Business Review* (March-April 1974): 137–145.

Stern, L. W., and A. I. El-Ansary, *Marketing Channels* (Englewood Cliffs, N.J.: Prentice-Hall, 1977), p. 83.

Urban, G. L., "Preceptor: A Model for Product Positioning," *Management Science* **21** (April 1975): 858–871.

Wilkie, W. L., and E. A. Pessemier, "Issues in Marketing's Use of Multi-Attribute Attitude Models," *Journal of Marketing Research* **10** (November 1973): 428–441.

ENVIRONMENTAL ANALYSIS WORKSHEET

Environmental elements	Facts	Assumptions or research needed	Conclusions

Organizational values,
objectives, and
policies (4)

Organizational
design (5)

Situation
   Generic demand (6)
   Brand demand (7)
   Competition (9)
   Public policy (10)

Opportunities (2)

Problems

MARKETING PLAN (CONSUMER PRODUCT)

Current performance
Recommendations
Effect of recommendations on income
Situation analysis
Opportunities and problems
Strategies
Tests and research
Supporting documents
   Comparative budgets
   Media allocation schedule
   Promotion control sheet

STRATEGY WORKSHEET

Opportunities and problems in rank order to importance

1.
2.
.
n.

	Current strategy	Alternatives and recommended strategy	Estimated Effect

Demand strategy
    Generic
    Brand

Strategic goals
    Financial
    Marketing

Marketing-mix strategies
    Product (12)
    Pricing (13)
    Channel and logistics (14)
    Advertising and promotional (15)
    Sales management (16)

Research (3)

Profit plan

Evaluation and control (19)

CHAPTER 8

CHAPTER **8**

Industrial Market Analysis

LEARNING OBJECTIVES   After studying this chapter you should:

1. Be aware of the similarities and differences between industrial and consumer marketing.
2. Know the techniques that are frequently used for a generic-demand analysis for an industrial product.
3. Appreciate the complexity of the industrial buying process.
4. Understand brand analysis for an industrial product.
5. Understand the role of planning in industrial marketing.
6. Be able to define and use the following concepts:

Buying process
Reciprocity
Technical forecasting
Industrial product life cycles
Product segmentation
Technology life cycles
Experience curves
Delphi method
Application segmentation
Input-output analysis

Standard Industrial Classification (SIC) analysis
County Business Patterns
"Survey of Industrial Purchasing Power"
Buyer-behavior segmentation
Industrial success factors
Horizontal and vertical product/market
   matches
Technological change
Value added
Vendor evaluation

SOME ANALYTICAL QUESTIONS FOR OPENERS

1. Where is the product in its life cycle? What is the state of technology?
2. What is the market potential for our product? What is our share?
3. From what industries is the demand for our industrial product derived? What are the trends and cycles in these industries?
4. Who are the buying influences? What benefits do they seek?
5. Can a segmentation strategy be used?
6. How can we improve our ranking in a vendor analysis?

WHAT IS INDUSTRIAL MARKETING?   "Industrial marketing is the marketing of goods and services to commercial enterprises, governments, and other nonprofit institutions for resale to other industrial customers or for use in the goods and services that they, in turn, produce."[1] Consumer marketing is for individual or family consumption. The primary distinction between industrial and consumer marketing, therefore, is the intended customer. The products also differ. Few families need *heavy equipment* (e.g., machine tools and blast furnaces), *light equipment* (e.g., laboratory equipment), *construction* (e.g., highways and docks), *component parts* (e.g., motors and gears), *raw materials* (e.g., iron ore and potash), *processed materials* (e.g., plastic sheeting and plywood), *consumable supplies* (e.g., cutting fluids and small tools), and *services* such as design and consulting.[2]

Because the buyers and products are different, industrial marketing *methods are different* from those used in consumer marketing. In industrial marketing the channels are often shorter, because they are direct from the manufacturer to the user. Personal selling is used more than in consumer marketing. Trade shows, where manufacturers exhibit their products, are very important in the industrial selling process. Industrial pricing is frequently a complex process of negotiation. The price may include special financial arrangements, such as financing or leasing with an option to buy. Service after the sale is extremely important. It is easy to see, therefore, that industrial marketing *strategies are quite different* from consumer marketing strategies. It is surprising to note, however, that the concepts used in analyzing consumer demand have many counterparts in the processes used for analyzing industrial demand.

SIMILARITIES OF CONSUMER AND INDUSTRIAL ANALYSES Many of the concepts used in *consumer* generic- and brand-demand analysis apply to *industrial* demand analysis as well. For instance, the questions of *who*, *what*, *where*, *when*, *how*, and *why* will help the industrial marketer to focus on correct data. *Market segmentation* by *usage rate* or *user profile* is used in industrial marketing. Quantitative techniques that are used in consumer marketing can apply also to industrial marketing.[3]

TABLE 8.1   **Comparison of industrial and consumer buying steps**

Buying steps	Industrial-fleet auto	Consumer auto
1. Anticipation or recognition of need	*Plans* for purchase on a routine basis	*Reacts* to needs when they arise
2. Determination of characteristics	Extensive, objective cost-benefit analysis	A limited analysis of benefits; concern with total cost
3. Description of product attributes	Precise, technical description	Description more in terms of benefits than technical product attributes
4. Search for sources	Extensive search, extending to manufacturer	Search limited to commuting area
5. Acquisition of proposals	Formal if purchase is for large volume	May be verbal or a completed order form
6. Evaluation of proposals and selection of supplier(s)	Extensive analysis of objective information	Limited analysis, with subjective information influencing the decision heavily
7. Selection of an order routine	Routinized time and place of delivery and financing	Not routinized
8. Performance feedback and evaluation	Extensive basis for comparison	Little basis for comparison

The sequence of events in the industrial buying process has many similarities with the consumer's buying process.[4] To illustrate, we will compare the buying process that would be used by a company buying a fleet of automobiles for its salespeople with the process used by a consumer (Table 8.1). The steps in this buying process are those generally used in industrial buying.[5] Note that the comparison in Table 8.1 illustrates that industrial and consumer buying processes are very similar, but that there is greater depth and objectivity in the industrial process.

We must note, however, that the complexity of the industrial buying process will vary across products within a single firm. Thus the purchase of a computer will get more consideration than the purchase of paper towels. Furthermore, this complexity lessens as buyers become more familiar with their needs and with available suppliers. An initial purchase of typewriters, for example, may require an extensive search. Subsequent purchases may be a simple reorder process. Industrial purchases are sometimes classified as new tasks, modified rebuys, and straight rebuys to reflect the amount of effort that goes into the decision.[6]

DIFFERENCES BETWEEN CONSUMER AND INDUSTRIAL ANALYSES

Differences in Emphasis The nature of buyer needs and product characteristics requires differences in analytical methods, but these differences are *more those of emphasis than of content*. For instance, risk, specification of features, and information search are part of all buying-decision processes, but since they are more extensive in the industrial buying decision, they must be given greater attention in the industrial demand analysis. The buying unit is frequently a group, so it is necessary to consider group behavior.

Some industrial buying decisions require *long-term* planning. In the chemical industry, for instance, the time between the planning and completion of a plant can be ten years. Demand analysis for the chemical industry therefore requires the analysis of long-term economic conditions. (See the planning outline for the Celanese Corporation, Table 2.5.)

Complexity The complexity of the industrial buying decision distinguishes consumer and industrial buying. For example, among the many influences in the buying decision for an electrical motor for a refrigerator could be inputs from such departments as design, engineering, production, consumer relations (for safety and power consumption), international (for export products), finance, and purchasing. Thus the purchasing manager must satisfy the needs of all of these buying influences.

The complexity of the industrial decision process is illustrated in Sheth's integrative model of industrial buyer behavior (see Fig. 8.1).[7] This model indicates that each person with buying influence is in turn influenced by his or her background (1a), information sources (1b), active search (1c), perceptual distortion (1d), and satisfaction with previous purchases (1e). The *complexity* of the buying process (2) tends to increase as the *complexity of the product* (2a) and the *complexity of the organization* (2b) increase. Meeting all of these individual and organizational needs requires some *system of conflict resolution* (3). The result of this resolution should be organizational consonance and the choice of a supplier. The final choice will be moderated by *situational factors* (4) such as shortages, inflation, strikes, mergers, recessions, and foreign-trade conditions.

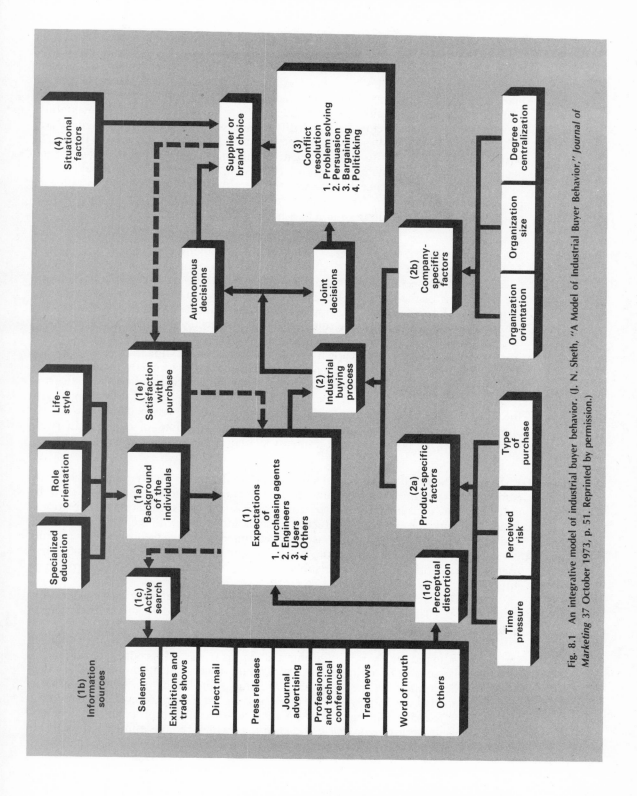

Fig. 8.1   An integrative model of industrial buyer behavior. (J. N. Sheth, "A Model of Industrial Buyer Behavior," *Journal of Marketing* 37 October 1973, p. 51. Reprinted by permission.)

The complexity of the industrial buying process increases when we consider the dynamics of organizational buying behavior.[8] Furthermore, each decision influential has a different set of criteria and various levels of influence. For example, Amercoat Corporation isolated the buying influences for its corrosion-control plan. The general manager, interested primarily in results, left details to others, but made the final decision. The plant manager was unlikely to have the authority to buy, but his recommendations were important, and therefore his goodwill was necessary. The corrosion engineer was an important influential, so his recommendation was very important too. The purchasing agent tended to have a negative influence on the purchase of corrosion plans, but it was frequently necessary to see him first. The research department tended to have a negative influence with regard to operating costs, but a positive influence in product development. The paint foreman usually followed "the line of least resistance"; he was unwilling to accept a new method if it required more work.[9]

Buyer/Seller Relationships *Buyer/seller relationships* in industrial buying are frequently long-term and complex. Buyers and sellers may *cooperate* in areas such as joint technical development. On other matters the relationship may be a *struggle for power* to gain the best terms of the negotiation. The buyer may regularly buy from at least three sources in order to bargain one supplier off against another. This policy also reduces the risks associated with a single source of supply, especially during times of shortages.

The stronger party may suggest reciprocity, e.g., "I'll buy from you if you'll buy from me." Reciprocity, also known as *trade relations*, is questionable on both ethical and legal grounds, however. The Justice Department and the Federal Trade Commission have viewed the collection of comparative sale and purchase data as the heart of *coercive reciprocity*.[10] Similarly, mergers and acquisitions are illegal if they could give the power of coercive reciprocity that would substantially lessen competition.[11] In short, the buyer/seller relationship must be one of a freedom of choice; otherwise, there is the strong possibility that antitrust legislation will be violated.[12]

GENERIC-DEMAND ANALYSIS An industrial demand analysis uses many methods that are common to consumer demand analyses. For example, survey research is used by industrial and consumer researchers to determine buyer usage rates. The National Lead Company, for example, conducted personal interviews with technical, marketing, and purchasing directors of major users to determine the *usage factor* of a new product per gallon of paint, per ton of plastic, etc. The company mailed questionnaires to small users, distributors, dealers, and jobbers who were too numerous for personal interviews.[13]

Research techniques that are used in industrial *and* consumer research were discussed in Chapter 3. The discussion in this chapter will be limited to methods unique to industrial marketing.

The stage in the life cycle of a product determines the methods appropriate for an industrial demand analysis.[14] During the *early stages* of product development, *technological forecasting* is important because the success of a new product's introduction is determined by the superiority of its attributes. The *geographic location* of users is important during these early stages because the firm must evaluate the cost of reaching the market. During the *growth stage*, when competition enters, the demand analysis must concentrate on *end-use applications*, which require a fuller knowledge of customers' technical needs. In the *mature stage* of the life cycle the successful industrial-

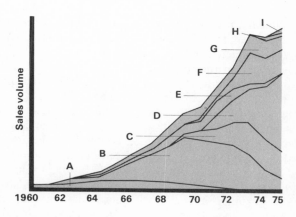

Fig. 8.2. Product life cycles within a chemical family. This is an example of product evolution in a urethane chemical family of products—the Dow Voranol® polyglycols. Products H and I are in the early stages of the life cycle. Products E, F, and G have relatively stabilized sales, whereas A has declined completely, B and C are declining rapidly, and D is growing dramatically. (1975 Dow Annual Report to Stockholders, p. 21. Used by permission.)

marketing strategies require an understanding of *buyer behavior* because by this point, the competitive differences among products have become minor. The marketing strategies over the industrial product life cycle, therefore, must shift from *product segmentation* to *application segmentation* and finally to *buyer-behavior segmentation*.[15] The methods for analyzing generic demand must follow these shifts in strategy.[16]

The industrial product life cycle is more complex than that of a consumer product (see Fig. 8.2). Overall sales in the urethane chemical family grew rapidly from 1960 to 1972, then flattened from 1973 to 1975. This "family" life cycle is made up of the life cycles of many individual products, each at a different stage in its life cycle. Products H and I are in the early stages. Product D is increasing dramatically, and products C, F, and G have stabilized sales, whereas A has declined completely, and B and C are declining rapidly.

Analysis for Product Segmentation Industrial demand analyses must be sensitive to rapid developments in technology. A computer manufacturer, for example, failed to detect a rapid development in technology. As a result, developmental costs for a recent computer model had to be charged to one year's profits rather than amortized over several years. During the mid-1970s the less profitable manufacturers of pocket calculators went bankrupt because of rapid developments in electronics technology. "Technically volatile" industries require early-warning devices, e.g., *technology life cycles*, *experience curves*, and the *Delphi method*.

Some analysts believe that *technology* has a *life cycle*, so that the time of appearance of new developments may be anticipated even when their form is unknown. Sprague Electric Company used this approach in 1965 when it was estimating the demand for integrated circuits. The life cycles of receiving tubes and transistors were analyzed. It was expected that the steady decline in the demand for tubes would continue and that there would be a sharp decline in the demand for transistors in 1968. Integrated circuits would fill the voids and open new markets. Sprague Electric anticipated that a new, unknown technological development would appear in the early 1970s.[17]

Experience curves are based on the total output of an industry. The patterns of these curves reflect conditions within an industry when there is a high probability of price competition. (The use of experience curves in pricing is discussed in Chapter 13.) The concept behind experience curves is that as an industry gains technological and production expertise, its production costs will decline. Firms that have not gained this expertise will become unprofitable when price competition begins. Experience curves were used to predict the shakeout in the pocket-calculator industry.[18]

The *Delphi method* is frequently used to predict future technologies. This method, which was developed by the Rand Corporation, gathers *unbiased* opinions from experts individually through a series of questionnaires that are handled impersonally by a coordinator. The effects of group pressures are thereby eliminated. At the end of each round, the coordinator summarizes the results and reports them to the experts anonymously. The experts then are permitted to revise their original estimates. Convergence tends to occur after five rounds.[19]

The Delphi questions tend to ask experts their prediction of some event. For example, "When will hydrogen made from water become an economical source of energy?" The accuracy of the Delphi method "has generally been relatively good" and "can also be used with reasonable accuracy in predicting when turning points will occur."[20]

Analysis for Application Segmentation   Application-segmentation analysis focuses on the *identification of a need*, an estimate of the *size of the potential market* for a product that will meet the need, and the *geographic location* of this market. Analytical methods leading to *application segmentation* in industrial market analysis include *input-output analysis*, *Standard Industrial Classifications* (SIC), and *buyer expectations*.

Input-output analysis.   Input-output analysis recognizes that there are many intermediate transactions before a product reaches the final consumer. The magnitude of the intermediate transactions varies among industries. For example, in Table 8.2 we see that only 6 percent of the total demand in the livestock and livestock products industry goes to the final consumer $(1,811/30,638 = 6\%)$, whereas 93 percent represents intermediate demand. The furniture industry (SIC 22) provides a marked contrast: 75 percent is the demand of personal consumption, and 18 percent is intermediate demand. The intermediate demand for the paper industry (SIC 24) is 84 percent, but only 35 percent for the motor vehicle industry (SIC 59). Of the 78 industries reported in the entire table, 45 sold more than half of their output to intermediate users. If we fail to understand intermediate markets, we overlook a very substantial part of marketing.

Input-output analysis reveals all of the intermediate industries that contribute to the output of a specific industry. To study the demand for an industry, a marketer needs to know two types of information: (1) how much of the industry's product is used by every other industry; and (2) the total product demand for each industry that uses the product. The following example illustrates the mechanics of input-output analysis and how the results relate to marketing strategy.[21]

TABLE 8.2 Intermediate outputs and final demand, by industry, in the United States economy, 1967 (selected examples)

For the distribution of output of an industry, read the row for that industry.

For the composition of inputs to an industry, read the column for that industry.

Standard Industrial Classification (SIC) number	Industry	Intermediate outputs, total	Personal consumption expenditure	Gross private fixed capital formation	Net inventory change	Net exports	Federal government purchases			State and local government purchases			Total final demand	Total	Transfers	Industry no.
							Total	Defense	Nondefense	Total	Education	Other				
1	Livestock and livestock products	28,620	1,811		129	55	8	5	4	15	1	13	2,018	30,638	2,453	1
8	Crude petroleum and natural gas	14,692			257	82							339	15,031	1,138	8
14	Food and kindred products	24,540	60,974		899	1,906	655	207	448	477	68	409	64,911	80,451	4,181	14
22	Household furniture	939	3,861	165	49	24	58	26	31	28	21	8	4,183	5,122	182	22
24	Paper and allied products except containers	14,060	1,502		228	649	116	62	55	179	93	85	2,673	16,733	1,251	24
37	Primary iron and steel manufacturing	30,395	4		514	519	290	286	4	2	2	2	1,328	31,723	2,048	37
51	Office, computing and accounting machines	1,659	112	3,352	156	710	533	243	291	160	119	42	5,023	6,682	521	51
59	Motor vehicles and equipment	15,464	15,822	9,054	−310	1,976	1,002	847	155	731	182	549	28,276	43,740	1,674	59
67	Radio and TV broadcasting	3,176											7	3,183	3,071	67

Bureau of Economic Analysis, U.S. Department of Commerce, "The Input-Output Structure of the U.S. Economy: 1967," *Survey of Current Business* **54** (February 1974): 42–43.

The Unlimited Data Research Company[22]

1. **Problem.** Unlimited Data was engaged by a manufacturer to estimate the market potential for paper and allied products for merchant wholesalers and the retail trade industry to 1980. First, since the company had sales representatives, it wanted to know the quantity of paper and allied products consumed directly by these trades in order to determine the size of the sales force. Second, Unlimited Data was asked to project, both directly and indirectly, the total requirements to the wholesale and retail trades for the same time period. Furthermore, the research organization was requested to project the total manufacturer's share of the market, given the fact that based on past history, the manufacturer normally accounted for 15 percent of the total market for paper and allied products.

2. **Source of data.**
   a) "Input-Output Structure of the U.S. Economy, 1967," *Survey of Current Business* (February 1974).
   b) *U.S. Industrial Outlook 1974 with projections to 1980.*

3. **Assumptions.**
   a) The relative demand for paper and allied products to the wholesale and retail trades will remain the same in 1980.
   b) In order to compute both direct and indirect use of paper and allied products by the wholesale and retail trades, Unlimited Data used gross profit, or gross margin, which is estimated to be about 25 percent of sales. Specifically, to demonstrate the links between producing and consuming industries on final markets in the input-output tables, commodities are shown as if moving directly from producer to user, bypassing intermediaries. Therefore, the output of trade is measured in terms of total margins, that is, operating expense plus profit.

4. **Procedure.** According to the *Outlook* (source b), merchant wholesaler sales in 1980 will be $613 billion, and retail sales should be no less than $722 billion. The combined total in 1980 will be $1335 billion.
   Since the manufacturer wanted to know the amount of paper and allied products consumed directly by wholesale and retail trades, Unlimited Data first took 25 percent (gross profit) of $1335 billion, or $334 billion. Then, from Table 8.3, reproduced from Table 2 of the input-output study of source (a), it found that for each dollar of gross profit of wholesale and retail trades, they consumed .006 cents of paper directly. This represents only the cost of paper products used directly by the two trades and does not include products used indirectly by the manufacturers of food and kindred products or by nonfood merchandise distributed via the wholesale and retail methods. Therefore, the total amount consumed directly by the wholesale and retail trades is $2 billion ($334 billion × .006 cents).
   In addition, the research company computed estimates of total requirements of paper and allied products, including those used by processors of other materials consumed by manufacturers. This was measured by using the direct and indirect costs shown in Table 8.4 (reproduced from Table 3 of the input-output study), or .015 cents. Total requirements in 1980 were estimated to be $5.0 billion ($334 billion × .015 cents).
   The paper manufacturer indicated that the company's share of the total market for paper and allied products to the wholesale and retail trades was about 15 percent.

TABLE 8.3 Direct requirements per dollar of gross output, 1967

Industry no.	For the composition of inputs to an industry, read the column for that industry	Communications; except radio and TV broadcasting 66	Radio and TV broadcasting 67	Electric, gas, water and sanitary services 68	Wholesale and retail trade 69	Finance and insurance 70
1	Livestock and livestock products	—	—	—	—	—
2	Other agricultural products	—	—	—	0.00006	—
3	Forestry and fishery products	—	—	—	—	—
4	Agricultural, forestry and fishery services	—	—	—	.00085	—
5	Iron and ferroalloy ores mining	—	—	0.00001	(*)	—
6	Nonferrous metal ores mining	—	—	.00002	(*)	—
7	Coal mining	0.00002	0.00009	.02399	.00002	0.00003
8	Crude petroleum and natural gas	—	—	.06756	—	—
9	Stone and clay mining and quarrying	—	—	(*)	.00003	—
10	Chemical and fertilizer mineral mining	—	—	(*)	—	—
11	New construction	.02934	—	—	—	—
12	Maintenance and repair construction	—	.00195	.03047	.00322	.00282
13	Ordnance and accessories	—	—	.00001	.00023	—
14	Food and kindred products	—	—	.00004	.00546	—
15	Tobacco manufacturers	—	—	.00001	.00006	—
16	Broad and narrow fabrics, yarn and thread mills	—	—	.00005	.00012	—
17	Miscellaneous textile goods and floor coverings	—	—	.00018	.00033	—
18	Apparel	.00027	—	.00022	.00082	—
19	Miscellaneous fabricated textile products	—	—	—	.00049	—
20	Lumber and wood products, except containers	—	—	.00002	.00056	—
21	Wooden containers	—	—	—	.00065	—
22	Household furniture	—	—	(*)	.00015	—
23	Other furniture and fixtures	—	—	—	.00016	—
24	**Paper and allied products, except containers**	**.00110**	**.00013**	**.00091**	**.00616**	**.00525**
25	Paperboard containers and boxes	.00001	.00006	.00008	.00350	.00932
26	Printing and publishing	.00210	.00031	.00020	.00232	.00932
27	Chemicals and selected chemical products	.00003	—	.00150	.00132	.00002

TABLE 8.3 (cont.)

	Transportation and warehousing 65	Communications; except radio and TV broadcasting 66	Radio and TV broadcasting 67	Electric, gas, water and sanitary services 68	Wholesale and retail trade 69	Finance and insurance 70
28 Plastics and synthetic materials	—	—	—	.00006	.00015	—
29 Drugs, cleaning and toilet preparations	—	—	—	(*)	.00168	—
30 Paints and allied products	.00005	.00003	—	.00001	.00031	—
31 Petroleum refining and related industries	.00336	.00016	—	.00737	.00842	.00192
32 Rubber and miscellaneous plastics products	.00123	.00016	—	.00061	.00437	.00028
33 Leather tanning and industrial leather products	—	—	—	(*)	.00001	—
34 Footwear and other leather products	—	—	—	—	.00024	—
35 Glass and glass products	—	—	—	—	.00079	—
36 Stone and clay products	.00001	—	—	.00002	.00097	—
37 Primary iron and steel manufacturing	—	—	—	.00109	.00023	—
38 Primary nonferrous metal manufacturing	.00052	—	—	.00029	.00026	—
39 Metal containers	—	—	—	—	.00066	—
40 Heating, plumbing and structural metal products	—	—	—	(*)	.00110	—

Bureau of Economic Analysis, U.S. Department of Commerce, *Survey of Current Business* **54** (February 1974).

TABLE 8.4 Total requirements (direct and indirect) per dollar of delivery to final demand, 1967

Industry no.	Each entry represents the output required, directly and indirectly, from the industry named at the beginning of the row for each dollar of delivery to final demand by the industry named at the head of the column	Transportation and warehousing 65	Communications; except radio and TV broadcasting 66	Radio and TV broadcasting 67	Electric, gas, water and sanitary services 68	Wholesale and retail trade 69	Finance and insurance 70
1	Livestock and livestock products	0.00341	0.00147	0.00918	0.00169	0.00502	0.00388
2	Other agricultural products	.00368	.00133	.01341	.00170	.00418	.00335
3	Forestry and fishery products	.00037	.00020	.00043	.00032	.00043	.00040
4	Agricultural, forestry and fishery services	.00040	.00018	.00184	.00027	.00130	.00038
5	Iron and ferroalloy ores mining	.00086	.00019	.00022	.00055	.00031	.00019
6	Nonferrous metal ores mining	.00058	.00023	.00025	.00043	.00028	.00018

7	Coal mining	.00163	.00060	.00120	.03657	.00124	.00117
8	Crude petroleum and natural gas	.02414	.00374	.00464	.09534	.00772	.00439
9	Stone and clay mining and quarrying	.00097	.00059	.00047	.00139	.00055	.00040
10	Chemical and fertilizer mineral mining	.00036	.00012	.00024	.00044	.00028	.00022
11	New construction	—					
12	Maintenance and repair construction	.04070	.03341	.01697	.07628	.01269	.01316
13	Ordnance and accessories	.00032	.00018	.00019	.00010	.00037	.00010
14	Food and kindred products	.00859	.00366	.01744	.00385	.01350	.00978
15	Tobacco manufacturers	.00021	.00021	.00103	.00021	.00044	.00056
16	Broad and narrow fabrics, yarn and thread mills	.00284	.00079	.00087	.00134	.00223	.00118
17	Miscellaneous textile goods and floor coverings	.00172	.00031	.00045	.00071	.00106	.00053
18	Apparel	.00091	.00057	.00036	.00070	.00138	.00032
19	Miscellaneous fabricated textile products	.00226	.00018	.00025	.00031	.00080	.00025
20	Lumber and wood products, except containers	.00276	.00166	.00151	.00308	.00344	.00284
21	Wooden containers	.00010	.00006	.00013	.00006	.00077	.00007
22	Household furniture	.00012	.00023	.00013	.00008	.00023	.00005
23	Other furniture and fixtures	.00010	.00004	.00004	.00007	.00022	.00004
24	**Paper and allied products, except containers**	**.00717**	**.00604**	**.00677**	**.00544**	**.01549**	**.02214**
25	Paperboard containers and boxes	.00203	.00074	.00147	.00104	.00517	.00143
26	Printing and publishing	.01044	.01339	.01786	.00840	.01838	.04696
27	Chemicals and selected chemical products	.00892	.00311	.00709	.01132	.00762	.00563
28	Plastics and synthetic materials	.00319	.00122	.00151	.00196	.00270	.00165
29	Drugs, cleaning and toilet preparations	.00105	.00071	.00120	.00108	.00271	.00133
30	Paints and allied products	.00334	.00151	.00102	.00325	.00119	.00081
31	Petroleum refining and related industries	.05030	.00655	.00597	.01846	.01343	.00675
32	Rubber and miscellaneous plastics products	.00941	.00312	.00314	.00403	.00748	.00352
33	Leather tanning and industrial leather products	.00007	.00006	.00014	.00005	.00014	.00009
34	Footwear and other leather products	.00012	.00019	.00051	.00010	.00042	.00020
35	Glass and glass products	.00174	.00057	.00103	.00073	.00153	.00052
36	Stone and clay products	.00288	.00163	.00136	.00412	.00233	.00110
37	Primary iron and steel manufacturing	.01673	.00356	.00397	.01016	.00582	.00355
38	Primary nonferrous metal manufacturing	.00822	.00340	.00334	.00536	.00361	.00231
39	Metal containers	.00087	.00040	.00082	.00062	.00150	.00086
40	Heating, plumbing and structural metal products	.00311	.00204	.00119	.00495	.00213	.00094

Bureau of Economic Analysis, U.S. Department of Commerce, *Survey of Current Business* **54** (February 1974).

Unlimited Data therefore projected the manufacturer's share of the total market to be $750 million ($5.0 billion × 15 percent).

5. Conclusion. Based on projected demand for paper and allied products to the trade, the manufacturer drafted a proposal for enlarging the plant, adding more salespeople, redefining sales territories, and expanding other facets of business operations.

Applications and Limitations of Input-Output Analysis. Applications of input-output analysis have not been extensive in industrial marketing. First, the method is more appropriate for large firms whose products are practically undifferentiated commodities, such as in the chemical industry and public utilities. Second, the data-gathering problems are extensive, so the tables tend to be out of date. Third, the method assumes that technology is the same among all firms in the industry, which is an inappropriate assumption for industrial marketers. Fourth, the method also assumes linearity; in other words, it does not consider production situations in which there are increasing or decreasing economies of scale. Linearity assumptions could result in an under- or overestimation of demand.[23]

Standard Industrial Classification analysis. Input-output analysis identifies all of the industries that use the product being analyzed, but does not identify the *geographic location of the demand.* Many strategic marketing decisions require an estimate of potential demand by geographic areas. The location of branches, the number of salespeople and their territories, and the selection of advertising media all require measures of *geographic* potentials. Industrial marketers frequently use the Standard Industrial Classification (SIC) approach for such measures.

The SIC numbers that appear in Tables 8.2 and 8.3 are part of the industry classification scheme used by the federal government for its annual survey of manufacturers.[24] These numbers are also used on all forms for reporting social security taxes. These tax records provide an annual, reliable source of data on total payrolls, number of employees, and number of establishments arranged by industry groups and counties and are reported in *County Business Patterns.* The following example illustrates how an industrial sales manager can use these data to allocate sales effort according to the market potential.

Ready Made Containers, Inc.[25]

1. Problem. The sales manager for a manufacturer of corrugated and solid-fiber boxes in one of the Mountain States decided to intensify the company's efforts in Arizona, one of the states the firm served. In the Phoenix Standard Metropolitan Statistical Area (Maricopa County), for example, the firm's sales totaled $850,000 in 1971— $680,000, or 80 percent, to firms within the food and kindred products industry, and the remaining $170,000, or 20 percent, to firms manufacturing electrical equipment and supplies. The sales manager felt that this was a very poor sales record, considering the diversity of industry in the Phoenix area.

In view of this preliminary analysis, the sales manager decided to determine the market potential for fiber boxes in the Phoenix area as the first step in establishing the firm's sales potential (or market share) and setting a realistic sales quota for the area.

2. Source of data.

a) *County Business Patterns, 1972;*

b) *1973 U.S. Industrial Outlook;*

c) *Fiber Box Statistics 1972.*

3. Procedure.
In order to estimate the total market potential for corrugated and solid-fiber boxes on an industry-by-industry basis, the sales manager concluded that the initial analysis should be based on "end use," or consumption statistics, as a means of determining the extent to which various industry groups use such products. Consumption per employee was determined by applying national employment data of each two-digit SIC industry to the level of corrugated and solid-fiber boxes used by each industry. The potential for Maricopa County was then determined by applying county employment data to arrive at the market potential for each using industry in the county. The five-step procedure is shown below, and the results appear in Table 8.5.

a) Value of the fiber container shipments by industry was arrived at by applying end-use percentage data from source (a) to total United States shipments of the fiber-box industry from source (c). The resulting dollar values appear in column 1 of Table 8.5.

b) Total United States and Maricopa County employment in each of the using industries were determined from source (b). Columns 2 and 4 of Table 8.5 show these data.

c) Consumption per employee in each of the using industries was calculated by dividing data in column 1 by column 2. The results appear in column 3.

d) An estimate of the value of fiber-box use by each industry in Maricopa County was then obtained by multiplying the consumption per employee data in column 3 by county employment in column 4. The resulting dollar estimate for each two-digit industry in Maricopa County appears in column 5.

e) Total market potential in Maricopa County was obtained by adding the potential for individual industries.

4. Conclusion.
With a market potential for corrugated and solid-fiber boxes totaling $14,098,000 in the Phoenix area, the sales manager concluded that the company's sales of $850,000 in Phoenix constituted six percent of the total market potential, considerably less than the figure originally estimated.

More important, the sales manager learned that the firm had no sales in a number of two-digit industries that used a considerable quantity of corrugated and solid-fiber boxes. The lumber and wood products industry (SIC 24), for example, was consuming approximately $1,259,000 of such boxes, yet the firm had no sales in this industry group. The stone, clay, and glass products industry (SIC 32) was an even larger untapped market, with a corrugated shipping container consumption of $1,407,000.

In light of these and other findings, the sales manager decided that the sales potential for the Phoenix area should be based on the company's sales accomplishment in the food and kindred products industry, where its market share was 17.9 percent ($680,000 ÷ $3,793,000). Thus the initial sales quota for the Phoenix area was set at $2,523,542 ($14,098,000 × 17.9 percent), or about triple the sales of the preceding year. Each industry group in turn was assigned a sales quota equal to 17.9 percent of

TABLE 8.5 Estimated market for corrugated and solid-fiber box by industry groups, Phoenix, Arizona, Standard Metropolitan Statistical Area, 1972

SIC major group code	Consuming industries	Value of box shipments by end use[1] ($1000) 1	Employment by industry group[2] 2	Consumption per employee by industry group (1 ÷ 2) (dollars) 3	Maricopa County Employment by industry group[2] 4	Maricopa County Estimated market (3 × 4) ($1000) 5
20	Food and kindred products	1,171,800	1,536,307	763	4,971	3,793
21	Tobacco manufacturers	29,400	63,919	460	—	—
22	Textile mill products	121,800	935,925	130	—	—
23	Apparel and other textile products	54,600	1,349,000	40	3,158	126
24	Lumber and wood products	42,000	579,037	725	1,736	1,259
25	Furniture and fixtures	147,000	468,311	314	1,383	434
26	Paper and allied products	567,000	631,588	898	284	255
27	Printing and publishing	58,800	1,056,336	56	4,346	243
28	Chemicals and allied products	260,400	849,969	306	1,133	347
29	Petroleum and coal products	33,600	139,228	241	—	—
30	Rubber and miscellaneous plastics products	163,800	555,539	295	779	230
31	Leather and leather products	21,000	277,371	76	—	—
32	Stone, clay, and glass products	365,400	588,897	620	2,270	1,407
33	Primary metal industries	42,000	1,144,327	37	2,036	75
34	Fabricated metal products	184,800	1,312,595	141	3,271	461
35	Machinery, except electrical	105,000	1,769,738	59	14,691	867
36	Electrical equipment and supplies	256,200	1,698,725	151	23,788	3,592
37	Transportation equipment	109,200	1,700,723	64	2,484	159
38	Instruments and related products	29,400	383,585	77	D	—
39	Miscellaneous manufacturing industries	403,200	411,967	979	868	850
90	Government	33,600	—	—	—	—
	Total[3]	4,200,000	—	—	—	14,098

D Data withheld to avoid disclosure of individual reporting units.
[1] Based on data reported in *Fibre Box Industry Annual Report 1972*, Fibre Box Association.
[2] *County Business Patterns, 1972*. U.S. Department of Commerce, Bureau of the Census.
[3] *U.S. Industrial Outlook 1973—With Projections to 1980*. Bureau of Domestic Commerce, U.S. Department of Commerce.

its market potential; the apparel group (SIC 23), for example, was assigned a sales quota of $22,554 ($126,000 × 17.9 percent).

(Table 8.5 illustrates only the two-digit classification, which is very broad. Classifications running to seven digits provide a finer definition of industries. For example, SIC 20 includes "food and kindred products," whereas SIC 2011 identifies meatpacking plants. These finer classifications make it possible to identify applications with greater precision.)

Limitations of SIC Analysis. SIC numbers, like all classification schemes, are subject to some limitations. The first limitation occurs with multiproduct firms; it is impossible to determine how many of their employees are accounted for by the several standard industrial classifications assigned to the firm. Assigning all the employees to a single SIC number will overestimate sales.[26] Thus analysts should expect that the potentials for multiproduct firms will require refinements after the SIC approach is applied.

A second limitation is the problem of *interplant transfers*, which can lead to double counting. The Census Bureau provides *industry* estimates of these transfers so that some adjustment can be made.

A third limitation is based on the fact that the data are collected in the county of *production, not* the county where the *buying decision* is made. Thus additional research will be necessary to avoid sending the salespeople to the wrong counties.

The most serious limitation of the *County Business Patterns* data is the nondisclosure rule, which prevents publication of data by the Census Bureau that can identify a specific establishment or company. Thus if there are two companies in a county, one could learn the sales of the other by subtracting its own sales from the total reported for the county. Commercial research firms are not constrained by this government rule. For instance, the "Survey of Industrial Purchasing Power," published by *Sales and Marketing Management*, is not subject to this rule. Returning to Table 8.5, for SIC 38 we find a letter *D* for Maricopa County. In the "1976 Survey of Industrial Purchasing Power," we find that SIC 3811, "Engineering and Scientific Instruments," includes two plants in this county which account for 4.2 percent of this industry's total shipments. If *County Business Patterns* had been used, sales would have been underestimated by 4.2 percent.

The SIC analysis method shown in Table 8.5 makes two assumptions that are inherent in the input-output approach. It assumes that all establishments have the same level of technology with regard to the product in question and that establishments are identical with regard to production efficiencies.

Even with these limitations, however, the SIC method of estimating potential demand among manufacturers is very useful and widely used. It should be used in conjunction with other market information, and adjustments should be made to refine the data for specific industrial marketers.[27]

Buyer expectations. The input-output and the SIC methods analyze demand at one point in time. Industrial market researchers sometimes use surveys of *industrial buyer* expectations to project demand into the future. Surveys of businesspeople include their expectations of their sales and their capital expenditures. These data are tabulated by the two-digit SIC number. The major sources of capital spending and sales anticipation data are the surveys of the Bureau of the Census and the Bureau of Economic Analysis (both in the United States Department of Commerce) and the McGraw-Hill Publications Company.[28]

Sales data are collected by the Bureau of the Census for forecast horizons that are one and two quarters into the future. One-year anticipations of sales are collected by the Bureau of Economic Analysis and McGraw-Hill, which also collects sales anticipations for four-year horizons.

Capital-spending expectations are collected by the Bureau of Economic Analysis for one-quarter, two-quarter, and one-year horizons. McGraw-Hill uses horizons that are one, two, three, and four years into the future.

Although expectations data are the *subjective* opinions of businesspeople, they do represent knowledgeable, even self-fulfilling, predictions. "Although there has been no overall study of all these data series, the general conclusion from analyses of some of the individual surveys is that they are quite accurate predictors of sales and capital spending."[29]

The accuracy of buyer-expectations data, however, is at the aggregate level of an industry. Predictions for the individual firm are more difficult. Predictions at the *industry level* are always easier, regardless of the type of data, because errors tend to be offsetting. When planning for an individual *firm*, the industrial market analyst will frequently use buyers' expectations data as one reference point for the forecast. Good forecasting, like good navigation through dangerous waters, requires many reliable reference points.

Analysis for Buyer-Behavior Segmentation   Market segmentation is a search for a classification scheme that will permit generalizations about the needs of buyers. Earlier industrial classifications schemes were based on product classes, such as capital goods, fabricating materials, raw materials, accessory equipment, and services. Customers were classified according to end-uses, such as manufacturing, construction, trade, government, and institutions. "Tying this diversity of products and customers together is the concept of a buying process that is common to all. This process consists of logical steps that can be studied and analyzed just as the buying behavior of individual consumers can be studied and analyzed."[30] Therefore, industrial market researchers have started to use behavioral science approaches to segment their markets according to *buyer behavior*.

When the industrial product reaches the mature stage and the quality and service offered by competitors tend to be similar, *buyer-behavior segmentation* dominates the marketing strategy. "The critical element in marketing success at this stage is knowing customer buying processes and the relative emphasis they place on factors such as price, availability of supply, business entertaining, and trade relations."[31]

Steps in the buying process.   Earlier in this chapter we saw that the industrial buying process has been divided into eight steps, beginning with recognition of a need and ending with evaluation. These steps represent generalizations that summarize many companies and many industries. Industrial marketing researchers find that large buyers have steps that are unique to their respective companies. For instance, a survey of the major manufacturers of wire and cable revealed that their decisions to buy sheathing varied from three to seven steps. Furthermore, the order of these steps differed in almost every case.[32] In such a situation it is difficult to have a single marketing strategy and a single marketing program of action. Industrial marketing strategies must be adaptable, which explains why in industrial marketing, salespeople are more important than advertising; the sales message can be adapted to the buying process of the individual industrial buyer. (The persons in this process are frequently called the decision-making unit—DMU.)[33]

Segmentation of the market according to buyer-behavior dimensions is still in its early development, so there are few published examples. The complexity of the research required for this segmentation is apparent from the Sheth model of industrial buyer behavior (Fig. 8.1). Other appropriate behavioral models have been summarized by Webster and Wind.[34]

The diffusion model has been applied to the industrial buying process.[35] The interpersonal relationships between insurance salespeople and their customers revealed that the probability of making a sale increased when the salespeople's characteristics were similar to those of their prospects.[36]

Research on the behavioral dimensions of industrial buyers is new, so there are few generalizations available for developing marketing strategies. The effectiveness of various methods of communication has been studied by Levitt.[37] He found that the prestige of the company and the quality of the presentation influences the industrial buyer, but that these influences wear off over time. Wilson studied the influence of personality variables on the decision-making styles of 132 purchasing agents.[38] He found that their *need for certainty* was a good predictor of their decision styles, which he classified as either normative or conservative. Measures of their *self-confidence* and their *need to achieve* did not predict their decision styles.

An Example of a Complex Purchase Process. The industrial purchase can involve many individuals and many separate organizations. Buying influences frequently are outside the buying organization and cannot be reached by the salesperson. Purchases by a state hospital illustrate a complex purchase process.

The purchase process required of a 500-bed state hospital is illustrated in Fig. 8.3. The decision process involved three separate organizations—the hospital, the comprehensive health-planning agency, and the state. In this example the product was new X-ray equipment costing $105,000.

The need for additional equipment was identified by the hospital's department of radiology. The initial request was in the department's annual budget (1). After evaluating the requests and priorities of other departments, the hospital administrator informed the department that its request was approved, asked for technical specifications, and sent them to the comprehensive health-planning agency (4). This state agency coordinates all purchases greater than $100,000 among hospitals in the state. (This coordination is required of all hospitals that receive federal funds from sources such as Medicare.) After approval, the administrator sent the purchase requisition to the state's department of purchasing and contracts (6), which then requested bids from vendors (7). These bids were forwarded to the administrator (9), who evaluated them in terms of the specifications and made recommendations to the state department of purchasing and contracts (10). The recommendations were forwarded to the state board of awards, which supervises all major contracts (11). The contract was awarded to supplier E, who installed the equipment (13). The entire process took eight months, a short time relative to many industrial selling processes.

BRAND-DEMAND ANALYSIS Because industrial demand is *derived* from the demand for other goods and services, a brand-demand analysis must begin with an understanding of the determinants of generic demand. For instance, the demand for earth-moving equipment will depend on the building of highways, the construction of homes, and economic development in foreign countries. The federal highway program requires an understanding of the political process. Interest rates will determine the demand for new

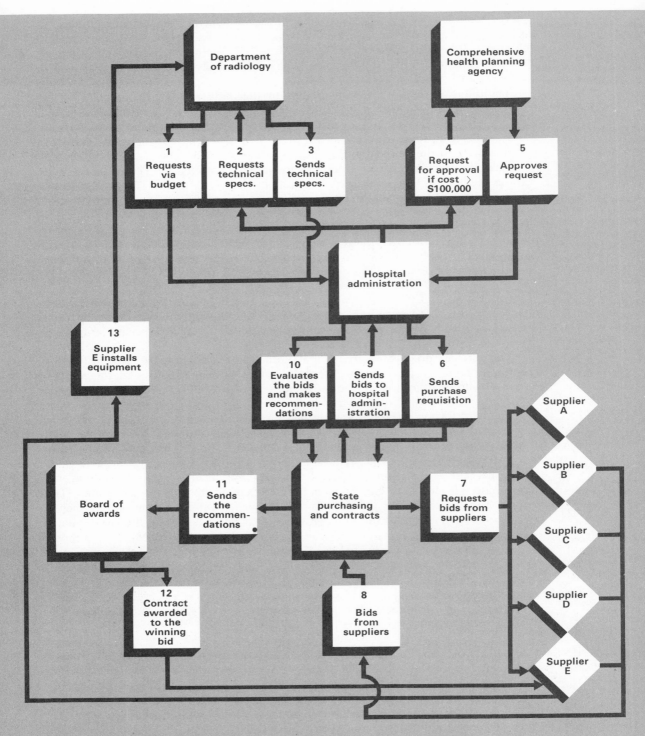

Fig. 8.3 Purchasing process of X-ray equipment for a state hospital. (Developed by Metin N. Gurol.)

homes. The demand in developing countries will be determined by world politics, monetary exchange rates, and world competition. Thus the broad economic, political, and social dimensions of generic demand create the environment for industrial brand-demand analysis and strategies.

Industrial brand strategies, like consumer strategies, must be built on an understanding of the *success factors* of the industry. Clark Equipment Company, a manufacturer of material-handling equipment, identified seven factors critical to the effectiveness of its worldwide marketing program:

1. Effective product planning, innovation, and timing;
2. A team marketing effort, with a balance of effort among the manufacturing, engineering, and marketing departments;
3. Involvement of all departments in product planning;
4. Many simultaneous merchandising programs;
5. A strong distribution network with initial sale and aftersale service;
6. Investment of resources in areas of growth and volume;
7. Setting profitability and market penetration as dual objectives.[39]

During the petroleum shortage of 1974–75, a success factor in the chemical industry was the *certainty of supply*. Buyers sometimes favored suppliers who were vertically integrated to the oil well, thereby ensuring a source of raw materials. Such a supplier needs, or maybe is forced to use, a *marketing allocation strategy* for the division of scarce products to its customers. This stategy must consider the past, present, and future buyer-seller relationships. The allocation strategy may also consider the entire mix of products that are bought and the previous quantity of purchases of the scarce product.

An evaluation of an industry's success factors leads logically into an analysis of the strengths and weaknesses of the companies in the industry. Some industrial researchers survey buyers to identify competitors' weaknesses. These weaknesses then become the basis for a new product service, method of distribution, or financial arrangement, such as leasing.

Matching Products and Markets for Brand Strategies   A *business* was defined in Chapter 4 as a product, a market, a connection between the two. The same product sold to a different market is a different business. Development of an industrial marketing strategy requires a careful matching of products to markets. This matching is difficult because industrial markets occur along two dimensions—the horizontal and the vertical market structures.[40]

Horizontal segments for an air conditioning manufacturer, for example, include "residential-tract builders, small 'stick' builders, and commercial contractors."[41] Vertical segments divide the production process into discrete markets. Broadly speaking, these include raw materials, semifabricated materials, components, and final end-products. Industrial brand-marketing strategy requires a complex analysis because of this two-dimensional segmentation.

Crown Cork & Seal Company.[42]   The Crown Cork & Seal Company case is an excellent example of a marketing strategy based on product/market matching. In 1957 the company was on the verge of bankruptcy; seven years later it had been turned around and had a higher return on sales than its two larger competitors. In analyzing the company's success, Corey concluded that the turnaround was due to an *understanding of marketing strategy.*[43] This strategy was supported by a changed organizational structure, a modified control system, overhead reduction, and top-management leadership.

The container industry had gone through a *high degree of technological change*— from glass, through aluminum, fiberfoil, and plastics—all of which competed with tinplate to serve the needs of 135 industries. *Competition* came from other can manufacturers, such as American Can Company and Continental Can, and from end-users who manufactured their own cans, such as Campbell Soup. The *value added* to cans by Crown Cork was only 35 percent of the value of shipments. This meant that there was little room for cost-reduction programs that would permit a low-price strategy. This value added was being threatened by rising material and labor costs on one hand and reduced prices on the other due to new low-cost materials, larger competitors, and self-manufacturers. This *analysis* of the situation clearly indicated that Crown Cork & Seal Company had to decide which markets it would serve and with which products.

The horizontal product/market selection made by Crown Cork was based on an analysis of the company's *strengths* and *weaknesses* and the *needs* of the market. The company's *strengths* included the technical ability to design and manufacture metal containers for "hard-to-hold" applications, such as beer, soft drinks, and aerosols. It had good working relationships with metal suppliers and was a major supplier of filling equipment for soft drink and beer cans. Crown Cork's *limitations* were a small market share, limited resources for research and development, outmoded manufacturing plants, and locations away from concentrations of market potential.

The markets Crown Cork decided to consider were beer, soft drinks, aerosol containers, and motor-oil cans. Technological change convinced the company not to concentrate on the motor-oil can market, even though it had introduced the first aluminum oil can and at one time had 50 percent of the market. Fiberfoil had emerged as the dominant packaging material for this end use, and the economics of paper gave the paper companies a significant cost advantage. Furthermore, the probability of self-manufacture was high, and manufacturing technology was low, so Crown's best resource would not be used.

The best match of products to markets for Crown Cork was in the beer, soft drink, and aerosol container industries. Each of these industries was characterized by a high growth rate, a need for high-strength containers (probably metal), low research and development needs, a low probability of self-manufacture, high service needs (e.g., delivery, can-filling technology, and lithographing of can surfaces), and customers' desires to have at least two sources of supply. These markets were a good match for Crown's strengths and limitations, except for the customers' need for rapid delivery. To serve these markets, Crown would need to locate its plants closer to concentrations of potential customers.

When a company is considering diversifying into new markets, it should ask four questions.[44] Is there a high potential for growth? Is the market dominated by powerful competitors, or is it still possible to claim a large share of the market? Is entry easy, or does it require large investments of capital, research and development, field sales, and management leadership? Is the value added high enough to give control over the final price of the product? Favorable answers to these questions suggest that the company should consider diversifying by developing new products.

When an industrial company is matching its strengths and weaknesses to markets, it should consider the *market as fixed* and the *product as a variable*. Given the technological needs of industrial markets, it is not possible to "create" needs through mass advertising, as *may* be possible in consumer markets.

Benefit Segmentation The concept of *benefit segmentation* applies to industrial marketing as well as to consumer marketing, with some differences. In industrial marketing heavy emphasis is given to service before and after the sale, to product performance, and to technological needs. For highly technical equipment the important benefits may be unique to each buyer. In such cases benefit segmentation would result in one customer in each segment. Such uniqueness prevents a generalized strategy. There are, however, some benefits that are common to most industrial purchases. These benefits include price, terms of sale, performance, quality maintenance, integrity, service after the sale, deliveries according to schedule, and efficient handling of complaints. The term *vendor evaluation* describes the process that buyers use to rate sellers along these benefits. (Included in this evaluation is the decision to buy the product or make it within the firm.)

Some industrial purchasing decisions are made with the aid of a *benefit-weighting* scheme. A study of the *military market* identified the scheme shown in Table 8.6 for the evaluation of contracts for base management in the missile program.[45] It is important to note that "cost and fee" accounts for only eight percent of the decision to award a contract. This illustrates that industrial and even military contracts do not necessarily go to the lowest bidder; there are many nonprice considerations in the decision process.

Value analysis, which gained stature during the 1960s, consists of *buying the necessary functions at the lowest cost*. It attempts to eliminate specifications for components that are overdesigned because they perform unnecessary functions. It searches for new products that will perform the same function for a lower cost. Thus a nut and bolt may be replaced by a clamp, or a clamp may be replaced by a glue. A complete value-analysis system will challenge the existing product specifications, its design, and even production methods.[46]

TABLE 8.6   **Benefit-weighting scheme in the military market**

Factor	Weight
Understanding scope of work	8%
Management control in government practices	8
Management availability and capability	10
Management philosophy and experience	10
Resources, skills, and manpower	10
Weapon-system knowledge and experience	8
Prior experience and performance	8
Labor relations, understanding human factors	8
Quality control	10
Acceptance of the conditions of contract	7
Acceptance of statement of work	5
Cost and fee	8
Total	100%

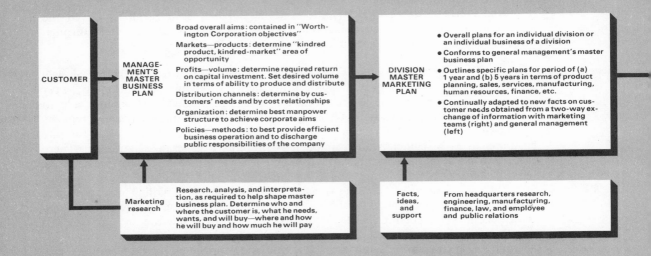

Fig. 8.4. Worthington Pump Corporation's marketing process. *(The Development of Marketing Objectives and Plans: A Symposium,* New York: The Conference Board, Experiences in Marketing Management, No. 3, 1963, p. 8. Reprinted by permission.)

Why Have the Behavioral Sciences Lagged? Application of the behavioral sciences came first to consumer marketing and then to industrial marketing. This explains why most textbook discussions of buying behavior focus on consumer behavior. This development is probably due to the nature of industrial marketers, who have technical, not behavioral science, backgrounds. Convincing them that these sciences can help in technical sales has been a slow process.

A second reason for the lack of behavioral science applications in industrial marketing is the nature of industrial marketing. Channels of communication are shorter than in consumer marketing, so there is less need for studies of consumer behavior. The salesperson gathers market information and immediately modifies the content of the presentation. In consumer marketing, market research may be a prerequisite to a change in advertising copy.

A third reason may be the slow maturation of industrial products. Industrial buyer-behavior segmentation has replaced end-use segmentation only recently. Many industrial marketers have yet to recognize the need to shift to a behavioral strategy, because they are not yet aware that their products have reached the mature stage and that they should be shifting away from a strategy of end-use segmentation.

AN INDUSTRIAL MARKETING-PLANNING PROCESS: WORTHINGTON CORPORATION Many of the marketing concepts discussed in earlier chapters were illustrated with examples from consumer marketing. The planning process for Worthington Corporation appears in Fig. 8.4 to illustrate that these concepts apply to the industrial marketing plan as well.

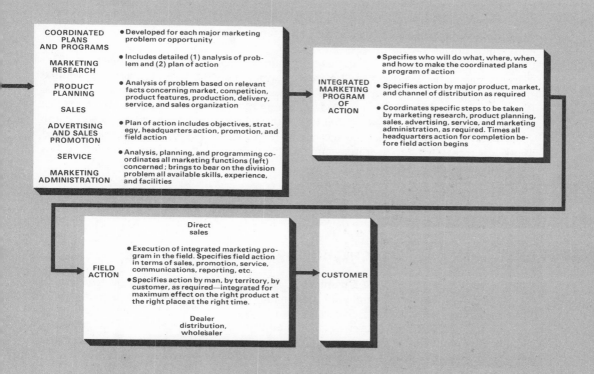

COORDINATED PLANS AND PROGRAMS	• Developed for each major marketing problem or opportunity
MARKETING RESEARCH	• Includes detailed (1) analysis of problem and (2) plan of action
PRODUCT PLANNING	• Analysis of problem based on relevant facts concerning market, competition, product features, production, delivery, service, and sales organization
SALES	
ADVERTISING AND SALES PROMOTION	• Plan of action includes objectives, strategy, headquarters action, promotion, and field action
SERVICE	• Analysis, planning, and programming coordinates all marketing functions (left) concerned; brings to bear on the division problem all available skills, experience, and facilities
MARKETING ADMINISTRATION	

INTEGRATED MARKETING PROGRAM OF ACTION

- Specifies who will do what, where, when, and how to make the coordinated plans a program of action
- Specifies action by major product, market, and channel of distribution as required
- Coordinates specific steps to be taken by marketing research, product planning, sales, advertising, service, and marketing administration, as required. Times all headquarters action for completion before field action begins

FIELD ACTION

Direct sales

- Execution of integrated marketing program in the field. Specifies field action in terms of sales, promotion, service, communications, reporting, etc.
- Specifies action by man, by territory, by customer, as required—integrated for maximum effect on the right product at the right place at the right time.

Dealer distribution, wholesaler

CUSTOMER

A manufacturer of industrial pumps and compressors, Worthington's marketing-planning process begins and ends with the customer. Market research is used to ask the same kinds of questions that are asked in consumer research. *Top management's master business plan* includes a discussion of customer needs; the *division master marketing plan* translates the business plan into the coordinated plans and programs for marketing research, product planning, sales, advertising and sales promotion, service, and marketing administration. These plans and programs are reduced to a program of action that specifies who will do what, where, when, and how in order to implement the master marketing plan. The final implementation of the plan occurs when the salespeople call on users or wholesalers.

SUMMARY Industrial marketing focuses on the intermediate demand for goods and services from commercial enterprises, governments, and nonprofit institutions. The concepts developed in consumer marketing apply to industrial marketing, but with different emphases, greater complexity, and a long-term buyer/seller relationship.

The position of the product in its life cycle determines the appropriate method for generic-demand analysis and the method for market segmentation. During the early stages methods such as technology life cycle, experience curves, and the Delphi method are used for *product segmentation*. During the growth stage the appropriate methods for *applications segmentation* include input-output analysis, Standard Industrial

Classification analysis, and surveys of buyers' expectations. At the mature stage, *buyer-behavior segmentation* is appropriate. This stage requires an understanding of the steps in the buying-decision process, organizational behavior, and the influences on the individuals in the buying process.

Brand-demand analysis requires the matching of products and markets. The markets may be both vertical and horizontal, which increases the marketer's alternative strategies, but which also increases the complexity of the industrial demand analysis. Benefit segmentation requires an understanding of the weights that the buyer applies to the decision criteria. *Vendor analysis* and *value analysis* are used to position the vendor and the product along the decision criteria. When a complex industrial demand analysis is translated into a strategy and finally into a marketing plan, many similarities to a consumer plan are evident.

DISCUSSION CASELETTE

INTERNATIONAL MINERALS AND CHEMICALS COMPANY (IMC)

The International Minerals & Chemicals Company (IMC) has asked you to evaluate its planning process, focusing your comments on its objectives and environment forecasts. The content of its five-year plan appears in Table 8.7; its structure of objectives, in Table 8.8; and its environment audit/forecast, in Table 8.9. IMC products include phosphate, potash, fertilizer, industrial chemicals, bonding and fire clay, cattle feed, foundry sand additives, refractories, and manganese ore.

1. What would you change and what would you leave alone? (Your answer should reflect on the first eight chapters of this text.)
2. Do you prefer the IMC or the Celanese plan (Table 2.5)? Explain your preference.
3. What methods would you recommend for IMC's audit/forecast of customer profiles, technological trends, and market trends?

DISCUSSION QUESTIONS

1. What are the major differences between consumer and industrial buying behavior? Why is the role of the salesperson so important in industrial marketing?
2. How do industrial marketing strategies shift over the product life cycle? What strategy should be emphasized in each of the following life-cycle stages: (a) product development, (b) early introduction, (c) growth stage, (d) mature stage?
3. What is meant by the term *family life cycle?*
4. How have technology life-cycle analysis, experience-curve analysis, and the Delphi method been used to predict future technology trends?
5. What are the purpose and limitations of input-output analysis?
6. What kinds of information can be derived from Standard Industrial Classification analysis? What are some limitations of SIC analysis?

TABLE 8.7   The International Minerals and Chemicals Company (IMC) five-year-plan

Objectives

    Creed and ethics
    Grand design
    Stakeholder expectations
    Social responsibility
    Managerial
    Economic goals
    Present and potential missions
    "Capsule" strategy

Environment forecasts
    U.S. and world economy
    User needs and demand
    Technology
    Competition
    Regulation

Key attributes

    Strengths
    Weaknesses

Key challenges

    Problems and opportunities

Momentum summary

    Sales
    Earnings
    Price   } Projections
    Volume

Internal development plan

    Research and development
    Logistics
    Overseas
    Mineral reserves exploration

Capital expenditure plan

    Proposed five-year budget
    Ex-plan projects

Acquisition program

    Selection criteria
    Priorities and top candidates

Financial plan

    Cash flow   }
    Balance sheet } Projections
    Performance }
    Funds source } Analysis

D. J. Smalter, "Anatomy of a Long-Range Plan," *What Industrial Marketing Management Should Know about Long-Range Planning*, American Marketing Association Industrial Division Annual Seminar, Cleveland, Ohio, March 31–April 1, 1966, pp. 31, 35, 43. (Reprinted by permission.)

NOTES

1. E. R. Corey, *Industrial Marketing: Cases and Concepts*, 2d ed. (Englewood Cliffs, N.J.: Prentice-Hall, 1976), p. 1.

2. *Ibid.*

3. R. W. Hill and A. Meidan, "The Use of Quantitative Techniques in Industrial Marketing," *Industrial Marketing Management* 4 (1975): 59–68.

4. J. N. Sheth, "A Model of Industrial Buyer Behavior," *Journal of Marketing* 37 (October 1973): 50–56.

5. P. J. Robinson, C. W. Faris, and Y. Wind, *Industrial Buying and Creative Marketing* (Boston: Allyn & Bacon, 1967).

TABLE 8.8 IMC structure of objectives

Statement of creed

Ethical aims and practices with respect to:
- Customers
- Suppliers
- Employees
- Shareholders
- Government
- Community

Stakeholder-relations objectives

Investors
- Earnings growth
- Dividend payout
- Stock value
- Financial control
- Stockholder service

Government, e.g., contractual

Lenders, e.g., financial leverage, access to capital markets

Employee, e.g., opportunity for increased compensation

Customer, e.g., product quality and availability

Supplier, e.g., dependability and service

Economic objectives

Mission(s) in the world economy—scope of purpose and service
- Financial risk taking
- Investment opportunities
- Adaptability to change
- Continuity and/or survival
- Stability
- Corporate image

Economic mission goals

Profitability performance
Market standing:
- Product quantity and growth
- Geographical scope
- Product characteristics
- Product-line compatibility

Productivity and efficiency
Resource position

Social-responsibility objectives

- Enlightened self-interest, e.g., world hunger
- Philanthropic and/or humanitarian
- Educational
- Community service
- Democratic and/or political
- Regulatory

Managerial objectives

- Authority and control over employee actions
- Stimulation of initiative, vigor, innovation, and creativity
- Perpetuation of control
- Utilization of management techniques
- Performance quality
- Development of skills
- Degree of employee communication
- Promotion practices
- Compensation and rewards
- Prestige in professional circles

TABLE 8.9   The IMC environment audit/forecast

Industry structure	*Technological trends*
Source of earnings	User needs research
Channels and costs	Technological forecast
Transport costs	Opportunities and threats
Innovative opportunities	
	Market trends
Regulatory constraints	
	Geographical outlook
Macroeconomic factors	Product-mix changes
	Demand expectations
Competitive situation	
	Momentum share
Position audit	
Attributes and strategies	*Potential for more effective participation*
Likely new activity	
	Penetration
	Development
Customer profile	Integration
	Innovation
Position audit	
Present sales strategy	

NOTES

6. *Ibid.*

7. Sheth, *op. cit.*

8. F. E. Webster and Y. Wind, *Organizational Buying Behavior* (Englewood Cliffs, N.J.: Prentice-Hall, 1972).

9. G. Risely, *Modern Industrial Marketing* (New York: McGraw-Hill, 1972).

10. Corey, *op. cit.*, pp. 359–360.

11. *Ibid.*, p. 359.

12. F. R. Finney, *We Like to Do Business with our Friends* (Cambridge, Mass.: Marketing Science Institute, 1969).

13. M. B. MacDonald, Jr., *Appraising the Market for New Industrial Products*, Conference Board Studies in Business Policy No. 123 (New York: Conference Board, 1967), pp. 77–80.

14. Corey, *op. cit.*, pp. 6–7.

15. *Ibid.*

16. R. N. Cardozo, "Segmenting the Industrial Market," in *Marketing and the New Science of Planning*, ed. R. L. King (Chicago: American Marketing Association, 1968), pp. 433–440; and R. E. Frank, W. F. Massy, and Y. Wind, *Marketing Segmentation* (Englewood Cliffs, N.J.: Prentice-Hall, 1972).

17. MacDonald, *op. cit.*, p. 91.

18. *Perspectives on Experience* (Boston: The Boston Consulting Group, 1968).

19. G. T. Milkovich, A. J. Annoni, and T. A. Mahoney, "The Use of the Delphi Procedures in Manpower Forecasting," *Management Science* **19,** Part I (December 1972): 381–388.

20. J. C. Chambers, K. M. Satinder, and D. D. Smith, *An Executive's Guide to Forecasting* (New York: Wiley, 1974), p. 50.

21. For more details, *see* M. F. Elliot-Jones, *Input-Output Analysis: A Nontechnical Description* (New York: Conference Board, 1971); and W. Leontief, *Input-Output Economics* (New York: Oxford University Press, 1966).

22. *Measuring Markets: A Guide to the Use of Federal and State Statistical Data* (Washington, D.C.: Government Printing Office, Stock Number 003 025 00031; Catalog Number C 57.8: M34, 1974).

23. J. Rothe, "The Reliability of Input-Output Analysis for Marketing," *California Management Review* **14**, 4 (1972): 75–81.

24. For a complete list of industries, *see Standard Industrial Classification Manual: 1972* (Washington, D.C.: Government Printing Office).

25. *Measuring Markets*, *op cit.*, pp. 45–46.

26. Some adjustment can be made to industry data by using the ratios of primary product specialization available from the Census of Manufacturers, but this adjustment does not apply to individual firms.

27. For an additional discussion of the limitations of SIC methods, *see SIC: The Increasing Misapplication of a Useful Tool* (Washington, D.C.: Machinery and Allied Products Institute, 1974).

28. R. Rippe, M. Wilkinson, and D. Morrison, "Industrial Market Forecasting with Anticipations Data," *Management Science* **22** (February 1976): 639–651.

29. *Ibid.*, p. 644.

30. D. B. Curll, III, "Inside Industrial Marketing," *Marketing News*, May 7, 1976, p. 3.

31. Corey, *op. cit.*, p. 7.

32. Proprietary research findings.

33. A. Wilson, *The Assessment of Industrial Markets* (London: Hutchinson, 1968).

34. Webster and Wind, *op. cit.*, Chapter 2.

35. F. E. Webster, Jr., "New Product Adoption in Industrial Markets: A Framework for Analysis," *Journal of Marketing* **33** (July 1969): 35–39.

36. F. B. Evans, "Selling as a Dyadic Relationship—A New Approach," *American Behavioral Scientist* **6** (May 1963): 76–79.

37. T. Levitt, *Industrial Purchasing Behavior—A Study of Communications Effects* (Boston: Division of Research, Harvard Business School, 1965).

38. D. T. Wilson, "Industrial Buyers' Decision-Making Styles," *Journal of Marketing Research* **8** (November 1971): 433–436.

39. R. H. Braun, Jr., "Correct Pricing, Suitable Products, Standardization Spur Worldwide Marketing," *Marketing News*, September 26, 1975, p. 9.

40. R. E. Corey, "Key Options in Marketing Selection and Product Planning," *Harvard Business Review* (September-October 1975): 119–128.

41. *Ibid.*, p. 121.

42. *Ibid.*

43. *Ibid.*, p. 119.

44. *Ibid.*, pp. 124–125.

45. M. L. Weidenbaum, *The Military Market in the United States* (Chicago: American Marketing Association, 1963), p. 33.

46. For a discussion of value and vendor analysis, *see* R. M. Hill, R. S. Alexander, and J. S. Cross, *Industrial Marketing*, 4th ed. (Homewood, Ill.: Richard D. Irwin, 1975), Chapter 6.

SUGGESTED READINGS

Fischer, L., *Industrial Marketing* (New York: Brandon/Systems Press, 1970).

Hummel, F. E., *Market and Sales Potentials* (New York: Ronald Press, 1961).

Industrial Marketing Management (a journal of industrial marketing and marketing research).

Lehmann, D. R., and J. O'Shaughnessy, "Difference in Attribute Importance for Different Industrial Products," *Journal of Marketing* **38** (April 1974): 36–42.

Piersol, R. J., "Accuracy of Estimating Markets for Industrial Products by Size of Consuming Industries," *Journal of Marketing Research* **5** (May 1968): 147–154.

Stacey, N. A. H., and A. Wilson, *Industrial Marketing Research* (London: Hutchinson, 1963).

Vinson, D. E., and D. Sciglimpaglia, eds., *The Environment of Industrial Marketing* (Columbus, Ohio: Grid, 1975).

Wind, Y., and H. J. Claycamp, "Planning Product Line Strategy: A Matrix Approach," *Journal of Marketing* **40** (January 1976): 2–9.

ENVIRONMENTAL ANALYSIS WORKSHEET

Environmental elements	Facts	Assumptions or research needed	Conclusions
Organizational values, objectives, and policies (4)			
Organizational design (5)			
Situation			
Generic demand (6)			
Brand demand (7)			
Competition (9)			
Public policy (10)			
Opportunities (2)			
Problems			

MARKETING PLAN (CONSUMER PRODUCT)

Current performance
Recommendations
Effect of recommendations on income
Situation analysis
Opportunities and problems
Strategies
Tests and research
Supporting documents
   Comparative budgets
   Media allocation schedule
   Promotion control sheet

STRATEGY WORKSHEET

Opportunities and problems in rank order to importance

1.
2.
.
n.

	Current strategy	Alternatives and recommended strategy	Estimated Effect

Demand strategy
   Generic
   Brand

Strategic goals
   Financial
   Marketing

Marketing-mix strategies
   Product (12)
   Pricing (13)
   Channel and logistics (14)
   Advertising and promotional (15)
   Sales management (16)

Research (3)

Profit plan

Evaluation and control (19)

CHAPTER **9**

Analyzing Competition

LEARNING OBJECTIVES   After studying this chapter you should:

1. Be sensitized to the dynamic interactions of competitive behavior.
2. Be aware of methods for identifying potential competitors and planning for their reactions.
3. Know the most common approaches for developing competitive strategies.
4. Be aware of the need for competitive contingency planning.
5. Be aware of the models and measures that are used for a competitive analysis.
6. Be able to define and use the following concepts:

Competitive interaction	Build, hold, harvest strategies
Counterstrategies	Product-portfolio strategies
Industry excess capacity	Cash cows
Potential competition	High market-share strategies
Experience curves	Competitive contingency planning
Product life-cycle strategies	Competitive information systems

SOME ANALYTICAL QUESTIONS FOR OPENERS

1. What are the success factors in this industry?
2. What are the strengths and weaknesses of our competitors?
3. Is the market structure competitive or oligopolistic?
4. Which marketing-mix variables do competitors emphasize?
5. Does industry capacity exceed demand? Is entry easy?
6. How will competitors react to a change in our strategy? How will we react to their reaction?

"The ultimate reason for going through the demanding process of developing a statement of corporate strategy is not to produce a document but to attain superior competitive performance."[1] *Superior competitive performance* is dependent on an understanding of competition, which is why the planner must analyze competition during the planning process.

A competitive analysis is basically an examination of the *strengths and weaknesses* of a firm's marketing mix relative to its competition. An understanding of these strengths and weaknesses becomes the basis for developing marketing strategies. In this chapter we will examine some examples of classic competitive strategies and counterstrategies in order to gain an appreciation of the dynamics and excitement of marketing competition. We will then examine methods that are appropriate for identifying competitive strengths and weaknesses, early-warning signals for anticipating competitive behavior, and competitive strategies that are appropriate for various life cycle/competitive situations.

CLASSIC COMPETITIVE STRATEGIES

Kodak versus Polaroid   The concept of instant photography was created by the Polaroid Corporation, which had the entire instant-photography market until 1976, when Kodak introduced its version of instant cameras and film. Also in 1976, Berkley Photo test-marketed its version, and there were rumors that Japanese manufacturers planned to enter the instant-photo market.[2] The strategies used by Kodak and the counterstrategies of Polaroid will become classic examples of competitive interaction.

The market situation was excellent for the Kodak introduction in the spring of 1976. The timing was perfect. The United States was celebrating its bicentennial, and Canada was hosting the Olympics. Summer is also the time when retail buyers place orders for the Christmas season. It was estimated that one-half of the 48 million households owning cameras would be good prospects for an instant camera priced around $50.[3] Kodak priced its instant cameras at $53.50 and $69.50. Film was priced at $7.45 for ten prints, slightly above Polaroid's $6.99. (Comparable Kodak print costs for its other cameras were 27¢ to 45¢ each.)

Polaroid had demonstrated the size and expansiveness of the instant-photography market. There were 22 million Polaroid cameras in use around the world. Polaroid had sold two million cameras that used the company's advanced SX-70 process. It used the classic *skimming* pricing strategy by introducing successively less expensive SX-70 models. The Deluxe model was introduced at $180 in 1972. In 1974 Model 2 was introduced, listing for $150; Model 3 was introduced in 1975, with a suggested price of $100. Model 4, called "Pronto," was introduced early in 1976, with a suggested price of $66.

Discount stores liked to discount Polaroid cameras to build store traffic. This retail policy had hurt Polaroid's relations with camera specialty stores, which try to sell at list price. The discounted price of Pronto brought it close to cannibalizing the older Polaroid lines, such as the $25 Square Shooter. The Kodak introductions at $53.50 and $69.50 were probably responsible for Polaroid's early introduction of its Pronto at $66.

What was behind the Kodak pricing strategy? The reasons behind such strategies are confidential, but the press has supplied some reasonable guesses. Foremost among these is that the camera was priced to reach the mass market.[4]

The film cost would not cannibalize Kodak's other film, and it would provide a margin for dealers who were losing processing business because of the new instant process. By pricing the film above that of Polaroid, Kodak would avoid a price war. The Antitrust Division of the Justice Department had been investigating Kodak for years, so Kodak would not want to appear to be a predatory price cutter.[5] Kodak also had the policy of selling its cameras at a low price and making its profits on film. (It licensed other camera manufacturers to use its films, such as its quick-loading film cartridges called Instamatic, thereby gaining additional film profits.)

Polaroid's counterstrategy seemed to be an earlier-than-planned introduction of the Pronto and a program to improve dealer relations. The dealer program for specialty stores included a "Special Edition" camera, which had a five-year warranty and a higher price. Dealers also received year-end bonuses for expanded sales. A 24-hour toll-free telephone number provided photographic information and follow-up on orders. There was some improvement in dealer relations, but Polaroid was still bothered by high salesforce turnover, which reduced dealer rapport.[6] Thus channel strategy was still a problem for Polaroid.

Datril versus Tylenol One of the most exciting and dynamic cases of competitive interaction occurred during the year ended May 1976. The generic product was acetaminophen, a nonaspirin analgesic. McNeil Laboratories' Tylenol dominated the market until Bristol-Myers introduced an identical product, Datril, in June 1975. *Price* was to be the theme of the Datril strategy; the product would sell for $1.85, whereas Tylenol was selling for $2.85.

In 1971 the Federal Trade Commission encouraged the television networks to allow competitive advertising; specific competitive brands could be compared. The Datril print and broadcast advertisements showed Datril and Tylenol and stated that the only difference was the price. This copy strategy resulted in the following chronology of competitive strategies and counterstrategies:

Approximate dates	*Events*
June 1975	Datril advertised that it was $1.00 cheaper. McNeil notified Bristol-Myers that it had cut the price of Tylenol, but the Datril advertisements were run stating that it was $1.00 cheaper than Tylenol.[7]
	McNeil Laboratories (a division of Johnson & Johnson) spent $20 million reducing the price of Tylenol by 30 percent. Four hundred McNeil detail men and 330 salesmen from other divisions were used to "reduce the price on every Tylenol package we could find."[8]
	Johnson & Johnson complained to the ABC and NBC television networks. (CBS had previously refused to run the Datril commercial.) The networks finally refused the ads.[9]
	It appeared that Bristol-Myers did not think that the Tylenol price would be reduced.[10]
	Johnson & Johnson was shipping all of the Tylenol it could make. The Datril advertisements seemed to acquaint the public with Tylenol, which had not been advertised to the consumer, but only to doctors and pharmacists.[11]
	Two other acetaminophen products, by American Home Products and Enderin Company, increased their promotional efforts.[12]
July 1975	NBC established the policy of rejecting commercials that compare prices at retail when prices fluctuate widely.[13]
	Sterling Drug rolled out nonaspirin Bayer, an acetaminophen. Miles Laboratories test-marketed Actron, a nonaspirin pain reliever. Thompson Medical was selling its version, Dantol.[14]
Aug. 1975	The acetaminophen market was $75 million, a 45 percent increase over the previous year. The total analgesic market was $650 million.[15]
	Bristol-Myers' *aspirin* products, Bufferin and Excedrin, had "substantial gains," so Datril did not cannibalize other Bristol-Myers products.[16]

Sept. 1975	The Federal Trade Commission took a hands-off policy toward Johnson & Johnson's allegation of Datril's false-advertising claim, because the advertisement benefited the consumer by lowering the price of Tylenol.[17]

Sept. 1975 — The Federal Trade Commission took a hands-off policy toward Johnson & Johnson's allegation of Datril's false-advertising claim, because the advertisement benefited the consumer by lowering the price of Tylenol.[17]

Oct. 1975 — Tylenol offered $1.00 rebates, which were similar to Datril's rebate, at the end of the summer.[18]

Datril readied a children's version for entry into the $30 million (at factory) children's cold-market segment.[19]

Jan. 1976 — Datril resumed its $1.00 rebate.

March 1976 — Datril had gained 15 percent of the nonaspirin analgesic market, which was growing at a rate of 40 percent. Datril had only 2 percent of the total analgesic market.[20]

Tylenol scored "remarkable share increases" during the competitive battle and enjoyed good shelf space. Market studies by Neilsen revealed that Tylenol was cheaper in more stores than Datril.[21]

Tylenol's profit margin before the price war was estimated by financial analysts to be between 30 and 40 percent of sales.[22]

Part of the Tylenol counterstrategy was to bolster its sales force. McNeil salespeople were experienced in calling on doctors and drug stores, not food stores; therefore, it borrowed salespeople with this experience from other divisions of Johnson & Johnson.[23]

April 1976 — Datril changed its copy theme to: "Datril delivers more pain relief faster than Tylenol." McNeil charged that the difference was based on how tightly the tablets were pressed. McNeil quietly reformulated Tylenol so that it was packed more loosely, enabling the tablets to dissolve more quickly.[24]

McNeil asked television networks to stop running the "Datril is faster" campaign, but it was still being approved for airing.[25]

May 1976 — One year after the Datril introduction, Tylenol advertised to the consumer for the first time by introducing an extra-strength tablet. Datril sales were now $9 million, one-sixth of the Tylenol sales. The price of both products in New York City ranged from 79¢ to $2.00 for a bottle of 100 tablets.[26]

There were four segments in the analgesic market—regular strength ($300 million), extra strength ($150 million), sinus headache remedies, and pediatric products. The regular tablets were 325 mg; the extra-strength tablets contained 400 to 500 mg of ingredients. The Food and Drug Administration (FDA) was pushing for a uniform 325-mg tablet.[27]

Thus at the end of one year, the competitive activity of one new brand had involved all nonaspirin analgesic manufacturers, the major aspirin manufacturers, the media, and two regulatory agencies. This scenario illustrates why the competitive analysis is so important. But competitive analysis cannot reduce the uncertainty of competition, because it is impossible to know how competition will react. Some observers feel that Datril underestimated Tylenol's reaction.[28]

There are doubts about the effectiveness of comparative-advertising campaigns. Some observers conclude that such advertising helps the competitor and confuses the consumer. Others conclude that the way to chip away the market share of a leader is to create confusion and doubts about the leader's brand.[29]

Procter & Gamble versus Everyone Working as a product manager at Procter & Gamble (P&G) has been described as "a post-graduate course in marketing management." P&G

is expert in all phases of marketing management and market research. Its marketing expertise, its proven strategies (extensive product development, heavy promotion in the form of cents-off and couponing, heavy advertising, and aggressive selling), and its financial staying power have made P&G a threat to all others in the packaged-grocery industries. It has diversified from soaps and detergents to paper products, deodorants, coffee, potato chips, and cake mixes.

P&G uses a multiple-brand approach to cover many market segments and to bracket its competition. In the heavy-duty laundry detergent market, its ten brands held a 54 percent market share in 1975.[30] Three P&G light-duty liquid detergents held 36 percent of the market. Seven P&G brands had 35 percent of the bath- and toilet-soap market in 1975.[31] These market shares attest to the success of P&G's marketing strategies. But they also attract the attention of antitrust enforcers, who want to make certain that large shares do not lead to monopolies. Perhaps this is why P&G has aggressively diversified.

In 1957 P&G entered the paper-products market by acquiring Charmin Paper Mills, "a small and largely obsolete operation."[32] By 1971 P&G had almost the entire disposable-diaper market, because Scott Paper decided to discontinue its disposable diaper and take a $12.8 million write-off. P&G held 16 percent of the toilet-tissue market and 14 percent of the paper-towel market.

In Chapter 7 we saw that Aim toothpaste was cutting into P&G's Crest toothpaste. Crest had 40 percent of the market in 1974, but lost a point to Aim in 1975. Crest's counterstrategy included most of the familiar P&G strategies—an improved product (flavor), a flurry of promotional activity, new television commercials, and cents-off coupons.[33]

P&G had only one brand of coffee, Folger's. Perhaps this is why it had only 21 percent of the regular coffee market and 7 percent of the instant market. But 20 percent in 1974 put it in second place, with Maxwell House holding 25 percent. (The generic demand for coffee decreased in 1974 by 4.7 percent,[34] which added to the challenge for coffee marketers.) Thus P&G captured a major share of the coffee market without using its usual strategy of brand proliferation.

COUNTERSTRATEGIES   In Chapter 7 we discussed several brand-marketing strategies. Now we will examine how competitors reacted to these strategies and how the original brand countered the reaction. These examples will illustrate the dynamics of competition and the difficulties in measuring and modeling competitive reactions.

McDonald's Reacts to Burger King   The Burger King "Have it your way" theme provided four years of rapid growth. This theme forced McDonald's to a more service-oriented theme: "We do it all for you." When McDonald's outspent Burger King four to one in advertising media, Burger King decided to stress other benefits—faster service, fresher products, and higher-quality service.[35]

The original Burger King goal was to gain a larger market share than McDonald's. In 1975 Burger King had increased sales over 1974 by 32 percent, and it had 5.3 percent of the market. McDonald's increased sales 26 percent and had a 19.6 percent market share.[36] Burger King then decided to rethink its goals. It changed its goal to being the leader in sales per store.

After four years of rapid growth, Burger King faced another problem—maturation. Growth had come from opening new stores, which required an organizational emphasis on operations. As the market approached saturation, Burger King had to shift to the strategy of increasing sales per store, which emphasizes marketing. This shift in emphasis required a reorganization of the marketing department.

McDonald's countered Burger King's Whopper with a McFeast. Burger King, in turn, followed McDonald's innovations by testing breakfasts and chicken. Thus the competitive interaction in the fast-food industry is likely to continue for a long time. A large and growing market, it accounted for 27 percent of the "eating out" expenditures in 1975, or 4 percent of disposable income.[37] But will this market continue to grow? There is some early evidence that the fast-food field is becoming saturated.[38]

Gillette Reacts to Bic   In Chapter 7 we saw how Schick used a strategy against Gillette that Gillette could not use because it would cannibalize its own double-edge market. We also learned that the Gillette pricing strategy had been to sell the razors at a low price and make money on the blades. Thus a twin-blade disposable razor would be counter to product and pricing strategies. But in 1976 Gillette seems to have been forced into introducing "Good News," a 25¢ twin-blade disposable razor for men. It was a reaction to the European introduction of a comparable product by Bic Pen Corporation.[39]

Gillette had been competing heavily with Bic in writing instruments and disposable butane lighters. Some observers thought that the "Good News" introduction was a message to Bic to stay out of the American market.[40]

NONRETAIL COMPETITION   The examples presented so far suggest that competition exists only at the retail level. However, it is also useful to look at competition among advertising agencies and industrial marketers.

Advertising Agencies Compete for the Toyota Account   A casual reading of *Advertising Age* reveals that there is extensive competition among agencies. For example, in 1975 three advertising agencies—Dancer-Fitzgerald-Sample (DFS), Wells, Rich, Greene, and Ted Bates & Co.—were competing for the $30 million account of Toyota Motor Sales. Toyota selected DFS after an extensive review of proposals. Consumer research done by the agency was credited with contributing the winning theme: "Toyota: The premium economy car."[41]

Competition in Minicomputers   The 40 percent annual growth rate in minicomputers during 1972 attracted many competitors. Capital needs were low and technology was simple. But by 1975 at least 12 of the 50 companies that had entered the market had dropped out. It looked as though only a dozen competitors would remain, with the top four accounting for 70 percent of the market.[42]

The industry strategy was one of sharp price cutting; some units were cut more than 50 percent in one year. While the marketing was growing, industry capacity grew even faster, because technology was readily available to anyone who wanted to enter the field. The marginal firms could not cover all costs and were driven from the business. The minicomputer industry illustrates that easy entry leads to excess capacity, which leads to price cutting, which eliminates the marginal firms from the field.

MAPPING COMPETITORS' STRENGTHS AND WEAKNESSES   The process of analyzing our strengths and weaknesses relative to those of competitors is greatly facilitated by the process of brand mapping, which was illustrated in Chapter 7.[43] Analysis of these maps can help the strategist to identify opportunities and potential competition and to develop competitive strategies.

Identifying Opportunities Brand maps (see Chapter 7) help to identify *holes in benefit space* where no brand is meeting a perceived need. An alert strategist will reposition present brands or develop new ones to meet an unmet need. For example, Fig. 7.2 suggested that soft drink brands should be repositioned toward the tart and sociable segments of the brand map to make them more attractive to the teenage market segment.

Identifying Potential Competition Brand and concept maps may be used to identify *potential* competition for new products or for new-product concepts. When a new concept is tested, a description of the product is given to the respondent, and she or he is asked to compare it with existing products.

Maps that position new concepts and existing brands suggest which products would compete if a new product were introduced near them. Figure 9.1 illustrates which existing brands are likely to compete if a new diet product is introduced. For

Fig. 9.1. Positioning new diet products among existing food products. (Y. Wind and P. J. Robinson, "Product Positioning: An Application of Multidimensional Scaling," in R. I. Haley, ed., *Attitude Research in Transition,* Chicago: American Marketing Association, 1972, p. 165. Reprinted by permission.)

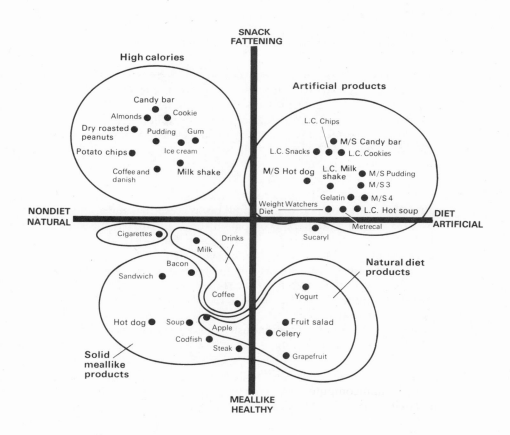

example, if the concept with the code name "M/S 4" is introduced, it will probably cut into the markets of gelatin, Metrecal, and Weight Watchers Diet. The marketing strategy for M/S 4 should include an estimate of the response of these competitors. Will they cut price or increase promotion? How would we respond to their reactions?

Developing Competitive Strategies Brand maps are not limited to grocery products. Figure 9.2 illustrates how mapping can be used for positioning a new bank financial service. This map positions respondents' perceptions of the new services *and* the occupations of persons who are likely to use each service, which is why it is called a *joint*-space map.

A comparison of the services and the perceptions of the occupations of persons who will use them reveals that there are prestige and nonprestige services. Investment evaluation is perceived as applicable to a physician, whereas monetary counseling would be used by a restaurant waitress. These joint-space maps provide useful insight for the development of copy and media strategies.

Fig. 9.2. Joint-space configuration of eight financial services and twelve occupations. (Y. Wind and P. J. Robinson, "Product Positioning: An Application of Multidimensional Scaling," in R. I. Haley, ed., *Attitude Research in Transition,* Chicago: American Marketing Association, 1972, p. 170. Reprinted by permission.)

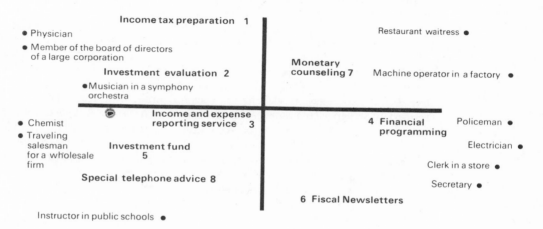

ANTICIPATING COMPETITIVE BEHAVIOR The examples earlier in this chapter illustrate that marketing strategies should anticipate competitors' behavior as conditions change in the marketplace. Some companies study competitors' past reactions to changes in price or new-product introductions for clues in predicting future behavior. Economic theory suggests two early-warning measures when there are few sellers in the market. (In economic terms this is the oligopolistic situation.) Excess productive capacity and declining product costs create a competitive environment that is volatile, especially with regard to declines in price. Marketing strategists, therefore, should include measures of industry capacity and costs of production in their competitive analyses.

Excess Capacity The minicomputer industry illustrates the need to estimate the capacity that exists in an industry. Failure to do so proved fatal for 70 percent of the firms in that industry. Most firms make some rough estimate of the generic demand for a product and a rough estimate of its market share, but few firms estimate the *future productive capacity of the industry*. Some firms never consider the importance of future capacity. Those that recognize its importance find it difficult to measure.

Measuring the future capacity of an industry requires estimates of the plans of present producers and those of firms not in the industry at present. For example, Bic Pen Company's movement into the razor industry would have been almost impossible to detect without commercial espionage or the observation of a test market. (Test markets are reported in *Advertising Age*.) Planned expansion of capacity for existing products may be even more difficult to detect until a new building is erected.

Ease of entry, because of low capital and technological requirements, results in a rapid buildup of excess capacity, as was the case in minicomputers. The chemical and petroleum industries have a different problem. In these industries capital and technical requirements are substantial, so new plants require five or ten years of preparation. Several firms may identify excess demand and start expanding capacity, unknown to other firms. When they come "on stream," the shortage suddenly turns to a glut.

Competitive behavior during periods of *excess capacity* generally takes on some form of *price cutting* if the market is operating freely, or *price collusion* if the market is not competitive. The latter is illegal under the antitrust laws, as we will see in the following chapter.

Declining Product Costs Accountants have long known that per unit *direct labor* costs decline a given percent each time cumulative total output is doubled. This is known as the "learning curve." The Boston Consulting Group (BCG) observed that *total unit costs* declined by 20 to 30 percent each time cumulative production doubled.[44] This held true for the industry as well as for the individual producer. This relationship was termed the "experience curve." BCG found that *prices* followed this same pattern when markets were competitive. A volatile situation for price cutting exists when the *industry* price does not follow the slope of the total-cost curve. Perhaps a price leader holds the price high and one oligopolist breaks ranks and cuts prices. Others follow and, according to the BCG, will stop price cutting when the price parallels the downward slope of the total-cost curve, as is shown in Fig. 9.3.

Fig. 9.3. The competitive kink in experience curves. (W. E. Cox, Jr., "Product Portfolio Strategy: A Review of the Boston Consulting Group Approach to Marketing Strategy," in *Combined Proceedings: 1975 American Marketing Association*, Chicago: American Marketing Association, 1975, pp. 465–475.)

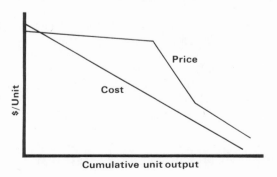

The marketing strategist can plot the "experience curve" for an industry and identify periods of competitive volatility. The BCG has identified experience curves for 24 industries. These curves help explain the rapid shakeout of firms in the integrated-circuit industry. By the end of 1964 accumulated total 1964 production was two million units and the price was $16.91 per unit. By the end of 1968 the accumulated industry volume was 242 million units and the price per unit (in constant dollars) was $1.87.[45]

(Critics of the learning- and experience-curve strategies feel that they can lead to narrowly specialized work groups that reduce the stimulation for innovation. Furthermore, they argue, experience curves disregard product or process design changes that were introduced during the period considered.[46])

Models of Competitive Behavior   Models of competitive behavior tend to borrow from the fields of game theory, econometrics, and simulation. Formal theories of competition may be found in the classical economic models and the more recent theories of games and economic behavior, but these are of only limited use in the practical world of marketing strategy.[47]   Instead, marketers tend to find econometric modeling and simulation modeling more appropriate. Some recent researchers have combined the approaches.[48] These combinations use econometric models to predict generic demand and simulation to test the effect of various competitive strategies on market share.

COMPETITIVE STRATEGIES   The development of successful competitive strategies is not a mechanical process that uses models or ratios. Competitive strategies require an understanding of generic demand, brand demand, the behavior of competitors, and the legal environment. But different combinations of these four elements suggest that some strategies have a higher probability of success than others. Here we will examine three situations—product life-cycle strategies, product-portfolio strategies, and high market-share strategies.

Product Life-Cycle Strategies   In Chapter 4 we saw that the PIMS project led the researchers to the conclusion that companies with the largest market share had the highest profits. This study recommended three strategies through the product life cycle. During the introduction of a new product the strategy should be to *build* a market share, which requires heavy investment in advertising and promotion. Once the share has been established, these expenditures may be reduced to a level that will *hold* the market share in the face of competitive brands. When the product has reached its mature state, where generic demand is constant and perhaps declining, the best strategy may be one of *harvesting*. This strategy reduces advertising and promotional expenditures and costs on previous expenditures, thereby increasing profits. In order to choose one of these strategies, it is necessary to first identify the product's position in the product life cycle.

Product-Portfolio Strategies   *Life-cycle strategies* focus on the *rate of growth* of a new product. *Product-portfolio strategies* add the *competitive dimension* by examining market share.[49] This creates a two-dimensional matrix, as shown in Fig. 9.4. Rates of growth and market share are divided simply into high and low, thereby creating four cells, each with a different strategy. Each of these cells is viewed as an investment; hence the term *product-portfolio strategies*. The goal of the portfolio strategies is to move products into the *cash cow* classification, where the market share may be maintained

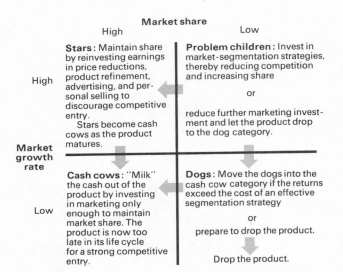

Market share

	High	Low
High	**Stars:** Maintain share by reinvesting earnings in price reductions, product refinement, advertising, and personal selling to discourage competitive entry. Stars become cash cows as the product matures.	**Problem children:** Invest in market-segmentation strategies, thereby reducing competition and increasing share or reduce further marketing investment and let the product drop to the dog category.
Low	**Cash cows:** "Milk" the cash out of the product by investing in marketing only enough to maintain market share. The product is now too late in its life cycle for a strong competitive entry.	**Dogs:** Move the dogs into the cash cow category if the returns exceed the cost of an effective segmentation strategy or prepare to drop the product. Drop the product.

Market growth rate (vertical axis label, High to Low)

Fig. 9.4. Product-portfolio strategies. (W. E. Cox, Jr., "Product Portfolio Strategy: A Review of the Boston Consulting Group Approach to Marketing Strategy," in *Combined Proceedings: 1975 American Marketing Association*, Chicago: American Marketing Association, 1975, pp. 465–475. Reprinted by permission.)

with the minimum investment in marketing effort. This amounts to "milking" the product for cash; hence the term *cash cow*.

Product-portfolio strategies require decisions in the areas of market share, pricing, promotion, existing products, and new products. Table 9.1 summarizes marketing strategies that are appropriate for investment, earnings, and immediate cash flow. Product managers are reluctant to suggest the strategies associated with managing for immediate cash. Foregoing market share, reducing volume, and avoiding promotion run counter to their thinking—and counter to the criteria for rewarding product managers. (Another version of the portfolio strategy appeared in Table 4.2.)

High Market-Share Strategies Companies with large market shares may make larger profits, but they are also larger targets for competition and antitrust action by the Federal Trade Commission, the Justice Department, or consumer-interest groups. Marketing strategists can be frustrated when economies of scale in production and promotion suggest a larger share of market than is possible, given the potential reactions from competitors and public-policy groups. Marketing strategists, therefore, must identify that market share which is likely to elicit an unfavorable response and then develop strategies to meet this situation. Perhaps the product will be treated as a "cash cow" just prior to its marketing share reaching the critical point. The cash may be used to diversify into new products that are in different industries, thereby avoiding antitrust action.

Identifying the market share that will result in antitrust action is difficult. In the next chapter we will see that antitrusters have continuously lowered the percentage of market share that they consider monopolistic.

A strategy of *demarketing* has been recommended as a means for reducing dangerously high market shares.[50] This strategy is essentially a passive one of letting

Table 9.1   Marketing portfolio strategies

	Strategy adopted for division or product line		
Marketing decision area	*Invest for future growth*	*Manage for earnings*	*Manage for immediate cash*
Market share	Aggressively build across all segments	Target efforts to high-return/high-growth segments Protect current franchises	Forego share development for improved profits
Pricing	Lower to build shares	Stabilize for maximum profit contribution	Raise, even at expense of volume
Promotion	Invest heavily to build share	Invest as market dictates	Avoid
Existing product line	Expand volume Add line extensions to fill out product categories	Shift mix to higher-profit product categories	Eliminate low-contribution products/varieties
New products	Expand product line by acquisition, self-manufacture, or joint venture	Add products selectively and in controlled stages of commitment	Add only sure winners

Louis V. Gerstner, Jr., "Can Strategic Planning Pay Off?" *Business Horizons*, December 1972, p. 15. Copyright, 1972, by the Foundation for the School of Business at Indiana University. Reprinted by permission.

competition gain share. The strategy of ReaLemon Foods, a subsidiary of Borden, is an example of demarketing.[51] ReaLemon held approximately 90 percent of the reconstituted–lemon juice market in 1970, when it began to allow competitors to make inroads. By 1972 ReaLemon considered the gains of one competitor to be too large, so it reacted. In 1974 the Federal Trade Commission filed a complaint, charging ReaLemon with predatory pricing and sales tactics. The marketing-management problem here is distinguishing between aggressive competition and the Federal Trade Commission's view of predatory tactics.

COMPETITIVE CONTINGENCY PLANNING   A good marketing plan includes answers to many "what if" questions. What will we do if there is a shortage of material? What will be our reaction to a sudden change—either an increase or decrease—in demand for our product? Competitive "what if" questions need to be asked in all areas of the marketing mix. What will we do if competitive new products cut into our market share? What is our strategy for a competitive price cut? How will we react to a competitor's copying our promotional strategy? Contingency planning is more important to a competitive analysis than during an analysis of demand or public policy, because the competitive scene changes so quickly.

It is impossible to identify all contingencies. Furthermore, limited resources prevent developing a plan for every contingency. Thus contingency planning must be limited to those one or two events that could destroy the entire marketing strategy. Beyond planning for the one or two major contingencies, the marketing planner must rely on *flexibility* to cope with additional, less critical contingencies.

Horizontal competition, the most familiar situation, occurs when two firms compete at the same level in the channel of distribution. Thus Burger King and McDonald's compete at the retail level; Datril competes with Tylenol at the manufacturing level, depending on advertising to reach the consumer. McDonald's and Tylenol did not seem to have a contingency plan for the strategies of their competitors. But Burger King and Datril did not seem to have a contingency plan for the *reactions* of their competitors. Thus contingency planning should include answers to: "What is our strategy if competition reacts this way or that way to our initial strategy?"

An example of a contingency plan for horizontal competition is reported by Gerstner.[52] A packaging company selling a commodity-type product was caught off guard by a small competitor when the latter increased its market share through a sharp price cut. Now the packaging company regularly reviews the potential prices of the smaller firm and meticulously plans a contingency strategy. When the smaller firm made its second move, the packaging firm "responded immediately and effectively."[53]

Vertical competition frequently takes place within a channel of distribution between members at different levels within the channel. For example, a large retail chain such as A&P integrates backward until it owns bakeries and other food processors. Thus A&P is then competing with wholesalers, food brokers, and producers in the bakery industry.

A contingency plan for vertical competition has been reported by Gerstner.[54] An electronics manufacturer made 30 percent of its sales to a single customer. Management asked, "What if this customer integrates backward into the manufacturing function?" The manufacturer did a detailed economic analysis of the risks and disadvantages that the customer would face if it integrated backward. One year later the analysis was used to convince the customer that this tentative step toward backward integration would be unwise.

MODELS AND MEASURES FOR COMPETITIVE ANALYSIS

Competitive Models   As important as competitive analysis is to the success of a marketing strategy, there is little formal theory to aid the marketing planner. Economics contributes the oligopolistic model of competitive behavior. This model states that when there are few competitors in the market, a price drop by one will be followed by others, but a price increase will not be followed. This competitive behavior produces the well-known kinked-demand curve.

The oligopolistic model has several limitations. It focuses on price competition, but much of marketing competitive behavior is nonprice. Furthermore, competitors may not compete directly on the same variable. For example, if one company increases advertising, another company may choose to have a contest for its salespeople. Modeling these competitive reactions is extremely difficult.[55] The second limitation is that the model does not describe competitive behavior during periods of shortages and inflation. Many competitors are happy to follow a price *increase* during these conditions.

The traditional oligopolistic model yielded to a new approach for studying competitive behavior—*game theory*.[56] Game theory analyzes payoffs under varying corporate alternative strategies and competitive reactions. A simple game may be expressed in a two-by-two matrix. For example, assume that a coffee roaster is considering introducing a new product that will have some noncoffee ingredients, such as grains, to reduce the cost of the total product. The payoff matrix may look like the following:

		Competitor	
		Does not introduce	Introduces
Company	Do not introduce	$0	− $15 million
	Introduce	$30 million	$10 million

The decision of whether or not to introduce will be based on the company's estimate of the competitor's reaction, the personal-risk functions of the company's executives, and whether it has other alternatives that will produce a payoff greater than $10 million if competition does introduce a comparable product.

Competitive Information Systems   Analysis of competitive behavior requires some form of competitive information system. Few business firms have a systematic procedure for collecting competitive information, most of which is readily available in public sources.[57] The type of information needed includes all that we can learn about a competitor's marketing mix, research and development, production methods and costs, organizational designs, financial status, and strengths and weaknesses.

Unethical means of intelligence gathering will probably be counterproductive for a variety of reasons, including the possibility that the agent may be a double agent. In buying information a firm may unknowingly be supplying information by indicating those areas of greatest interest to it. Some of the usual ethical sources are business periodicals, financial reference services, field salesforce, purchasing department, banks, our key executives, suppliers to the research and development department, government sources, customers, professional associations, financial analysts, and annual reports.

Planning for Competitive Reactions   A marketing strategist will want to evaluate the effect of competitive reactions when strategic alternatives are being considered. This may be accomplished easily by adding columns to the tree diagram for evaluating alternatives (see Chapter 3). These additional columns would require estimates of competitive reactions and the effect on future profits. A simple diagram is as follows:

	Alternative strategies this period	Expected profit this period	Competitor's reaction next period	Effect on our profit next period
Opportunity or problem	Cut price	$0.7 m	Cut price	− $0.3 m
	Advertise	$0.5 m	Advertise	$0.1 m
	Use premiums	$0.4 m	No reaction	$0.3 m

The use of premiums will maximize profit over two periods, whereas cutting price would maximize it for one period. In a highly competitive industry the strategist may want to think through for several periods the likely reactions and counterreactions that an initial strategy might precipitate.

SUMMARY   An analysis of competitive strengths and weaknesses is the basis for a competitive marketing strategy. The competitive strategies used by Kodak, Datril, and Procter & Gamble illustrate the dynamics of competition. But competitors react when attacked, so their reaction must be anticipated when developing a marketing plan. Competitive counterstrategies were illustrated by the cases of Polaroid, Tylenol, McDonald's, and Gillette.

Brand maps help us to visualize the strengths and weaknesses of competitors. This visualization helps marketers to develop new strategies for existing products as well as to identify opportunities for new products. The positioning of new-product concepts on a map with existing brands helps us to anticipate the competition.

There are few theories that will help us to anticipate how competition will react. The economic theory of oligopoly (few sellers) alerts us to measure industry capacity, and experience curves urge us to consider declining industry total costs. Excess capacity and high prices when costs have declined create situations that lead to competitive price cutting.

Competitive strategies should vary over the product life cycle. When a company has a large number of products, it may take an investment-portfolio approach toward competitive strategy. Firms with a high market share tend to be larger targets for competition, antitrust action, and consumer complaints. Therefore, they should have a strategy of diversification when their share reaches a critical level.

A good plan provides for the one or two contingencies that could destroy a strategy. Flexibility must be used to cope with the less critical events.

DISCUSSION CASE: SCOOP ICE CREAM'S PLAN FOR 1972

The 1971 Scoop marketing plan was implemented as recommended (see Chapter 2). Generic-demand projections were accurate. Scoop attained its goal of 2.4 million cases and a 2.4 percent market share. The trial rates were 35 percent of the 40 percent of the housewives who were aware of Scoop and its attributes. One-fourth of the triers made repeat purchases.

The focus-group interviews revealed that families in the Southeast served fewer desserts and that they reserved ice cream for special occasions. This was especially true in the lower income groups. The Nielsen index showed that Scoop had a distribution rate of 80 percent in supermarkets, 5 percent in ice cream stores, and 10 percent in drug stores.

In May 1971 blind product-taste tests revealed that Scoop was preferred by 69 percent of the housewives, whereas 19 percent preferred existing brands. Reasons for preferring Scoop included the following: better flavor, 61 percent; better taste, 76 percent; doesn't crystallize, 73 percent; and overall quality, 71 percent. In June 1971 market research studies showed that 58 percent of the housewives thought that Scoop took too much time and trouble to make. Of those housewives who had not tried Scoop, 33 percent did not believe that it could taste better than regular ice cream. The trade preferred Scoop because it carried a higher margin than ice cream and did not require refrigeration for stocking and display. Recall tests showed 40 percent recall of Scoop's low price among housewives.

During 1971 Admiral Foods test-marketed in Kansas City a competitive mix, "Confectionery Ice Cream Mix," and achieved a 2.9 percent share of dollar volume.

This case is abstracted from the "Scoop Ice Cream Mix" case, which was developed for the Association of National Advertisers (ANA) by Booz, Allen & Hamilton, Inc., for use in ANA Seminars on Creative Advertising. The case material is copyrighted by the ANA and appears in its publication *Effective Marketing Management*, by F. Beaven Ennis, copyrighted 1973. Permission to abstract the case and use parts of the marketing plan in the above text has been granted by Herbert A. Ahlgren, Vice-President of ANA. This permission is gratefully acknowledged. Some data have been modified to emphasize particular points of marketing.

Scoop's advertising agency projected the Kansas City spending to national levels as follows:

| | Confectionery spends, in $ millions | | |
	First six months	Second six months	Total
Media	$4.0	$2.5	$6.5
10¢ mailed coupon	1.2	—	1.2
Other promotion	1.1	0.8	1.9
Totals	$6.3	$3.3	$9.6

These spending rates were considerably higher than Scoop's during 1971, when it was introduced. The advertising budgets of the three largest ice cream producers were less than $400,000 each. Promotion on new flavors is generally a 50¢ case allowance to the trade. The trade is very price sensitive. A consumer survey in Kansas City indicated that consumers perceived that the benefits and disadvantages of Scoop and Confectionery Ice Cream Mix were about equal. Confectionery sold for an average of $1.05 per gallon.

Production capacity will be adequate for 1972, but not for 1973.

ASSIGNMENTS

1. Develop an Environmental Analysis Worksheet for 1972, similar to the one in Chapter 2.
2. Develop a Strategy Worksheet for 1972. Since this is the second year for this product, the 1972 Strategy Worksheet should have three columns—current strategy, recommended strategy, and estimated effect. An example appears in Fig. 2.1.
3. Prepare a 1972 marketing plan for Scoop.

DISCUSSION QUESTIONS

1. If you were a marketing planner for Schick, how would you react to the 25¢ disposable razor introductions by Gillette and Bic?
2. Assume that as marketing manager for a company that sells vodka, you are trying to develop contingency plans to respond to possible horizontal competitive situations. Develop a reactive strategy for each of the following situations. (Your only competitor markets a product with the same benefits, but at a higher price than your product.) In your answers, consider the effects that your strategy may have on (a) generic demand, (b) brand demand, (c) gross margin, and (d) overall profit for your product.

Situation 1: Your competitor lowers the price (consider your competitor's new price to be the absolute lowest that a product can be priced and still be profitable).

Situation 2: Competitor increases price.

Situation 3: Competitor introduces another vodka (same benefits) with a different name and at a price slightly under your current price.

Situation 4: Competitor increases advertising and offers (via mail) a free booklet on mixing vodka drinks.

3. Explain the difference between the learning curve and the experience curve. What significance do these declining product-cost theories have with regard to (a) competitive pricing strategies, (b) generic demand, and (c) product-line extensions via a skimming strategy?

4. Give an example for each of the four cells of the product-portfolio strategies (Fig. 9.4). How do the different stages in a product's life cycle relate to the four portfolio strategies?

NOTES

1. S. Tilles, "Making Strategy Explicit," Boston, Massachusetts: Boston Consulting Group, 1966, excerpted in *Business Strategy*, ed. H. I. Ansoff (Baltimore: Penguin, 1969), pp. 180–209.

2. B. Donath, "New Polaroid SX-70 Ready; Kodak Entry Near?" *Advertising Age*, January 5, 1976, pp. 1, 49.

3. "Kodak vs. Polaroid, Finally," *Sales & Marketing Management*, May 10, 1976, pp. 10, 12.

4. *Ibid.*

5. *Ibid.*; and W. M. Carley, "Polaroid Seen Wary, Worried as It Girds for Kodak Arrival in Instant-Photo Field," *Wall Street Journal*, April 16, 1976, p. 4.

6. *Ibid.*

7. *Advertising Age*, July 14, 1975.

8. *Advertising Age*, March 29, 1976, and July 28, 1976.

9. *Advertising Age*, July 28, 1975.

10. *Ibid.*

11. *Ibid.*

12. *Ibid.*

13. *Advertising Age*, August 11, 1975.

14. *Advertising Age*, August 11, 1975, and September 1, 1975.

15. *Advertising Age*, October 6, 1975.

16. *Ibid.*

17. *Advertising Age*, October 13, 1975.

18. *Advertising Age*, November 3, 1975.

19. *Ibid.*

20. *Advertising Age*, March 29, 1976.

21. *Ibid.*

22. *Wall Street Journal*, May 24, 1976.

23. *Ibid.*

24. *Advertising Age*, April 26, 1976.

25. *Ibid.*

26. *Wall Street Journal*, May 24, 1976.

27. *Advertising Age*, May 17, 1976.

28. W. Copulsky, "Tylenol-Datril 'Poker Game' Analyzed from Marketing Strategy Viewpoint," *Marketing News*, March 12, 1976, p. 7.

29. "Comparative Ads a 'Disaster'?" *Advertising Age*, October 20, 1975, p. 14.

30. J. C. Maxwell, Jr., "Soap, Detergent Trend: Dollars Up, Volume Down, Maxwell Report Says," *Advertising Age*, June 21, 1976, p. 80.

31. *Ibid.*

32. J. Hyatt and J. E. Conney, "How Procter & Gamble Put the Big Squeeze on Scott Paper, Co.," *Wall Street Journal*, October 20, 1971, pp. 1–2.

33. N. Giges, "P&G's Crest Efforts Taking Aim against Growing Lever Share," *Advertising Age*, January 26, 1976, p. 2.

34. J. C. Maxwell, Jr., "GF Boosts Coffee Share in 1974: Maxwell," *Advertising Age*, September 8, 1975, pp. 24, 26.

35. "Reshuffled Burger King: Giving Marketing Their Way," *Advertising Age*, May 24, 1976, p. 1.

36. "McDonald's Stretches Lead in Fast Foods," *Advertising Age*, June 7, 1976, p. 30.

37. *Ibid.*

38. N. Howard, "Market Saturation Specter Looms over Fast-Foods," *Advertising Age*, March 21, 1977, pp. 3, 82.

39. J. J. O'Connor, "Did Gillette Rush Intro of Good News to Avert the Bad?" *Advertising Age*, February 23, 1976, pp. 3, 139.

40. *Ibid.*

41. "D-F-S Wins Toyota Account over Ted Bates, Wells, Rich," *Advertising Age*, October 27, 1975, p. 1.

42. "Bowling over the Minis," *Forbes*, May 1, 1975, p. 42.

43. For a discussion of techniques, *see* P. E. Green and V. R. Rao, *Applied Multidimensional Scaling: A Comparison of Approaches and Algorithms* (New York: Holt, Rinehart and Winston, 1972); and R. M. Johnson, "Market Segmentation: A Strategic Management Tool," *Journal of Marketing Research* **8** (February 1971): 13–18.

44. W. E. Cox, Jr., "Product Portfolio Strategy: A Review of the Boston Consulting Group Approach to Marketing Strategy," in *Combined Proceedings: 1975 American Marketing Association* (Chicago: American Marketing Association, 1975), pp. 465–475.

45. *Ibid.*

46. W. J. Abernathy and K. Wayne, "Limits of the Learning Curve," *Harvard Business Review* (September-October 1974): 109–119.

47. R. L. Schultz and J. A. Dodson, Jr., "An Empirical-Simulation Approach to Competition," Institute for Research in the Behavioral, Economic and Management Sciences, Krannert Graduate School of Industrial Administration Working Paper No. 420, July 1973.

48. *Ibid.*; J. J. Lambin, "Optimal Allocation of Competitive Marketing Efforts: An Empirical Study," *Journal of Business* **43** (October 1970): 468–484; and J. D. C. Little, "A Model of Adaptive Control of Promotional Spending," *Operations Research* **14** (November-December 1966): 175–197.

49. Cox, *op. cit.*

50. P. N. Bloom and P. Kotler, "Strategies for High Market-Share Companies," *Harvard Business Review* (November-December 1975): 63–72.

51. *Ibid.*, p. 70.

52. L. V. Gerstner, Jr., "Can Strategic Planning Pay Off?" *Business Horizons* (December 1972): 9–11.

53. *Ibid.*, p. 11.

54. *Ibid.*

55. R. E. Quandt, "Estimating the Effectiveness of Advertising: Some Pitfalls in Econometric Methods," *Journal of Marketing Research* **1** (May 1964): 51–60.

56. J. VonNeumann and O. Morgenstern, *Theory of Games and Economic Behavior*, 3rd ed. (New York: Wiley, 1953).

57. D. I. Cleland and W. R. King, "Competitive Business Intelligence Systems," *Business Horizons* (December 1975): 19–28.

SUGGESTED READINGS

Buzzell, R. D., B. T. Gale, and R. G. M. Sultan, "Market Share—A Key to Profitability," *Harvard Business Review* (January-February 1975): 97–105.

Fruhan, W. E., Jr., "Pyrrhic Victories in Fights for Market Share," *Harvard Business Review* (September-October 1972): 100–107.

Kotler, P., "Competitive Strategies for New Product Marketing over the Life Cycle," *Management Science* (December 1965): B 104–119.

———, "The Competitive Marketing Simulator—A New Management Tool," *California Management Review* **7**, 3 (Spring 1965): 49–60.

Naylor, T. H., *Corporate Simulation Models* (Reading, Mass.: Addison-Wesley, 1978).

Wall, J. L., "What the Competition Is Doing: Your Need to Know," *Harvard Business Review* (November-December 1974): 20–24, 28.

ENVIRONMENTAL ANALYSIS WORKSHEET

Environmental elements	Facts	Assumptions or research needed	Conclusions

Organizational values, objectives, and policies (4)

Organizational design (5)

Situation
   Generic demand (6)
   Brand demand (7)
   Competition (9)
   Public policy (10)

Opportunities (2)

Problems

MARKETING PLAN (CONSUMER PRODUCT)

Current performance
Recommendations
Effect of recommendations on income
Situation analysis
Opportunities and problems
Strategies
Tests and research
Supporting documents
   Comparative budgets
   Media allocation schedule
   Promotion control sheet

STRATEGY WORKSHEET

Opportunities and problems in rank order to importance

    1.
    2.

    n.

	Current strategy	Alternatives and recommended strategy	Estimated Effect

Demand strategy
  Generic
  Brand			

Strategic goals
  Financial
  Marketing			

Marketing-mix strategies
  Product (12)
  Pricing (13)
  Channel and logistics (14)
  Advertising and promotional (15)
  Sales management (16)			

Research (3)			
Profit plan			
Evaluation and control (19)			

CHAPTER **10**

Analyzing the Public-Policy Environment

LEARNING OBJECTIVES   After studying this chapter you should:

1. Understand the evolution of United States public policies toward business and their influence on marketing strategies.
2. Understand how public policy is an aid to business.
3. Know how public policy creates marketing opportunities as well as constrains strategies.
4. Know how *antitrust* policies constrain product, price, channel, and advertising strategies.
5. Understand the opportunities and problems created by the consumer movement and the concern for the environment.
6. Be able to define and use the following concepts:

Public policy	Shared monopoly
Antitrust	Costs and benefits of regulations
Atomistic competition	Consumerism
Price flexibility	Environmentalism
Per se violations	

SOME ANALYTICAL QUESTIONS FOR OPENERS

1. How does public policy affect our marketing strategy?
2. Does our marketing plan violate existing public policies?
3. How will changes in public policy affect our plan?

The topic of public policy could be introduced at many points in the planning process. The ethical dimensions, such as illegal political contributions, could be discussed under the topic of corporate policies. Antitrust policies influence the organizational design of firms. The demand for products that conserve energy and do not pollute the environment is a suitable topic for the discussion of generic demand. Reactions to competition must consider the possibility of charges of predatory behavior. Thus public policy is part of each step in the analysis of the company's environment.

Public policy strongly influences each of the elements in the marketing-mix strategy. Products must not be harmful. Price fixing is illegal. Channels of distribution must be competitive. Advertising cannot be deceptive. Sales tactics in door-to-door selling are subject to legal action. Thus the marketing manager must be aware of the public-policy implications of his or her strategy.

This discussion of the public-policy environment has not been dispersed throughout these many chapters, so that you may see the philosophy of public policy as a unit. This chapter is positioned at the end of the situation analysis because public policy is very much part of this analysis. In fact, some marketing chief executives spend one-half of their time on public-policy matters. Placing this discussion before the discussion of strategy will help you to keep public-policy constraints in mind as the marketing-mix strategy is developed.

PUBLIC POLICY AS AN AID TO BUSINESS It is easy to think only of the negative business effects of public policy. But in fact many federal agencies and laws are designed to help businesspeople. For example, the United States Department of Commerce aids businesspeople with information and assistance for foreign trade. The department's Bureau of Census collects valuable data on population, housing, manufacturers, wholesalers, retailers, and transportation. Laws for patents, trademarks, and trade names protect businesspeople's investments in new-product development. The Bureau of Standards provides uniform measurements, the absence of which would lead to chaotic marketing. Contract law facilitates marketing transactions. Thus the federal government should not be regarded as antibusiness. Neither can it be accused of being anti-advertising; in 1975 it was the tenth largest advertiser in the United States ($113 million), positioned between R. J. Reynolds and Colgate-Palmolive.[1]

PUBLIC POLICY TO PRESERVE, PROTECT, AND CONSERVE Public policy in the United States has been designed to *preserve competition*, *protect the consumer*, and *conserve natural resources and the environment*. Historically, legislation was concerned first with competition (late nineteenth century), then the consumer (early and midtwentieth century), and finally natural resources and the environment (late twentieth century). The three sections that follow are designed to give the planner a working knowledge of marketing law and public policy as they relate to the planning process. The planner should search for the marketing opportunities as well as the constraints that they place on strategies.

The discussion of antitrust is extensive because of recent trends toward stricter enforcement in this area of public policy. Furthermore, antitrust policy affects all of the elements of the marketing mix, so a marketing manager must have a working knowledge of the subject.

Preserve Competition (or, Antitrust Caveats for the Marketing Planner)[2] Until recently "antitrust" seemed hardly relevant to the marketing planner's daily problems of *profit, market share, product-line extensions, advertising expenditures, copy themes, channel strategies,* and *rates of return*. Antitrust was thought of as *pricing* practices involving competitors and was the concern of corporate counsel or someone else. But the scene has changed. New tests of competition are being expounded by the Federal Trade Commission (FTC), the Department of Justice, and private plaintiffs and are being adopted by the courts. These tests include profit, market share, product-line extensions, advertising expenditures, channel strategies, and rate of return—the very heart of the marketing plan; and now the FTC *specifies* copy for "corrective advertisements." Some antitrust laws have become more relevant to today's planners now that penalties for corporate violations have been increased to $1.0 million and for individual violations to $100,000 and three years in jail. The trend for stronger enforcement should give all planners cause to be careful. For example, in a recent case where a national sales director was charged with price fixing, the head of the Antitrust Division made a special plea for a long jail term. Thus all levels of the corporate structure are becoming targets for antitrust enforcement.

The purpose of this chapter is to provide planners with a view of the current antitrust situation so that they may understand the constraints that antitrust policy places on their choice of marketing strategies. The discussion cannot hope to convey all of the antitrust dimensions of the marketing plan, but it should serve to encourage the planner to seek legal advice early if he or she is in doubt.

The enduring nineteenth-century model. To understand antitrust legislation and its implementation, it is helpful to look at the political-economic model on which it is built. Antitrust policy in the United States has been an economic analogue of the political model that states that power should be distributed among many units—in a word, pluralism. In the political model the unit is the *individual voter*. In the economic model the unit is the *small, competitive firm*, so small that its actions can have no perceptible impact on market price. *Atomistic competition* (large numbers of small firms) will, according to the theory, allow the market mechanism to allocate resources in everyone's best interest in the aggregate. The goal of antitrust policy, therefore, is to maintain atomistic competition. Since the economic model assumes a standardized product, competition is defined as *price flexibility*. Thus freedom to change price, like freedom to vote, is taken as the measure of a successful economic democracy.

The economic model of atomistic competition, which undergirds the Sherman Act of 1890 and subsequent antitrust legislation and uses price flexibility as the primary barometer of competition, is being questioned by economists and lawyers who are experts in antitrust. Their basic argument is that this nineteenth-century model does not fit the environment of the twentieth century. For one thing, the atomistic model assumes mobility of labor and ignores the federal policy of full employment. Other changes in the times are greatly increased economies of scale, environmental-protection concerns, rapidly diminishing natural resources, consumerism (a collective demand), social activism, technological development, and big government. The hypo-thetical homogeneity of the product in the atomistic model (which was much closer to the reality of the nineteenth century) is today translated into a rejection of product variety as unnecessary brand proliferation. The model defines away as *irrational* all competition that is not price competition. Yet in the twentieth century the buyer is very rational in his or her consideration of nonprice attributes such as style, product improvement, services, warranties, credit, and availability. Updating the atomistic model will be a slow process.

The nineteenth-century model and the judiciary. With rare exception the trend of recent Supreme Court decisions has been to hold all trade restraints illegal. Although the original Sherman Act had indeed condemned "every" restraint of trade, the Court at an early date had interpreted the statute to forbid only unreasonable restraints. The reasonable-unreasonable dichotomy necessitated a judicial inquiry into the economic effect of a particular practice on competition. Then as the Court felt more knowledgeable in antitrust, some practices were conclusively presumed to be illegal without inquiry into their effect on competition. This is the doctrine of per se illegality. A few cases will illustrate how the Court has extended its use.

White Motor Co. granted its dealers an exclusive territory and confined them to their own territory. While one obvious effect of this arrangement was to eliminate competition among dealers, another effect, White contended, was to strengthen its competitive position vis-à-vis the trucks of other manufacturers. In 1963 the Supreme Court ruled that this practice *might* be reasonable and that only a trial could resolve the issue.

Only four years later the question of distributor confinement was before the Court again. Arnold, Schwinn & Co. distributed its bicycles to wholesalers and retailers under an arrangement the Court found to limit sales within a specified territory. This time the Court adopted a conclusive presumption that confinement of dealers to specified territories, the manufacturer having parted with title to the goods as is usually the case, is illegal. Thus the elimination of intrabrand competition became a per se offense, with no inquiry into competitive effect. Schwinn had argued unsuccessfully that its distribution system was necessary to compete with mass merchandisers of bicycles, e.g., Sears, Roebuck & Co. The response of the Schwinn planners was to eliminate independent wholesalers in its channel of distribution.

This case foretold trouble for all manufacturers and suppliers who want to confine their outlets to a specified geographical area. Later, in 1972, the Topco Associates, Inc., system of confining outlets for its branded grocery goods was to fall under the per se label.

In *United States* v. *Topco Associates, Inc.* (1972), the Supreme Court struck down as per se illegal an arrangement by competing grocery chains to restrict territories for the Topco brand to permit economies of scale that would enable them to compete with large, fully integrated competitors. There is the real possibility that such arrangements would increase competition at the retail level rather than reduce it, but to demonstrate the possibility would require complex economic analysis that would go beyond the nineteenth-century model.

There are many unresolved issues surrounding the use of price flexibility as the sole criterion for price fixing. For instance, there is no clear distinction between predatory price cutting and vigorous competition. Millstein concluded that "we've glorified the means—price flexibility—and forgotten the end, namely, *that* resource allocation which promises the greatest good for the economy as a whole."[3] Although the United States courts have used *competitive price flexibility* as the single criterion for determining price-fixing antitrust policy, the Canadian courts have broadened the criterion to include the *effects* of a decision on *competition, economies of scale,* and *the consumer.*[4]

The use of per se criteria makes for judicial efficiency, because there is no need to perform extensive economic analysis, but the cases cited above suggest that excessive use is counterproductive, because it can reduce competition. There is some evidence that the courts are changing their opinions on some territory arrangements, as is evidenced in the Sylvania case.

In 1962 Sylvania had less than two percent of the television market. To improve its share, it decided to adandon its policy of saturation distribution and use selective distribution, hoping that fewer loyal distributors would promote more aggressively. Sylvania phased out the wholesale distributors and its own factory distributorships and instead sold directly to franchised dealers who sold to consumers. The franchise was for a location, and dealers agreed not to move merchandise to a new location without the approval of Sylvania. Sylvania remained competitive by not giving an exclusive dealership for an area and by authorizing at least two dealers in major areas. This policy and the growth of color television improved Sylvania's position to a five-percent share.

Continental TV was one of the largest Sylvania dealers in the country. Continental wished to enter the Sacramento, California, market, but Sylvania denied permission because it considered the present distribution adequate for the market potential. Nonetheless, Continental opened in Sacramento and moved merchandise from other stores. For this and other reasons, Sylvania terminated the contract and Continental sued Sylvania. The District Court decided in favor of Continental, under Section 1 of the Sherman Act, citing the per se rule established in the Schwinn case. The Ninth Circuit Court of Appeals reversed the decision, stating that the trial judge was too literal in his application of the Schwinn decision and had not considered the environment of the present case. The majority opinion in the Sylvania case closely paralleled the dissenting opinion in the Schwinn case.

In 1977 the Supreme Court affirmed the decision of the Court of Appeals, concluding "that the appropriate decision is to return to the rule of reason that governed vertical restrictions prior to Schwinn," and stating that "under this rule, the fact finder weighs all of the circumstances of a case in deciding whether a restrictive practice should be prohibited as imposing an unreasonable restraint on competition. Per se rules of illegality are appropriate only when they relate to conduct that is manifestly anticompetitive."[5]

The rejection of the per se rule returns the planner to a state of uncertainty in developing a channel strategy. The desire of a company to reduce intrabrand competition in an attempt to improve interbrand competition could result in expensive litigation in the attempt to prove that the net effect of reducing intrabrand competition is to increase competition. The measuring of this net effect on competition, and therefore the benefits to society, has eluded the courts. Legal thinking is moving toward a position between the per se rule and the rule of reason, but the rate of convergence is very slow.

The costs and benefits of existing enforcement.   What are the benefits associated with the costs of maintaining competition? The usual response to this question is to appeal to the face validity of the nineteenth-century model, which assumes that atomistic competitive units are the best method for resource allocation. No federal agency is assigned the task of estimating the short- and long-run impact of antitrust public policy. It is clear, however, that the social costs of enforcing competition should be considered.

One social cost of antitrust policy is the failure of an efficient company to pass along savings to consumers in the form of price cuts. "The efficient company, for example, will ease off on price competition rather than take too much business away from the potential plaintiff-competitor. A manufacturer will tolerate inefficiency in a distributor rather than run the risk of being penalized for putting a more efficient one in his place. And the free market system and the consumer will suffer."[6]

Short-run costs to a firm come from the way that antitrust laws are implemented. "The generality and ambiguity of the antitrust laws has always meant that the kinds of cases brought largely determine the direction in which competition policy evolves. Private enforcement, however, has too often led to anti-competitive policy determination and has produced a juridical climate of antitrust uncertainty and caprice."[7] Private enforcement, in this context, refers to the treble-damage suits, where the goal is not necessarily a concern for the working of the free market, but for the fees for the plaintiff's counsel.[8] An increase in private, treble-damage suits, therefore, does not necessarily reflect an increase in violations. Treble damages, which were originally intended as a stimulus for reporting violators, can direct the thrust of antitrust away from the best interests of the public. Nitschke concluded that enforcement should be by public officials, not by private suits.

A second cost to the defending firm comes from the fact that there is a strong incentive for a nuisance settlement, because the counsel's time for the defendant will generally exceed that of the plaintiff.[9] A third cost comes from a certain asymmetry in the use of precedents in suits by the Justice Department. A company can be a defendant in two Justice Department cases covering the same ground—one criminal and one civil. "If he loses *either one* there is a *prima facie* case for private plaintiffs. If the defendant wins *both* government cases, he derives no evidentiary benefit at all for future cases."[10]

The legal costs of the defending firm appear as higher prices to the consumer, which is a social cost. Unfortunately, there does not seem to be a mechanism or an incentive for lowering these costs to the defendant. In effect, they have become part of the punitive element of antitrust, even when the defendant is innocent.

The nineteenth-century model ignores the fact that technology has brought about economies of scale and that these economies require capital to buy the necessary equipment. The capital, in turn, requires profits which can generate internal financing and attract external funds. If corporate and industry profits are ever used as a per se violation of antitrust laws, the result would be a return of the production methods of the nineteenth century. Thus by a strange reordering of the facts, the nineteenth-century model would be proved correct, but resources would be allocated inefficiently, which is the obverse of the intent of the whole antitrust policy.

In summary, present antitrust legislation and implementation suffer from being based on a nineteenth-century *theoretical* model of how an *atomistic* economy *should* work. Existing interpretation of the *legislation* often ignores the technological, financial, political, and social environment of the late twentieth century. Within this rather confusing antitrust environment the planner must develop a marketing strategy.

Antitrust and the marketing mix.   To help the planner avoid marketing-mix strategies that violate antitrust laws and to encourage the early seeking of legal advice, Table 10.1 relates antitrust laws and important cases to the four elements of the marketing mix. After developing a marketing plan, the planner may read down the columns of this table to check each section of the plan for possible violations.

Reading down the columns for marketing strategies, we see that the impact of the Sherman Antitrust Act (1890) has been largely in the areas of price and channel strategies. The recent Coors and Topco cases suggest that the courts regard any territorial restriction as a per se violation, regardless of its effect on horizontal competition, but the Sylvania case modified this clear interpretation and leaves the planner confused.

TABLE 10.1   The impact of antitrust laws and recent cases on the marketing mix

Marketing laws and recent cases	Product	Price	Channel	Advertising
Sherman Antitrust Act (1890)				
Section 1: Price fixing is prohibited. (Vertical price fixing was permitted between 1937 and 1976 under the Miller-Tydings Amendment, 1937, and the McGuire Act, 1952. These "Fair Trade" acts were repealed on March 11, 1976).		×		
Recent cases:				
1. The Court (1975) found that Adolph Coors Co. controlled prices of its beer by terminating distributors who did not follow company pricing policy. Exclusive geographic territories prevented dealers from using alternative sources of Coors. Coors argued that exclusive territories were necessary to justify the dealers' investment in refrigerated warehouses to maintain the quality of Coors beer, which is not pasteurized.[11]		×	×	
2. Topco was a cooperative of independently owned local grocery chains which was formed in 1940 to compete with the larger chains. By 1967 Topco had sales of $2.3 billion and was fourth after A&P, Safeway, and Kroger. Members agreed not to sell Topco-brand products outside their assigned territories. The Supreme Court (405 U.S. 596 (1972)) held that this was a per se violation of Section 1 because it was a horizontal territorial limitation.			×	
3. In 1926 the Supreme Court approved General Electric's consignment system for setting the retail prices of lamp bulbs. In 1966 the Antitrust Division of the Justice Department charged GE with price fixing. In 1973 the district court concluded that the system should be outlawed in the future. (*JM*, January 1974, p. 72).		×	×	
4. The Supreme Court (1967) found Arnold, Schwinn & Co. in violation of Section 1, per se, because of its vertical restrictions on the distributors and reailers of its bicycles. Distributors were limited to dealing with franchised dealers, and dealers were limited to dealing only with consumers. (*JM*, January 1968, p. 73)		×	×	
Section 2: Monopolization, attempts to monopolize, and conspiracies to monopolize are forbidden. The seminal monopolization case may well be *Standard Oil Co.* v. *United States* (1911); a collection of firms, which first dominated the beginning oil industry through the device of a common-law trust and later through a New Jersey holding company, was held to be an illegal monopoly and was ordered dissolved.		×	×	

TABLE 10.1 (cont.)

Marketing laws and recent cases	Product	Price	Channel	Advertising
1. The Justice Department (1976) dropped its antitrust suits against Goodyear Tire & Rubber Co. and Firestone Tire & Rubber Co. because it could not prove its charge that the companies were using predatory price cutting to drive competitors out of the replacement-tire market. The Justice Department spent $1 million on pretrial work. The suit charged that price cuts were predatory because they were made when material and labor costs increased. The suit failed to consider the fact that new manufacturing operations offset some of these costs. Furthermore, consumers had switched to lower-priced grades. Thus the companies seemed to be taking a short-term profit-maximizing course that reflected changes in costs and demand. (*Wall Street Journal*, March 3, 1976, p. 3)		×		
2. The Supreme Court (1967) found three national frozen-pie makers in violation of the Robinson-Patman Act for predatory price cutting in the Salt Lake City market. It rejected the defense that there was no competitive injury to the Utah Pie Company, because it was able to cut prices, increase sales volume, and maintain profits. (*JM*, October 1967, p. 74)		×		
Clayton Act (1914)				
Section 2: As amended by the Robinson-Patman Act (1936), this section prohibits price discrimination that may substantially lessen competition. This discrimination may take the form of direct price differences, differential discounts, a brokerage allowance to a phantom broker, or advertising allowances that are not given proportionally to all buyers in competition with each other. Furthermore, the section makes it unlawful to knowingly induce or receive a price discrimination.		×		
Recent case:				
The Great Atlantic & Pacific Tea Company, Inc. (A&P) was found in violation of Section 2(f) of the Robinson-Patman Act and Section 5 of the FTC Act by an FTC administrative law judge (1975) for knowingly inducing discriminatory prices for dairy products from Borden, Inc. A&P induced from Borden an offer that was much better than the competitive offer. Furthermore, the competitive offer was not operative, because A&P could not meet the required volume and the competitor could not meet the delivery schedule. The Borden offer would be justified only on the grounds of meeting competition, not on a cost saving. (*JM*, April 1976, p. 92)		×	×	
Section 3: This section prevents tying contracts and exclusive dealership arrangements when they may substantially lessen competition.	×		×	

TABLE 10.1 (cont.)

	Product	Price	Channel	Advertising
Marketing laws and recent cases				

A *tying* contract may occur when a manufacturer requires a retailer to carry the full line of its products. Oil companies have violated this act when they required a retailer to sell their products exclusively.

Classic cases in tying contracts:[12]

1. In 1949 American Can Company was found in violation of Section 3 because it required food-processing lessees of its can-closing machinery to buy all of their cans from American Can on a five-year contract. To encourage this purchase the machines were leased at low rentals. × × ×

2. International Business Machine (IBM) was prevented (1936) from tying the leasing of business machines to the purchase of tabulating cards. ×   ×

Classic cases in exclusive dealerships:[13]

1. Standard Fashion Co. was prohibited (1922) from exclusive dealership arrangements in the sale of its dress patterns because it controlled 40 percent of the market. ×   ×

2. Carter Carburetor Corporation's exclusive dealership arrangement violated (1940) Section 3 because it had a 30 percent market share. ×   ×

Clayton Act

Section 7: This section prohibits mergers that would reduce the number of producers or distributors of a product, thereby substantially lessening competition. ×   ×

Classic cases:

1. In 1967 the Supreme Court ordered Procter & Gamble Co. to divest itself of Clorox Bleach. The original FTC complaint was in 1957; the key issues were that P&G was a potential competitor of Clorox, that Clorox had a 40 percent market share, and that P&G could "command one third more advertising per dollar of expenditure" than competitors because it received large discounts from the mass media as the largest user of advertising. The relevant criteria were the effect that the Clorox acquisition would have on competition by raising the barriers to entry by new competitors and eliminating P&G as a potential competitor.[14] ×   ×

2. The Supreme Court (1962) held that Brown Shoe Co.'s acquisition of G. R. Kinney Co., Inc., might substantially lessen competition ×   ×

TABLE 10.1 (cont.)

Marketing laws and recent cases	*Product*	*Price*	*Channel*	*Advertising*

even though Kinney had only a 0.5 percent share and Brown had a 4 percent share. (Each had larger shares in specific markets.) The Court concluded that because this was a fragmented industry, rank, not share, was important. Brown was the fourth largest and Kinney was the twelfth largest producer. (There were vertical aspects of the case, because Brown had retail outlets.)[15]

Federal Trade Commission Act (1914)

Section 5: As amended by the Wheeler-Lea Act (1938), "unfair methods of competition in commerce, and unfair or deceptive acts or practices in commerce, are hereby declared unlawful." This section, among other things, prohibits deceptive advertising and pricing arrangements that treat transportation costs in ways that result in unfair competition.

            ×   ×   ×   ×

Recent cases in deceptive advertising:

1. The Great Atlantic & Pacific Tea Co., Inc. (A&P) was found by the Federal Trade Commission (1975) to be advertising deceptively, because an FTC survey of newspaper advertisements and store checks revealed that 9.3 percent of the items were not available in the stores and 3.7 percent were priced higher than advertised. The administrative law judge found nothing intentional or willful. The cease-and-desist order provided for the future defenses of sufficient quantities ordered and received, but sold out; ordered but not delivered for reasons beyond the control of A&P (but A&P must immediately revise the advertisement); and offer "rain checks." (*JM*, July 1975, p. 90)

                            ×   ×

2. The television advertising for Chevron F-310 gasoline was found to be deceptive by the FTC (1974) because it used illustrations that conveyed the message that its gasoline emissions did not pollute the air. A before-and-after demonstration used a balloon on the exhaust pipe. The deception occurred because the "before" exhaust came from specially formulated dirty gasoline. Furthermore, most pollutants are invisible. Standard Oil of California and its advertising agency— Batten, Barton, Durstine & Osborn—were ordered to cease and desist. (*JM*, July 1975, pp. 88–89)

                                              ×

3. The FTC (1976) ordered the Fedders Corp. to cease and desist from advertising that its air conditioners had a unique "reserve cooling power"; in fact, there was no technical advantage over competitors. (*JM*, July 1976, pp. 102–103)

                                              ×

4. The J. B. Williams Co. paid $302,000 in fines, penalties, and interest when the U.S. Court of Appeals (1976) found the Fem-Iron

                                            ×

TABLE 10.1 (cont.)

Marketing laws and recent cases	*Product*	*Price*	*Channel*	*Advertising*

advertisements deceptive because they failed to disclose that most people do not feel and tired and run down because of an iron deficiency. (*JM*, July 1976, p. 103)

5. The FTC (1973) dismissed the complaint against Coca-Cola that its Hi-C drink advertisements were false, misleading, and deceptive. This case was unique in that it examined *implied*, as distinct from *expressed*, product claims. The majority of the commission concluded that there was not persuasive evidence that Hi-C had been claimed to be equivalent to citrus juices in general or to orange juice in particular. (*JM*, April 1974, pp. 81–82)				×

Recent cases requiring corrective advertising:

1. ITT Continental Baking Co. was required to devote 25 percent of its media budget for one year to correct the claim that Profile bread is effective for weight reduction. (The bread is sliced thinner.) (*JM*, October 1971, p. 76)				×
2. Two sugar-trade associations were required to advertise to correct the misconception in previous advertisements that eating sugar before a meal will help in weight reduction. (*JM*, January 1973, p. 80; *JM*, April 1973, p. 85)				×

A recent case in channels:

An FTC administrative law judge ruled that exclusive territories for Coca-Cola and Pepsi Cola distributors did not restrain trade, because the restrictions protected smaller bottlers who would be eliminated without this protection, thereby reducing the number of competitors. He concluded that additional benefits were: that returnable bottles would not be used by large bottlers, thus raising prices and damaging the ecology; that market power would increase, resulting in higher prices to the consumer; and that the territories encourage the development of marketing effort. He concluded further that there was sufficient interbrand competition to offset the lack of intrabrand competition. (*JM*, April 1976, pp. 94–95)

The concept of *shared monopoly* is a new and untested development. The FTC has charged Kellogg, General Foods, General Mills, and Quaker Oats with monopoly control over the ready-to-eat cereal market. The monopoly existed, according to the FTC, because marketing activities, expecially large advertising expenditures, represented a barrier to entry for small competitors. In 1974 these four manufacturers are reported to have spent a total of $95 million advertising cereals.[16] The FTC charged that there was tacit agreement not to cut prices but to compete with advertising and promotion to attain shelf space. The FTC began its investigation in 1970, but a final decision may not be reached until the end of the decade.[17]

The term *shared monopoly* seems to be the FTC's word for *oligopoly*, which does not convey the evil connotation of *shared monopoly*. If the FTC is successful in the "cereal case," then we may expect to hear of *shared monopolies* in automobiles, oil, steel, etc.

For the marketing planner, the Clayton Act (1914) and the Robinson-Patman amendment (1936) have their greatest impact on price and channel strategies. The planner should note that in the decisions in the A&P/Borden case and frozen-pies case, hard bargaining and competitive pricing produced charges of knowingly including a discriminatory offer and predatory price cutting. Thus the Court has a view of the marketplace quite different from the planner's.[18]

The case of the Justice Department against Goodyear and Firestone is interesting because it made a basic error in logic. Price cuts that were highly correlated were not predatory, but rather reactions to the external factors of lower-cost production methods and a downward shift in consumer demand.

The Clayton Act (1914) regulates tying contracts, exclusive dealerships, and mergers. Therefore, it constrains the alternatives available to the planner for product diversification, product promotion, and channel relationships. It is useful to note that it was necessary to use "classic" rather than "current" cases to illustrate applications of this act. There are two points of view for the lack of recent action under this act. Businesspeople think that government is no longer pursuing this charge, or that cases are easier to prove under the vague Section 5 of the Federal Trade Commission Act. Government concludes that it has solved the major problems in this area and set precedents for the lower courts to follow. "A finding of illegality will subject a company to the risk of many private treble-damage actions. Moreover, the public image of a company found to be operating in violation of the antitrust laws is likely to be seriously impaired. These risks compel the conclusion that tie-in sales and exclusive dealing arrangements should be avoided if at all possible."[19] The lack of recent cases in this area suggests that businesspeople are following this advice.

The Clorox case is important because the decision considered not only the large market share of Clorox, but also the ability of Procter & Gamble to command large media discounts. The Brown Shoe case emphasizes the point that market share may not be an important criterion in fragmented industry. A new criterion, rank order of size, was a key factor here. It is important to note that economic efficiencies that could result in lower prices to the consumer were *not* relevant in these two classic cases.

Section 5 of the Federal Trade Commission Act (1914) has been called the omnibus act, because it can be applied to a variety of charges. In Table 10.1 we see that its thrust recently has been against deceptive advertising. These cases emphasize several important developments. First, charges have been leveled against the advertising agency as well as the advertiser. Second, an order of cease and desist is no longer the final action. *Corrective advertising* to correct false impressions has been ordered. The copy to be used in the advertising and the amount of the budget for media have been specified by the FTC.

A recent development that planners will find interesting is the Hart Bill,[20] which was also known as the "Industrial Reorganization Act." Rebuttable monopoly power would have been presumed when two or more firms had an average rate of return exceeding 15 percent for five consecutive years and when four or fewer firms accounted for 50 percent or more of sales in any year. Kramer concluded that this would give top priority to the reorganization of seven industries—chemicals and drugs, computing equipment, electrical machinery, energy, steel, autos, and nonferrous metals.[21] A new Industrial Commission would have taken cases before a new Industrial Court. Kramer noted that "our experience over the last 40 years, in my view, demonstrates that the administrative agencies, with few exceptions, have failed to achieve their purposes."[22] This bill did not pass and is not likely to reappear.

Anticipating changes in antitrust emphasis. The antitrust laws are enforced largely by the Antitrust Division of the Justice Department and the Federal Trade Commission (FTC). An examination of recent events strongly suggests that emphasis on antitrust is sensitive to the current political and economic environment. A few examples will illustrate this point.

The Response of the FTC. To illustrate the sensitivity of the FTC to the political and economic environment, we will examine its *Program Justification to the Congress,* for fiscal year 1977, prepared in February 1976. Previously there had been double-digit inflation, an energy crisis, and a recession. In the public's mind these three events overshadowed its earlier concern with consumerism.

The shift in the emphasis of the FTC may be seen in its budget. In 1975 consumer protection accounted for 45 percent of the FTC budget; the estimate for 1977 was 35 percent. The budget for maintaining competition was 32.7 percent of the total budget in 1975. It was increased to 43.8 percent in 1977. Energy and medical costs were major contributors to the double-digit inflation. Between 1976 and 1977 the FTC budget for maintaining competition was shifted from 23.5 percent to 34.5 percent for the energy program and from 2.8 percent to 4.6 percent for health-care costs. Thus budget data must be examined with great care to determine if shifts represent a change in emphasis, the completion of programs, a shift of programs to other agencies, more productive methods of enforcement, or a shift of the enforcement costs to industry.[23] In the case of the FTC, there seems to have been a major shift in emphasis.

The Response of the Justice Department. The response of the Antitrust Division of the Justice Department was similar to that of the FTC. The number of antitrust cases pending at the end of 1973 was 134; the number estimated for the end of 1977 was 194. For this same period the pending consumer cases declined from 1113 to 626.

Earlier Warning Signals. Agency program budget justifications give the marketing manager a warning period of about one year. Earlier warnings may be found by analyzing speeches of key people in these agencies and Congress. Speeches given in 1976, for example, indicated that service industries will receive more scrutiny, small companies will be examined as well as large ones, the antitrust implications of payoffs in foreign countries will be examined, and there may be a renewed interest in the enforcement of the Robinson-Patman Act.

The mounting private costs of public policy. There are no data available to permit a cost-benefit analysis of antitrust policy where the costs for industry and the government are concerned. Data are becoming available that help us to assess the mounting private costs of public policy. For example, a survey by the National Association of

Manufacturers shows that the Occupational Safety and Health Act involved an initial cost of $33,000 for manufacturers with 100 or fewer employees.[24] "There are other dangers of injustice that can result from official haste and arbitrariness. Some time ago, the cranberry industry suffered a tremendous loss of sales when one agency announced—incorrectly as it later turned out—that the entire cranberry crop had been sprayed with a cancer-inducing pesticide. The result was that the Department of Agriculture finally made indemnification payments of $8.5 million to the industry."[25]

The private costs of public policy have led observers to suggest that federal agencies should be required to make an *economic-impact statement* of the effect of their actions. Furthermore, perhaps individual members of agencies should be held individually accountable for their haste and arbitrariness. One of the businessperson's frustrations in dealing with governmental agencies is the facelessness of the dealings. In so many cases the faces change every few years.

Another way of looking at the mounting private costs of public policy is to examine the cost ratio between the cost to industry and the cost to the federal agency. Line-of-business reporting, as required by the Bureau of Economics of the Federal Trade Commission, provides an example. Recently the FTC has made an effort "to improve the effectiveness of its law enforcement resource allocations for antitrust and consumer protection. One consequence has been a shift toward investigations and cases which are industry-wide in scope. To choose as wisely as possible which industry-wide investigations best serve the public interests, accurate industry-by-industry performance is needed."[26] Financial reporting methods by companies that are in more than one industrial classification do not reveal the amount of their sales by industry.

In 1975 the FTC sent questionnaires to 345 firms, requiring them to report data by industrial classifications. There was considerable controversy regarding the costs of complying. The FTC estimated that it would cost the average firm $24,000 to comply and that some large firms might spend up to $100,000.[27] Using the $24,000 estimate, to be conservative, we see that compliance would cost these 345 firms $8.28 million. The FTC budget for collecting, processing, and publishing the data was $305,000. Thus the regulatee/regulator ratio was 27 to 1; it would cost industry at least $27 for each dollar spent by the FTC. Federal agencies will appear to be more efficient by shifting the burden to industry. It does seem unreasonable to require agencies to provide *independent* estimates of such cost ratios. This could be part of the *economic impact statement*.

Protect the Consumer Laws to protect the consumer are not new and are certainly not unique to the United States. Hammurabi's law, the first recorded law, contained many standards of conduct for producers, sellers, and buyers. The Aztecs had judges in the market-place to ensure honest measures, and capital punishment was considered appropriate for violations. In the United States the consumer movement arose in the mid-nineteenth century.

The origins of consumerism. The popularity of *consumerism* may preclude the need to define the term, but there is also the danger that this popularity may blur its meaning. *Consumerism*, as used here, means the efforts of groups to ensure that consumers receive *value* in the marketplace. The groups may range from self-appointed experts, who need a rallying point for their militancy, to formal organizations that objectively test products and publish impartial results. The difficult part of this definition is the word *value*. In its nineteenth-century context the term meant the physical, or functional, ability of a product to perform as promised. But the physical needs are only the first of a hierarchy of needs that also include social and psychological needs. Thus modern-day consumerists are faced with a more difficult problem than that of their nineteenth-century counterparts, because measuring the ability of a product to meet a social or psychological need is a very subjective process. In fact, these measures may be biased by the personal value of the measurer. To understand the criticism of consumerists, therefore, we must know something of their personal values.

The roots of consumerism are in the Industrial Revolution that brought us affluence, the remoteness of mass production, and higher levels of education, leisure, and pollution. The early consumer movement began in England during the mid-nineteenth century with cooperative buying and banking organizations. It was an attempt to bring economies of scale to consumption and to provide an equitable basis by which the individual could interface with large organizations.[28]

All of these results of the Industrial Revolution contributed to the forces that produced consumerism as we know it today. Mass production has created a great void between producer and consumer. The dialogue between the artisan and the consumer has been replaced by an advertising monologue, thereby creating the consumers' demands to be heard. Mass production has contributed to pollution. Affluence has met our basic physical needs so that we can concentrate on social and psychological needs. Higher levels of education make our needs more complex and make us aware of more ways of meeting them. Education also makes us aware that it is possible to bring change that will favor the individual. Mass production frees some people so they can be full-time consumerists, regulators, and testers.

The Industrial Revolution, affluence, and education provide an underlying environment for a consumer movement, but they do not explain the sudden upsurge of the movement. This recent surge of interest is probably related to the lack of confidence in existing institutions. There is a distrust of all large organizations—public and private.[29] People feel that they are being generally deceived and that their position is not represented. Much of this distrust can be traced to governmental manipulation of information during the Vietnam war and Watergate. Perhaps individuals shifted their scale of trust. When they could not trust the government, which had been relatively high on the scale, they then shifted everything else downward, so they increasingly distrust the marketer, who was already low on the scale.

The *marketing concept* stresses the need to understand and meet the needs of the consumer. Drucker concluded that consumerism exists because firms have not practiced the marketing concept.[30] Andreasen concluded that only 25 percent of consumers' complaints are satisfied.[31]

The consumer movement has become an outlet for hostilities. "It turns out that over half the people in the country agree that when people complain about the quality of products, they are not really complaining about the products so much as expressing their unhappiness at the way things are going in general right now."[32] But why should marketing take the brunt of these hostilities? Perhaps it is because of the frequency with which the individual interacts with the marketing system. She or he must make hundreds of buying decisions a year, and there are millions of advertisements to which a person may be exposed. The frequency of the exposure increases the hostility. A person's interaction with institutions such as political parties, labor unions, Congress, and the Supreme Court are infrequent, so there is less opportunity to transfer hostilities.

Much of the consumer movement is concerned with providing the consumer with better information. The consumer needs two kinds of information: (1) what criteria to use when evaluating a product; and (2) the impartial rank of each brand along these criteria. For infrequently purchased products, such as automobiles and household durable goods, experience is an extremely costly way of gathering information. Yet consumers are unwilling to buy relevant information. An unpublished study by the author revealed that the people who had just moved all of their household furniture were not willing to pay more than $1.00 for information about the moving company at the receiving end of their move, despite the fact that there were many horror stories. Many respondents thought that the government should provide such information.[33]

Consumer legislation. In 1962 President John F. Kennedy sent a special message to Congress on protecting consumer interests. This message contained the now famous four consumer rights—to safety, to be informed, to choose, and to be heard. These consumer rights captured much of the spirit of the consumer movement and gave direction to the consumer legislation that followed. The right to *safety* means protecting consumers against hazardous products. The right to be *informed* means eliminating fraudulent, deceitful, or misleading information, advertising, or labeling. The right to *choose* exists when competition is preserved, so that the consumer can select from among a number of brands. The right to be *heard* in government means a willingness to accept consumer input during policy formulation.

Safety Legislation. There was considerable existing legislation dealing with protecting the consumer from unsafe products when President Kennedy sent the special message to Congress, but the message was the stimulus for additional consumer legislation. For example, the consumer is protected from unsafe and adulterated food, drugs, and cosmetics by the Federal Food, Drug, and Cosmetic Act (1906, amended 1938, 1958). The Kefauver-Harris Amendment (1962) to this act requires that drugs be tested for safety and efficacy. The inspection of conditions for the processing and packaging of meats and poultry was the subject of acts in 1906, 1967, and 1968. Health warnings on cigarette labels and in advertising were required by the Cigarette Labeling Act (1966).

Safety in nonfood and nondrug products has been the focus of the Flammable Fabrics Act (1953, amended 1967), the Hazardous Substances Labeling Act (1960), and the National Traffic and Motor Vehicle Safety Act (1966). Children's safety too has been the subject of legislation. The Child Protection and Toy Safety Act (1966, amended 1969) banned toys that pose electrical, mechanical, or thermal hazards. The Poison Prevention Packaging Act (1970) established standards for child-resistant packaging for drugs and other hazardous substances. The Consumer Product Safety Commission was established by the Consumer Product Safety Act (1972).

Legislation for Better Information. The public is not an experienced purchasing agent in the wide variety of goods that it must buy. The need for better information expanded as the number of brand choices increased and as self-service stores replaced salesclerks. In the grocery field, for example, the corner store with a clerk and several hundred products was replaced by a supermarket with shopping carts and

8000 items. Advertising and lables took on a new importance as they became the consumer's only sources of information.

The desire to make consumers better-informed buyers has been the subject of considerable consumer legislation. The Wheeler-Lea Amendment (1938) to the Federal Trade Commission Act (1914) made deceptive advertising illegal. The consumer also needs help in buying products that go beyond his or her technical knowledge. Misleading names on labels have been used to make the buyer think that he or she is buying a higher-quality product than is the case. Accurate labels in clothing are the result of the Wool Products Labeling Act (1939), the Fur Products Labeling Act (1941), and the Textile Fiber Products Identification Act (1958). The Fair Packaging and Labeling Act (1966) is conerned with deceptive packaging and labeling of consumer goods.

Consumer finance has been replete with complex documents and true-interest rates that are understood only by the lender. The Consumer Credit Protection Act (Truth-in-Lending) of 1968 (amended 1970) requires full disclosure of credit terms and regulates the maintenance and dissemination of consumer credit records.

Product warranties have been one of consumers' leading complaints. Documents that seemed to be warranties were meaningless because of hidden disclaimers. The Magnuson-Moss Warranty/Federal Trade Commission Improvement Act (1975) empowers the FTC to make rules regarding consumer-product warranties and methods for redress.

Right-to-Choose Legislation. Providing the consumer with a choice in the marketplace is the goal of antitrust legislation. Competition provides the consumer with a choice of products, brands, services, and channels of distribution.

The Right to be Heard. The right to be heard is not a subject for legislation, but rather a philosophy for running a government or a business. Governmental policies regarding prompt replies to consumers reflect this policy. Business has responded with free long-distance telephone lines for consumer complaints. During the early 1970s several companies advertised that they "listened better."

Consumerism has been popular with politicians.

> With every voter also a consumer, talk or action on high prices, shoddy merchandise, misleading advertising or poor service was certain to be received sympathetically. Furthermore, the topics could be worked nicely into discussions of the problems of poverty. With the Vietnam war, the space program and other high priority demands on federal funds generating such enormous demands, consumer issues were especially appealing since the remedies, e.g., the introduction of federal standards for automobile tires, were, for the most part, cheap.[34]

Governmental agencies protecting the consumer. Consumerism has had its impact on marketers largely in two planning areas—product and advertising. There have been 19 separate pieces of legislation on product safety. The best-known laws are the Automobile Safety Act of 1966 and the Consumer Product Safety Act of 1972. Implementation of the latter act occurs through a five-member board which can set safety standards; require warnings by producers and resellers; seize, ban, or recall merchandise; give consumers their money back; and send offenders to jail.

Many federal and state agencies are concerned with safeguarding the consumer and the environment. The Environmental Protection Agency is concerned with air and water pollution, pesticide regulation, noise abatement, radiation, solid-waste management, and oil and hazardous substances. The Federal Administration has noise abatement among its responsibilities. The Federal Trade Commission protects the consumer against fraud, deceptive practices and deceptive advertising. The Interstate Commerce Commission regulates the movement of household effects. The National Highway Transportation Safety Administration is concerned with automobile safety. The United States Department of Agriculture is responsible for meat and poultry surveillance. The United States Food and Drug Administration protects the consumer in the food and drug fields. State officials are responsible for food and drug surveillance, weights and measures, land-sales regulations, insurance, pollution, pesticides, and noise abatement.[35]

The United States Office of Consumer Affairs processes 30,000 complaints per year. The major complaint is about automobile repair service. Other areas of complaint include mail order, housing-related problems, appliance repair, business practices, credit, food, prices, and insurance.[36] There are also more than 350 state and local consumer officers. With all of these agencies looking after the consumer's interests, it is no surprise that a marketing vice-president may spend one-half of his or her time on matters of public policy.

Strategic opportunities. The rise in consumerism provides opportunities for the alert marketer. Oscar Mayer & Co., a meatpacker, provides an example. It was among the first, if not the first, meatpacker to date its packages, list the meat's nutrients on the package, and provide a clear window on the package so consumers could see what they were buying. Product quality was stressed, which permitted a higher margin. Catering to consumerism proved to be financially successful. Oscor Mayer's return on capital was 13 percent versus the industry median of 9 percent.[37]

Strategic constraints. Consumerism constraints on marketing-mix strategies fall largely in the areas of product and advertising. In addition to the many agencies that try to protect and inform the consumer about product characteristics, the Magnuson-Moss Warranty/Federal Trade Commission Improvement Act of 1975 provides minimum disclosure standards for written consumer-product warranties on products costing more than $5.00. Consumer-product firms that *elect* to offer written warranties must disclose the terms in simple and easily understood language. The FTC will issue rules regarding the implementation of the act.[38]

Some strategic constraints come from consumers. For instance, Allstate Insurance Company found that its $5 million promotion of automobile air bags between 1971 and 1974 failed to generate strong public demand for them. A previous $1 million campaign on drunk driving and better bumpers proved to be successful. One bumper advertisement generated 30,000 letters to the Department of Transportation; the five-year air-bag campaign generated only 1950 positive letters.[39] We must conclude, therefore, that not all safety measures will sell.

Public-policy constraints on advertising focus on the problem of deception. Some practices are undoubtedly deceptive. For example, the FTC found deception in the visual presentations for television commercials. In one soup commercial, marbles had been added to the soup to make it look thicker. Similarly, a window that showed the superiority of plate glass was really a picture of a window frame without glass. A shaving system that claimed it could shave sandpaper was actually shaving only shaving cream on plexiglass.

The more difficult cases are those where there is no intent to deceive. The FTC found that the A&P food chain was guilty of deceptive advertising because its stores did not carry all of the items advertised. The fact that "rain checks" were available was not an adequate defense. During the FTC hearings an A&P executive testified that local managers were pressured to keep inventories low to conserve working capital. A policy of not automatically shipping advertised items from the A&P warehouse to each store seems to have contributed to the unavailability and therefore the deceptive advertising.[40] The culprit in this case was a policy on working capital, not an advertising policy.

The marketing planner faces the problem of a clear definition for deceptive advertising. None presently exists.[41] *Deception* is a personal matter that is determined by an individual's personal values, such as good taste, offensiveness, and intelligence. Thus an ad that is *deceptive* for one market segment may be quite acceptable to another. Some companies, especially pharmaceutical firms, pretest advertisements to be certain that the illustration and the copy are not deceptive. "One of the more far-reaching new undertakings of the FTC is its program for the substantiation of advertised claims. Announced in 1971, this program requires advertisers to submit on demand by the commission data supporting advertised claims relative to product safety, performance, efficacy, quality, or comparative price."[42]

Advertising may be declared as deceptive and unfair where no "reasonable basis" for a claim exists. The FTC may take one of four courses of action against the advertiser. The advertiser may be ordered to *cease and desist* from such advertising. This order may be accompanied by a fine.

A second course of action is to require *affirmative disclosure*, the addition of information in subsequent advertisements. For example, advertisements for three computer schools misrepresented career opportunities for their graduates. An FTC consent order required them to disclose placement percentages and starting salaries in subsequent advertisements.[43]

Corrective advertisements require that a part of the advertising budget be used to correct the residual effects of misleading advertising. The FTC required Continental Baking Company to spend 25 percent of its media budget for one year stating that its Profile bread is not effective for weight reduction, as previous advertisements indicated.

The fourth and most controversial course of action is the FTC proposal to the Federal Communications Commission to permit *counteradvertising* to counteract controversial product claims.[44]

Organizing for consumerism. Many companies have established formal corporate organizations to handle consumer affairs, and these departments can have extensive power within an organization.[45] Gillette has a vice-president for product integrity who is a Ph.D. in medical science. He has the authority to pull products off the market, veto new-product introductions, stop advertising claims, require package changes, and stop proposed acquisitions.[46]

Organizing for product recalls can be extensive if the firm has long channels of distribution. There are complex questions such as the legal status of the product resellers, product-identification records, methods for notification, and possible alternatives to full-scale product recall.[47]

Conserve the Environment   Public policy directed toward conserving the environment and resources is the last of the three major thrusts of public policy. This lag stems from the fact that the environment has been external to economic analysis and that resources, especially energy, fresh air, and clean water, were regarded as cheap and abundant.

Businesspeople frequently ask, "Can a free-enterprise system be concerned about the environment?" Quinn concluded that the answer is a strong yes.[48] Furthermore, he thinks that improving the environment may be the next big industry.

The concern for the environment can provide new marketing opportunities. The demise of aerosol cans led to a return to pump sprays and roll-on antiperspirants. Plastic containers that are destroyed by bacteria are being developed. When buried, such a container is converted by the bacteria into water, soil, and carbon dioxide.[49]

The concern for the environment does not affect all firms favorably, however. If there was a return to refillable glass bottles for soft drinks and malt beverages, 80,000 persons in container manufacturing would lose their jobs. On the other hand, 100,000 workers would be added to retailing and distribution to handle the returns.[50]

In the short run, the marketing strategist will want to examine product strategies such as labels that report the energy use of a product. The Federal Energy Administration and the National Bureau of Standards have developed voluntary energy-use labels for many appliances.[51]

PUBLIC POLICY THROUGH PRIVATE MANAGEMENT   The growing concern with preserving competition, protecting the consumer, and conserving the environment raises the question: "Can these public policies be pursued in a private-enterprise system?" The answer seems to be yes, but it will require a new type of manager. "As a result of a gradual process of socialization, the notion is now very widely accepted that private business organizations are, in some general sense, involved in the larger society and have some responsibility to take into account their general social impact."[52]

There are three stages of business socialization. First, there is the corporate philanthropy and passive citizenship role. Second, there is an attempt to bring neglected considerations into the managerial process. Finally, there is the formulation of positive proposals about areas that concern management. But business socialization is just one of the many elements in the dynamic process that creates a public-policy agenda.[53]

"The modern large corporation is clearly a prominent institution—some would say the *dominant* institution—in our society."[54] Society has witnessed shifts in economic power from the church, to the state, and now to large corporations. In each case the institution losing power has resisted the change. Some of the current public policies seem to be a recognition by the federal government that it may be a declining institution. However, the broad social concern should not be who has the economic power, but rather how the new institution fits the democratic economic model and whether it does so better than the old institution. Then one must ask: "What institution will replace the corporation and what are its social values?"

SUMMARY   Public policies dealing with preserving competition, protecting the consumer, and conserving the environment require careful consideration when a planner develops a marketing strategy. They provide opportunities for new products, but they also place constraints on strategic alternatives on each element in the marketing mix.

To understand the antitrust law, the planner must understand the economic model on which it is built. Some limitations of the nineteenth-century model used in United States antitrust policy raise questions about its viability in the twentieth century.

The recent shift in antitrust enforcement requires the marketing planner to weigh the antitrust implications of marketing strategies. Failure to do so may cost the firm $1.0 million in fines, a three-year jail term and a $100,000 fine for executives, or a substantial corrective-advertising budget. The trend has been toward more strict enforcement of antitrust, a trend that is likely to continue.

The sole criterion for implementing antitrust policy in the United States is the effect on competition, which is a rather limited criterion. It fails to consider economies of scale, the effect on the price of the product, and the effect on the consumer. Some of the new methods for increasing "regulatory efficiency" simply pass the cost of regulating to industry, which passes it to the consumer as a higher price. It has been suggested that agencies be required to file an *economic-impact statement* that would estimate the cost to industry and the consumer resulting from a new action.

The planner can reduce some of the uncertainty of antitrust policy by anticipating shifts in emphasis. This emphasis is very sensitive to the political-economic environment. Short-range shifts may be detected by examining an agency's program budget justification to Congress. Long-range predictions will require an analysis of speeches by key persons in the FTC, the Justice Department, Congress, and consumer-action groups.

Laws designed to protect consumer safety began in 1906 in the United States with the Food and Drug Act, but the origins of the consumer movement can be traced to nineteenth-century political and economic forces. Consumer legislation was stimulated by President Kennedy's consumer message, which identified four consumer rights—to safety, to be informed, to choose, and to be heard. The popularity of the consumer movement yielded to the realities of shortages and inflation in the mid-1970s.

This chapter cannot hope to inform a planner of all of the things that he or she needs to know about public policy, because the policy is in a continuous state of development. Rather, the goal of this chapter is to help the planner identify the questions that need to be asked and the strategic implications of the answers.

DISCUSSION QUESTIONS

1. What is the atomistic model of competition? In what ways does this model no longer fit the twentieth-century competitive environment?

2. What is meant by a per se violation? Give examples.

3. Which areas of the marketing mix have been most affected by each of the following antitrust legislation: (a) Sherman Act, (b) Clayton Act and the Robinson-Patman amendment, and (c) Section 5 of the Federal Trade Commission Act?

4. Describe some ways of anticipating developments in antitrust legislation.

5. Prepare a checklist that will help brand planners evaluate the public-policy implications of their marketing plans. Compare and contrast a checklist for the following two products: a ten-speed bicycle and color television.

6. In what ways does government aid business?

7. What do you think will be the important public-policy issues five years from now? Ten years from now?

8. Give examples of marketing opportunities created by public-policy requirements.

NOTES

1. *Advertising Age*, August 23, 1976, p. 1.

2. The author acknowledges the comments of William S. Stewart, Professor of Business Law, School of Business Administration, and Paul Verkuil, Professor of Law, Law School, both of the University of North Carolina. Dr. Betty Bock, Director of antitrust research of the The Conference Board, provided material and comments. The author is grateful for this assistance, but he remains responsible for any errors. Parts of the section discussing antitrust appeared in the author's article entitled "Antitrust caveats for the marketing planner," *Harvard Business Review*, March–April, 1978. The author is indebted for permission to republish some of this material.

3. I. M. Millstein, "Antitrust in Search of an Identity: Images and Classical Models Under Crossfire, *Proceedings of the Twelfth Conference on Antitrust Issues in Today's Economy* (New York: Conference Board, 1973), p. 16.

4. P. C. Warnke, "Trade Regulation as a Tool for Social Change?" *Proceedings, op. cit.*, p. 22.

5. *GTE Sylvania Inc.* v. *Continental T.V., Inc.*, 537 f. 2d 980 (9th Cir. 1976), *cert. granted*, 97 S. Ct. 252 (1976), and *United States Law Week*, Extra Edition no. 2. Supreme Court Opinions, vol. 45: no. 49, June 21, 1977, p. 4834."

6. R. A. Nitschke, "Toward a National Antitrust Policy?," *Proceedings of the Fifteenth Conference on Antitrust Issues in Today's Economy* (New York: Conference Board, 1976), pp. 3–9.

7. *Ibid.*, p. 4.

8. *Ibid.*

9. *Ibid.*, p. 6.

10. *Ibid.*, p. 5.

11. *Journal of Marketing* (*JM*) (July 1975): 84–85. Citations are the *JM* feature section, "Legal Developments in Marketing," which provides a quarterly summary in nonlegal terms. This section provides an updating of legal developments.

12. These classic cases are based on M. C. Howard, *Legal Aspects of Marketing* (New York: McGraw-Hill, 1964), pp. 99–102.

13. *Ibid.*, p. 97.

14. B. Bock, *Mergers and Markets*, 6th ed., Studies in Business Economics, No. 100 (New York: Conference Board, 1968), pp. 70–74.

15. Howard, *op. cit.*, p. 81.

16. R. L. Gordon, "Big Ad Spending a Prime Target in FTC's Cereal Industry Case," *Advertising Age*, March 29, 1976, pp. 3, 118.

17. *Marketing News*, May 7, 1976, p. 11.

18. R. Bauer and S. Greyser, "The Dialogue that Never Happens," *Harvard Business Review* (November-December 1967): 2–12.

19. E. W. Kinter, *An Antitrust Primer*, 2d ed. (New York: Macmillan, 1973), p. 59.

20. S. 1167, 93d Congress, March 12, 1973.

21. V. H. Kramer, discussant on "Trade Regulation as a Tool for Social Change?" *Proceedings*, 1973, *op. cit.*, pp. 25–26.

22. *Ibid.*, p. 26.

23. A more detailed discussion may be found in G. D. Hughes, "Anticipating Antitrust Trends," in John F. Cady (ed.), *Marketing and the Public Interest: Proceedings of the Symposium in Honor of E. T. Grether* (Cambridge, Mass: Marketing Science Institute), in press.

24. R. L. Werner, "Antitrust, Social Responsibility and Changing Times," in *Antitrust and Shifting . . .* (New York: Conference Board, 1974), pp. 5–12.

25. *Ibid.*, p. 8.

26. Senate Hearings before the Committee on Appropriations, State, Justice, Commerce, the Judiciary and Related Agencies Appropriations, Fiscal Year, 1976, 94th Congress, First Session, HR 8121 US GPO, 1975, p. 638.

27. *Ibid.*, p. 648–649.

28. S. A. Greyser, "Advertising: Attacks and Counters," *Harvard Business Review* (March–April 1972): 22–28, 140–146.

29. J. Elliot, "How Far Can You Stretch Your Coffee Break?" (Talk before the AAF Public Affairs Conference, Washington, D.C., May 15, 1972); and Daniel Yankelovich, Inc., *The Changing Values on Campus* (New York: Washington Square Press, Pocket Books, 1972).

30. P. F. Drucker, *Management: Tasks, Responsibilities, Practices* (New York: Harper & Row, 1974), p. 64.

31. A. R. Andreasen, "Consumer Movement, Government, and Business . . . ," *Marketing News*, July 16, 1976, p. 9.

32. Elliot, *op. cit.*

33. W. L. Wilkie, *Public Policy and Product Information: Summary Findings from Consumer Research.* Report prepared for the National Science Foundation, Washington D.C.: Superintendent of Documents, Government Printing Office, 1975.

34. R. H. Holton, "Forward," in *Consumerism: Search for the Consumer Interest*, ed. D. A. Aaker and G. S. Day (New York: Free Press, 1971), p. xviii.

35. D. Sprecher, *Directory of Government Agencies Safeguarding Consumer and Environment*, 5th ed. (Alexandria, Va: Serina Press, 1973).

36. H. C. Hall, "U.S. Office of Consumer Affairs Plans National Survey," *Marketing News*, July 16, 1976, pp. 9–11.

37. "Help from Betty Furness," *Forbes*, November 1, 1975, p. 58.

38. D. Cohen, "New Consumer Product Warranty Law also Broadens FTC Jurisdiction," *Marketing News*, March 28, 1975, p. 7.

39. T. Rowan, "Hefty Ad Outlays Failed to 'Sell' Air Bags: Allstate," *Advertising Age*, September 8, 1975, p. 73.

40. FTC Docket No. 8916, January 24, 1975.

41. D. M. Gardner, "Deception in Advertising: A Conceptual Approach," *Journal of Marketing* (January 1975): 40.

42. R. E. Wilkes and J. B. Wilcox, "Recent FTC Actions: Implications for the Advertising Strategist," *Journal of Marketing* (January 1974): 55–61.

43. *Ibid.*, p. 59.

44. *Ibid.*

45. E. P. McGuire, *The Consumer Affairs Department: Organization and Function*, Conference Board Report No. 609 (New York: Conference Board, 1973).

46. R. Martin, "Gillette's Giovacchini Rules on the Quality, Safety of 850 Products," *Wall Street Journal*, December 12, 1975, pp. 1, 20.

47. G. Fisk and R. Chandran, "How to Trace and Recall Products," *Harvard Business Review* (November–December 1975): 90–96; and *Managing Product Recalls* (New York: Conference Board, 1974).

48. J. B. Quinn, "Next Big Industry: Environmental Improvement," *Harvard Business Review* (September–October 1971): 120–131.

49. *British Record*, October 18, 1975.

50. "Washington Wrap-Up," *Marketing News*, December 19, 1975, p. 7.

51. "FEA/FTC Set to Work on Product 'Efficiency' Labels," *Advertising Age*, December 29, 1975, p. 4.

52. L. E. Preston and J. E. Post, *Private Management and Public Policy* (Englewood Cliffs, N.J.: Prentice-Hall, 1975).

53. *Ibid.*, p. 86.

54. *Ibid.*, p. 151.

SUGGESTED READINGS

Areeda, P., *Antitrust Analysis: Problems, Text, Cases*, 2d ed. (Boston: Little, Brown, 1974).

Bock, B., "Data, Information and Antitrust: An Introduction," *Proceedings of the Fifteenth Conference on Antitrust Issues in Today's Economy* (New York: Conference Board, 1976), pp. 1–2.

Bork, R. H. "A Law Professor's View; Antitrust and the Judicial Process, The Bench as an Economic Forum," *Proceedings of the Seventh Conference on Antitrust Issues in Today's Economy* (New York: Conference Board, 1968), pp. 12–16.

Brozen, Y. "The Antitrust Task Force Deconcentration Recommendation," *Journal of Law and Economics* 2 (October 1970): 279–292.

Busch, P., "A Review and Critical Evaluation of the Consumer Product Safety Commission: Marketing Management Implications," *Journal of Marketing* (October 1976): 41–49.

The Challenge of Consumerism: A Symposium (New York: Conference Board, 1971).

Cunningham, W. H., and I. C. M. Cunningham, "Consumer Protection: More Information or More Regulation?" *Journal of Marketing* (April 1976): 63–68.

Edwards, C. D., *Maintaining Competition Requisites of a Governmental Policy* (New York: McGraw-Hill, 1969).

Feldman, L. P., "New Legislation and the Prospects for Real Warranty Reform," *Journal of Marketing* 40 (July 1976): 41–47.

———, *Consumer Protection: Problems and Prospects* (St. Paul, Minn.: West, 1976).

Howard, M. C., "Government, the Retailer, and the Consumer," *Journal of Retailing* 48 (Winter 1972–73): 48–62.

"Introduction to *Antitrust and Shifting National Controls Policies: Impact on Differently Positioned Companies*," *Proceedings of the Thirteenth Conference on Antitrust Issues in Today's Economy* (New York: Conference Board, 1974), pp. 1–3.

"Introduction to *Antitrust in a Rapidly Changing Economy*," *Proceedings of the Fourteenth Conference on Antitrust Issues in Today's Economy* (New York: Conference Board, 1975), pp. 1–3.

Kotler, P., "What Consumerism Means for Marketers," *Harvard Business Review* (May–June 1972): 48–57.

Myers, J. G., *Social Issues in Advertising* (New York: A.A.A.A. Educational Foundation, 1971).

Peterson, E., "Consumerism as a Retailer's Asset," *Harvard Business Review* (May–June 1974): 91–101.

Rockefeller, E. S., and J. G. Van Cise, *The FTC in Action* (New York: Practicing Law Institute, Corporate Law and Practice Course Handbook Series, Number 107, 1972).

Singer, E. M., "Antitrust in Search of an Identity: Images and Classical Models Under Crossfire—1," *Proceedings of the Twelfth Conference on Antitrust Issues in Today's Economy* (New York: Conference Board, 1973), pp. 3–9.

Steiner, R. L., "The Prejudice Against Marketing," *Journal of Marketing* 40 (July 1976): 2–9.

Part IV. Marketing-Mix Strategies

A marketing strategy is the link between a product and its market. A strategy (based on the Greek word for leadership) provides the direction for allocating the marketing effort. The strategy is translated into an action plan (tactics) through the tools of marketing management—the product, price, channels of distribution, advertising, and personal selling. These tools are known as the marketing mix.

Chapter 11 provides an overview of strategy development. It discusses the creation of alternatives, contingency planning, and criteria for choosing among alternatives. Chapters 12, 13, 14, 15, and 16 discuss the development of strategies for product, price, channels, advertising, and personal selling, respectively. (Chapter 15 includes a discussion of career opportunities in advertising.) Chapter 17 examines marketing strategies from the viewpoint of one member in the channel of distribution, the retailer. This chapter meets several needs. It provides the marketing manager with insights into the concerns of retailers. It also illustrates how marketing concepts may be used by members in the channel of distribution. Career opportunities in retailing are also discussed.

Chapter 18 explores the opportunities and problems in international marketing. The marketing manager must appreciate those situations which will require a different marketing strategy for each country. Various organizational strategies for international marketing are examined.

The evaluation of the success of a marketing strategy and the control of its implementation are the subjects of Chapter 19. Measures and models for evaluation and control are discussed and illustrated.

ENVIRONMENTAL ANALYSIS WORKSHEET

Environmental elements	Facts	Assumptions or research needed	Conclusions
Organizational values, objectives, and policies (4)			
Organizational design (5)			

Situation
  Generic demand (6)
  Brand demand (7)
  Competition (9)
  Public policy (10)			

Opportunities (2)			
Problems			

MARKETING PLAN (CONSUMER PRODUCT)

Current performance
Recommendations
Effect of recommendations on income
Situation analysis
Opportunities and problems
Strategies
Tests and research
Supporting documents
  Comparative budgets
  Media allocation schedule
  Promotion control sheet

STRATEGY WORKSHEET

Opportunities and problems in rank order to importance

1.
2.
.
n.

	Current strategy	Alternatives and recommended strategy	Estimated Effect

Demand strategy
   Generic
   Brand

Strategic goals
   Financial
   Marketing

Marketing-mix strategies
   Product (12)
   Pricing (13)
   Channel and logistics (14)
   Advertising and promotional (15)
   Sales management (16)

Research (3)

Profit plan

Evaluation and control (19)

CHAPTER **11**

CHAPTER **11**

Introduction to Creating Marketing-Mix Strategies

LEARNING OBJECTIVES After studying this chapter you should:

1. Have a fuller understanding of the process for creating alternative strategies.
2. Understand how and when contingency planning should be used.
3. Know how alternatives are shown on the Strategy Worksheet.
4. Understand how alternative strategies are linked to opportunities and problems.
5. Know some of the criteria for evaluating strategies.
6. Be able to define and use the following concepts:

Marketing-mix strategies   Marketing audit
Uncontrolled variables   Cannibalization
Controlled variables   Contingency planning

SOME STRATEGIC QUESTIONS FOR OPENERS

1. Are the alternatives realistic?
2. Do they solve the problems or tap the opportunities that have been identified?
3. Are the alternatives consistent with corporate goals, policies, and available resources?
4. Have present successes kept us from searching for new opportunities?
5. What are the financial goals? Is marketing performance judged by sales, market share, or profits? Have we been meeting past goals?
6. Which of the marketing-mix elements have we emphasized in past strategies?
7. How do public and corporate policies constrain strategic alternatives?

The previous chapters have provided the background necessary to develop a marketing-mix strategy. The situation analysis identifies a brand's strength, weaknesses, opportunities, threats, and problems. The next step is the creative process—developing a brand strategy.

Marketing strategy is the path through which marketing resources are matched to market opportunities and problems. The marketing strategist must operate in an environment of influences that are largely *uncontrollable*—the values and philosophy of the firm, the generic demand for the product type, the brand demand for competitive products, competitive behavior, and public policy. Analysis of these influences yields marketing opportunities and problems.

The strategist also deals with decision variables that are *controllable* within the bounds of corporate and public policy—product, price, channels of distribution, advertising, and personal selling. (Some authors refer to the four P's—product, price, pipelines (channels), and promotion (advertising and personal selling.) The strategist "mixes these ingredients"[1] to create a broad battle plan for a product. Each mix is unique to the product and its environment. The influence of this mix on demand and the cost of each element in the mix determine whether the strategy is profitable.

We have already seen how the Strategy Worksheet helps to organize the strategy and the profit plan (Chapters 2 and 9). In this chapter we will discuss refinements in the Strategy Worksheet to emphasize the creation of alternatives and the need for contingency planning. We will also examine the need to create clear links between the elements of the strategy and the opportunities and problems that were rank-ordered at the top of the Strategy Worksheet.

THE IMPORTANCE OF IDENTIFYING A STRATEGY

"The key to understanding marketing today is an understanding of strategy."[2] *Strategy is what* you are going to do; *tactics are how* you are going to do it. Note that we generally refer to strategy in the singular and tactics in the plural. This emphasizes an important point, namely, that there should be a single strategy, but may be many tactics. Thus there is one selling proposition, but many ways to state it to the consumer. An example will clarify this point.

Almost 90 years ago John S. Pemberton created a patent medicine to soothe upset stomachs and headaches. Consumers loved the taste, so he increased advertising, added carbonation, and repositioned it as a drink—Coca-Cola. This represents a shift in strategy—from a medicine to a drink. During the ensuing years Coca-Cola has never changed its strategy from the theme of a "refreshing drink." It has had many different tactics to express this theme, such as "the real thing" or "things go better with coke." But the strategy has never changed.

This example stresses the importance of developing a winning strategy and then sticking with it. This is sometimes described as finding the *unique selling proposition* (USP). Once this has been identified, the remaining task is to effectively communicate the USP to the target audience.

A strategic product repositioning may be required when the initial target market segment is found to be too small. Miller's High Life beer provides an example. Initially it was positioned as the "champagne of bottled beer." This positioning yielded a narrow market of infrequent beer drinkers. The strategy was changed to stress quality and leisurely enjoyment. The message then became: "If you've got the time, we've got the beer."[3]

Being first with a new product, however, does not ensure success unless the product is supported by an effective marketing strategy. There are many examples of second-entry products which became the leaders because of a superior marketing strategy. As late as 1955, for example, Sperry Rand's Univac computer had the largest market share. In the next decade, IBM took more than 75 percent of the market by using the strategy of helping the businessperson solve his or her problem. "IBM was essentially a data processing company; Sperry Rand was essentially a manufacturing company, strong in electronics know-how, but with a weak organization for marketing data processing equipment. What counted was that IBM sensed a major need and tailored the whole company to fit it. That others came along *first* with the hardware hardly counted."[4]

BUILDING A MARKETING STRATEGY What is the sequence of events in building a marketing strategy? It depends on the analysis of the situation. The events for the development of L'eggs panty hose appear in Fig. 11.1 as a series of building blocks. The L'eggs strategy was built on the base of product development and market research. These two elements created the basis for defining the opportunity. Once the opportunity was known, the package, the display, and the name were developed as an integrated unit, based on an egg. The next step was to develop a strategy. To solve the problems of out-of-stock and dealer resistance, a strategy of rack distribution by L'eggs was established. (A detailed discussion of this strategy appears in Chapter 14.) Media and advertising strategies were then developed as a unit. The final strategic element was promotion, which appears in the figure at the top of the L'eggs package.

Of course, the L'eggs sequence is not the only one for a successful strategy. In another case the advertising strategy may be developed earlier because of a particular communication problem. In yet another case a redesigned package may be the beginning for a new strategy.

Fig. 11.1 Developing the L'eggs strategy. (Courtesy Barry Boyd, L'eggs Product Manager.)

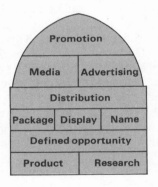

CREATING ALTERNATIVES Creating alternative strategies begins with a clear definition of the opportunities and problems. Developing these strategies is a creative leap, a shift in thinking from the logical process of deduction in the Environmental Analysis Worksheet to the creative process of induction in the Strategy Worksheet.

The Marketing Audit If a product is not new, it will have had a previous strategy. This should be examined for its strengths and weaknesses. Furthermore, the strengths and weaknesses of competitive strategies should be studied. This evaluation of a brand's strengths and weaknesses, as well as those of a competitor, is frequently known as a *marketing audit.*

Each element of the marketing mix will have its own strategy, which must be consistent with the entire marketing strategy, which in turn will reflect the corporate philosophy. For instance, a pharmaceutical firm with a corporate philosophy of "detecting and treating illness in people and animals" could accomplish this with several different *product* strategies. It could license the rights to manufacture a drug from another manufacturer. It could have another manufacturer produce it in bulk and package the drug under its own label. It could wait for the patent to run out on competitor's products. Or it could invest in research and development to make its own discoveries. Having selected a *product* strategy, the next problem may be a *channel* strategy. Should the firm sell directly to retailers, or should it require chains to buy from wholesalers?

If each of the five elements in the marketing mix had only three alternative strategies, there would be a possibility of 125 total strategies ($5^3 = 125$). Working out the expected revenue and costs for each of these strategies would be a costly and time-consuming task. The task is simplified by the fact that many of the alternatives are eliminated because they fall outside corporate policy. (See Fig. 4.2.) Furthermore, executive judgment will "prune" the decision tree to a few alternatives.

The final few strategies that are considered are selected according to the planner's experienced judgment and by decision theory. Decision trees are used to help organize estimates of revenue, costs, and competitive reaction. Subjective probabilities are associated with each of these estimates to yield an *expected value* for each alternative. The alternative that should be selected is the one with the highest expected value. (See Chapters 3 and 13 for examples.) The validity of the decision may be challenged by rerunning the analysis, using different dollar estimates and revised subjective probabilities of occurrences of events. This is known as a sensitivity analysis.

Showing Alternatives on the Strategy Worksheet To keep the initial discussion of the Strategy Worksheet simple, no attempt was made to show alternative strategies. Now we must illustrate where and why alternatives appear on the worksheet.

Table 11.1 is a refinement of the Scoop 1971 Strategy Worksheet (Table 2.2). Here we focus on three elements of the marketing strategy—product, package, and price. The major refinement of the Strategy Worksheet appears in the second column, which has been changed from "Recommended strategy" to "Strategic alternatives in rank order." The first alternative is the one that was recommended in Table 2.2. The other alternatives were considered to be viable, but not the best.

Each alternative includes an estimate of its effect on demand, costs, competition, and public policy. In practice, each of these estimates would be supported with an appendix that gave details. Ideally, these details would include the expected value of each alternative. An examination of each of the alternatives illustrates how difficult it is to choose from among strategic marketing alternatives. It is necessary to make trade-offs among the costs and benefits.

There are two reasons why a product manager should identify the alternatives considered. First, this identification will help the group product manager to evaluate the young planner's ability to create viable alternatives. Second, these alternatives serve as *contingency plans.*

TABLE 11.1   Refinements of the Scoop 1971 Strategy Worksheet

Rank-order of problems:

1. Create buyer awareness of Scoop's benefits
2. Achieve high distribution rates
3. Increase trial rate
4. Increase repeat-purchase rate

Decision areas in marketing-mix strategies	Strategic alternatives in rank order	Estimated effect
Product	1. Available flavors are vanilla and chocolate (1, 2, 3, 4)*	1. This will cover 60% of the preferences
	2. Available flavors are vanilla, chocolate, and strawberry (1, 3, 4)	2. This will cover 75% of the preferences and require $800,000 for developing the strawberry flavor
	3. Available only in chocolate (1)	3. This will meet only 35% of the preferences, but will reduce variable costs from 12% to 9% and fixed costs from 38% to 33% (see Appendix for details)†
Package	1. A reusable half-gallon plastic container (1, 4)	1. The reuse factor will appeal to the price conscious and the environmentalists
	2. A paperboard container in lithographic color illustrations of Scoop ice creams, milk shakes, and puddings (4)	2. This container would make it easier to promote other uses; the savings would permit a price at a retail of 97¢
Price	1. Retail at $1.00/gallon (1, 2, 3, 4)	1. Should be attractive to consumers because it is 12¢ less than they are paying
	2. Retail at $0.95/gallon (1, 3, 4)	2. This would be more attractive to consumers and would discourage competition, but would also reduce the dollar margin to retailers
	3. Retail at $1.05 and drop to $1.00 when competition enters (2)	3. This price is still a saving for the consumer; the higher price permits a faster repayment of the investment for product development and also gives the channel more of a dollar margin (see Appendix for details)†

* Numbers refer to the problems that this alternative will help solve.
† The Appendix is not included in this illustration.

CONTINGENCY PLANS   Contingency planning has long been a part of military planning, but few business firms practice it. It is impossible to have a contingency plan for every event that does not work out as planned. Some of the minor deviations from a plan must be handled by retaining flexibility in the plan. But for the key elements in the marketing mix, there should be a contingency plan when that element is vital to the success of the entire marketing strategy. The second and third strategic alternatives, as shown on the Strategy Worksheet, become the contingency plan. They have been thought through, and their costs and benefits have been evaluated. They can be implemented quickly, without extensive committee meetings to establish a new strategy.

There are many reasons why the first-choice strategy may not be usable. The final estimated *costs may exceed the budget*. The new planner may not be aware of all *corporate policies*, and the plan may have violated them. The alternative that is best for a brand may not be the best for the company, because it would *cannibalize another company brand*. Simultaneous inspiration is not uncommon in marketing. Just prior to launching a new advertising campaign, a *competitor may launch a campaign with a similar theme*. *Public policies* may have been violated because the planner was not aware of the policy or because a policy was introduced after the plan had been approved. When a marketing goal has not been met, the planner could pump more money into the first strategy or introduce additional strategies. Thus it may be necessary to have a *contingency plan for underachieving* when reaching a specific goal is vital to the success of the firm.

LINKING THE STRATEGIES TO OPPORTUNITIES AND PROBLEMS   The planner can easily get carried away in the creativity of strategies and forget that the reason for the strategy is not creativity itself, but to tap an opportunity or to solve a problem. A further refinement in the Strategy Worksheet will help the planner to keep the opportunities and problems in focus.

The top of the revised Strategy Worksheet (Table 11.1) has repeated the rank order of problems that appeared in Table 2.2. The numbers in parentheses after each strategic alternative refer to the problem that this alternative will help solve. For instance, the availability of vanilla and chocolate flavors will contribute in varying degrees toward solving each of the four problems. The existence of the product makes it possible to experience the benefits of Scoop (problem 1). Retailers want a minimum number of flavors, but not too many because of limited shelf space. Thus limiting the introduction to two flavors may improve the distribution rate (problem 2). Two flavors will cover more of the customers' preferences than one flavor, which should increase the trial rate (problem 3) and the repeat-purchase rate (problem 4). Note that in Table 11.1 each of the strategies ranked first contributed to the solutions of more problems than those given lower ranks. It is difficult to quantify this benefit when evaluating the alternatives, but it certainly should be considered.

A PRIORI **EVALUATION OF STRATEGIES**   The final test of a strategy is whether it meets the goal in the assigned time. This can occur only after the strategy has been implemented. There is a need to evaluate strategies before they are implemented to ensure a higher probability of success. The six criteria Tilles presents for the evaluation of corporate strategies are also applicable to marketing strategies.[5]

1. Is the strategy internally consistent among the elements of the marketing mix and the goals of the firm?

2. Is the strategy consistent with the environment? The answer to this criterion will be affirmative if the environmental analysis has been completed.

3. Is the strategy appropriate in view of the available resources? *Resources* in marketing must include capital, productive capacity, management capacity, and capacities in advertising, personal selling, and channels of distribution.

4. Does the strategy involve an acceptable degree of risk? To answer this question, one must consider the amount of resources that are required, the time period to which they must be committed, and the proportion of all corporate resources that these resources represent. A strategy that requires all of the resources a firm can accumulate certainly is a risky strategy.

5. Does the strategy have an appropriate time horizon? Strategies, like goals, must have a time for completion. Delay may allow competition to enter, which will require a new strategy.

6. Is the strategy workable? To answer this question, it is necessary to have criteria that can be measured. The final criterion in marketing may be sales, share, or profit, but intermediate criteria are needed also. A reduction in marketing crisis could be one measure of a workable strategy.

SUMMARY   The marketing strategist must match marketing resources to market opportunities and problems. The strategy may include adapting to the *uncontrollable* variables—corporate policy, generic demand, demand for competitors' brands, competitive behavior, and public policy. Market segmentation is a strategy of adapting to existing environments. Most marketing strategies emphasize the *controllable* variables of the marketing mix—product, price, channels of distribution, advertising, and personal selling.

A single successful strategy may be used for decades by changing only the tactics for executing it. The sequence of events for building a strategy will vary across brands and environments.

The identification of alternatives is a creative leap from the opportunities and problems. Each element in the marketing mix has its own strategy. Second- and third-ranked strategies may be used as a contingency plan when the first alternative cannot be implemented. The final marketing strategy should be evaluated for its consistency among the marketing-mix elements, with corporate values and external environments; for its appropriateness with regard to resources, risk, and time; and for its workability.

DISCUSSION QUESTIONS

1. How can there be one strategy but many tactics or action plans for the same brand?
2. What determines where one begins the process of developing a market strategy?
3. What are the criteria for selecting one of the alternatives for implementation?
4. Why should rejected alternatives be reported?
5. How extensive should contingency planning be?

NOTES

1. J. E. Culliton, *The Management of Marketing Costs* (Boston: Division of Research, Graduate School of Business Administration, Harvard University, 1948); and N. H. Borden, "The Concept of the Marketing Mix," *Journal of Advertising Research* (June 1964): 2–7.

2. This paragraph and the next one are based on a conversation with James Hind, Group Product Manager, R. J. Reynolds Company, January 15, 1975.

3. J. McAllister and R. T. Davis, "Marketing Strategy (B)," Teaching Note S-M 163/B (Stanford, Calif.: Leland Stanford Junior University, 1975).

4. "Of Pioneers and Winners," *Forbes*, April 1, 1964, p. 5.

5. S. Tilles, "How to Evaluate Corporate Strategy," *Harvard Business Review* (July–August 1963): 111–121.

SUGGESTED READINGS

Gerstner, L. F., Jr., "Can Strategic Planning Pay Off?" *Business Horizons* (December 1972): 5–16.

Lambin, J.-J., "A Computer On-Line Marketing Mix Model," *Journal of Marketing Research* **9** (May 1972): 119–126.

Newstrom, J. W., W. E. Reif, and R. M. Monczka, *A Contingency Approach to Management: Readings* (New York: McGraw-Hill, 1975).

ENVIRONMENTAL ANALYSIS WORKSHEET

Environmental elements	Facts	Assumptions or research needed	Conclusions
Organizational values, objectives, and policies (4)			
Organizational design (5)			
Situation			
Generic demand (6)			
Brand demand (7)			
Competition (9)			
Public policy (10)			
Opportunities (2)			
Problems			

MARKETING PLAN (CONSUMER PRODUCT)
Current performance
Recommendations
Effect of recommendations on income
Situation analysis
Opportunities and problems
Strategies
Tests and research
Supporting documents
   Comparative budgets
   Media allocation schedule
   Promotion control sheet

STRATEGY WORKSHEET

Opportunities and problems in rank order to importance

   1.
   2.
    .
   n.

	Current strategy	Alternatives and recommended strategy	Estimated Effect

Demand strategy
  Generic
  Brand			

Strategic goals
  Financial
  Marketing			

Marketing-mix strategies
  Product (12)
  Pricing (13)
  Channel and logistics (14)
  Advertising and promotional (15)
  Sales management (16)			

Research (3)			
Profit plan			
Evaluation and control (19)			

CHAPTER 12

Product Strategies

LEARNING OBJECTIVES   After studying this chapter you should:

1. Know the importance of a product strategy to a corporate strategy.
2. Be aware of the changing location of critical product decisions.
3. Understand the concept of a "product" from the consumer's viewpoint.
4. Know what causes products to have a life cycle.
5. Know the different ways for repositioning a product.
6. Know common product strategies during market and technological change.
7. Know how new-product ideas are generated and screened.
8. Be aware of the complexity of new-product development.
9. Know how industrial new-product strategies differ from consumer new-product strategies.
10. Know the strengths and weaknesses of the various ways for organizing for new-product development.
11. Know some of the reasons why new products fail.
12. Be able to define and use the following concepts:

Product-portfolio strategies	Product improvement	Concept tests
Differentiated and undifferentiated product strategies	Product extensions	Net present values
	Horizontal, vertical, and conglomerate diversification	National brands
		Private brands
Product repositioning	Product elimination	Mixed branding strategy
		Focus-group interviews

SOME STRATEGIC QUESTIONS FOR OPENERS

1. Where is the generic product in its life cycle?
2. Do the product attributes meet perceived needs?
3. Does the product need repositioning?
4. How should we organize for new-product ideas?
5. Can product costs be reduced?
6. Should products be dropped?

WHY A STRATEGY APPROACH   Many forces have changed the criteria for evaluating product strategies. During the late 1970s a shortage of capital awakened many firms to the need to evaluate their product mixes as they would a portfolio of investments. This portfolio approach has led to a variety of matrices for the classification of products. Thus the Shell Company uses the dimensions of *outlook for profitability* and *competitive capabilities* (see Chapter 4). The Boston Consulting Group uses *market growth rate* and *market share* as its dimensions (see Chapter 9). General Electric prefers *industry attractiveness* and *business attractiveness*.[1] Although the dimensions vary among companies, the strategic product decisions are very similar—invest, retain selectively, and divest. In managing product decisions, therefore, the marketing manager will be required to use financial criteria, such as return on investment.

The location of product decisions is also changing. The new criteria, heightened competition, legal implications, and the increasing complexity of the product levels of management are all factors in this shift. In an earlier chapter we saw that the H. J. Heinz Company moved product strategy decisions from product managers to corporate-level managers. To reflect these trends in the development of product strategies, this chapter takes the broader, corporate view of product decisions rather than brand-level decisions.

THE IMPORTANCE OF A PRODUCT STRATEGY   "The end product of strategic decisions is deceptively simple; a combination of products and markets is selected for the firm. This combination is arrived at by the addition of new product-markets, divestment from some old ones, and expansion of the present position."[2]

"To be effective, therefore, a product strategy or product line policy must arise from a thorough and objective appraisal of the company's situation and a sensitivity to market needs. It must derive from a full recognition of the firm's strengths and weaknesses as well as from a careful and continual monitoring of consumer requirements."[3]

"Knowledge that a product yields significant and unique benefits to a sizable segment of consumers does not, unfortunately, ensure its success. The actions of the competitors and of intermediaries in the distribution process can prevent the attainment of satisfactory volume and profits. It is important, therefore, that the definition of market opportunity be based not only on consideration of consumer or user wants but also on careful consideration of the desires of distributive organizations and the behavior of rivals."[4]

The planner who has completed the Environmental Analysis Worksheet and ranked the opportunities and problems is well prepared to develop a product strategy. The planner's analysis of the organization will have answered basic questions about corporate objectives, policy constraints, and organizational design. The generic-demand analysis will have identified unmet consumer needs, new market segments, product life cycles, and trends in old markets. The brand-demand analysis will have answered questions about a product's strengths and weaknesses. It will have positioned a brand against competitors' brands according to consumers' perceptions of product benefits. The planner will have learned something about the innovators in the market in order to direct new products toward this important group. Public policies that provide opportunities as well as those that are constraints on product policy will have been identified. In short, if the environmental analysis has been done well, the planner may turn to the next task—the development of a product strategy. This requires a creative leap from analysis, and creativity does not come easily.

Because creativity cannot be taught, we must limit the discussion of product strategy to the *identification of alternative product strategies* that have been successful for many firms. It is hoped that these alternatives will stimulate the planner to develop his or her own winning strategies.

WHAT IS A PRODUCT?   To the consumer, a product is a bundle of perceived benefits that will meet his or her needs. The manufacturer views the product as a bundle of attributes that, *ideally*, will meet consumers' needs. To the product manager, the product is a way of life. Most of the product manager's waking hours, and some sleepless ones as well, are spent thinking about *the* product. The advertising agency sees the product as a communication challenge. The corporate treasurer sees it as a source of funds.

The term *product* will be used here to mean more than the physical attributes of the product. It will also include the features of the package, such as a pouring spout on a detergent box, that make the product easier to use. *Product* will also mean the services provided before and after the sale. These services are very much a part of the product/service mix in the sale of industrial products. *Product* may also include the prestige associated with the product's brand name, because this prestige contributes to consumer's satisfaction with the product.

The marketing of a *service*, such as health care or insurance, is frequently recognized as the most difficult kind of marketing, because the consumer is buying an intangible and therefore has nothing to show for his or her purchase. Space limitations prevent a separate discussion of the marketing of services; Rathmell has provided a very good discussion of the problems of service marketing.[5] Many of the strategies that are appropriate to product marketing have their counterparts in service marketing. Therefore, the term *product* in this chapter is defined broadly to include services.

During the discussions of the situation analysis (Chapters 6–9) several concepts were introduced that are extremely important in the development of a product strategy: segmentation, benefit segmentation, product positioning, and the life cycle of the product. We saw the relevance of the product life cycle in the information system (Chapter 3), in the organizational design (Chapter 5), and in competitive strategies (Chapter 9). It is a widely used market concept, but there is also a controversy about its existence.

DOES THE PRODUCT LIFE CYCLE EXIST?   Attempts to derive the S-shaped curve of the life-cycle phases of introduction, growth, and maturing have not been convincing.[6] Indeed, some authors suggest that the product life-cycle concept should be forgotten entirely.[7] Complete rejection of this concept misses the point, however. A conceptual model helps to organize our thinking and, in the case of marketing, our strategies. Similarly, the concept of an atom proved to be a very powerful analytical tool in physics, even though nobody had seen one.

Although the shape of the curve may be unknown, there are many examples of successful product life-cycle strategies. For example, in 1969 the E. & J. Gallo Winery added carbonation to its slow-selling Boone's Farm apple wine. By early 1971 sales had jumped from 2500 cases to 720,000 cases a month. When the "pop" wine boom peaked in 1972, Gallo had 88 percent of the market. Gallo then "milked" this product so that it could shift to a strategy of upgrading its product line into the higher-price wines. It stopped advertising Boone's Farm, and its market share fell to 33 percent.

The advertising effort was shifted to Hearty Burgundy, which more than tripled its sales. The *total* case sales for *both* product lines stayed flat, around 20 million cases, but the upgrading of the line boosted brand image and profits.[8]

Some of the confusion about the product life cycle exists because users of the concept often fail to differentiate the generic product-type life cycle from the specific brand life cycle. "Pop" wines are a product type; Boone's Farm is a brand. Although the life cycle for the product type may be beyond the control of the product planner, he or she can adapt a strategy to the product life cycle, as Gallo so clearly demonstrated. The product manager, therefore, should think in terms of *managing* the *brand* life cycle and *adapting* to the *product-type* life cycle. (When a company dominates the market, it may be able to manage the product-type life cycle, but only until competition is able to react.)

Competitive activities will shorten a product life cycle. A good example is the leisure industry, e.g., golf, tennis, and skiing. In the early 1970s Wilson could sell as many steel-framed tennis rackets as it could make. By 1975, 35 percent of the rackets were steel framed, but competition was so intense that prices had dropped to one-third of the previous levels. Everyone was caught with expanded productive capacity, excess inventories at all levels of distribution, and commitments to import from Taiwan. The shakeout included Chemold, an early metal-racket manufacturer, which filed for a Chapter 11 bankruptcy.

Many nonsports conglomerates moved into the manufacturing of sporting goods, e.g., Victor Comptometer, Colgate-Palmolive, S. C. Johnson & Sons (waxes), and American Brands (foods).[9] This diversity of entries made the identification of competitors and the measurement of industry capacity difficult, if not impossible.

Golf grew at the rate of ten percent per year, until its popularity resulted in overcrowded courses. But the high cost of new courses prevented expansion. Ski equipment and apparel businesses too had their shakeout. AMF's Head Ski, the inventor of metal skis, went from a 70 percent to a 12 percent market share. Manufacturers seemed to have overlooked the fact that their growth is limited by the fact that people have only so many leisure hours to spend on sports.[10]

Product life cycles, therefore, are the result of *economic* and *competitive* forces. They are also of a *social-psychological* nature. A style becomes a fashion when society accepts it, not when a manufacturer promotes it. Bass reasoned that the product life cycle could be related to the diffusion of innovation (see Chapter 6) by measuring the numbers of innovators and imitators and their rates of adoption. He successfully identified the peak years and the peak unit sales for home freezers, television, water softeners, power lawnmowers, and automatic coffee makers.[11] Nevers verified the Bass model by applying it to color television, boat trailers, Holiday Inn Motels, Howard Johnson Motor Lodges, Ramada Inns, McDonald's Restaurants, hybrid corn, and industrial chemical processes.[12] We conclude, therefore, that the planner must understand the economic, competitive, and social-psychological forces that shape the product life cycle for an industry.

To implement the product life-cycle concept, it is necessary to include competition, profit considerations, and the effect of marketing effort. Wind and Claycamp provide a matrix for such a procedure.[13] The product life cycle is not a model that should be followed blindly, but rather a concept that should help us to ask the right questions during the development of a product strategy.

A firm's point of entry in the product life cycle should reflect its strengths. If it is strong in technological development or promotion, it should enter early. If its strengths are distribution, it should enter in the middle of the cycle. If engineering and cost cutting are its strengths, it may even consider entering late in the product life cycle.

STRATEGIES FOR EXISTING PRODUCTS The product-portfolio approach reminds us that most product strategies are concerned with existing products—those in the growth, mature, or declining phase of their life cycles. The product planner has a variety of alternative strategies for products, even though they have been part of the product mix for a long period of time.

Differentiated and Undifferentiated Product Strategies Market segmentation leads to two product strategies—differentiation and undifferentiation. Differentiated product strategies require that separate products be designed to meet the needs of each segment. An undifferentiated strategy uses a single product, but differentiates the promotional strategy. Floor polishes illustrate both strategies.

Market research discovered that there are two market segments for floor-polishing products. One segment will use a labor-saving floor polish because it dislikes the chore and wants to use its time in other ways. The other segment thinks that it is "cheating" not to get down on the floor and work at the job of floor polishing.[14] A *differentiated product* strategy would develop a product for each of these market segments; an *undifferentiated product* strategy would develop a single product, but then differentiate its advertising message. For instance, to reach the second group with a labor-saving product, one could advertise: "Spend more time with your children by using our labor-saving product." Such a copy theme would reinforce this second segment's basic values about its role in the family.

No Product Change The glamour and excitement of new-product introductions make us overlook the fact that the majority of marketing plans do not make changes in the product. A successful product does not need to be changed. Furthermore, a successful marketing plan may require only some fine tuning, e.g., replacing a worn-out copy theme or improving the media mix. Thus one product strategy that should not be overlooked is to leave the product unchanged.

Product Repositioning Product repositioning does not always require changes in the attributes of the product, but instead may require changes in consumers' perception of the benefits. Repositioning can also be accomplished by finding *new uses* for old products. We have already seen how Lysol, Vaseline, and Arm & Hammer Baking Soda successfully repositioned their brands by identifying and promoting new uses (see Chapter 7). Success comes from repositioning a brand in a growing market.

Another form of repositioning a product requires moving consumers' perception of the brand closer to their perception of an ideal brand or moving their perception of the ideal brand closer to the brand being promoted. The second strategy may be very difficult, however, because it requires consumers to change their basic values toward the product type.

Product Improvement Product improvement may take many forms. There may be minor *changes in the attributes* of a product, such as a more pleasant flavor in a toothpaste or the substitution of a new glue for a clamp. These changes are reactions to changes in the marketplace and in technology.

Product improvement also occurs when a *package is redesigned* to be more convenient or to provide better protection. Packaging changes raise many questions about appropriate material, legal requirements, disposability, trade acceptance, design, consumer recognition, ease of use, and buying habits. The shape of the package may enhance brand recognition. For example, the "Gibson Girl" shape of Coca-Cola bottles made them easy to recognize. Conversely, a household cleaner packaged in a soft drink-type container violated child-safety laws.

New services, before or after the sale, represent a product improvement. The Buyer Protection Plan for American Motors Corporation cars represents a product strategy. This warranty has now been joined by a Service Protection Plan, which guarantees the price of service and customer satisfaction.[15] Thus warranties can be an important part of product strategy.[16]

Product Extensions   The motive for product extensions may be to fill gaps in the product line, use excess capacity in marketing and production, and meet competition. During periods of tight money markets, such as 1973 to 1975, many manufacturers in the grocery package-goods industries used product extensions rather than new products, because extensions gave a shorter payback period.

Product extensions may include a new-flavored cake mix, a larger-size soft drink, or a shampoo for dry hair. Product extensions, product repositions, and minor product improvements account for approximately 80 percent of the new offerings to supermarkets. These introductions tend to follow the business cycle. Thus there were 9252 in 1972, 6776 in 1973, 6465 in 1974, and 6688 in 1975.[17]

Product-line extensions are less risky, because they represent a line of business that the company presently knows, there are many marketing efficiencies in using the same brands and the same distribution system, and there are production economies of scale. They can be used as a competitive strategy to "cover our flanks" and keep out competition.[18]

Extensions are not without risks, however. A product extensions that fails can damage the brand image, weaken trade relations with retailers, and discourage salespeople and product managers. An extension may also cannibalize an existing brand. For instance, a coffee producer carefully positioned a new decaffeinated coffee for young people to avoid cannibalizing its existing brand, which appealed to older persons.

Diversification through New Products   When a firm decides to diversify through new products, it may move in three directions—horizontally, vertically, and in all directions (conglomerate diversification). Horizontal diversification occurs when new products are added which have a close relationship to old products. For example, Bemis Bag Company began in 1858 by producing paper and cotton bags. By 1959 its markets were threatened with new materials, and it also had an image problem; it was the "bag company." Bemis diversified horizontally by introducing packages made of new materials. It introduced blow-molded plastic containers for food, plastic-strip packages for pharmaceuticals, polyethylene self-service packages, and polystrene cushioning for packaging industrial products.[19]

Vertical diversification occurs in a product line when a company produces products that it previously purchased. A company may integrate to the source of supply to lower costs or to ensure a source of supply during periods of shortages. Chemical companies with their own sources of petroleum have a tremendous competitive advantage during petroleum shortages. Raw-material producers may integrate forward to ensure a market for their products. Supermarket chains may integrate backward to food processing or baking to gain greater margins.

Conglomerate diversification is motivated solely by a desire to increase the return on investment. There is no direct relationship between the new product and the present business. Present ties with customers, production, and distribution are not relevant.[20]

The strategy of new products is so risky and complicated that an extensive discussion will follow shortly. But first we must consider the strategy of dropping products.

Product Elimination Most marketing strategists are familiar with the 80/20 rule, which states that 80 percent of our profit comes from 20 percent of our products. A product strategy should include answers to such questions as: When should a product be considered for elimination? What criteria should we use? Can unprofitable products be made profitable by using a different strategy (e.g., sell through distributors rather than direct)?

A survey of manufacturers of drugs, major appliances, food, clothing, and minor appliances identified the following variables as those most frequently used to identify weak products: sales, profit, or share did not reach a required minimum level; share did not compare favorably with that in previous years; sales did not reach the level forecasted; and the contribution to total company sales was insignificant.[21]

The analysis of existing data will identify weak products and suggest appropriate strategies, such as dropping the product, selling it to another firm, or reducing marketing costs. The strategies of reducing sales calls, marketing through wholesalers, and dropping products must be tested before implementation. Sevin has demonstrated that such tests can produce strategies that will greatly increase profits.[22]

When Is a Change in Product Strategy Required? The primary forces that require a change in product strategy are changes in the market and technology. Top management will want to consider appropriate strategies for these changes. Table 12.1 illustrates appropriate strategies for three market states (no market change, a strengthened market, and new markets) and three technological states (no change, improved technology, and new technology). The cell entries illustrate strategies that are consistent with a corporate policy. By providing marketing planners with such a table, a marketing manager will provide a unified corporate response to changes in the market and in technology.

DEVELOPING NEW PRODUCTS

The Motivation for Innovation There are many incentives for developing new products. For example, the desire for internal growth has led to new products, accounting for 7 to 50 percent of annual sales across major industries.[23] There is the desire to offer a full product line, thereby preventing competition from entering some markets. There may be excess capacity in production or marketing facilities. Seasonal lows may be offset by new products, e.g., an outboard motor manufacturer introducing a line of snowmobiles. Diversification may be necessary because further growth would increase

TABLE 12.1   Strategies during market and technological change

		Technological state	
Market state	*No change*	*Improved technology*	*New technology*
No market change	No action	Reformulate the product for optimal balance of product quality and cost	Replacement with new and better ingredients in present products
Strenthened market (exploit existing markets more fully)	Find more customers for present uses by remerchandising existing products	Improve the product	Extend the product line to present customers
New markets (increase market segments)	New product uses to present and new customers	Modify present products for new uses	Diversify by developing new products to appeal to new market segments.

Adapted by permission from Samuel C. Johnson and Conrad Jones, "How to Organize for New Products," *Harvard Business Review* (May–June 1957): 52. Copyright © 1957 by the President and Fellows of Harvard College; all rights reserved.

market share to a point that would bring antitrust action. The desire to "be first" in a new field is a great incentive to new-product development efforts. Being first reduces the promotional costs of introducing a "me too" product. A successful track record of introducing new products builds enthusiasm and confidence within the marketing organization and the channels of distribution. Industrial and consumer-product manufacturers agree that the benefits of new-product introductions more than offset the risks.[24]

The economist J. A. Schumpeter considered innovation and its diffusion a prime mover in an economy because of its encouragement to investment.[25] In 1974 firms listed on the New York Stock Exchange reported the introduction of 4754 new products. The industry leaders in new products were computers (144), communications (132), pharmaceuticals (118), photographic equipment (90), toiletries (80), and surgical and medical instruments (52).[26]

Some authors see a slowing in the rate of new-product introduction in the late 1970s due to the high cost of capital; the high cost of introductions, especially in areas that require government approval; the lack of a national energy policy; and the end of many growth industries. There seems to be a decline in innovation just when it is needed to give the American economy an international comparative advantage. It is easy to see why executives, operating in an environment of such uncertainty, cited "unavailability of market information" and "fear of failure" as the primary bars to innovation.[27]

Generating New-Product Ideas

Definitions of the business reexamined. New-product ideas should begin with a reexamination of a firm's definition of its business and policies. Thus the corporate strategy of Burroughs Wellcome Company, a pharmaceutical firm, states that it will manufacture and market "products that contribute to good health through the prevention, detection, or treatment of disease in humans and animals" (see Chapter 4). This statement of corporate strategy limits the type of new products that will be appropriate. For example, a new cosmetic would not be acceptable unless it is related to the prevention, detection, or treatment of disease.

Some companies have found that their businesses have been defined so narrowly that there is no hope of growth. Other companies have found that their definitions have placed them in a declining industry. For instance, the declining birth rate forced Gerber to change its long-standing policy: "Babies are our only business," and Coca-Cola was very slow to diversify out of the soft drink business into other beverages.[28]

A new definition of corporate strategy should build on the strengths of the company. For instance, Hertz excels in renting equipment, Corning Glass excels in glass technology, and Procter & Gamble excels in promotion. Research and development tend to be the strengths of firms in the fields of industrial chemicals, pharmaceuticals, and industrial electronics. Marketing tends to be the strength of companies that manufacture personal-care products, food, and beverages.[29]

Inventors. Many new products are the result of a creative person's seeing an unmet need. Clarence Birdseye was a biologist, a fur trader, and an investigator for the United States Fisheries Association, which led to his desire to develop a method for preserving fish for market. In 1923 he put packages of fish between two refrigerated metal surfaces, thereby beginning the frozen-foods industry. His pioneering companies are now divisions of General Foods. Gail Borden invented condensed milk when he observed children dying from infected fresh milk. Dr. Joseph C. Muhler, while he was a sophomore in the Indiana University School of Dentistry in 1945, found that stannous fluoride prevents tooth decay.[30]

Managing creative people can be a real challenge. McGuire suggests that they require a management style that is "indirect and participatory rather than direct and authoritarian."[31] Creative people may cause misunderstandings and friction in an organization because they refuse to conform and because they place a high value on their work time; they resent having to expend time on extraneous tasks. On the other hand, the creative person is a superior problem solver with extraordinary powers of observation and imagination; the management problem is identifying and unlocking this creativity.[32]

In solving problems the creative person finds new ways of arranging common elements. Brainstorming and synectics are two techniques that have been used to encourage small groups of people to seek new insights into solving problems. The basic philosophy of these approaches is to encourage new ideas by not being critical of any idea that a person advances.

Internal and external sources. Internal sources for ideas include employees, product complaint files, salespeople, and of course the research and development and market research departments. External sources for ideas include customers, user panels, retailers, distributors, materials suppliers, advertising agencies, market research firms, venture capital firms, patent attorneys, licensors, patent brokers, and the results obtained by monitoring competitors' test markets.[33] One source that may be over-looked is the register of patents available for license.

The validity of methods such as brainstorming has been questioned by some researchers. Tauber has tried to remedy their weaknesses by developing a technique he calls HIT (heuristic ideation technique).[34] The technique requires the identification of the salient factors associated with the product area. Then the task is to identify all of the combinations of these factors and evaluate their potential as a new idea. For example, if the product area were a dog food, salient factors would include *form* and *package*. A table such as the following would then be created:

| | Package | | | |
Food form	Aerosol	Bag	Boil in bag	Bottle
Biscuit	1	2	3	4
Bread	5	6	7	8
Burger	9	10	11	12

The task then becomes one of evaluating each of these 12 product ideas for a new dog food.

Urban illustrates how a computer model may be used to design frequently purchased consumer products.[35] He links physical and psychological product attributes to trial and repeat-purchase rates to estimate long-run market shares. Urban notes that many models have been built to screen and test new-product ideas, but few models exist to design a new product.

Acquisitions. The high risk and delay involved in new-product introduction have caused many companies to diversify through acquisition of products rather than through internal development of new products. Some of the most famous acquisitions have been made by Procter & Gamble (Duncan Hines Cake Mixes), General Foods (Kool Aid, SOS Cleanser, and Good Seasons), Campbell Soups (Swanson and Pepperidge Farm), Corn Products (Knorr Soups and Skippy Peanut Butter), and Gillette (Toni and Papermate).

The biggest problem in acquisition strategies is finding products that are compatible with the company's present policies and capacities. When the Singer Sewing Machine company decided to go the acquisition route, it identified its strengths as: a favorable image, an ability to operate abroad, engineering and production skills in the manufacture of precision electro-mechanical products, a strong worldwide marketing network, a strong working-capital position, and worldwide experience in the financing of consumer receivables.[36] Its capital far exceeded what it could profitably invest in the sewing machine industry. To improve return on investment, therefore, Singer would have had to become a conglomerate. The search procedure led Singer to conclude that business machines would be a compatible match, and so it acquired the Friden company, whose major product is electro-mechanical desktop calculators. This acquisition proved less than successful, however, because electronic calculators were soon to replace mechanical ones.[37] In this case, acquisition was not risk-free.

Cooper Industries used the "toolbox theory" when acquiring new companies. Until 1967 Cooper was a one-product, one-market company that sold engines and compressors to energy companies. To offset this cyclical business, Cooper chose to diversify into hand tools that were used throughout the year. The idea was to offer hardware dealers a variety of tools from a single source. In 1971 the downturn in the energy market was worse than expected, but the hand-tool acquisitions produced 81 percent of earnings. The "toolbox theory" worked.[38]

Licensing.   Licensing may be a good source of product ideas. Frequently a company will develop a new product that has applications outside its definition of its business. For example, the National Cash Register Company developed a new type of carbon-less paper for making duplicate copies in its accounting machines. The process encapsulated minute bits of ink on the back of a piece of paper. This capsule of ink would break under the pressure of a pencil or typewriter, making a duplicate copy. This process of encapsulation was licensed to pharmaceutical companies for time-released drugs, because pharmaceutical marketing was not within National Cash's definition of its business. Licenses are also available from foreign companies which do not wish to expand their operations beyond their present geographic boundaries.

Screening New-Product Ideas

Criteria.   New-product ideas must be screened according to marketing, production, and financial criteria. Marketing criteria include compatibility with the present product line, methods of distribution, and promotional methods. Market-growth potential is a crucial criterion; a firm would not want to diversify into a dying market. The product should be compatible with production technology, raw-material sources, and purchasing expertise.

A survey of 85 large firms revealed that 47 percent used return on investment (ROI) as the primary financial criterion, 24 percent used the payback period, and 7 percent used some form of subjective rating scale.[39] Other financial criteria that can be used include net present value, internal rate of return, and accessory income, such as income from film if cameras are sold.

Concept tests.   In concept tests the potential consumer is presented with the product attribute or benefit. This presentation may take one of several forms: a written description, a picture, a mock-up of the product, or a simulation of the advertisement. The respondents may be a group of employees, laboratory test panels, focus groups, or consumers at central locations, e.g., a shopping center. Concepts have the advantages of being quick, cheap, reducing the risk of a big blunder, and minimizing disclosure to competition. Their disadvantage is that the result cannot be projected into the total market.[40] There is also the problem that the concept and the method of presentation may confound the results, so that it is difficult to know exactly what has been measured.[41] However, refinements have been suggested so that concept tests can measure the size of the market and the interaction of product attributes.[42]

Mathematical models.   The high cost of new-product introduction and the complexity of analysis have led to the development of mathematical models to screen new-product ideas. The inputs reflect the interests of the developers. For instance, the NEWS (*new-product early warning system*) model developed by the advertising agency of Batten, Barton, Durstin and Osborn, Inc., attempts to predict the number of triers, the repurchase rates, and the usage rates in test markets, given brand awareness, advertising dollars spent, the number of persons exposed to advertising, and the number of advertising exposures per person.[43]

Researchers at the advertising agency of N. W. Ayer developed a new-product screening model that used product positioning media impressions, copy execution, consumer promotion, and category interest to predict *knowledge about the product.* Distribution rates, packaging, family brand, consumer promotion, product satisfaction, and category usage were used to predict *initial trial rates.* Relative price, product satisfaction, and purchase frequency were used to predict *repeat purchases.*[44]

Other models emphasize different variables. For example, Eskin and Malec model *trial rates* as a function of distribution rates, promotional spending, and the size of the product class. The model estimates repeat purchase rates from the repeat rates of similar products.[45] A decision model of the go, no-go format has been developed to maximize profits under various conditions of price, advertising, distribution, and competition.[46]

The Post Division of General Foods uses a model to decide if a proposal meets the financial criteria of ROI, share, and net profit contribution. This model consists of four submodels—a volume forecasting model, a business evaluation model, a portfolio evaluation model, and a decision-analysis model. The last submodel gives payout estimates under various market and manufacturing conditions.[47]

General Mills uses a new-product screening model that gives the probability distribution for the net present value of new-product concepts. An example of the distributions for six product concepts appears in Fig. 12.1. The data are generated by the computer in response to information supplied by the product planner. The

Fig. 12.1 An application of the General Mills concept screening program for six product concepts. (W. L. Etter, Manager, Quantitative Analysis, Consumer Services, General Mills, personal communication, October 26, 1976.)

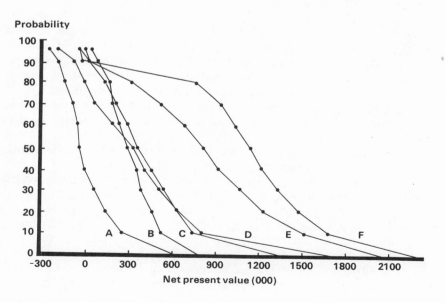

planner estimates the time periods until technical success, interest rates, developmental costs, capital investments, marketing expense, competitive reactions, margins, and volumes. Many of these variables require estimates of the probability distribution.[48] In Fig. 12.1, for example, we see that concept F is the clear winner because it has the highest probability of attaining the highest net present value.

A computer program is used at Bristol-Myers to create a "national payout plan" for various new product programs.[49] The program calculates the likely annual sales level, the probability of present values, and the number of years to break even.

These various models must be regarded as in the developmental stage. The cost of developing them tends to limit them to companies that introduce a large number of new products. It is difficult to compare the results of the models, because they have been developed in very competitive markets where a company is unwilling to reveal a competitive advantage such as a good screening model.

Brand Strategies   The decision to introduce a new product raises numerous questions about branding strategies. Should we use a new brand name or one that is used for existing products? If we use an existing brand name, the new product can ride on the success of the existing product. On the other hand, if the new product fails, it may hurt the image of the existing brand.

Should we use our own brand or should we sell to a retailer, such as Sears, and let Sears promote the product under its own brand name? This is the question of the national (i.e., manufacturer's) brand versus the private (i.e., distributor's) brand. Some companies use a mixed-branding strategy. They use their own brand for their products, but use excess productive capacity to sell to distributors for private branding.

The mixed-branding strategy leads to some difficult questions about the retail-price differentials between the manufacturer's and the distributor's brands. The gasoline industry provides an example. A large refinery that sells through its own stations and to independents permits the independent distributors to sell at a price about four cents less per gallon. If the independent distributor exceeds this price spread, the national-brand refinery reacts by cutting its price. A study of the relationship between branding policies and net profit after taxes indicated that a manufacturer's brand policy led to the highest profit, whereas the mixed policy ranked second and the straight private-branding policy was third.[50] "Branding policy affects the entire stance of a company, from product development and production to finance and the price of corporate securities. A decision to produce, or not produce private brands can change the firm's market standing and affect its earnings for years to come."[51]

A brand can add many benefits to a product, such as familiarity, confidence, differentiation, identification, and prestige. Although these benefits are to the advantage of the manufacturer, branding can also be a liability. For example, since the manufacturer is held responsible for damages from product malfunctions, the private brand also carries certain expressed or implied warranties.

Some recent branding strategies illustrate the importance of a good brand strategy. Canada Dry ginger ale was concerned about its slipping market share. The drink did not appeal to the younger market, because it had been positioned as a mixer. One problem was that the old package did not emphasize the brand name Canada Dry. The nonprotectable, generic "ginger ale" was more prominent than "Canada Dry." A redesigned package reversed this emphasis.[52]

The Burger King/McDonald's competitive interaction led to both companies' promoting their large hamburgers (see Chapters 7 and 9). McDonald's called its version "Big Mac"; Burger King called its "The Whopper." McDonald's may have made the better choice because its name was closely linked to the name of the parent company, whereas "The Whopper" had no such link and was confused with Burger King's competitor, Burger Chef.[53]

A branding policy can be so successful that the brand name becomes the generic name. Aspirin, nylon, cellophane, and cola were brand names at one time. Kleenex, Xerox, Scotch Tape, Kodak, and Frigidaire have almost become generic names.

An Example of a New-Product Introduction—Pampers   The effort, time, and cost of a new-product introduction can be appreciated best by tracing a product from the idea to the profitable conclusion. Pampers disposable diaper provides an excellent example.[54]

The Pampers story begins when a grandfather changed diapers for his first grandchild and decided that there must be a better way than cloth diapers or the disposable diapers then on the market. The grandfather happened to be a Procter & Gamble engineer. Before the company could make any investment in the idea, however, it had to ask three basic questions. Was there a real need? Did P & G have the technical ability to develop the product? Would the product be profitable?

Thousands of mothers were interviewed, and a real need was identified. Present methods of diapering were uncomfortable for babies, cloth diapers bunched up and did not keep the baby dry, and plastic pants irritated the baby's skin. These unmet needs answered the first questions and identified the attributes that were needed in the new product.

The company concluded that the second question could be answered in the affirmative. It had experience in inventing and manufacturing absorbent paper products for paper towels and tissues.

The profitability question was the most difficult one. It was not answered in the affirmative until after a major investment had been made in the product. The generic demand ($N \times R$) was estimated to be 15 billion diaper changes per year. The unknown variable was the proportion (P) of users who would use the new product. The only way to determine this was to make the product and measure consumer acceptance.

The product attributes were to be comfort (a better fit and keeping the baby drier), ease of storage, disposability, competitive price with cloth diapers, and materials that would be safe for the baby and that would not harm the environment when disposed. Nine months of research produced a diaper pad that was rejected in a Dallas test market because it required the wearing of plastic pants. P & G did not know that Dallas babies do not wear plastic pants because they are too hot. Six months later a new attribute had been developed—a thin sheet of plastic across the back to keep the moisture in but permit some circulation. To keep the babies drier, a one-way porous sheet was also added between the baby and the absorbent material.

To test the new diaper, 37,000 of them had to be made by hand. Consumer reaction was overwhelmingly favorable. But the question of profitability still had not been answered. Before it could be answered, there was much more work to be done by a variety of persons. Engineers had to design equipment that would mass produce enough of the product for a test market. This required inventing a new manufacturing process. After one year the engineers were able to produce enough Pampers so that P & G could establish the same level of consumer acceptance with the machine-made product as it had with the hand-made ones.

Concurrent with the engineers' work, market researchers worked on the problem of a product name. Pampers won over Tenders, Dri-Wees, Winks, Tads, Solos, and

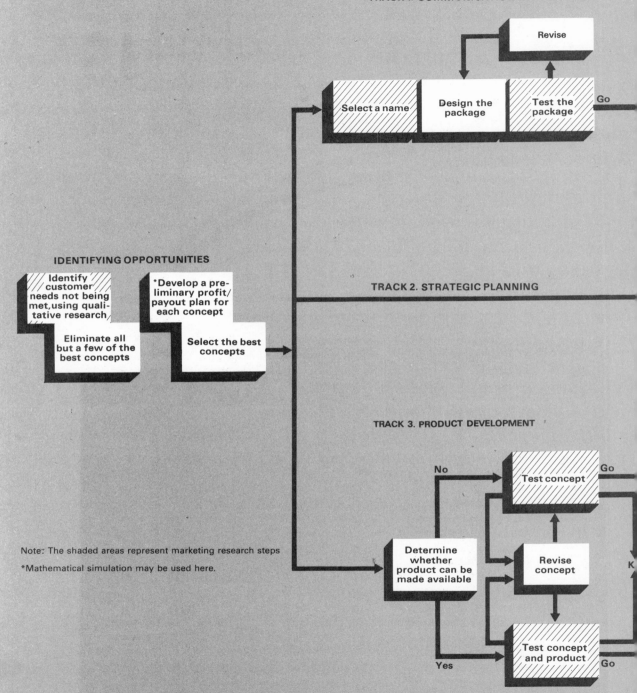

Fig. 12.2 A process for new-product development. (Joy E. Klompmaker, G. David Hughes, and Russell I. Haley, "Test Marketing in New Product Development," *Harvard Business Review* (May–June 1976): 128–138. Copyright © 1976 by the President and Fellows of Harvard College; all rights reserved.)

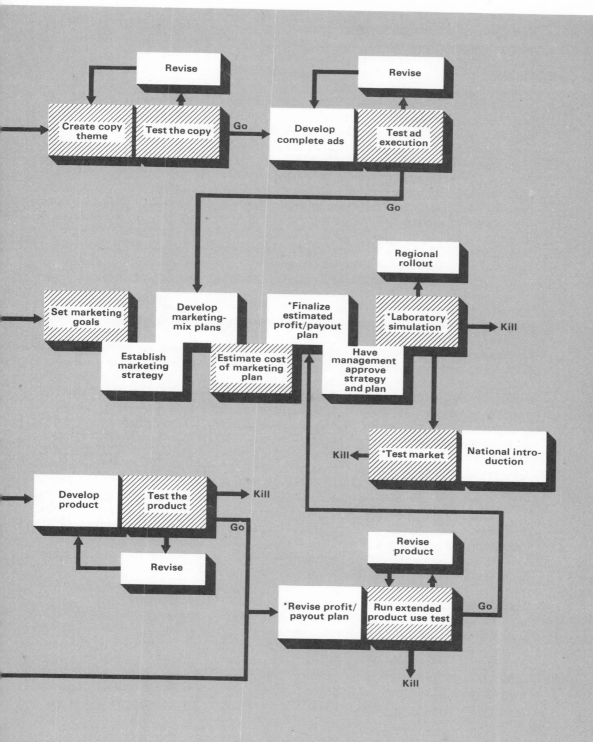

Zephyrs. Packaging experts worked on a package design that would meet the requirements of easy storage, content protection, and attractiveness. The brand manager and the advertising agency worked on the problem of communicating Pampers' benefits to consumers. Distribution experts had to solve logistics problems. Technical experts and purchasing managers focused on the problem of locating vast quantities of the materials that would be needed.

The brand manager and the accountants decided that a price of 10 cents per diaper would be appropriate and that they could sell 400 million diapers annually at this price. But a market test in Peoria, Illinois, indicated that the company could not attain one-half of this goal. Additional market research indicated that the price was too high. The benefits were not worth the cost.

P & G sought ways to reduce the cost, but savings in raw materials, production costs, and delivery costs could not reduce total costs enough to lower the price. The company decided that the only way to lower costs was to increase the volume to one billion diapers, thereby spreading the fixed costs over more units. This would make it possible to sell the product at six cents per diaper. A test market in Sacramento, California, was a success. Production facilities were opened around the country, but they could not keep up with the initial demand.

A Process for New-Product Development The Pampers case illustrates that many marketing activities occur simultaneously as a new product is developed. Figure 12.2, which diagrams this process, is a synthesis of the experiences of 32 persons who are experts in new-product introduction.[55]

There are many procedures for generating new-product ideas, as we have already seen. The approach shown in Fig. 12.2 is some form of qualitative research. Focus-group interviews are frequently used to identify unmet needs. Small groups of about eight persons are led through a discussion of their needs and problems with existing products. The goal of these focus-group sessions is to identify problems and produce ideas. However, because the responses are not quantifiable, they cannot be generalized into estimates of market potential. Rather, these needs may be verified through more structured interviews, as was the case with Pampers. Product attributes that will meet these needs are then developed. A product concept is a hypothetical product that contains some of these attributes. A preliminary profit plan is developed for each concept, and the most promising concepts are selected for further development.

Further development proceeds down three tracks simultaneously. The communication track develops all of the elements that are related to communicating the concept's benefits. These elements include the product name, the package, the message (known as the copy theme), and the visuals in print or television that are associated with communicating the message. The test of the final advertising execution is to provide estimates of the probability of success of the communication strategy and the cost of the strategy. These estimates are inputs to the profit plan.

The lower track in Fig. 12.2 focuses on developing the product. This track branches into two paths according to whether or not the product can be made for testing. If the concept is a product-line extension, such as a new flavor or a new size, it may be possible to make sufficient quantities of the product to test the product directly. If the product is quite technical, which would require a great investment for a small quantity, concept tests may be used. If concept tests are favorable, a product will be developed for further testing. The profit plan will be revised on the basis of these product tests.

The middle track begins the strategic-planning process by setting the marketing goals. Input from the communication track helps in the development of the marketing mix. Cost estimates for these plans, along with the estimates of product costs, serve as inputs to a final estimated-profit plan. If management approves this plan, the product will proceed to one of several final stages. Ideally, it would go to a laboratory simulation before going to a test market or a regional rollout. A laboratory simulation exposes respondents to test commercials and allows them to buy test products in a simulated store. These data, plus follow-up interviews, are used to estimate the market share of the new product.

It is important to note that the test market is the last step in a new-product introduction. There are at least three reasons for its being last. First, a test market tests the entire marketing plan, not just the product. Second, test markets are very expensive. The minimum test for a new grocery product would be a two-city test, and the cost at 1976 prices would be at least $500,000. Finally, a test market reveals vital information to a competitor.[56]

The shaded areas in Fig. 12.2 represent the need for marketing research during the new-product development process. The need is extensive.

INDUSTRIAL NEW-PRODUCT STRATEGIES Throughout this text the point has been emphasized that the concepts developed in consumer-goods marketing can be applied to industrial marketing, with suitable adjustments. For example, we have seen that the success factors in industrial marketing tend to be related to technology; in consumer-goods marketing, to be marketing factors. The industrial marketing mix emphasizes personal selling over advertising. To continue the comparison of the similarities and differences between these two types of marketing, we will examine the planning process in an industrial-products company.

Product strategies in industrial firms are tied more closely to engineering functions than consumer products are. This fact is illustrated by comparing the flow chart for introducing a consumer product (Fig. 12.2) with a chart for introducing a new industrial product (Fig. 12.3). In Fig. 12.3 we see that a rough marketing plan does not appear until the middle of the process; in the consumer-products field a rough plan and a pro forma financial statement appear very early, at the concept stage of development. In the consumer-goods process, communication has a separate track, which begins after the concept has been selected. In the industrial case advertising does not enter until after the product has been field tested. This positioning of advertising illustrates the point that advertising's role is more dominant in consumer-goods marketing than in industrial-goods marketing. The salespeople play a key role in the industrial marketing mix.

In both industrial and consumer marketing the management of existing product lines requires trade-offs. A line that is too limited weakens a competitive position, economies of scale, distributor support, and the enthusiasm of the salespeople.[57] A line that is too broad adds unnecessary costs for inventories, product-line change-over costs, confusion of the distributors and salespeople, and order-processing costs. Finding the optimal balance of products for the line is no easy task.

ORGANIZING FOR NEW-PRODUCT DEVELOPMENT Organizational systems for *existing products*, such as the product-management system, were discussed at length in Chapter 5. Here we will focus on the decisions that must be made to organize for *new-product development*.

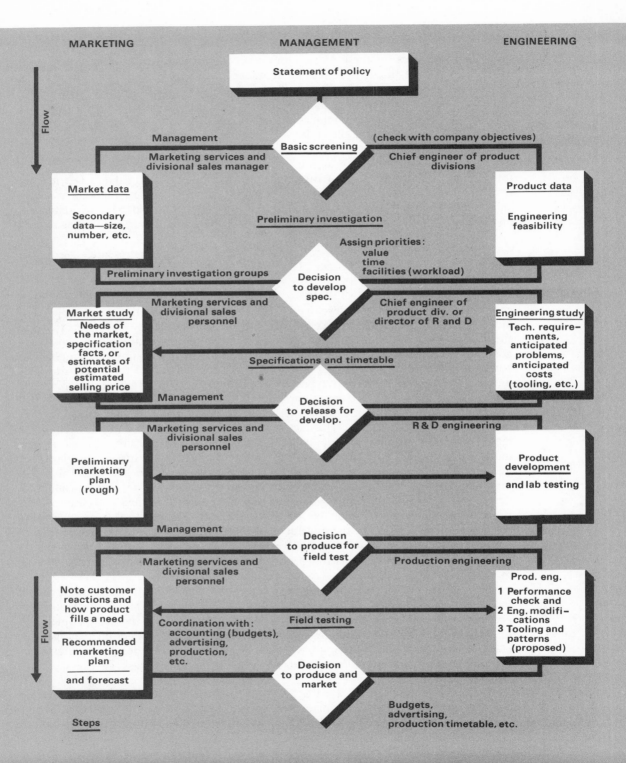

Fig. 12.3 Flow of product planning—an industrial-products company. (E. P. McGuire, *Evaluating New-Product Proposals*, New York: Conference Board, 1973, p. 3. Reprinted by permission.)

Organizing for product innovation raises many organizational questions. "How can we get research people to be more responsive to the needs of the market? What can we do to get our salesmen more involved in selling new products and seeking new applications? How can we get sales, research, and production people to pull in the same direction on product development?"[58]

Centralization versus Decentralization The multidivision company faces the question of centralizing new-product development or decentralizing development to the divisional level. Centralization of new-product development provides better coordination with corporate policies, and it conserves resources by eliminating duplication of facilities. Placing it at the divisional level, however, moves new-product development closer to the market-place. It increases new-product success because it involves in the development those persons who will be responsible for selling the new product, thereby ensuring their support.[59]

Functional Jurisdiction There are three strategies for placing new-product responsibilities in functions. They may be placed in the marketing department, in research and development, or in a separate staff function that reports to top management. Location within the marketing function moves new-product development closer to the market, but there is the danger of being too sensitive to the market so that there are "me-too," short-range, and hurried product introductions. Location within R & D or other technical units is appropriate when the product is a technical innovation, but this organizational design can lead to the development of technically fascinating products that are unrelated to the market demand or to corporate objectives. A separate staff function reporting to top management provides objectivity and top-management support, but it may become impractical, isolated, and elitist.[60]

Project Teams and Venture Groups A project team or a venture group is like a minicompany in that it has specialists from the functions of marketing, R & D, finance, and production. These units are placed outside the corporate organizational structure so that they will be independent in their thinking. The project-team and the venture-group approaches differ in that venture groups tend to have a long-range orientation, taking the company into areas outside its present definition of its business.

The two approaches free new-product development from the biases of present thinking. They assemble the "best and the brightest" talent. Incentive and commitment are high because the teams or groups become the nucleus for new divisions if the product is a success.

These approaches do have limitations, however. One may be the difficulty of assembling qualified people and their working together to overcome the biases of highly trained specialists. Another limitation is that vested interest in the new idea may be so strong that the group is unwilling to terminate a poor product.[61]

New-Product Committees The utility of a new-product committee is controversial. Because they cut across all departmental and functional boundaries, such committees can be efficient for communication and coordination purposes. On the other hand, they are ineffectual in decision making. A creative new idea can be reduced to a mediocre one. If a committee is used, it should be formed at a high management echelon with a clear charter and a strong leader. It should be kept small and manageable.[62]

ANALYZING FAMOUS FAILURES How many new products fail? This is a hard question to answer, because of variations in classification of what constitutes a new product and if it failed. One frequently used figure is that 90 percent of all new products fail. In many companies the failure rate is as low as 25 percent because of extensive testing prior to a market introduction. The percentage is quite high if test markets are counted as product introductions.

A recent analysis of cigarette brands indicated that of 105 brand introductions, including test markets, 33 brands went national, but only 13 were classified as successful.[63] "Success" in the cigarette industry can be a market share as low as 0.5 percent, because the market is so large. The ban on television cigarette advertisements is given as the reason for the low success ratio. One company had 7 successful brands out of 15 introductions. Another company had no successes in 28 introductions. Thus generalizations about product success rates are difficult because of definitional problems and because of great variances among companies.

Most of the details of product failures are buried in corporate files, so little can be learned by outsiders that would help to avoid similar mistakes. Several recent products were so famous that they have been documented in the public press, however. These famous flops include the most unusual combination of cases—diapers, Corfam, the Edsel, and Frost 8/80 whisky.

Disposable Paper Diapers By 1972 Procter & Gamble (P & G) had invested over $100 million into its disposable diaper, Pampers. The company enjoyed more than a 25 percent after tax return on its investment.[64] Competitors could not resist this attractive return. Johnson & Johnson, Kimberly-Clark, Colgate-Palmolive, Georgia-Pacific, International Paper, Scott Paper, and even Union Carbide invested heavily in product development. But getting a diaper that does not leak seems to be a real technological problem. Scott invested $15 million in its effort. Only Kimberly-Clark and Johnson & Johnson had market shares in 1976 that seemed viable.[65]

Corfam The leather substitute Corfam cost duPont over $100 million before it sold the process to a foreign firm.[66] The basic problem was that the product's consumer benefit did not offset its disadvantages. When made into shoes, Corfam's primary benefit was ease of care. The disadvantages were that it did not feel good, it seemed to be hot, it did not "give" like leather, and it was costly.[67] Consumers concluded that the costs exceeded the benefits, and they rejected Corfam shoes.

The Edsel Why did the Ford Motor Company's Edsel automobile fail in the mid-1950s? Analysts have different opinions. Some feel that there was insufficient forecasting, so the effects of a recession were not considered. Others point out that Ford and Mercury extended their product lines, thereby cannibalizing the market in which Edsel was to be positioned. Some marketers think that the name "Edsel" and the design of the car made it difficult to sell.

Whatever the cause, the experience cost Ford $500 million.[68] The lessons to be learned, according to Reynolds, are that new products should be marketed through existing divisions using existing dealers and that marketing research should be used instead of the personal preferences of chief executives.[69] The Edsel is now a collector's item.

Frost 8/80   Brown-Forman Distillers invested $6 million on Frost 8/80, a "dry, white" whisky, for the young, affluent market. The product, it was hoped, would gain that segment of the market that was buying Scotch and Canadian whiskies and vodka at increasing rates. But the public was not willing to shift its tastes when no real benefits were offered. Drinkers of Scotch and Canadian whisky were not about to give up the prestige of these brands. Martini drinkers saw no reason to switch from gin or vodka. Bourbon drinkers would not shift their preference for a heavier taste.[70] In short, the product seemed to be positioned between whisky and vodka, with no consumers at this position. It seems to have been a classic "squat between the stools" error in product strategy.

Some Generalizations on Why Products Fail   The 125 members of the Conference Board's Senior Marketing Executives Panel were asked to report on products that had been introduced within the previous five years that had not met original expectations. Fifty percent of the companies in industrial products or the service industries had a failure rate of 20 percent or less. The comparable rate for the consumer-products industry was 40 percent or less. The causes for failure were inadequate market analysis, product defects, inadequate marketing effort, high costs, competition, poor timing, and technical or production problems.[71] These causes verified earlier studies that identified similar causes and almost the same rankings.[72] In addition, one study of 75 new-product failures adds to this list "vague product differences" and "poor product positioning."[73]

There are three strategies for timing a new-product introduction—too soon, too late, and just right.[74] In a fast-moving market, a few weeks may be too late. The Chrysler Airflow automobile design of 1934 was decades too soon. Henry Ford was too late in shifting from the black Model-T as Chevrolet offered a more stylish car. Ford's slowness opened the market for Plymouth's move into the low-priced market.[75] General Electric showed excellent timing when it introduced the 14-inch portable television. The industry had just stabilized on 17- and 21-inch screen sizes. An earlier introduction would have been counter to the move to larger and larger screens. A later introduction may have resulted in another firm's introducing the portable size. Timing an introduction requires a feel for the market and estimates of competitors' reactions. The speed of a competitive reaction can be devastating.

In closing the discussion of product strategy, we should note the warning given by Machiavelli: "It must be remembered that there is nothing more difficult to plan, more uncertain of success, nor more dangerous to manage than the creation of a new order of things. For the initiator has the enmity of all who would profit by the preservation of the old institutions, and merely lukewarm defenders in those who would gain by the new ones."[76]

SUMMARY   A company's product strategy is a logical extension of its definition of its business. A product, in the mind of the consumer, is not the physical attributes of the product, but its perceived benefits, its package, its brand, and associated services. Thus a product strategy must include strategies for packaging, branding, and warranties. The product life cycle is a useful analytical tool for developing the product strategy, especially the crucial decision of *when* to enter the market with a new product.

Strategies for existing products include undifferentiated strategies, no product change, repositioning, improvements, extension, and dropping products. The desire for growth is probably the strongest motivation for developing new products. The sources for new-product ideas vary, but they reduce to the elusive process known as creativity, which is difficult to recognize and even more difficult to manage. Procedures for screening new-product ideas vary from very subjective methods to complex mathematical programs. New-product introduction in industrial marketing puts considerable emphasis on engineering and the salesperson.

There is no perfect organizational scheme for coordinating new-product development. Basic decisions include whether to locate new-product development in decentralized divisions and whether they should be located in functional units. Project teams, venture groups, and new-product committees each have their advantages and disadvantages.

Failure to understand the market seems to be the most common reason for a new-product failure. Vague product differences, poor positioning, poor timing, economic downturns, and competitive reactions represent dimensions of a failure to understand the market.

DISCUSSION QUESTIONS

1. What forces shape the product life cycle? What is the difference between a brand life cycle and a product life cycle? When can they be considered the same?

2. Differentiate the following strategies for existing products: (a) differentiated products; (b) undifferentiated product, differentiated promotion; (c) product repositioning; (d) product improvement; (e) product extensions. Give examples for each of these strategies.

3. What is product cannibalization?

4. Differentiate horizontal, vertical, and conglomerate diversification. Give examples for each.

5. In what ways does the industrial product–planning process differ from consumer product planning?

6. What are some advantages and disadvantages of functional jurisdiction in new-product development? What are new-project teams and new-venture groups? What advantages and disadvantages do they have?

NOTES

1. D. S. Hopkins, *Business Strategies for Problem Products* (New York: Conference Board, 1977), p. 48.

2. H. I. Ansoff, *Corporate Strategy, An Analytic Approach to Business Policy for Growth and Expansion* (New York: McGraw-Hill, 1965), p. 12.

3. T. L. Berg and A. Shuchman, eds., *Product Strategy and Management* (New York: Holt, Rinehart and Winston, 1963), p. 97.

4. *Ibid.*, p. 99.

5. J. M. Rathmell, "What Is Meant by Services?" *Journal of Marketing* (October 1966): 32–36; and *Marketing in the Service Sector* (Cambridge, Mass.: Winthrop Press, 1974).

6. W. E. Cox, Jr., "Product Life Cycles as Marketing Models," *Journal of Business* (October 1967): 375–384; and R. Polli and V. Cook, "Validity of the Product Life Cycle," *Journal of Business* **42** (October 1969): 385–400.

7. N. K. Dhalla and S. Yuspeh, "Forget the Product Life Cycle Concept!" *Harvard Business Review* (January–February 1976): 102–112.

8. "Their Cup Runneth Over," *Forbes*, October 1, 1975, pp. 24–39.

9. "Repent at Leisure," *Forbes*, December 15, 1975, pp. 20–21.

10. *Ibid.*

11. F. M. Bass, "A New Product Growth Model for Consumer Durables," *Management Science* 15 (January 1969): 215–227.

12. J. V. Nevers, "Extensions of a New Product Growth Model," *Sloan Management Review* 13 (Winter 1972): 77–91.

13. Y. Wind and H. J. Claycamp, "Implementing the Product Life Cycle Concept," working paper, rev. August 1974.

14. J. A. Lunn, "Empirical Techniques in Consumer Research," in *Industrial Society*, ed. D. Pym (Baltimore: Penguin, 1968), pp. 401–425.

15. "AMC Extends Warranty with Service Plan," *Advertising Age*, November 3, 1975, p. 72.

16. C. L. Kendall and F. A. Russ, "Warranty and Complaint Policies: An Opportunity for Marketing Management," *Journal of Marketing* (April 1975): 36–43.

17. S. Scanlon, "Calling the Shots More Closely," *Sales and Marketing Management*, May 10, 1976, pp. 43–48.

18. H. Zeltner, "Product Line Extensions Can Spur Profitable New Volume," *Advertising Age*, April 26, 1976, pp. 60, 62.

19. B. Hake, *New-Product Strategy* (London: Pitman, 1971).

20. *Ibid.*, p. 27.

21. J. T. Rothe, "Product Elimination Decision," *MSU Business Topics* 18 (Autumn 1970): 45–52.

22. C. H. Sevin, *Marketing Productivity Analysis* (New York: McGraw-Hill, 1965).

23. E. A. Pessemier and H. P. Root, "The Dimensions of New Product Planning," *Journal of Marketing* 37 (January 1973): 10–18.

24. D. S. Hopkins and E. L. Bailey, "New-Product Pressures," *Conference Board Record* (June 1971): 16–24.

25. J. A. Schumpeter, *Business Cycles*, Vol. 1 (New York: McGraw-Hill, 1939).

26. "Marketing Briefs," *Marketing News*, January 30, 1976, p. 2.

27. E. D. Phelps, "Study Finds Unavailability of Market Information and Executives' Fear of Failure Bar Innovation," *Marketing News*, May 1, 1974, p. 1.

28. M. Crawford, "Strategies for New Product Development," *Business Horizons*, December 1972, pp. 49–58.

29. E. A. Pessemier, "Managing Innovation and New-Product Development," Report No. 75–122 (Cambridge, Mass.: Marketing Science Institute, December 1975), p. 5.

30. "Some Who Dared," *Printers Ink*, May 29, 1964, p. 47.

31. E. P. McGuire, *Generating New-Product Ideas*, Conference Board Report No. 546 (New York: The Conference Board, Inc., 1972).

32. *Ibid.*, pp. 3–4.

33. *Ibid.*, pp. 29–35.

34. E. M. Tauber, "HIT: Heuristic Ideation Technique—A Systematic Procedure for New Product Search," *Journal of Marketing* 36 (January 1972): 58–70.

35. G. L. Urban, "Preceptor: A Model for Product Positioning," *Management Science* 21, 1 (April 1975): 858–871.

36. M. H. Pryor, Jr., "Anatomy of a Merger," *Michigan Business Review* 16 (July 1964): 28–34.

37. "How the Directors Kept Singer Stitched Together," *Fortune*, December 1975, pp. 100–103ff.

38. Advertisement in *Wall Street Journal*, Thursday, August 28, 1975, p. 9.

39. L. J. Konopa, "New Products: Assessing Comercial Potential," Management Bulletin No. 88 (New York: New York Management Association, 1966), pp. 8–9.

40. E. P. McGuire, "Concept Testing for Consumer and Industrial Products," *Evaluating New Product Proposals* (New York: Conference Board, CBR 604, 1973), pp. 33–75.

41. R. I. Haley and R. Gatty, "The Trouble with Concept Testing," *Journal of Advertising Research* (June 1968): 23–35; and E. M. Tauber, "What Is Measured by Concept Testing?" *Journal of Advertising Research* (December 1972): 35–37.

42. Y. Wind, "A New Procedure in Concept Evaluation," *Journal of Marketing* **37** (October 1973): 2–11.

43. McGuire, *op. cit.*, p. 89.

44. H. J. Claycamp and L. E. Liddy, "Prediction of New Product Performance: An Analytical Approach," *Journal of Marketing Research* (November 1969): 414–420.

45. G. J. Eskin and J. Malec, "A Model for Reestimating Sales Potential Prior to Test Market," in *Marketing: 1776–1976 and Beyond*, ed. K. L. Bernhardt (Chicago: Proceedings of the American Marketing Association, Series 39, Memphis, 1976), pp. 230–233.

46. G. L. Urban, "SPRINTER Mod III.: A Model for the Analysis of New Frequently Purchased Consumer Products," *Operations Research* **18** (September-October 1970): 805–853.

47. McGuire, *op. cit.*, pp. 96–97.

48. W. L. Etter, "Concept Screening Risk Analysis Program," personal communication, September 7, 1976. (W. L. Etter is Manager, Quantitative Analysis, General Mills, Inc.)

49. A. S. Pearson, "How to Compare New Product Programs," *Journal of Advertising Research* (June 1971): 3–8.

50. V. J. Cook and T. F. Schutte, *Brand Policy Determination* (Boston: Allyn and Bacon, 1967).

51. *Ibid.*, p. 1.

52. W. Margulies, "Brand Marketing Power: How to Differentiate Your Product from Competitors," *Advertising Age*, September 6, 1976, pp. 45–46.

53. *Ibid.*

54. Adapted from "P & G Uses Pampers Story to Teach the Consumer About Marketing," *Advertising Age*, April 4, 1977, pp. 41, 44.

55. J. E. Klompmaker, G. D. Hughes, and R. I. Haley, "Test Marketing in New Product Development," *Harvard Business Review* (May-June 1976): 128–138.

56. See *ibid.*, for a further discussion of these and other costs of test marketing.

57. B. P. Shapiro, "Industrial Product Policy: Viewpoints and Issues," Report No. 76–101 (Cambridge, Mass.: Marketing Science Institute, 1976).

58. J. W. Lorsch and P. R. Lawrence, "Organizing for Product Innovation," *Harvard Business Review* (January-February 1965): 109–122.

59. D. S. Hopkins, *Options in New-Product Organization* (New York: Conference Board, 1974), pp. 6–15.

60. *Ibid.*, pp. 16–32.

61. *Ibid.*, pp. 33–45.

62. *Ibid.*, pp. 44–48.

63. J. J. O'Connor, "RJR Monitors 105 New Brands, Classifies 13 as Successful," *Advertising Age*, July 12, 1976, p. 3.

64. "All Those Leaky Diapers," *Forbes*, February 15, 1976, pp. 49–50.

65. *Ibid.*

66. "Exit Corfam: duPont Reaffirms that the Top Is a Slipppery Place," *Barron's* March 22, 1971, p. 1.

67. "$100 Million Object Lesson," *Fortune* **83** (January 1971): 109.

68. J. N. Brooks, *The Fate of the Edsel and Other Business Adventures* (New York: Harper & Row, 1963).

69. W. H. Reynolds, "The Edsel Ten Years Later," *Business Horizons* (Fall 1967): 39–46.

70. F. C. Klein, "An Untimely End," *Wall Street Journal*, January 5, 1973, p. 1; and "Light Whiskey Comes at Maybe the Wrong Time," *Business Week*, March 11, 1972, p. 101.

71. Hopkins and Bailey, *op. cit.*, p. 20.

72. H. Lazo, "Finding a Key to Success in New Product Failures," *Industrial Marketing* (November 1965): 74–77.

73. T. L. Angelus, "Why Do Most New Products Fail?" *Advertising Age*, March 24, 1969, pp. 85–86.

74. E. A. Malling, "Timing: How Marketing Masters It," *Printers Ink*, April 20, 1962, pp. 60–63.

75. *Ibid.*

76. Machiavelli, *The Prince*, quoted in Hopkins, *op. cit.*, p. 2.

SUGGESTED READINGS

Davidson, J. H., "Why Most New Consumer Brands Fail," *Harvard Business Review* (March-April 1976): 117–122.

Eskin, G. J., "Dynamic Forecasts of New Product Demand Using a Depth of Repeat Model," *Journal of Marketing Research* (May 1973): 115–129.

Johnson, S. C., and C. Jones, "How to Organize for New Products," *Harvard Business Review* (May-June 1957): 49–62.

Kotler, P., "Phasing Out Weak Products," *Harvard Business Review* (March-April 1965): 107–118.

Lantis, T., "How to Generate New Product Ideas," *Journal of Advertising Research* **10** (June 1970): 31–35.

Levitt, T., "Exploit the Product Life Cycle," *Harvard Business Review* (November-December 1965): 81–94.

Luck, D., *Product Policy and Strategy* (Englewood Cliffs, N. J.: Prentice-Hall, 1972).

Massy, W. F., "Forecasting the Demand for New Convenience Products," *Journal of Marketing Research* (November 1969): 405–412.

McGuire, E. P., *Evaluating New-Product Proposals* (New York: Conference Board, 1973).

Pessemier, E. A., *Product Management: Strategy and Organization* (New York: Wiley, 1977).

Scheuing, E. E., *New Product Management* (Hinsdale, Ill.: Dryden Press, 1974).

Shocker, A. D., D. Gensch, and L. S. Simon, "Toward the Improvement of New Product Search and Screening," *1969 Fall Conference Proceedings of the American Marketing Association*, ed. P. R. McDonald, pp. 168–175.

Shocker, A. D., and V. Srinivasan, "A Consumer-Based Methodology for the Identification of New Product Ideas," *Management Science* **20** (February 1974): 921–937.

Twedt, D. W., "How to Plan New Products, Improve Old Ones, and Create Better Advertising," *Journal of Marketing* **33** (January 1969): 53–57.

Wasson, C., "What Is New About a New Product?" *Journal of Marketing* (July 1960): 52–56.

ENVIRONMENTAL ANALYSIS WORKSHEET

Environmental elements	Facts	Assumptions or research needed	Conclusions
Organizational values, objectives, and policies (4)			
Organizational design (5)			
Situation			
Generic demand (6)			
Brand demand (7)			
Competition (9)			
Public policy (10)			
Opportunities (2)			
Problems			

MARKETING PLAN (CONSUMER PRODUCT)

Current performance
Recommendations
Effect of recommendations on income
Situation analysis
Opportunities and problems
Strategies
Tests and research
Supporting documents
   Comparative budgets
   Media allocation schedule
   Promotion control sheet

STRATEGY WORKSHEET

Opportunities and problems in rank order to importance

1.
2.
.
n.

	Current strategy	Alternatives and recommended strategy	Estimated Effect

Demand strategy
   Generic
   Brand

Strategic goals
   Financial
   Marketing

Marketing-mix strategies
   Product (12)
   Pricing (13)
   Channel and logistics (14)
   Advertising and promotional (15)
   Sales management (16)

Research (3)

Profit plan

Evaluation and control (19)

CHAPTER 13

Pricing Strategies

LEARNING OBJECTIVES   After studying this chapter you should:

1. Understand how the environment determines pricing policies and strategies.
2. Understand why the final pricing strategy is made at the top corporate levels.
3. Understand how the other elements in the marketing mix influence pricing strategy.
4. Be able to explain why industrial pricing strategies differ from consumer pricing strategies.
5. Understand why it is necessary to know how the market and competitors will react to a price change.
6. Be able to use tree diagrams to evaluate competitive reactions to price changes.
7. Be able to compute break-even levels in units and dollars.
8. Know a general procedure for developing a pricing strategy.
9. Be able to define and use the following concepts:

Demand curve	Experience curves	Leverage
Delivered prices	Target pricing	Payback period
Demand-based strategies	Social pricing	Skimming and pricing
Elasticity	Psychological pricing	strategies
Marginal cost	Elastic and inelastic	Incremental cost-pricing
Cross elasticity	generic demand	strategies
Substitution effect	Elastic and inelastic	Price lining
Cost-based price	brand demand	Customary prices
strategy	Sensitivity analysis	Characteristics of goods
Cost-plus pricing	Predatory pricing	Seasonal discounts
Markup pricing	Bona fide prices	Trade-position discounts
Joint costs	Break-even analysis	Chain discounts
Transfer costs and	Target rate of return	Functional discounts
prices	Return on investment	Promotional allowances
Learning curves	Turnover	Push money
		Trade deals

SOME STRATEGIC QUESTIONS FOR OPENERS

1. Are corporate goals consistent with pricing strategies?
2. How will the product's life cycle determine the pricing strategy?

3. How will competition react to our price change?

4. How will the channel of distribution react to our price change?

5. How will product differentiation strategies affect pricing strategies?

6. What are the price elasticities for generic and brand demand?

7. Do our pricing strategies violate antitrust policies?

8. What price must we charge to break even? For a given return on investment?

A good pricing strategy is simple: Sell the product for more than it costs. Implementing such a strategy is not easy, however. Will the product be bought at that price? How much "more" is desirable? What are the costs? How will competition react? Does the resulting pricing strategy violate public policy? The elements in the Environmental Analysis and Strategy Worksheets provide the structure for answering these questions. This chapter will follow the organization of these worksheets. At the conclusion of the chapter a procedure for developing a pricing strategy will be recommended that is consistent with the flow of thinking in the worksheets.

Pricing is important to the *economy* and the *firm*. In the *economy* it is the *mechanism for allocating resources* and reflecting degrees of both risk and competition. In the *firm* it is the *basis for generating profits*. Price reflects corporate objectives and policies and is an important part of the marketing mix. Price is often used to offset weaknesses in other elements in the marketing mix. Price changes can be made more quickly than product, channel, and personal-selling changes. A price change is easily understood, so communicating to the buyer is easy. For these reasons price changes are frequently used for defensive and offensive strategies.

ANALYZING THE PRICING ENVIRONMENT

Values, Objectives, and Policies Corporate values, objectives, and policies provide the thrust and constraints for a pricing policy. One company may want to convey the image of quality, whereas another has a policy of "We will never be undersold." The pricing strategies for these companies will be quite different.

An examination of corporate goals will frequently reveal inconsistencies. The most frequent one is a statement of the dual goals of maximizing profit and sales (or market share). Figure 4.1 illustrated that these two goals cannot occur simultaneously. Profit is maximized at point OQ_2, while revenue is maximized at point OQ_4.

To sell more units it will be necessary to lower the price. This is illustrated in Fig. 13.1, where reducing the price from $1.00 to $0.90 increases the quantity from 100,000 to 120,000 units.

Figure 4.1 may have seemed theoretical, but it has very practical implications. For instance, a new industrial marketing firm had the dual goals of maximizing profit and market share (which was analogous to maximizing revenue). Its sales force was on a straight commission on dollar sales. It quickly attained its target level of market share, but it operated at a loss. The compensation scheme of a commission on dollar sales stimulated the salespeople to sell to customers who required excessive sales calls, thereby increasing expenses. It also stimulated price cutting. A diagram like Fig. 4.1 illustrates this inconsistency, which amounted to "buying market share at the expense of profit." The salespeople's compensation scheme was modified to encourage them to shift their efforts from the small, quick sales to the more profitable sales which

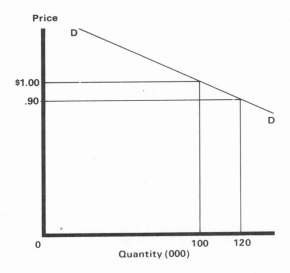

ig. 13.1 A price-demand curve.

take longer to develop. The new compensation scheme rewarded them for developing new, larger accounts.

Pricing goals may change at different stages in a product's life cycle. The initial goal may be market share and later change to profit. This desire for a good market share is explained by the dynamics of the marketplace. The brand that is the first to gain a large market share does not have to spend as much on promotion at later stages as does the second or third brand to enter the market.

Pricing strategies may be determined by financial strategies, such as a given return on investment, assets, or equity. The relationship between price and these returns will be illustrated later in this chapter. A firm that has a policy of extensive research and development will have a pricing strategy that will be high enough to recover its investment.

A company with conservative values may choose to be a price follower, but it may avoid cut-throat price competition because it is "unethical." We saw such a case in Table 4.1. The president of a small manufacturer of office duplicating equipment ranked high on social value, security, welfare of employees, and aesthetic values and refused to compete on price.

Preserving the favorable image of one brand may require the development of a "fighting brand" to test how competition will react to a price cut. The decision to use one channel of distribution may constrain pricing flexibility because of "traditional discounts" in that channel.

These limited examples should emphasize the point that the development of a pricing strategy requires a clear understanding of the values, objectives, and policies of the organization. Some of these philosophical values are made operational by expressed and implied objectives, such as to make a profit, experience growth, stabilize markets, desensitize customers to price, discourage entrants, maintain price leadership, speed the exit of marginal firms, avoid government investigation and control, maintain loyalty of middlemen and get their sales support, avoid excessive demands from suppliers (especially labor unions), improve the image, be regarded as fair, create interest and excitement, be considered trustworthy, discourage others from cutting prices, and build traffic.[1]

A classic study by Lanzillotti revealed that well-known firms cited quite different principal pricing goals.[2] Some form of *return on investment* was the pricing goal of Alcoa, duPont, Esso, General Electric, General Motors, International Harvester, Johns-Manville, Union Carbide, and U.S. Steel. *Market share* was the pricing goal of American Can, A & P, Kroger, Sears, Standard Oil (Indiana), and Swift. A one-third gross *profit margin* was the principal pricing goal of General Foods. *Meeting competition* guided Goodyear's pricing decisions. Gulf Oil and National Steel chose to be *price followers*. Kenecott wanted to keep *prices stabilized*. Although this classic study is now two decades old and companies may have changed their pricing goals, it is useful to see the variety of pricing goals and the preference for return on investment.

Organizational Design   The organizational design of the marketing effort will determine *where* the pricing strategy will be developed. Because pricing strategies are so closely related to basic policies, these strategies tend to be centralized. Thus a multidivision company will decentralize the authority for minor product changes, advertising, and personal selling, but it will centralize major product decisions, pricing decisions, and major channel decisions. Firms that use the product-manager system frequently do not allow the product-manager to make the final pricing decision, but that person is expected to make recommendations.

A firm that operates in a highly competitive market may decentralize the pricing strategy all of the way through the organization to the salesperson. The salesperson may be given a price range within which to sell, but he or she is permitted to make adjustments to meet changing competitive and demand situations. To ensure that the salesperson will operate at a profit, his or her compensation scheme will be related to the profitability of the business generated. This tends to be the practice in industrial marketing more so than in consumer marketing.

One of the most common ways for decentralizing the pricing decision is to use decentralized profit centers. This approach decentralizes pricing authority and responsibility, but holds the profit center responsible for attaining a level of profit or a return on investment.

SITUATION ANALYSIS

Generic Demand   The disciplines used for a generic-demand analysis—demography, economics, sociology, and social psychology—provide insights that lead to pricing strategies.

Demographic price strategies.   Age-segmented markets may provide the basis for price differentials. Thus airline "youth fares" encourage college students to develop the habit of flying. Similarly, senior citizen rates are common for many goods and services.

Geographic pricing takes many forms. "Slightly more west of the Rockies" is sometimes seen on price lists of East Coast manufacturers. Some manufacturers quote *delivered prices*, which means that the manufacturer pays the freight. FOB means "free on board" the vehicle: the buyer pays the cost of shipping and unloading.

Economic price strategies

Demand-Based Strategies.   Economic theory provides many insights for the development of price strategies. The most frequently used concept is *price elasticity*, or the ratio of the percentage change in sales (in units) associated with a given percentage change in price. In Fig. 13.1 a reduction in price from $1.00 to $0.90 is a 10 percent decrease in price $(0.10/1.00 = 0.10)$. The quantity increased 20 percent $(20/100 = .20)$. The price elasticity is 2.0 $(.20/.10 = 2.0)$. In simple mathematical terms, elasticity is computed as follows:

$$\text{Price elasticity} = \frac{\text{Percentage change in sales}}{\text{Percentage change in price}}$$

$$= 20/10$$

$$= 2.0.$$

The term *price elastic* is used to describe elasticity greater than 1.0. This means that the percentage increase in sales is greater than the percentage decrease in price. A price is *inelastic* when the percentage change in sales is less than the percentage change in price. In such cases the numerical value will be less than 1.0. *Unit elasticity* describes the case when the elasticity is exactly 1.0.[3]

Maximization of sales may be the best short-run pricing strategy in a competitive industry, where it is necessary to establish brand loyalty and a large promotional expenditure later in the product's life cycle. To maximize sales the price must be lowered to that point where price elasticity is 1.0.[4]

To *maximize profit* the concept of marginal cost must be introduced into the pricing rule. *Marginal cost* is the *change in total costs that is required to produce an additional unit.* The following pricing rule can be derived from the economists' model that states that profit will be maximized when marginal revenue equals marginal costs:

$$\text{Price} = \frac{\text{Price elasticity } (E)}{1 + \text{Price elasticity } (E)} \text{ (Marginal cost)}. \tag{13.1}$$

The first part of the equation $(E/1 + E)$, is the markup that will maximize profits. Thus if the elasticity is -4, the markup for profit maximization is $-4/(1 - 4) = 1.333$. If the marginal cost of the product is $10, a price of $13.33 $(= \$10 \times 1.333)$ will maximize profit.[5] (In practice, the marginal cost is unknown. The average cost may be substituted for small changes in sales.)

Cross elasticity is a useful economic concept for measuring the effect of a change in price for one product on the sales of competitive products. Cross elasticity is the ratio of the percentage change in the sales of product B, to the percentage change in price of product A $(\% \Delta S_B/\% \Delta P_A)$.

Cross elasticities may be computed when the two products are from competitive firms or when they are part of the product offering of a single firm. In the latter case there is a concern for a *substitution* (or *cannibalizing*) effect; one brand may gain, but the total company revenue may suffer. The substitution effect helps to explain why the final pricing strategy is handled higher than the product-manager level. Only top management can be objective about substitution effects due to price changes.

Price elasticities may be computed by using regression techniques on historical data, experiments in a laboratory situation, or surveys.[6] All of these methods have limitations. Regression techniques face the problem of joint costs and joint revenues. Experimental and survey techniques raise questions about realism. Will the subject or the respondent behave this way in the marketplace? Market tests may be used by varying the prices in stores, but the costs of such tests are extremely high. The subjective opinions of executives and members of the channel of distribution can be useful.

Economic theory helps to guide our thinking, but it does not provide mechanical approaches to price determination. Oxenfeldt attributes the gap between the pricing literature and pricing practice to the fact that authors lack practical experience in the competitive and complex business environment.[7] They do not consider the large number of products, the lack of reliable information about product demand, and the dynamic nature of technology. "Little has been written on innovative approaches to pricing—approaches designed to *increase* demand, rather than *adapt to existing* demand. Attention must be given to measures that alter these elasticities in his firm's favor."[8]

Price-elasticity calculations tend to assume that the product is sold directly to the consumer by the manufacturer. However, these calculations fail to consider the sensitivity of the channel (distributors, wholesalers, and retailers).

Estimates of elasticity vary through time and over geographic areas. Experimental methods and analysis of historical data have shown marked variation in elasticity of brands. Brands priced close to the average price in a product category are highly price elastic. Brands priced above or below this average are less price elastic.[9] This reduction in elasticity is the goal of product differentiation.

Cost-Based Price Strategies. Using costs as a basis for a price strategy may be the result of an inability to estimate demand, or there may be only one buyer. For example, *cost-plus pricing* is common when selling weapons to the Defense Department. A single *markup pricing ratio* may be a matter of convenience or tradition. For decades drugstores used traditional markups. A standard markup policy was considered necessary because the traditional drugstore might carry 5000 or more items. Later in this chapter we will see how discount retailers chose to take a lower margin and turn their inventory over more often, thereby generating return on investment.

There are some rules of thumb, e.g., "The retail price should be three times the cost at the end of the production line" or "Cost plus 50 percent." Such rules are easy to apply when costs can be calculated. But these calculations can be very difficult when production facilities are shared with other products. This *joint cost* is even more difficult when there are *transfer costs* among several divisions of a firm. International production facilities complicate the transfer costs. Some foreign governments have charged international companies with false *transfer prices* to other divisions.[10] The allegations stated that companies report high costs in countries with high tax rates and low costs in countries with low rates.

The major criticism of cost-based pricing strategies is that they ignore demand and competition. In addition, it is extremely difficult to estimate the costs of goods in manufacturing. Costs of goods purchased are easier to estimate for wholesalers and retailers. This is one reason why they make extensive use of cost-based pricing strategies.

In computing the cost of a product, we must not forget the effects of the learning and experience curves on total costs. As noted in Chapter 9, failure to consider declining total costs as *industry experience* accumulates can lead to some rapid price cuts that will eliminate the high-cost, marginal producer.

A variation of cost-based price strategies is *target pricing*. The target is usually a fixed amount of profit or a given rate of return on investment. Later in this chapter, during a discussion of break-even analysis, we will see that target profits or returns are simply treated as other fixed costs. Thus the usual break-even computation is modified only slightly.

Social pricing strategies. Sociological variables are more concerned with identifying needs and the diffusion of innovations than with matters related to price. Social class, however, may be the basis for a pricing market-segmentation strategy. Thus products with snob appeal or those consumed conspicuously may command a higher price than products with less social visibility.

Psychological pricing strategies. Psychological pricing may take many forms. Selling the product for $5.98 instead of $6.00 is thought to be desirable because the buyer thinks of the price as "being in the $5 bracket." Research, however, has not supported such "psychological pricing."[11]

Another form of psychological pricing is the relationship between the price and the buyer's perception of product quality. Research seems to indicate clearly that price is used as a measure of quality *only* when price is the only variable given. Gardner, for example, found that when additional cues were provided, such as the merchandise itself, brand information, and some product information, the *price-quality* relationship was replaced by a *brand-quality* relationship.[12] Rao found that the price-quality relationship was no longer supported when additional variables were added, such as prior knowledge and personality.[13] When a price-quality relationship does exist, it is not linear; McConnell found that the perception of quality increased at a lower rate than the increase in price.[14]

Brand Demand   Selecting a pricing strategy for a specific brand is part of the strategy of *positioning* a brand (see Chapter 7). What is the image of the brand to be? Are we positioning it as a high-quality one or as a fighting brand? Brand maps frequently include an image of price as one dimension. Thus beer-brand maps, for example, may have one dimension labeled "popular price/premium price."[15] These maps help the strategist to position his or her brand along the price dimension so as to attract an adequate market share without also attracting a devastating competitive reaction.

Industrial Pricing Strategies   Pricing strategies in industrial markets differ from those in consumer markets because there are fewer buyers in industrial markets and they tend to be more sophisticated buyers. Industrial and government buyers frequently provide prospective sellers with detailed technical specifications. Sellers are then asked to submit bids, which may be quite complex. For instance, the bid for earth-moving equipment may include the selling price for the new equipment, the service costs for five years, the trade-in allowance for old equipment, and in some cases a guaranteed trade-in for the new equipment in five years. The bid must include technical descriptions of the equipment and its attachments. Government bidding procedures frequently require a "performance bond" that guarantees that the product will meet government specifications. Competitive-bidding models have been developed to help the strategist formulate a bid that will maximize expected profit, given estimates of competitive behavior.[16]

Industrial marketing in the chemical industry can become "commodity marketing." This occurs when the product becomes so standardized that price is the only basis for competition. The pricing strategy in such a case is to find *values* that can be added to the basic product that will justify a *premium price* over competition. Marketing researchers at duPont identified six attributes associated with one of their chemicals for which buyers would pay a premium price. Their research also indicated how much each of the product and service attributes contributed to the premium price. If the base price was $100, the total premium differential of $5.30 included the following elements: rate of product innovation for the industry, $2.00; product quality (purity), $1.70; system versus product supplier, $0.80; plant personnel retraining policies, $0.40; speed of troubleshooting service, $0.25; and speed of delivery, $0.15.[17]

Identification of the elements of the premium differential does more than help set a pricing strategy for an industrial product. It also helps to determine the upper limit on how much should be spent on maintaining that differential. In the example above, the upper limit for an expenditure for an improvement in the speed of delivery seems to be $0.15 per $100 of the base industry price for the product.

A company that tracks the decline in the perceived value of attributes in its offer has an early-warning device that alerts it to the need to change either its price or the attributes of the offer. Procedures for "monetizing" these attributes are not difficult.[18]

Competition The competitive environment raises many questions about ethics. Are we willing to drive competitors out of business? Are we willing to violate the *spirit* of the law to increase sales? Should we shake out the weak firms to stabilize profits? Should we be a price leader or a follower?[19] Answers to these questions trace back to the values of the executives, their corporate objectives, and the policies they set and enforce for marketing strategists.

Competitive reactions. Competitive pricing strategies require estimates of how competitive firms will react. A drop in price is one of the clearest signals that can be communicated to a competitor. Price can be changed more quickly than any of the other variables in the marketing mix. Thus the strategist must examine how *competitors* will react *and* how the *market* will react. These estimates must be based on an estimate of the price elasticities of brand and generic demands. Figure 13.2 illustrates the need to estimate these elasticities. The first example illustrates the case of *elastic brand demand* and *inelastic generic demand*. The second example illustrates the situation when *both demands are elastic*.

The size of the circle in Fig. 13.2 represents total *dollar* sales for the industry. The wedges of the circle represent the market shares of three competing firms—A, B, and C. The upper two circles illustrate the case when generic demand is *inelastic*. The lower circles represent the case of elastic generic demand.

Turning to the upper left-hand circle in Fig. 13.2, we see that the initial effect of a cut in price by firm A is an increase in share, because brand demand is taken as elastic for this illustration. This gain by A has been at the expense of the market shares of firms B and C. The competing firms cut their prices to regain share. The final effect of this price war appears in the upper right-hand circle; all firms have

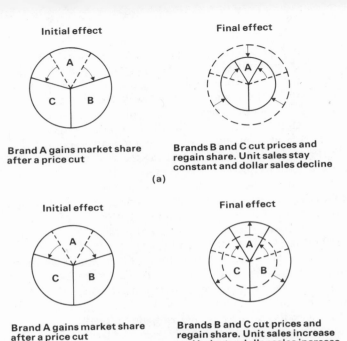

Initial effect

Final effect

Brand A gains market share after a price cut

Brands B and C cut prices and regain share. Unit sales stay constant and dollar sales decline

(a)

Initial effect

Final effect

Brand A gains market share after a price cut

Brands B and C cut prices and regain share. Unit sales increase and industry dollar sales increase

(b)

Note: The size of the circle represents industry dollar sales.
The size of each wedge represents market share.

Fig. 13.2 Reaction of the market when brand demand is elastic and generic demand is inelastic or elastic: (a) inelastic generic demand; (b) elastic generic demand.

returned to their initial market shares, but all have less sales revenue because they are selling the same *number* of products at a *lower price*. This is true because the generic demand for the product is inelastic. This illustration could easily represent the automobile industry. The generic price elasticity for automobiles has been estimated to be approximately 0.7.[20] It could also represent commodities such as salt, where the demand will not increase if price is lowered.

The lower two circles in Fig. 13.2 represent the case when brand demand *and* generic demand are elastic. Initially firm A gains market share. Competitors react, regaining their share. The total dollar market expands because buyers buy more of the industry's product at these lower prices. A classical example of this situation occurred on August 6, 1940, when Columbia Recording Company reduced the price of classical records from $1.50 to $0.75. RCA Victor, which dominated the market, met this price three days later. Much to the surprise of RCA Victor and others, the market expanded dramatically.[21] A similar case occurred in 1975, when price cutting expanded the market for hand-held electronic calculators. The pricing strategists who gained in the calculator industry were those who understood the competitive-pricing implications of experience curves (see Chapter 9).

Economic textbooks frequently discuss the "kinked-demand curve case." These discussions generally state that oligopolists will follow a competitor down but not up. Some of the assumptions behind this analysis do not seem to apply to the real world, however.[22] Worldwide inflation, for instance, has made this theory irrelevant. Rather, oligopolists seem anxious to follow price increases in anticipation of higher costs.

Some firms state their competitive-pricing rules, e.g., "We will never be undersold." The large refineries allow a four-cent differential between their price and independent gas stations to arise before reacting. A discount store may attempt to maintain a fixed interval between its prices and those of the traditional department store. Some industries use *efficacy* pricing rules to introduce a new product. Thus if the effectiveness of a new drug or the speed of a new computer is 150 percent of the product presently on the market, the initial price may be set at 150 percent of the current market price.

Modeling competitive price reactions. *Tree diagrams* and *expected-value calculations* can be useful when estimating the effects of competitive reactions to a price cut. The Scoop Ice Cream Case, 1972 (see Chapter 9) illustrates how subjective and objective data may be combined in a tree diagram to help a planner decide if a competitive price cut is the best strategy. Prior to the introduction of a competitive product, Scoop Ice Cream Mix was retailing for $1.00. Admiral Foods' competitive introduction included extremely high advertising expenditures. If Admiral decides to go national with its product, should Scoop lower its price to $0.90? The tree diagram in Fig. 13.3 helps to answer this question.

Scoop has two choices at the first decision node—retain the $1.00 price or lower it to $0.90. If Scoop chooses to keep the $1.00 price, it must estimate the actions that Admiral will take. For illustrative purposes we will consider three possible responses—

Fig. 13.3 Tree diagram for a competitive strategy decision.

Scoop pricing strategy (1)	Admiral's competitive reaction (2)	Subjective probability of occurrence (3)	Effect on Scoop's contribution (4)	Expected value (3) x (4) (5)
Scoop retains $1.00 price	No response	0.70	$4.0 million	$2.8 million
	Admiral cuts price	0.20	$1.5 million	$0.3 million
	Admiral cuts price and increases advertising	0.10	$-0.5 million	$-0.05 million
	Totals	1.00		$3.05 million
Scoop lowers price to $0.90	No response	0.50	$5.0 million	$2.5 million
	Admiral cuts price	0.30	$2.0 million	$0.6 million
	Admiral cuts price and increases promotion	0.10	$-2.0 million	$-0.2 million
	Totals	1.00		$2.9 million

no response, Admiral cuts the price, and Admiral cuts the price and increases advertising. We must then estimate the subjective probability of Admiral's taking each of these actions (column 3). Then we must estimate the effect of these reactions on Scoop's contribution (column 4). By multiplying these probabilities times the estimated contribution, we arrive at an *expected value* (column 5). Adding the expected values for the three alternatives, we see that the total expected value for the strategy of "keep the price at $1.00" is $3.05 million.

The lower branch of the tree diagram estimates the expected value for a strategy of cutting the price to $.90. In this case there is a 0.50 probability that Admiral will not respond with a price cut and a 0.30 probability that it will cut price. If Admiral does not respond, Scoop is expected to have a contribution of $5.0 million. This increase would come from increases in generic and brand demand. If Admiral cuts price, Scoop's contribution is estimated to drop to $2.0, because Admiral's price cut and heavy advertising would shift customers to Admiral. The total expected value for the cut-price strategy is $2.9 million.

The diagram indicates that the decision is a close one, but the decision to retain the $1.00 price has a slight edge of $0.15 million. Because the decision is so close, the strategist will want to do the calculations again, using different estimates of subjective probabilities, different estimates of the effects on generic and brand demand, and different estimates of the costs of production at these various levels of output. Tracing through the effects of different estimates in the decision model is known as a *sensitivity analysis*.

Public Policy In Chapter 10 we saw that the philosophy of public policy with regard to pricing was originally based on the classical economic model of the nineteenth century, namely, that the best allocation of resources depends on prices that move only in response to supply, not to manipulation by buyers and sellers. The flexibility of price, therefore, became the test of whether buyers and sellers were engaged in antitrust behavior. You may have been surprised to learn that the antitrust laws preserve competition, frequently at the expense of a lower price to the consumer. Therefore, in fact, antitrust policies are not in the best interests of the consumer.

To preserve competition. The antitrust law and its interpretation by the courts, the Justice Department, and the Federal Trade Commission have attempted to maintain price flexibility. Any arrangement that reduces price flexibility is generally regarded as a violation of the antitrust laws, without the need to prove that competition was lessened. This is the *per se violation* of the law. Examples of per se violations are horizontal agreements where the retailer must stock an unwanted product to get the one wanted.

Three common categories of price discrimination are:

1. The failure to give *like quantity discounts* to all buyers;
2. *Unequal functional discounts*, e.g., a promotional discount given to a large supermarket chain must be given also to the small independent grocery store;
3. *Geographic price differentials* through regular freight absorption.

The defense that the price discrimination was the result of cost savings must be proved by the defendant, using extensive cost accounting procedures. In recent years the courts have not been willing to accept these data, however.

Price-fixing conspiracies are not limited to giant firms. Excess capacity in an industry and price cutting have led many companies to decide to "stabilize prices." Ready-mixed concrete suppliers in a medium-sized city provide an example.[23] Wet-concrete hauling is a local business, limited to a 15-mile radius. It is a competitive business in that everyone tends to charge the *going price.* Entry is easy because there is little technology, and capital for a "portable" plant can be as low as a few thousand dollars.

Firms in the city under study tended to be small, with the largest grossing $1 million. Everyone knew one another, so there were no secrets about who got which job. Before the building boom there were only a few producers, and you had to schedule a day for concrete. If it rained, you went to the bottom of the list. Then about ten new producers entered the industry. The building boom slackened, there was a recession, and nobody made a profit.

The industry had a local trade association that cleared credit ratings and worked on quality control. At one association meeting the problem of deteriorating prices was discussed. After a lengthy discussion the firms decided to "stabilize prices" because they "would rather go to jail than starve." A three-person enforcement committee maintained the arrangement for 18 months until uncontrollable deals appeared. A producer with excavating equipment would hold the concrete price but lower the bid for excavation. Discounts were offered on other services. Then price conspiracy ended, prices declined another 20 percent, and many producers could not make contributions to fixed costs.

Penalties for price fixing now include fines *and* jail sentences. The Justice Department has argued that only stiff jail sentences will deter executives from price fixing. In 1976 the Assistant Attorney General appeared in a federal court to ensure that price fixers were given stiff sentences. The defendants were 48 officials of 23 paperboard-box companies who pleaded "no contest" to price-fixing charges between 1960 and 1974. The Justice Department listed seven criteria that should be considered during sentencing: the rank of the official, the size of the company, the length of the official's participation, the degree of remorse and rehabilitation demonstrated by the officer, the officer's net worth and salary, and significant mitigating circumstances. The Justice Department clearly wanted to set examples in this case, because it was the largest price-fixing case that it has ever filed.[24]

Another important price-fixing case in 1976 charged five paper-product manufacturers with conspiring since 1950.[25] Seven executives were indicted, including several general sales managers. Each company faced a maximum fine of $1.0 million. Each *executive* faced a maximum fine of $100,000 and three years in prison. These stiffer penalties were the result of Congress changing the law so that all criminal price-fixing cases are felonies, which carry higher penalties. It is important to note that the volume of business was not large. Total industry sales were estimated to be $42 million. One company reported the business involved represented less than one percent of its total sales.

Predatory pricing refers to strategies based on low prices to drive competitors from the market so that the resulting monopolist can then raise prices. In 1976 the H. J. Heinz Company charged the Campbell Soup Company with predatory marketing practices which threatened to eliminate Heinz from the canned soup market. Heinz asked for $315 million in treble damages. The complaint alleged that Campbell maintained its 80 percent market share by using brand proliferation to gain shelf space and that it used predatory pricing, advertising, and promotional practices. According to Heinz, Campbell maintained competitive prices where it faced competition, but it raised prices where it did not have competition. Campbell was also charged with "saturation advertising" in test markets selected by competitors.[26] The outcome of this case will have important implications for pricing and promotional strategies.

To protect the consumer. Consumer protection from deceptive pricing does not come from antitrust legislation, but rather from legislation that deals with truth in advertising. The A & P supermarket chain lost to the Federal Trade Commission in 1975 because it failed to have products on the shelf as advertised, which constituted deceptive advertising.

In 1964 the Federal Trade Commission issued a guide against deceptive pricing to assist retailers in making pricing decisions.[27] The guide listed four common violations. (1) *Former price comparisons* must be *bona fide* prices that existed for a reasonable period of time. Inflated prices that are shortly lowered to have a "sale" constitute deception. "Formerly sold at ..." must be supported by substantial sales at that price. (2) *Retail-price comparisons* must represent comparable products and selling situations, e.g., a discount store comparing prices with another discount store, not with a small, isolated jewelry store. (3) *Manufacturer's list-price comparisons* may be deceptive if a substantial part of the sales do not occur at the list price. (4) *Bargain offers based on the purchase of other merchandise*, such as "Buy one, get one free" or "1¢ sale," may be deceptive if the seller increases the price of the regular product, lowers its quality, or attaches other strings.

More recently, the consumer movement has led to the use of unit pricing in retail grocery stores. The prices of all brands are reduced to a common price per unit, such as one ounce, so that the consumer may make direct price comparisons easily.

To conserve resources and preserve the environment. Public policies toward the conservation of resources and the preservation of the environment are just beginning to have their impact on pricing strategies. Antipollution devices on automobiles have raised automobile prices and led to the development of engines that do not require these devices. The environment has always been a "free good," so that it did not enter pricing decisions. But now the environment is rapidly entering production costs as companies are required to add devices to their production systems that will reduce the pollution of air and water.

Conservation of resources enters pricing decisions as states require soft drink and beer bottlers to use returnable bottles. Conservation may also enter the variable-costs elements of pricing as tax advantages are given to manufacturers who switch from oil to coal. Today pricing strategists should have a feel for the environment in which they are operating, so they will be ready to turn to the development of the pricing strategy.

DEVELOPING A PRICING STRATEGY

Demand Strategy   The analysis of price elasticities, market structure, and the pricing patterns of competitors will help us to determine if we should try to expand the generic demand, the brand demand, or both.

Strategic Goals   The *financial goals* for the product are important inputs to the pricing decision. Break-even analysis, return on investment, target rates of return, and payback calculations are an important part of pricing strategies.

Break-even analysis.   The break-even model can be derived very easily as follows:

$$\text{Product total profit} = \text{Product total revenue} - \text{Product total cost}, \qquad (13.2)$$

which may be expanded to the elements of revenue and cost:

$$\text{Profit } (\pi) = (Price \times Quantity) - [Fixed\ Costs + (Variable\ Costs \times Quantity)],$$

or

$$(13.3)$$

$$\pi = PQ - (FC + VC \times Q). \qquad (13.4)$$

By definition, total profit at break-even is zero; thus the break-even equation is as follows:

$$0 = Q(P - VC) - FC \qquad (13.5)$$

$$- Q(P - VC) = -FC. \qquad (13.6)$$

Dividing both sides of Eq. (13.6) by $-(P - VC)$ yields

$$Q = \frac{FC}{P - VC}, \qquad (13.7)$$

which is the break-even equation for quantity in units.

Break-even analysis is not a complicated concept. It simply answers the question: What must our sales be, at a given price, to cover our fixed costs? Sales may be expressed in units or dollars. The equation, in words, is as follows:

$$\text{Sales quantity (in units) to break even} = \frac{\text{Fixed costs}}{\text{Price} - \text{Variable costs}}. \qquad (13.8)$$

For example, assume that the *total* fixed costs to produce a product are $150,000 and the variable costs per *unit* are $5.00. If we are considering selling the product for $8.00, how many units must we sell to break even? Using Eq. (13.8), we see that

$$\text{Break-even quantity in units} = \frac{\$150,000}{\$8 - \$5} \qquad (13.9)$$

$$= \$150,000/\$3$$

$$= 50,000 \text{ units.}$$

If we were to sell the product at $10, the dollar margin would increase to $5, so we would break even at a lower quantity. Specifically, the break-even point would be 30,000 units ($150,000/$5).

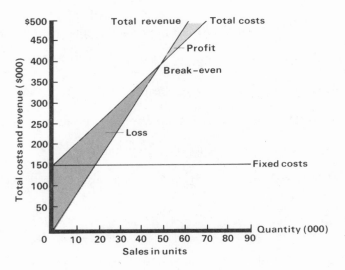

Fig. 13.4 A break-even analysis for Eq. (13.9).

The break-even analysis in Eq. (13.9) is illustrated graphically in Fig. 13.4. Total cost and total revenue are expressed as straight lines. Straight lines ignore diminishing returns in production, which will increase costs, and market saturation, which requires lower prices to attract marginal buyers. Figure 4.1 illustrated curvilinear cost and revenue functions. The latter functions illustrate an important concept—there can be two break-even points. In Fig. 4.1 the second break-even point occurred below the point where sales were maximized, so a strategy of maximization of sales would result in a loss.

Break-even in terms of *dollar sales* may be computed in two ways. When the break-even in units is known, the dollar level of break-even is simply a matter of multiplying the number of units times the price. Thus at a selling price of $8 in the example above, a dollar sales volume of $400,000 is required to break even ($8 × 50,000). At a selling price of $10, the dollar volume break-even is $300,000 ($10 × 30,000). The dollar volume to break even is used when estimating cash flow.

The second way to compute dollar break-even is to divide fixed costs by percent markup where the price is the base.

$$\text{Break-even in dollars} = \frac{\text{Fixed costs}}{\text{Markup on selling price}}. \tag{13.10}$$

In other words, we have multiplied both sides of Eq. (13.7) by price:

$$Q \times P = \frac{FC}{P - VC} \times P, \tag{13.11}$$

which is the same as:

$$QP = \frac{FC}{(P - VC)/P}. \tag{13.12}$$

The quantity $(P - VC)/P$ is the markup based on price, and QP is the sales revenue in dollars.

For example, when the price in the example above is $8, the margin is .375 ($8/$3). Thus break-even in dollars is $400,000 ($150,000/.375). Similarly, break-even in dollars for a price of $10 is $300,000 ($150,000/.5).

What costs should we include as fixed costs? This is generally a subject for debate. Some authors argue that in addition to production fixed costs, we should include the initial costs for a new product, such as market research, test marketing, initial new-product promotion, and initial inventory.[28]

Target rate of return. A more likely financial goal than just break-even is a *target rate of return on investment*. This rate, times the investment, enters the break-even model as a fixed cost. Thus if the investment in the case in Eq. (13.4) was $5000,000 and the desired return on investment was 10 percent, we must add $50,000 to the fixed costs in this equation. Thus

$$\text{Break-even for a target 10 percent ROI} = \frac{\$150,000 + \$50,000}{\$8 - \$5} \qquad (13.13)$$
$$= \$200,000/\$3$$
$$= 66,667 \text{ units.}$$

Return on investment. The concept of return on investment needs to be refined over that which appeared in Eq. (13.13). We need to be clear on the definition of "investment." From the finance point of view, we must distinguish between return on assets and return on equity.

A rate of return is specific to a definite time period, generally a year. The more times the investment is used during a year, the higher the rate of return. For instance, if we earn 8 percent on our investment every six months, we are earning 16 percent per year because we are *turning our assets over* twice a year. Turnover, a very important concept for pricing strategies, was the basis for the success of the discount stores. They lowered the price margins on products that were highly price elastic. Their increased volume enabled them to turn over their assets many times per year, which more than offset the lower margins.

We may see how this works by using the following equations:

$$\text{Turnover} = \frac{\text{Sales}}{\text{Total investment}} \qquad (13.14)$$

$$\text{Earnings as a percent of sales} = \frac{\text{Earnings}}{\text{Sales}} \qquad (13.15)$$

$$\text{Return on investment} = \text{Earnings as a percent of sales} \times (\text{Turnover}) \qquad (13.16)$$

$$= \frac{\text{Earnings}}{\text{Sales}} \times \frac{\text{Sales}}{\text{Total investment}}. \qquad (13.17)$$

To illustrate, assume that a retailer had earnings (sales less cost of sales) of $250,000 on an annual sales volume of $2.5 million. Thus earnings as a percent of sales were 10 percent ($250,000/2.5 million = 0.10). If the total investment (inventories, accounts receivable, cash, and permanent investment) was $2.5 million, the retailer's investment turnover for the year was 1.0 ($2.5 million/$2.5 million = 1). The rate of return on *investment* is 10 percent ($0.10 \times 1 \times 100 = 10\%$). Recognizing the price elasticity of the products, the retailer lowers the margin to 8 percent of sales. Sales double to $5.0 million per year. The retailer's turnover is now 2.0 ($5 million/$2.5 million = 2), and the *annual* return on investment is now 16 percent because the investment is being used twice per year.

To increase the return on equity, the retailer may use borrowed capital. Continuing the example above, by borrowing $500,000 at 8 percent, the retailer will reduce annual revenue by $40,000 to $360,000, or 7.2 percent of sales. Equity turnover will increase to 2.5 ($5 million/$2.0 million), and return on *equity* will be 18 percent (2.5×7.2). This process is known as *leverage*.

Leverage is computed as follows:

$$\text{Leverage} = \frac{\text{Total investment}}{\text{Stockholders' equity}}. \tag{13.18}$$

Return on equity may be calculated as follows:

$$\text{Return on equity} = \text{Earnings} \times \text{Turnover} \times \text{Leverage}. \tag{13.19}$$

In our example we may compute return on equity as follows:

$$\text{Return on equity} = \frac{\$360,000}{\$5.0 \text{ million}} \times \frac{\$5.0 \text{ million sales}}{\$2.5 \text{ million invest.}} \times \frac{\$2.5 \text{ million invest.}}{\$2.0 \text{ million equity}} \tag{13.20}$$

$$= 0.072 \times 2.0 \times 1.25$$

$$= 0.18 \text{ or } 18 \text{ percent.}$$

In this case the retailer has used *price elasticity* and leverage to increase return on equity from 10 percent to 18 percent.

This increase in the retailer's return on equity also increases the risks. The marketing risk comes from the inability to be certain that a lower price will double sales. The financial risks include the addition of a fixed charge and the lowering of borrowing capacity to meet emergencies.

Payback period. Many companies require the new-product proposal to estimate how long it will take before the original investment is paid back. The *payback* concept combines the estimates of demand and break-even units. The equation is simply:

$$\text{Payback period (in years)} = \frac{\text{Break-even (in units)}}{\text{Annual demand (in units)}}. \tag{13.21}$$

If the break-even is 100,000 units and the annual demand is 50,000 units, the payback period is two years. If the break-even can be lowered to 75,000 units, the payback period would be reduced to 18 months. (For a full financial analysis of the payback period, we expand Eq. (13.21) to terms of net present value, discounted cash flow, or internal rate of return.)

Marketing-Mix Strategies   The pricing strategy must reinforce the overall marketing strategy of the firm. The desire for a quality image and a full-service operation would preclude a discount pricing strategy, for example. This quality image may require greater product research and development costs, higher quality retail outlets, and more expensive promotion. The consumer may be willing to drive farther, pay cash, and carry the product home if the price is discounted enough. Thus a pricing strategy must be related to all of the elements in the marketing mix.

Product/price strategies.   The two best-known pricing strategies, *skimming* and *penetration*, are associated with the *product life cycle*. *Skimming* means a high margin and therefore a high price, so that the seller is skimming the cream off the market. *Penetration*, in contrast, is a strategy of a lower margin, a lower price, and a penetration into the market to reach down into those segments which have a high price elasticity.

Early in the life of a new product there are few competitors, research and development costs are high, and initial promotional costs are high. The initial adopters of the new product tend not to be sensitive to price, so price is inelastic. Therefore, the *skimming* strategy is possible early in the life cycle of the new product. The higher margins will help to cover the initial research, development, and promotional costs. When the initial demand has been met, however, it is time to reduce the price, thereby tapping that market segment which is price elastic. If the timing of the price reduction is correct, it will attract new market segments and discourage competitors who have been attracted by the large margin.

Incremental cost pricing states that the price should cover the variable costs and make some contribution to fixed costs and profits. Incremental cost pricing assumes that any contribution to fixed costs is better than no contribution. This tends to be a short-range strategy, because in the long run fixed costs must be covered.

Price lining is a strategy frequently used in retail department stores and mail-order catalogs. For example, in department stores, women's dresses may appear in four departments, each with a price range that will not cut into another department. Thus prices may range as follows: in the basement department, $12 to $19; daytime dresses, $20 to $39; "better" dresses, $40 to $79; and the fashion department, $80 and higher. The buyer for each department must buy merchandise to sell within a specific range and maintain the department's assigned average margin. A buyer who adds a high-cost item "to sweeten the line" must pick up a bargain with a big margin to maintain the assigned average margin.

Failure to maintain the price ranges in a price-lining situation can result in a firm's cannibalizing other products in its line. One reason cited for the demise of the Edsel automobile was the fact that it was originally positioned between the Ford and Mercury brands. Prior to the introduction of the Edsel, Ford introduced a higher-priced model, and Mercury introduced a lower-priced model. Thus other Ford brands cut into the Edsel market.

Customary prices were frequently illustrated by the nickel candy bar. Because of inflation this illustration is now the 20¢ candy bar. So that candy could be sold in vending machines, prices were increased at intervals of five cents, and inflation was reflected in a smaller candy bar. When the minimum acceptable size was reached by one candy manufacturer in 1976, it raised the price from 15¢ to 20¢ and *increased* the size of the candy bar by 12 percent. Thus the price was increased 33 percent, but the net effective increase was 21 percent.

The product-pricing strategy must include consideration for *warranties* and services offered after the sale of the product. A product such as an automobile may be profitable when sold, but it could become unprofitable if warranty costs, due to poor quality control, exceed the original estimates.

The *characteristics of the good* will establish a price range that is acceptable to the customer. Of course, these characteristics also determine the appropriate channel of distribution. A *convenience good*, such as a bar of soap, must be conveniently located and competitively priced. A *specialty good*, such as a high-quality perfume, may be located in exclusive shops and priced high.

Seasonal discounts occur because styles become out of date or it is costly to carry nonstyle inventories to another season. We are all familiar with "end of season" clothing sales. In the clothing trade there is also frequently a discount *before* the season begins. The manufacturer attempts to induce the retailer to stock heavily before the season begins by giving a discount or delaying billing.

Channel/price strategies. The selection of a channel of distribution may also determine channel discount structure. Some channels have "*traditional*" discounts. In the pharmaceutical industry the "ethical" channel is through the wholesaler to the retailer, not directly to the retailer. For decades, the standard margins in this channel have been $16\frac{2}{3}$ percent for the wholesaler and $33\frac{1}{3}$ percent for the retailer.

Discounts to brokers, wholesalers, and retailers are known as *trade-position* discounts because the middlemen are compensated according to the activities they are expected to perform at their *position* in the *trade*. Thus a broker may get 5 percent, the wholesaler may receive 15 percent, and the retailer may receive 25 percent for services. This series of discounts is known as a *chain discount*.

The chain discount illustrated above does not add to a total discount of 45 percent, because the discount is taken at the price at each level. Thus the base is reduced as the calculation moves from the retailer backward through the chain. For example, assume that the retail price of the product is $1.00. The retailer pays $0.75, or $1.00 less $0.25. The wholesaler pays $0.6375, which is $0.75 less $0.1125. The wholesaler's discount is computed as 0.15 times $0.75, or $0.1125. The broker, in turn, pays $0.605625; this reflects the 0.5 discount on the broker's selling price of $0.6375. The discount is $0.31875 (.05 × $0.6375). The total discount is $0.394375, or 39.4 percent of the retail selling price. The manufacturer need not go through this long calculation to determine the net from a *chain discount*, however. Rather, net can be calculated directly by multiplying the complement of each percent (1.00 less the trade discount). Thus in this example, if we multiply .95 × .85 × .75, we get the net receipt to the manufacturer, which is 0.605625. Multiplying this figure times the retail selling price of $1.00 gives us $0.605625, which is the dollar receipt to the manufacturer, which is the same as the price paid by the broker.

The chain discount makes it convenient to change prices without reprinting catalogs. The catalog gives the list price, and a reprinted insert with the trade discounts states what discount each member of the channel is entitled to receive.

Functional discounts may be included in the chain discount to reimburse the channel member for additional marketing functions performed. For instance, carrying a complete stock, stocking service parts, building window displays, maintaining a repair department, and advertising may entitle a retailer to additional discounts.

Promotional allowances are a temporary price cut to reimburse channel members for promoting the product. These allowances are common when new grocery products are introduced. In the Scoop Ice Cream case (Chapter 2) we saw that a 50¢ per case allowance was given for promotion during the ice cream season. Promotional allowances may appear as a temporary addition to the chain discount.

When giving brokerage discounts and promotional allowances, the pricing strategist must not forget the provisions of the Robinson-Patman Act (see Chapter 10). It is illegal to give a brokerage discount to a retailer who has established an in-house, or phantom, brokerage organization that is simply a means for gaining an additional discount. An equitable promotional discount must be given to all retailers, not just to the large retail chains which exert market power.

Wholesalers probably have the most difficult pricing problems. They must buy from sophisticated sellers and sell to sophisticated buyers. Perhaps this is why wholesale prices respond so quickly to conditions in the marketplace. Wholesalers must perform a balancing act between two sets of price elasticities.

Vertical pricing competition within the channel of distribution consists of trying to gain the largest share of the margin. In the terms of game theory, this is a *zero-sum game*—what one channel member gains, another member loses. Game theory has been used to examine the dynamics of this vertical channel competition.[29]

A form of promotional allowance that is questionable on ethical grounds is PM, or *push money*. These are bonuses given to salespersons who "push" a specific brand. The salesperson may be a retailer's agent or a wholesaler's phone order salesclerk. PM seems counter to the best interest of the buyer when the buyer is relying on the salesperson's advice, which is no longer objective.

Nonprice channel arrangements frequently amount to a discount. For instance, an extra case of merchandise may be given for stocking a product before the season. Long payment terms may be granted a retailer for early stocking by either extending the due period to 90 days or by post-dating the invoice. These arrangements, along with PM and promotional discounts, are known as *trade deals*.

Advertising/price strategies. The strong interactions between advertising and pricing strategies can be explained by the fact that price changes must be advertised. Furthermore, advertising is most effective when the message it communicates is easily understood. A price cut is the most easily understood change in the marketing mix.

During the early stages of the product's life cycle there can be a strong relationship between pricing and advertising strategies. At this stage it is frequently necessary to charge a high price to cover the initial advertising expenditures that are necessary for introducing a new product.

Personal selling/price strategies. The relationship between personal selling and pricing strategies depends on whether the salespeople can control prices or whether prices are used to control the salespeople. Industrial marketing represents the first case. In many forms of industrial selling the price is negotiated by the salesperson either through the pricing of the product or by altering the offer for a trade-in. In such a case the pricing decisions are decentralized.

When the pricing decisions are centralized, the pricing strategy may be used to control the salespeople. Compensation methods may be based on margins, so that the salespeople do not sell only the easy, low-margin product. Similar compensation-pricing methods can encourage the salespeople to spend their efforts on profitable customers and profitable order sizes.

A PRICING PROCEDURE Figure 13.5 summarizes the pricing procedure that has been outlined in this chapter. The first step is to establish a price range that is consistent with corporate values, objectives, and policies. The range of prices will be defined by the desire to establish a discount image or a quality image. Similarly, the policy to use "ethical channels" of distribution in the drug industry will determine channel discount structures. The pricing policies of top executives who are risk takers may be different from those of risk averters.

Given some estimate of the demand curve for the target market segment, the price strategist attempts to identify the price that will maximize sales. This price is then positioned against competitive prices to determine expected market share. If this share is too small, the strategist will recycle to the generic demand and select a new price.

Once a price is selected which provides what seems to be an acceptable sales volume, the next task is to estimate how competitors will react. A very low price may cause a price war in an oligopoly. An exceptionally high price will attract competitors. If either of these responses would destroy the basic marketing strategy, the strategist must recycle and select a new price.

Unfavorable reactions from the public may take many forms. The Federal Trade Commission and the Justice Department may look on a given price strategy as inflexible and therefore subject to antitrust regulations. Consumerists may regard a price as excessive and boycott all of the company's products. Labor unions may regard a price increase as an indication that the company can now afford to raise wages.

The next test for the pricing strategy is to see if it will meet financial goals such as return on investment, target rate of return, or a payback period. Failure to meet the financial goal sends the pricing strategist back to the generic-demand curve to select a new price. In actual practice, the strategist would probably have tested the price against the financial goals before proceeding to the positioning of the price among other brands, because rough calculations can be based on previous experience. In Chapter 12 we saw that pro forma profit plans were made as early as the concept stage during new-product development; then further research was used to refine the original estimates.

The selected price must then be evaluated in terms of the product, channel, advertising, and personal-selling strategies that will be used in the market segment in question. Any inconsistencies must be reconciled by altering the price or one of the other strategies.

A low price is appropriate when the product is at the mature stage in its cycle, perhaps having reached the point of being a commodity. A low price is also used when there is little promotion, the product is mass-produced, market coverage is intense, production is capital-intense, technological change is slow, the product is for limited application, the product is needed to complete the product line, few services are offered, the product is disposable, or the life cycle is short.[30]

The cost of producing the product and the cost of the marketing-mix strategy *at the estimated sales level* provide inputs for the profit plan. An inadequate profit may send the strategist back to the setting of a new price *or* to the reduction of the cost of the strategies of other elements in the marketing mix.

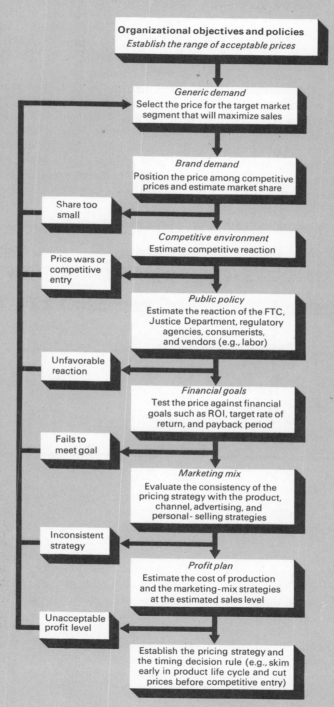

Fig. 13.5   Flow chart of a pricing procedure.

The pricing procedure is a process that attempts to reduce the range of possible prices until a final price is identified. If it were possible to identify the total cost and total revenue functions, it would be possible to use the *marginal pricing* approach by using calculus or an equation such as (13.1) to set a price that would maximize profit. The procedure described in Fig. 13.5 approximates this theoretically ideal approach by using an estimate of elasticity to maximize sales and then testing this sales level against costs. Although the procedure in Fig. 13.5 is not as neat as the theoretical model, it is more realistic. The theoretical model ignores many important elements of pricing, such as competitive reactions, public policy, and channel reactions.

The process of reducing the range of acceptable prices is illustrated in Fig. 13.6. We see many conflicts that require compromises when setting a price. Maximizing market share may not be consistent with the desire for a quality image and the use of exclusive distribution. A discount image may trigger a price war. Maximization of long-run profits may require a different price than the maximization of short-run profits. It will be a rare situation when the final price does not require some trade-offs.

Fig. 13.6 How corporate objectives and strategies limit pricing alternatives.

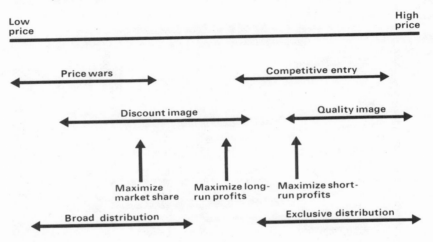

SUMMARY Economic theory provides us with a precise decision rule for a pricing strategy: To maximize profit, set the price so that marginal revenue equals marginal cost. This ideal model can serve only as a guide in the real world, for many reasons. First, there are many strategic pricing goals other than profit. Second, the problem of joint costs and joint revenues makes it impossible to estimate the marginal revenue and marginal costs for a single product. Finally, the model does not include competitive effects, public policy, and channel reactions. Although it may be possible to adapt the model so that these environmental variables are reflected in the revenue and cost estimates, these estimates are even more doubtful than the estimates for the product revenue and costs. The approach in this chapter, therefore, has been to present a practical procedure that keeps the ideal model in mind and approaches it as best as possible by circling around the pricing decision process many times. The elements in this pricing procedure are familiar. They are the elements in the two planning worksheets.

DISCUSSION QUESTIONS

1. What are some reasons why price changes are frequently used in defensive and offensive strategies?

2. What is price elasticity? Differentiate elasticity, inelasticity, unit elasticity, and cross elasticity. With reference to price elasticity, how would a goal of sales maximization be reached?

3. What should be the pricing strategy to maximize profits?

4. Differentiate incremental pricing, target pricing, price lining, and customary pricing.

5. Why is sensitivity analysis important for pricing decisions?

6. Describe three common categories of per se violations in price discrimination.

7. How is the break-even point calculated for units and for dollars?

8. Explain the difference in return on investment and return on equity.

9. How do skimming and penetration strategies relate to the product life cycle?

10. How do corporate policies determine prices? Give examples of conflicting policies and how you would resolve them with regard to pricing.

NOTES

1. A. R. Oxenfeldt, "A Decision-Making Structure for Price Decisions," *Journal of Marketing* **37** (January 1973): 48–53.

2. R. F. Lanzillotti, "Pricing Objectives in Large Companies," *American Economic Review* (December 1958): 921–940.

3. The minus sign is dropped for the sake of convenience. In calculating the percentage change in price, two approaches may be used. If the change is slight, the original price (P_1) may be used as the base. When the change is large, it is common practice to use the average of the original price (P_1) and the new price (P_2). The quantity is also averaged. Thus

$$\text{Elasticity} = \frac{\dfrac{Q_2 - Q_1}{(Q_1 + Q_2)/2}}{\dfrac{P_2 - P_1}{(P_1 + P_2)/2}}.$$

4. H. W. Boyd, Jr., and W. F. Massy, *Marketing Management* (New York: Harcourt Brace Jovanovich, 1972), pp. 332–335.

5. *Ibid.*

6. E. A. Pessemier, "An Experimental Method for Estimating Demand," *Journal of Business* (October 1960): 373–383.

7. Oxenfeldt, *op. cit.*

8. *Ibid.*, p. 50.

9. W. T. Moran, "Insights from Pricing Research." (Paper delivered at the 1976 Marketing Conference, New York, October 21, 1976.)

10. W. M. Carley, "Investigations Beset Multinational Firms, with Stress on Pricing," *Wall Street Journal*, December 19, 1974, pp. 1, 20.

11. For citations, *see* K. B. Monroe, "Buyers' Subjective Perceptions of Price," *Journal of Marketing Research* (February 1973): 70–80.

12. D. M. Gardner, "Is there a Generalized Price-Quality Relationship?" *Journal of Marketing Research* (May 1971): 241–243.

13. V. R. Rao, "Salience of Price in the Perception of Product Quality," *Proceedings of the American Marketing Association*, 1971, pp. 571–577.

14. J. D. McConnell, "The Price-Quality Relationship in an Experimental Setting," *Journal of Marketing Research* **5** (August 1968): 330–333.

15. R. M. Johnson, "Market Segmentation: A Strategic Management Tool," *Journal of Marketing Research* **8** (February 1971): 13–18.

16. Boyd and Massy, *op. cit.*, pp. 336–340.

17. I. Gross, "Prices and Values: Insights through Research." (Paper delivered at the 1976 Marketing Conference, New York, October 21, 1976.)

18. G. D. Hughes, "Monetizing Utilities for Product and Service Benefits," in *Consumer and Industrial Buying Behavior*, ed. A. G. Woodside, J. N. Sheth, and P. D. Bennett (New York: Elsevier North-Holland, 1977).

19. Oxenfeldt, *op. cit.*, p. 50.

20. G. C. Chow, "Statistical Demand Function for Automobiles and Their Use for Forecasting," in *The Demand for Durable Goods*, ed. A. C. Harberger (Chicago: University of Chicago Press, 1960), p. 158; T. R. Dyckman, "An Aggregate-Demand Model for Automobiles," *Journal of Business* **38** (July 1965): 252–267.

21. "Columbia Record Case," Harvard Business School, 1940.

22. For a discussion of the unfounded assumptions, *see* E. Mansfield, *Microeconomics: Theory and Applications* (New York: Norton, 1970), pp. 311–312.

23. "The anatomy of a price-fixing conspiracy," *Business Week*, September 8, 1962, pp. 72–73.

24. T. D. Schellhardt, "Justice Agency Bids for Stiffer Penalties, Including Jail, on Corporate Price-Fixers," *Wall Street Journal*, October 20, 1976, p. 2.

25. "Five Paper Bag Firms Charged in Price Fixing," *Wall Street Journal*, November 1, 1976, p. 3.

26. "Heinz is Boiling ...," *Advertising Age*, December 6, 1976, p. 2.

27. Federal Trade Commission, *Guides Against Deceptive Pricing* (Washington, D.C.: Government Printing Office, 1964).

28. C. Raymond, *The Art of Using Science in Marketing* (New York: Harper & Row, 1974).

29. D. L. Harnett, G. D. Hughes, and L. L. Cummings, "Bilateral Monopolistic Bargaining Through an Intermediary," *Journal of Business* **41** (April 1968): 251–259.

30. W. J. E. Crissy and R. Boewadt, "Pricing in Perspective," *Sales Management*, June 15, 1971, p. 44.

SUGGESTED READINGS

Alpert, M. I., *Pricing Decisions* (Glenview, Ill.: Scott, Foresman, 1971).

Corey, E. R., *Industrial Marketing*, 2d. ed. (Englewood Cliffs, N.J.: Prentice-Hall, 1976), pp. 157–178.

Cox, K. C., and B. M. Ennis, *Experimentation for Marketing Decisions* (Scranton, Pa.: International Textbook, 1969), pp. 82–85.

Dean, J., "Pricing Policies for New Products," *Harvard Business Review* (November-December 1976): 141–153.

Edelman, F., "Art and Science of Competitive Bidding," *Harvard Business Review* (July-August 1965): 53–66.

"Flexible Pricing," *Business Week*, December 12, 1977, pp. 78–88.

Howard, J. A., and W. M. Morgenroth, "Information Processing Model of Executive Decision," *Management Science* (March 1968): 416–428.

Knox, R. L., "Competitive Oligopolistic Pricing," *Journal of Marketing* **30** (July 1966): 47–51.

Lere, J. C., *Pricing Techniques for the Financial Executive* (New York: Wiley, 1974).

Nevin, J. R., "Laboratory Experiments for Estimating Consumer Demand: A Validation Study," *Journal of Marketing Research* (August 1974): 261–268.

Palda, K. S., *Economic Analysis for Marketing Decisions* (Englewood Cliffs, N.J.: Prentice-Hall, 1969), Chapter 7.

Shapiro, B. P., "Price Reliance: Existence and Sources," *Journal of Marketing Research* (August 1973): 286–294.

ENVIRONMENTAL ANALYSIS WORKSHEET

Environmental elements	Facts	Assumptions or research needed	Conclusions
Organizational values, objectives, and policies (4)			
Organizational design (5)			
Situation 　Generic demand (6) 　Brand demand (7) 　Competition (9) 　Public policy (10)			
Opportunities (2)			
Problems			

MARKETING PLAN (CONSUMER PRODUCT)

Current performance
Recommendations
Effect of recommendations on income
Situation analysis
Opportunities and problems
Strategies
Tests and research
Supporting documents
　Comparative budgets
　Media allocation schedule
　Promotion control sheet

STRATEGY WORKSHEET

Opportunities and problems in rank order to importance

   1.
   2.
   .
   n.

	Current strategy	Alternatives and recommended strategy	Estimated Effect
Demand strategy Generic Brand			
Strategic goals Financial Marketing			
Marketing-mix strategies Product (12) Pricing (13) Channel and logistics (14) Advertising and promotional (15) Sales management (16)			
Research (3)			
Profit plan			
Evaluation and control (19)			

CHAPTER **14**

Channel and Logistics Strategies

LEARNING OBJECTIVES   After studying this chapter you should:

1. Know how the environmental analysis guides the channel strategy.
2. Be able to trace and anticipate shifts in the locus of channel power.
3. Be able to develop a channel strategy based on a knowledge of the functions performed by middlemen.
4. Understand the interrelationships between channel strategies and other marketing-mix strategies.
5. Understand why different channels have different costs.
6. Understand the effect of channel cooperation and conflict on channel management.
7. Understand the interrelationships between production and marketing logistics.
8. Recognize how logistics strategies represent a trade-off between selling costs and customer satisfaction.
9. Be able to define and use the following concepts:

Channels	Functional middlemen
Wide and narrow distribution	Manufacturer's agent
Full-function wholesaler	Logistics
Drop shipper	Production logistics
Cash-and-carry wholesaler	Marketing logistics
Truck jobber	Logistics costs
Franchise wholesaler	

SOME STRATEGIC QUESTIONS FOR OPENERS

1. Is a new channel strategy needed?
2. Which channels are the most productive?
3. What do we expect from the members of our channel of distribution? What do they expect from us? What does the customer expect from the channel?
4. Is the channel compensation appropriate for the number of functions performed and the quality of performance?
5. Are competitors developing new channel strategies?

Marketing is sometimes defined as "having the right product, at the right price, in the right *place*, at the right *time*." Channel and logistics strategies perform the functions of determining *place* and *time*. In this chapter we will see how the channel and logistics strategies require an environmental analysis. The channel strategist must also have a sense of channel history to be able to detect shifts in the locus of channel power. These shifts create opportunities and problems in channel strategies.

DETERMINANTS OF CHANNEL STRATEGY

The development of a channel strategy is less frequent than strategy development for other elements in the marketing mix. Traditions in the channels are longstanding. For example, the "ethical" channel for drugs is through the wholesaler. Strong pressures are brought to bear against manufacturers who develop channels that bypass this middleman. Consumer habit may make it difficult to change channel strategies. Conversely, as we will see in the L'eggs example, changes in buying habits may make it possible to develop a new channel.

The Environmental Analysis

The determinants of a channel strategy include the elements in the environmental analysis. The *corporate policy* of using "ethical" channels of establishing a low-price image will limit the number of alternative strategies. The components of *demand*, especially that of geography, will determine whether we use a short channel with few intermediaries or a long channel with many intermediaries. *Competition* may force us to reach part of our market through a new channel. The L'eggs channel strategy illustrates this point. Hosiery manufacturers that had not used supermarkets quickly changed their strategy as they lost market share to L'eggs. *Public policy* limits channel strategies when public health and safety are in question. The distribution of drugs and alcohol, for example, is controlled by federal and state agencies. Horizontal agreements violate antitrust agreements.

The channel strategy, like all marketing-mix strategies, begins with an understanding of consumers' needs. *When* and *where* is the product bought? Where is it consumed? How much effort will the consumer expend in search of the product? Which segments of consumers will search for a store that carries a specific brand, and which segments will switch rather than search?[1]

Identification of the characteristics of these consumers—where they are located, whether they are heavy buyers, etc.—will help to determine the kind of channel that should be used. For example, if heavy users have low brand loyalty, meaning that they will not search for stores carrying our brand, we must have a channel strategy that will distribute our brand *widely*, so it will be available when the consumer has a need. Conversely, if there is a need for self-actualization, the buyer will want to feel that his or her purchase is unique. The channel strategy in the latter case would be a *narrow* one that emphasizes the fact that the brand can be found only in exclusive stores.

In industrial marketing, in contrast, the buyers' needs when buying a computer or materials-handling equipment will require a short channel of distribution. Thus products may be designed to fit the specific application, and service may be provided after the sale.

Consumers are willing to change their buying habits—for a lower price. Discount houses succeeded because consumers were willing to forgo in-store service and delivery in exchange for a lower price. The convenience of one-stop shopping made the shopping malls a success. Working women, inflation, convenience, and the gas shortage may help to explain the fact that mail-order marketing has grown more than retail stores have in recent years.[2]

The environmental analysis will reveal other factors that will determine channel strategy. For example, if the corporate goal is to maximize profit, it may integrate forward and perform as many functions as are profitable. Economies of scale may discourage integration if the manufacturer cannot build sufficient sales volume to take over the wholesaling or retailing functions. Tradition plays an important role in channel strategy. Channel relations are human ones that have been developed over many years, so companies will be reluctant to change. Favors, such as extending credit during lean years or providing products during periods of scarcity, will also influence channel decisions.

Channel alternatives may be limited because one member of the channel is in a position of power. The poultry and egg industries illustrate this point. In Fig. 14.1 we note that there are a large number of producers, processors, wholesalers, and retailers, so few could dominate the channel. In comparison, there are few feed mills, and they perform functions that cannot be assumed easily by other members of the channel. During periods of grain shortages, they may be in control of the channel through their pricing and allocation policies.

The Shifting Locus of Channel Power   The locus of channel power shifts in the channel of distribution. The strategist must be aware of trends in the movement of power as the channel strategies are developed. An understanding of the economic history of marketing channels will help the marketing manager to anticipate changes in channels in the United States. He or she will also gain insights into the development of channels in emerging countries.

During the colonial period the foreign trader dominated the channel, because the American colonies were viewed as part of the British Empire. Local manufacturing was strongly discouraged. The traders exchanged American raw materials and furs for English manufactured goods. The traders were social and political leaders as well as business leaders.

Following the American Revolution, the United States was free to develop its own manufacturing capabilities. New England became a center for textile, shoe, and metal manufacturing. The excess capacity of these new industries led to the development of the merchant wholesaler. The westward expansion created the need for the general store, which dominated the economic life of small Western communities.

From the midnineteenth to the early twentieth century the Industrial Revolution expanded productive capacity and strengthened the position of the manufacturer. In the midnineteenth century a new force emerged—large retailers. In 1859 the Great Atlantic and Pacific Tea Company (A & P) was established. Montgomery Ward was founded in 1872, F. W. Woolworth was established in 1879, and Sears Roebuck began in 1886. The early chain shoe stores of Melville, Florsheim, Kinney, and Endicott-Johnson were founded in the 1890s.[3] These large retailers became a threat to the wholesalers because they were large enough to buy directly from the manufacturer. The general-line, full-service wholesalers declined and were replaced by more specialized wholesalers, some of whom performed only limited marketing functions.

The period beginning about 1920 saw the rise of the mass media—print and electronic—which freed the manufacturer from dependence on the retailer to communicate to the consumer. The depression years of the 1930s were used by

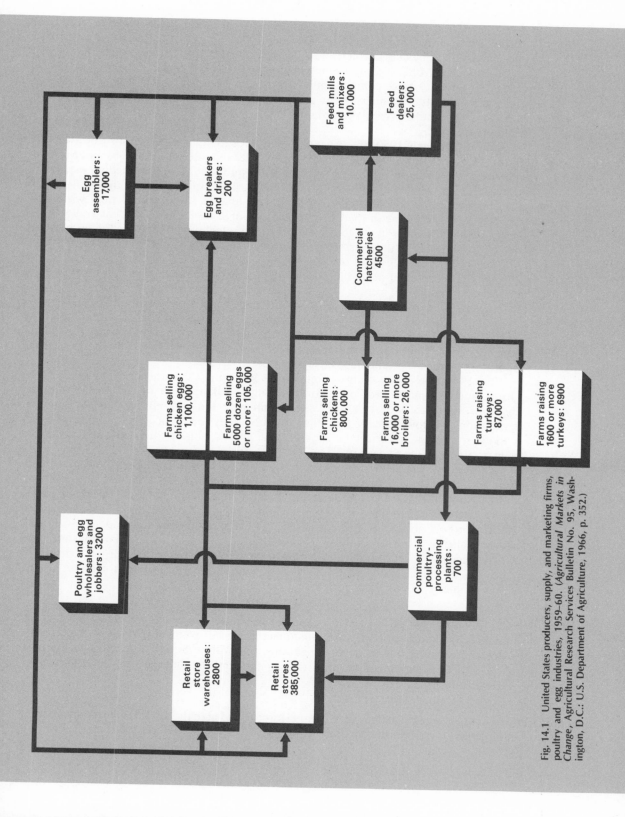

Fig. 14.1 United States producers, supply, and marketing firms, poultry and egg industries, 1959–60. (*Agricultural Markets in Change*, Agricultural Research Services Bulletin No. 95, Washington, D.C.: U.S. Department of Agriculture, 1966, p. 352.)

wholesalers and small retailers to retain some of their dwindling channel influence through legislative means. Their argument was that price cutting drove small merchants out of business, which added to unemployment. The Robinson-Patman Act (1936) and the Miller-Tydings Amendment (1937) to the Sherman Act (1890) were designed to reduce price competition. As noted in Chapter 10, the Robinson-Patman Act prevented large retailers from receiving special discounts. The Miller-Tydings Amendment permitted resale price maintenance ("fair trade") by manufacturers through to the consumer.

During the early 1950s the pent-up demand for many durable goods not available during World War II was released, and there was also the postwar baby boom. This increased demand, a more highly educated public, the mass media—especially television—and the availability of automobiles all led to the rise of discount stores. Consumers knew what they wanted. They were able to pay cash and were willing to carry the product home in the car, in exchange for a discount. The "fair trade" laws were tested many times in the courts, but most manufacturers abandoned them in favor of a higher inventory turnover. (The Miller-Tydings Act was not repealed until 1976.)

The rise of the regional, one-stop shopping centers led to the demise of some 75-year-old department stores that would not move from the decaying central cities. The typical new shopping center had a large *anchor* department store at each end, with many specialty stores located along the mall connecting them.

Retailing in the late-1970s reflects changing life-styles and the search for an identity. There are many small specialty shops and gourmet cookware stores. Sensing this trend, some department stores are reducing the breadth of their product lines and are now appealing to more specific market segments.

The evolution of new forms of retailing is known as "the wheel of retailing." New stores, such as pineboard food stores during the depression of the 1930s and the discount appliance stores in the 1950s, begin with the minimum of facilities and a reputation for low prices. "As they mature, they often acquire more expensive buildings, provide more elaborate services, impose higher margins, and become vulnerable to new competition."[4]

Economies of scale in production, brought on by the Industrial Revolution, created time and place voids between the producer and the consumer. Channel strategies are designed to fill these voids. The channel also performs the function of taking large, homogeneous outputs from many sources and breaking them into small, heterogeneous assortments of goods for the consumer. These assortments are made available at concentrations of retail outlets, like shopping centers, which make consumption more efficient. Unfortunately, our economic system does not measure consumer efficiency, so the costs of performing the distribution functions are not compared with the consumer costs without marketing channels.

DEVELOPING A CHANNEL STRATEGY   The development of a channel strategy requires a matching of the functions that the manufacturer needs to have performed in order to reach the consumer with the organizations that will perform the functions. Because of the variety of organizations, one must understand the functions that are performed by each one.

Functions Performed by Selected Middlemen   Channel forces that led to the development of specialized middlemen increased the alternative strategies for the marketing planner. Table 14.1

summarizes the functions performed by several merchant wholesalers and functional middlemen.

The *full-function wholesaler* performs the functions of storage (including sorting large, homogeneous lots into smaller, heterogeneous lots), transportation, risk taking (physical and economic), selling, buying, financing, and market research. The *limited-function wholesaler*, by not performing all of the functions, can therefore operate at a lower margin. The *drop shipper* passes the customer's order to the manufacturer, who ships directly to the customer. The drop shipper's functions are limited to selling, passing the order to a source of supply, and possibly arranging for transportation and financing. Drop shippers are used when the goods are sold in bulk.

Cash-and-carry wholesalers are used by small grocery stores that cannot buy in large lots. They drive to the wholesalers, pay cash, and carry the product back to their stores.

Truck jobbers are wholesalers who carry most of their inventory on their trucks. This form of middleman is seen in products such as candy, sundries, and auto parts.

A *rack jobber*, such as a potato chip wholesaler, owns the inventory that is on the rack in the supermarket. In addition to performing all of the middleman functions, the rack jobber also physically places the product on the shelf or rack. Other rack-jobbed items in the supermarket are magazines, clothing (such as L'eggs hosiery), and household items such as cookware. A chain store may use a rack jobber until the market is established, then switch to buying the product and carrying inventory so as to gain a wider margin.

A *franchise wholesaler* is a voluntary chain of independent grocery stores that uses a common buying source to compete with large chains. As franchised stores they may be required to paint the store front a standard color and carry the franchise brands. A retail-owned cooperative wholesaler is another approach for competing with the large chains. As with most cooperatives, the motive is to pool purchases to gain quantity discounts.

Functional middlemen differ from merchant wholesalers in that since the former do not own the inventory, they operate on a commission rather than a profit margin. Real estate brokers are probably the most familiar form of brokers. The food broker is frequently used in the food industry.

The *manufacturer's agent* is really the manufacturer's sales force. The agent carries several noncompeting lines, which makes it possible for several manufacturers to have a more effective sales effort than their volume would support on an individual basis. A manufacturer will have many independent agents, each handling a specific territory. A *selling agent*, in contrast, will handle the entire output of the manufacturer and is free to negotiate prices, terms, and territories. A selling agent is frequently used by a manufacturer who does not have a strong position in the marketplace.

Commission (or factor) merchants receive goods on consignment and have full power to negotiate. The use of such a middleman suggests that the manufacturer is weak both in the marketplace and financially.

The margins or commissions charged by middlemen reflect the number of services provided; the more services they perform, the greater the compensation. The challenge for planners is to develop a channel strategy that will perform only those services that they do not want to perform themselves, so that channel costs are as low as possible. Vertical conflict in the channel occurs when channel members are competing to perform more functions to gain a larger margin.

TABLE 14.1 Functions performed by selected middlemen

Type of middleman	Storage (including sorting)	Transportation	Risk taking (physical and economic)	Selling	Buying	Financing	Market research
Merchant wholesalers (own inventory)							
Full-function	Yes	Yes	Yes	Yes	Yes	Yes	Yes
Limited-function							
Drop shipper	No	Yes	No	Some	Passes order on to supplier	Yes	No
Cash-and-carry	Yes	No	Yes	Some	Yes	No	No
Truck jobber	Yes	Yes	Yes	Yes	Yes	Yes	No
Rack jobber	Yes	Yes	Yes	Rack setup	Yes	Yes, consignment	Yes
Franchise wholesaler (voluntary chain)	Yes	Yes	Yes	Some	Yes	Yes	Yes
Retail-owned cooperative	Yes	Perhaps	Yes	Little	Yes	Using members' capital	Perhaps
Functional middlemen (do not own inventory)							
Brokers	No	No	Economic only	Yes	No	Yes	Some
Manufacturers' agent (limited territory and activities)	No	No	No	Yes	No	No	No
Selling (sales) agent (unlimited activities)	No	No	Economic if financed	Yes	No	Perhaps	No
Commission merchants	On consignment	Perhaps	Economic if financed	Yes	No	Yes	No

Creating a Channel Strategy   The marketing manager may use Table 14.1 to determine the types of middlemen that are most appropriate for the functions that are to be performed by others. The most profitable strategy may be a mixed strategy that uses more than one channel. For instance, industrial marketers frequently use their own sales forces for large accounts and manufacturers' agents for smaller accounts. (This point, as well as how to calculate when agents should be used, is discussed in Chapter 16.)

The first task facing the channel strategist is to determine which of the functions listed in Table 14.1 to perform. This decision will be determined by the profits, risks, and economies of scale associated with each function. For instance, a manufacturer who did not want to perform any channel functions would choose a full-function wholesaler or a rack jobber.

The Irreducible Minimum Functions   In the 1930s the Russians learned the hard way that "you can eliminate the middleman, but you cannot eliminate his functions." The Russians eliminated the wholesalers, only to find that the railroads had to take over the functions of inventory and breaking bulk lots into smaller lots for retailers. The result was inefficient transportation and retailers who did not know where to get supplies.[5]

A new institution enters a channel when it can perform a function more efficiently than existing institutions can. The automobile channel provides an example. One of the primary functions of the automobile *distributor* was to solve the financing needs of the manufacturer and the retailer. Banks entered the channel with a financing plan known as "floor planning"—the bank actually owns the car on the showroom floor. Given this shift, the automobile manufacturers started shipping directly to dealers, eliminating the distributor.

The evolution of the channel illustrates that its basic task is to collect large, homogeneous assortments of goods, break them down into small, heterogeneous assortments, and make these assortments available to the ultimate consumer. Economies of scale within the channel make it cheaper for the channel member, rather than the manufacturer or the consumer, to perform the function. Competition within the channel will alter the types of institutions performing the function, with the newer institution being the cheaper one.

Relationships Between the Channel and Other Strategies   The interrelatedness of the elements in the marketing mix will limit channel strategies. We will see that the shelf life of the *product* required a short channel for potato chips until Pringle's lengthened the shelf life. A low-*price* policy will yield a different channel strategy than a high-price strategy.

Industrial equipment and computer manufacturers generally use their *own sales force* because it is necessary to adapt their products to the unique needs of the buyers. A manufacturer who is extremely effective in *advertising and promotion* will not choose a channel that is also strong in these functions. Conversely, a manufacturer may need the channel's expertise in advertising.

The *profit plan* raises the questions of who will perform which functions. *Where are the economies of scale?* In *advertising?* In *physical distribution?* In *working capital?* A firm whose volume does not permit it to handle its own warehousing, for example, puts itself at a competitive disadvantage if it does not use a wholesaler or a public warehouse. Limited working capital may limit options such as direct distribution, vending machines, and using one's own retail stores.

The focus of promotional effort leads to *push* and *pull* channel strategies. The *push* strategy consists of promoting to the channel and relying on it to promote the product to the final consumer. The *pull* strategy promotes to the consumer and relies on consumer demand to pull the product through the channel. Most firms use a combination of push and pull strategies.

Examples of Successful Channel Strategies   To illustrate that channel strategies can be exciting as well as important, we will examine recent changes in the channel strategies for women's hosiery and snack foods. The first example illustrates a change in retail institutions. The second group of products illustrates how a change in the product characteristics permitted manufacturers to perform the wholesaling function.

"Our L'eggs Fit Your Legs."   In 1969, when the Hanes Corporation, producers of hosiery, knitwear, and foundation garments, investigated the sale of women's hosiery through supermarkets and drug stores, it discovered some startling facts.[6] There was a $1.5 billion retail hosiery market through supermarkets and drugstores. A marketing research study costing about $400,000 revealed that there were more than 600 different brands, none of which had more than a four-percent share. Promotion was based solely on price. Stockouts were frequently as high as 25 percent, and inventory turnover was low. Consumer research disclosed that product quality was low and inconsistent and that no consumer loyalty existed.

The *product* strategy developed by Hanes was a one-size stretch panty hose which took the shape of the woman's leg; hence the copy theme "Our L'eggs fit your legs." In test market the product had more than a 30 percent share, and in two years the brand became a $100,000,000 business.

Hanes's *marketing* strategy was based on the shape of an egg for the package, the store display, and the name. The unique part of the channel strategy was the fact that the display unit, which took only $2\frac{1}{2}$ square feet of floor space, was owned by Hanes. The inventory was on consignment, so the retailer had no investment in inventory. The display unit was kept stocked by a L'eggs route woman, thereby solving the out-of-stock problem. Computerized inventory methods were used to analyze the turnover rates of colors by stores so that the inventory in each store would match the local demand, thereby reducing out-of-stocks.

This channel strategy was a tremendous gamble for Hanes because it required a large investment in production equipment, displays, in-store inventories, delivery trucks, and inventory systems, as well as the substantial advertising investment. The success of the gamble is now history. L'eggs has expanded the product line to hosiery for men and for the entire family. Many competitors have copied the L'eggs product and marketing strategy.

Snack foods.   Potato chips have a shelf life of about three days. This product characteristic requires frequent deliveries by a myriad of producers who use their own delivery trucks or who use rack jobbers as wholesalers. On the receiving end, the grocer has the time-consuming task of supervising the delivery, monitoring the inventory, and checking the return of merchandise. It is estimated that this type of delivery adds 25 percent to the cost of the product.[7]

The usual distribution channels for firms such as General Mills use chain stores, food brokers, and independent grocery warehouses. In order for General Mills to compete in the $600 million potato chip, corn curls, and cheese curls market, change would be needed either in the channel of distribution or in the length of the shelf life of the product. General Mills chose the latter strategy. It defined the *product concept* as a product that was equal or superior to store-delivered products, had a unique shape, provided adequate margins for grocers, and provided a comparable value for the consumer. The result was Bugles, Whistles, and Daisy's—shelf-stable snacks. These products captured over ten percent of the market. The grocers were pleased to have delivery from their regular warehouses.

Procter & Gamble introduced Pringle's potato chips in 1968, after ten years and $70 million in development costs. Pringle's are uniform chips made from a dehydrated potato mash and packed in a can. By 1975 Pringle's had 13 percent of the market.[8] Competitors fought back by advertising that their products did not have artificial preservatives and by giving grocers a 25 percent margin versus Pringle's 15 to 17 percent margin. In Chicago this counterstrategy limited Pringle's to a five-percent share.

These channel success stories can be matched by stories of not-so-successful products that had ineffective channel strategies. For example, Berg traced the failure of Dow and duPont to gain a market share of the antifreeze market from Prestone and the failure of General Foods' Gourmet Foods line to a poor channel strategy and a failure to understand consumer motivation.[9]

CHANNEL COSTS One frequently heard complaint about marketing is that the channel of distribution costs too much. Table 14.2 uses data from the input-output structure of the

TABLE 14.2   Industrial composition of personal-consumption expenditures

Personal-consumption expenditure category	Percent of allocation to personal-consumption expenditure		
	Producers' prices	Transport and warehousing	Wholesale and retail trade
Food purchased for off-premise consumption	68.2%	2.4%	29.4%
Shoes and other footwear	56.1	0.8	43.1
Women's and children's clothing and accessories	55.3	0.7	43.9
Jewelry and watches	48.1	0.6	51.3
Furniture	53.9	2.0	44.1
Kitchen and other household appliances	65.0	2.3	32.7
Drug preparations and sundries	53.1	0.8	46.1
New cars and net purchases of used cars	73.8	1.9	24.3
Tires, tubes, accessories, and parts	47.9	1.7	50.4
Nondurable toys and sport supplies	52.1	1.5	46.3
Radio and TV receivers, records, and musical instruments	60.1	1.0	39.0
Flowers, seeds, and potted plants	46.4	2.6	51.0

"The Input-Output Structure of the U.S. Economy: 1967," *Survey of Current Business* **54** (February 1974): 24–56.

United States economy to examine the percentage of allocation to personal-consumption expenditures of producers' prices, transport and warehousing, and wholesale and retail trade. Relating these percentages to the previous discussion of functions, we can easily see why the channels in some industries require a higher margin than others do. Flowers, seeds, and potted plants, for example, are highly perishable, so a 51 percent margin is needed to cover the physical risks of this industry. In contrast, the new-car channel requires only 24.3 percent. The manufacturer dominates this industry, using mass advertising to bypass the dealer. The financial risk is assumed by the banks. Thus the auto dealer is left with few functions to perform. Some observers conclude that this channel needs revision.[10]

Are these marketing costs excessive? This is a difficult question to answer, because these percentages are *relative* to the selling price of the product. We know nothing of the *absolute* cost of the product. Economies of scale lower the cost of producing a product, but they may increase the cost of marketing the product because the producer is moved farther from the consumer as production becomes more capital-intense. The void must be filled by increased costs for market research, advertising, selling, buying, and transportation. It is possible that we have assumed that large economies of scale in production result in a lower price to the consumer, when in fact there is a middle point where a higher cost of production would be more than offset by a reduction in marketing costs.

MANAGING THE CHANNEL: POWER AND CONFLICT There has been considerable interest in the dual questions of who has the power and why there is conflict in the channel of distribution. Most of the approaches have been exploratory, either examining theoretical models or measuring conflict within a channel through a survey approach.[11]

In a study of sources of power Lusch concluded that coercive sources of power increase automobile dealer conflict.[12] These sources of power include national and local advertising, training (executive, sales, and mechanics), supply of service manuals, service and sales representatives, warranties, inventory rebates, slow delivery, slow payment on warranty, threat of termination, and red tape. Areas of automobile dealer disagreement include vehicle and parts availability, product quality, sales contests, warranty work, new-vehicle inventory, and sales responsibility. The small margin for new-car dealers indicated in Table 14.2 suggests that the dealers do not hold a strong position in the channel. Perhaps this contributes to the fact that automobiles and their repair are the number-one complaint of consumers.

The legislative activities of trade associations support the Bentley group hypothesis that governmental action is the result of struggle and compromise among groups to secure political redress for economic grievances.[13] The National Automobile Dealers Association tried to balance the power in the channel by urging legislation favorable to the dealers on matters such as inventory forcing by manufacturers, unwarranted franchise cancellation, antibootlegging provisions, direct factory sales that eliminate the dealer, and legalization of territorial security clauses.[14]

Emphasis on the competition and conflict in the channel of distribution has overshadowed the fact that there is also extensive *cooperation* in the channel. The channel shares a common goal—profitably meeting the needs of the consumer. "Internal cooperation is required if a behavior system is to act as a unit."[15]

The channel relationships can be examined as a bargaining process. The subject of the bargain is economic—price, margin, commission, advertising allowances, freight costs, credit, delayed billings, etc. Laboratory experiments suggest that members of a channel will reach agreements that will optimize the *total* channel profit, but the *division* of the profit among the channel members is influenced by the position in the channel. The wholesaler may be at a disadvantage because of the need to bargain in two directions. Bargaining within the channel appears to be a process of information gathering about an opponent's economic situation and bargaining style, particularly yield points. Increases in transaction costs may cause harder bargaining.[16]

So far our discussion of channel competition has been limited to *vertical competition*, which is aimed at gaining a larger share of the margin by performing additional channel functions. *Horizontal competition* exists among channel members of the same type, e.g., retailers. Attempts to reduce this competition will generally violate antitrust legislation, however (see Chapter 10).

In developing a channel strategy, therefore, the strategist must recognize that a channel is a behavioral system composed of individuals, not a collection of institutions whose behavior is always predictable. Like any behavioral system, the channel is a complex set of conflicting and cooperating roles.

LOGISTICS MANAGEMENT Logistics management consists of the decisions regarding the flows of goods, services, and information that are necessary to produce the product and get it to the consumer. The term *logistics*, as used here, means more than *physical distribution*, because logistics also includes the movement of *nonphysical information*. This distinction becomes important when it is possible to move information instead of the product, because it is generally cheaper to move information. For instance, a grain merchant can telephone a customer and state the price of "Number 2 winter wheat." Without uniform standards for wheat grading, it would be necessary for the merchant to physically get the wheat to the customer. This would result in considerable cost and delay. Logistics managers, therefore, should search for opportunities to move information and delay the movement of goods as long as possible. The goal of logistics management is the optimization of the trade-offs among the cost of carrying inventory, storage costs, transportation costs, and the degree of customer service.

The Activities of Logistics *Business* logistics management can be divided into two components—*production logistics* and *marketing logistics*. Production logistics may include the activities of sales forecasting, production planning, purchasing, production scheduling, distribution planning, inventory control, and customer-order processing.[17] Marketing logistics may include sales forecasting, order processing, inventory control, transportation, and customer satisfaction with delivery schedules. By comparing these two types of logistics, we see that there is a possible duplication of effort. Many firms have found that they can reduce their overall *business* logistics costs by developing a single, integrated logistics system. A single system has the potential of reducing the overlap between production and marketing logistics in areas of order processing, inventory control, and transportation. Optimizing only one part of the logistics system may result in a saving in one area being shifted to another area as a cost. For example, a more efficient inventory system may increase the costs of production.

In making the logistics system efficient, we must consider the trade-offs with customer efficiency. An efficient inventory system may result in delays that cause a loss in customers and sales.

Figure 14.2 shows a *business* logistics system. The dashed lines trace the production

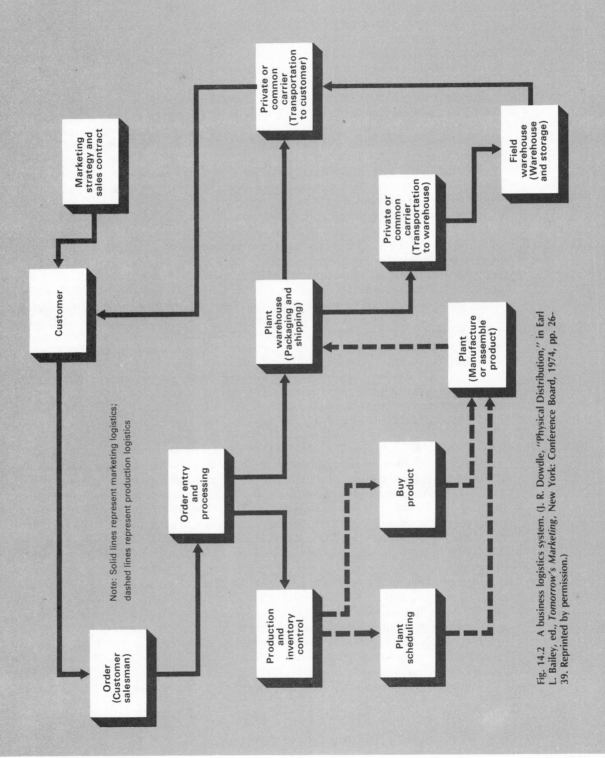

Note: Solid lines represent marketing logistics;
dashed lines represent production logistics

Fig. 14.2 A business logistics system. (J. R. Dowdle, "Physical Distribution," in Earl L. Bailey, ed., *Tomorrow's Marketing*, New York: Conference Board, 1974, pp. 26–39. Reprinted by permission.)

logistics, and the solid lines identify the marketing logistics. Tracing through the marketing logistics will illustrate the kinds of logistics decisions that must be made by the channel strategist.

Management of Logistics   Once the salespeople have received the orders, how do they communicate them into the marketing logistics systems? Should they be mailed or phoned in to the plant? Sometimes orders are collected at regional offices and checked against regional inventories before being forwarded to the home office. Some companies have the salespeople phone in the orders every Monday morning, so that production schedules can be adapted accordingly.

Should inventories be centralized to reduce inventory carrying costs, or should they be decentralized to speed delivery and increase customer satisfaction? An alternative is to use a single warehouse and faster transportation, such as air freight. The channel strategist must consider the trade-offs between the inventory savings and the higher costs of air transportation.

The warehouse and transportation decisions require "make or buy?" decisions. Should we build our own warehouses or use a public warehouse? Or, should we give a larger margin to a distributor who will carry our regional inventories? Should we buy or lease our trucks, or should we use common carriers? These decisions must be reexamined as costs and rate structures change.

Logistics Costs   The operating costs for warehousing, transportation, handling, and order processing appear in a company's expense statement as *distribution expenses*. But other logistics costs go unidentified, e.g., the indirect costs of "communications, data processing, administrative overhead, inventory investment, property taxes and insurance, and inventory obsolescence and spoilage."[18] There are also subtle costs that affect profits, but are rarely traced to the channel strategy. These are "the *lost profit opportunities* because of products not shipped on time, canceled orders, a customer dissatisfaction, which, in turn, affect field sales morale and often require significant management attention to solve."[20]

The more direct and measurable costs of distribution are summarized in Table 14.3. We see that 13.8 percent of the chemical-sales dollars go to physical distribution,

TABLE 14.3   The cost of physical distribution for selected industries

Physical distribution function	Percent share of costs					
	Chemicals, plastics, and glass	Distribution firms	Food processors	Pharmaceuticals and health care	Consumer products	Machinery and industrial equipment
Inventory	20%	20%	10%	15%	15%	28%
Order processing	15	25	5	15	5	10
Warehousing	15	20	15	20	25	18
Transportation	45	10	65	45	50	35
Miscellaneous	5	25	5	5	5	9
Total	100%	100%	100%	100%	100%	100%
Physical distribution costs per $100 of sales	$13.80	$13.70	$9.50	$8.30	$7.50	$5.20

Adapted from Herbert W. Davis & Co.; Sales & Marketing Management's 1976 Survey of Selling Costs, as quoted in "Physical Distribution: The Right Time, The Right Place," *Sales & Marketing Management*, June 14, 1976, p. 47. Reproduced by permission.

whereas only 5.2 percent of machinery sales are spent on distribution. We note also that there are great variances across industries in the amount spent on a particular function.

Methods for the reduction of physical-distribution costs can be divided into five categories: (1) computer models to aid in the balancing of inventory, warehousing, and transportation costs; (2) data transmission via telephone; (3) computerized control of distribution operations; (4) industrial engineering methods applied to the physical handling of materials; and (5) analyses of transportation rates to identify lower-cost methods such as new routes, new modes, or methods for aggregating shipments. These methods may not yield long-range savings for the total system, because many of the trade-offs cannot be quantified, the answers are too complex for execution, and market dynamics place continuous new demands on the logistical system.[20]

Logistics strategies represent a trade-off between costs and customer satisfaction. Industrial purchasing managers rated physical distribution second only to product quality in the criteria influencing their decisions.[21] But rapid deliveries will add costs to the entire logistics system. The channel strategist must consider three trade-offs—the cost of added service, the expected value of the loss of sales because of poor service, and the *cost of replacing a lost customer*. The last cost is rarely considered. In some cases it may be cheaper to increase the marketing effort to gain new customers than to raise an inventory in-stock situation from 95 percent to 99 percent to retain customers whose contribution to profit is marginal.

Examples of Logistics Strategies[22] A grocery manufacturer used 60 public and company-owned warehouses to ship 450 million pounds of products valued at $300 million. A separate sales organization was used for each product line. The alternative channel strategy was to use a single sales force. It was estimated that savings would occur in the handling of orders and transportation, but that inventory costs would increase. The estimated net savings was $0.5 million on a total distribution cost of $20 million.

A pharmaceutical company distributed 50 million pounds of goods, representing $150 million in sales, through its field branches at a cost of $15 million. Its major promotion was a twice-a-year program. The bulge in orders resulted in overtime payments at its public warehouses and delays in regular orders. "The alternative was a coordinated distribution and marketing strategy calling for the forwarding of advance orders to the plant, building truckload shipments and using commercial break-bulk services, with a resulting cost reduction of $200,000 and an improvement in service."[23]

Both of these examples illustrate the interrelationships between channel strategies and other marketing-mix strategies. They emphasize the point that a channel strategy cannot be made independently of the product, pricing, advertising, promotional, and personal-selling strategies.

SUMMARY Channel strategies begin with an understanding of where and when consumer needs occur so that the product can be at the right place at the right time. The Environmental Analysis Worksheet will identify channel opportunities as well as constraints. A channel strategist must understand the locus of channel power as she or he bargains with channel members for the best services at the lowest prices. To understand the dynamics of channel power, it is necessary to understand the economic history of channels.

The power in the channel rests with the institution having the greatest economies of scale. In the eighteenth century it was the wholesaler. In the nineteenth century the power went first to the manufacturer and then to the large retailer. Power returned to the manufacturer early in the twentieth century, when the mass media made it possible for the manufacturer to advertise directly to the consumer, thereby reducing dependence on the retailer. New institutions will appear as more economical ways are found to reduce the costs of the irreducible channel functions. The old institutions seek legislative support for their dwindling power.

The functions performed by the middlemen include storage, transportation, risk taking, selling, buying, financing, and market research. The goal of the channel strategy is to have these functions performed at the lowest cost and still maintain adequate service to customers.

Vertical relations in a channel are a balance of *cooperation* to sell to the consumer and *conflict* to gain a larger share of the margin by performing more functions. The division of the margin among the channel members seems to be determined by a member's location within the channel, the bargaining styles of opponents, and the bargainers' personalities. Although *vertical* competitors may seek legislation to reduce competition within the channel, *horizontal* competitors are forbidden by antitrust laws to take any action that will reduce competition.

After gaining an understanding of the historical and political environment in which he or she operates, the channel strategist must develop specific channel strategy alternatives. The elements in the Environmental Analysis and Strategy Worksheets will guide the development of profitable channel strategies.

Business logistics systems require trade-offs among cost of production, inventory, storage, transportation, customer satisfaction, and the cost of replacing customers who were lost due to inadequate service. Many of the operations research approaches to business logistics have failed to yield expected savings, because some trade-offs cannot be measured, solutions are too complex for implementation, and market dynamics require a dynamic logistics system.

Channel and logistics strategies may not require the continuous evaluation and revision that product and advertising strategies require, but channel and logistics strategies need more attention than they receive in most firms.

DISCUSSION QUESTIONS

1. What are the differences between merchant wholesalers and functional middlemen?
2. Differentiate the functions of the following merchant wholesalers: full-function wholesaler, drop shipper, cash-and-carry wholesaler, truck jobber, rack jobber, franchise wholesaler, and retail-owned cooperatives.
3. Where do you think the locus of channel power will move in ten years?
4. To keep cost as low as possible, what services does the planner want to include in a channel strategy?
5. What is the marketing danger of large economies of scale in production?
6. Differentiate push and pull channel strategies. Think of examples of each.
7. What is logistics management? What are some important trade-offs involved in developing a logistics strategy?
8. What is the crucial factor that determines which institution in the channel has the most power?

9. Visit local retailers and wholesalers to determine what functions they perform.

10. Make a generalized flow chart like that in Fig. 13.5 that will establish a procedure for a channel strategy.

NOTES

1. For a discussion of the classification of goods, *see* L. P. Bucklin, "Retail Strategy and the Classification of Consumer Goods," *Journal of Marketing* **27** (October 1962): 50–55.

2. M. Sroge, "11 Publicly-owned Consumer Mail Order Companies Outperform Major Retailers," *Marketing News*, November 19, 1976, p. 6.

3 E. H. Lewis, *Marketing Channels: Structure and Strategy* (New York: McGraw-Hill, 1968).

4. S. C. Hollander, "The Wheel of Retailing," *Journal of Marketing* (July 1960): 37–42.

5. M. I. Goldman, *Soviet Marketing* (New York: Free Press, 1963).

6. This discussion is based on H. Singer and F. S. DeBruicker, "L'eggs Products, Inc. (A), (B), and (C)," (Boston: Intercollegiate Case Clearing House, 1974, 1974, and 1975, ICH order numbers 9-575-065, 9-575-066, and 9-575-090, respectively); H. W. McMahan, "Alltime Ad Triumphs Reveal Key Success Factors Behind Choice of '100 Best,'" *Advertising Age*, April 12, 1976, pp. 72–78.

7. C. W. Plattes, "Strategic and Tactical Decision Making in Marketing," in *Decision Making in Marketing* (New York: Conference Board, 1971), pp. 14–20.

8. "The Great Potato-Chip War," *Forbes*, September 15, 1975, pp. 24–25.

9. T. L. Berg, *Mismarketing* (Garden City, N.Y.: Doubleday, 1970).

10. M. S. Moyer and N. M. Whitmore, "An Appraisal of the Marketing Channels for Automobiles," *Journal of Marketing* **40** (July 1976): 35–40.

11. L. P. Bucklin, "A Theory of Channel Control," *Journal of Marketing* **37** (January 1973): 39–47; A. I. El-Ansary and L. W. Stern, "Power Measurement in the Distribution Channel," *Journal of Marketing Research* **9** (February 1972): 47–52; S. D. Hunt and J. R. Nevin, "Power in a Channel of Distribution: Sources and Consequences," *Journal of Marketing Research* **11** (May 1974): 186–193; L. J. Rosenberg and L. W. Stern, "Conflict Measurement in the Distribution Channel," *Journal of Marketing Research* (November 1971): 437–442.

12. R. F. Lusch, "Sources of Power: Their impact on Intrachannel Conflict," *Journal of Marketing Research* (November 1976): 382–390.

13. J. C. Palamountain, Jr., *The Politics of Distribution* (Cambridge, Mass.: Harvard University Press, 1955).

14. H. Assael, "The Political Role of Trade Associations Distributive Conflict Resolution," *Journal of Marketing* (April 1968): 21–28.

15. W. Alderson, "Cooperation and Conflict in Marketing Channels," *Dynamic Marketing Behavior* (Homewood, Ill.: Richard D. Irwin, 1965).

16. D. L. Harnett, L. L. Cummings, and G. D. Hughes, "The Influence of Risk-Taking Propensity on Bargaining Behavior," *Behavioral Science* (March 1968): 91–101; D. L. Harnett, G. D. Hughes, and L. L. Cummings, "Bilateral Monopolistic Bargaining Through an Intermediary," *Journal of Business of the University of Chicago* (April 1968): 251–259; G. D. Hughes, J. B. Juhasz, and B. Contini, "The Influence of Personality on the Bargaining Process," *Journal of Business of the University of Chicago* (October 1973): 593–604.

17. For a discussion of the design and limitations of production and inventory systems, *see* H. M. Wagner, "The Design of Production and Inventory Systems for Multifacility and Multiwarehouse Companies," *Operations Research* **22** (1974): 278–291.

18. J. R. Dowdle, "Physical Distribution," in *Tomorrow's Marketing*, ed. E. L. Bailey (New York: Conference Board, 1974), pp. 26–39.

19. *Ibid.*

20. *Ibid.*

21. W. D. Perreault and F. A. Russ, "Physical Distribution Service in Industrial Purchase Decisions," *Journal of Marketing* (April 1976): 3–10.

22. These examples are taken from Dowdle, *op. cit.*, pp. 35–36.

23. *Ibid.*

SUGGESTED READINGS

Baligh, H. M., *Vertical Market Structures* (Boston: Allyn and Bacon, 1967).

Ballou, R. H., *Business Logistics Management* (Englewood Cliffs, N.J.: Prentice-Hall, 1973).

Bowersox, D. J., "Planning Physical Distribution Operations with Dynamic Simulation," *Journal of Marketing* (January 1972): 17–25.

Bucklin, L. P., *Competition and Evolution in the Distributive Trades* (Englewood Cliffs, N.J.: Prentice-Hall, 1972).

Cox, R., *Distribution in a High-Level Economy* (Englewood Cliffs, N.J.: Prentice-Hall, 1965).

Davis, H. W., *Workbook for a Physical Distribution Audit* (Washington, D.C.: Marketing Publications, 1976).

El-Ansary, A. I., and R. A. Robicheaux, "A Theory of Channel Control: Revisited," *Journal of Marketing* **38** (January 1974): 2–7.

Geoffrion, A. M., "Better Distribution Planning with Computer Models," *Harvard Business Review* (July-August 1976): 92–99.

Heskett, J. J., N. A. Glaskowsky, Jr., and R. M. Ivie, *Business Logistics*, 2d ed. (New York Ronald Press, 1973).

Magee, J. F., *Physical-Distribution Systems* (New York: McGraw-Hill, 1967).

Mallen, B. E., *The Marketing Channel, A Conceptual Viewpoint* (New York: Wiley, 1967).

ENVIRONMENTAL ANALYSIS WORKSHEET

Environmental elements	Facts	Assumptions or research needed	Conclusions
Organizational values, objectives, and policies (4)			
Organizational design (5)			

Situation
  Generic demand (6)
  Brand demand (7)
  Competition (9)
  Public policy (10)			

Opportunities (2)			
Problems			

MARKETING PLAN (CONSUMER PRODUCT)

Current performance
Recommendations
Effect of recommendations on income
Situation analysis
Opportunities and problems
Strategies
Tests and research
Supporting documents
  Comparative budgets
  Media allocation schedule
  Promotion control sheet

STRATEGY WORKSHEET

Opportunities and problems in rank order to importance

1.
2.
.
n.

	Current strategy	Alternatives and recommended strategy	Estimated Effect

Demand strategy
   Generic
   Brand

Strategic goals
   Financial
   Marketing

Marketing-mix strategies
   Product (12)
   Pricing (13)
   Channel and logistics (14)
   Advertising and promotional (15)
   Sales management (16)

Research (3)

Profit plan

Evaluation and control (19)

CHAPTER 15

Advertising and Promotional Strategies

LEARNING OBJECTIVES   After studying this chapter you should:

1. Understand the function of advertising in the communication mix.
2. Know the common communication goals for advertising, promotion, and institutional advertising and be able to define them in precise terms.
3. Understand the criteria for developing media strategies.
4. Understand media timing strategies.
5. Know some of the common ways for measuring advertising effectiveness.
6. Be able to evaluate the most frequently used methods for budgeting advertising.
7. Be aware of careers in advertising agencies and the importance of matching personalities.
8. Know both sides of some common criticisms of advertising.
9. Be able to define and use the following concepts:

Advertising ✔	Reach and frequency	Institutional advertising
Promotion ✔	Media	Trademarks
Communication mix	Vehicles and units	Recall ✔
Communication goals	Broadside approach	Panel
Hierarchy of effects ✔	Profile matching	First-brand awareness
Cognitive dissonance ✔	Marginal (high-assay)	Breakdown and buildup
Copy strategy	principle	budgets
Copy segmentation	Pulse strategies	Competitive parity
Comparison advertising	Consumer purchase cycle	Marginal-approach budgets
Copy research	Cost per thousand (CPM)	Objective-and-task budgets
Media segmentation	Effective CPM	Account executives

SOME STRATEGIC QUESTIONS FOR OPENERS

1. What is the relative role of advertising in the communication mix for the product? For the industry?
2. What are the goals of advertising? Of promotion? Of institutional advertising? Are they stated in measurable terms?
3. Do the copy and media strategies need to be changed?
4. How should the effectiveness of advertising be measured?
5. How should budgets be established and controlled?

Defining advertising would seem to be simple, because most of us are exposed to hundreds of advertisements each day. In broad terms, advertising is selling through print or electronic media. Any *sponsored communication* designed to influence buying behavior is advertising. The familiar media include television, newspapers, magazines, radio, outdoor advertising, transit advertising, direct mail, telephone directories, etc. But there are other forms of sponsored communication which do not use these media, such as trade shows, exhibits, coupons, samples, premiums, case allowances, contests, free goods, rebates, and point-of-purchase material.[1] These communications are known as *promotions. Packaging* plays an important role in the communication mix and is sometimes known as *three-dimensional advertising*.

COMMUNICATION GOALS The *goals* for the communication strategy are identified by the environmental analysis and summarized in the statement of opportunities and problems. The Strategy Worksheet, it will be recalled, begins with a rank-ordering of the most important opportunities and problems.

The Scoop Ice Cream case illustrates how the opportunities and problems change, causing communication goals to change. The initial opportunity was to introduce a new process for making ice cream. Advertising had as its task making housewives aware of the new product and convincing them to try it. The second year, Scoop had new communication tasks: nontriers had to be convinced to try the product, and initial triers had to be persuaded to continue to buy and use it. The introduction of Admiral brand required a competitive advertising strategy. The key elements in the Scoop buying process, therefore, were the percentage of the target consumers who were aware of the new process and its benefits, their trial rate, and their usage rate. The Scoop *advertising* strategy will have as its goal changing the percentage of target customers who are aware, the percentage who have tried Scoop, and the repurchase rate of users. The *promotional strategy to the trade* will attempt to improve the distribution rate.

The key elements in the buying process will vary according to the product, the market, and consumer habits. During the discussion of brand-demand analysis (Chapter 7), we saw a matrix that could be used to develop a brand strategy for soft drinks. The generic demand was composed of the number of teenagers in the target market, the percentage of this group who drank soft drinks, and their weekly consumption rate. The key variables for the brand demand were the percentage of users who were aware of our brand, the percentage of this group who made our brand their first choice, and the percentage of stores that carried our brand. A *generic*-advertising strategy would focus on changing the percentage using the product type and their consumption rate. A *brand*-advertising strategy would state its goals in terms of altering the percentage of users who were aware of our brand and the percentage who made our brand their first choice. A *channel* strategy would use advertising and promotion to improve the distribution rate.

Making Goals Measurable Advertising researchers use a variety of variables and measures to identify the communication effect of advertising. For instance, Dunn states that the advertising agency of Benton & Bowles uses four variables to test copy strategies—recall, communication, belief change, and purchase-intent change.[2] *Recall* of an advertisement measures the ability to attract attention and be memorable. *Communication* measures what message was actually conveyed. *Belief change* measures the ability to change attitudes in the desired direction. *Purchase-intent change* measures "the ability to create more willingness to purchase the advertised brand."[3]

A strategy for industrial advertising will focus on the opportunities and problems that are unique to the industry and the product. For instance, the key decision variables may be price, delivery schedule, technological superiority, and service after the sale. The position of our brand along these key dimensions will determine our advertising strategy.

Communication Models   Advertising strategists have used a variety of models to identify the components of their target markets' buying processes. Lavidge and Steiner, for example, identified six stages in the buying process: awareness, knowledge, liking, preference, conviction, and purchase.[4] The DAGMAR (Defining Advertising Goals for Measured Advertising Results) model identified four stages—awareness, comprehension, conviction, and action.[5] These models reduce to the basic model of awareness, attitudes, and behavior.

Some researchers have been confused about using these "hierarchy of effects" models, assuming that advertising must begin by changing awareness, then attitudes, and then behavior. This is not the case, however. Research has shown that advertisements may change awareness *and* attitudes simultaneously.[6] Also, the model may work backwards. A change in behavior without a change in attitudes will create a *cognitive dissonance*. To avoid this uncomfortable state, an individual will change his or her attitudes after the behavior. For instance, a person may read automobile advertising *after* purchasing a specific brand, as reassurance that she or he has made the correct choice, thereby reducing cognitive dissonance.

A precise definition of the advertising goal makes it possible to trace the effectiveness of the advertising strategy. To be measurable, a goal must be defined in terms of *magnitude* of some variable *and* the *time* in which the goal is to be achieved. For instance, the advertising goals for Scoop in 1971 were to attain a 60 percent recall of Scoop's quality and price (see Table 2.2). The magnitude is explicit—60 percent. The time period of one year is implicit, because this is a one-year plan. Given this precision, this strategy may be evaluated at the end of the year before the strategy for 1972 is developed.

What should our benchmark be when setting advertising goals? General Motors used as a benchmark the attitudes of people who would consider the brand. GM's advertising goal, therefore, was to move the attitudes of those who would not consider the brand to equal the level of those who would consider the brand. A strategy matrix like the one shown in Table 7.4 helps to organize the goals and test their relationship to sales.

ADVERTISING STRATEGY   The creation of an advertising strategy begins after an analysis of the facts has ended. The leap from the facts to the strategy is a creative one, not a scientific one. *Strategy*, from the Greek word meaning *generalship*, is an "ingenious design for achieving an end."[7] The creative strategist finds new ways for looking at an old problem. Mary Wells, president of a very successful advertising agency, stated that her talent is putting together information and coming up with a better way to sell a product.[8]

A good strategy requires simplicity, because it is difficult for consumers to understand more than one concept in an advertisement. For instance, "It's the real thing"

(Coke), "Come to Marlboro country," and "We try harder" (Avis) all convey a concept with great graphic simplicity. This simplicity makes it easier to execute the strategy. A complex strategy is useless if it cannot be translated into copy and media strategies.

In Chapter 6, after analysis of the beverage and mixer market segments for an orange soft drink, we concluded that the product should not be differentiated, but that the advertising should be. Furthermore, because the demographic profiles were the same for both segments, we concluded that the media strategy could be undifferentiated, but that the copy would be differentiated. Thus we could take advantage of quantity discounts in media and communicate with the two segments by using different copy themes.

In Chapter 7 we saw that brand maps help to identify product and advertising strategies. In some cases it will be necessary to reformulate the product to move it closer to an ideal brand. In other cases a communication strategy can be used to correct misperceptions about the brand. We also saw that the goals of the strategy could be established by using brand maps.

Brand positioning is a new-product strategy. An existing product may be *repositoned* by reformulating the product, changing the advertising strategy, or finding new uses for the product. Lysol, Vaseline, and Arm & Hammer were three very old brands that were repositioned successfully, as we saw in Chapter 7.

Advertising strategies must relate to other elements in the marketing mix. For instance, an efficient mass media advertising strategy would be less than optimal if the channel strategy called for exclusive outlets. One or the other strategy must be changed.

COPY STRATEGIES The *copy* is the selling message of an advertisement. It should communicate memorably and convincingly the advantages of the product. The copy strategy for Anheuser-Busch's Budweiser beer stresses *fun, fellowship,* and *quality.* Busch, another Anheuser-Busch brand, stresses *quality* and *price.* A third Anheuser-Busch brand, Michelob, emphasizes *superior quality* and *social acceptability.* This differentiated copy strategy helps to prevent one brand from cannibalizing the sales of another brand. All three brands stress *quality,* but each is positioned differently. Michelob is the super premium beer, Budweiser is the premium beer, and Busch is positioned as the popular brand.[9]

The execution of the copy strategy in print, such as a magazine advertisement, includes the illustration and the layout. The elements of execution can make or destroy a good copy theme. Figure 15.1 illustrates a layout that seems to be designed to focus attention on the brand. The product is located in the point of central focus, which is in the center of the page, two-thirds up from the bottom. Mountains, reeds, all eyes, and other parts of the bodies in the picture bring the viewer's eye motion toward the product.

The copy themes in *industrial* advertising reflect the fact that the target audience is looking for information that will help them on their jobs. Industrial copy, therefore, stresses information, product benefits, problem solving, and demonstrations.[10] One research study of industrial advertising managers concluded that most managers do not understand the major elements in their customers' buying process.[11]

Copy Segmentation Markets are frequently segmented according to the different consumer benefits. The most frequently used example of benefit segmentation is the toothpaste market.

Haley identified four benefit segments—sensory (children), sociable (young people), worrisome (large families), and independent (the economic person).[12] Why bother with benefit segmentation when the media profiles are along demographic, economic, and sometimes life-style dimensions? Haley points out that *benefit copy segmentation* improves communication with a target group, thereby increasing the impact of advertising two- or threefold.[13]

Copy segmentation helps the advertiser cut through the selective perception of the target audience. The average individual perceives no more than ten percent of the advertisements to which he or she is exposed. *Creative* copy and execution will penetrate this perceptual screen. Haley suggests than another solution is *benefit information*, which he defines as copy that offers you something you want.[14] Haley presents evidence to support his conclusion that *message differentiation is as important as product differentiation.*

Where does the copy writer get the creative insights for effective benefit segmentation? The copy writer in the Schlitz beer case went tavern hopping. Life-style research and focus-group interviews are frequent sources for identifying consumer needs. Other group techniques include brainstorming and synectics (a more structured group technique). Effective copy will focus attention on the needs of the buyer, without drawing attention to itself. By contrast, many clever or humorous advertisements did not sell the product because the consumer remembered the humor, not the brand.

The statistical methods for identifying benefit segments are new, but benefit copy is not. A 1927 advertisement for the RCA Radiola drips with benefits: "The music reaches to the fartherest corner of the great barn. Yet it is clear and true. The songs reach the couples who sit outside in the shadows by the lake. And the voices are full and real. The Radiola gives a summer function [a barn dance] new possibilities."[15]

In writing benefit copy, the copy writer must remember that the benefits must be supported by product facts. Firestone made safety claims "without disclosing that there is no such thing as a completely safe tire."[16] The civil penalty included a $50,000 fine and Firestone's agreeing to fund $750,000 in advertising on tire-care information.

Comparison Advertising   Prior to 1971 advertisers avoided direct mention of a competitive brand in an advertisement because they feared a charge of unfair competition under Section 5 of the Federal Trade Commission Act. This changed in 1971, when the FTC stated that it thought that it was in the best interest of the consumer to have direct brand comparisons in advertisements. In 1974 the American Association of Advertising Agencies established policies and guidelines for comparative advertising. We have already seen the competitive interaction between Tylenol and Datril that resulted from Datril's competitive price comparisons (Chapter 9).

Is comparative advertising effective advertising? Is it a passing fad? It is too early to answer these questions, but there has been an examination of the pros and cons.[17]

One study of comparative television advertising was conducted by the advertising agency of Ogilvy & Mather. It concluded that comparative television advertising does not offer any advantage to a package-goods advertiser. Brand identification is not increased. Consumers are made more aware of competitive brands. Belief in claims is lowered. It is not persuasive. Miscommunication and confusion are increased.[18] The Tylenol experience in the marketplace seems to support this research conclusion, because its share rose almost 4 percent, to 14.7 percent of the overall analgesic market, whereas new Datril established about 2 percent of the market.[19] (The nonaspirin market expanded also.) It is not possible to tell whether the Tylenol share increased because of the Datril comparative advertisements or because Tylenol made two other changes—increasing its personal-selling effort and adding the package-goods channels to its channel strategy (see Chapter 9).

Copy Research and Testing Because of the importance of copy strategies, many methods have been developed to *pretest* copy for its ability to attract attention, be memorable, be comprehensible, and to motivate. Some very imaginative devices have been used, many of which are adaptations from psychological experiments. For example, galvanic skin response and eye dilation have been used to measure the respondent's interest in an advertisement. Theaters have been arranged so that respondents could turn a dial to report their interest in a particular section of a commerical. Split runs are used in magazines and community antenae television systems (CATV) to test different strategies or executions. Sample advertisements are placed in a portfolio and respondents are asked to report their preferences; this is known as a *folio test*. In other cases respondents are asked to evaluate a single ad. Such a test is known as the *monadic test*. Gross developed a mathematical model to determine how much to spend for research on the generation and evaluation of alternative advertising campaigns.[20] All of these tests measure the communication effect of a copy strategy, not sales. Sales are dependent on other variables, such as media, product characteristics, and distribution rates—all of which are beyond the control of the copy writer.

Many copy researchers stress the need to test copy within the media that will be used. Thus test advertisements will be embedded in a magazine or television show. These researchers feel that the media are part of the message and will affect the productivity of an advertisement.

The variety of pretest research methods attests to the fact that no one method has been found to be the best. Longman, an experienced advertising researcher, concluded, "For obvious reasons, copy-testing in all its current forms is extremely imprecise."[21] Light, the senior vice-president for research at the advertising agency of BBD&O, concluded that copy-testing techniques "have an inherent degree of unreliablity"; he found that when he paired different testing techniques, different methods picked different advertisements 77 percent of the time.[22]

For *posttesting* advertisements, many advertisers and agencies use syndicated services that measure some dimension of an advertisement's ability to gain attention.[23] Starch, Nielsen, and Gallup & Robinson are three of the available syndicated services that permit an advertiser to buy into an ongoing survey. Figure 15.1 illustrates a magazine advertisement that has the Starch ratings for various parts of the layout. Three measures are reported—the percentages of respondents who noted, advertiser associated, and read most of the copy. Persons are classified as having *noted* the advertisement if they report having seen it in the issue of the magazine that is being studied. *Associated* means that they read some part of the advertisement which clearly indicates the brand or advertiser. *Read most* classifies persons who read half or more of the written material.

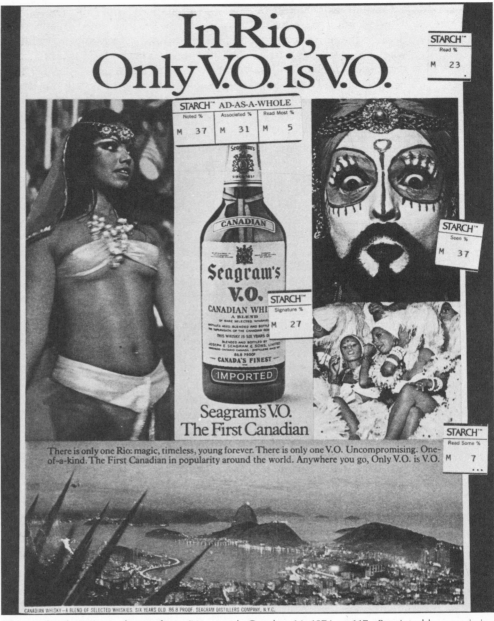

Fig. 15.1 A layout that focuses on the product. (*Newsweek*, October 14, 1974, p. 117. Reprinted by permission of Joseph E. Seagram & Sons, Inc., and Starch Inra Hooper Inc.)

MEDIA STRATEGIES   One of the most complex marketing decisions is the development of media strategies. It is a mix of art and science. Science has entered in the form of models to estimate coverage and operations research techniques to help the strategist select from among the astronomical number of combinations of media that could form a media strategy.

Reaching the Target Audience   The basic task of the media strategy is to reach the target audience with the message (i.e., the copy strategy) in order to achieve the communication goal at the lowest media cost. Segmentation strategies for media include segmentation by editorial content. This subtle distinction can be illustrated with the Anheuser-Busch strategy. All of the Anheuser-Busch beers used televised *sports*, but the segmentation occurred in the type of sport portrayed. Busch used baseball, Busweiser used football and hockey, and Michelob used "country club" sports, such as golf.

Once the demand analysis has identified the target audience, the media strategist must consider what percentage of the audience to *reach* and the *frequency* with which it should receive the message. Scheduling, message wearout, media efficiencies, budget limitations, and competitors' use of media must all be considered. Creative elements in the copy strategy must be reflected in the media strategy. For instance, a long message can be used in magazine advertising, but not in outdoor advertising. Some strategies need visual presentations, which would eliminate radio. Strategies requiring visual demonstrations would consider the dynamics of television for a first choice and print media as a second choice. The use of print media has the advantage of future reference. A buyer may refer back to a printed advertisement, but an electronic one is gone once it is broadcasted.

A large number of combinations of strategies is illustrated by the choices available to the media strategist. First, a decision must be made as to which *media* to use—newspapers, magazine, television, etc. Then the strategist must select from among the *vehicles* in a medium. For example, if television has been selected, the media strategist may choose sports programs, comedy, mystery, news, etc. The profile of the target audience will help the strategist make this choice. Some profile data, such as Simmons and the Target Group Index, provide the media habits of product users, which permits the strategist to identify specific programs. A *vehicle* choice in magazines would include specific magazines such as *Time, Psychology Today*, and *The New Yorker*. To give some idea of the magnitude of the choice, note that there are approximately 700 television stations, 7500 radio stations, 3200 cable television stations, 1800 daily newspapers, 640 Sunday newspapers, 13,000 farm magazines, 17,600 industry periodicals, 20,000 general magazines, and 1500 business periodicals.[24]

The choice is not complete, because the strategist must choose a *unit* of the vehicle. If it is a magazine, the strategist may decide to use a half page, four-color, run-of-the-press location, with *monthly* insertions, or the more costly inside back cover (if available) in full color *once per quarter*. An alternative strategy would be to use a regional edition of a magazine if the target population has geographic concentrations. The vast combination of unit alternatives can be appreciated only by examining *Standard Rate and Data*, which is the catalog of media alternatives and costs.

Matching the media to the target audience may be accomplished through a variety of media strategies. Longman, for example, illustrates the *broadside approach, profile matching*, and the *high-assay principle* (Table 15.1).[25] The broadside approach gives all market segments equal coverage, regardless of the number of prospects in each segment. The profile method allocates the coverage in proportion to the number of prospects in each segment. For example, Segment A in Table 15.1 has 45 percent of the prospects ($90/200 = 45\%$), so it gets a coverage of 18 messages ($.45 \times 40 = 18$). The profile

TABLE 15.1   The methods for matching media and markets

Market segment	Population	Prospects	Broadside approach Coverage	Broadside approach Prospects reached	Profile matching Coverage	Profile matching Prospects reached	High-assay principle Coverage	High-assay principle Prospects reached
A	100	90	10	9	18	16.2	40	36
B	100	60	10	6	12	7.2	0	0
C	100	30	10	3	6	1.8	0	0
D	100	20	10	2	4	.8	0	0
Total	400	200	40	20	40	26.0	40	36

K. A. Longman, *Advertising* (New York: Harcourt Brace Jovanovich, 1971), p. 209. Reprinted by permission.

method is an improvement over the broadside method because it reaches six more prospects.

The high-assay principle is based on the gold miner's strategy to send the entire crew to the mine with the most gold. When this mine's assay drops below the next available mine, the crew moves to the next mine. Thus all messages are allocated to the A market. This approach reaches 36 prospects, a great improvement over the other two methods.

The high-assay principle has several limitations, however. First, it is difficult to measure the assay (i.e., profits) that each vehicle would produce. Second, territorial claims may be placed on a gold mine, but not on potential customers. Failure to promote to a market may leave it open to competitors, thereby preventing our entry at a later date.

Time Strategies   The media strategy must consider some obvious timing factors, such as a seasonal demand or the length of time in which a competitor will react, but it must also consider many less obvious factors. For instance, should the insertions appear in a short period of time as a *burst* or *pulse* of effort, or should they be *spaced* over a long period of time? Research indicates that when initial levels of brand awareness are low, a pulse strategy produces higher cumulative levels of awareness than does a spaced strategy.[26] Factors that must be considered when choosing between these two timing strategies are the rate of decay of awareness without advertising and the impact of competitive advertising on the awareness level of our brand. Longman has identified six types of media schedules—steady, seasonal pulse, periodic pulse (regular intervals), erratic pulse (irregular intervals), start-up pulse (new campaign), and promotional pulse (tie-in with sales promotion).[27]

A third time pattern that must be considered is the consumer's usual purchase cycle. "Generally, the longer the purchase cycle, the more inclined we will be to pulse our advertising."[28] Pulsed advertising may be used with products that have high brand loyalty and those that are purchased after lengthy deliberation. Conversely, steady, high-frequency advertising must be used for products that are bought on impulse, have a short repurchase cycle, and have low brand loyalty.

Another timing strategy is concerned with the *planned frequency* of message duplication to the same audience. A new product or the correction of an incorrect image may require many duplications to accomplish the communication goal. One researcher has concluded that there are upper and lower thresholds of frequency.[29] Below the lower limit the advertisement is not effective; above the upper limit, it is a waste of resources.

The total number of exposures generated by a media strategy is determined by the percentage of the market that is reached by the strategy (known as *reach*) and the average number of times that each prospect is exposed to the message (known as *frequency*). A media schedule that uses many media and vehicles will duplicate the audiences reached. Media researchers have developed models to estimate the amount of this duplication or to estimate the total exposures in a media schedule.[30] The media planner must make trade-offs between reach and frequency, because an increase in one will be accompanied by a decrease in the other, given a fixed budget. The planner will consider many combinations of schedules to attain the optimal reach and frequency patterns.[31]

Additional timing considerations when selecting media are mechanical requirements and discount structures. The use of network television requires the purchase of time six to twelve months in advance because of the limited number of networks. Magazines, in contrast, can add pages to accommodate additonal advertisers. Mechanical requirements in printing also limit media strategies. For instance, the decision to use four colors may require more lead time to prepare the color negatives.

The number of vehicles chosen in a specific medium will be influenced by the discount structure for quantity purchases. The planner must consider discount structures when deciding whether to buy two units in two different vehicles or two units in one vehicle.

Selecting Media, Vehicles, and Units   The forming of a specific media schedule has been an art until recently, when operations researchers have brought some of their tools to the task. These tools include linear programming, iteration (i.e., marginal analysis) models, dynamic programming, heuristic programming, and simulation.[32] But the artistic element has not been completely removed. The user of these models must supply subjective weights for factors such as target population, vehicle appropriateness, exposure, effectiveness, and frequency.[33]

Many media models and refinements have taken place during the 15 years since the first model was developed. An excellent comparison of the models is provided by Longman.[34] Most of the models have difficulty handling the timing objectives *and* the discount opportunities. Figure 15.2 shows a flow chart for a simple iterative media model that begins with a fixed dollar budget and builds a media schedule by locating the medium with the lowest cost per thousand weighted prospects. After one unit of this medium has been bought, the model adjusts the remaining media vehicles to show the net unduplicated audience from vehicles selected for time period *t*. It continues the iterative search process until it completes the budget for a period, such as a month, and finally until the total annual budget is exhausted.

The concept of *cost per thousand prospects* (CPM) is frequently used as a first approximation of a medium's productivity. An example appears in Table 15.2. The two right-hand columns show the cost per thousand *total audience* for *Reader's Digest* and *Newsweek*. (The *total* audience for a magazine includes subscriptions, newsstand sales, and pass-along readers.)

Column 5 shows that *Reader's Digest* has the lower CPM, $1.44 versus $1.71. If our target market is households with an annual income greater than $20,000, the total audience must be adjusted for the percentage of readers with this income. The

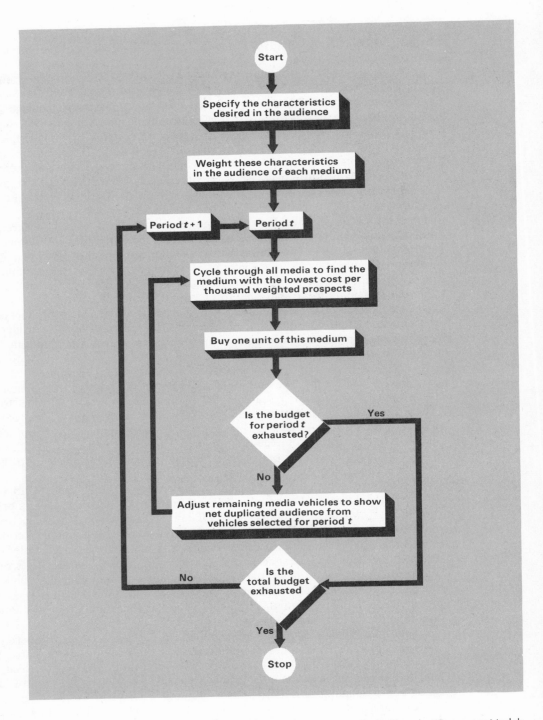

Fig. 15.2 An iterative media allocation model. (Adapted by permission from D. H. Gensch, "Computer Models in Advertising Media Selection," *Journal of Marketing Research,* **5**, November 1968: 414–424.)

TABLE 15.2 Computing cost per thousand (CPM) for a target audience (1975)

Vehicle	Total audience* (000)	Target audience: households with incomes $20,000+ %	Target audience: households with incomes $20,000+ No.	One-page cost, four colors	CPM Total audience	CPM Target audience
	(1)*	(2)*	(3)* (1 × 2)	(4)*	(5) (4/1)	(6) (4/3)
Reader's Digest	44,123	24	10,590	$63,620	$1.44	$6.01
Newsweek	19,013	34	6,464	32,565	1.71	5.04

* Doyle Dane Bernbach, Inc. *Media Guide*, 1976.

adjustments appear in columns 2 and 3. The *effective CPM* for our target audience shows that in this case *Newsweek* has the more favorable CPM, $5.04 versus $6.01. This calculation does not complete the schedule, because we have not considered other criteria such as total audience and frequency. The *Reader's Digest* reaches 10.59 million persons in our target market, whereas *Newsweek* reaches only 6.464 million. If we want to reach more than six million persons, we must supplement the use of *Newsweek* with other vehicles. When considering frequency, we must recognize that the *Reader's Digest* is a monthly magazine, whereas *Newsweek* is a weekly. Thus the *Reader's Digest* advertisement is likely to have a higher frequency rate, because it will be read many times throughout the month.

PROMOTIONAL STRATEGIES "Many companies do not keep records on couponing, premiums, trade allowances, bonus packs, sampling, sales incentives, and trade shows—the elements that make up promotion."[35] This statement helps to explain why dollar estimates are not available for the total promotional expenditures. Estimates indicate that the 1975 expenditures on promotion were $27 billion, which equals the expenditures for advertising.[36] Strang concluded that sales promotion is managed poorly in most manufacturing firms and advertising agencies.[37] The agencies frequently assign promotion to the youngest, most inexperienced staff member. The concern for measuring and modeling productivity in advertising has not been reflected in promotional decisions. Yet the fact that coupon-redemption rates range from 2 to 25 percent stresses the importance of pretesting.

In the consumer package-goods field, cents-off coupons account for the largest share of promotional expenditures—26 percent. Additonal expenditures include premiums, 16 percent; sales meetings, 12 percent; 10 percent each for trade shows and direct mail; and 7 percent for point-of-purchase promotion.[38]

The goals of a promotional campaign are similar to those for media campaigns and are coordinated with them. Some of the *promotional goals* include attracting *attention* by *breaking* through the *competitive noise* level, getting *trial*, expanding *share*, and promoting *new uses*. A goal of *loading* encourages consumers to stock up for future needs. *Loading* is also used to remove customers from the market just as a competitor is about to introduce a new or improved product. *Loading* increases the usage rates for convenience products such as snacks.[39] Consumer premiums generate *excitement* at the consumer level and *enthusiasm* among salespeople and dealers.[40]

Most of us are familiar with premium promotions, which represent a $5 billion industry (and a unique channel of distribution). These are the products that we may buy at reduced prices for sending a coupon with two labels from the sponsoring brand's package. Recent premiums in this category included a poncho (Hormel Chilli), a wool hat with "M'm! M'm! Good!" across the band (Campbell Soup), and a super lounge shirt (Winston Super Kings). But these consumer premiums are not the largest category for premiums. Dealer and salespeople premiums, which are used as incentives, are the largest premium categories.[41] Hard goods, such as a color television, are used as *sales incentives*.

Consumer premiums were used to reposition Canada Dry Ginger Ale in the soft drink market.[42] The newly redesigned can appeared on drinking glasses, a Tiffany-type lamp, a book bag, a cap, etc., as shown in Fig. 15.3.

Fig. 15.3 Premiums for repositioning Canada Dry Ginger Ale. (*Product Management* (September 1976): 36. Reprinted by permission of Canada Dry Corporation.)

INSTITUTIONAL ADVERTISING AND PUBLIC RELATIONS Institutional advertising (which promotes a company, not a product) and public relations are used to create an image, correct an image, and communicate a corporate philosophy. Three cases will illustrate each application.

When the capital-goods manufacturer Eaton, Yale & Towne shortened its name to Eaton, there was a corporate identity crisis. The important audiences did not know the company. So Eaton mounted a corporate communications campaign to make its publics aware of the fact that it was more than a maker of locks, automotive parts, and fork lift trucks. It wanted to convey the image of being a well-diversified capital-goods producer. It used television to communicate a message of social responsibility. One of its television programs, on juvenile justice, won awards. Programs on China were coordinated with a visit to China by the United States president.[43]

After the 1973 oil embargo, Mobil Oil Corporation wanted to correct the impression that it was part of a conspiracy to raise oil prices. It used two distinctly different media—"Masterpiece Theatre" on public television and editorial-type advertisements in the *New York Times*. The public broadcasting was a goodwill umbrella. The newspaper advertisements stressed the need for a national policy on energy. Mobil thinks that it made progress in the following ways: It established credibility in Washington, it established a constituency of people who recognize that it is different, it established a leadership position in oil industry communications, and it established a policy of speaking out on issues. Mobil executives even took courses on how to debate on television talk shows.[44]

The corporate advertising campaign of St. Regis Paper Company began with the development of a new corporate logo (a graphic symbol that is unique to a company). During the next ten years, the campaign went through three distinct stages. The first stage was a print campaign which artfully told about forest husbandry. The campaign generated one-half million requests for reprints and was eventually published as a book. The second stage was an ecology campaign which explained the benefits of forest management as practiced by St. Regis. The third stage used print and television to discuss its products for the publishing and packaging fields. Having established its image, the company then used a hard-hitting marketing campaign built on the theme of informativeness.[45]

TRADEMARKS There is always the danger that an advertising and promotional campaign will become so successful that the trademark becomes the generic name for the product. Aspirin, nylon, cellophane, and cola were proprietary trademarks at one time. The trademarks of Kodak, Kleenex, Xerox, and Frigidaire are generic names in the minds of some consumers, despite the companies' strong promotional efforts to the contrary.

After losing cellophane as a trademark in 1936, duPont learned its lesson. Since then the company has been careful to protect its legal rights in Teflon and its annual investment of $3 million in advertising. It won a case against a Japanese firm for using the trademark "Eflon." DuPont won the case in what became a battle of opposing research. The duPont survey established that 68 percent of the respondents identified "Teflon" as a brand name and that only 31 percent thought it was a generic term.[46] DuPont has a trademark-protection program that involves its legal department, its advertising department, and its advertising agency.

MEASURING ADVERTISING EFFECTIVENESS The measurement of advertising effectiveness begins with a precise statement of advertising goals. For advertising results to be measurable, the goal must be expressed in terms of magnitude and time, and it must be capable of being measured. A full discussion of the topic includes the psychological effects of advertising, the reliability and validity of measuring instruments, experimental designs, syndicated sources of data, and the major methods for gathering data. Here we will focus on the methods for gathering data. Many texts discuss the other topics.[47] The methods for gathering advertising effectiveness data may be classified as survey, experimental, laboratory, and historical.

Surveys

Surveys may be commissioned by the advertiser or the agency, or they may be syndicated services. Starch and Gallup & Robinson are two syndicated sources for measuring readers' *recall* of magazine advertisements. (Figure 15.1 shows a sample of Starch measurements of an advertisement.)

Telephone, personal interviews, and mail surveys may be used to measure the effects of advertising on *brand awareness*, *attitudes*, *brand choice*, *probability of buying*, and *actual purchase*. When the same respondents are measured several times over a period of weeks or months, it is possible to track the effect of advertising on specific psychological dimensions, such as awareness. Such a survey design is known as a *panel*. Some panels are syndicated and some are proprietary.

The psychological dimensions can be refined for greater precision. For example, brand awareness has been refined to *first-brand awareness*. This is the brand listed first when respondents are asked to name the brands for a specific product category. It has been found that *first-brand awareness* is a better correlate of sales than just *brand awareness.*

The Convair division of General Dynamics Corporation used a scaling approach to pretest its advertising. The pretest attempted to estimate the Starch ratings of its advertisements in business publications. Points were assigned to each of the following criteria: illustration, caption, color, ad size, ad layout, copy length, type size, type selection, copy layout, general theme, timeliness, suitability for schedule media, and position in the publication.[48]

Experiments

To establish a cause-and-effect relationship between advertising effort and some change in the buyer, it is necessary to control the conditions of advertising exposure. This requires some form of experimental design. The simplest is a two-group design, whereby one group is measured before the advertisement and the other is measured after exposure. A comparison of the two measures indicates the effectiveness of the advertisement. One advantage of this design is that the group that received the "after" measurement has not had a "before" measurement, which may make the group more receptive to the advertisement.[49] More complex designs permit the use of analysis of variance that will indicate the effectiveness of *interactions*, such as color *and* size, as well as the *individual* effects of color *or* size.

One classic study of advertising experimentation was done by duPont on the effect of television advertising on the sale of cookware coated with Teflon.[50] The study identified the carry-over effects of advertising, the upper and lower levels for dollar expenditure, and the tendency of the advertisements to shift future sales back to the period of heavy advertising.

Another famous experimental study is the research on Budweiser beer.[51] As a result of the experiment, advertising strategy was changed, with the following results: volume doubled, market share increased from 8.14 to 12.94 percent, and advertising expenditures were reduced from $1.89 to $0.80 per barrel. In addition, the advertising agency's compensation scheme was changed from that of a percentage of media expenditures to a percentage of increased sales. These strategic changes were based on the research findings that there were lower and upper advertising thresholds, below and above which funds were wasted. Pulsing was possible because of strong carry-over effects. The effectiveness of advertising was related to the position of a product in its life cycle. There were also variations in advertising effectiveness among different market segments.

Laboratories Laboratories are frequently used to test advertising effectiveness for new products. The method is cheaper than test markets, and it keeps a new product or advertising strategy a secret while it is being tested. Syndicated laboratories are available from firms such as Daniel Yankelovich, Inc., and Elrick and Lavidge, Inc. To illustrate the steps in a laboratory test, we will describe the COMP system developed by Elrick and Lavidge.

COMP (A Comprehensive System for Predicting Sales of New Products) is used as the final screening step before a test market or a product rollout (see Fig. 12.1) to evaluate the strategies for the product, the package, the copy, the media, and distribution. COMP integrates research that is usually conducted separately. The results are fed into a computer model to predict the market share.

The COMP approach consists of the following nine steps:

1. Respondents who are logical product prospects are screened.
2. Participants are given money after initial screening and before an "initial interview" as a reward for participating.
3. During an initial interview, measures are made of respondents' brand awareness, the importance of product benefits and attributes, competitive ratings, prior purchase and use, brand-purchase intentions, and demographic characteristics.
4. Participants are exposed to advertising messages for the test product and its competitors.
5. After shopping in a simulated store setting, the respondents rate the new product and its competitors along selected product benefits and attributes.
6. Customers who do not purchase the test product are given a sample for home use.
7. Personal interviews are conducted in the participants' homes. A variety of options for repurchase is available.
8. After an appropriate period of time (depending on the product-use cycle), a follow-up personal interview measures participants' satisfactions, dissatisfactions, purchase intensions, and attitudes toward all brands in the study.
9. The data from these steps are fed into a computer model which predicts the purchase behavior of each participant. Market share is computed at each possible level of awareness and distribution that the new product may experience.

With a two-week use period, a COMP analysis is available in about ten weeks. The basic cost for a test involving a panel of 300 qualified consumers is $22,000.[52]

Historical Data A variety of methods is available for testing advertising effectiveness by analyzing historical data. If the goal of the campaign was to generate traffic in the showroom, simple counts of customers will provide measures of productivity. Print media that use coupons can be evaluated by counting coupons which have been keyed to "Department WSJ 3″ to indicate that this was the coupon in the third advertisement that appeared in the *Wall Street Journal*, for example. Catalog and direct-mail advertising can use frequency counts of orders to test advertising strategies.

Econometric methods have been used to analyze the effect of advertising on sales. (Econometrics is the science of estimating and testing economic models.) There have been many econometric models built to measure advertising effectiveness.[53] These studies use the Koyck lagged-variable model to measure the cumulative effect of advertising.[54]

Econometric models of advertising effectiveness have provided many useful insights. Some researchers have extended the method into a system of simultaneous equations to determine the optimal level of advertising.[55] A technical discussion of econometric methods as they relate to advertising effectiveness is readily available in other texts.[56] The planner should, however, be aware of some of the problems in implementing these models.

One of the major problems in econometric model building in advertising is the measurement of units of advertising. Dollars are not a good proxy measure for advertising effort, because of the creativity factor. Two advertisements costing the same may differ in productivity because of the creativity element in copy, execution, and media strategies. Another problem is the direction of causality. In one case advertising may be used on a sales upswing to increase sales, and in another case it may be used to slow a downward trend. The accounting data do not distinguish these different strategies, so combining all sales and advertising data would probably result in a coefficient in the model that was *not significant*. Advertising during months when sales are seasonally low to keep our name before the buyer can result in a *very significant* coefficient with a *minus* sign. The planner will want to guard against quick and easy models in which the variables are poorly specified. Another major problem is the incompatibility of data with regard to time frame or geographic distribution. Media coverage may be quite different in our sales districts, which makes it difficult to build models of advertising effectiveness in different market segments.

BUDGET STRATEGIES The subjectivity and creativity of advertising help to explain why it is so difficult to determine the level of an advertising budget. Central to this budgeting decision is the difficulty of relating advertising expenditures to profits. Advertising is only one element in the marketing mix which creates a sale. Furthermore, the time lag between advertising and sales varies across products and market segments, which makes it difficult to link advertising effort to profit.

There are two basic budget strategies—the *breakdown* and the *buildup* methods. The *breakdown* method requires two steps. First, the size of the budget must be determined, and then it must be broken down into the copy and media strategies. The *buildup* method estimates the costs to *execute* all of the advertising strategies. These costs are added to *build up* to a total budget.

The breakdown methods include percent of dollar sales, a fixed amount per unit, competitive parity, return on investment, and the marginal approach. A brief description of each is in order.

The *percent of dollar sales* approach seems like one of the easiest methods to implement until the question is asked, "Which sales figure do we use?" If *historical* sales are used, then it is a simple method. To use historical sales, however, makes advertising dependent on sales, the opposite of the intended relationship—that of advertising determining sales. The approach of *forecasted* sales makes it more difficult and introduces the uncertainty of forecasting. The most logical sales figure to use is *potential* sales, because this relates the advertising budget to market opportunity. But estimating sales potential is difficult and requires research.

A *fixed amount per unit* is used in those industries in which the advertiser has considerable experience and therefore can estimate how much advertising will be required to sell a unit of the product. The package grocery and the automobile industries use this method when giving trade allowances for cooperative advertising. Using units rather than dollar sales makes the advertising effort independent of changes in price. Otherwise, a decision to change the price would automatically change the advertising budget in the same direction, which may be unrelated to the advertising task at hand.

Competitive parity starts with a competitor's advertising budget and either matches it or adjusts to it according to some predetermined percentage. This approach is used in oligopolistic industries where the advertiser *thinks* that market share is determined by advertising share. This method ignores the market potential, however. It also assumes that the competitor is a better judge of market opportunities.

Return-on-investment approaches view advertising strategies as investment portfolios. The strategy is sound, but the implementation is difficult except when advertising is the sole determinant of sales and when sales can be linked directly to advertising effort. Direct-mail marketing is one of the few situations that meet these two conditions. Sales can be linked to a specific promotional piece or catalog.

The *marginal* approach is based on the sound economic theory that advertising effort should be added in small increments until the cost of the additional unit of advertising and the profit generated by this unit are equal. This economic concept states that profit will be maximized when the marginal cost equals the marginal revenue. The theory cannot be questioned, but the implementation is possible only in the case of a single-product firm that uses easily measured units of advertising effort. Few real-world advertising budgets meet these criteria.

The *buildup* method is also known as the *objective-and-task* method because it begins with a statement of the advertising objective and estimates the costs of the tasks to meet the objective. The most common objectives are communication ones—changes in brand recall, benefit awareness, attitudes, etc. Direct-action advertising, such as direct-mail advertising, may define the objective in terms of sales. Trade advertising may define the objective in terms of percent of distribution or the number of point-of-purchase displays used. The buildup method seems more logical than the breakdown methods, but it suffers from the cost and delay in establishing the costs to perform the tasks. Unless adequate research has been performed, the costs reduce to subjective estimates.

We must conclude, therefore, that a budget strategy may require as much creativity as a copy strategy. In practice, both buildup and breakdown methods are used. The advertising department uses a buildup approach to estimate its needs, and top management uses breakdown methods to set a rough advertising budget. The differences are then reconciled.[57]

CAREERS IN ADVERTISING AGENCIES So far we have viewed marketing management from the viewpoint of the manufacturer, as seen through the eyes of a product manager. But product management is only one of many career paths in marketing. In this section we will briefly examine careers in advertising agencies. We begin by examining the position of the *account executive*.[58]

Account Executive   The account executive (AE) is the advertising agency's counterpart of the product manager. Both analyze the environment, develop a strategy, and develop a plan. The AE also performs many different roles, including those of business manager, marketing consultant, and agency salesperson. The client looks to the account executive for advice on marketing and advertising strategies. The creative people in the agency depend on the AE for product information, market analysis, and a timetable. Agency management holds the AE responsible for account profitability. The AE must be a capable organizer with a good business mind for facts and must be able to communicate well with agency colleagues (the writer, the art director, and the market researcher), outside suppliers (for research, graphic arts, and media), and of course the client and its staff. The AE, therefore, must have an analytical mind and be able to communicate effectively.

The educational preparation for becoming an account executive is usually a bachelor of arts (B.A.) with a major in business or a master's in business administration (M.B.A.). Work experience may include retailing or the advertising department of a large advertiser.[59]

When asked what it takes to be a success in advertising, David Ogilvy, one of the giants in advertising, stressed the need to write: "It's no use going out into the world with a knowledge of marketing, accounting, and all the other things you get in business schools unless you can put your ideas on paper in a lucid, well-organized manner."[60] Ogilvy recommends that persons should specialize in some area of advertising, such as research, media, or copy writing before moving to the generalist's role of an account executive. He also concludes that an M.B.A. is not a prerequisite to being a success in an agency and that it may be harmful to have one in some advertising roles. "The mere fact that you become an M.B.A. is *prima facie* evidence that you are *not* creative."[61]

Assistant Account Executive   The assistant account executive is expected to acquire a maximum knowledge of the functions of account management and to provide assistance to the account executive. Specific duties include the following:[62]

1. Administration—budgets, conference reports, and factory shipments;
2. Marketing—market research (e.g., Nielsen analysis), business review, specific assignments in the annual marketing reports and analysis;
4. Creativity—coordination of special projects, competitive copy reports and analysis, attendance at copy meetings, and attendance at preproduction meetings and shootings;
5. Research—consumer research and analysis, research design planning, and attendance at focus-group sessions.

This job description illustrates the variety and excitement of accountant mangement, as well as the need to be analytical and able to communicate.

Other Careers in Advertising Agencies   There are many careers in advertising agencies that may be overlooked. For example, a person who is interested in marketing and finance could combine these talents to work in the management and financial aspects of the agency. Indeed, many high-flying, creative agencies have been brought down to reality because they failed to practice good management.

Figure 15.4 shows the typical organizational chart of an advertising agency. The major departments, which are headed by vice-presidents, are creative services, account

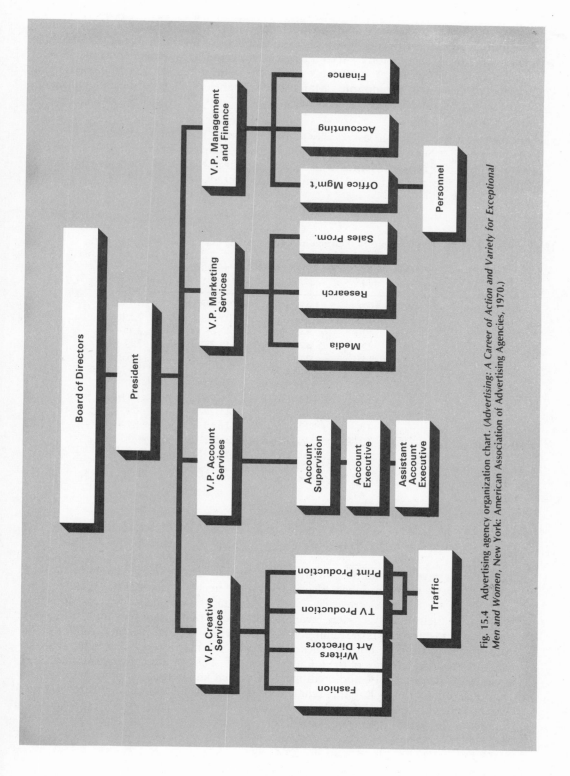

Fig. 15.4 Advertising agency organization chart. (*Advertising: A Career of Action and Variety for Exceptional Men and Women*, New York: American Association of Advertising Agencies, 1970.)

services, marketing services, and management/finance. The creative services include fashion, writers, art directors, television production, print production, and traffic (which controls media production). Account services include account supervision, account executives, and assistant account executives. Marketing services include media, research, and sales promotion. Management/finance includes office management, accounting, finance, and personnel.

Locating an Agency   A robber who was asked why he robbed banks replied, "Because that is where the money is." Searching for a career in advertising requires going where the agencies are. Table 15.3 ranks 15 cities which have the largest gross receipts in advertising. These cities are marketing and communication centers.

TABLE 15.3   **Agency receipts, employment by metropolitan areas, 1972**

	No.	Receipts ($000)	Payroll ($000)	Employment
New York	1038	3,957,557	372,548	25,169
Chicago	471	1,165,705	105,213	7,596
Detroit	130	543,056	40,152	3,114
Los Angeles	421	473,347	48,951	3,883
San Francisco	151	220,251	21,861	1,635
Philadelphia	203	211,463	27,284	2,175
Cleveland	100	148,749	15,843	1,253
Minneapolis	140	143,865	16,560	1,316
St. Louis	94	136,169	11,774	931
Boston	176	125,886	16,633	1,290
Houston	107	122,225	10,019	759
Dallas–Fort Worth	158	112,671	10,988	979
Atlanta	118	104,614	9,537	778
Milwaukee	85	78,120	9,721	699
Pittsburgh	67	77,299	9,547	980

Bureau of the Census, as reported in *Advertising Age*, July 21, 1975, p. 52.

Agencies have personalities, which means one must match one's personality to that of the agency. Comaford has identified several agency personality types.[63] The *entrepreneurship* agencies are early in their organizational life cycles and are still managed by their founders. They have loose control, opportunities for innovation and creativity, and little organizational constraint. Detail-oriented persons would not fit in such an organization, however, despite the fact that it will need such individuals as it matures and the energies of the founders dwindle. The *establishment* agency searches for stability, predictability, and credibility. Research and consensus precede all major decisions. Innovation is less apparent. "This is the place for the well-adjusted middle-class person who wants a life balanced among work, home and social responsibility; who tends to avoid risk; who can accept a certain amount of office politics."[64]

Decadent establishment agencies become bureaucracies. "As the entrepreneurial flame dies over a period of years, the emphasis shifts first to risk control, then to risk avoidance, and finally, to elimination of risk altogether. At this point, the promotion goes to the person who best avoids decisions, manipulates his peers or subordinates, and positions himself to take credit for the ideas that work."[65] An *autocracy* may arise by founding the agency or capturing the power system, but it remains in the control of a single person who rules through manipulation and dominance. The autocratic atmosphere is one of insecurity, a lack of solid information, hot rumors, and the assignment of similar tasks to several individuals to create internal competition. "One of the worst things you can do in an autocracy is to prove the autocrat wrong. You may be thanked, but never forgiven."[66] (The concept of matching your personality to that of the company is good advice in any career, not just advertising.)

The Ever-Evolving Agency In Chapter 14 we saw that mass advertising permits the manufacturer to gain control over the channel of distribution by promoting directly to the consumer. One agency executive thinks that the power is shifting in favor of distribution.[67] The proliferation of brands in the supermarkets has given the retailer the power to determine who gets the scarce resource of shelf space. Computerized inventory systems give the large chains the advantage of information: They can analyze the characteristics of products that sell and can use this information when bargaining with manufacturers. He concludes that this shift in power from the manufacturer to the retailer will result in less advertising, especially the advertising of minute differences in products which have become practically commodities.

Changes in consumers will reduce the effectiveness of advertising. "When they perceive that products are the same, they increasingly tire of being told that they are different. Advertising money spent this way will become less and less productive."[68] As we saw in Chapter 10, some government officials feel that the advertising of parity products is deceitful. The reduced productivity of advertising and governmental pressures will reduce parity advertising. When this occurs, the role of the advertising agency will shift to that of strategic planning and new-product introduction.[69]

These social, economic, and political forces will greatly change the advertising agency. We have already seen that the United States government is the tenth largest advertiser (Chapter 10). The Postal Service, Amtrak, and the volunteer armed services may be just the beginning of the federal government's need for the services of advertising agencies.

BOTH VIEWS OF CRITICISM The brief discussion in this section cannot hope to capture the centuries of criticism and counterarguments that have centered on advertising. The purpose of this section is to present some of the major criticisms and counterarguments to illustrate the complexity of advertising in a mass-production economy. Samples of the criticisms and counterarguments are given in Table 15.4.[70]

The attacks and counterarguments have gone on for many centuries. It is unlikely that these attacks and counterarguments have caused a reader to change any opinion about advertising. They have probably only provided additional points for previously held positions. There is an irony in the fact that the same advertising which can alter attitudes and change images for clients cannot do the same for itself.

TABLE 15.4 Views on advertising

Criticism	Counterargument
Advertising persuades people.	Parents, professors, preachers, and politicians are persuaders, but nobody criticizes them for trying to influence behavior.
Advertising sells things that people don't need.	Needs are very complex. Social needs are as important as physical needs, so to some people cosmetics may be as important as food.
Advertising is a waste of money.	If advertisers could measure the part that is a waste, they would eliminate it. It is still the cheapest way to communicate. Marketers would abandon it if a cheaper way were available.
Cut the consumer advertising and lower the price to the consumer; price elasticity will offset the lack of advertising.	This has not proved to be the case for those products which tried. "Active" brand detergent eliminated consumer advertising, used public relations and trade advertising, and lowered the price, but decided not to expand beyond the New England test-market area.[71]
Advertising causes a proliferation of brands.	True, because we have learned how to identify the needs of market segments more precisely and to make products to fit the needs of the segment. This permits a choice in the marketplace. Brand proliferation is part of the competitive system that antitrust preserves. When does *competition* become *proliferation*?
Advertising is just another cost, so it raises prices.	Advertising permits mass production, which spreads the fixed costs over more units, thereby lowering costs.
Advertising is false or misleading.	Sometimes this is true. Respectable advertisers have organizations such as the National Advertising Review Board to provide the industry with self-regulation.[72]
Advertising intrudes.	This is true of the electronic media because television and radio commercials must be waited out, not skipped over as in printed media. Waiting out a commercial is the price that one must pay for free entertainment. The alternative is paid, taxed, or subscription television.
Advertising presents only one side of the story.	This is true. It is also true of other persuaders, and it is the heart of the adversary system in law.

SUMMARY Advertising and promotion are the central elements in a company's communications strategy. The communication goals may be *behavioral* (e.g., sales, visits to the showroom, or requests for information) or *cognitive* (awareness, attitudes, or buying intentions). These goals must be stated in terms of magnitude, time, and concepts that are measurable. *Communication models* of the buying decision vary across products, but they reduce to the basic elements of *awareness*, *attitudes*, and *buying intentions*.

Advertising strategies include *copy strategy* (the selling message) and *media strategies* (the vehicles that will carry the message). Segmentation strategies apply to copy and media as well as to product strategies. Media strategies require decisions regarding *reach* (i.e., coverage) and *frequency* of message exposure to the target audience. Media timing strategies must consider the seasonality of demand, the consumers' purchase cycle, competitive reaction times, pulsing effects, and the need for frequency of exposure. Operations research methods are aiding the development of media strategies and execution, but they have not eliminated the need for creative input.

Promotional strategies (e.g., cents-off, coupons, and premiums) may be directed toward the sales force, dealers, or consumers. Promotional expenditures are about equal to media expenditures, but they have not received management's attention or the research that media strategies have received.

The need to measure advertising effectiveness introduces many complex problems, such as the psychological effect of advertising, the reliability of measuring instruments, experimental designs, and sources of information. Sources of information include surveys, experiments, laboratories, and historical data.

Budget strategies are a combination of the *breakdown* and the *buildup* methods. Although the breakdown method is easier to apply, it tends to ignore the communication opportunities and the cost to achieve advertising and promotional goals.

Careers in advertising may be within the advertising department of an advertiser, in retailing, or in an advertising agency. The *account executive* is the agency's counterpart of the product manager. The position requires an analytical mind and the ability to communicate effectively. Agencies also need business managers, financial experts, accountants, and computer experts. The future needs of agencies will be determined by their changing position in the continuously evolving power struggle among marketing institutions.

The criticisms of advertising have been going on for centuries. Generally, they reflect differences of opinion in how the economic, political, and social systems should be managed.

DISCUSSION QUESTIONS

1. Why and in what ways must a product manager make advertising goals specific? What are examples of the different variables researchers have used to measure advertising effectiveness?

2. Glance for three seconds at a print advertisement in a popular magazine. Turn the page. What do you remember about the ad? Go back and look at the ad again and notice the product's position in the ad, where other copy elements direct your attention, and whether the color scheme makes the ad's message more visible. Repeat this process with several more advertisements.

3. Differentiate the following media strategies: broadside approach, profile matching, and the high-assay principle. What are some strengths and weaknesses of each strategy?

4. What is meant by reach and frequency in media strategy?

5. Describe several ways for gathering data on advertising effectiveness.

6. Differentiate the breakdown and the buildup budget strategies. Describe the different breakdown methods. What are the strengths and weaknesses of these two strategies?

7. Predict areas where the Federal Trade Commission will direct its advertising investigations in the future.

NOTES

1. R. A. Strang, "The Relationship Between Advertising and Promotion in Brand Strategy," Report No. 75–119 (Cambridge, Mass.: Marketing Science Institute, 1975).

2. T. F. Dunn, "PREP, A Copy Research Technique, Helps Cope During Change Periods," *Marketing News*, August 15, 1974, p. 8.

3. *Ibid.*

4. R. J. Lavidge and G. A. Steiner, "A Model for Predictive Measurements of Advertising Effectiveness," *Journal of Marketing* **25** (October 1961): 59–62.

5. R. H. Colley, *Defining Advertising Goals for Measured Advertising Results* (New York: Association of National Advertisers, 1961).

6. D. A. Aaker and G. S. Day, "A Dynamic Model of Relationships Among Advertising, Consumer Awareness, Attitudes and Behavior," *Journal of Applied Psychology* **59**, 3 (1974): 281–286.

7. "A Point of View on Advertising Strategy," White Paper I (New York: McCann-Erickson, 1972), p. 2.

8. *Ibid.*

9. "Three Marketing Elements Combine to Make and Sell Three Distinctive Buyers," *Marketing News*, September 26, 1975, p. 9.

10. W. D. Tyler, "Top Industrial Ads Feature Product Benefits, Demos, Problem Solving," *Advertising Age*, July 14, 1975, pp. 91–92.

11. G. McAleer, "Do Industrial Advertisers Understand What Influences Their Markets?" *Journal of Marketing* **38** (January 1974): 15–23.

12. R. I. Haley, "Benefit Segmentation: A Decision-Oriented Research Tool," *Journal of Marketing* **32** (July 1968): 30–35.

13. ———, "Beyond Benefit Segmentation," *Journal of Advertising Research* **11** (August 1971): 3–8.

14. *Ibid.*

15. H. E. Agner and G. B. Hotchkiss, *Advertising Principles* (New York: Alexander Hamilton Institute, 1927).

16. "Firestone to Spend $750,000 for Ads in FTC Order," *Advertising Age*, February 16, 1976, p. 1.

17. A. G. Kershaw, "The Mischief of Comparative Advertising," paper delivered at the 1976 annual meeting of the American Association of Advertising Agencies, May 12–15, 1976; S. I. Tannenbaum, "Comparative Advertising: "The Advertising Industry's Own Brand of Consumerism," paper delivered at the 1976 annual meeting of the American Association of Advertising Agencies, May 12–15, 1976; S. M. Ulanoff, "Comparison Advertising: An Historical Retrospective," working paper of the Marketing Science Institute, Cambridge, Mass., February 1975; and S. L. Wilkie and P. Farris, "Comparison Advertising: Issues and Prospects," working paper of the Marketing Science Institute, Cambridge, Mass., August 1974.

18. "Comparative Ads Ineffective: O&M Study," *Advertising Age*, October 13, 1976, p. 16.

19. "Finally, Tylenol Campaign Set for National Debut," *Advertising Age*, July 12, 1976, p. 3.

20. I. Gross, "The Creative Aspects of Advertising," *Sloan Management Review* (Fall 1972): 83–109.

21. K. A. Longman, *Advertising* (New York: Harcourt Brace Jovanovich, 1971), p. 324.

22. "Copy Testing Is Still a Nebulous Area," *Advertising Age*, December 1, 1975, p. 54.

23. Longman, *op. cit.*, p. 323.

24. *U.S. Statistical Abstract*, 1975.

25. Longman, *op. cit.*, p. 209.

26. W. T. Moran, "Does Flighting Pay?" (Paper delivered at the twenty-second annual meeting of the Advertising Research Foundation, New York, October 19, 1976.)

27. Longman, *op. cit.*, p. 371.

28. *Ibid.*, p. 214.

29. H. E. Krugman, "What Makes Advertising Effective?" *Harvard Business Review* (March-April 1975): 96–103.

30. R. S. Headen, J. E. Klompmaker, and J. E. Teel, Jr., "Predicting Audience Exposure to Spot TV Advertising Schedules," *Journal of Marketing Research* (February 1977): 1–8; and J. M. Agostini, "Analysis of Magazine Accumulation Audience," *Journal of Advertising Research* **2** (December 1962): 24–27.

31. For a discussion of this problem, with illustrations, *see* Longman, *op. cit.*, Chapter 18.

32. D. H. Gensch, "Different Approaches to Advertising Media Selection," *Operational Research Quarterly* **21**, 2 (June 1970): 193–219; and ———, *Advertising Planning: Mathematical Models in Advertising Media Planning* (Amsterdam: Elsevier Scientific Planning Company, 1973).

33. ———, "Media Factors: A Review Article," *Journal of Marketing Research* **7** (May 1970): 216–225.

34. Longman, *op. cit.*, p. 384.

35. R. A. Strang, "Sales Promotion—Fast Growth, Faulty Management," *Harvard Business Review* (July-August 1976): 115–124.

36. L. J. Haugh, "What's in a Name? Premium Ad Association Views Name Change, Expanded Role," *Advertising Age*, December 20, 1976, pp. 27–29.

37. Strang, "Sales Promotion," *op. cit.*, p. 122.

38. Haugh, *op. cit.*

39. This discussion is based on T. Conlon, "Six Promotion Objectives to Help You on Your Way," *Advertising Age*, December 8, 1975, p. 44.

40. For a discussion of the advantages and disadvantages of the 12 basic promotional techniques, *see* W. A. Robinson, "12 Basic Promotion Techniques: Their Advantages—and Pitfalls," *Advertising Age*, January 10, 1977, p. 50, 55.

41. E. Mahany, "Dealer, Salesman Incentives Lead Premium Growth," *Advertising Age*, September 2, 1975, pp. 1, 30.

42. C. Schleier, "Premiums and Incentives, Tools for Repositioning," *Product Management* (September 1976): 37–39.

43. D. Ritzel, "The Eaton Corporation." (Paper delivered at the Eastern Annual Conference of the American Association of Advertising Agencies, 1975.)

44. R. D'Argenio, "Mobil Oil Corporation." (Paper delivered at the Eastern Annual Conference of the American Association of Advertising Agencies, 1975.)

45. M. Biondo, "St. Regis Paper Company." (Paper delivered at the Eastern Annual Conference of the American Association of Advertising Agencies, 1975.)

46. S. A. Diamond, "DuPont's Teflon Trademark Survives Attack," *Advertising Age*, July 14, 1975, p. 93.

47. *See* D. B. Lucas and S. H. Britt, *Measuring Advertising Effectiveness* (New York: McGraw-Hill, 1963); and P. J. Robinson *et al.*, *Advertising Measurement and Decision Making* (Boston: Allyn & Bacon, 1968).

48. E. Frye, "A Practical Checklist Developed by One Company to Evaluate its Advertisements," *Laboratory of Advertising Performance* (New York: McGraw-Hill, 1958), Report No. 9071.

49. For a discussion of experimental designs, *see* P. E. Green and D. S. Tull, *Research for Marketing Decisions* 3rd ed. (Englewood Cliffs, N.J.: Prentice-Hall, 1975), Chapter 11; and K. K. Cox and B. M. Enis, *Experimentation for Marketing Decisions* (Scranton, Pa: Intext, 1969).

50. J. C. Becknell and R. W. McIsaacs, "Test Marketing Cookware Coated with Teflon," *Journal of Advertising Research* **3** (September 1963): 2–8.

51. R. L. Ackoff and J. R. Emshoff, "Advertising Research at Anheuser-Busch, Inc. (1963–1968)," *Sloan Management Review* (Winter 1975): 1–15.

52. The description of the COMP is from a 1977 promotional brochure supplied by Elrick and Lavidge, Inc., and correspondence with R. J. Lavidge, August 8, 1977.

53. D. G. Clarke, "Econometric Measurement of Duration of Advertising Effect on Sales," *Journal of Marketing Research* (November 1976): 345–347; J. J. Lambin, "Measuring the Profitability of Advertising: An Empirical Study," *Journal of Industrial Economics* 27 (April 1969): 86–103; and K. S. Palda, *The Measurement of Cumulative Advertising Effects* (Englewood Cliffs, N.J.: Prentice-Hall, 1964).

54. For a discussion of the applications and limitations of this model, *see* G. D. Hughes, *Demand Analysis for Marketing Decisions* (Homewood, Ill.: Richard D. Irwin, 1973), pp. 98–100.

55. L. J. Parsons and F. M. Bass, "Optimal Advertising-Expenditure Implications of a Simultaneous Equation Regression Analysis," *Operations Research* (May-June 1971): 822–883.

56. P. Kotler, *Marketing Decision Making: A Model Building Approach* (New York: Holt, Rinehart and Winston, 1971); D. B. Montgomery and G. L. Urban, *Management Science in Marketing* (Englewood Cliffs, N.J.: Prentice-Hall, 1969); Chapter 3; and L. J. Parson and R. L. Schultz, *Marketing Models and Econometric Research* (New York: North-Holland, 1976).

57. For case examples of advertising budget practices, *see* D. L. Hurwood and J. K. Brown, *Some Guidelines for Advertising Budgeting* (New York: Conference Board, 1972).

58. For a discussion of the history of advertising agencies between 1776 and 1976, *see Advertising Age*, April 19, 1976.

59. *See* "Advertising: A Guide to Careers in Advertising," a brochure published by the American Association of Advertising Agencies, 1975.

60. "David Ogilvy: More Confessions," *MBA* (March 1970): 12.

61. *Ibid.*

62. These duties are based on the job description of the assistant account executive at Dancer-Fitzgerald-Sample, 1973.

63. C. M. Comaford, "How to Land an Ad Job: Match Your Personality with the Agency," *Advertising Age*, February 2, 1976, pp. 31–32.

64. *Ibid.*, p. 31.

65. *Ibid.*

66. *Ibid.*, p. 32.

67. P. C. Harper, Jr., "The Agency Business in 1980," *Advertising Age*, November 19, 1973, pp. 1, ff.

68. *Ibid.*

69. *Ibid.*

70. For a more detailed discussion, *see* Longman, *op. cit.*, 80–116; and S. A. Greyser, "Advertising: Attacks and Counters," *Harvard Business Review* (March-April 1972): 22–28; 140–146.

71. "No-Ad Strategy Failed," *Advertising Age*, May 3, 1976, p. 11.

72. R. A. Purdon, "Advertising Self-Regulation—A New Reality." (Paper delivered at the Annual Meeting of the American Association of Advertising Agencies, 1972.)

SUGGESTED READINGS

Aaker, D. A., ed. *Advertising Management: Practical Perspectives* (Englewood Cliffs, N.J.: Prentice-Hall, 1975).

Aaker, D. A., and J. G. Myers, *Advertising Management* (Englewood Cliffs, N.J.: Prentice-Hall, 1975).

Aaker, D. A., "A Probabilistic Approach to Media Selection," *Journal of Advertising Research* 8 (September 1968): 46–54.

Bass, F. M., and R. T. Lonsdale, "An Exploration of Linear Programming in Media Selection," *Journal of Marketing Research* 3 (May 1966): 179–188.

Gundee, H. N., "Prediction Systems Really Work; Outdo Market Testing," *Marketing News*, September 9, 1977, p. 5.

Hurwood, D. L., and J. K. Brown, *Some Guidelines for Advertising Budgeting* (New York: Conference Board, 1972).

Kaplan, R. S., and A. D. Schocker, "Discount Effects on Media Plans," *Journal of Advertising Research* 11 (June 1971): 37–43.

Little, J. D. C., and L. M. Lodish, "A Media Planning Calculus," *Operations Research* 17 (January-February 1969): 1–35.

Schutte, T. F., "The Semantics of Branding," *Journal of Marketing* (April 1969): 5–11.

Simon, J. L., *The Management of Advertising* (Englewood Cliffs, N.J.: Prentice-Hall, 1971).

————, "A Simple Model for Determining Advertising Appropriations," *Journal of Marketing Research* 2 (August 1965): 285–292.

————, "Expenditure Policy for Mail-Order Advertisers," *Journal of Marketing Research* 4 (February 1967): 59–61.

Wheatley, J. J., *Measuring Advertising Effectiveness* (Homewood, Ill.: Richard D. Irwin, 1969).

Wolfe, H. D., J. K. Brown, and G. C. Thompson, *Measuring Advertising Results* (New York: Conference Board, 1962).

Wolfe, H. D., J. K. Brown, S. H. Greenberg, and G. C. Thompson, *Pretesting Advertising* (New York: Conference Board, 1963).

Zufryden, F. S., "Media Scheduling: A Stochastic Dynamic Model Approach," *Management Science* 19, 12 (August 1973): 1395–1406.

ENVIRONMENTAL ANALYSIS WORKSHEET

Environmental elements	Facts	Assumptions or research needed	Conclusions
Organizational values, objectives, and policies (4)			
Organizational design (5)			

Situation
   Generic demand (6)
   Brand demand (7)
   Competition (9)
   Public policy (10)			

Opportunities (2)			
Problems			

MARKETING PLAN (CONSUMER PRODUCT)

Current performance
Recommendations
Effect of recommendations on income
Situation analysis
Opportunities and problems
Strategies
Tests and research
Supporting documents
   Comparative budgets
   Media allocation schedule
   Promotion control sheet

STRATEGY WORKSHEET

Opportunities and problems in rank order to importance

   1.

   2.

    .

   n.

	Current strategy	Alternatives and recommended strategy	Estimated Effect
Demand strategy			
Generic			
Brand			
Strategic goals			
Financial			
Marketing			
Marketing-mix strategies			
Product (12)			
Pricing (13)			
Channel and logistics (14)			
Advertising and promotional (15)			
Sales management (16)			
Research (3)			
Profit plan			
Evaluation and control (19)			

CHAPTER **16**

Sales Management Strategies

LEARNING OBJECTIVES   After studying this chapter you should:

1. Understand the changing roles of sales representatives.
2. Know the strengths and weaknesses of various sales force organizations.
3. Know how sales management goals are expressed.
4. Know the duties of field sales managers.
5. Know how to determine if a direct sales force should be used.
6. Understand the steps that are required to build and maintain a sales force.
7. Know criteria for allocating selling effort.
8. Know the advantages and disadvantages of various compensation schemes.
9. Know procedures for motivating and evaluating sales representatives' performances.
10. Be able to define and use the following concepts:

Sales representative	Position description
Account representative	Detail representative
(or manager)	Return-on-assets management

SOME STRATEGIC QUESTIONS FOR OPENERS

1. What is the relative role of the sales force in the marketing mix? In the communication mix of the firm? In the industry?
2. How should we recruit, train, and motivate the sales force?
3. Does the compensation scheme reward the sales representatives for the selling tasks which have been assigned to them?
4. Does the compensation scheme encourage the representatives to maximize corporate goals as well as their own goals?
5. What is the sales representative's role in planning?

It was the homecoming football weekend at an Ivy League campus. A recent M.B.A. looked up his marketing professor and said, "You and the other marketing professors have been making a mistake by not telling students about opportunities in sales management. My company's training program requires that we sell. Now I find that

I love it and want to make it my career. I am a district manager with seven salespeople under me and I love it. I must use all the knowledge that I learned as an M.B.A., especially how to deal with people." This was in the late 1960s. The student was sensing the rapid change in the role of salespeople and, therefore, the sales manager. In this chapter we will examine these changes and the elements of sales management strategies.

THE CHANGING ROLES OF SALESPEOPLE

"To many novelists, playwrights, sociologists, college students, and many others, he [the salesman] is aggressively forcing on people goods that they don't want. He is the drummer, with a dubious set of social values—Willy Loman in the Arthur Miller play [*Death of a Salesman*]."[1] People who hold this view of selling have probably never spent a day with a professional salesperson or tried to sell. The general public has little contact with professional sales representatives. Rather, its image tends to be based on retail salesclerks and automobile salesmen, two selling roles that have been diminished because of mass media advertising.

The roles of selling have become more complex because products have become more technical, buyers are more sophisticated, competition has become more intense, and the trend toward large, integrated customers requires that selling take place at many levels in the customer's organization. The representative is no longer out there alone. Today this "account manager" links the research, engineering, marketing, and upper-management members of the company with their counterparts in the prospect's firm. In many industries, the fast-talking, flashy-dressing, heavy-entertaining personality has been replaced by an analytical individual who can converse on a wide range of subjects, including finance, interest rates, macro- and microeconomics, and world affairs that influence the business of the prospect. Thus the new salesperson requires a broad knowledge. He or she must be able to communicate effectively, get along with people, and be creative in identifying and solving problems. He or she must be patient and persistent, because many selling opportunities require months or years of work before an order is written, e.g., the sale of a computer or industrial equipment (see Chapter 8). A few examples will illustrate the complexity of the new role for salespeople.[2]

To sell plastic film, one may be required to help a packager sell the present equipment, purchase the new equipment, and work out the details of amortization. A representative must be able to demonstrate that the investment in the proposition will give the prospect the best return on investment.

The growth of supermarket chains dramatically changed the role of representatives in the packaged-goods field. Del Monte foods has an *account representative* to call on retailers and write orders. The *sales representative*, who is one level below, works with store managers on inventories, shelf management, and merchandising. Gillette uses women who work part-time to handle retail displays, distribution, and stock replenishment. As a result, Gillette salespersons have been able to increase the selling time spent with buyers from 30 percent to 85 percent. Dow Chemical created 14 *corporate account managers*, who are one level above the salespeople. The new managers handle all 1200 Dow products for potential multimillion-dollar customers.

The need for creativity in selling is illustrated by the case of Owens-Corning Fiberglass Corporation. A customer considered switching to a competitor when it cut prices $1\frac{1}{2}$ cents per pound. Freight costs would be less because the competitor was closer to the customer. Owens-Corning countered by developing a new package for shipping materials that the customer could use to ship the finished product. The saving to the customer was two cents per pound, and Owens-Corning retained the customer.

Perhaps the greatest change in the roles of sales representatives and sales managers is the change in their positions in the planning process. Today's representatives and sales managers play an active role in developing plans for themselves and their companies.

The basic elements of sales management are identical to those for management roles. *Planning* includes forecasts, objectives, organization, policies, and strategies. *Procedures* require programs, schedules, standards, and budgets. *Directing* implements the strategies through supervision, delegation, motivating, coordinating, counseling, staffing, and training. *Controlling* measures, evaluates, and corrects.[3] Elaboration of each of these elements of management would require a text on general management principles. The remainder of this chapter will focus only on the elements that are part of the selling strategy. Thus we will not discuss the tactical details of sales management. Instead, our focus will be on the broad issues of planning, selecting and training candidates, allocating the selling effort, and supervising the sales force.

PLANNING Planning the sales force requires decisions in organizational arrangement, goals, duties, and sales force size.

Organizational Designs A sales manager who accepts the fact that there is no perfect organizational design (see Chapters 4 and 5) will be less frustrated by the difficulty of organizing the sales force. The "pure" designs are by geography, product, and industry.

Geographic organizations have regional sales managers, who in turn supervise about five district sales managers. Each district manager will have five to seven salespeople. A sales force of 150 people, therefore, will require 25 district managers and 5 regional sales managers.

Product designs are used when the products are very technical and require specialization in the sales force. Before using this design, the sales manager must weigh the benefits and costs. The benefit of a product-specialized sales force is a salesperson who is an expert in the product. Training costs will be less than those required to train all salespeople in all products. These efficiencies may be more than offset by the costs of duplication, because several salespeople will travel the same territories and call on the same customers. Furthermore, customers may be annoyed by the confusion created by several salespeople representing the same company.

Industry designs require the salespeople to know the problems of specific industries, such as automobiles, air lines, banks, insurance, steel mills, etc. In the computing field, for example, the needs of each of these industries are quite different. By concentrating on an industry, the salesperson can better identify problems and speak the language of the industry. If the company has a wide line of products, however, the salesperson may need assistance in identifying the appropriate product to meet the need. In highly technical fields, such as computers, the salesperson will have product experts, with titles such as systems engineer, to assist in the sale. Thus the gain in efficiency in identifying the customer's problem is offset by the cost of staff support personnel.

Combination organizations attempt to maximize the benefits and minimize the costs of several designs. Thus, for example, Hewlett-Packard shifted from a product-oriented structure to a *product/market*-oriented structure. In this case, the salesperson for electronic products will specialize in the electrical manufacturing, aerospace, communication, or transportation equipment industries. The selling team for each industry includes salespeople, application engineers, and software specialists.

The organizational trend is toward a market-oriented structure. This shift reflects the increasing complexity of customers' needs, the technology of the products, and the greater domestic and foreign competition in every field.[4]

Sales Management Goals The goals for the sales manager are determined by the corporate goals (Chapter 4) and the situation analysis (Chapters 6–10). *Sales management goals* are expressed in terms of desired levels of sales, profits, contribution, distribution rates, and new accounts. Implementing these strategic goals requires *tactical goals* expressed in terms of reduced levels of expenses, call rates, close ratios (ability to get the order), recruiting rates, lowered days of open territories, greater training-effectiveness rates, and improved motivation. These goals must be accomplished within the limits of corporate resources and public policy.

The *communication goals* assigned to the sales force will vary according to the products being sold and the role of personal selling in the marketing mix. Sales representatives who sell a product or service that does not require a long and complex decision process may have a communication model containing four stages—attention, interest, desire, and action (AIDA). The sale of complex equipment requires selling at many levels within the firm, where the needs at each level differ. The AIDA approach may still apply, but the salespeople must adapt it for each level and know when to call in staff persons to assist at each stage in the selling process. This is the type of selling required of the *acount manager.*

Professional salespersons perform many functions other than "getting the order." Technical service, delivery, and service after the sale are major elements in the selling job. These elements yield long-term partnerships between the representative and the client, which in turn lead to future sales. Representatives also perform the function of gathering market information about unmet customer needs.

The goals of the salesperson should match those of the company. A person who is interested in selling as a career should select a company in an industry in which personal selling is an important *success factor* (see Chapter 4). If the competitive norm in the industry is heavy media advertising, the person who aspires to a career in selling will want to consider another industry.

Duties of a Field Sales Manager The field sales manager, the first level of sales management, will have about five to seven salespeople reporting to him or her and will generally report to a branch or regional sales manager. An aggressive salesperson with management potential may become a field manager in as short a period as three years. The duties of a field manager are quite broad and in many companies are a scaled-down version of the regional and general sales managers' duties. To illustrate this point we will examine the *position description* of the *district sales manager* for Burroughs Wellcome Company, a pharmaceutical firm with a sales force of 550 persons.[5] This description is divided into three parts—key objectives, critical objectives, and organizational relationships.

Key objectives.
1. To plan, organize, lead, and control the activities and personnel of the district sales staff in order to achieve the planned level of sales within the approved levels of expenses;

2. To promote the prestige of the company and to make appropriate contribution to the social climate of the communities in which we operate;

3. To provide stable employment with opportunity for the district sales staff.

Critial objectives.

1. To prepare projections for expenditures, equipment, services, and personnel required for the district sales staff;

2. To collect and present field marketing data and current marketing information and to recommend programs and procedures to the regional sales manager and appropriate departments;

3. To maintain an adequate district sales staff;

4. To develop and implement a district recruiting program to ensure the continuing availability of sales personnel;

5. To train and develop the district sales staff to ensure capable management succession;

6. To train and motivate the personnel of the district sales staff to work efficiently together and with other departments of the company to:
   a) achieve the sales objectives
   b) control expenses in order to maximize profits
   c) promote the prestige of the company and the pharmaceutical industry
   d) make appropriate contributions to the social climate of the communities in which the company operates
   e) provide stable employment with opportunity for district personnel

7. To establish performance criteria and to regularly evaluate, review, and report performance of the district sales staff to:
   a) recognize and reward achievement
   b) detect unsatisfactory trends and deviations from planned performance at an early stage and ensure that prompt and corrective action is taken when necessary

8. To apply within the district sales staff all standard company procedures, programs, and policies, including those pertaining to relevant statutory regulations governing labor relations, equal employment opportunities, fair employment practices, and safety and to ensure that such compliance is within state and federal regulations;

9. To recommend to the regional sales manager such programs, policies, and procedures as would improve the company's performance; to inform the regional sales manager immediately and to recommend changes for approval as soon as possible when conditions arise which indicate that an approved plan is unlikely to be achieved;

10. To keep the district sales staff informed of company objectives and programs;

11. To communicate the needs, concerns, and achievements of the district sales staff to the regional manager and appropriate departments;

12. To adequately compensate the district sales staff within company guidelines.

Organizational relationships.

1. Responsible to regional sales manager;

2. Direct line responsibility for district sales staff;

3. Staff liaison with other district sales managers.

Structuring the Sales Force   A crucial sales management strategy is the structure of the sales force. Should the sales force be direct factory-controlled, or should it be manufacturers' representatives' selling agents? (See Chapter 14 for a definition of these terms.) Perhaps it should be a mixed structure that uses both types of salespeople. Or should it be a sales force that is shared with another division or even another company? Fogg and Rokus developed a quantitative approach to help answer these questions when the *industrial* sales manager is faced with the problem of building a new sales force or restructuring an old one, as is the case when corporations are merged.[6] The output from the system is the number of salespersons who are needed for each type, the management system needed to control them, and the potential profits from each type of sales force.

The decision to use either a direct sales force or representatives is determined by the *contribution to profit that is associated with accounts of various sizes.* Above a break-even account size, the direct selling force normally has a higher contribution.[7] The task, therefore, is to identify the break-even point below which representatives should be used and above which a direct sales force should be used. The detailed illustration provided by Fogg and Rokus leads to Fig. 16.1, which illustrates the break-even chart that will help to make the decision.

The vertical axis in Fig. 16.1 is the contribution to the operating profit per account. The horizontal axis is the potential account size, expressed in thousands of dollars. To create a break-even chart, one must segment the market into subgroups according to their sales potential. The *contribution to operating margin* (COM) is

Fig. 16.1   Finding the potential account size required for a direct sales force. (C. D. Fogg and J. W. Rokus, "A Quantitative Method for Structuring a Profitable Sales Force," *Journal of Marketing* **37** (July 1973): 8–17. Reprinted by permission.)

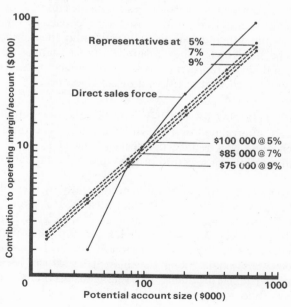

then calculated for each segment, first using a direct sales force, and then using representatives. For n classification of accounts, the two equations are as follows:

$$\text{Direct COM} = \sum_{1}^{n} \begin{array}{l} \text{(Account potential} \times \text{Number of accounts} \times \\ \text{Estimated share} \times \text{Percent gross margin)} - \\ \text{(Number of accounts} \times \text{Calls/year} \times \text{Cost/call)} \end{array} \qquad (16.1)$$

$$\text{Representative COM} = \sum_{1}^{n} \begin{array}{l} \text{(Average account potential} \times \text{Number of accounts} \times \\ \text{Estimated share} \times \text{Percent gross margin)} - \\ \text{(Sales} \times \text{Commission rate).} \end{array} \qquad (16.2)$$

The figure shows break-even levels at three commission rates for representatives. A *mixed sales structure* is one that uses direct salespeople for large accounts and representatives for small accounts. Under such an arrangement, the representatives will want a higher commission. In this example it was assumed that a five-percent commission would be adequate if representatives were given accounts with potentials less than $100,000, but that seven percent would be necessary if accounts were limited to those under $85,000, and nine percent would be required for accounts with a potential less than $75,000.

Once the break-even point is identified, it is possible to estimate the number of direct salespeople and the number of representatives that are needed. This is accomplished by the following ratio:

$$\frac{\text{Number of salespeople/}}{\text{Representatives needed}} = \frac{\text{Total calls required/year}}{\text{Salesperson's call capacity/year}}. \qquad (16.3)$$

This equation should be regarded as a rough estimate because of our inability to measure precisely the calls required and the salesperson's capacity to make them.

Fogg and Rokus continued their calculations by estimating the number of field sales managers that would be necessary. They assumed that a manger could supervise five direct salespeople and seven representatives. (This higher management cost for direct selling should be included in the cost of a direct sales force.)[8]

BUILDING AND MAINTAINING THE SALES FORCE Building and maintaining the sales force includes the closely interrelated activities of recruiting, selecting, and training. The earlier steps, when done well, reduce the costs of the later steps. Thus a good recruiting program will simplify the selection process and reduce the need for training.

Recruiting The type of candidate to be recruited will be influenced greatly by the selling task to be performed. A few examples will illustrate the contrast in tasks and therefore the differences in recruiting. *Inside* salespersons, such as store clerks and wholesalers' phone clerks, essentially are order takers. The sale has already taken place in the mind of the buyers, and placing the order is a confirmation of that decision. In contrast, the *outside* salesperson does "missionary" selling to help the prospect identify problems and then solve them with particular products. This selling task is one of creating the sale. Selling *tangible* products (books, typewriters, oil drilling equipment, etc.) is generally regarded as easier than selling intangibles (insurance, consulting services, educational systems, etc.). The *outside* selling tasks vary greatly. For example, the soft drink driver-salesperson is largely an order taker, whereas the commercial banker who sells a new banking service must create the sale.

Having identified the selling tasks that are required of the salespeople, the manager must identify the profiles of individuals who will perform the tasks. The criteria are generally expressed in terms of education, selling experience, character, health, communication abilities, and appearance.

The recruiting program will take on many forms. Some programs are highly centralized; the home office does all recruiting. Decentralization may be at the regional level or at the district and salesperson level. Some firms require salespeople to make presentations to college seniors. When candidates have been identified, the district sales manager screens the candidates before passing the candidate on to the regional manager.

The sources of candidates vary according to the job description and the strategies of sales management. The job title can be misleading, however. For example, candidates for industrial selling are no longer limited to engineers. The changing role of selling that has produced account managers backed up by a selling team of technical staff requires a broad individual. Some industrial firms have been recruiting liberal arts majors and business students.

The sales management strategy will determine whether the search will be for experienced or inexperienced candidates. The experienced salesperson arrives ready to sell, but may have acquired bad selling habits or be a prima donna, not fitting in with the rest of the organization. The experienced salesperson costs more. Other companies would rather invest in training programs and start with fresh candidates who can be trained in their methods.

There are many obvious sources of candidates, such as educational insitutions and employment agencies. Less obvious sources include upgrading an employee within the firm. This provides the advantage of a fresh person to sales, but one who is familiar with the company and its products.

Hiring from competitors probably has more dangers than advantages. In some cases this may be regarded as unfair competition, which would violate the Federal Trade Commission Act (see Chapter 10). Furthermore, the practice does not ensure a good salesperson. One may hire someone who was about to be fired. Also, a salesperson who was willing to be hired away once will be willing a second time. The second time it is *our* secrets that the person leaves with.

Selecting[9] Selecting from among the candidates who were recruited requires selection tools. The *structured background questionnaire*, which records the applicant's hobbies, school performance, and attitudes toward past performance, has shown the greatest success in screening good salespersons.[10] *Intelligence tests* have yielded mixed results. These tests give an indication of a candidate's ability to learn, so they are important when there is a need for extensive training. "A dismal history has been recorded by *personality tests*," however.[11] Such tests fail because they measure interest, not ability; can be faked; favor conformity, not creativity; and identify fractional traits, not the whole person.[12] Two traits that have been found to predict a good salesperson are empathy and ego drive.[13] Empathy is the ability to feel as the other person does. Ego drive is the force that makes the salesperson want to achieve a goal.

Many firms use an *interviewer rating sheet* to summarize the interviewer's impression of the candidate. The candidate will score high if she or he has clear, consistent career goals, has shown initiative and leadership in past activities, and is persistent. Conversely, a history of being a follower and one of changing career goals several times will result in a low rating.

The questions on application blanks and the use of tests are being limited by the Equal Employment Opportunities Commission, which enforces federal civil rights legislation. It is no longer possible to ask questions that could discriminate unfavorably with regard to sex, age, or race. Questions about marital status, home ownership, and finances were once used to measure candidates' ability to manage their personal affairs, but such questions have been eliminated as discriminatory. No questions about physical characteristics may be asked. Many firms have eliminated the social security number on personnel forms to protect employees from being traced to data banks. Aptitude tests may not be used unless their ability to predict performance on the specific job for which the candidate is being hired has been validated. It is still possible to check references that have been given by the candidate. The emphasis of equal opportunity legislation on the hiring of salespeople has placed greater emphasis on the personal interview and less emphasis on the paperwork. Some sales managers have extended the interview process to include having the candidate ride with a salesperson so that the candidate can decide if his or her personality will fit the job.

Many sales recruiters are finding that the loss of data from tests and application blanks has not altered their ability to develop quality salespersons. This seems to be explained by two events. First, higher-quality people have been interested in selling, so there is a high probability of success for any candidate, regardless of test scores. Second, firms have improved the quality of their training programs. Thus the important criterion for many sales positions is the ability to learn.

Training   The goals of a training program change over the life cycle of the salesperson. Early in a career, training should emphasize selling, corporate policies, and procedures. Once these have been established, new problems arise, such as motivating the mature salesperson who has no potential for promotion to management. Training goals vary among products and industries. The most common goals include the following: increasing volume or profit; reducing costs, supervision, and turnover; introducing new products, markets, channels, and promotional campaigns; improving morale, motivation, and customer relations; and training for management. These goals answer the question: Why should we have a training program? The development of a training program requires answers to the additional questions of who, what, where, when, and how.[14]

Who should be trained and *who* should do the training? The answer to these questions will depend on the sales management strategy. A company with the policy of hiring experienced salespeople will answer them differently from a firm that hires college graduates with no experience. Some companies will use a field sales manager as a trainer; others will have a staff trainer who has specialized in developing training materials. Other firms will use outside organizations that specialize in selling training programs. The choice will be determined to a large extent on the number of salespersons to be trained per year.

Many firms have training programs for all of their salespeople, not just recruits. For example, Armour-Dial, Inc., a consumer-goods firm, evaluated the effectiveness after salespeople attended a program. The result was an increase of 12 percent in the number of calls per day, 25 percent more new-product retail placements, a 100-percent gain in case sales, 62 percent more displays sold, and a 250-percent increase in direct-buying accounts.[15]

What will be the content of the program? The content will vary according to the needs of the salespeople and the company. The most common elements include: development of selling skills, product knowledge, analyzing buyer needs, corporate policies and procedures, time management, new governmental regulations, new technology, and motivation.

Where should the training be conducted? Should it be centralized at the home office in a special training facility, or should it take place in the field? The centralized approach makes it possible to use training equipment and expose salespersons to top executives, but centralization greatly increases the transportation costs associated with moving the salespeople. There is also the cost of having them away from their territories for several days. Conversely, decentralized training may not be efficient because of distractions from the pressures of the territory and family needs.

When should the training be conducted? There can be no generalized answer to this question because of the different needs among salespersons and companies. This question is closely linked with the *what* question. Clearly, the new salesperson needs *early* training in products, policies, and selling skills.

How should the material be communicated? Role playing is effective in teaching selling skills and analyzing buyers' needs. On-the-job training is effective in training the salesperson how to organize his or her territory and time. Technical material about products and customer needs are best communicated through lectures, demonstrations, and visuals such as movies or television.

A clear definition of training goals and methods will make it possible to evaluate the results of training programs. These evaluations will facilitate the development of more effective programs.

ALLOCATING THE RESOURCES OF THE SALES FORCE The selling effort can be measured in terms of salespeople's time, their compensation, and their expenses. The task of the sales manager is to make *optimal allocation* of this effort *across geographic territories, customers, and products* to maximize profits. The task of the salesperson is to achieve *optimal scheduling* and *routing of calls* to maximize personal income. The system of sales goals and rewards must be designed carefully to ensure that both the sales manager's and the salesperson's goals are being met.

Allocating Salespeople's Time The complexity of allocating selling time has attracted the attention of many management scientists. This "scheduling problem" has long fascinated them because of its difficulty. Although no one model provides an *optimal* allocation of effort for the firm and the salespeople, many of the models provide a *better* allocation than is being used presently.

Some of the analytical approaches include methods to equalize the call load in territories,[16] to maximize profit,[17] to maximize the expected value of customers,[18] to allocate sales calls with subjective inputs,[19] to allocate selling effort across products,[20] and to reflect differences in salespeople's ability and carry-over effects.[21]

We have already seen an allocation procedure based on market potential. In Chapter 8 we discussed a manufacturer of corrugated and solid-fiber boxes who estimated industry market potentials using the number of employees in selected standard industrial classifications (SIC). These potentials were used to establish sales quotas, which in turn guided the salespeople in directing their sales effort. The limitations of SIC approaches were discussed in Chapter 8. In Chapter 15 we learned that matching profiles is a *proportional* method that does not produce the *optimum* allocation of *advertising* effort. With the advertising example in mind, we can see that assigning sales quotas that are proportional to the potential of geographic or industrial segments is not an optimizing procedure. For this reason, many of the computer models for allocating sales efforts are heuristic models that search for solutions that approach the *marginal* allocation of effort. We saw a media scheduling model that used the marginal (i.e., the *high-assay*) approach to select that media vehicle that added the most net-unduplicated audience (Fig. 15.2). The sales allocation models search for the customer who will produce the largest unit of profit for an additional increment of selling effort.

Lodish developed a computer routine that can be used easily by salespeople or sales managers to make decisions on sales force size, territory boundaries, and call frequencies.[22] Input data are historical and judgmental. The computer first decides how many calls should be made on each account (or prospect) to maximize the contribution to profit. Then it generates what would happen to contribution if *selling time* were added or deleted from a territory. The maximum contribution occurs when the last *hour of selling* in each territory produces the same contribution. The computer program tests to determine if *salespersons* should be added to or deleted from the entire sales force. Companies that used the procedure to establish new-call policies estimated a nine-percent increase in contribution to profits.

Hess and Samuels used the legislative-apportionment analogue for equal voter representation to redraw sales and service territories.[23] The goal was to build better (not optimal) territories using the existing sales force. "The heuristic constructs a predetermined number of compact sales territories comprised of smaller geographical units (counties, five-digit zip code areas or a combination of both)."[24] These compact territories have approximately equal potential or work loads. Changes in territorial boundaries were minimized by starting the heuristic procedure with existing territories. The procedure was used by CIBA Pharmaceutical Company when it discovered that there was a great disparity in the distribution of physicians among its present territories. This reallocation of effort was credited with a large increase in sales.

Most computer sales force allocation models have used a combination of historical and subjective data to estimate customer potential and the number of sales calls needed to complete a sale. The computer, therefore, did not eliminate the subjectivity of sales force allocation. Instead, it made it possible to handle large quantities of data to create territories and then test the effect of changes in territories, call schedules, and sales force size.

Compensating Salespeople   The ideal compensation scheme will jointly maximize the goals of the firm and the individual salesperson. The compensation program begins with the job description. Some of the elements that are common to all job descriptions are: "sell for optimum volume and profit, forecast by product and customer, plan orderly exploitation of territory, manage time and expenses, consult with and develop customers, communicate, keep records, handle complaints, provide customer service, implement promotions, assist with credit and collection, bird-dog new accounts, recommend changes, develop himself, represent the company, and implement policy."[25] The importance of these functions will vary according to conditions of supply, demand, competition, corporate goals and policies, and the status of the territory development. Thus the *compensation scheme must be flexible so that it can change as these conditions alter the importance of the elements of the selling function.*

The goal of the compensation program scheme, therefore, is basically to stimulate and reward the salesperson for performing his or her job. The programs have the subgoals of attracting and retaining good salespeople and providing stable earnings. A good compensation program is equitable, based on factors controlled by the salespeople, is understood by them, is simple to compute, and provides a means for evaluation.

Webster suggested the following six steps for building a compensation plan:

1. Establish clear and consistent compensation objectives, such as guaranteed income, stimulation, *individual* sales incentives, *group* incentives, and flexibility for local modification.

2. Determine the level of income for each salesperson.

3. Establish the proportions of fixed and incentive income.

4. Select measurement criteria for each component. For example, the size of the fixed component may be determined by the amount of servicing, follow-up work, and prospecting required. The incentive component may be determined by some measure of sales volume, such as total sales in dollars, in units, or the gross margin.

5. Establish the compensation formula.

6. Pretest the formula.[26]

The two pure forms of compensation methods are straight salary and straight commission. There are also many variations. In Table 16.1 we see that the most common plan is a base salary plus either a commission or a bonus. This table also shows that the straight salary tends to be used more in industrial firms.

TABLE 16.1 **Alternative sales compensation and incentive plans**

	Percent of companies using—1975				
	All industries		*Consumer products*	*Industrial products*	*Other commerce/ industry*
Method	*1975*	*1974*	*1975*	*1975*	*1975*
Straight salary	25.5%	23.4%	14.1%	25.3%	52.4%
Straight commission	0.9	1.4	2.1	0.7	—
Draw against commission	5.3	4.6	9.9	3.9	4.8
Salary plus commission	25.6	23.6	23.3	27.7	15.8
Salary plus individual bonus	28.4	25.3	34.5	28.5	14.3
Salary plus group bonus	3.8	6.7	6.3	3.3	1.6
Salary plus commission plus individual or group bonus	7.2	6.9	4.9	7.8	7.9
More than one method of payment	3.3	8.1	4.9	2.8	3.2
Total	100.0%	100.0%	100.0%	100.0%	100.0%

American Management Association, Executive Compensation Service as published in *Sales & Marketing Management*, February 9, 1976, p. 61.

The direct costs of selling include the compensation to the salesperson, his or her automobile, and other expenses. These expenses are summarized in Table 16.2 for five different types of salespeople. (Note the different selling tasks that are represented across these salespeople types and the variance in compensation.) Table 16.3 shows the number of calls per day that can be made by each type of salesperson by two territory types—metropolitan and rural. These data can be very helpful when evaluating a sales force strategy.

The variety of compensation plans is extensive. One of the more imaginative ones was developed by Ormont Drug & Chemical Company, which compensates a salesperson's spouse $150 per month for handling customer orders and inquiries on the home phone. The compensation is tied to a bonus that could bring the total amount to $6000. Some spouses become so enthused about this team approach that they attend sales training programs.[27]

TABLE 16.2 Direct sales costs of salespeople's calls

	Range of yearly direct sales costs				
Type of salesman	*Compensation*	*Automobile*	*Entertainment, travel, food, and lodging*	*Total 1975*	*Total 1974*
Account representative[1]	$17,000–21,000	0–$4000	0–$5000	$17,000–30,000	$15,000–24,000
Detail salesman[2]	15,000–18,000	2000–3500	0–2500	17,000–24,000	14,000–20,000
Sales engineer[3]	20,000–23,000	2000–4000	2500–8000	24,500–35,000	23,000–32,000
Industrial products salesman[4]	16,000–21,000	2500–3500	1500–5500	20,000–30,000	19,000–26,000
Service salesman[5]	16,000–22,000	2500–4000	0–4000	18,500–30,000	17,000–26,000

Note: Base salary—commission or bonus ranges obtained from American Management Associations, "Sales Personnel Report," 1975 edition.

Source: Sales & Marketing Management survey.

[1] Account Representative—A salesman who calls on a large number of already established customers in, for example, the food, textiles, apparel, and wholesaling industries. Much of this selling is low key, and there is minimal pressure to develop new business.

[2] Detail Salesman—A salesman who, instead of directly soliciting an order, concentrates on performing promotional activities and introducing products. The medical detail man, for example, seeks to persuade doctors, the indirect customers, to specify the pharmaceutical company's trade name product for prescriptions. The firm's actual sale is ultimately made through a wholesaler or direct to the pharmacist who fills the doctor's prescription.

[3] Sales Engineer—A salesman who sells products for which technical know-how and the ability to discuss technical aspects of the product are extremely important. The salesman's expertise in identifying, analyzing, and solving customer problems is another critical factor. This type of selling is common in the chemical, machinery, and heavy-equipment industries.

[4] Industrial Products Salesmen, Nontechnical—This salesman sells a tangible product to industrial or commercial purchasers; no high degree of technical knowledge is required. Industries such as packaging materials or standard office equipment rely on these salesmen.

[5] Service Salesman—A salesman who sells intangibles, such as insurance and advertising. Unlike the four preceding types of salesmen, those who sell service must be able to sell effectively the benefits of intangibles.

Reprinted by permission from *Sales & Marketing Management*, February 9, 1976, p. 30. Copyright 1976.

TABLE 16.3 Typical salespeople's call patterns

Type of salesman		Average calls per day — Territory A	Average calls per day — Territory B	Estimated days in field per year	Average calls per year — Territory A	Average calls per year — Territory B
Account representative	R*	4–6	2–3	239[1]	956–1434	478–717
	M†	5	2.5		1195	598
Detail salesman	R	6–10	4–6	239[1]	1434–2390	956–1434
	M	8	5		1912	1195
Sales engineer	R	4–7	3–4	190[2]	760–1330	570–760
	M	5.5	3.5		1045	665
Industrial products salesman	R	6–8	3–5	239[1]	1434–1912	717–1195
	M	7	4		1673	956
Service salesman	R	8–10	4–6	239[1]	1912–2390	956–1434
	M	9	5		2151	1195

* R: Range of calls.
† M: Mean number of calls.
Source: Sales & Marketing Management survey.
Note: [1] Based on 5 days, 52 weeks per year, less 6 holidays and 15 days for vacation and sickness.
Note: [2] Based on 239 workdays less 1 day per week in office (49 days).
Territory definition: A—Usually a metro area where customers are concentrated, the salesman can make several calls at one location, or the sales manager's philosophy emphasizes maximum calls per day. B—Customers are dispersed and longer sales calls are required to sell a product or service.
Reprinted by permission from Sales & Marketing Management, February 9, 1976, p. 30. Copyright 1976.

Several researchers have explored the problem of developing a compensation scheme that would optimize the goals of the firm and the salesperson. Farley, for example, demonstrated mathematically that when marginal costs are constant, salespeople who are paid a percent of gross margin will allocate their time so as to maximize the contribution to profit.[28] Weinberg extended this analysis to demonstrate that when these conditions are met, the salespeople may be given control over prices and that these prices will be optimal to the firm and the salespeople.[29]

When a bonus is used as the incentive component of compensation, it is based on goals such as sales volume, reducing expenses, encouraging balanced selling across all products, promoting new business, and servicing customers. It averages around 12 to 15 percent of the base salary.[30]

There are many dangers in having the wrong compensation scheme. Salespersons on a straight commission regard themselves as almost self-employed, so they are unwilling to complete paperwork or service accounts that they did not sell. Conversely, representatives who are on a straight salary may give more service than the accounts justify.

SUPERVISING THE SELLING EFFORT The supervision of the selling effort is accomplished through recruiting, selecting, training, and compensating the salesperson. Weaknesses in any of these steps make supervision difficult or, in the extreme cases, impossible. Although everything the sales manager does is directed toward supervision, the topics of *motivation* and *evaluation* deserve some elaboration.

Motivating Motivation of the sales force begins with an understanding of the personal needs of the salespeople. They, like all individuals, have a hierarchy of needs. Maslow identified five levels of needs—physiological, safety, belongingness and love, esteem, and self-actualization.[31] A higher-order need emerges as the preceding lower-order need is met. Thus a sales force will have a complex need pattern, which means that it will require a variety of motivators.

Churchill, Ford, and Walker studied the motivators of salespeople in two large industrial firms.[32] They found that salespeople want more than money. They also want their self-fulfillment needs met through opportunities for accomplishment and personal growth. Most sales management motivation programs are based on financial rewards, however. Few programs even consider the self-fulfillment factors. Measuring these needs is difficult, but systems can be developed to permit the achievement of self-fulfillment. Salespeople can be included in the setting of objectives and in planning. Special positions, such as a sales trainer, recognize a salesperson's ability to teach others. This gives the individual a special feeling of being needed. Liberal use of lower-level management positions, such as district sales manager, provides opportunities for promotion and for testing a person's potential as a manager.

These researchers also found that security and the social rewards of recognition and respect were not important to the salespersons studied. They concluded that this may be due to a self-selection process; persons with these needs do not go into selling.

The study found that there are diminishing returns for financial rewards, but not for self-fulfillment. This means that as salespersons reach a satisfactory pay level, they are not strongly motivated by additional pay, but the attainment of one accomplishment does not diminish the attractiveness of additional accomplishments. Thus opportunities within the sales force for career and personal development are an extremely important element of the motivation system.

A survey of 1761 salespeople concluded that more freedom should be given to salespeople to counter the trend toward unionization.[33] The biggest complaints were about "rah-rah" sales contests, cutting sales territories, paperwork, and preimposed sales priorities. Salespeople see themselves as entrepreneurs, so they want a role in developing objectives and strategies. In short, they want to participate in sales planning. Furthermore, they want to be treated as professionals.

Churchill, Ford, and Walker found that the importance of motivators varied among salespersons according to their age and family obligations. Financial rewards were highly valued by older salespeople and those who were married and had large families. Promotion and opportunities for accomplishment and growth were most valued by younger, less experienced, and highly educated salespeople. The fact that older salespeople want higher pay may be explained by the fact that these are the only rewards that are left, since they have chosen not to move into management positions.

Given the complexity of the needs structure of a medium to large sales force, a sales manager must design his or her own system of motivators rather than simply copy the system of another company or buy a standard package. It is extremely unlikely that the motivators would fit the sales manager's need patterns. The complexity of the need structure also explains why the reward structure requires many motivators. A sales force will have members at all levels of the need hierarchy.

Charles H. Singler, General Sales Manager of Burroughs Wellcome Company, uses an *open system of management* to motivate salespeople.[34] He begins by noting that salespeople work to satisfy their needs; they motivate themselves. Management must find ways to encourage them. Sincerity is what differentiates motivation from manipulation. Manipulation is a win-lose situation; motivation is a win-win situation in which everyone gains—the salesperson and the company.

The open-management approach, as presented by Kafka and Schaefer, stresses the need to see the salesperson's needs through his or her eyes.[35] Thus the task of the sales manager is to identify the salesperson's needs without judging them. This may be done by identifying the symbols that are important to the individual, such as a car, a boat, or travel, and relating reward systems to these symbols. Motivation, therefore, meets the needs of the company and the salesperson simultaneously. To accomplish motivation through open management, Singler believes that in addition to considering the human or psychological needs of the individual, the following management steps are critical:

1. Describe precisely the job and the performance standards;
2. Hire qualified or qualifiable candidates by establishing clear hiring standards;
3. Train candidates through a training program;
4. Provide proper supervision through a performance-appraisal system that is *mutually* agreeable to the salespeople and the sales manager;
5. Pay equitably;
6. Have a program for personal development.

This Burroughs Wellcome system seems to meet the needs for a motivation program that were identified by Churchill, Ford, and Walker.

Evaluating The system for evaluating salespeople begins with a precise job description and mutually agreed on performance standards. The evaluation system must have clear goals of its own and must identify the methods that will be used to evaluate each item.

A study by the Conference Board identified three primary reasons for measuring salespeople's performance: job improvement, determining compensation, and determining promotability.[36] The study identified three basic methods for judging salespeople's performance: analyzing data on the person's sales volume, observing the person at work, and analyzing the person's sales expenses and business income. Most companies use a combination of these methods. The Conference Board study found that the following criteria were used most frequently: attained sales volume, met objectives in promoting specific products or accounts, new-account development, profitableness of sales, expense-to-sales ratio, knowledge (products, prices, advertising, promotional programs, etc.), time management, diligence and accuracy in reporting, cutomer relations, and personal qualities (appearance, speech, intelligence, interest in work, etc.).

Return-on-assets management (ROAM) has been suggested as a variable for evaluating a territory or a salesperson.[37] This system has several advantages. First, it provides a means for analyzing weaknesses in salespeople. Recalling that the return on investment (or assets) is the product of margin times turnover (see Chapter 13), the sales manager can analyze a territory according to these two variables. A salesperson may be selling only the products with a low margin because they are easy to sell. Perhaps turnover of assets managed is low because the salesperson requires a high inventory or gives extended credit to customers, which requires more working capital for accounts receivable.

Proponents of this approach argue that forcing the salesperson to think in terms of return on assets is useful training for top-management positions, where thinking in these terms is required. It also helps the salesperson communicate with customers who frequently buy his or her products on the basis of a return on investment.

Measuring the productivity of salespeople is difficult when the sale takes a long period of time, which is the case with many types of industrial selling. A field study showed that it is possible to use measures of changes in belief and changes in attitudes to evaluate selling effectiveness prior to a sale.[38]

The actual instruments used to collect the data to evaluate salespeople's effectiveness vary greatly across industries and companies. In the Burroughs Wellcome Company case in Chapter 20 we will see several forms for such evaluation during field training and on the job and a simplified computerized call report that minimizes paperwork.

Because the call report is common to most sales-evaluation programs, a discussion of its applications and weaknesses is important. A well-designed call report can provide management with important information. It reveals the status of accounts; monitors individuals' performance; provides market information on customers' needs for new products, service problems, and competitive activities; and provides measures of the effort required to sell specific products to specific industries. In short, the call report provides a wealth of information for evaluating the sales force and for sales planning. Approximately 40 percent of the industrial and consumer-products firms require a call report on *each* customer call.

Despite their advantages, however, call reports have the inherent weakness of requiring paperwork, which most salespeople abhor. In addition, salespeople tend to use them as a means of communicating with the home office on other matters, such as credit adjustments. Call reports may be subject to embellishment or excessive detail. They are oriented toward the past instead of the future. They tend to be sent in late, a problem one firm solved by printing the call report on the back of the expense sheet.[39]

SUMMARY The expanded role of personal selling is due to higher product technology, greater buyer sophistication, greater competition in the marketplace, and the need for decentralized planning. The development of a sales management strategy requires a decision about its organizational design. The trend in design has been away from one that is solely geographic toward one that is market-oriented. This shift is necessitated by the growing complexity in the selling task.

The field sales manager is the first level of sales management, and his or her duties tend to be a scaled-down version of those of the general sales manager. When choosing a sales force structure, the sales manager must decide whether to create a sales force, use sales representatives or agents, or use the sales force of another division or company that sells related, but not competitive, products.

Building and maintaining a sales force requires programs of recruiting, selecting, and training. The recruiting program requires a precise job description. Selection requires instruments to evaluate the selling potential of a candidate. Personality profiles have not proved to be a good predictor. The Equal Employment Opportunity Commission prevents the use of any instrument which discriminates according to age, sex, race, or physical disability. This has removed many items from the application blank and limited aptitude tests to measuring the abilities that are required for the entrance-level job.

Training needs vary over the life cycle of the salesperson and across industries. Training goals can be classified broadly into two categories—making salespeople more productive and introducing new marketing strategies to the sales force. Who, what, when, where, and how questions will help the sales manager design an effective training program.

The sales manager attempts to achieve an optimal allocation of the resources of the sales force across geographic territories, customers, and products to maximize profits. The salesperson attempts to maximize personal income by an optimal scheduling and routing of sales calls. Computerized models have not developed the optimal solution to these complex allocation problems, but they have developed improved solutions.

The compensation program should jointly optimize the goals of the firm and the salespeople. It should compensate them for their performance of the elements of the job, as noted in the job description. The program should be flexible so that it can be modified as the importance of these elements changes. The most common compensation scheme is a base salary plus a commission or a bonus.

Motivation and evaluation are key elements in supervising the sales force. Motivation is based on an understanding of the needs of the salespeople. A large sales force will have a complex need structure because of the diversity of economic demands on the salespeople and their various needs for self-fulfillment. When the need structure is complex, the motivation program too must be complex. It must go beyond financial rewards to include opportunities for self-improvement and promotion. Self-fulfillment rewards do not seem to be subject to the diminishing returns of financial rewards.

An evaluation system requires a precise job description and mutually agreed on performance standards. Most companies use a combination of evaluation methods that are based on sales volume, management observations, sales expenses, and the profitability of sales.

DISCUSSION QUESTIONS

1. A salesperson explains that to get business in a foreign country, one must bribe public officials: "That is the way business is done here." How would you respond?

2. A conservative drug manufacturer had a man and a woman who were detailers. They met at a sales convention and decided to get married. They asked the company to move them to adjacent territories. After considerable rearrangement of territories, they were given adjacent territories in California. The couple decided not to marry, but to live together instead. What would you do as the general sales manager? Would your answer be the same if they were living in a small Southern town?

3. As a sales force planner, how would you decide whether to use a direct sales force, manufacturers' representatives, or a mixture of both? What conditions would have to exist for each of these sales strategies to be the best choice?

4. Describe the basic content of a sales training program. What factors in the sales candidates and company will affect the content of the sales training?

5. What is the goal of sales allocation models?

6. Describe the return-on-assets management model for evaluating a salesperson or territory and explain some of its advantages.

7. What is a call report? What are its advantages and disadvantages?

8. The Mutual Insurance Co. was able to recruit salespeople, but it could not retain them. A behavioral scientist suggested that a study be done to examine their attitudes

FIRST RUN

FILE NONAME (CREATION DATE = 07/03/74)

* MULTIPLE REGRESSION *

07/03/74   PAGE 15

DEPENDENT VARIABLE   PR $\overline{Y} = 637$

VARIABLE(S) ENTERED ON STEP NUMBER 9..   ATTM 35

MULTIPLE R	0.79291	
R SQUARE	0.62870	
STANDARD ERROR	1.63755	

ANALYSIS OF VARIANCE	DF	SUM OF SQUARES	MEAN SQUARE	F
REGRESSION	9-	231.56778	25.72975	9.59503
RESIDUAL	51-	136.76009	2.68157	

------- VARIABLES IN THE EQUATION -------

$\overline{Y}$ VARIABLE	B	BETA	STD ERROR B	F
3.8 ATTM10	0.81829	0.43694	0.17856	21.002
4.0 ATTM09	0.60560	0.22969	0.28886	4.404
3.2 ATTM29	0.47467	0.26343	0.17376	7.463
4.4 ATTM16	-1.01721	-0.48983	0.21992	21.395
3.1 ATTM30	0.54118	0.26781	0.20230	7.156
4.4 ATTM12	0.67112	0.35673	0.20390	10.834
4.0 ATTM27	0.97207	0.41148	0.30032	10.477
4.3 ATTM33	-0.68271	-0.25821	0.28342	5.803
4.3 ATTM35	-0.42075	-0.18573	0.27204	2.392
(CONSTANT)	0.32177			

---------- VARIABLES NOT IN THE EQUATION ----------

VARIABLE	BETA IN	PARTIAL	TOLERANCE	F
ATTM01	-0.07755	-0.11817	0.86210	0.708
ATTM02	-0.00517	-0.00714	0.70741	0.003
ATTM03	0.07216	0.09527	0.64719	0.458
ATTM04	-0.01998	-0.02751	0.70403	0.038
ATTM05	-0.00950	-0.01419	0.82851	0.010
ATTM06	0.10948	0.13566	0.57011	0.937
ATTM07	0.07712	0.09683	0.58524	0.473
ATTM08	-0.12903	-0.15277	0.52047	1.195
ATTM11	-0.05079	-0.05030	0.36417	0.127
ATTM13	0.04640	0.05375	0.49818	0.145
ATTM14	-0.01563	-0.02344	0.83513	0.027
ATTM15	0.01128	0.01420	0.58903	0.010
ATTM17	-0.03036	-0.03369	0.45734	0.057
ATTM18	0.17946	0.15354	0.27179	1.207
ATTM19	0.00904	0.00636	0.18372	0.002
ATTM20	0.04920	0.06650	0.67818	0.222
ATTM21	-0.05001	-0.05744	0.48987	0.166
ATTM22	-0.06957	-0.09979	0.76393	0.503
ATTM23	0.02265	0.03266	0.77243	0.053
ATTM24	-0.03748	-0.04989	0.65810	0.125
ATTM25	0.09791	0.12635	0.61833	0.811
ATTM26	-0.03769	-0.03510	0.32200	0.062
ATTM28	-0.06348	-0.08360	0.64400	0.352
ATTM31	-0.12082	-0.11171	0.31744	0.632
ATTM32	-0.03126	-0.03606	0.49382	0.065
ATTM34	-0.06363	-0.09168	0.77076	0.424
ATTM36	0.12185	0.14345	0.51463	1.050

Fig. 16.2 Regression of probabilities on 36 attitudinal dimensions, based on SPSS step-regression program.

toward the company and the probability of their recommending the Mutual Insurance Co. to a friend as a place to work. The attitude and probability data served a variety of uses in analyzing the retention problem. The behavioralist suggested that these probabilities and attitudes could be related through regression analysis in a way that may reveal the attitudinal dimensions of the probabilities. The probabilities were regressed on the 36 attitudinal dimensions, using the SPSS step-regression program. The appropriate computer printout appears in Fig. 16.2. The probabilities were measured on a ten-point scale; the attitudes, on a six-point semantic differential scale. The variables in the equation are as follows:

Variable number	Scale anchors
10	Good/Poor customer orientation of the company
9	Good/Poor leadership by immediate sales manager
29	Good/Poor communication with the home office
16	Good/Poor on-the-job training
30	Acceptable/Excessive paperwork
12	Easy/Hard to get assistance from home office
27	Good/Poor communications with customer billing
33	Good/Poor communications with promotions department
35	Good/Poor communications with underwriting department

The mean value (X) of these variables is shown in the left column of the printout.

Make recommendations to the sales manager that are consistent with the findings. Note limitations in the findings. Indicate how the sales manager might use these findings to improve the probability of salespeople's recommending Mutual to their friends.

9. Dean & Wilson, Inc., is a small 20-year-old firm that manufactures replacement parts for several models of broadcloth looms and markets them to the Southern textile industry. Initially Dean sold the shop's entire output, and Wilson managed the manufacturing end (which at first consisted of a small machine shop). The firm's policy had been to concentrate on those parts which wear out most frequently and to undersell the loom manufacturers while maintaining an acceptable level of quality. The firm has prospered, and now Dean manages a direct sales force of 15 and has retained two manufacturer's representatives who call on the textile industry. (The nature of the product and market is such that distributors are not an alternative in this case.)

Wilson has recently retired, selling his interest to Dean. Dean, concerned that sales management takes too much of his time away from the overall direction of the firm and sensing that the sales effort needs some redirection, hired Harris, who has extensive industrial sales management experience. Harris's first assignment is to restructure the sales force for maximum profitability.

Harris has elected to use the Fogg and Rokus method and has developed the data shown in Tables 16.4 and 16.5 for a typical minor territory.

TABLE 16.4 Direct sales force

Account potential ($1000)	Number of accounts	Sales potential ($1000)	Calls/account/ year	Average penetration in percent	Average percent gross margin
100–300	6	1200	45	40	41
50–100	7	525	35	40	41
25–50	22	825	35	35	41
12–25	14	259	20	35	41
6–12	18	162	10	30	43
3–6	28	125	6	30	43
1.5–3	25	56	6	30	43
0.5–1.5	21	21	6	30	43
0–0.5	80	20	6	30	43

A Dean & Wilson direct salesperson can average 440 customer location calls per year, at an average total cost per call of $95 (includes salary, direct sales management overhead, travel and expenses, fringe benefits, and average training costs).

TABLE 16.5 All-representative organization

Account potential ($1000)	Number of accounts	Average sales potential/account ($1000)	Average percent penetration	Average percent gross margin
100–300	6	200.0	30	39
50–100	7	75.0	30	41
25–50	22	37.5	30	41
12–25	14	18.5	30	41
6–12	18	9.0	25	43
3–6	28	4.5	25	43
1.5–3	25	2.25	25	43
0.5–1.5	21	1.00	25	43
0–0.5	80	.25	25	43

Assume that manufacturers' representatives can average approximately the same number of calls per year as direct representatives.

a) Estimate the COM (contribution to operating margin) for: (1) an all-direct sales force, and (2) an all-representative sales force at a seven-percent commission rate.

b) Assume that a mixed system is being considered and estimate the break-even account size—that is, the point at which COM is the same for both direct and representative forces—using a ten-percent commission rate for representatives.

c) How many direct salespeople will be required?

d) Assuming that a field sales manager can satisfactorily supervise either five direct salespeople or seven manufacturer's representatives, what management structure is required?

NOTES

1. C. Rieser, "The Salesman Isn't Dead—He's Different," *Fortune* **66** (November 1962): 124–127ff.

2. This discussion and the examples below are based on "The New Supersalesman: Wired for Success," *Business Week*, January 6, 1973, pp. 44–49.

3. R. O. Loen, "Sales Managers Must Manage," *Harvard Business Review* **42** (May-June 1964): 107–114.

4. For a detailed discussion of selling organizations, *see* W. J. Stanton and R. H. Buskirk, *Management of the Sales Force*, 4th ed. (Homewood, Ill.: Richard D. Irwin, 1974), Chapters 4 and 5.

5. Used by permission of Charles H. Singler, General Sales Manager, Burroughs Wellcome Co., Inc. For an example of the duties and goals of a sales representative, *see* the Burroughs Wellcome case, Chapter 20.

6. C. D. Fogg and J. W. Rokus, "A Quantitative Method for Structuring a Profitable Sales Force," *Journal of Marketing* **37** (July 1973): 8–17.

7. *Ibid.*, p. 13

8. A switchover point is computed by C. E. Harris, Jr., and J. E. Hilliard, "Switchover for Bigger Profits," *Sales and Marketing Management*, November 8, 1976, pp. 47–48, using *units* per salesperson on the horizontal axis.

9. For a detailed discussion, *see* Stanton and Buskirk, *op. cit.*, Chapters 6 through 9.

10. R. S. Barrett, "Guide to Using Psychological Tests," *Harvard Business Review* **41** (September-October 1963): 138–146.

11. *Ibid.*, p. 140.

12. D. Mayer and H. M. Greenberg, "What Makes a Good Salesman?" *Harvard Business Review* **42** (July-August 1964): 119–125.

13. *Ibid.*

14. For a discussion of training programs and an elaboration of these questions, *see* Stanton and Buskirk, *op. cit.*, Chapters 11 and 12.

15. *See* "The New Supersalesman," *op. cit.*

16. C. Easingwood, "Heuristic Approach to Selecting Sales Regions and Territories," *Operations Research Quarterly* **24** (December 1973): 527–534.

17. L. M. Lodish, "Sales Territory Alignment to Maximize Profit," *Journal of Marketing Research* **12** (February 1975): 30–36.

18. W. J. Talley, "How to Design Sales Territories," *Journal of Marketing* **25** (January 1961): 7–13.

19. L. M. Lodish, "CALLPLAN: An Interactive Salesman's Call Planning System," *Management Science* **18** (December 1971): 25–40.

20. D. B. Montgomery, A. J. Silk, and C. E. Zaragoza, "A Multiple-Product Sales Force Allocation Model," *Management Science* **18** (December 1971): 3–24.

21. A. Parasuraman and R. L. Day, "A Management Oriented Model for Allocating Sales Effort," 1976, working paper.

22. L. M. Lodish, "'Vaguely Right' Approach to Sales Force Allocation," *Harvard Business Review* **52** (January-February 1974): 119–124.

23. S. W. Hess and S. A. Samuels, "Experiences with a Sales Districting Model: Criteria and Implementation," *Management Science* **18**, 4, Part II (December 1971): 41–54.

24. *Ibid.*, p. 43.

25. S. A. Washburn, "The Case of the Missing Incentive," *Sales and Marketing Management*, Special Report: Sales Force Compensation, August 23, 1976, pp. 5–9.

26. F. E. Webster, Jr., "Rationalizing Salesmen's Compensation Plans," *Journal of Marketing* **30** (January 1966): 55–58.

27. J. D. Snyder, "Ormont Espouses Compensation for Spouses," *Sales and Marketing Management*, Special Report: Sales Force Compensation, August 23, 1976, pp. 50–55.

28. J. U. Farley, "An Optimal Plan for Salesmen's Compensation," *Journal of Marketing Research* **1** (May 1964): 39–43.

29. C. B. Weinberg, "An Optimal Commission Plan for Salesmen's Control over Price," *Management Science* **21**, 8 (April 1975): 937–943.

30. D. A. Weeks, *Incentive Plan for Salesmen*, Personnel Policy Study No. 217 (New York: Conference Board, 1970).

31. A. H. Maslow, *Motivation and Personality*, 2d ed. (New York: Harper & Row, 1970).

32. G. A. Churchill, Jr., N. M. Ford, and O. C. Walker, Jr., "Motivating the Industrial Salesforce: The Attractiveness of Alternative Rewards," Report No. 76-115 (Cambridge, Mass.: Marketing Science Institute, October 1976).

33. A survey conducted by Roy W. Walters & Associates, as reported in the *Wall Street Journal*, December 28, 1976, p. 1.

34. This discussion is based on lectures given at the School of Business Administration, University of North Carolina, February 27 and November 4, 1976.

35. V. W. Kafka and J. H. Schaefer, *Open Management* (New York: Pitti Wyder, 1975).

36. *Measuring Salesmen's Performance*, Business Policy Study No. 114 (New York: Conference Board, 1965).

37. J. S. Schiff and M. Schiff, "New Sales Management Tool: ROAM," *Harvard Business Review* (July-August 1967): 59–66. Return on assets managed is used rather than return on investments to differentiate the active role of management from the role of the investor seeking a return from funds risked. See Chapter 13 for a discussion of return on investment.

38. G. D. Hughes, "A New Tool for Sales Managers," *Journal of Marketing Research* (May 1964): 32–38.

39. This discussion of call report is based on E. P. McGuire, *Salesmen's Call Reports* (New York: Conference Board, 1972).

SUGGESTED READINGS

Beswick, C. A., "Allocating Selling Effort Via Dynamic Programming," *Management Science* **23** (March 1977): 667–678.

Beswick, C. A., and D. W. Cravens, "A Multistage Decision Model for Salesforce Management," *Journal of Marketing Research* **14** (May 1977): 135–144.

Davis, O. A., and J. U. Farley, "Allocating Sales Force Effort with Commissions and Quotas," *Management Science* **18**, 4, Part II (December 1971): P-55–63.

Goodman, C. S., *Management of the Personal Selling Function* (New York: Holt, Rinehart and Winston, 1971), pp. 78–80.

Idelson, E. M., *Affirmative Action and Equal Employment: A Guidebook for Employers* (Washington, D.C.: United States Equal Employment Opportunity Commission, Volume 1, January 1974).

Lucas, H. C., C. B. Weinberg, and K. S. Clowes, "Sales Response as a Function of Territorial Potential and Sales Representative Workload," *Journal of Marketing Research* **12** (August 1976): 298–305.

Robinson, P. J., and B. Stidsen, *Personal Selling in a Modern Perspective* (Boston: Allyn and Bacon, 1967).

Sales Analysis, Business Policy Study No. 113 (New York: Conference Board, 1965).

Shapiro, B. P., "Manage the Customer, Not Just the Sales Force," *Harvard Business Review* (September-October 1974): 127–136.

————, *Sales Program Management: Formulation and Implementation* (New York: McGraw-Hill, 1976).

Shapiro, B. P., and R. S. Posner, "Making the Major Sale," *Harvard Business Review* (March-April, 1976): 68–78.

"Survey of Selling Costs," *Sales and Marketing Management*, February 21, 1977. (This survey is an annual feature.)

Webster, F. E., Jr., "Interpersonal Communication and Salesman Effectiveness," *Journal of Marketing* **32** (July 1968): 7–13.

Wotruba, T. R., *Sales Management: Planning Accomplishment and Evaluation* (New York: Holt, Rinehart and Winston, 1970).

CHAPTER 17

Marketing Strategies of an Intermediary – Retailers

LEARNING OBJECTIVES After studying this chapter you should:

1. Be aware of career opportunities in channels of distribution, particularly in retailing.
2. Know how department stores are organized.
3. Better understand the role of the retailer in the execution of a manufacturer's marketing strategy.
4. Understand how concepts such as benefit segmentation and success factors apply to retail establishments.
5. Understand the forces that keep retailing in a continuous state of development.
6. Be able to define and use the following concepts:

Merchandise management	Department store success	Off-balance sheet lease
Open-to-buy position	factors	financing
Benefit segmentation	Gravitational models	Regional shopping center
Store promotion	Profile of the population	Discount department store
Store operations	Characteristics of the site	Variety chains
Store personnel	Internal and external	Specialty mail-order houses
Store finance and control	shrinkage	Wheel of retailing

SOME STRATEGIC QUESTIONS FOR OPENERS

For the retailer:

1. Do our success factors meet the needs of our market? If not, should we change the factors or our location?
2. How will the dynamics of retailing affect our strategies?
3. Can we apply new marketing concepts, such as benefit segmentation, to retailing?

For the manufacturer:

1. Do the retailers in our channels meet our needs? Have they kept up with changes in the market?
2. Do the retailers perform all the functions we need, such as personal selling, delivery, installation, and service?

CAREERS IN RETAILING One of the many stories told about Ben Franklin is that his father took him on a tour of all the trades so that he might find his career. Given his success in so many areas, he must have liked them all. In a small way we have been on a tour of careers in marketing management. Like most textbooks on the subject, we have spent most of our time on the marketing activities of the manufacturer, as viewed through the eyes of the marketing planner. We have differed in that in Chapter 15 we saw the career opportunities in advertising agencies. But this still neglects the marketing career opportunities in 1.5 million service establishments, 276,000 wholesale establishments, and 1.7 million retail establishments.[1] Rather than treat all these establishments superficially, this chapter will examine the marketing activities and strategies of one group, retailers. To further sharpen our focus, we will examine the department store because it is so familiar and accounts for ten percent of retail sales.

The rapid development of the department store in the last two decades has made it an exciting career opportunity for business students. In this chapter it will become apparent that careers in retailing are not limited to marketing. Majors in accounting, finance, personnel, and operations management may enjoy the excitement and creativity of retailing as well.

To help us understand the complexity of department stores we begin with a discussion of several typical organizational forms. In examining the functional areas of these forms, we will see that the marketing principles we learned in earlier chapters apply to retailing. An examination of the *success factors* of retailing will help to explain recent developments in department stores and suggest future changes.[2]

DEPARTMENT STORE ORGANIZATIONAL STRUCTURES The basic task in the management of a department store is the efficient use of people, merchandise, creativity, and property to produce a profit. In 1974 it was a $52 billion industry that employed 1.7 million people.[3] We will examine how these tasks are accomplished by single- and multiunit stores.

Single-Unit Organizations The single-unit store is generally organized around two broad functional areas—merchandising/promotion and store operations. The director of merchandising and promotion supervises the merchandising manager, who is responsible for merchandise management, which includes buying, selling, personal shopping, comparison shopping, unit control, and merchandise budget supervision. The merchandising manager also supervises the manager of promotion/publicity, who is responsible for advertising, store displays, special publicity, and press releases. The remainder of the store's activities—workrooms, adjustments, delivery, receiving, stockrooms, protection service, nonmerchandise purchasing, and expense budget supervision—are under the director of store operations.[4] In a small department store the president is likely to handle financial matters, and the merchandising/promotion director will be responsible for personnel matters. In a larger single-unit store these two activities will have their own directors, who will report to the president.

Medium-Size and Multiunit Department Stores The medium-size multiunit department store structure begins to show the specialization that is necessary to run the modern, complex department store. The organizational charts for the very large department stores represent further refinements on the organization chart that appears in Fig. 17.1.[5] Each of the five functions in this figure will be examined briefly.

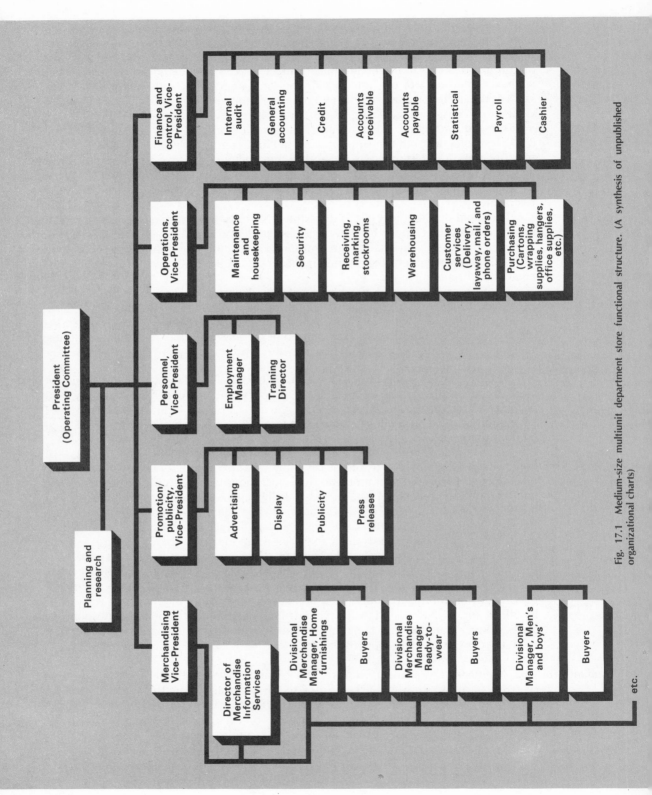

Fig. 17.1 Medium-size multiunit department store functional structure. (A synthesis of unpublished organizational charts)

Merchandising.   Merchandising is the central activity of a department store. The retail buyer is the counterpart of the product manager in manufacturing and the account executive in advertising. Buyers are responsible for assessing the market, positioning the department, selecting sources for goods, buying, arranging the display of merchandise, setting prices, and determining markdowns. Thus the buyer is the marketing planner for a department. The department will probably be run as a profit center on a season-by-season basis, so the buyer will be held accountable for a profit goal. The buyer reports to a divisional merchandise manager, who is the retail counterpart of the group product manager.

The buyer must be aware of fashion and price trends. He or she gathers information externally from buying trips to domestic fashion centers and foreign markets and from trade publications. Internally, the buyer is supported with management information systems and feedback from sales personnel. Competitive information is provided by merchandise information services, which supervise comparison shopping. Comparison shoppers gather data on styles, color, and prices of similar merchandise in competitive stores, usually every two weeks.

The buyer develops a budget plan which controls the activities of the department. The heart of the plan to the buyer is his or her open-to-buy (O-T-B) position, which is that dollar amount of the merchandise buying commitment allocated to the department. As merchandise is bought, the O-T-B is reduced. When the merchandise is sold, the O-T-B is increased. The O-T-B is reviewed monthly with the divisional merchandise manager.

Sales and gross margin goals will be planned by the buyer and the divisional manager. In a more sophisticated store, the budget typically includes space charges for the sales floor and stockrooms and an interest charge for the investment in inventory and receivables. Operating within these constraints, the buyer adjusts the merchandise, the advertising, and the selling effort to reach the assigned goal.[6]

Some of the demand-analysis concepts that have been used by manufacturers (see Chapters 6 and 7) are being applied to the development of department store strategies. Benefit segmentation, which has been widely applied to the marketing of package goods, has been applied to a department store. In Table 17.1 we see that a store using this approach identified four segments—store-loyal, convenience shopper, compulsive

TABLE 17.1   Retail store customer benefit segments

Segment name	Store-loyal	Convenience shopper	Compulsive shopper	Price buyer
Principal benefit sought	High-quality merchandise	Fast shopping	Recreation	Good value
Personality or life-style	Conservative	Sociable	Hedonist	Cognitive
Behavioral characteristics	Shops predominantly at one or two stores	Shops at stores near home	Shops in a wide variety of stores	Usually tries several stores
Stores favored	Old, established stores	Stores with ample parking and fast service	New stores	Discount stores
Demography	Older/upscale	Middle class	Young married	Upper education

Based on private communication with Russell I. Haley, June 1976.

shopper, and price buyer. Each of these segments has a different profile for the benefit sought, life-style, behavioral characteristics, stores favored, and demographics. This information could be very important to the positioning of a new store or the repositioning of an old store. It could also help buyers in their complex decisions.

Benefit segmentation analysis will probably replace the concepts of convenience shopping and specialty goods, which were used for years to describe the behavior of consumers in the marketplace. McNair and May, two experts on emerging trends in retailing, concluded that this classification of goods was no longer useful because it could not handle the complexity of buying motives and because the dynamics of channels required too many exceptions to make it fit reality.[7] They concluded that instead of having classifications of goods or stores there should be categories of consumers' buying attitudes. In Table 17.1 the goods-classification concept has been replaced by the benefit sought.

The buyer's job has become so complex that there are good reasons to consider dividing it into more homogeneous functions.[8] Buying and selling require different abilities and personalities. In the present arrangement, buying tends to overshadow selling. Modern merchandise-control systems can coordinate these activities instead of depending on coordination through a single person. Specialization permits economies of scale in buying and selling. Splitting these functions, however, makes it difficult to use the department as a profit center.

Promotion/publicity. The promotion/publicity department is responsible for store promotion, advertising, and display. It coordinates special events, fashion shows, exhibits, and general programs to build store image. It works closely with the buyers on designing and placing advertising. Its creative staff is responsible for window dressing, store displays, and shelf designs.

Personnel. The employment manager is responsible for establishing uniform policies across stores with regard to hiring, compensation, benefits, evaluation, and record keeping. The training director is responsible for all training policies, standards, and program development. In a large multiunit firm, each of these activities will have its own manager.

Operations. The operations identified in Fig. 17.1 are self-explanatory. In brief, the operations department is responsible for the merchandise from the moment it arrives at the receiving dock until it is accepted by the customer. In addition, this department provides support services such as maintenance, security, and purchasing.

Modern materials-handling methods, computerized inventory control, and the high cost of space at store locations have resulted in the emergence of centralized receiving and distribution centers. Such a center minimizes the cross-shipment of merchandise among stores and reduces improper deliveries. Economies of scale at the central location are possible, thereby reducing the handling costs for each branch store.

Finance and control. Some of the activities of the finance and control department have characteristics that are unique to retailing. Internal auditing verifies sales and inventory reports. General accounting is concerned with budgets, forecasts, daily summaries, and tax reports. The credit department is concerned with billing, customer credit, collections, and adjustments. Accounts receivable activities include billing charge customers. Accounts payable functions include the matching of invoices, shipping documents, receiving documents, and original store orders. The computer has greatly facilitated the development of statistical reports to guide the buyer. Payroll and cashier functions are self-explanatory.

Planning and research. The planning and research department examines trends in population, income, and buying habits that may affect the stores' location and operation. These studies will affect site locations, buying decisions, advertising, and operations.

SUCCESS-FACTOR STRATEGIES The concept of success factors, which was discussed in Chapter 4, applies to department stores as well as to manufacturing and service organizations. After extensive interviews with the chief operating officers of major retail department stores, Applebee and Nitzberg identified six success factors: location, merchandising, personnel, layout, general management, and finance.[9]

Location of Stores The population density and income level of the neighborhoods around a store are the most crucial factors in determining the traffic through the store. A typical department store will draw 75 percent of its sales from a radius of 15 miles. The radius of a discount store is five miles. To succeed, the store must satisfy the needs of a target market segment in the area. This segment must be large enough to support the store.

As population, income, and needs change, the department store must change its merchandising strategy or abandon the location. In Chicago Heights, Illinois, for example, stores lowered their price and quality strategies to match a shift in population. If such a strategy is counter to the store's image, it may decide to sublet the location to a retailer who can better meet the needs of the market.

The single, free-standing store seems to be a strategy of the past. Today a successful department store must be located in a complex of complementing stores that constitute a major drawing area for shoppers. The most successful concept has been the regional mall, which contains several anchor department stores, such as Sears Roebuck & Co. and J. C. Penney Co., surrounded by specialty and service stores.

Stores that have failed to get good locations face crises. Because many metropolitan areas have more shopping malls than the market will support, stores' needs cannot be met by building a new mall. Instead, they must buy into a mall through the acquisition of existing companies or their locations. The crucial nature of location as a success factor became apparent when W. T. Grant went bankrupt. The two major reasons were poor locations and a poor merchandising strategy.[10]

The selection of store locations is a combination of art and science. Mathematical geographers have contributed gravitational models that measure the attraction of a store to its trading area. The size of the trading area has been related to the square footage of selling area, the mileage from the store,[11] the driving time, and the psychologically perceived distance.[12] Surveys are used to locate buyers on trading-area maps.[13] Many locational decisions are based on an experienced executive's judgment after driving around the trading area. This approach is based on the assumption that many of the subtleties of an area cannot be reduced to measures and models.

The criteria for selecting a site include the *profile of the population* as measured by its age distribution, the size and stability of its income, buying habits (e.g., willingness to travel to shop), and needs (e.g., position in the family life cycle). *Characteristics of the site* include the progressiveness of local government, competition, and present and future traffic patterns.[14]

Operations research methods are being used by retailers to aid in the controlling and scheduling of new stores. PERT (Program Evaluation and Review Technique), which finds the most time-consuming path in a network of tasks, is used to control building projects. PERT enables the retailer to plan the purchase and delivery of fixtures, equipment, and merchandise inventories to coincide with the completion of sections of the store.[15]

Merchandising   *Merchandising* is the selection and promotion of goods to meet the needs of the market. *Price*, *location*, and *timing* are important elements of merchandising, which is sometimes described as having the *right goods at the right time at the right price.*

Many of the merchandise techniques that we now take for granted were great innovations at one time. John Wanamaker, a Philadelphia dry-goods merchant, introduced the concept of fixed prices for his goods because he was unable to hire clerks who could bargain. Prepackaged grocery products in consumer sizes represented an advancement from the use of cracker barrels, butter tubs, flour bins, and potato sacks. Aaron Montgomery Ward gained farmers' confidence in his mail-order business with the innovation of a money-back guarantee. In 1875 a stockroom boy named F. W. Woolworth suggested an improved display of merchandise so that the customer could see and handle the goods. People responded by buying more of the products they could see and handle. When he opened his own store, Woolworth introduced another innovation—departmentalization. The logical extension of these innovations was taken by a cost-conscious food merchant, Clarence Sanders. In 1916 he moved the combination cash register and wrapping desk from the side of his Piggly Wiggly Memphis store to the front door. This became the first checkout counter and the beginning of self-service.[16]

Communication with consumers, vendors, and other branch stores is a vital element in a merchandising strategy. Rapid shifts in consumer tastes must be detected to avoid overstocking and costly price markdowns. New sources of supply must be sought so that the best values will be available. Because fads and fashions vary among branches, rapid communication among branches is needed to permit the shifting of inventory. Daily branch sales reports are now possible with computerized inventory control. These reports and centralized distribution make it possible to match colors and styles to regional demand patterns.

Timing is important in the pricing element of merchandising strategies. Taking the markdown too soon forgoes profit. An insufficient markdown or one taken too late may not clear the inventory soon enough for the new merchandise, thereby increasing investment and space charges and requiring a final markdown at distress prices.

A clear store *image* is grounded in a clear merchandising strategy. The W. T. Grant image became blurred when the chain attempted to shift from an image of limited-price items in smallwares, wearing apparel, and soft goods to that of a department store. Customers who viewed Grant as a variety store were not willing to buy big-ticket items such as furniture and appliances.[17]

A successful merchandising strategy must attack the problem of shrinkage—paper, internal, and external. *Paper shrinkage* occurs when markdowns, returns, and transfers are not recorded properly in inventory records. This shrinkage can be reduced by simplifying the inventory documents and training sales clerks.

Internal shrinkage requires a system to properly identify employees, vendors, guests, and persons in the stock and loading areas. Some retail organizations require store employees to take a lie detector test. Other stores attempt to instill loyalty in their employees.

External shrinkage due to shoplifting was estimated to be worth $4.8 billion in 1973.[18] The best defense seems to be full prosecution of the professional shoplifter. Detective agencies, closed-circuit television, and radioactive markings have been used to reduce shoplifting. This reduction is necessary in many competitive fields of retailing where both the profit margin and the shrinkage rates are three percent of sales.[19]

Quantitative and computer methods have been used to develop better merchandising strategies. Rapid changes in product assortments, the opening of branches, and competition forced merchandisers to abandon old rules of thumb and to adopt more rigorous methods of analysis. Cash registers that are tied to computers simplify the daily reporting of sales, margins, inventory turnover, markups, reorder points, and inventory status, as well as financial and accounting functions.

Decision models are used to help the buyer estimate future sales under various states of the environment. Buyers at Dayton's, a division of Dayton-Hudson Department Stores, concluded that a decision model helped them to forecast the outcome of their decision.[20] Decision models have also been applied to the strategies of the allocation of shelf space to products[21] and the selection of suppliers.[22] A *retail patronage model* has been developed to estimate the effects of promotional strategies on new and old customers.[23]

Personnel "There probably isn't a major industry around where management and people are more important than in retailing."[24] The effective utilization of people is necessary because 70 percent of the operating expenses go to personnel costs. Sales clerks, if properly motivated, can perform the expanded roles of detecting shifts in needs and styles, thereby providing vital information for the buyer.

Store Layout The store layout, an extension of the merchandise strategy, helps to create the store image. The store layout should match the self-image and mood of the shopper. The image quickly conveys the store value of quality, discount, or cheap. Some store designers think that the design should mirror the living room of the store's target market so that the customer feels comfortable, not threatened, while shopping.

The store layout will determine the traffic pattern, which in turn will determine the location of merchandise. The items with the greatest sales per square foot tend to be the convenience items that require little deliberation on the part of the shopper. These items will be placed on the high-traffic aisle on the main floor. Customers do not want to be hurried when purchasing high-fashion clothing or furniture, so these can be located on the upper floors; customers are willing to spend the search time for such major purchases. Credit and collection offices are usually on the top floor, thereby taking the customer through many departments, with the hope that this induced traffic will create additional sales.

General Management The successful management of a department store must excell in satisfying customer needs, recognizing competitive behavior, and *being unique*. A store is unique if it meets the needs of its target market better than any other store does. When Tiffany's changed owners, it had a giant sale. Chauffeur-driven limousines arrived at the front door to carry away expensive silver pieces that had been in stock for years. This merchandise did not fit the self-image of the target market for Tiffany's. In this case the uniqueness was merchandise assortment. In other stores it may be location, services, or price.

Competition must be defined carefully and monitored frequently. Comparative shopping provides input. Buyers watch competitors' buyers (or their agents) at the buying market. Some stores have a "battleground map" which locates competitors and their behavior along the main traffic patterns to the store.

Finance   Department stores require efficient capital management through capital budgeting, working-capital management, inventory control, and trade-offs between risk and return. Property-lease financing and captive-finance companies have been key strategies for some firms.

Property-lease financing occurs when the buildings and fixtures are built by a developer and leased to the store. This removes the mortgage debt from the store's balance sheet, giving it an apparent healthier debt level. This *off-balance sheet lease financing* has contributed to the rapid expansion of many retailers. Internally generated capital can then be used for expanded inventories and accounts receivable. The negative side of the leasing arrangement is that the store may be committed to a long-term arrangement when its target population moves to another area. Downgrading its merchandising strategy will create inefficiencies and blurred images. If the store were owned instead of leased, it might be possible to sell the location to a retailer whose strategy is directed toward the entering population.

Leading banks and other financial institutions are now asking for the "true debt level" of department stores. A study of 20 of the 50 largest department stores revealed that long-term leases were almost triple the long-term debt levels that appeared on the balance sheet.[25] Recently the Financial Accounting Standards Board, in its Statement number 13, requires firms to capitalize the present value of their minimum annual lease obligation on their balance sheets.

The captive-finance company is typically a nonconsolidated, wholly owned subsidiary of the parent retailer. Its assets are largely the customer accounts receivable of the partner retailer, which it buys with funds borrowed from banks. The retailer can then use the cash to invest in inventories and other working-capital needs. The banks are willing to lend funds at a higher leverage ratio because the receivables are liquid and are good collateral.[26]

The computer has played an important role in the management of department store finances. Abraham & Strauss, a New York department store chain, uses two IBM 370/145 computers to handle 800,000 charge and credit customer accounts and to provide daily sales reports for 200 departments by product categories. All of these reports are accomplished in a few hours at night, a task that would be impossible without the computer. These reports enable merchandising managers to make key inventory, pricing, and buying decisions. Computer simulations have been developed to enable merchandise managers to test the effect of their decisions on return on investment.[27]

THE CONTINUOUS DEVELOPMENT OF RETAILING   The dynamics of retailing can be illustrated with a few statistics. During the period from 1939 to 1972, the population of the United States increased 62 percent, but the number of retail stores increased only 9 percent, from 1.76 to 1.91 million.[28] This small increase is the net change of many dramatic increases and decreases. For example, increases were posted by department stores (88 percent), automotive dealers (102 percent), apparel and accessory stores (21 percent), furniture and home furnishings stores (110 percent), sporting goods stores (643 percent), mail-order houses (2000 percent, from 400 to 8000 houses), and direct-selling organizations (2700 percent, from 5200 to 141,300 organizations). Food stores declined from 546,000 to 267,000, a reduction of 51 percent. The general store went from 40,000 to zero.[29]

The dynamics of retailing from the late 1940s to 1978 can be traced to a variety of forces. On the demand side, the early 1950s represented the release of pent-up demand following World War II and a rapid increase in the rates of marriage, births, and housing starts. There was the movement toward the suburbs. Television shifted the marketing power back to the manufacturer (see Chapter 14). Thus personal selling by the retailer was greatly reduced, which added to the impetus of self-service stores. The availability of automobiles made possible the regional shopping center and discount stores. The car was important in the latter case, because discount stores do not deliver. Anticipation of future changes in retailing requires an understanding of the changes from 1950 to 1978.

Selected Developments from 1950 to 1978.[30] Because we are focusing on the development of department stores, we will first examine changes that took place among stores that sold shopping goods and general merchandise. The most dramatic changes were the advent of department store branches, regional shopping centers, discount department stores, and variety chains. Then we will briefly examine the rapid growth in specialty mail-order houses and in-home selling.

Department store branches. Many department stores were reluctant to open branches in the suburbs because their organizations and operations were based on the concept of a single, centralized store that had a monopoly advantage by being located along routes of public transportation. The movement of the population to the suburbs, the increase in the number of automobiles, and the demise of public transportation changed the buying habits of the public, however. Nonetheless, many central-city department stores were unwilling to change their organizations and operations. As a result, some 75-year-old firms went out of business. Combining the buying and selling functions under the buyer made it extremely difficult to decentralize to branches. Thus the movement to the suburbs required new organizational designs that would either separate these functions or make it possible to coordinate them at the branch level. These forces led to the development of regional department store chains. Stores had 70,000 to 250,000 square feet of floor space, about one-third that of the central-city store. Buying and merchandising were centralized, but selling was decentralized to the branch and thereby separated from the buying function. Branches from these regional department stores served as anchors in the next development, the regional shopping center.

Regional shopping centers. There are three strategies in building a shopping center. The first, most familiar one is to build to match the existing population and traffic patterns. The second strategy builds its own population and traffic pattern by building the community as well as shopping facilities. The third strategy reuses existing locations. In each case site-location criteria include population demographics, purchasing power, population density, driving time, and media availability, especially newspaper circulation.

Columbia, Maryland, illustrates the second strategy. Its shopping center is the nucleus for residences, schools, offices, professional services, recreational facilities, and industrial and trade establishments.

The strategy of reusing present locations takes many forms. In some cases the urban renewal of downtown areas means tearing down existing structures and rebuilding a system of shopping facilities, offices, hotels, restaurants, and tourist attractions.

Another approach is to build a mall around existing downtown department stores, as was done successfully in Rochester, New York. Another reuse strategy is to turn nonretailing structures into stores. The Ghiradelli chocolate factory became the focus for Ghiradelli Square in San Francisco. The Cannery, also in San Francisco, was transformed from an old canning factory into a collection of specialty shops, boutiques, and restaurants. Both facilities have become tourist attractions.

The Johns Landing Project in Portland, Oregon, differs from the Rochester and San Francisco reuse projects in that when it is completed, it will include a community of 2500 persons, a captive market for the retail facilities. The project includes the old Portland Furniture Building, which contained 100,000 square feet of floor space. The building was turned into specialty shops, gourmet food stores, and restaurants.

New shopping centers, which are built on previously vacant land, continue to evolve. The pattern now is to have two or three anchor department stores. The malls tend to range from one-half million to one and one-half million square feet of selling space. The newer malls also serve as community centers. Eastridge Shopping Center in San Jose, California, has an ice skating rink; the Galleria in Houston, Texas, includes an athletic club.

Discount department stores.   There were many forces in the early 1950s that produced the rapid development of discount department stores. Supermarket food stores had trained the consumer in the concepts of self-service, rapid checkout, cash payment, and no delivery, in exchange for a lower price. In addition to the postwar pent-up demand, education, the mass media, more leisure, and geographic and social mobility had expanded buyers' expectations to the point where expectations exceeded income. Thus buyers were anxious to get more for their money. Inflationary forces in the early 1950s also contributed to the desire to shop for lower prices. Geographic mobility had reduced loyalty to stores that the family had patronized for generations. Once the young family was out of the range of previous stores, it was free to shop as it pleased. The new life-style was a busy one, so time became a factor. One-stop shopping and rapid checkouts became important. By the 1970s, the discount department stores had an annual volume exceeding that of the national and regional department stores (excluding Sears, Ward, and Penney).[31]

The earliest discount department stores followed a strategy of volume sales at low prices and did not give priority to the quality of merchandise, location, or store furnishings. This image changed quickly when firms such as S. S. Kresge Company entered the discount field with its K-Mart division. It became the largest discount department store through a strategy that included careful market research and site selection, aggressive pricing, merchandising "value," strong customer service, and intensive management training.[32]

Discount department stores that want to compete with the leaders—Kresge, Gibson's, Zayre's, and King's—are following all or part of the following strategies. They offer quality items, primarily nationally advertised brands at a value. Storewide discounts are offered at all times. Stores are clustered in a market to gain economies of scale in advertising, distribution, and supervision. Liberal refund policies are offered.

By following these strategies, the discount department store is approaching the strategy of the regular department store. But there is one noticeable difference— location. The discount department stores tend to be single, free-standing stores near major thoroughfares. This locational strategy lowers overhead and keeps the discounter free from merchandising restrictions in the shopping center lease, but it means that the retailer must generate traffic. To accomplish this, the store may have to advertise extensively, thereby drawing traffic from shopping centers. The discount department store typically will team up with a strong grocery outlet adjoining the facility.

Variety chains. The early variety chains, such as Woolworth's and Grant's, limited themselves to merchandise that would sell for under a dollar, but inflation made this merchandising strategy obsolete, and consumer demand had expanded to large items—television, driers, and hi-fi sets. Merchandising these large items is quite different from selling small household items. Thus the old organizations were obsolete. Kresge responded by moving into the discount department store field with its K-Mart chain. Woolworth responded with its Woolco discount department stores. At first the regular department stores underestimated the success of this movement into their field of retailing. Those variety-chain operations that did not make this shift have a very doubtful future.[33]

Specialty mail-order houses. The large growth in the mail-order houses can be traced to sporting goods, outdoor equipment, gifts, gadgets, apparel, fruits, gourmet foods, seeds, and other items that are not readily available to consumers. The rapid growth of this form of retailing suggests that it is meeting a special need for the consumer.[34] Indeed, the leisure market seems to explain much of this growth.

In-home selling. The term "in-home selling" is used because it covers more than door-to-door selling. "Party selling" is used in the fields of health and beauty aids and cookware. A customer acts as a hostess for the salesperson's presentation and receives a commission on all sales. Party selling has contributed to the rapid growth in selling in the home.

Food stores The population increased 62 percent, the number of items increased from a few hundred to 8000 per store, but the number of food stores decreased by 51 percent. The explanation for this seeming inconsistency is larger stores and self-service.

Recent developments in food retailing have included food discounting and 24-hour stores. The mid-1970s saw the development of "hypermarket" stores. Meijer, Inc., had a 245,000-square-foot supermarket that used bins to hold the food and metal racks to stack higher. A 6600-square-foot furniture department had carpets displayed on a conveyor that works like a Ferris wheel.[35]

Take-out food departments were added to supermarkets in response to the rapid growth in franchised food retailers such as Hardees and McDonald's.[36] Thus the supermarkets have attempted to continue their success by building larger stores, carrying nonfood items, and adding departments to meet competition head-on. This movement toward a "superstore" is a strategy aimed at reducing distribution costs, finding competitive advantages in food offerings, and diversifying into nonfood items in an effort to reverse the down-trend in profits and return on net worth even though sales have been increasing.[37]

During this discussion of the life cycles of retail institutions, the term "wheel of retailing" has been avoided. In the early stages the new institutions are low-service, low-cost operations. Costs and services increase as competition increases. "Wheel of retailing" was used to describe this evolution by Professor Malcolm P. McNair. Recently he concluded that the term is too narrow and too superficial to explain the changes among retail institutions. "Such a change is clearly an amalgam of many factors and an integral part of an evolving competitive economy."[38]

SUMMARY   Retailing provides many diverse career opportunities because competition has forced retailers to adopt more sophisticated management techniques. The proliferation of store branches has produced the need for decentralized decision structures, which require more broadly trained managers at the local level. This chapter focuses on strategies in department stores. The management task in these stores is the efficient use of people, merchandise, creativity, and property to produce a profit.

Five basic functions—merchandising, publicity, personnel, operations, and finance/control—are performed by all department stores. The arrangement of these functions, however, varies according to the size of the store and the number of branches.

The traditional organizational designs have placed buying and selling under the control of the buyer. When branch stores are opened, the selling function tends to be decentralized to the branch, but the buying function remains centralized. The department store buyer performs many of the same planning activities as the brand manager. Techniques that were developed in the packaged-goods industry, such as benefit segmentation, have been applied to retail analysis as well. Benefit segmentation may replace the goods classification as a means for explaining shopping behavior.

The success factors for department stores have been identified as location, merchandising, personnel, layout, general management, and finance. Stores having good competitive strategies for each of these factors have enjoyed profitable growth during the last 25 years. The failure to compete on one or two key factors has driven some department stores out of business, however.

The competitive nature of retailing has kept it in a continuous state of development. Some of the changes prior to 1950 were examined in Chapter 14. Changes came rapidly from the late 1940s through the mid-1970s because of changes in the characteristics of demand and competition within retailing. A burst of demand followed World War II and was accompanied by new family formations, inflation, and heightened expectations. Self-service, the movement toward the suburbs, the automobile, and the loss of the selling function to television stimulated major changes in the organization and operations of retailing. These forces led to the development of department store branches, regional shopping centers, discount department stores, and new forms of variety chains. The rapid rise in the specialty mail-order houses and in-home selling was probably due to a desire for more convenience and an assortment of goods that were not available through other means. Self-service and larger stores were the major innovations in food retailing. During the mid-1970s the movement was toward "superstores" in an attempt to reverse a downward trend in supermarket profits.

DISCUSSION QUESTIONS

1. How does centralization of buying and distribution affect the organizational structure of the department store?

2. How can management centralize activities into a limited group of people and remain flexible in its operations?

3. As economic conditions change, such as the recession of 1974–75, how will the six success factors need to be adapted by management?

4. As a consumer, you probably shop in a regular full-fashion and/or discount department store. How do you evaluate the trade-offs between service and price?

5. What quantitative techniques have you been exposed to that could be implemented in a retail department store environment? What would be the benefits relative to the cost of implementation?

6. What will be the next major development in retailing? How will present institutions be affected?

7. What sources of long-term capital are available to retailers to help finance expansion?

8. What are the issues involved in separating buying and selling activities?

9. What are the success factors in operating a retail department store? How do merchants control them?

10. How do regional shopping centers influence the communities in which they are situated?

NOTES

1. *U.S. Bureau of the Census, Statistical Abstract for the United States: 1976*, 97th ed. (Washington, D.C.: Government Printing Office, 1976), p. 798.

2. The author is indebted to Stanley Nitzberg, M.B.A., for sharing his research and retail and banking experiences for this chapter.

3. *Standard and Poors Industrial Survey*, 1974, p. R 127.

4. D. J. Duncan, C. F. Phillips, and S. C. Hollander, *Modern Retailing Management*, 8th ed. (Homewood, Ill.: Richard D. Irwin, 1972), p. 160.

5. For a detailed discussion of organizational structures, *see ibid.*, Chapter 7.

6. For an example of the use of regression and linear programming techniques to aid in this allocation, *see* G. D. Hughes and W. R. Bishop, Jr., "Some Quantitative Aids to Merchandise Management," *Journal of Retailing* (Fall 1967): 39–49.

7. M. P. McNair and E. G. May, *The Evolution of Retail Institutions in the United States*, Report 76-100 (Cambridge, Mass.: Marketing Science Institute, April 1976).

8. Duncan, Phillips, and Hollander, *op. cit.*, p. 169.

9. E. Applebee and S. Nitzberg, "Factors Contributing to the Successful Operation of a Retail Department Store." (Research paper, August 16, 1974.)

10. S. Slom and K. Rothmyer, "Retailer on the Rocks," *Wall Street Journal*, October 3, 1975, p. 28.

11. W. J. Reilly, *Methods of Study of Retail Relationships*, Research Monograph No. 4., Bulletin No. 2944 (Austin: University of Texas, Bureau of Business Research, 1929); A. F. Jung, "Is Reilly's Law of Retail Gravitation Always True?" *Journal of Marketing* (October 1959): 62–63.

12. D. B. MacKay, R. W. Olshavsky, and G. Sentell, "Cognitive Maps and Spatial Behavior of Consumers," *Geographical Analysis* 7 (January 1975): 19–34.

13. W. Applebaum, "Methods for Determining Store Trade Areas, Market Penetration, and Potential Sales," *Journal of Marketing Research* 3 (May 1966): 127–141.

14. For additional discussions and citations, *see* Duncan, Phillips, and Hollander, *op. cit.*, Chapter 4; J. E. Sueflow, *Market Potential—Its Theory and Application*, Wisconsin Commerce Papers, Vol. III, No. 3 (Madison: Bureau of Business Research and Service, 1967); D. L. Huff, "Defining and Establishing a Trading Area," *Journal of Marketing* 28 (July 1964): 34–38; L. W. Stern and A. I. El-Ansary, *Marketing Channels* (Englewood Cliffs, N.J.: Prentice-Hall, 1977); and W. Applebaum, *Store Location Strategy Cases* (Reading, Mass.: Addison-Wesley, 1968).

15. M. S. Moyer, "Management Science in Retailing," *Journal of Marketing* 36 (January 1972): 3–6.

16. J. J. Kiety, "8 Great Innovations in Modern Merchandising," *Sales Management*, December 6, 1963, pp. 41–43.

17. Slom and Rothmyer, *op. cit.*

18. "To Catch a Thief," *Newsweek*, September 23, 1974, p. 27.

19. *Fairchild Financial Manual—Retail Industry, 1974* (Chicago: Fairchild Publications, 1974), pp. 1–5.

20. W. Rudelius, J. Saraph, and B. Sonne, "A Computer Assisted Planning System to Aid Retail Buyers," Working Paper No. 18 (Minneapolis: Center for Experimental Studies in Business, University of Minnesota Graduate School of Business, December 1973).

21. R. C. Curhan, "Shelf-Space Allocation and Profit Maximization in Mass Retailing," *Journal of Marketing* 37 (July 1973): 54–60.

22. J. S. Berens, "A Decision Matrix Approach to Supplier Selection," *Journal of Retailing* (Winter 1971–72): 47–53.

23. D. B. Brown, "Retail Patronage Modelling," working paper (Cambridge, Mass.: Arthur D. Little, April 23, 1974).

24. "25th Annual Industry Report," *Forbes Magazine*, January 1, 1973, p. 166.

25. Unpublished study by Stanley Nitzberg of the 10-K reports, as filed with the Securities and Exchange Commission, January 1975.

26. This point is examined by W. G. Lewellen, "Finance Subsidiaries and Corporate Borrowing Capacity," *Financial Management* 1, 1 (Spring 1972): 11, 21–31.

27. D. J. Sweeney, "Improving the Profitability of Retail Merchandising Decisions," *Journal of Marketing* 37 (January 1973): 60–68.

28. McNair and May, *op. cit.*, p. 6.

29. For a discussion of the economic forces of retailing, *see* D. J. Dalrymple and D. L. Thompson, *Retailing, an Economic View* (New York: Free Press, 1969).

30. This section draws on the report by McNair and May, *op. cit.*, research conducted by Stanley Nitzberg, and unpublished research by the author.

31. McNair and May, *op. cit.*, p. 47.

32. "Keeping Up with Kresge," *Business Week*, October 19, 1974, p. 70.

33. McNair and May, *op. cit.*, p. 48.

34. *Ibid.*, pp. 49–50.

35. "America's 1st hypermarket," *Chain Store Age Executive* (March 1975): 25–27.

36. P. E. McGuire, *Franchised Distribution*, Report No. 523 (New York: Conference Board, 1971).

37. W. J. Salmon, R. D. Buzzell, and S. G. Cort, "The Super-Store—Strategic Implications for the Seventies" (Cambridge, Mass.: Marketing Science Institute, 1972), commissioned by *Family Circle Magazine*.

38. McNair and May, *op. cit.*, p. 145.

SUGGESTED READINGS

Dickinson, R. A., *Retail Management: A Channels Approach* (Belmont, Calif.: Wadsworth, 1974).

Larson, C. M., R. E. Weigand, and J. S. Wright, *Basic Retailing* (Englewood Cliffs, N.J.: Prentice-Hall, 1976).

Lowden, J. A., "Valuation of Shopping Centers," *Appraisal Journal* 35 (April 1967): 232–243.

Montgomery, D. B., "New Product Distribution: An Analysis of Supermarket Buyer Decisions," *Journal of Marketing Research* (August 1975): 255–264.

CHAPTER 18

International Marketing Strategies

LEARNING OBJECTIVES After studying this chapter you should:

1. Understand the incentives for international marketing.
2. Know the various ways in which a firm may engage in international marketing.
3. Be aware of how the situation analysis differs for international marketing.
4. Be aware of differences in public policy among countries.
5. Appreciate how marketing-mix strategies need to be adapted to each country.
6. Know how the performance in each country must be adjusted before international marketing strategies are compared across countries.
7. Know the advantages and disadvantages associated with the various organizational strategies for exporting and for foreign investment.
8. Be able to define and use the following concepts:

   International marketing   Combination export manager (CEM)
   Dumping strategies   Export department
   Transfer pricing   Assembly
   Domestic international sales   Contract manufacturing
   Piggyback   Licensing
   Indirect exporting   Joint venture
   Direct exporting   Wholly owned subsidiary

SOME STRATEGIC QUESTIONS FOR OPENERS

1. Must we use a differentiated product and promotional strategy for each country?
2. Do our strategies violate local cultures and public policies?
3. Is our international marketing organization meeting our present needs? Will it meet future needs?

THE INCENTIVES FOR INTERNATIONAL MARKETING[1] The incentives for international marketing are the same as those for domestic marketing—opportunities and competition. The opportunities appear as unmet needs and a potential for rapid growth. Competition may require having a presence in a market or merely exporting; both require competitive strategies. The success of international marketing strategies is measured in the same terms as domestic strategies are—sales, profit, return on investment, etc. In 1970 foreign markets were responsible for more than 50 percent of the sales of Caterpillar Tractor, Colgate Palmolive, and Massey Ferguson and 40 percent of the sales of IBM, J. H. Heinz, NCR, and Chas. Pfizer.[2] A large portion of the profits of these corporations came from foreign operations. The potential is large. International business was estimated to be 25 percent of the gross world product in 1973.[3]

International marketing, as used here, is the marketing of goods and services outside the home country. This marketing may take many forms. There can be several forms of exporting, which will be discussed shortly. A foreign subsidiary may sell within its country and export to a third country. Each of these types of international marketing must begin at the same origin—an adequate analysis of the market. Thus we begin our discussion of international marketing strategies with an examination of examples of special problems that occur during a situation analysis for international marketing. Then some common pitfalls of marketing-mix strategies will be examined. Finally, alternative strategies for organizing the international marketing effort will be examined.

SITUATION ANALYSIS

Analyzing the Market Generic demand is analyzed using demographic, economic, social, and social-psychological variables (see Chapter 6). These same variables are used in international marketing to identify unmet needs and develop products to meet these needs. The task is made difficult, however, by the lack of reliable data that are comparable across countries.[4] The differences in culture, religions, life-styles, and customs make the planner vulnerable to serious marketing blunders. A study of international blunders revealed that they were more likely to occur in marketing than in any other functional area.[5]

A few examples will illustrate the need to weigh cultural differences heavily when conducting a demand analysis. Benefit segmentation backfired for Pepsodent toothpaste when it promised white teeth to users in Southeast Asia. Since betel nut chewing is an elite habit there, however, black teeth signify prestige.[6]

The benefits of Campbell's *condensed* soups were not explained to English housewives, who were accustomed to Heinz's *ready-to-eat* soups. The small cans of Campbell's soups suggested that they were unjustifiably more expensive. "It was two years before Campbell attempted to make the necessary explanations and to sell English housewives on the idea and various other uses of 'condensed soups.'"[7] An adequate demand analysis would have revealed that English cooking traditions do not include adding liquids to canned soups.

General Foods removed its powdered Jell-O brand gelatin from the British market after substantial losses. Although gelatin is an established product, the British were accustomed to using a different form—solid cakes—and felt that Jell-O took too much shelf space.[8]

Traditional eating habits in Japan have prevented the introduction of many new food products. H. J. Heinz Company found that ketchup, a ubiquitous staple in American kitchens, could not cut into the use of soy sauce in Japan. Similarly, a joint venture by General Mills and Morinaga Confectionery Co., Ltd., in Japan was unable to popularize cornflakes because the public was accustomed to a different morning breakfast.[9] Coca-Cola Foods, however, demonstrated that if the same research and analytical methods that are successful elsewhere are applied to Japan, new food products can be introduced successfully. It proved the point with a successful introduction of Hi-C fruit drinks.[10]

Folk beliefs can limit the acceptance of a new food product. Facing small sales of carbonated beverage, a manufacturer discovered that carbonated beverages were thought to lower male sexual potency. But sales zoomed when advertisements showed admiring women around a handsome man who was drinking the product.[11]

International marketers, like their domestic counterparts, search for clusters of market segments that have similar needs, in the hope that a single product strategy can be applied to many countries. Cluster analysis has been used to group countries with similar characteristics.[12]

The environment for international investment is in a continuous state of change. From 1946 to 1971 the environment was favorable, but it became uncertain between 1971 and 1975, when economic growth turned to stagnation.[13] Real income declined as major countries experienced double-digit inflation.

During this same period multinational corporations were the subject of widespread criticism, especially after the bribery of public officials was revealed. Technology ran into costly obstacles. There were increased demands for local ownership. The United States dollar declined in value. There were worldwide shortages of resources, especially energy. The general mood was one of pessimism. These conditions required a careful analysis of the changing environment in order to adapt international marketing strategies. A decline in international investment opportunities may require a shift in marketing strategies that would emphasize exporting from the home plant rather than investing in foreign plants. A decline in the value of the dollar would encourage exports over foreign investment.

Public Policy The response of many countries toward multinational corporations has not been all negative. A Conference Board study supported by the State Department interviewed leaders in Canada and Italy. These leaders credited multinational corporations with "spurring modernization, increasing wages, mobilizing capital, spreading technology, developing managerial skills, and opening up overseas markets."[14] The study revealed two strong negative responses from these leaders. They want a greater voice in the operation of the multinational corporations on their soil, and they resent the efforts of the United States government to apply its antitrust laws to them. Unusual payments to government officials and "trading with the enemy" laws also were said to make life difficult for the manager of the affiliate company.[15]

Product-warranty legislation varies greatly across Belgium, Denmark, France, and Germany.[16] This variation may require different strategies for products, promotion, and service, thereby raising the cost of marketing to these countries.

We may conclude that the planning process embodied in the analysis and strategy worksheets applies to international marketing. The differences in planning for domestic and international marketing are not in the planning process, but in the differences in cultural customs, currency, laws, government regulations, weather, attitudes, institutions, language, etc. The planner must weigh the cost of adjusting for these differences against the size of the market opportunity. International marketing provides a real test of the marketing concept. There will be times when the size of the market does not justify the costs of a unique product or promotional strategy, but the export of the home strategies will produce some profitable sales.

INTERNATIONAL MARKETING-MIX STRATEGIES Faced with differences among international markets, the planner has two basic approaches—product differentiation and promotional differentiation. These strategies must be applied without tactical blunders within each of the elements of the marketing mix.

Product Strategies Exporting the standard product that succeeded in the United States market did not work for Campbell's soups, but it did work for PepsiCo. The PepsiCo. product and advertising message are the same worldwide.[17] Foreign consumers are not the only ones who will not change their cooking habits. Corn Products Co. attempted to introduce Knorr dry soups in the United States, but they were rejected because they took 15 to 20 minutes to cook, whereas canned soups could be ready in a few minutes.[18] Soup is not as important to the United States consumer as to the European consumer; therefore, it is not worth the extra effort. A soup powder sold in the United States for use in a sauce or a chip dip was very successful.

The product life cycle has been used to explain strategies for exporting products.[19] As the product matures, marketing costs go up and demand goes down at home; the opposite occurs in less-developed countries. At this point in the product's life cycle it is advantageous to shift production to the less-developed country, thereby extending the product life cycle.[20] An improved cash flow can be used to develop new products. Foreign competitors are discouraged from the country that is the new producer. The life-cycle concept has been used to explain world trade in the petrochemical industry.[21]

The same product will meet different needs in *developing* countries than in *developed* countries. In developed countries outboard motors and garden tractors are recreational items. In less-developed countries they are industrial products to be used by fishermen and small-acreage farmers. In the developed country these products must be marketed as consumer products, but in the less-developed countries they must be marketed as industrial products.

Coffee roasters and cigarette manufacturers too have found it necessary to fit their products to local tastes. Ford Motor Company was successful in Europe when it marketed European-styled autos, but it lost market share when it switched to Detroit styling. The European market rejected Detroit-styled cars as being too wide, long, heavy, and expensive.[22]

International marketers must consider changes in packaging for export. Besides the obvious changes, such as language, there may be a need for a stronger container that will protect the product during shipment and will keep it fresh during long shelf lives.

Pricing Strategies Pricing strategies require careful coordination among all countries and with the production facilities. Some exporting companies use *marginal pricing* when their production facilities have excess capacity. This means that the export products need to cover only the marginal costs associated with their production. Thus they may be sold at a lower price. The effect of this on foreign producers can be unfavorable if they do not have comparable economies of scale. This pricing policy frequently results in accusations of *dumping* excess goods on foreign markets just for a contribution to fixed costs.

Maintaining the f.o.b. plant price and then adding shipping, insurance, agent's costs, and tariffs, can easily result in a retail price that exceeds the price in the United States market. This becomes a problem in most international markets, since most of the per capita incomes are less than those in the United States. If the price is lowered to meet local economic conditions, the exporting company may face the problem of the transshipping of the product by distributors in the low-priced countries to those in the high-priced countries.

Transfer pricing (intracompany pricing) is a difficult problem when all producing units are in the same country. It becomes more difficult when the producing units are in different countries, all with different tariffs and tax structures. Many countries have complained that companies adjust their transfer prices so that their profits are low in countries with high taxes, letting the profits appear in those countries with low tax rates.[23]

Not all international marketing errors have been made by United States firms. Hitachi Sales Corporation of America made many mistakes in marketing its line of consumer electronic products. The most serious strategy was a pricing one. The firm entered the United States market in the 1950s through a trading company. In 1964 it established a direct sales subsidiary to compete with Sony. The product line was inadequate. The channels of distribution included "distributors" who were largely retailers and performed little of the usual distributor's functions of advertising and establishing a sales force. But they did receive a larger discount. This provided an incentive to cut prices, which they did. The four selling regions were semiautonomous, so there was little control over pricing. When a price cut spread through one region, there was pressure on all of the other regions. When it was clear that the United States operation was in trouble, Hitachi hired a new United States executive vice-president who had 25 years experience in United States marketing of consumer electronic products. He changed the strategy by redesigning the product line, overhauling the price structure, naming new people to top sales positions, replacing 5 of the 22 independent sales representative firms, cancelling the entire distributor network, and centralizing most of the functions of the four regions. The company then began to show a profit.[24]

Channel Strategies Channel strategies in other countries face a variety of unique problems. Retailers tend to be small operations with only a few employees. In some developing countries retailing is a means for reducing unemployment. Thus inefficient retailing is a matter of public policy. In countries without many refrigerators, daily shopping is a way of life. Thus small, conveniently located retail stores will not be replaced by large supermarkets. Shopping is also a social activity, with shoppers discussing the affairs of the day with friends and merchants.

Reaching these small, scattered retailers may require several layers of intermediaries, all adding to the cost and problems of control. Some channels may be closed to outsiders unless they agree to the terms of a cartel.[25]

Problems of entry may be simply a matter of long-term relationships. A United States manufacturer of feed and poultry set up operations in Spain by establishing a wholly owned subsidiary. Only when it could not sell its products did it realize that existing relationships between buyers and sellers were like a closed family. Using a joint venture may have avoided this problem. To solve the problem the company bought chicken farms, only to find that no one would buy its chickens. It then started to buy restaurants instead.[26]

Advertising Strategies The most obvious blunders in international marketing occur in advertising. Failure to understand the subtleties of culture and language have cost many marketers a market opportunity. Articles on international blunders tend to cite the same cases (e.g., "Body by Fisher" became "corpse by Fisher" in translation). This tends to suggest that the few cases that are frequently cited represent only a small part of the thousands of advertising messages that are translated effectively. Successful translations are most likely when the English copy is written with a sixth-grade vocabulary.[27]

Although the blunders may be few, their effect can be substantial. Chevrolet Nova did not sell in Puerto Rico, because the spoken word "Nova" sounds like "no va," meaning "it does not go."[28] "Otis Engineering Company once raised Russian eyebrows with a poster at a Moscow trade show promising that its oil well completion equipment was just dandy for improving a person's sex life."[29]

Color too can be a problem. In Malaysia green is a symbol for the dangers and diseases of the jungle; thus it conveys a negative connotation.[30] Colors for mourning vary among countries and may be red, black, white, purple, or blue.

A picture of a man and a woman in an advertisement may violate cultural norms. This would be true especially in those cultures where women have a lower status than men.

Whether to use the same advertising strategy in all countries or to develop a strategy for each country has been the subject of much debate. "Companies such as Exxon and Shell, Pepsi-Cola and Coca-Cola, Estée Lauder and Revlon are often given as examples of companies which have successfully employed standardized advertising worldwide."[31] But a standardized approach may not be the best strategy for all companies. To ensure quality control over advertising decisions, Light recommends a common procedure for developing all advertisements.[32] His approach includes the following steps: (1) knowing the prime prospect, (2) knowing the prime prospect's problem, (3) knowing your product, and (4) breaking the boredom barrier. The last step is a matter of executing the strategy, and it must be done locally so that it will reflect local culture and be memorable and convincing.

The execution of a strategy at the local level will vary according to available media. For example, television commercials are not permitted in many European countries, but there are commercials in the movie theaters. As noted earlier, some countries limit the amount of advertising that may be spent on some products, such as drugs.

Personal-Selling Strategies Restrictions on advertising cause greater emphasis to be placed on personal-selling strategies. There is a second reason for emphasizing the sales force in developing nations: the low wages make this an economical marketing strategy. Personal selling is especially important for industrial marketers, who also make heavy use of industrial trade fairs.

Job descriptions and criteria for recruiting and training salespeople may be controlled from the home office, but they will almost always be from the country in which they will sell. In some countries they must be recruited from specific religions or tribes. When Simmons-Japan built a sales force to sell its beds in Japan, it had problems with the class system. A salesperson from a lower class could not sell to someone in a higher class. Furthermore, no one had ever slept on an American-style bed.[33]

In concluding this discussion of international marketing strategies, it is useful to note the factors which limit the standardization of strategies across countries. Buzzell has identified eight factors.[34] *Physical environmental* factors include the climate and the dispersion of customers. *Stages in economic and industrial development* will determine needs and income levels. *Cultural factors* will determine acceptable means for meeting the needs, symbolism, their attitudes toward shopping, and different patterns of adoption of new products. The *stage of the product life cycle* in each market will determine the extent of product differentiation and the amount of education that will be required. *Local competition* may require a joint venture, matching quality levels, and matching prices. *Distributive systems* may dictate the channels, margins, and prices. The *unavailability of advertising media and agencies* may preclude a pull strategy. *Legal restrictions* will regulate product standards, patents, tariffs, taxes, antitrust, trademark laws, and restrictions on advertising and personal selling. Given the influence of all of these factors on the marketing mix, it is easy to see why a completely standardized international marketing strategy is unusual.

Evaluating International Marketing Strategies Conceptually each market may be viewed as an investment, so the basis for evaluating performance would be something that is comparable to return on investment. But direct comparison is difficult because of differing risks of currency and political interventions. Henley suggests five dimensions that should be considered when the international product-line performance is evaluated.[35] *Market share* will be influenced by costs, location of manufacturing, pricing, tariff, and tax structures. The *degree of product differentiation* to meet local needs and customs will determine how much selling effort is required. The *stage of the product life cycle* in each country will determine the productivity of each element in the marketing mix. *Public policy toward competition* will determine the degree of competition and therefore the amount of marketing effort that will be required. The *extent of the market support system* (media, retailers, wholesalers, agents, service facilities, warehousing, transportation, and credit) will determine the size of the investment and the cost of operating within a country. Comparisons of the performance of a product strategy across countries must make adjustments for these differences.

ORGANIZATIONAL STRATEGIES FOR INTERNATIONAL MARKETING Organizational strategies for international marketing may be arrayed along a continuum of commitment, from the least to the maximum commitment of resources. Exporting products produced in home plants is a minimal commitment; a 100-percent investment in a plant abroad is a maximum commitment. Within the broad strategies of exporting and investing there are many strategic alternatives that represent degrees of commitment. The most common alternatives will be considered briefly.

Alternatives for Exporting

Domestic sales. The minimum of exporting effort occurs when domestic sales are for shipment and resale in foreign markets. The buyers may be American agents, foreigners who represent wholesalers or retailers who will resell the product, or manufacturers who need subassemblies. This indirect form of exporting relies on the buyer's market analysis. All other forms of exporting require the seller or the seller's agent to perform a market analysis.

Piggyback. Another form of indirect exporting is known as *piggyback*. When Bendix parts are used in Ford automobiles, Bendix parts are distributed through the Ford overseas parts-distribution system. Thus the demand for the parts is a derived demand, and the channels of distribution are established. Bendix, in this instance, is involved in international marketing with a minimum of international effort. Piggyback will occur also when an exporting firm adds the product of another company to broaden the line of products that it exports.

In *indirect exporting* the tasks of market research, physical distribution, channel strategies, pricing, export documentation, etc., are assumed by the buyer. *Direct exporting* describes those cases in which these functions are performed by the seller or the seller's agent.[36]

Noncompetitors' facilities. To minimize commitment, a manufacturer may use the channels of noncompeting manufacturers, wholesalers, distributors, or an agent that has been formed to perform the export functions. The American export agent available to a manufacturer may be known as an export merchant, an export broker, a combination export manager, a manufacturer's export representative, a commission agent, or an export distributor. An American manufacturer may work through a foreign agent, such as a Japanese trading company.[37]

Of special interest is a combination export manager (CEM), who operates as the export department for a manufacturer on a continuing assignment. The term *combination* derives from the fact that this type of agent has a continuing relationship with several manufacturers, like a manufacturer's representative in domestic marketing. The CEM performs four general functions—developing sales, arranging financing, handling shipping and documentation, and recommending and assisting in negotiations with prospective licensees.

Export department. The decision to establish an export department must be followed with a decision on how extensive the commitment should be. The corporate exporting unit may be a part-time activity of an individual, a department within the domestic organization, a separate organization in the United States that is established solely for exporting, or a foreign subsidiary operating as an international sales division.[38] The decision to establish an export department rather than use an agent will be determined by economic factors such as the potential sales volume in the foreign market, the company's knowledge of the market, local traditions in distribution, and the ability to perform the functions cheaper than the commission that would be paid to the agent. The decision to use an export department is very similar to the decision in the domestic market of whether to use a direct sales force, a manufacturer's agent, or some combination of the two systems. (The analytical methods that were presented to aid in the sales force decision in Chapter 16 could be adapted to the export department decision.) The alternative of an export department is a commitment that requires capital and management resources and risks.

Alternatives to Foreign Investment Exporting is the preferred strategy because it has lower risks than does investing in foreign production facilities. The decision to invest abroad must go beyond the market analysis to an analysis of the costs of production, the political environment, and cultural restrictions. The costs of shipping, insurance, tariffs, etc., may require a price that is too high for the local market, but a lower price could be charged if the product were produced in the foreign country. The foreign government may require local production or assembly, and it may require a local partner. Traditional channels of distribution may not be available to outsiders, so it will be necessary to establish a joint venture with a local company. A local company may dominate the market, so the best strategy may be to acquire the local company.

Assembly.   The marketer has a range of options for foreign supply. An assembly plant is less than full manufacturing because it simply assembles parts that have been shipped to it. Transportation costs and tariffs make assembly plants attractive. Some countries require at least an assembly plant, so that there will be local employment. Automobile assembly plants, pharmaceutical "mixing" operations, and the shipment of Coca-Cola syrup for local bottling all represent assembly plant operations.

Contract manufacturing.   Contract manufacturing requires a local producer who can supply a product to specifications—quality and quantity. This is an attractive alternative when the comparative advantage of the international firm is in the areas of engineering, marketing, and financing, not in production. Some of the problems with contract manufacturing include the training of a potential competitor, the difficulty of maintaining quality, and foregoing the profits in production. It has the advantage of avoiding labor and culture problems. Also, it is easier to terminate a contract than to close a foreign plant.

Licensing.   A licensing arrangement can divide rights into those to manufacture a product, to use a component part, or to sell the product. (The license to manufacture only is known as a *manufacturing contract*.) The rights may be based on patents, trademarks, copyrights, or production technology. The licensor usually receives a percent of sales in return. Licensing is a rapid way to enter a market with no capital outlay. The primary disadvantage is that the international firm may be establishing a future competitor.

Joint venture.   A joint venture injects equity ownership into the relationship abroad with a partner who may also be a licensee. The venture may be formed to produce the product, to sell it, or both. When the venture includes selling, the local firm may prefer to sell the new product under its own brand while the foreign firm sells the identical product under its brand. A third local company may be brought into the selling part of the venture to round out a line or to take advantage of its access to the market. Thus there are many possible combinations of joint ventures.

The joint venture has the advantage to the American company of a greater return, more control, and better market information than licensing. The disadvantage, however, is the conflict that the international and national managers face in terms of pricing, products, and allocation of profits.

Wholly owned subsidiary.   The wholly owned foreign subsidiary has the advantage of a management with a point of view that is consistent with the international firm that owns it. There are no conflicts of interest with national partners. The gains in control and uniform strategies are at the cost of additional capital and management resources, local hostilities, and the cost of gathering information about the local market and labor conditions. The wholly owned subsidiary, contract manufacturing, and assembly place the responsibility for knowing the market on the manufacturer.

SUMMARY   Opportunities and competition provide the incentives for international marketing. An analysis of a foreign market requires the same procedures as analyzing domestic markets, but care must be exercised to reflect subtle differences in culture and language. The environment for international investment has changed because of inflation, energy shortages, the unpopularity of multinational corporations, and the decline of the dollar.

Rarely can marketing-mix strategies be exported without changes. In some countries it will be necessary to differentiate the product; in others it may be possible to use a standard product and differentiate the message. Pricing strategies based on the marginal concept may produce criticisms of dumping surpluses on foreign markets. Transfer pricing has been criticized by governments as a means for dodging taxes.

Channel strategies are difficult in those countries where there are large numbers of small retailers. No one distribution system will reach them all. A new firm may not be able to break into the long-term relationships that have been established in some channels.

The most frequent marketing blunders occur in advertising, where errors in culture and translation can convey some unsavory meanings. Some companies have been able to use a standardized message in all countries, but this has not been possible for products that are complex in their use. Single messages worked for gasoline and soft drinks, but not for foods, which are tied more closely to the complexities of the culture. While an advertising strategy may not be used in all countries, the procedure for developing a strategy can be exported.

Personal-selling strategies may be controlled from the home office by supplying job descriptions and criteria for recruiting and training. There will still be major problems in the field due to differences in culture and class barriers.

With so many factors affecting the productivity of the marketing mix, it is extremely difficult to develop a standardized strategy. Furthermore, it is difficult to evaluate the strategies across countries.

APPENDIX 18.1: COMPARATIVE ADVANTAGE—THE BASIS FOR TRADE

To understand international marketing opportunities, it is necessary to understand the concept of *comparative advantage*. Both countries can gain from an exchange of goods if there is a relative price differential in the two markets. This price differential is partly explained by the concept of comparative advantage in production and differences in the relative demand of the goods. A simplified example will clarify the concept.

Assume that two developing nations, both with simple agricultural economies, are exploring the advantages of trade. Each is considering allocating one million persons and ten million acres of tillable land to the much-needed commodities of cotton and wheat. Each nation conducted experiments to determine the level of output when one person cultivates ten acres of land. The results were as follows:

Output in Aurora		Output in Batavia
70	Cotton	15
35	Wheat	30

In Aurora the price of wheat is twice that of cotton because the output of wheat is half that of cotton. In Batavia the opposite is the case, so the price of cotton is twice that of wheat. Based on the experiments, Aurora has an *absolute advantage* in both cotton and wheat and, it would appear, has no reason to trade with Batavia. But a comparison of the exchange ratios (i.e., relative prices) of the two products in both countries shows that an opportunity for trade exists. An Auroran exporter could ship 70 units of cotton to Batavia and exchange it for 140 units of wheat. The imported wheat would be worth 280 units of cotton. The gain from exchange is 210 units of cotton, less the costs of transactions, shipping, and risk. The explanation for the fourfold increase in the exporter's holding is found in the relative price structure of the two commodities.

The allocation decision for each country is obvious. The two countries should specialize to that point where changes in costs and demand bring prices into equilibrium. As a result, more cotton and wheat will be available in each country than if each attempted to produce both commodities.

Having established that *comparative advantage* is a basis for trade among groups, we must determine the origins of these advantages. The comparative advantages for Aurora and Batavia might be explained by differences in growing conditions. In other examples the advantages might be those of mineral resources (e.g. coal, oil, or iron) or natural advantages such as a warm-weather port, a superior educational system that provides technical and managerial comparative advantages, or cultural differences that stimulate a motivation for achievement that yields higher rates of productivity. Although these forces provide a theory for international marketing, data are not available to apply them. In practice, price differentials and shifts in demand trigger most shifts in international marketing. Shifts in exchange rates will alter relative prices, so the basis for trade extends beyond the economic conditions in the trading countries to include world economics.

DISCUSSION QUESTIONS

1. What have been some of the negative and postive responses from leaders of foreign countries toward multinational corporations?
2. How does an analysis of a foreign market differ from that of an American market?
3. Differentiate indirect exporting from direct exporting.
4. Give some reasons why an international marketer would choose to establish a foreign assembly plant, a contract manufacturing arrangement, a licensing arrangement, joint ventures, and a wholly owned foreign subsidiary.
5. How has the product life cycle been used to explain exporting strategies?
6. Why would export opportunities increase as foreign investment opportunities declined?
7. What are the characteristics of products that have been able to export product and promotional strategies?

NOTES

1. The author is indebted to Dr. Jack N. Behrman, Professor of International Business, University of North Carolina, for assistance in writing this chapter.

2. V. Terpstra, *International Marketing* (New York: Holt, Rinehart and Winston, 1972), p. 12.

3. W. J. Keegan, "Multinational Product Planning: New Myths and Old Realities," *Multinational Product Management*, Report No. 76-110 (Cambridge, Mass.: Marketing Science Institute, August, 1976), p. I-3.

4. R. Moyer, "International Market Analysis," *Journal of Marketing Research* (November 1968): 353–360.

5. D. A. Ricks, M. Y. C. Fu, and J. S. Arpan, *International Business Blunders* (Columbus, Ohio: Grid, 1974).

6. *Ibid.*, p. 15.

7. *Ibid.*, p. 16.

8. *Ibid.*

9. *Ibid.*, p. 20.

10. J. R. Thomson, "How Coca-Cola's Hi-C Scored Success in Japan," *Advertising Age*, November 29, 1976, pp. 44–46.

11. D. H. Swett, "Anthropology and the Business Community" (Berkeley: Northern California Business Liaison Committee, University of California, Berkeley, February 25, 1967).

12. S. Prakash Sethi, "Comparative Cluster Analysis for World Markets," *Journal of Marketing Research* **8** (August 1971): 348–354.

13. Keegan, *op. cit.*

14. "U.S. Multinationals: The Pressure Is On," *The Conference Board Focus* (November, 1976): 4–7.

15. *Ibid.*

16. S. E. Permut, "Consumer Product Warranty Legislation," *Multinational Product Management* (Cambridge, Mass.: Marketing Science Institute, Report No. 76-110, August 1976), pp. XV-1-23.

17. W. J. Keegan, "Multinational Product Planning: Strategic Alternatives," *Journal of Marketing* (January 1969): 58–62.

18. *Ibid.*

19. L. T. Wells, Jr., "A Product Life Cycle for International Trade?" *Journal of Marketing* **32** (July 1968): 1–6.

20. W. V. Rapp, "Strategy Formulation and International Competition," *Columbia Journal of World Business* (Summer 1973): 98–112.

21. Robert Stobaugh, "The Product Life Cycle and World Trade Patterns," working paper (Cambridge, Mass.: Marketing Science Institute, November, 1970).

22. Ricks, Fu, and Arpan, *op. cit.*, p. 18.

23. Terpstra, *op. cit.*, Chapter 14.

24. A. Detman, Jr., "The Americanization of Hitachi," *Sales and Marketing Management*, May 10, 1976, pp. 31–34.

25. Terpstra, *op. cit.*, Chapter 11.

26. Ricks, Fu, and Arpan, *op. cit.*, p. 25.

27. Terpstra, *op. cit.*, p. 357.

28. G. C. Hill, "More Firms Turn to Translation Experts to Avoid Costly, Embarrassing Mistakes," *Wall Street Journal*, January 13, 1977, p. 34.

29. *Ibid.*

30. Ricks, Fu, and Arpan, *op. cit.*, p. 14.

31. L. Light, "Common Discipline Approach Best for Multinational Advertisers," *Marketing News*, April 9, 1976, p. 9.

32. *Ibid.*

33. Ricks, Fu, and Arpan, *op. cit.*, p. 21.

34. R. D. Buzzell, "Can You Standardize Multinational Marketing?" *Harvard Business Review* (November-December 1968): 102–113.

35. D. S. Henley, "Evaluating International Product Line Performance: A Conceptual Approach," *Multinational Product Management*, pp. II-1–II-19.

36. Terpstra, *op. cit.*, pp. 274–284.

37. J. Greene, *Organizing for Exporting*, Business Policy Study No. 126, (New York: Conference Board, 1968).

38. For examples of these various organizations, *see* Greene, *op. cit.*, Chapter 2.

SUGGESTED READINGS

Boddewyn, J., *Comparative Management and Marketing* (Glenview, Ill.: Scott, Foresman, 1969).

Britt, S. H., "Standardizing Marketing for the International Market," *Columbia Journal of World Business* (Winter 1974): 39–45.

Gestetner, D., "Strategy in Managing International Sales," *Harvard Business Review* (September-October 1974): 103–108.

Moyer, R., and S. C. Hollander, *Markets and Marketing in Developing Economics* (Homewood, Ill.: Richard D. Irwin, 1968).

Thorelli, H. B., *International Marketing Strategy* (Baltimore: Penguin, 1973).

Wind, Y., P. S. Douglas, and V. H. Perlmutter, "Guidelines for Developing International Marketing Strategies," *Journal of Marketing* 37 (April 1973): 14–23.

ENVIRONMENTAL ANALYSIS WORKSHEET

Environmental elements	Facts	Assumptions or research needed	Conclusions
Organizational values, objectives, and policies (4)			
Organizational design (5)			
Situation			
Generic demand (6)			
Brand demand (7)			
Competition (9)			
Public policy (10)			
Opportunities (2)			
Problems			

MARKETING PLAN (CONSUMER PRODUCT)

Current performance
Recommendations
Effect of recommendations on income
Situation analysis
Opportunities and problems
Strategies
Tests and research
Supporting documents
   Comparative budgets
   Media allocation schedule
   Promotion control sheet

STRATEGY WORKSHEET

Opportunities and problems in rank order to importance

   1.
   2.
    .
   n.

	Current strategy	Alternatives and recommended strategy	Estimated Effect
Demand strategy			
Generic			
Brand			
Strategic goals			
Financial			
Marketing			
Marketing-mix strategies			
Product (12)			
Pricing (13)			
Channel and logistics (14)			
Advertising and promotional (15)			
Sales management (16)			
Research (3)			
Profit plan			
Evaluation and control (19)			

CHAPTER **19**

Evaluation and Control

LEARNING OBJECTIVES   After studying this chapter you should:

1. Know how the marketing plan performs the functions of allocation, communication, and coordination.
2. Understand why evaluation and control systems require goals that are stated precisely and in measurable terms.
3. Know the methods that are commonly used for evaluating marketing effectiveness and efficiency.
4. Know the steps for controlling the marketing systems.
5. Know the control techniques commonly used in marketing.
6. Be able to define and use the following concepts:

Evaluation	Marketing budgets
Control	Brand budget
Effectiveness	Media budget
Efficiency	Promotional budget
Distribution cost analysis	Bar (Gantt) charts
Functional-cost groups	Critical-path method (CPM)
Bases of allocation	Decision analysis
Variance analysis	Marketing information systems
Productivity analysis	Planning information
80/20 rule	Control information

SOME EVALUATION AND CONTROL QUESTIONS FOR OPENERS

1. Are all marketing goals subject to evaluation and control procedures?
2. Do we need distribution cost analysis to identify the products and customers which should be dropped as well as to identify the channels of distribution which are more profitable?
3. Do we need to change the compensation scheme for sales representatives and channel members to redirect their effort?
4. Do our systems adequately control time and money?
5. Is our marketing information system adequate for planning and control?

The marketing plan performs many functions. Its strategies give direction to the marketing effort. It *allocates* resources. It is the basis for *communication* and *coordination* of effort among those persons who will execute the strategy. The plan must also provide for its own *evaluation* and *control*. These last two functions are the subject of this chapter. These functions are necessary because strategies and their executions are never perfect.

Evaluation consists largely of systems for measuring the output of a system to determine if it has met the desired goals. *Goals*, it will be recalled, must be stated in terms of *magnitude* and *time*, and they must be *measurable*. Therefore, the means for evaluating the marketing plan begins with the statement of the strategic goals. *Evaluation* is also based on the assumption that the criteria for evaluation are *effectiveness* and *efficiency*. (Effectiveness, as used here, means whether the goal was achieved. Efficiency means the ratio of the input of effort to the output.)

Although these criteria are readily accepted for systems which deal with economic outputs, they have been questioned by philosophers who feel that they have been misapplied to systems whose outputs are largely social, social-psychological, and artistic. Thus Weisskopf concluded that "the 'economic man' is the prototype of alienated man. He is confined to conscious, deliberate action. All spontaneous, emotional, non-utilitarian behavior is suppressed.... This resulted in the reduction of human behavior to a small segment of its total potentialities and dimensions, that is, in alienation."[1] Because marketing systems deal with social, social-psychological, and artistic matters, it is easy to see why the criteria of effectiveness and efficiency are not always appropriate. These criteria tend to be physical ones. Their inappropriateness helps to explain some of the conflicts between the marketing department and other functional departments.

Control systems attempt to keep the marketing system along a trajectory that will bring it toward its goal. A deviation that exceeds some acceptable range will require one of three actions. When a goal has not been met, it will be necessary to add resources. If it is above the goal, it may be possible to remove excess resources and reassign them to other projects. If the original goal was inappropriate, it may be necessary to restate the goal.

A control system must begin with the understanding that accomplishments are made through people, so control requires working with people. Budgets, schedules, monitors of performance, and corrective actions are all concerned with people. Control systems, therefore, must be designed to detect human errors, correct them on a continuing basis, and plan to prevent them in the future.

MARKETING EVALUATION

The overall goal of marketing effort is to influence buyer behavior within a competitive environment. This environment is external, which makes it harder to measure than activities which occur largely within the firm. Measures of buyers' responses to marketing effort are of two types—physical behavior (purchases, store visits, etc.) and mental behavior (change in awareness, buying intentions, etc.).

Measures of Buyer Behavior

One common measure of buyer behavior is sales. Thus many evaluations include measures of sales. These measures may be a comparison of actual and forecasted sales, sales by territories, sales by customer classification, advertising costs per dollar sales, personal-selling expenses per dollar sales, bad-debt expenses per sales dollar, etc. Another measure is the profitability of products, customers, and territories. These measures have led to a blend of accounting techniques and marketing to form *distribution cost analysis.*

Distribution cost analysis. Distribution cost analysis allocates costs and revenues to determine the profits (or losses) by products, customers, territories, channels of distribution, and methods of promotion. The problem of joint costs and revenues requires *bases of allocation.* Suggested bases for allocating the costs of marketing functions to products and customers appear in Table 19.1. Allocation of some of these costs requires extensive studies of time, duties, and space utilization.[2] Standardized costs and profits become a basis for comparison. Examining variations from these standards is known as *variance analysis.* Variances become the basis for action, e.g., dropping unprofitable products or customers. Less expensive channels of distribution may be utilized. Unprofitable salespeople may be replaced or receive additional training. Less expensive promotional methods may be substituted for expensive ones.

Distribution cost analysis does not lead directly to action. These data create hypotheses that must be tested experimentally. The results of these experiments are actionable. The combination of distribution cost analysis and experiments has been called *productivity analysis.*[3]

TABLE 19.1 **Allocation of distribution cost groups**

| | Bases of allocation | |
Functional-cost groups	To commodities	To customers
Investment in finished goods	Average inventory value	(not allocated)
Storage of finished goods	Floor space occupied	(not allocated)
Inventory control, finished goods	Number of invoice lines	(not allocated)
Order assembly (handling)	Number of standard handling units	Number of invoice lines
Packing and shipping	Weight or number of shipping units	Weight or number of shipping units
Transportation	Weight or number of shipping units	Weight or number of shipping units
Selling	Time studies	Number of sales calls
Advertising	Cost of space, for example, of specific product advertising	Cost of space, for example, of specific customer advertising
Order entry	Number of invoice lines	Number of orders
Billing	Number of invoice lines	Number of invoice lines
Credit extension	(not allocated)	Average amount outstanding
Accounts receivable	(not allocated)	Number of invoices posted

"Distribution Cost Analysis," Bibliography No. 34 (Washington, D.C.: Small Business Administration, 1970).

The 80/20 rule. Marketers frequently refer to the 80/20 rule (a variation is known as the "ABC" concept in inventory control). This rule states that 80 percent of the profit comes from 20 percent of the products or customers. Distribution cost analysis has verified this rule many times.

Sevin reported that a manufacturer of 12 products found that three of them accounted for 81 percent of the total profit.[4] Two of the products *lost* 15 percent of the profit. An analysis of salespeople's time revealed that they were spending too much time on the unprofitable products and not enough time on the profitable ones. A controlled experiment revealed that sales of an unprofitable product remained stable even after cutting the salespeople's time on it. The product then become profitable when selling costs were lowered. A product that had contributed 16 percent of the profit contributed 31 percent after it received the additional salespeople's time that had been taken from the unprofitable product.

Another company had 635 unprofitable products in a line of 875 products.[5] An analysis failed to reveal any way that these products could be made profitable. Salespeople argued that these items were needed to have a complete line or to keep customers who bought the profitable products. A controlled experiment in several territories resulted in the elimination of 592 of the 635 unprofitable products. The net profit contribution increased 24 percent.

A manufacturer used company branches to distribute a long product line to retail stores in the United States.[6] An analysis revealed that half of the accounts created a loss equal to 44 percent of the company's profit. The company considered the alternatives of shifting selling effort to the profitable customers, charging more for small orders, using a lower-cost channel, and dropping unprofitable customers. It ran an experiment to test whether mail-order and wholesale distributors could handle small accounts profitably. The mail-order approach showed a profit of 10 percent and the distributors showed a profit of 28 percent. All small accounts were then given to wholesale distributors.

A company that produced raw material used in more than 3000 different forms found that about ten percent of the forms accounted for all of the profits.[7] Marketing management refused to drop the unprofitable items or raise the prices to cover costs because it did not want to antagonize those customers who bought the profitable items. Two approaches were considered. An *optimizer* constructed a model of the production-inventory-sales system to lower costs by improving the production schedule. An *adaptivizer* found that these savings could be matched by eliminating four percent of the least profitable items. The adaptivizer turned to the marketing problem, not the production one, and modified the salespeople's compensation plan. The previous plan had been a base salary plus a percentage of total dollar sales. The new plan paid a commission on profit. The plan was designed to pay the same compensation if the salespeople sold the same product mix, but to pay an increased compensation if the mix was shifted to a more profitable one. After the first year, sales of about one-half of the unprofitable items virtually stopped, and sales of the profitable items increased significantly.

Measures of marketing productivity must consider time. Price promotions, for example, may not increase total sales for the year, but they may shift the timing of purchases. This shift in the timing of demand may be used to smooth demand and yield more even production runs.

Measures of Buyers' Mental Activities A good part of marketing effort is concerned with communicating information that may not lead to an immediate change in buyer behavior. To evaluate this effort, it is necessary to measure the communication effects. The three most commonly used intermediate variables are awareness, attitudes, and buying intentions. The communication effect, therefore, is measured in terms of changes in buyers' awareness of a brand, their attitude toward a brand, and their probability of buying a brand. The instruments for making these measures have been discussed at great leangth in the literature and are beyond our concern with strategy.[8] Our present concern is simply whether they are a good intermediate measure for buying behavior.

Achenbaum, a market researcher and former advertising agency executive, has concluded that awareness and attitude measures are strongly related to buying behavior.[9] In one study of brand switching among 19 brands in 7 product categories, he found that switches in awareness and attitudes were closely related.[10]

This study revealed another point that should be remembered when evaluating marketing strategies: considerable switching goes on even within a brand share that has remained constant. While the shares of these 19 brands remained at 20 percent over a six-month period, only 14 percent of the buyers remained constant; 6 percent of them shifted out of the brand, and 6 percent shifted into the brand.[11] Thus a great deal of marketing activity lies behind a seemingly stable market share.

Evaluating Potential Competitors   In previous chapters we have seen that potential competition may be identified with brand maps, by studying past competitive behavior, and by observing test markets. These methods reveal competitors who are generally in the product category. It is extremely difficult to identify those competitors who are outside the category but have the technical, production, and marketing capacities to enter the market.

One way to anticipate competition is to search the patent files. Clusters of patents will reveal a theme that a company is pursuing, thereby giving an early warning. A study of the patents registered by Procter & Gamble, for example, has revealed their activities in four product areas—carbonation at point of use, skin care, coffee, and agricultural chemicals.[12] Carbonation at the point of use would permit the creation of a soft drink by using water and a device such as a tea bag or swizzle stick. The patent reads: "It has now been discovered that by employing readily available molecular sieves which contain absorbed carbon dioxide and which readily release such carbon dioxide upon contact with water, the ... objectives can be accomplished."[13] Patents on coffee have surrounded the problem of extracting more beverage from a pound of coffee. A patent issued in 1972 described methods for getting up to 30 percent more beverage from the coffee beans. In January 1977 Procter & Gamble announced that new Folger Flaked coffee would make up to 25 percent more coffee, thereby providing consumers some relief from recent marked increases in coffee prices.

CONTROLLING MARKETING SYSTEMS   Control, which is the evaluation of strategic decisions once they have been implemented, consists of the following four steps: predicting the outcomes of the decision, gathering information on actual performance, comparing the predicted and the actual performance, and correcting the procedure that produced the variation.[14] "It should be apparent that control, decision, and management-information systems are strongly interrelated and are merely subsystems of what might be called the *management system*."[15] "Controls are neither objective nor neutral," because they reflect the value of the executives.[16] Executives control those variables which they feel are important. A variety of techniques has been developed as control devices. Those which have been applied to control marketing systems include budgets, critical-path methods (CPM), decision analysis, management information systems, and mathematical models. Each of these will be considered briefly.

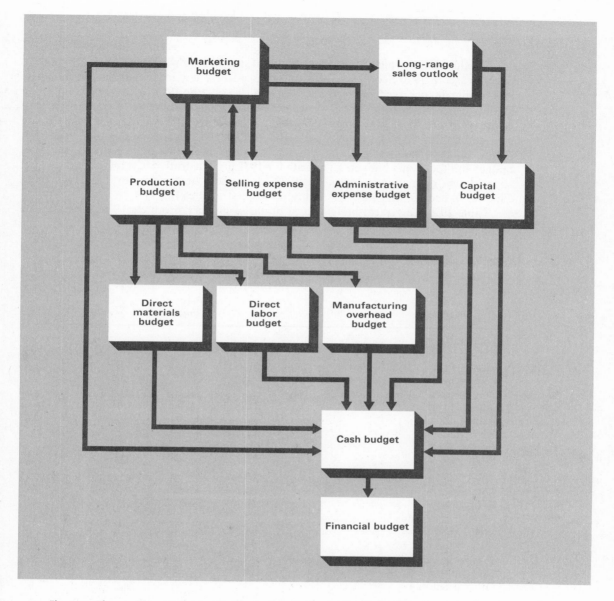

Fig. 19.1 The position of the marketing budget in the corporate budget. (C. L. Moore and R. K. Jaedicke, *Managerial Accounting*, 4th ed., Cincinatti, Ohio: South-Western, 1976, p. 576. Reprinted by permission.)

Marketing Budgets Marketing budgets provide important inputs for many of the other budgets in the corporation. In Fig. 19.1 we see that the marketing budget inputs directly into the cash, production, selling expense, administrative expense, and long-range sales budgets. Through these budgets it inputs into the direct materials, direct labor, and manufacturing overhead budgets. Thus the planner must develop a budget with great care.

To illustrate a typical marketing budget for a brand, we return to the Scoop Ice Cream case. In 1970 Scoop was introduced as a freeze-dry ice cream mix in chocolate and vanilla flavors (see Chapter 2). At this time we saw the 1971 Scoop Marketing Plan in the "executive read-and-run" form. No supporting documents were shown. We returned to Scoop at the end of 1971 when it was planning for the next year, facing new competition (see Chapter 9). At the end of 1972 Scoop is planning for 1973. At this point we will not examine the details of the marketing plan, but only the total budget and the media budget. (The data for 1972 are illustrative of a budget that would support one of many strategies for 1972. It is not the answer for the problem in Chapter 9, because this case has many possible strategies.)

Table 19.2 is a typical budget for a brand of grocery products. The rows are the major elements in the marketing budget. The columns compare the present and the

TABLE 19.2 Scoop Ice Cream Mix 1973 budget (,000)

	1972 Current year	(Percent sales)	1973 New year	(Percent sales)
1. Total market:				
Value (millions)	$1,232.0		$1,250.5	
Cases	—		—	
Percent increase/decrease	1.5%		1.5%	
2. Brand share:	2.7%		2.9%	
3. Brand shipments:				
Value (millions)	$ 28.0	100	$ 30.0	100
Cases (millions)	2.8	—	3.0	—
4. Cost of goods				
Fixed cost	$ 10.6	38	$ 11.1	37
Variable costs	3.4	12	3.6	12
Total costs	$ 14.0	50	$ 14.7	49
5. Gross margin:	$ 14.0	50	$ 15.3	51
6. Marketing expenses:				
Media/production	$ 4.1	15	$ 4.5	15
Advertising reserve	0.1	—	0.2	1
Sampling/couponing	1.2	4	0.1	—
Trade allowance	1.1	4	0.8	3
Other promotions	0.5	2	1.9	6
Total marketing expenses	$ 7.0	25	$ 7.5	25
7. Other expenses:				
Market research	$ 0.1	—	$ 0.2	1
Sales force cost	1.5	5	1.6	5
Distribution cost	1.2	4	1.2	4
Administration	0.6	2	0.6	2
Miscellaneous income and expenses	—	—	—	—
Total other expenses	$ 3.4	12	$ 3.6	12
8. Profit contribution	$ 3.6	13	$ 4.2	14
Increase/decrease	5.9%		16.7%	

new year in dollars and percentages. This format highlights the changes that are recommended.

The *brand budget* is supported by additional detailed budgets, such as the *media budget*, which appears in Table 19.3. The brand budget shows a total figure of $4.5 million for media. The media budget shows how this expenditure is allocated among television and print media. The expenditures are shown for the year and by quarters. The quarterly figures reflect the seasonal strategy. The media budget is related to the planned quarterly shipments, which reflect the seasonal demand.

The *promotional budget* must be controlled each month of the year and by region to be certain that the promotion effort reaches the right place at the right time. The *brand budget* requests $2.8 million for sampling/coupon, trade allowances, and other promotions. This amount is allocated according to the strategy in Table 19.4, the *promotional budget*. This budget reflects the promotional strategy to spend at the following case rates: North, $0.95; South $1.03; Central, $0.99; and West, $0.81.

Managing Time Time is a critical factor in a marketing plan. Two common methods for managing time are bar (Gantt) charts and the critical-path method (CPM). Both of these will be illustrated briefly.

TABLE 19.3 Scoop Ice Cream media allocation schedule, 1973 budget

	Current Year (000)	%	New Year (000)	%	Difference ±000
I. NATIONAL EXPENDITURES					
Television					
Network TV	$1,075	26	$1,003	22	$ −72
Spot TV	1,550	38	2,007	45	+457
Production	150	4	100	2	−50
Total TV	$2,775	68	$3,110	69	$ +335
Print					
Magazines	$ 680	17	$ 665	15	$ −15
Newspapers	330	8	487	11	+157
Supplements	265	6	208	4	−57
Preparation	50	1	30	1	−20
Total Print	$1,325	32	$1,390	31	$ +65
Other media	$ —	—	$ —	—	$ —
Total media expenditures	$4,100	100	$4,500	100	$ +400

II. QUARTERLY EXPENDITURES

	1st qtr.	2nd qtr.	3rd qtr.	4th qtr.	Total
Television	$362	$ 992	$1,273	$383	$3,010
Print	168	445	597	180	1,390
Other	—	—	—	—	—
Total working media	$530	$1,437	$1,870	$563	$4,400
% of year	12%	33%	42%	13%	100%
Planned shipments (000)	417	889	1,139	555	3,000
% of year	14%	30%	38%	18%	100%

TABLE 19.4 Scoop Ice Cream Mix promotion control spread sheet, 1973 budget (,000 omitted)

	Jan.	Feb.	Mar.	1st qtr.	April	May	June	2nd qtr.	1st half
Region—North									
Shipments	37	47	55	139	83	102	111	297	436
Type of promotion	—	—	—	—	—	60¢/ Cs. & Prem.	60¢/ Cs. & Prem.	—	—
Promotion cost	—	—	—	—	—	$201	$219	$420	$420
Region—South									
Shipments	18	23	28	69	42	51	56	149	218
Type of promotion	—	—	—	—	Free Coupon Test	60¢/ Cs. & Prem.	60¢/ Cs. & Prem.	—	—
Promotion cost	—	—	—	—	$50	$99	$108	$257	$257
Region—Central									
Shipments	23	31	37	91	57	68	73	198	289
Type of promotion	—	—	—	—	—	60¢/ Cs. & Prem.	60¢/ Cs. & Prem.	—	—
Promotion cost	—	—	—	—	—	$140	$152	$292	$292
Region—West									
Shipments	33	38	47	118	68	84	93	245	363
Type of promotion	—	—	—	—	Mail Sample Test	60¢/ Cs. & Prem.	60¢/ Cs. & Prem.	—	—
Promotion cost	—	—	—	—	$50	$130	$144	$324	$324
Total shipments	111	139	167	417	250	305	333	889	1,306
% of year	3.7%	4.6%	5.5%	13.8%	8.3%	10.2%	11.2%	29.7%	43.5%
Total cost	—	—	—	—	$100	$570	$623	$1,293	$1,293
% of year	—	—	—	—	4%	20%	22%	46%	46%
Cost per case	—	—	—	—	$0.44	$1.87	$1.87	$1.45	$0.99

Bar (Gantt) charts.   Bar charts, or Gantt charts, show the time required to complete an activity along a time line. The flow chart for the mail survey (Fig. 3.1) could be expressed as a bar chart, such as Fig. 19.2. The bars show the starting and stopping times, and the length indicates the time to complete the activity. The right-hand columns can be used to record the persons with the primary responsibility for the activity and the amount of money that has been budgeted. The dates, the person responsible, and the budget figure make it possible to control the research project. Overlapping time bars reveal activities which could be performed concurrently. These charts have several limitations. They become difficult to read when the projects become complex. More important, they do not reveal the effect of delays in particular tasks on the total project completion time. The critical-path method was designed to reveal this effect.

TABLE 19.4 (cont.)

	July	Aug.	Sept.	3rd qtr.	Oct.	Nov.	Dec.	4th qtr.	Total year
Region—North									
Shipments	129	139	111	379	92	56	38	186	10,000
Type of promotion	60¢/ Cs. & Prem.	60¢/ Cs. & Prem.	—	—	—	—	—	—	—
Promotion cost	$254	$274	—	$528	—	—	—	—	948
Region—South									
Shipments	64	69	56	189	46	28	19	93	500
Type of promotion	60¢/ Cs. & Prem.	60¢/ Cs. & Prem.	—	—	—	—	—	—	—
Promotion cost	$125	$135	—	$260	—	—	—	—	$517
Region—Central									
Shipments	86	92	74	252	62	37	27	126	667
Type of promotion	60¢/ Cs. & Prem.	60¢/ Cs. & Prem.	—	—	—	—	—	—	—
Promotion cost	$177	$191	—	$368	—	—	—	—	$660
Region—West									
Shipments	110	117	92	319	76	47	28	151	833
Type of promotion	60¢/ Cs. & Prem.	60¢/ Cs. & Prem.	—	—	—	—	—	—	—
Promotion cost	$170	$181	—	$351	—	—	—	—	$675
Total shipments	389	417	333	1,139	277	167	111	555	3,000
% of year	13.0%	13.9%	11.1%	38.0%	9.2%	5.6%	3.7%	18.5%	100%
Total cost	$726	$781	—	$1,507	—	—	—	—	$2,800
% of year	26%	28%	—	54%	—	—	—	—	100%
Cost per case	$1.87	$1.87	—	$1.32	—	—	—	—	$0.93

The critical-path method (CPM). The critical-path method (CPM) of management control makes planning and scheduling two distinct steps. The sequence of events is planned first, and then time schedules are worked out for the implementation of the plan. There are three essential steps in CPM—list all activities required to complete the project, estimate the time required to complete each activity, and arrange all the jobs in a logical sequence according to which one must be completed before the next can begin. Furthermore, one should schedule as many jobs concurrently as possible.[17] There will be many paths of activities that must be done in a technological sequence. For example, if the project is the building of a house, the roof cannot be put on until the framing is completed, which in turn must be preceded by the foundation. The *critical path* is that path with the longest time to complete all of its activities.

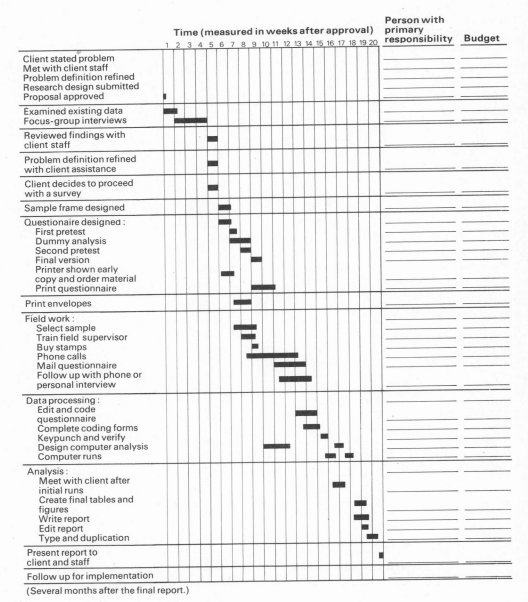

Fig. 19.2 A control sheet for a survey of nurses.

Expediting activities that are *not* along this path will not shorten the time required to complete the total project. CPM analysis will often reveal ways that activities may be made concurrent, thereby saving time.

CPM control methods include project graphs and manual analysis procedures for simple projects and computer routines for more complex projects. These methods improve communication among departments on controversial topics, such as responsibility and the relative importance of a completion time. They identify where replanning is necessary while there is still time to replan. For instance, the Diamond Alkali Company used CPM to plan the introduction of proprietary chrome-plating compounds. The first estimate was that the plan would require 76 weeks. But the goal was a major trade show in 36 weeks. Through CPM the 36-week deadline was met, and the product introduction was a success.[18]

Figure 19.3 illustrates how a CPM graph was used for the introduction of a new industrial product. In this graph the circles represent the activities and the departments that are responsible. The activity is described on the arrow to the left of the circle. The numbers along the arrows are the estimated number of weeks the activity requires. The numbers in the circles show the technological sequence of activities. For example, drafting the operations manual (activity 9) must be preceded by the new-product definition and development of tentative specifications (activities 2 and 3). The critical path, shown in the darker line, consists of events 2, 5, 12, and 19, because this sequence of activities requires the longest completion time—22 weeks. Expediting events such as developing the advertisement or developing the maintenance manual will have no effect on the project completion time, because these events are not along the critical path.[19]

Decision Analysis   Decision analysis, complete with decision trees, probabilities, and payoffs, can be very useful when sorting out alternative strategies. An example of a decision tree appeared in Chapters 3 and 13.[20]

Formal decision analysis is being accepted slowly in many companies, but other companies, such as Pillsbury, require that a recommendation be supported by a decision tree. General Electric requires that some recommendations be accompanied by a value distribution, such as return on investment.[21] The structure of decision analysis requires the planner to have explicit assumptions. The executive can then challenge these assumptions. One means for controlling a plan is to monitor the assumptions and make adjustments when they do not come true. Thus a system of formal decision analysis can be useful during the stages of selecting an alternative strategy and controlling its implementation.

Marketing Information Systems   Marketing information systems are necessary for the development of strategies and for evaluating and controlling them. Figure 19.4 illustrates the information system for a manufacturer of prescription and nonprescription drugs.

The information used for planning may differ from that which is necessary for control. Daniel observed that *planning information* transcends organizational lines, covers long time periods, lacks minute details, and is future-oriented. *Control information*, in contrast, follows organizational lines, covers short time periods, is very detailed, and is past-oriented.[22]

The availability of the computer may have turned the information revolution into an information inundation. It is too easy to generate data that will make only a slight contribution to the planning process. There may be substantial investment of executive time to determine whether the information is valuable. There is the additional problem of executives not understanding the information system. Some executives assume that the data are better because they came from the computer; others discount its value when it is computerized. Ackoff concluded that "no management-information system should ever be installed unless the managers it serves understand how it operates well enough to evaluate its performance."[23]

Ackoff has noted that the deficiencies in management information systems (MIS) are the result of assumptions that are not justified. MIS designers assume that

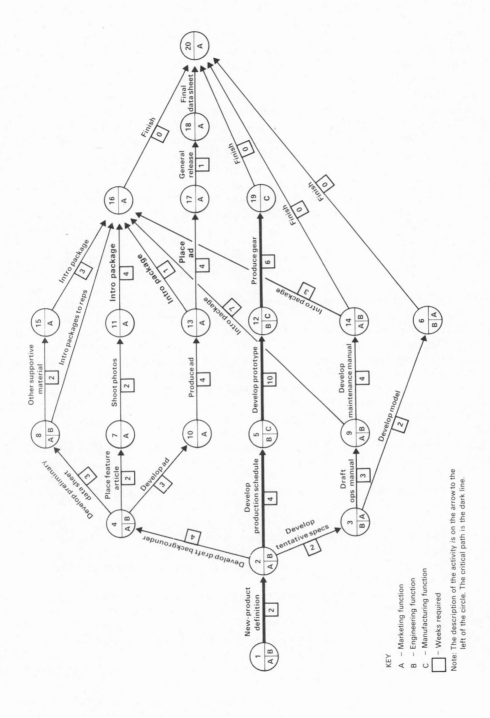

Fig. 19.3 CPM graph for an industrial product introduction. (Adapted from G. A. Marken, "New Product Introduction Schedule Yields 'Fantastic Results,'" *Marketing News*, April 15, 1974, p. 4. Reprinted by permission.)

KEY

A – Marketing function
B – Engineering function
C – Manufacturing function
☐ – Weeks required

Note: The description of the activity is on the arrow to the left of the circle. The critical path is the dark line.

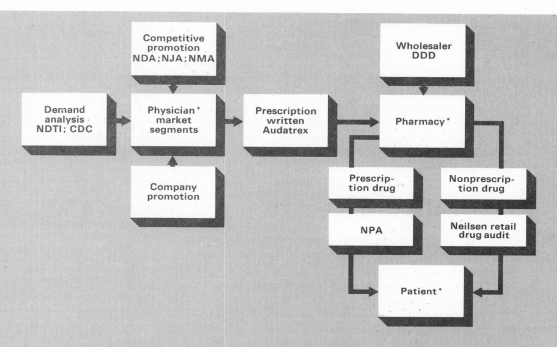

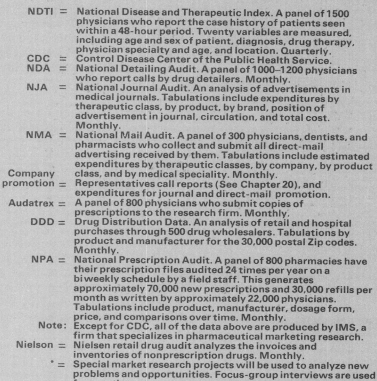

NDTI = National Disease and Therapeutic Index. A panel of 1500 physicians who report the case history of patients seen within a 48-hour period. Twenty variables are measured, including age and sex of patient, diagnosis, drug therapy, physician specialty and age, and location. Quarterly.

CDC = Control Disease Center of the Public Health Service.

NDA = National Detailing Audit. A panel of 1000–1200 physicians who report calls by drug detailers. Monthly.

NJA = National Journal Audit. An analysis of advertisements in medical journals. Tabulations include expenditures by therapeutic class, by product, by brand, position of advertisement in journal, circulation, and total cost. Monthly.

NMA = National Mail Audit. A panel of 300 physicians, dentists, and pharmacists who collect and submit all direct-mail advertising received by them. Tabulations include estimated expenditures by therapeutic classes, by company, by product class, and by medical speciality. Monthly.

Company promotion = Representatives call reports (See Chapter 20), and expenditures for journal and direct-mail promotion.

Audatrex = A panel of 800 physicians who submit copies of prescriptions to the research firm. Monthly.

DDD = Drug Distribution Data. An analysis of retail and hospital purchases through 500 drug wholesalers. Tabulations by product and manufacturer for the 30,000 postal Zip codes. Monthly.

NPA = National Prescription Audit. A panel of 800 pharmacies have their prescription files audited 24 times per year on a biweekly schedule by a field staff. This generates approximately 70,000 new prescriptions and 30,000 refills per month as written by approximately 22,000 physicians. Tabulations include product, manufacturer, dosage form, price, and comparisons over time. Monthly.

Note: Except for CDC, all of the data above are produced by IMS, a firm that specializes in pharmaceutical marketing research.

Nielson = Nielsen retail drug audit analyzes the invoices and inventories of nonprescription drugs. Monthly.

* = Special market research projects will be used to analyze new problems and opportunities. Focus-group interviews are used frequently.

Fig. 19.4 A marketing information system for a pharmaceutical firm.

managers critically need more relevant information, when the real need is to reduce irrelevant information. Instead of needing more information, managers need better decision models to use present information.[24]

Control Models Mathematical models are beginning to make contributions to many areas of marketing. We saw how they are used to predict the market share of a new product using laboratory data, to choose the best product concepts, to set a price, to develop a media mix, and to develop a sales force strategy. But it is difficult to find examples of models that are used to control the marketing strategy and its execution. Most of the examples are models which were used to develop the strategy. For instance, if break-even analysis is used to choose a pricing strategy, it will probably be used to evaluate and control the pricing strategy, but it is difficult to find an example of a model assigned exclusively to *control* the marketing system.

At first one is tempted to conclude that control models do not fit the marketing system because so many variables are not measurable. Another possible explanation is that marketing planners do not think in mathematical terms and therefore shy away from models. A third explanation may be a general distrust of models because "the optimizer tends to ignore goals that he cannot quantify. This can distort the value of his work and produce justifiable discomfort in the consuming managers who must moderate quantitative results with their own qualitative judgments on important problems that have not been taken into account."[25] A fourth hypothesis is that there is a general disenchantment with some of the models because they promised more than they delivered. Available data support this fourth hypothesis.

Many of the control models were developed during the early 1960s by operations researchers who were working on problems of production and inventory control. Because the variables in this area are much more quantifiable and controllable than in marketing, we would expect wide adoption of these models by engineers in these fields. A survey of the members of the American Production and Inventory Control Society, in 1973, however, revealed that this was not the case.[26]

> Of the eight techniques surveyed from 1961 to 1973, only two—the "ABC" principle of inventory classification, and the Economic Order Quantity concept—demonstrated any significant growth in percentage use over this 12-year period. In contrast, the use of more sophisticated techniques like Linear Programming (LP), Queuing Theory (QT) and Probability Theory (PT) remained at very low levels of 10% or less. Only one of these techniques—Queuing Theory—showed a significant gain between 1961 and 1973. The others remained relatively constant or actually declined in use.[27]

Marketing planners should learn two lessons from the experience of their counterparts in production and inventory control. First, given the low adoption rate of production and inventory control models, marketers should not feel guilty about the lack of marketing control models. Second, in borrowing concepts and models from other fields, marketers should check back into the literature of the field from time to time to determine which methods have proved to be successful and which were passing fads.

The lack of control models reported in the literature does not necessarily mean that there are no control models in marketing. The very nature of a successful model makes it a competitive asset, so companies are reluctant to report a successful model. Conversely, researchers do not want to report unsuccessful models because this suggests that they are incompetent. As a result, if applications are reported at all, they tend to be mediocre ones.[28] Marketers who are considering developing control models should consider the experience of model builders.[29] The crucial points to remember are that management should be involved in the development and implementation of the model; the model should supplement the management decision process, not replace it; the model objectives and conditions to be portrayed must be defined clearly; there must be a commitment from management, and it must be involved in the planning and coordination of events leading to the model development; and finally, decision makers should be warned of the uncertainties in modeling so that they do not place too much reliance on the output.

SUMMARY   Evaluation and control are part of the marketing plan. They begin with the definition of objectives and goals that are measurable. Marketing evaluation measures changes in buyers' behavior or their mental states (awareness, attitudes, and buying probabilities). Distribution cost analysis and controlled experiments estimate the profitability of products, customers, and channels of distribution to identify more profitable marketing strategies.

Marketing budgets are one of the key mechanisms for controlling a marketing plan. The total budget will be supported by detailed budgets for media, promotion, personal selling, and marketing research. The marketing budget provides input to other key budgets in the firm.

The critical-path method (CPM) helps to control for the scarce resource of time. CPM sequences events so that the longest time path can be established and ways identified which will shorten the path. CPM identifies the departmental responsibility for completing an activity. It also emphasizes the importance of this activity to the entire completion time.

Decision analysis is generally thought of as a means of choosing among alternatives. It can serve also as a control device because it forces the planner to identify the relevant details of a decision and specify the assumptions. One means for controlling a plan is to periodically check on the validity of the assumptions.

Information for control differs from information for planning in that control information tends to be more internal, follow organizational lines, cover shorter time periods, and is historical. The computer has created a problem of information inundation as well as distorted the validity of the data that were fed it.

There are few examples of pure marketing control models in the literature. This does not necessarily mean that good control models do not exist, because such a model would be a competitive asset. The trend in control models for inventory and production control has been away from the mathematically sophisticated models to the simpler procedures. Marketers should note this trend when developing control models.

DISCUSSION QUESTIONS

1. Where do evaluation and control systems begin in the planning process?
2. What is the importance of the 80/20 rule in the evaluation of the product mix and the allocation of selling effort?

3. Identify the variables that are used to measure the productivity of each element in the marketing mix.

4. What control functions does a bar (or Gantt) chart perform? What is the advantage of CPM over a bar chart?

5. Discuss the marketing information system for the pharmaceutical firm in Fig. 19.3. How does it relate to the worksheets? What question would it answer in Table 3.1?

NOTES

1. W. A. Weisskopf, "Existence and Values," in *New Knowledge in Values*, ed. A. H. Maslow (New York: Harper & Brothers, 1959), pp. 107–118.

2. For additional discussion, *see* D. R. Longman and M. Schiff, *Practical Distribution Cost Analysis* (Homewood, Ill.: Richard D. Irwin, 1955); C. H. Sevin, *Marketing Productivity Analysis* (New York: McGraw-Hill, 1965); and "Distribution Cost Analysis," Bibliography No. 34 (Washington, D. C.: Small Business Administration, 1970).

3. Sevin, *op. cit.*

4. C. H. Sevin, "Marketing Profits from Financial Analysis," *Financial Executive*, May, 1966, pp. 22–30.

5. *Ibid.*

6. *Ibid.*

7. R. L. Ackoff, *A Concept of Corporate Planning* (New York: Wiley-Interscience, 1970), pp. 19–20.

8. D. B. Lucas and S. H. Britt, *Measuring Advertising Effectiveness* (New York: McGraw-Hill, 1963); H. D. Wolfe, J. K. Brown, and G. C. Thompson, *Measuring Advertising Results*, Studies in Business Policy, No. 102 (New York: National Industrial Conference Board, 1962).

9. A. A. Achenbaum, "Knowledge is a Thing Called Measurement," in *Attitude Research at Sea*, ed. L. Adler and I. Crespi (Chicago: American Marketing Association, 1966), pp. 111–126.

10. A. A. Achenbaum, "Relevant Measures of Consumer Attitudes." (Speech delivered at the Conference of the American Marketing Association, June 21, 1967.)

11. *Ibid.*, p. 6.

12. L. Edwards, "P & G Watcher Sees Lots of New Products Ahead," *Advertising Age*, January 24, 1977, pp. 1, 78.

13. *Ibid.*, p. 78.

14. Ackoff, *op. cit.*, p. 112.

15. *Ibid.*

16. P. F. Drucker, *Management* (New York: Harper & Row, 1974), p. 494.

17. W. Dusenbury, "CPM for New Product Introductions," *Harvard Business Review* (July-August 1967): 124–133.

18. *Ibid.*

19. CPM has largely replaced PERT because of the biases in the three time estimates required in PERT. For more detailed discussions and applications of CPM, *see* E. W. Davis, *Project Management: Techniques, Applications and Managerial Issues* (Norcross, Georgia: American Institute of Industrial Engineers, 1976); F. K. Levy, G. L. Thompson, and J. D. West, "The ABCs of the Critical Path Method," *Harvard Business Review* (September-October 1963): 98–108. The author is indebted to Professor E. W. Davis for advice on these paragraphs on CPM.

20. For a nontechnical discussion of decision trees, *see* J. F. Magee, "Decision Trees for Decision Making," *Harvard Business Review* (July-August 1964): 126–138. For applications of decision

analysis in marketing, *see Decision Making in Marketing: A Colloquium* (New York: Conference Board, 1971).

21. R. Brown, "Decision Analysis in the Organization," working paper (Cambridge, Mass.: Marketing Science Institute, December 1974).

22. D. Ronald Daniel, "Management Information Crisis," in *Management Control Systems*, ed. R. N. Anthony, J. Dearden, and R. F. Vancil (Homewood, Ill.: Richard D. Irwin, 1965), p. 114.

23. Ackoff, *op. cit.*, p. 119.

24. *Ibid.*, pp. 126–127.

25. *Ibid.*, p. 12.

26. E. W. Davis, "A Look at the Use of Production-Inventory Techniques: Past and Present," *Production and Inventory Management* (Fourth Quarter, 1975), pp. 1–19.

27. *Ibid.*, pp. 8–10.

28. G. L. Urban, "Building Models for Decision Makers," *Interfaces* (May 1974): 1–11.

29. *Ways to Improve Management of Federally Funded Computerized Models*, Report to the Congress. LCD-75-111 (Washington, D.C.: Comptroller General of the United States, August 23, 1976).

SUGGESTED READINGS

Crawford, C. M., "The Trajectory Theory of Goal Setting for New Products," *Journal of Marketing Research* **3** (May 1966): 117–125.

Dean, J., "Does Advertising Belong in the Capital Budget?" *Journal of Marketing* **30**, 4 (October 1966): 15–21.

Grayson, C. J., Jr., "Management science and business practice," *Harvard Business Review* (July-August 1973): 41–48.

Hamilton, W. F., and M. A. Moses, "A Computer-Based Corporate Planning System," *Management Science* **21**, 2 (1974): 148–159.

Urban, G. L., "Building Models for Decision Makers," *Interfaces* (May 1974): 1–11.

Ways to Improve Management of Federally Funded Computerized Models, Report to the Congress. LCD-75-111 (Washington, D.C.: Comptroller General of the United States, August 23, 1976).

Part V. Strategic Decision Cases

The cases in this section were collected to meet the need for cases in strategic planning as well as to cover contemporary topics not generally available in marketing cases. These topics include information systems to control the sales force (the Burroughs Wellcome case, Chapter 20), an energy product that preserves the environment (the methane generator, Chapter 21), a health-care service for lower-income families (Wake Health Services, Inc., Chapter 22), the effect of inflation and shortages of material on strategies (April Showers, Chapter 23), and coordinating the marketing planning for new acquisitions (S & L, Chapter 24). The relationship of these cases to preceding chapters and to the cases within the chapters and the text material are noted in the preface. The cases in Part V may be used to supplement cases presently being used.

CHAPTER **20**

Information Systems for Sales Management: Burroughs Wellcome Company, U.S.A.

HISTORY Burroughs Wellcome Company was founded in London in 1880 by two young American pharmacists—Henry A. Wellcome of Wisconsin and Silas M. Burroughs of New York. London was then the export center of the world, and the two Americans acted as agents for American drug firms in marketing their products in other parts of the world. The new Burroughs Wellcome Company set up its own manufacturing facilities and began pioneering in compressed medication and in pharmaceutical research. Burroughs died in 1895, leaving Wellcome as the sole owner.

In 1906 the United States branch was established in New York City. In 1924 Henry Wellcome linked together all of his varied enterprises, some 30 associated companies and 68 subsidiaries, into one corporate body called The Wellcome Foundation Limited. Under the terms of his will, all of the shares of the foundation were transferred to The Wellcome Trust, which was established as a philanthropic organization. Under the terms of the trust, the trustees are required to use the dividend income from the foundation for the support of research anywhere in the world, in human and veterinary medicine and the allied sciences, and in the establishment or endowment of research museums and libraries.

Burroughs Wellcome Company, U.S.A., is comprised of the corporate headquarters and research laboratories, employing some 500 people, located at Research Triangle Park, N.C., and the production plant, employing another 925 people, located at Greenville, N.C. An additional 500 men and women make up the field force of service representatives, also known as "detail" men and women.

SALES REPRESENTATIVES Company sales representatives, or "detail" men and women, are used heavily in the pharmaceutical industry and represent the bulk of the marketing effort promoting sales of ethical drugs. Products in the pharmaceutical industry are basically separated into two categories—ethical drugs and proprietary products. Ethical drugs are advertised and promoted only to the medical profession and are usually sold by

---

Case material is prepared as the basis for class discussion. Cases are not designed to present illustrations of either effective or ineffective handling of administrative problems.

Written by Jesse W. Meyers, Jr., under the direction of G. David Hughes, Burlington Industries Professor of Business Administration, University of North Carolina. All rights reserved.

prescription. Proprietary products are advertised directly to consumers and do not require a prescription.

"Detail" representatives are trained to make highly professional product presentations to physicians and paramedical personnel in an effort to persuade them to prescribe the company's products. They work on a straight salary basis with no commissions. They do little or no selling and are highly trained in the technical aspects and characteristics of the drugs they sell. Their activities consist mainly of promotional presentations, responding to inquiries, and distributing promotional materials.

THE PHILOSOPHY OF MANAGING THE REPRESENTATIVES Late in 1975 Charles H. Singler, General Sales Manager of Burroughs Wellcome Company, U.S.A., was trying to decide if he should spend $300,000 for a new marketing research service to help him direct the selling effort. He tried to relate the utility of the new information to his function as a general sales manager.

"My main task as General Sales Manager is to motivate the representatives in the field force. If I can recruit the right people, train them properly, give them competitive tools with which to work, and then *motivate* them to sell our products to the best of their abilities, then sales will take care of themselves. I think I am more of a Sales Personnel Manager than a Sales Product Manager."

Under this sales philosophy, the sales of Burroughs Wellcome have gone from around $60 million in 1970 to a projected $135 million in 1975.

GENERAL SALES MANAGER As General Sales Manager (GSM), Mr. Singler must function as a sales strategist, sales tactician, and personnel manager. He is directly responsible to the Vice-President for Marketing and is responsible for the entire field sales force, Wellcome Reagents Division (the company's diagnostic sales unit), and the Sales Administration Department.

As a *sales strategist*, the GSM sits on the Marketing Policy Committee (MPC), the Distribution Committee, and the Management Coordinating Committee. Within these committees, marketing policy for the company is developed, guidelines are established, and objectives are defined and set.

As a *sales tactician*, Mr. Singler takes the guidance from these committees and the sales promotion plans from the Sales Promotion and Training Department and, with his staff, implements the company's sales strategy. The Sales Promotion and Training Department, headed by Jack Munroe, continually works in close coordination with the Sales Department in the areas of both planning and training, which will be discussed later. The major goal of the sales department is to achieve sales forecasts within budgetary constraints. The achievement of this goal is the overriding objective that governs the actions of every member of the department, from GSM to representative. Mr. Singler monitors execution, implements changes and corrections when necessary, and recommends changes to the Vice-President for Marketing when it appears that company objectives cannot be met within established policies.

As a *personnel manager*, he is responsible for the recruiting program which provides continuing availability of qualified personnel within the sales staff, the sales department, and the Wellcome Reagents Division. He is also responsible for the training and development of his staff to ensure capable management succession at all levels. He establishes performance criteria for his staff and is responsible for reviewing their performance regularly. Finally, he is responsible for motivating his personnel to achieve the sales objectives of the company, to promote the prestige of Burroughs Wellcome, and to make appropriate contributions to the social climate of the communities in which the company operates.

REGIONAL SALES MANAGERS   Below the GSM in the managerial hierarchy are eight regional sales managers (RSM), each in charge of a separate sales region. RSMs are responsible for planning, organizing, leading, and controlling the regional sales staff. In doing so, the duties of the RSMs closely parallel and support those of the GSM.

The RSM acts both as a sales tactician and a personnel manager. As a *sales tactician*, the RSM develops plans for the regional sales staff that support the general sales plan, annually preparing a one- and three-year plan covering projections for expenditures, equipment, services, and personnel requirements for the sales region. The RSM collects and presents field marketing data to the GSM and the marketing policy committee, monitoring plans, and provides feedback to the GSM on the plan's performance.

As a *personnel manager*, the RSM supports the GSM's plans for training by providing trainer personnel and feedback on trainees' performance. Each RSM has the authority to hire and fire in other regions and supervises the recruiting activities of the regional sales staff. The RSM supports the performance evaluation through the district sales managers.

DISTRICT SALES MANAGER/FIELD SUPERVISOR   Within the eight sales regions, there are a total of 51 sales districts, each headed by a district sales manager (DSM) or a field supervisor. After being promoted to a DSM position, a representative goes through a probationary period and is known as a field supervisor. Upon successful completion of this probationary period, the field supervisor's title is changed to DSM.

The DSM's duties parallel and support those of the RSM. However, the DSM is more of an implementer.

As a personnel manager, the DSM is responsible for implementing the recruiting program and making it work in order to ensure a constant supply of qualified sales personnel for the company. Once representatives have been recruited, the DSM takes an active role, sometimes being called on to instruct a group of new representatives at corporate headquarters. At other times the DSM may supervise the special representative-trainer in training new representatives. Finally, the DSM conducts some training of new representatives in one-on-one field situations.

The DSM is also charged with reviewing and reporting the performance of the district sales staff, both to recognize achievements and to detect unsatisfactory trends and deviations from planned performance at an early stage. When marginal performance is detected, the DSM must ensure that prompt and appropriate action is taken.

The DSM is a communications medium, being responsible for seeing that the district sales staff is kept informed of company objectives and programs and that feedback is provided to the RSM on their needs, concerns, and achievements.

Finally, the DSM prepares projections for expenditures for services, equipment, and personnel required for the district sales staff and provides it as input to the RSM's annual and three-year plans.

FIELD REPRESENTATIVE   The focal point of the organization is the 510 field representatives (commonly referred to as reps) who detail Burroughs Wellcome products across the United States. They are reponsible to their respective DSM or field supervisor. A summary of their activities would not do justice to the requirements and reponsibilities placed on these individuals. Following is the official job description used by the GSM and intermediate managers in evaluating representatives.

The representatives are responsible for:

1. Developing excellence in product knowledge, planning, selling skills, and acquiring the proper attitude toward the job requirements and company goals.

2. Detailing doctors and dentists to persuade and encourage them to prescribe, recommend, and use Burroughs Wellcome products.

3. Calling on leading retail stores to make certain they have in stock sufficient quantities of Burroughs Wellcome products, take care of demand created by detail work, inform retailers of products being detailed, actively sell and help educate pharmacy personnel to sell those products ordinarily purchased by the lay customer, obtain prescribing and marketing information.

4. Calling on all assigned hospitals and medical centers to actively detail and sell Burroughs Wellcome products for use in the institution; cultivate staff members, residents, interns, and other hospital personnel; maintain adequate stocks of Burroughs Wellcome products in the hospital and assist the hospital in setting up contracts with wholesale distributors; and know the wholesalers from whom they usually buy.

5. Covering assigned wholesale distributors, with particular attention to maintenance of adequate stocks in clean condition, seeking of continual support from wholesaler's salespeople to check retailer's and hospitals' stocks, seeing that retailers place new items in stock as soon as released, speaking at wholesaler sales meetings.

6. Calling on personnel in medical, dental, pharmacy, and nursing schools, industrial and college health clinics, and military and other governmental health facilities to persuade and encourage them to prescribe, recommend, or use Burroughs Wellcome Company products.

7. Evaluating the territory properly in relation to leading prescribers, key stores, and hospitals; planning work to allow proper time to call on physicians, hospitals, and wholesale and retail druggists according to evaluation; keeping Work Plan Books and other records up to date and set up according to instructions.

8. Following the detailing and selling-program instructions.

9. Properly utilizing specimen material and selling aids.

10. Promptly submitting all reports requested by the office or supervisor.

11. Keeping the DSM or field supervisor informed about any unusual developments in their territorites.

12. Maintaining complete and easily available records and files of any information of future reference value and disposing of such records and files after they have ceased to be of value.

13. Working with fellow representatives on a team basis.

14. Conforming to legal and ethical requirements in the promotion of Burroughs Wellcome products.

15. Assisting in the recruiting of qualified applicants for positions as Burroughs Wellcome representatives.

SPECIAL REPRESENTATIVE-TRAINER In an effort to improve the training program and to motivate the trainers, the company created the position of special representative-trainer (SRT) in 1973. There are 51 SRTs, one SRT per district. The allocation is made on the basis of an average of one SRT per sales district within each sales region. If one district has two highly qualified representatives, both can be appointed SRTs; a district with less-qualified reps may not have an SRT. Since SRTs cross district and regional boundaries in executing their tasks, trainers are available to all districts.

SRTs are selected competitively by the RSM, based on the recommendation of the DSM and with the approval of the GSM. The assignment is for two years and carries with it a $50 monthly salary increase. At the end of the two-year period, the SRT can be (1) reappointed if still qualified and competitive; (2) placed on inactive status if still qualified; (3) demoted if judged to be no longer qualified.

SRTs hold down a regular sales territory and also spend up to nine weeks per year in training assignments. Before an SRT can exceed this nine-week limit, every other SRT in the nation must have met the nine-week requirement. These training assignments can include:

1. Providing week-long territory training of new representatives on the trainee's territories.
2. Working with a DSM (not necessarily his or her own) at corporate headquarters in a two-week basic training class.
3. Working as a representative training instructor with the sales training staff at corporate headquarters in the four-week advanced training class.
4. Undertaking special assignments in the field with other representatives who are no longer trainees but who need assistance.
5. Helping to screen interested applicants by having them spend two days in the field with the SRT working that territory. In this way the applicant sees the job of a sales representative in action, and the company has an opportunity to observe the applicant under prolonged exposure.
6. Presenting topics at district sales meetings.

SPECIAL REPRESENTATIVE: MEDICAL AND GOVERNMENT Two more special categories of representative are the special representative—medical center (SRMC) and the special representative—government (SRG). As their title suggests, SRMCs specialize in visiting hospitals and medical centers, whereas SRGs specialize in detailing Burroughs Wellcome products to government agencies. SRMCs and SRGs are highly qualified specialists who are promoted to their positions after demonstrating their capabilities while performing as representatives. There are 64 SRMCs and 11 SRGs spread throughout the United States; their territories are determined by the number and concentration of medical centers and government agencies.

SENIOR REPRESENTATIVES Some areas, such as Hawaii, are isolated, too large for one sales territory, but too small to be a sales district. In these instances the representatives are placed under the supervision of a *senior representative*, who performs the duties of a DSM and also services a small territory as a representative while supervising a lesser number of prepresentatives. There are currently two senior representatives functioning in this semisupervisory role.

WELLCOME REAGENTS   Wellcome Reagents Division, the company's diagnostic sales unit, has a total of 14 representatives selling its specialized products across the nation. This division has its own sales manager, who is responsible directly to Mr. Singler. Reagents can be thought of as chemical detectors because of their capacity to detect, examine, or measure other specific substances. These representatives primarily visit medical laboratories and detail their specialized products to these insitutions.

TOPS PROGRAM   TOPS is the acronym applied to the company's management development program: *T*emporary *O*ffice *P*ersonnel *S*ociety. Under this program, outstanding representatives and special reps are selected competitively to come to corporate headquarters on a temporary basis. There, they are given a functional job in one of the marketing division's four departments. These assignments are for two years and may be extended for an additional year if the need arises. While in a TOPS assignment, representatives are expected to broaden their background and outlook and begin to take a management viewpoint. TOPS people are thought of by management as having the potential to eventually move up to management jobs in the organization. Once the assignment is over, they can go back to their old positions, be promoted to DSM and given a new assignment, or remain at corporate headquarters in a permanent staff position.

NORMAL PROMOTION AND LINE OF PROGRESSION   In considering candidates for promotion, representatives are at the entry level. SRTs, SRGs, and SRMCs are all equal on the next level. The senior representative is at an intermediate level between the representative and DSM. Next up the ladder is the field supervisor, followed by the DSM and then the RSM. TOPS people are selected from the two lowest levels. Office staff personnel are selected from the TOPS people, the DSM ranks, and the RSM ranks. A model of the promotional track is depicted in Fig. 20.1.

Fig. 20.1   The promotional track at Burroughs Wellcome.

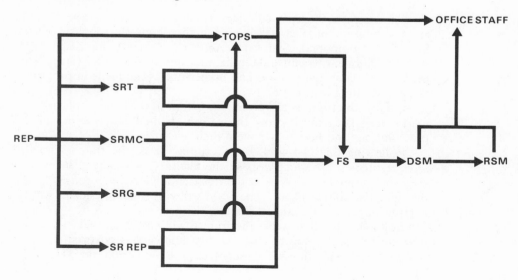

Recruiting   Recruiting is handled in a unique way at Burroughs Wellcome. Every representative, in addition to detailing the company's products, is also a recruiter. Representatives, as part of their duties, regularly visit college and university campuses in their territories to tell the Burroughs Wellcome story. Interested applicants are screened, and arrangements are made for qualified applicants to be interviewed by the DSM. The DSM may make arrangements for an applicant to spend a few days on the job with an SRT or a highly qualified representative to give the applicant a feel for the job as well as to give the company an opportunity to observe the applicant in a work environment. If the applicant is still interested and the DSM still feels that he or she would make a good representative, arrangements are made for the applicant to be interviewed by the RSM. The RSM has the authority to hire a new representative.

Throughout the recruiting process, the applicant is not being interviewed for a specific territory, but rather to determine whether he or she meets the high standard Burroughs Wellcome demands of its representatives. The RSM may be hiring an individual who will be employed in a territory in a completely different region. The fact that the RSM will be judged by other RSMs and will be receiving representatives hired by other RSMs helps keep the standard high and consistent among all RSMs.

Training   After being recruited and hired, the new representatives must be trained. Initial training consists of a two-week basic training class. During this period, they receive an introduction to sales techniques and instruction on several of the company's many products. One DSM and one SRT are selected to conduct the bulk of the training in classroom facilities at corporate headquarters.

This two-week training session includes parallel training in four areas, all conducted intermittently and all integrated. First, the representatives learn the mechanics of being a Burroughs Wellcome representative. They are taught the company's wholesale distribution system, are exposed to a selling plan, and are shown how to fill out expense account vouchers and other company reports. Next, they are exposed to basic selling skills and techniques and given numerous opportunities to practice them in mock situations using the Burroughs Wellcome products in which they are being educated.

Concurrently, the representatives are educated in the therapeutic actions, the market and competitors for such well-known, high-volume Burroughs Wellcome products as Empirin® Compound, Sudafed®, Actifed®, Septra®, Lanoxin®, Zyloprim®, Neosporin® Ointment/Cream and Opthalmics, and Cortisporin® Otics. This training takes the form of classroom lectures and homework assignments in programed texts known as basic training learning units.

Finally, the trainees are given instruction in the legal implications of ethical drug marketing. They must know the various United States codes affecting their sales presentations and how they govern their activities.

Following this two-week basic training class, the trainees go to their assigned sales territories. The first week in the territory is usually spent with the DSM, who assists in setting up an office at the representative's home, getting a company car, and outlining the sales territory. The DSM will visit some physicians with the trainee, who is given opportunity to detail some of the products.

Following the first week, the trainee will spend the next three weeks with three different SRTs. During this period, the emphasis is on products, policies, and procedures. Following this initial four-week training period, the SRT or DSM will spend three days with the trainee in the eighth week, two days in the twelfth week, two days in the sixteenth week, and two days in the twentieth week. Throughout the training period, the trainee maintains a copy of the territory training schedule (Fig. 20.2). This schedule lists all products and topics to be scheduled, as well as a time schedule for activities. In addition, the trainee maintains a schedule for special assignments (Fig. 20.3), which lists specialized topics to be covered.

While conducting training, the trainer maintains a log of daily training objectives and progress (Fig. 20.4) to ensure that all topics are covered. The trainer also keeps a territory training report (Fig. 20.5) for evaluating the trainee's progresss each week.

In addition to the field training, the trainee is also required to complete ten home-study correspondence courses on products to which he or she has not been exposed. Once the field training is satisfactorily completed and the ten correspondence courses have been completed and returned, the trainee is ready for the final phase of training.

This final phase, called the advanced training class, consists of a four-week course conducted by the office staff at corporate headquarters. This class uses much the same format as the basic training class, but also includes tours of all manufacturing and lab facilities, covers more products at a higher level, and offers opportunities to polish selling skills under the watchful eye of the sales training staff and experienced representatives now serving on the office staff. After completing this course, a trainee is fully qualified and takes his or her place alongside the other Burroughs Wellcome representatives. Postgraduate training will consist of course segments at sales meetings, home study courses for new products, sales promotion bulletins, and on-the-spot corrections during periodic DSM visits.

EVALUATION   Evaluation of a representative is done on two different forms. The first form (Fig. 20.6) is called the supervisory report. This report is filled out by the DSM each time a representative is visited. Sales promotion is done on the basis of a two-month cycle. A selling plan outlines instructions for each two-month cycle. There are six selling plans and six promotion cycles during each fiscal year. The company has a policy that the DSM will spend two days with each representative in the district during each promotion cycle. Consequently, a representative should receive six supervisory reports each year. These reports are discussed with the representative after they are completed. The DSM retains a copy of the report and forwards copies to the RSM and the GSM.

The second and more important form is the district sales manager's appraisal form (Fig. 20.7), which is completed once each year. The DSM completes a copy of the form and the representative too completes a copy for self-evaluation. The DMS and the representative then sit down together and compare and discuss the differences in the evaluations and how the representative can improve his or her performance. The DSM keeps one copy of the appraisal and forwards one copy to the RSM.

SALARIES AND BONUSES   All Burroughs Wellcome representatives work on a salary-plus-bonus basis. There are no commissions. The company establishes a bonus pool at the beginning of each sales year. This pool is broken up, with 40 percent going to the sales performance pool and 60 percent going to the merit evaluation pool.

ORIGINAL: TRAINEE'S DSM
TRAINEE
RSM
TRAINERS
TRAINERS' DSM's
TRAINING DEPT

TERRITORY TRAINING SCHEDULE *(Trainee to return to supervisor
after territory training. Trainer's copy to trainee's supervisor at end of week.)*

FROM: SALES TRAINING DEPARTMENT   TO:_____ DATE: _____

TRAINEE:
ADDRESS:
ASSIGNED TERRITORY:
TELEPHONE:

1st week dates		Trainer:
Monday		Address
Tuesday	Sudafed	
Wednesday		
Thursday	Actifed, Actifed-C	
Friday		Phone:

2nd week dates		Trainer:
Monday	Septra	Address:
Tuesday		
Wednesday		
Thursday		
Friday		Phone:

3rd week dates		Trainer:
Monday	Neosporin Ointment and Cream	Address:
Tuesday		
Wednesday	Neosporin Ophthalmic Solution and Ointment	
Thursday		
Friday	Empirin Compound c̄ Codeine, Empracet with Codeine, Ascodeen-30	Phone:

4th week dates		Trainer:
Monday	Cortisporin Otic	Address:
Tuesday		
Wednesday	Zyloprim	
Thursday		
Friday		Phone:

| *About 8th week* | Anectine | Trainer: |
| 3 days only | Neosporin G.U. Irrigant Neosporin Foil Packets Bacteriology Lab Contacts | Phone: |

| *About 12th week* | | Trainer: |
| 2 days only | Lanoxin, Cardilate, Wholesale | Phone: |

| *About 16th week* | | Trainer: |
| 2 days only | Zyloprim | Phone: |

| *About 20th week* | | Trainer: |
| 2 days only | Septra | Phone: |

After Triangle Training (IF NEEDED)

| *About 4th week after Triangle Training* | | Trainer: |
| Hospital | | Phone: |

| *About 8th week after Triangle Training* | | Trainer: |
| Retail | | Phone: |

TO CORRECT ASSIGNMENTS:

U.S.A. 1153A
Rev. 12/1/76

Fig. 20.2   The Burroughs Wellcome Territory Training Schedule.

FROM: _____ TO: TRAINING DEPARTMENT (ORIGINAL)
(TRAINER)   RSM, DSM, YOUR FILE (COPIES)

SPECIAL ASSIGNMENTS *(Trainee's copy to be initialed and dated by Territory Trainer and Trainee.)*

1ST WEEK   *Completed*
(Complete all for week unless previously
done.)
Obtain a map of territory, mark off
boundaries of sections, discuss Working
Order and prepare Forward Itinerary
(DSM/FS if possible).   _____
Review TIPS Operations Manual.   _____
Set up temporary office.   _____
Organize storage of samples, forms, litera-
ture in motel, car and detail bag.   _____
Review procedures binder and order addi-
tional stationery.   _____
Begin Retail Territory Training Course.   _____
Begin Hospital Territory Training Course.
Review Expense Account procedure and
advise trainee to save receipts (DSM/FS if   _____
possible).
If Expense Account is due in some other
week, it will be the responsibility of the
Territory Trainer working with the trainee   _____
at that time to do this.
Explain State Welfare, Medicare Programs   _____
and Sampling Laws (DSM/FS if possible).

2ND WEEK
Review Hospital Section of Procedures   _____
Manual.
Review Government Section of Procedures   _____
Manual.
Continue work on Retail Territory Training   _____
Course.
Continue work on Hospital Territory   _____
Training Course.

3RD WEEK
Review Auto Manual.   _____
Explain Selling Plan.   _____
Make Occupational Medicine calls (student   _____
health center, industrial clinic).
Continue work on Retail Territory Training   _____
Course.
Continue work on Hospital Territory   _____
Training Course.

4TH WEEK
Discuss procedure for completing Compre-   _____
hensive Assignments.
Help trainee plan for first day alone — next   _____
Monday.
Continue work on Retail Territory Training   _____
Course.
Continue work on Hospital Territory   _____
Training Course.

ABOUT 8TH WEEK   *Completed*
Coach trainee in promoting Anectine,
Neosporin G.U. Irrigant, and Neosporin
Foil Packets.   _____
Check hospital record cards.   _____
Continue work on Hospital Territory   _____
Training Course.

ABOUT 12TH WEEK
Coach trainee in detailing Lanoxin.   _____
Review progress with Retail Territory   _____
Training Course.
Review progress with Hospital Territory   _____
Training Course.
Review Wholesale Territory Training Course   _____
and make a wholesale call.

ABOUT 16TH WEEK
Coach trainee in detailing Zyloprim.   _____
Review progress with Retail Territory   _____
Training Course.
Review progress with Hospital Territory   _____
Training Course.

ABOUT 20TH WEEK
Coach trainee in detailing Septra.   _____
Review progress with Retail Territory   _____
Training Course.
Review progress with Hospital Territory   _____
Training Course.

_____

After Advanced Training (IF NEEDED)

_____

**ABOUT 4TH WEEK AFTER ADVANCED
TRAINING**
Work hospital projects.   _____
Coach trainee in other areas as needed.   _____

**ABOUT 8TH WEEK AFTER ADVANCED
TRAINING**
Work retail outlets.   _____
Coach trainee in other areas as needed.   _____

COMMENTS:

U.S.A. 1153B Rev. 7/77

Fig. 20.3 The Burroughs Wellcome Special Assignments Schedule.

TERRITORY TRAINER'S LOG OF DAILY TRAINING
OBJECTIVES AND PROGRESS U.S.A. 1077

TO: Training Department (original)
RSM, DSM, Your File (copies)

Prepare daily. Trainer and trainee to initial each day's objective. Please press pen down hard and write clearly.

MONDAY	
	Main Objective
Date _____	Progress
Initials	
_____ _____	

TUESDAY	
	Main Objective
Date _____	Progress
Initials	
_____ _____	

WEDNESDAY	
	Main Objective
Date _____	Progress
Initials	
_____ _____	

THURSDAY	
	Main Objective
Date _____	Progress
Initials	
_____ _____	

FRIDAY	
	Main Objective
Date _____	Progress
Initials	
_____ _____	

Specific recommendations made to trainee for further development

Fig. 20.4   The Burroughs Wellcome Log of Daily Training Objectives and Progress.

TERRITORY AND EXTENDED TRAINING REPORT   U.S.A. 1078 Rev. 12/76

WEEK # _____ TRAINEE _____   TO: Training Department (original)
                                                                   RSM, DSM, Your File (copies)
DATE _____ TRAINER _____

1. Report, evaluate and explain the trainee's performance in each of the major areas listed below.
    a. Rate the trainee overall in each major area by checking the appropriate box (5. Outstanding, 4. Above
       Average, 3. Satisfactory, 2. Marginal, 1. Unsatisfactory, 0. Unacceptable).
    b. The first column should be used as a memory jogger only to assist you in evaluating the trainee's performance
       in the major areas listed.
2. At end of Training Assignment, be sure to review trainee's performance with him or her.

KNOWLEDGE	5.	
1. Product*		
Depth	4.	
Sales Points		
Literature	3.	
Reprints		
2. Alternate Therapies	2.	
3. Customer		
*Please list and report	1.	
products scheduled for		
this assignment.	0.	
PLANNING	5.	
Alternate Calls		
Evaluation	4.	
Work Plan Booklet		
TIPS Cards	3.	
Call Backs		
Individual Calls	2.	
Personal Affairs		
Organization of	1.	
Supplies		
	0.	
SALES SKILLS	5.	
IBS's		
Benefits	4.	
Trial Closings		
Overcoming Objections	3.	
Closes		
Proving	2.	
Probing		
General Expressive	1.	
Ability		
Sales Aids	0.	
HOSPITALS	5.	
Please list and		
comment on all	4.	
completed tasks by		
code number	3.	
(HO-O/T-O)		
Other comments	2.	
	1.	
	0.	

Fig. 20.5 The Burroughs Wellcome Territory Training Report.

TERRITORY AND EXTENDED TRAINING REPORT (continued) U.S.A. 1078 Rev. 12/76

WHOLESALERS Return Goods Inventory Key Executive Personnel Salesmen	5. 4. 3. 2. 1. 0.	
RETAIL CALLS Please list and comment on all completed training tasks by code number (RO-O/T-O) Other Comments	5. 4. 3. 2. 1. 0.	
ATTITUDE Job Acceptance of Criticism Willingness to Work Self Improvement Conduct Punctuality Undesirable Mannerisms	5. 4. 3. 2. 1. 0.	
MISCELLANEOUS Moving Settled in home Personal problems Company Car		

Types of calls not made to date

MD/DO	HOSP	DENTAL	HEALTH CLINICS	W/S	GOV'T	OTHER

Would you be willing to share a territory with this new representative? Please explain why you feel as you do. (Use other side if necessary).

Fig. 20.5 (cont.)

SUPERVISORY REPORT

U. S. A. 91   5M

Representative_____ Date_____ Submitted by _____

PRODUCT KNOWLEDGE

DEPTH
SALES POINTS
LITERATURE
COMPETITION
REPRINTS

PLANNING

BALANCE
EVALUATION
WORK PLAN BOOKLET
PLANNED DETAIL
  AGAINST COMPETITION
CALL BACKS
INDIVIDUAL CALLS

SALES SKILLS

D & S
OPENINGS
F E C
2 WAY FLOW
OVERCOMING OBJECTIONS
CLOSINGS
USE OF REPRINTS AND
  SALES AIDS
PROBING

HOSPITALS

PLANNED PROGRAM
GETS TO DECISION
  MAKERS
SEES KEY RES., INT.,
  AND H.P. REGULARLY
PROG. SALES APPROACH

RETAIL CALLS

CHECK STOCKS
GETS Rx ING
  INFORMATION
DETAILS CLERKS
SELLS DEALS
NOTES MOVEMENT OF
  B.W. AND COMPETITION

ATTITUDE

SUPERVISORY COMMENTS
  AND SUGGESTIONS
COMPANY POLICIES
TEAM WORK
WILLINGNESS TO WORK
SELF IMPROVEMENT
TERRITORY MANAGEMENT

COMMENTS — USE BACK IF NECESSARY

Fig. 20.6   The Burroughs Wellcome Supervisory Report.

DISTRICT SALES MANAGER'S APPRAISAL OF REPRESENTATIVE -   USA 700A Revised 8/68

Prepare in duplicate - Once yearly on each Rep. Send 1 to Regional Mgr. Keep duplicate.

Name of Rep.   Territory   Date   NAME OF D.S.M. or F.S.

Show grade in each box: 1. Outstanding 2. Satisfactory 3. Unsatisfactory
                        X. Improving, - Backsliding.

	WORK PATTERN GRADE	Comments on important aspects of his performance and your course of action.
PRODUCT KNOWLEDGE		
Knowledge of physiology, pharmacology, therapeutics.		
Knowledge of sales points, user benefits, etc.		
Knowledge of content of detailing literature, R.G.'s, D & S program and reprints.		
Knowledge of competitive products and competitive activities.		
PLANNING		
Territorial knowledge.		
Maintains good balance in M.D., D.D.S., Hosp., Retail & Special Calls.		
Inquisitiveness re useful information.		
Use of written daily plan.		
Condition and up-to-dateness of Work Plan Book, including chronologic arrangement and U.S.A. 1040.		
Ability to make good evaluation on worth of calls based on information.		
Plans use of specimens. No undue shortage or surplus.		
Adequate number and proper scheduling of call-backs.		
Follows D & S & R.G. promotional activities -- uses D & S schedule card.		
SALES SKILLS		
Ability to discuss products intelligently.		
Ability to probe, quantify and get prospect into the discussion.		
Use of Fact, Explanation and Conclusion.		
Ability to overcome objections.		
Ability to "ask for the business."		

Fig. 20.7   The Burroughs Wellcome District Sales Managers' Appraisal of Representative Form.

SALES SKILLS (cont'd)	Grade	Comments
Skillful use of visualizers, literature, specimens, reprints and other selling tools.		
Uses 'Empirin' specimens as a calling card with receptionists.		
Shrewdness in judging how to handle difficult types of people. Not easily thrown.		
Imagination and resourcefulness in building good detailing and selling presentations, including good opening statements.		
Keeps himself well groomed.		
Keeps car, detail bag, etc. in good condition.		

HOSPITAL and/or MEDICAL SCHOOL COVERAGE		
Plans time well for contacting key personnel and departments indicated.		
Contacts pharmacology department at medical and dental schools.		
Cultivates residents.		
Contacts interns.		
Coordinates hospital work and detailing activity in his territory, contacting fellow Representatives when indicated.		
Ability to conduct hospital exhibit.		
Keeps complete and current information on hospital record cards.		
Regular contact with nursing schools.		
Keeps price lists up-to-date.		
Expands use of established products by getting to key people regardless of difficulties.		
Initiates and follows up hospital projects.		

RETAIL CALLS		
Check stocks and rotates dated items.		
Details pharmacists and clerks and leaves literature.		
Aggressively sells deals.		
Gets good placement of new items.		
Keeps price lists up to date.		

Fig. 20.7 (cont.)

WHOLESALERS	Grade	Comments
Maintains sound relationship with personnel on monthly basis.		
Speaks at sales meetings.		
Obtains maximum cooperation in promotion and placement of products.		
REPORTING		
Hospital exhibits reports.		
Punctual with reports and accounts.		
Keeps District Sales Manager informed.		
Keeps office informed.		
Accurate on expense reporting.		
ATTITUDE		
Toward Company.		
Toward The Job.		
Toward D& S Program.		
Toward Reporting.		
Toward Supervision.		
Toward Fellow Representatives.		
Industriousness.		
Self Improvement.		

PUT SUMMARY COMMENTS ON REVERSE SIDE OF SHEET.

Fig. 20.7   (cont.)

The sales performance pool is divided at the national level with an equal share allocated for each representative. Payment of this bonus is triggered when the company achieves 95 percent of forecast. If the company achieves 97 percent of forecast, each representative's allocation rises to 97 percent. If the company achieves 99 percent, each rep receives 99 percent, and so forth. If sales exceed 100 percent of forecast, additional money is added to the pool.

The merit evaluation pool is also divided at the national level, based on an equal share for each representative. The pool is then allocated to the sales districts according to the number of representatives in each district. Eleven shares go to a district with eleven reps, and ten shares go to a district with ten reps. At the end of the fiscal year, the DSM divides the pool among the district's representatives, based on their supervisory reports and their annual appraisal for the past year. Each representative receives a share proportionate to her or his relative merit. The bonus program is very important to representatives and for some amounts to more than $1000 per year.

The purpose of the bonus is to reward one year's performance. To reward long-term consistent performance, the company has the annual salary review, which takes into account long-term performance, salary ranges, and seniority.

TERRITORY INFORMATION PLANNING SYSTEM The *Territory Information Planning System* (TIPS) is a computer-based management system designed to assist the representatives by providing them with information about every physician in their territories, thereby making it possible for the reps to manage their time more effectively and concentrate their efforts on high-potential physicians. It also provides feedback to the marketing division to evaluate territory and district productivity.

The bases for the system are the physician call card (Fig. 20.8) and the weekly activity report (Fig. 20.9). Each representative receives a deck of physician call cards at the beginning of each two-month promotion period. Each card has printed on it the following information:

1. Physician's name and address
2. Representative's territory number
3. Section number
4. Medical education number—an identifying number for each physician, assigned by the AMA and made up of the following information:
   a) state
   b) medical school
   c) year of graduation
   d) sequential number within the graduating class
   e) a computer check digit
5. Burroughs Wellcome specialty, e.g., urologist, general practitioner, etc.
6. Call class—A, B, C, or E (a productivity measure assigned by representative based on access and prescriptions written)
7. Type of practice:
   a) PP—direct patient care
   b) STF—full-time hospital staff
   c) FAC—faculty
   d) INT—intern

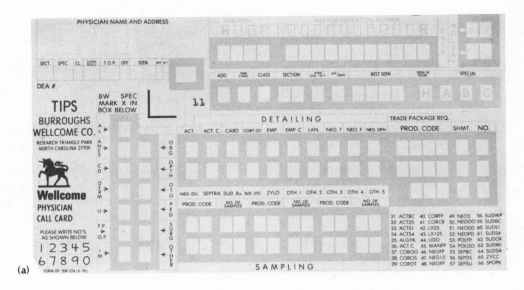

Fig. 20.8 The Burroughs Wellcome Physician Call Card: (a) front; (b) back.

8. Day off (shown as number 1 to 5, M to F)

9. Hour best seen

10. Appointment required (Y if yes, N if no)

11. Medical times listing (Y if yes).

This information is based on previous reports sent in by reps in the territory as well as other sources. The representative fills in both sides of this form when visiting the physician, noting which products were detailed and what samples were left with the physician. At the end of the week, the rep sends in all of the physician

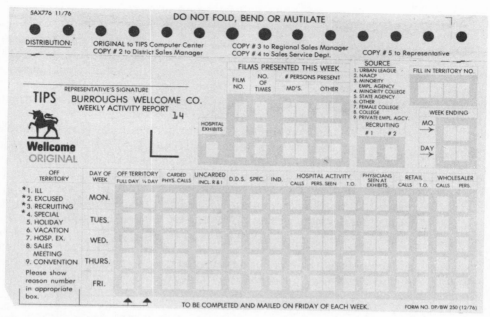

Fig. 20.9 The Burroughs Wellcome Weekly Activity Report.

cards for the physicians visited as well as cards for any new physicians visited for the first time. At the same time, the rep turns in a card for his or her weekly activity report.

The weekly activity report depicts a rep's activities for the week. The rep fills it out, showing how his or her time was spent each day. whether he or she was ill, vacationing, recruiting, on holiday, or at a sales meeting. For days spent working the territory, the report shows how the rep's visits were distributed.

These forms are processed by computer, and every two months reports are issued summarizing the activities of each representative, district, region, and the entire nation. Looking at this printout, a representative can compare his or her performance for the two-month period with past performance, with the average performance in his or her district, region, and the nation. The representative is then able to set individual goals for the next period.

BURROUGHS WELLCOME MANAGEMENT SYSTEM   In November 1972 a new management system was introduced to top management at Burroughs Wellcome. This system was an amalgam of the Louis A. Allen system and the Burroughs Wellcome system. Based on the well-recognized four functions and nineteen activities of management, this system involves establishing critical objectives, developing programs to support these objectives, and then measuring and evaluating performance and adjusting standards and programs to meet the objectives.

The program was initiated at the board level and then cascaded down to all levels of management and supervision. In the first year, sessions were conducted each Monday; 250 people received training, with each completing the required ten days of training. Following completion of this echelon, Mr. Singler conducted the formal phase of instruction to 8 RSMs and 51 DSMs during a series of ten four-day sessions. Participants from the sales management force were given the course outline and individual sections of the instructor's guide. Then participants were assigned responsibility for conducting portions of the course. They actually ran the course themselves.

Since then the participants have been engaged in developing their position descriptions. This is a slow process. The RSMs and the GSM are currently developing performance standards for the RSMs.

The heart of the program is the system of objectives. The GSM develops objectives from the marketing division's objectives. The RSM develops objectives from the GSM and those specifically for the region. The DSM develops objectives to support those of the RSM. Ultimately, the representatives derive their objectives to support the DSM.

When the entire program is implemented, every level is supporting the company objectives. Mr. Singler thinks it will be late 1977 before the program is implemented throughout the organization. The next step, of course, is to indoctrinate the representatives. The main problem would be in writing the performance standards for areas of critical objectives. In the past these activities had been observable rather than measurable. As these performance standards are developed, supervisory reports and appraisal forms will be changed to reflect the new standards.

DISTRIBUTION   In the ethical drug business, the normal sequence for marketing a drug product is to research the drug, develop a drug compound based on research findings, develop a dosage form, promote the drug, and turn the product over to wholesalers. Burroughs Wellcome has more than 400 franchised wholesalers and an additional 100 who are not franchised, but buy through other wholesalers.

In promoting products, a representative visits everyone in his or her territory involved with prescribing and selling ethical drugs. This includes wholesalers, retailers, hospitals, schools, pharmacists, physicians, nurses, and physicians' assistants.

Measuring the productivity of representatives and territories involves both subjective observable factors and objective measurable factors. Mr. Singler feels that the company has a good concept for the subjective factors and that this concept will be even better when the Louis Allen system has filtered down to the representatives' level. The problems are encountered in the objective factors.

These problems, particularly in the area of sales productivity, take three forms. First, there is the situation of the aggressive wholesaler. Some wholesalers are marketing nationwide and others regionally, but most market locally. For example, a New England wholesaler might be shipping to retailers in Texas. The sales in Texas are due to the efforts of the representative in that territory. However, because Burroughs Wellcome shipped the product to New England, the representative in that territory receives credit for the sale.

The second problem is the emergence of chains of retail drug stores. These chains are a central purchasing office. Products are shipped to a central warehouse for breakdown and redistribution nationwide. The representative in the territory where the purchasing office is located receives credit for the nationwide sales.

The third problem is in areas of high population concentration. Territories are broken down so that a representative will cover 275–300 physicians, 50–75 drugstores, and several hospitals in a two-month promotion cycle. In Los Angeles there are 10,000 physicians and three sales districts. Thirty-three representatives, three DSMs, and one RSM are located there. There are 17 wholesalers. A patient who lives in one territory may go to a physician in the second territory, receive a prescription from the physician, and get it filled in a neighborhood drugstore. To further confuse the issue, the druggist may buy from a wholesaler in the third territory.

THE UNICORN AWARD In 1971 the company initiated the Unicorn Award to be awarded annually to the top representative in the nation based on sales performance in his or her territory. The award was made for four consecutive years, but has been temporarily discontinued because of the backlash from representatives and DSMs on the fairness of the sales measures used in determining the recipient. Mr. Singler has no idea when the award will be reinstituted.

DRUG DISTRIBUTION DATA A new marketing research service is being offered Burroughs Wellcome for a price of between $400 and 500 thousand. This service is called *Drug Distribution Data* (DDD). Essentially, DDD takes the invoices on retail and hospital purchases from more than 500 drug wholesalers nationwide, breaks these shipments down by manufacturer and product, and totals these breakdowns by zip codes. There are 30,000 zip codes in the United States, so segregating territories by the zip codes in the territory gives a measure of retail sales by product and company for each territory. DDD would provide the company with not only sales by territory, but also the total market for the territory.

DISCUSSION QUESTIONS

1. Should Mr. Singler buy the DDD service?
2. Could DDD be used in other areas of marketing management?
3. Evaluate the BW sales management programs.

CHAPTER 21

Conserving Natural Resources: The Methane Generator

In the fall of 1973 a small group of North Carolina investors was talking about opportunities in converting organic waste into methane gas. The group decided to investigate the business potential.

ENERGY POTENTIAL FROM ORGANIC WASTE[1]   Energy needs in the United States are increasing at a very rapid rate and are expected to double in the next 15 years. In 1970, 96 percent of American energy requirements was supplied by oil, gas, and coal. The reserves of these fossil fuels, although formerly in abundant supply, are expected to decline severely in the next 30 years; some shortages have already occurred. Nuclear energy will provide a partial solution to the problem, with 23 percent of American energy needs predicted to be fulfilled by nuclear power in the year 2000. However, there does appear to be an ever-increasing void between the sources and uses of energy.

Enormous quantities of organic waste are produced each year in the United States. The total amount is in excess of 2 billion tons, and at least 880 million tons of this is moisture-free and ash-free organic material (dry organic solids), representing a potential energy source of significant magnitude that is not being utilized. The most abundant waste materials containing the organic solids are manure, urban refuse, and agricultural waste,[2] with manure and agricultural waste making up the largest portion.

The chief constituent of organic waste is cellulose; this material, continually made by photosynthesis from water and atmospheric carbon dioxide, is the most abundant raw material in the world. The cellulose produced by photosynthesis on the earth is the chief basis of all fossil fuels.

By special conditions and entrapment, coal, oil shale, petroleum, gas, and bituminous sands have been preserved. These fossil fuels, however, are only a small fraction of the living material that was formed in the past. Most of the organic material that formed in past ages has long since been converted by oxidation back to carbon dioxide and water. When this oxidation takes place in streams and rivers, water pollution results. When inefficient combustion of organic materials takes place, air pollution ensues.

This case was prepared by Robert D. Martin and W. Barry Schneider, second-year M.B.A. students, under the direction of G. David Hughes, Burlington Industries Professor of Business Administration, University of North Carolina, as the basis for class discussion only.

Research has shown that the slow process nature uses to create fossil fuels can be speeded up. Organic wastes can be converted fairly quickly to fuels—either oil or gas. In view of energy shortages facing the United States, the disposal problems presently created by organic waste and the continuously replenishable characteristic of organic waste, organic waste appears to be a very appropriate source for new energy.

THE METHANE GENERATOR

History The idea of taking the gas from farm waste is not a new concept. It was demonstrated at an exhibition in London in 1871, and in 1905 a very large plant designed to produce both gas and fertilizer from waste was installed in Bombay, India. During World War II the Germans built many methane generator plants for both the fertilizer and the methane that was made. Today, thousands of methane generator plants are in use in India, Algeria, South Africa, Korea, France, Hungary, and many other countries.

Description of the Process There are two kinds of organic decomposition: aerobic (requiring oxygen) and anaerobic (in the absence of oxygen). Any kind of organic material—animal or vegetable—may be broken down by either process, but the end products will be quite different. Aerobic fermentation produces carbon dioxide, ammonia, small amounts of other gases, considerable heat, and a residue which can be used as fertilizer. Anaerobic decomposition, on the other hand, creates combustible methane, carbon dioxide, hydrogen, traces of other gases, only a little heat, and a slurry which is superior in nitrogen content to the residue yielded by aerobic fermentation.

Anaerobic decomposition takes place in two stages as certain microorganisms feed on organic materials. First, acid-producing bacteria break the complex organic molecules down into simpler sugars, alcohol, glycerol, and peptides. Then, and only when these substances have accumulated in sufficient quantities, a second group of bacteria converts some of the simpler molecules into methane. The methane-releasing microorganisms are especially sensitive to environmental conditions.

Anaerobic digestion of waste material will occur at temperatures ranging from 32° to 156°F. The action of the bacteria responsible for the fermentation decreases rapidly below 60°F, however, and gas production is most rapid at 85° to 105°F and at 120° to 140°F. Different bacteria thrive in the two ranges, and those active within the higher limits are much more susceptible to environmental changes. Thus a temperature of 90° to 95°F is the most nearly ideal for stable methane gas generation.

The proper pH range for anaerobic fermentation is between 6.8 and 8.0, and an acidity either higher or lower than this will hamper fermentation. The introduction of too much raw material can cause excess acidity (a low pH reading), and the gas-producing bacteria will not be able to digest the acids quickly enough. Decomposition will stop until balance is restored by the growth of more bacteria. If the pH grows too high (not enough acid), fermentation will slow until the digestive process forms enough acidic carbon dioxide to restore balance.

Although bacteria responsible for the anaerobic process require both elements in order to live, they consume carbon about 30 to 35 times faster than they use nitrogen. Other conditions being favorable, then, anaerobic digestion will proceed most rapidly when raw material fed into a methane-generating plant contains a carbon-nitrogen ratio of 30 to 1. If the ratio is higher, the nitrogen will be exhausted while there is still a supply of carbon left. This causes some bacteria to die, releasing the nitrogen in their cells and eventually restoring equilibrium. Digestion proceeds slowly as this occurs. On the other hand, if there is too much nitrogen, fermentation (which will stop when the carbon is exhausted) will be incomplete, and the "left over" nitrogen will not be digested. This lowers the fertilizing value of the slurry. Only the proper ratio of carbon to nitrogen will ensure conversion of all available carbon to methane and carbon dioxide with minimum loss of available nitrogen.

The anaerobic decay of organic matter proceeds best if the raw material consists of about seven- to nine-percent solids. Fresh cow manure can be brought down to approximately this consistency by diluting it with an equal amount of water.

Design of the System Central to the operation and common to all methane generator plant designs is an enclosed tank called a digester. This is an air-tight tank which may be filled with raw organic waste and from which the final slurry and generated gas may be drawn. Differences in the design of these tanks are based primarily on the material to be fed to the generator, the cycle of fermentation desired, and the temperature under which the plant will operate. Tanks designed for the digestion of liquid or suspended-solid waste (such as cow manure) are usually filled and emptied with pipes and pumps. Circulation through the digester may also be achieved without pumps by allowing old slurry to overflow the tank as fresh material is fed in by gravity. An advantage of the gravity system is its ability to handle bits of chopped vegetable matter which would clog pumps. This is quite desirable, since the vegetable waste provides more carbon than the nitrogen-rich animal manure.

Complete anaerobic digestion of animal wastes, such as cow manure, takes about 50 days at moderately warm temperatures. Such matter, if allowed to remain undisturbed for the full period, will produce more than a third of its total gas the first week, another quarter the second week, and the remainder during the final six weeks. A more consistent and rapid rate of gas production may be maintained by continuously feeding small amounts of waste into the digester daily. The method has the additional advantage of preserving a higher percentage of the nitrogen in the slurry for effective fertilizer use. If this continuous feeding system is used, care must be taken to ensure that the plant is large enough to accommodate all the waste material that will be fed through in one fermentation cycle. A two-stage digester—in which the first tank produces the bulk of the methane (up to 80 percent) while the second finishes the digestion at a more leisurely rate—is often the answer.

Characteristics of the proposed generator. It will generate 6000 cubic feet of methane per month. The pump will require 360 cubic feet per month, and the heater will require about 400 cubic feet per month, depending on the climate and the insulation around the unit. The net production will be more than 5000 cubic feet per month.

When loaded with the proper carbon-nitrogen mixture, and if the temperature is maintained between 90° and 95°F, in 40 days the material will produce 95 percent of the gas that it is capable of producing.

The generator may be built of a variety of materials, including reinforced concrete and steel tanks. The approximate cost for materials in 1973 was about $400.

Conversion factors[3]

1. Five cubic feet of methane is produced from one pound of organic material.

2. One and one-quarter barrels of oil (net) from one ton of dry organic waste. This ratio excludes power used to stir, heat, and pump the waste.

3. The BTU values per cubic foot of gas are as follows: natural gas, 1100; methane from cow manure, 650; and gas from coal, 450.

4. One ton of the slurry that the system produced was equal to $7.00 worth of fertilizer, at 1973 prices.

Fig. 21.1   The proposed methane generator. (From L. L. Anderson and various copies of *Mother Earth News.*)

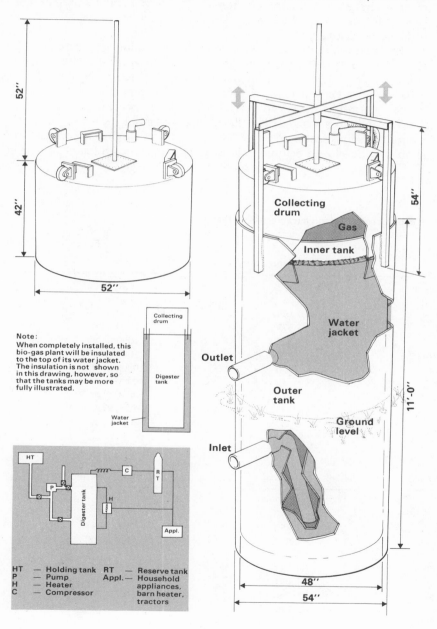

Feasibility   The students decided to look into the feasibility of producing and selling methane generators. They agreed that the initial market segment to investigate would be farmers. They also agreed that the preliminary analysis would be just for North Carolina, since they were all familiar with the state, which has a large farm population. Figure 21.1 shows the product they were considering. Some of the demographic data of North Carolina farms is given in Table 21.1. The breakdown of waste generated by farm animals is shown in Table 21.2, and Table 21.3 shows the energy requirements of an average 1800-square-foot home. It was generally thought that the methane generator could be used to satisfy the energy requirements of anything presently using propane or gasoline.

In determining the waste produced by farm animals, the students figured that the effective yield of manure would probably be much lower than that shown in Table 21.2. For instance, 100 percent of the manure would be recovered if the livestock is kept in a barn with a cement floor. However, if 50 percent of the stock is kept 50 percent of the time inside, the effective yield would be 25 percent.

The investors wondered if the market potential did exist in North Carolina for a product as presented in Fig. 21.1. If so, they felt that a complete marketing plan should be developed before attempts were made to gain financial backing.

TABLE 21.1   North Carolina farm characteristics (1969)

Farms with cattle and calves

No. cattle	No. farms
1–4	14,412
5–9	8,747
10–19	9,198
20–49	5,373
50–99	2,543
100–199	990
200–499	250
500–1000	19
over 1000	11

Farms with chickens

No. chickens	No. farms
1–99	16,761
100–399	1,120
400–1599	356
1600–3999	300
4000–7999	482
8000–15999	345
16000–29999	126
30000–59999	82
60000–99999	28
over 99999	10

Farms with hogs and pigs

No. hogs and pigs	No. farms
1–4	11,252
5–9	4,877
10–24	7,850
25–49	4,013
50–99	3,053
100–199	1,737
200–500	931
over 500	296

Farms with sheep and lambs

No. sheep and lambs	No. farms
1–24	253
25–99	85
100–299	20
300–1000	4

TABLE 21.1   (cont.)

	All farms*	Farms with sales of $2500 and over†
Poultry farms		4843
Dairy farms		2536
Livestock farms other than poultry and dairy		6479
Total	28,460	13,858

* only total given
† annual sales
United States Bureau of Census, Census of Agriculture, 1969, Volume Area Reports Part 26, North Carolina, Section 1. U.S. Government Printing Office, 1972.

TABLE 21.2   Wastes generated by major farm animals, 1971

Animals	Daily wastes, lb/animal*
Cattle	10.25 (9.5 to 11.4)
Hogs	1.2 (0.8 to 1.6)
Sheep	.56
Poultry	.06 (0.05 to 0.1)

* Figures in parentheses are ranges to account for the fact that the amount of manure produced by animals is dependent on such factors as confinement conditions, type of feed, size of animal, etc.
L. L. Anderson, "Energy Potential from Organic Wastes: A Review of the Quantities and Sources," Information Circular 8549 (Washington, D.C.: United States Department of the Interior, Bureau of Mines, 1972), p. 5.

TABLE 21.3   Energy requirements for 1800 sq ft home (in North Carolina)

	Gas heating (cu ft)	Gas water heating (cu ft)	Gas cooking (cu ft)	Electric general purpose (KWH)
January	28,600	2,500	800	400
February	23,900	2,500	800	400
March	15,500	2,500	800	400
April	7,200	2,500	800	400
May	—	2,500	800	400
June	—	2,500	800	400
July	—	2,500	800	400
August	—	2,500	800	400
September	—	2,500	800	400
October	4,800	2,500	800	400
November	15,500	2,500	800	400
December	23,900	2,500	800	400
Total	119,400	30,000	9,600	4,800

Conversion factors
1030 BTU per cubic ft gas (average)
3412 BTU per KWH
91.5 cubic ft gas = 1 gal propane
225 cubic ft gas = 1 gal gasoline

Prices, Fall 1973
Propane, 30¢ per gallon
Gasoline, 50¢ per gallon

DISCUSSION QUESTIONS

1. Would you recommend investing? Support your recommendation with facts.

2. Do a sensitivity analysis on the key variables in your analysis. Would these change your conclusion?

NOTES

1. L. L. Anderson, "Energy Potential from Organic Wastes: A Review of the Quantities and Sources," Information Circular 8549 (Washington D.C.: United States Department of the Interior, Bureau of Mines, 1972).

2. Field wastes generated by major agricultural crops, e.g., cornstalks, pea vines, sugarcane stalks, and leaves.

3. From L. L. Anderson, **op. cit.**, and various copies of *Mother Earth News*.

CHAPTER 22

Planning for a Nonprofit Health-Care Organization:
Wake Health Services, Inc.

In June 1976 the Wake Health Services, Inc. (WHSI) was writing its marketing plan for the next year. WHSI was formed as a private nonprofit corporation in April 1972. It was the only prepaid health plan in North Carolina. In 1976 it continued to receive funds from the Department of Health, Education and Welfare (HEW) to sponsor the Triangle Health Plan (THP). The purpose of the Triangle Health Plan (triangle: family-individual-community) is to provide primary health care to those individuals and families who would not otherwise have access to such services. The price structure is designed to provide health care, health maintenance, and preventive care to anyone, regardless of his or her income.

JUSTIFICATION FOR DEVELOPMENT OF WHSI

Wake County Medical Personnel   In December 1970 there were 153 practicing physicians per 100,000 civilian population in the United States. In Raleigh, which had a population of 121,577, there was a total of 208 physicians, for a physician-population ratio of 171 physicians per 100,000 population. Therefore, on the surface, it would appear that Raleigh was well supplied with medical practitioners. However, in Wake County, excluding Raleigh, there were 17 physicians, for a physician-population ratio of 15.9 physicians per 100,000 population. Grouping the Raleigh and Wake County physicians together for a total of 225, the physician-to-population ratio for the county as a whole was 98.5 physicians per 100,000 people, a figure well below the 1970 national ratio of 153/100,000.

   The physicians of Raleigh served not only the populations of Raleigh and most of Wake County, but also a good portion of the populations of the surrounding eastern

---

Case material is prepared as the basis for class discussion. Cases are not designed to present illustrations of either effective or ineffective handling of administrative problems.

Written by Douglas Behrman, under the direction of G. David Hughes, Burlington Industries Professor of Business Administration, University of North Carolina. All rights reserved.

North Carolina counties, including Granville, Franklin, Nash, Johnston, and Harnett counties. The population of these surrounding counties was approximately 230,000. Assuming that only 30 percent of the total population of these surrounding counties came to Wake County for health services, the ratio of physicians to population served becomes 75.6 physicians per 100,000. For the lower economic portions of the county population, the ratio was much lower.

Poverty as an Indicator of Need   In order to arrive at an understanding of the target population, HEW developed a socioeconomic (SES) index. The population in the 25–34-year-old classification was further divided into five equal-size strata according to the SES index. This stratification was thought to reflect the economic condition of county residents and to identify the age group most likely to receive the greatest benefit from the proposed medical services. Using this stratification, WHSI found that Wake County, including Raleigh, had a total of 24,344 families with incomes of less than $5000 (Table 22.1, column 4), and the total number of Wake County families in strata 1 and 2 (the lower SES strata) was 32,315 (column 2). The data indicated that the low-income population was approximately equally distributed among the four outlying towns of Apex, Fuquay, Zebulon, and Wake Forest, and southeast Raleigh (column 1).

TABLE 22.1   **Distribution of families in Wake County with annual incomes of less than $5000**

Town	Strata 1 and 2 population (1)	No. families in strata 1 and 2 (2)	Population with less than $5000 annual income (3)	Families with less than $5000 annual income (4)
Apex	10,112	3,066	7,617	2,310
Fuquay	12,326	3,679	9,285	2,771
Zebulon	17,036	5,416	12,833	4,080
Wake Forest	11,524	3,403	8,681	2,563
Southeast Raleigh	15,777	4,959	11,885	3,736
Raleigh	37,115	11,792	27,959	8,883
	103,890	32,315	78,260	24,343

	Family income by percent of families				
	0– $2999	$3000– 4999	$5000– 7999	$8000– 9999	$10,000 and over
Wake County	19.7	14.4	21.5	13.1	31.3

Experience at Wake Memorial Hospital confirms a large number of medically indigent. A recent study showed that 41 percent of the clinic patients were covered by Medicaid or Medicare, 4 percent were self-supporting, and 53 percent were classified as indigent, with no sponsorship, who could not afford to pay, but who did not qualify for Medicaid or Medicare.

Future Health Services Scarcity   The 1990 population projection for Wake County is 350,000 to 400,000, and the projection for Raleigh is 175,000 to 200,000. In 1970 health-care facilities and medical personnel would become totally inadequate by 1990.

Because Wake Memorial Hospital was initially operated by the Wake County

Hospital Authority, it was responsible for providing the service, equipment, and personnel necessary to care for the medically indigent outpatients of Wake County. Beginning in fiscal year 1969, Wake Memorial provided all hospital outpatient facilities, care, and support for Wake County.

The present health services for the indigent are inadequate. Wake Memorial Hospital bears the indigent load because the satellite hospitals do not accept patients unattended by a private medical practitioner. The services at Wake Memorial and those supplied by the various county health agencies are frequently inaccessible and, when they can be reached, often necessitate very long waits for patients.

The proposed operation of WHSI could provide services currently inaccessible to the indigent population and could reduce the inpatient demand by keeping the people well. An increase in demand for services at all levels is anticipated. Successful operation of the WHSI program would provide one alternative to the future problem of the delivery of a comprehensive primary medical service at reasonable cost to all elements of the population.

SERVICES PROVIDED BY WHSI The health services received by a member of the plan are as follows:

1. Office visits—by appointment
2. Health assessments
   a) physical and medical examinations
   b) X-rays
   c) laboratory tests
   d) Pap smears
3. Diagnosis and treatment:
   a) infections, illness, and routine injuries
   b) medications such as injections, treatment materials, supplies, dressings, and casts
   c) maternal and pediatric services
4. Referrals—for specialty care as prescribed by a WHSI physician
5. Physical therapy—when selected treatment would produce early improvement
6. Health education services
7. 24-hour on-call
8. Ambulance service when authorized by a family nurse practitioner.

The family health-center system designed for operation under Wake Health Services, Inc., is unique in three respects. It is a dispersed system with multiple entry points widely distributed across the geographic area served. The most important function of the program—the Family Health Center Operation—is under the direction of a family nurse practitioner (FNP). Each unit contains the staff required for delivery of primary health care.

Family nurse practitioners are trained at the University of North Carolina in Chapel Hill. This program trains registered nurses to make independent judgments and to assume principal responsibility for decision making in relation to health needs. The FNPs work collaboratively with physicians and other members of the health team.

CENTERS IN OPERATION In 1976 there were three centers in operation. The first center (102 N. Tarboro Road, Raleigh) opened in August 1973. The second center (3001

Falstaff Road, Raleigh) opened in October 1973. The Apex Center opened in April 1975 (Fig. 22.1). The first two sites were of modular construction; the third, of permanent construction. A very advantageous rental agreement has been reached on the land of the Tarboro site. The land for the Falstaff site is rented from the adjacent Wake Medical Center for one dollar a year.

The complete administrative and medical staff organizational structure is shown in Fig. 22.2. The clinic director is one of three general practitioners currently employed by WHSI. The Tarboro Center is directed by a black male assisted by three FNPs; the Falstaff Center, by a black female assisted by four FNPs; and the Apex Center, by a white male assisted by four FNPs.

The WHSI Board of Trustees, which establishes general policy, is composed of 27 members. Medical care providers, members of the health-care plan, and other responsible community members are evenly represented on this board. The administrative offices are located at a central office. Accounting, planning, marketing, and other administrative functions for all three centers are performed at this central location.

Fig. 22.1 Population by census tracts in Wake County, North Carolina, 1970.

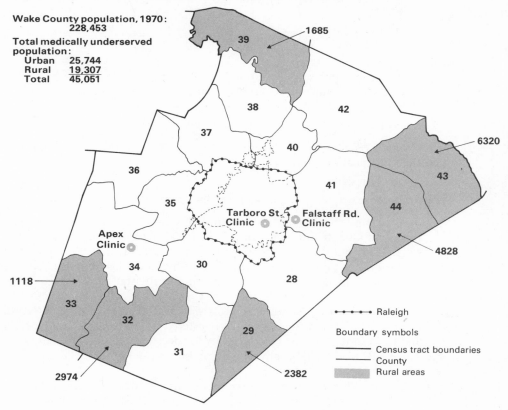

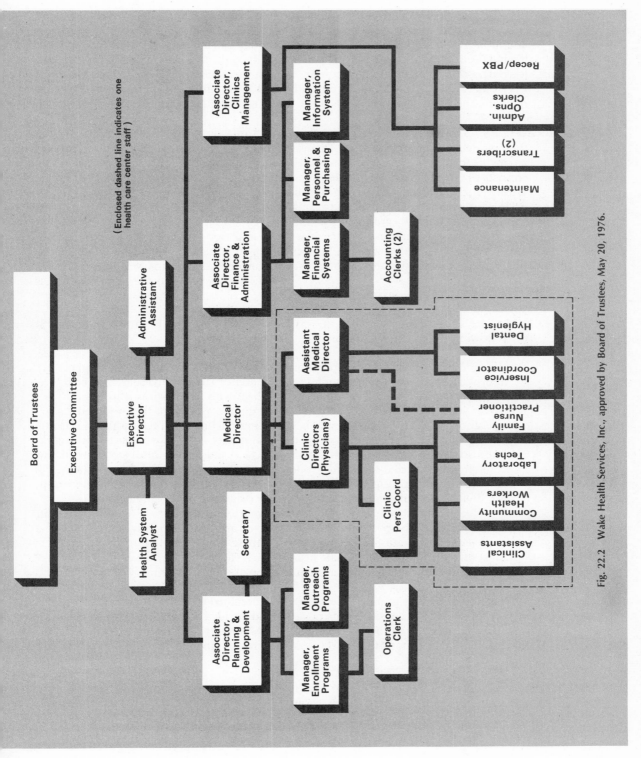

(Enclosed dashed line indicates one health care center staff)

Fig. 22.2   Wake Health Services, Inc., approved by Board of Trustees, May 20, 1976.

The patient-doctor relationship and patient visits are designed to be efficient and effective. Appointments are encouraged; however, walk-in members will also receive attention as quickly as possible. Many situations can be handled by the FNP, thus freeing the doctor for more difficult problems. Records on each patient are maintained for purposes of a complete medical file on each member. WHSI feels that the use of FNPs in conjunction with MDs has enhanced both efficiency and effectiveness, thus reducing the costs of patient visits and reducing the patient's time at the center.

PATIENT GROUPS The enrolled population consists of a mix of individuals and families from three designated groups. Group I consists of people who are eligible for third-party payments for health care, e.g., Medicaid/Medicare. Group II, the self-provider group, consists of individuals and families who can pay for services from personal resources. Group III, the medically indigent group, consists of individuals not included in Groups I or II who are members of families that do not have incomes in excess of the limits stipulated in the HEW grant.

A fourth classification of patients is the fee-for-service group. These are people seeking medical services who are not enrollees in the Triangle Health Plan. Many times such patients use the facilities more than once during the year, yet have not enrolled in the plan. These patients pay for medical services in the same manner as if they were visiting a private physician.

PROJECTED MARKET Within the text of the original proposal for the formulation of WHSI the following statement was made:

> When WHSI becomes fully operational, the enrolled population will number approximately 16,000 persons among six centers. These individuals will be distributed across the three groups of enrollees who will be drawn from both urban and rural environments. One of the unique aspects of the proposed operations of WHSI is that family health-center facilities will be installed in health service–scarcity areas in not only the major city of Wake County (Raleigh), but also in the health service–scarcity areas existing in the rural portions of the county. It is expected that the enrolled population will consist of approximately 20 percent from Group I, 20 percent from Group II, and 60 percent from Group III, divided approximately equally between rural and urban families.
>
> The proposed program is designed primarily for delivery of health services in scarcity areas. The populations of these areas are predominantly of the lower socioeconomic strata of the county. Also, these people are the ones who find it most difficult to obtain adequate health care. Therefore, the delivery function has been conceived with this lower-income population as the primary target.

The initial patient group percentages were designed to comply with HEW recommendations. HEW reconsidered its position and decided to permit WHSI to establish its own patient group ratios. WHSI is now considering restructuring its patient group ratios in order to attract the most members and be able to provide services to the medically indigent.

COST TO MEMBERS Monthly membership fees are determined by the group classification of the particular member. Group I is divided into the Medicare and Medicaid classifications. Medicare members are charged a flat $5.00 per month. Medicaid members are charged on the same scale as Group III members. Group II, the self-providers, are charged on the following scale: individual, $7.00/mo; two-person family, $12.00/mo; family, three or more, $15.00/mo. Group III, the medically indigent group, is charged according to the scale shown in Table 22.2. Medical charges for fee-for-service patients are comparable to those of local private physicians. However, these patients are encouraged to become full-time enrollees.

TABLE 22.2 Group III rates

Income Class	Ranges of income (in dollars) by family size							Monthly membership fee
	1	2	3	4	5	6	7 or more persons	
1	0–500	0–1,400	0–2,200	0–3,000	0–3,800	0–4,400	0–5,000	$0.00
2	501–1,000	1,401–2,000	2,201–2,700	3,001–3,500	3,801–4,300	4,401–4,900	5,001–5,500	$2.08
3	1,001–1,500	2,001–2,400	2,701–3,200	3,501–4,000	4,301–4,800	4,901–5,400	5,501–6,000	$2.92
4	1,501–2,000	2,401–2,900	3,201–3,700	4,001–4,500	4,801–5,300	5,401–5,900	6,001–6,500	$5.00
5	2,001–2,500	2,901–3,400	3,701–4,200	4,501–5,000	5,301–5,800	5,901–6,400	6,501–7,000	$10.00

All members are required to have a hospitalization insurance program membership or some sort of hospitalization contingency before they can enroll, except those enrollees classified as Group III. Wake County will defray the cost of their hospitalization due to their indigency. WHSI at this time does not have its own hospitalization insurance program, but it is examining the feasibility of including one in its package. This requirement for hospitalization insurance protects WHSI from spending all of its funds on specialists for a few serious cases.

ENROLLMENT SCHEDULE The following is a statement on enrollment projections found in the initial WHSI proposal:

It is anticipated that the clientele to be enrolled in this program will come from the three groups of individuals described above. Twenty percent of the program will be enlisted from Group I, 20 percent from Group II, and 60 percent from Group III. It is expected that of these enrollees 15 percent will be single individuals, 15 percent will be individuals plus one dependent, and 70 percent will be families. For purposes of estimation, it has been assumed that there are four persons to be served under each family certificate.

It is expected that approximately one quarter, or 4000 persons, will be enrolled by the end of the first operating fiscal year 1973–74. By the end of the second year, 1974–75, an enrolled population of 10,000 is projected. The third fiscal year, 1975–76, projection is for the fully enrolled population of 16,000 individuals. It is expected that the initial enrollment will be predominately among the Group III individuals, since these are those most heavily concentrated in the Southeast Raleigh sector, site of the first operational unit.

It is expected that Groups I and II will be the most difficult to enroll in this program due both to the currently available services to the Medicaid/Medicare patients of Group I and to the already established practices of most members of the Group II population. After a sufficient time for the Family Health Centers to become operational, accepted, and recognized by the Wake County community, however, it is expected that enrollments of the Group I and Group II people will proceed as projected.

Thus by the end of the second year of operation, it is expected that the mix of individuals in the overall program will be approximately the 20/20/60 ratio indicated above and that this ratio will be maintained throughout the operation of the system from that time forth.

Enrollment figures are shown in Table 22.3. Recent enrollment projections have been modified downward to show a projected enrollment of 2816 by June 30, 1976. From July 1, 1975, through April 15, 1976, WHSI reported a growth in enrollment from 1380 to 2141. A community education and information program initiated in March 1976 resulted in an increase of 255 members during that month, and it was

TABLE 22.3   Triangle Health Plan enrollment information

	Total enrollment	
7-1-75—1382	6-1-76—2556	7-1-76—2755

Enrollment by group category

	6-1-76	7-1-76
Group I	711 (27.82%)	744 (27.01%)
Group II	1324 (51.80%)	1410 (51.18%)
Group III	521 (20.38%)	601 (21.81%)
Total	2556	2755

Enrollment by race

	6-1-76	7-1-76
Black	1118 (43.74%)	1224 (44.43%)
White	1438 (56.26%)	1531 (55.57%)
Total	2556	2755

Enrollment by sex

	6-1-76	7-1-76
Male	1088 (42.57%)	1143 (41.49%)
Female	1468 (57.43%)	1612 (58.51%)
Total	2556	2755

Enrollment by center

	6-1-76	7-1-76
Tarboro	961 (37.60%)	989 (35.90%)
Falstaff	917 (35.88%)	972 (35.28%)
Apex	678 (26.52%)	794 (28.82%)
Total	2556	2755

New enrollees (June) by group

	6-1-76	7-1-76
Group I	61 (29.61%)	47 (19.03%)
Group II	86 (41.75%)	105 (42.51%)
Group III	59 (28.64%)	95 (38.46%)
Total	206	247

June enrollees by race and center

	Black	White
Tarboro	32 (27.12%)	30 (23.26%)
Falstaff	23 (19.49%)	43 (33.33%)
Apex	63 (53.39%)	56 (43.41%)
Total	118	129

June re-enrollees by group

Group I	3 (14.28%)
Group II	8 (38.10%)
Group III	10 (47.62%)
Total	21

Disenrollment by group

Group I	17 (24.64%)
Group II	27 (39.13%)
Group III	25 (36.23%)
Total	69

Date: July 9, 1976

TABLE 22.4 Actual and projected monthly enrollment

| | For FY 75–76 | | For FY 76–77* | |
Month	Number	% Increase	Number	% Increase
July	1380		2966	
August	1520	10.1	3116	5.1
September	1498	−1.44	3266	4.8
October	1570	4.8	3416	4.6
November	1668	6.2	3686	7.9
December	1784	7.0	3959	7.3
January	1968	10.3	4226	6.8
February	1886	−4.2	4496	6.4
March	2141	13.5	4766	6.0
April*	2366	10.5	5036	5.7
May*	2591	9.5	5306	5.4
June*	2816	8.7	4476	5.1

* Projected

TABLE 22.5 Annual cost per encounter

FY	Amount	% Decrease
73–74	$63.19	
74–75	$59.68	5.6
75–76	$39.68	33.5
76–77	$29.32	26.1

expected that this trend would continue for the rest of the fiscal year. Thus an enrollment of 2816 was anticipated for the end of fiscal year 1976. Projections for fiscal year 1976/1977 were 230 per month, for a total enrollment of 5576 by June 30, 1977 (Table 22.4).

Actual enrollment figures show that membership reached the level of 2755 by the fiscal year ending June 1976, and although an average of 230 new enrollees per month was projected for 1977, it was believed that the increase would be at the rate of 150 per month through October and at 270 per month for the remainder of the year, for an increase of 2760 members. Because of this slow growth rate the WHSI has remained at three centers. Cost per patient encounter dropped steadily from $63.19 in 1974 to $29.32 in 1977 (Table 22.5).

FUNDING WHSI began in 1972 with 100 percent of its funding from the Department of Health, Education and Welfare. The goal was complete financial independence. Independence has been a goal even with a growing budget (Table 22.6). The percent of federal participation for the fiscal year ending June 30, 1977, is projected to be 40.7 percent. WHSI indicates that the most obvious reason for the downward trend is that patient revenues have been increasing.

TABLE 22.6 Federal versus self-generated funds

FY	Amount		Percentage	
	Federal	Self	Federal	Self
72–73	248,747	0	100	0
73–74	403,314	45,610	89.8	10.16
74–75	687,072	145,300	82.5	17.5
75–76	429,829	264,354	61.9	38.1
76–77	349,527	509,190	40.7	59.3

Sources of income for WHSI, FY 1976–77, are shown in Table 22.7. The "other" income category is principally interest income. Enrollment fees comprise all of the monthly payments to be received from enrollees. The fee-for-service income comes from nonmember patients using WHSI medical services and HEW payments to WHSI for each visit made by Medicaid or Medicare enrollees. Tables 22.8 and 9 give a monthly income breakdown by enrollee, contract, and center for FY 1975–76. The final category, third-party income, will be that money collected through filing with the various hospitalization insurance programs when specialist treatment is required. Table 22.10 indicates the actual revenues and expenses for fiscal years ending June 30, 1974 and 1975.

TABLE 22.7 Income sources FY 1976–77

Other income	4,500
Enrollment fees	199,896
Fees for service	168,600
Third party	136,194
Total	509,190

TABLE 22.8 Income (July 1, 1975–March 31, 1976)

1. Monthly premium income

Group	Average monthly income	Income/enrollee month
I		
Medicare	$ 687.64	$4.91
Medicaid	106.22	.41
Other (Employees)	332.17	2.75
II	4281.11	5.27
III	477.02	2.26
Total		

2. Average premium/enrollee	$ 3.33
3. Average premium/contract	$ 6.34
4. Average income/visit (gross)	$14.56
5. Medicare reimbursement, average claim (includes premium)	$16.98
6. Medicaid reimbursement, average claim (includes premium)	$15.80

TABLE 22.9 Enrollment contract report—June 15, 1976

I. Contract distribution by center and percentages

	Totals	Tarboro	Falstaff	Apex
Medicare	242 (21.57)	74 (30.58)(6.60)	43 (17.77)(3.83)	125 (51.65)(11.14)
Medicaid	112 (9.98)	34 (30.36)(3.03)	20 (17.86)(1.78)	58 (51.79)(5.17)
Other	35 (3.12)	11 (31.43)(.98)	21 (60.00)(1.87)	3 (8.57)(.27)
Group II	600 (53.48)	258 (43.00)(22.99)	274 (45.67)(24.42)	68 (11.33)(6.06)
Group III	133 (11.85)	58 (43.61)(5.17)	17 (12.78)(1.52)	58 (43.61)(5.17)
Totals	1122 (100)	435 (38.77)	375 (33.42)	312 (27.81)

II. Distribution by family size and percentages

Family Size	Contracts	Tarboro	Falstaff	Apex
1	615 (54.81)	231 (37.56)(20.59)	168 (27.32)(14.97)	216 (35.12)(19.25)
2	182 (16.22)	81 (44.51)(7.22)	76 (41.76)(6.77)	25 (13.74)(2.23)
3	82 (7.31)	29 (35.37)(2.58)	38 (46.34)(3.39)	15 (18.29)(1.34)
4	94 (8.38)	40 (42.55)(3.57)	35 (37.23)(3.12)	19 (20.21)(1.69)
5	68 (6.06)	24 (35.29)(2.14)	27 (39.71)(2.76)	17 (25.00)(1.52)
6 or more	81 (7.22)	30 (37.04)(2.67)	31 (38.27)(2.76)	20 (24.69)(1.78)
Totals	1122 (100)	435 (38.77)	375 (33.42)	312 (27.81)

III. Contract income and percentages as of 5/31/76

	Totals	Tarboro	Falstaff	Apex
Medicare	$1137.92 (13.45)	$ 387.92 (34.09)(4.58)	$ 245.00 (21.53)(2.90)	$ 505.00 (44.38)(5.97)
Medicaid	136.16 (1.61)	40.84 (29.99)(.48)	38.32 (28.14)(.45)	57.00 (41.86)(.67)
Other	432.00 (5.11)	145.00 (33.56)(1.71)	242.00 (56.02)(2.86)	45.00 (10.42)(.53)
Group II	6303.00 (74.49)	2589.00 (41.08)(30.60)	2968.00 (47.09)(35.08)	746.00 (11.84)(8.82)
Group III	452.40 (5.35)	209.60 (46.33)(2.48)	45.84 (10.13)(.54)	196.96 (43.54)(2.33)
Totals	$8461.48 (100)	$3372.36 (39.85)	$3539.16 (41.83)	$1549.96 (18.32)

IV. Other information as of 5/31/76

Average premium income per contract	$ 7.54	Average premium income per other enrollee	3.22
Average premium income per Medicare contract	4.70	Average premium income per Group II enrollee	4.76
Average premium income per Medicaid contract	1.22	Average premium income per Group III enrollee	.87
Average premium income per other contract	12.34	Average family members per Medicare enrollment contract	$2.28
Average premium income per Group II contract	10.51	Average family members per Medicaid enrollment contract	1.05
Average premium income per Group III contract	3.40	Average family members per Medicaid enrollment contract	2.89
		Average family members per other enrollment contract	3.83
Average premium income per enrollee	$3.31	Average family members per Group II enrollment contract	2.21
Average premium income per Medicare enrollee	4.50	Average family members per Group III contract	3.92
Average premium income per Medicaid enrollee	.42		

NOTE: The first percentage column represents center distribution within a contract group, i.e.: Tarboro has 30.58% of all Medicare contracts. The second percentage column represents center distribution within the total number of contracts, i.e.: Tarboro has 6.60% of all contracts as Medicare contracts.

TABLE 22.10 Wake Health Services, Inc. Statements of revenues, expenses, and changes in fund balance—note 1 for the years ended June 30, 1975 and 1974

	1975	1974
Revenues:		
Grants from HEW	$654,027	$331,862
Other		
Fees for services	55,287	26,987
Membership fees	39,418	13,378
Medicaid/Medicare income	42,710	3,510
Other income, principally interest	7,885	1,734
Total revenue	798,327	377,473
Expenses:		
Program services		
Family health services	305,368	257,968
Supporting services		
Management and general	271,881	140,146
Total expenses	577,249	398,114
Excess (deficiency) of revenue over expenses	221,078	(20,641)
Fund balance at beginning of year	299,803	320,444
Fund balance at end of year	$520,881	$299,803

Sometime during FY 1976–77 WHSI expects to be receiving funds from HEW on a per capita basis. That is, HEW will allocate funds to WHSI based on the difference between a Group III enrollee and an equivalent Group II enrollee. This method of funds allocation will become the primary method through which WHSI will receive its funding.

CAPACITY WHSI has a medical staff complement of three physicians and eleven FNPs. HEW has calculated that a full-time equivalent (FTE) provider should be able to see 2.7 patients per hour. An MD is classified as an FTE provider; an FNP is equal to one-half of an FTE provider. In an effort to assess WHSI's service capacity, the corporation conducted an in-depth study and determined that based on HEW definitions for FTE providers, WHSI should request funding for nine FTE providers for FY 1975–76. During that year each provider was able to provide direct patient care for an average of 30 hours per 40-hour week. Ten hours a week were devoted to on-the-job training and other nonpatient care activities, such as clinical evaluation, marketing, home visits, administration duties, and sick and leave time.

Thus using the formula provided by HEW, encounter capacity is calculated to be 33,736 (Table 22.11). From July 1, 1975, through March 31, 1976, WHSI experienced 13,411 encounters. An additional 7010 encounters are projected through June 1976, producing a total encounter experience of 20,421. The encounters for FY 1974–75 totaled 9656; thus the FY 1975–76 encounters represent a doubling of growth in one year. If the FY 1975–76 projections are realized, WHSI will be operating at 61 percent of capacity with a rate of 1.63 patient encounters per hour. WHSI anticipates a strong growth situation in the coming fiscal year that will enable it to approach the national utilization average for FTE providers (Table 22.12).

TABLE 22.11 WHSI calculations from DHEW program indicators

Personnel	FTE
3 Physicians	3
11 Family nurse practitioners (FNP)	5.5
14 Totals	8.5

A = Full-time equivalent providers = 8.5
B = Total hours work per week = 40 excluding on-call
C = Total hours providing direct
  patient care per week = 30 excluding on-call
D = Total hours work per year
  40 hours × 52 weeks = 2080 excluding on-call
E = Average total hours vacation,
  holidays and sick per FTE per year = 120 excluding on-call
F = Net hours work per FTE per year = 1960
G = Adjusted FTE providers = 6.375
H = Minimum hourly productivity per FTE = 2.7
K = WHSI hourly capacity—productivity = 17.212
N = WHSI annual encounter capacity = 33,736

$(AC) \div B = G$
$G \times H = K$
$D - E = F$
$F \times K = N$

TABLE 22.12 Actual and projected monthly encounters

Month	For FY 1975–76		For FY 1976–77*	
	Number	% Increase	Number	% Increase
July	1398		2297	
August	1253	− 10.4	2360	2.7
September	1291	3.0	2423	2.7
October	1568	21.4	2486	2.6
November	1294	− 17.5	2549	2.5
December	1384	7.0	2612	2.5
January	1463	5.7	2675	2.4
February	1715	17.2	2738	2.4
March	2045	19.2	2801	2.3
April*	2175	6.4	2864	2.2
May*	2360	8.5	2927	2.2
June*	2475	4.9	2990	2.2

Annual average encounters per enrollee = 2.1
Annual average encounters per nonenrollee = 1.8

THE WHSI GOALS The WHSI goal statements are qualitative, not quantitative, because "management feels this reflects a 'real-world' fact that external and internal events occur in the 'life' of WHSI which alter strategies, policy, plans, and objectives toward obtaining goals."

The goals may be summarized as follows:

1. The quality of care and management will meet or exceed any locally or nationally recognized standard.

2. Wake Health Services, Inc., will be a self-sufficient community health center network.

3. Regardless of their sources or level of income, all patients receive the same quality of medical and health care.

4. All available community resources, facilities, and personnel will be used at optimal levels. We hope that our family nurse practitioners can meet productivity levels in this year of approximately two patient encounters per hour, and for the physicians approximately 3.5 patient encounters per hour. We also expect to reduce the ratio of administrative costs to medical care costs by approximately one-third.

5. In improving the health status of a large number of Wake County inhabitants, WHSI hopes to be able to measure effectiveness by seeing a statistically significant decrease in the number of nonemergency patients being seen at the emergency rooms of local hospitals. It is also WHSI's hope that the unit cost of such care shall be reduced by virtue of our enrollees being part of a prepaid system which provides a disincentive for the misuse of outside sources of care.

6. In the long term, WHSI strives to produce a network of primary care at a level of comprehensiveness that is aimed at prevention and early detection of disease and at the substitution of low-cost medical modalities in place of the more expensive hospital-oriented medical care.

COMMUNITY ACCEPTANCE AND SUPPORT The acceptance and support of the community for this concept is important to WHSI's survival. Indications of such support can be found from several sources. Transportation for Apex-area indigents who are Triangle Health Plan patients is provided on request through Wake County Opportunities, Inc. Referrals to WHSI are being made from the Wake County Department of Social Services, Wake Medical Center's emergency room and outpatient clinic, Wake County Health Department, Wake County Medical Society, private physicians, and the Trentman Mental Health Center. Continuing education for the medical staff has been provided through a number of agencies, including the University of North Carolina Schools of Nursing and Medicine, Area Health Education Center, Red Cross, private physicians, and Wake Medical Center Staff.

Consumer support has been exemplified by requests from communities for WHSI participation in four fairs and exhibitions sponsored by shopping center managements and community agencies during fiscal year 1975–76. Also, WHSI has received and responded to invitations from numerous religious, civic, social, and professional organizations and governmental agencies to make presentations about the services offered by WHSI. Finally, newspapers in Raleigh and Wake County have published articles about the Triangle Health Plan, and local radio and television stations have agreed to air spots and provide exposure through special interviews with WHSI staff.

PROBLEMS MANAGEMENT RECOGNIZES

Community Acceptance and Support Ever since its incorporation, WHSI's management has recognized that the concepts of prepaid medical care and the family nurse practitioner would meet community resistance, if only because these are relatively new concepts in this geographical area. In an article from the July, 3, 1974, *Wall Street Journal* the controversy surrounding FNPs was explored. Problems arise in establishing the educational program that should be required to obtain the status of FNP. Inconsistencies have led some doctors to conclude that FNPs are second-class doctors whose limited knowledge could actually make them dangerous to patients. This, however, has not been the national trend. The American Medical Association has generally supported the FNP system, except in the case of the FNP operating independently of advice and consultation of a licensed MD. Using an FNP instead, under a physician's supervision, has reduced costs and enabled the doctor to handle more serious cases.

WHSI has maintained high standards in selecting FNPs for its centers and additionally has an MD assigned to each center to provide the necessary consultation and supervision or to take over a case. Such precautions have virtually eliminated potential problems of inadequate medical attention. Though the FNP concept has not been accepted completely, community interaction projects and news reports have helped in explaining the role of the WHSI FNP.

An important facet of WHSI and its Triangle Health Plan is community support and participation. One-third of the board members consist of enrollees in the Plan, one-third are from other medical providers in the county, and the remaining third consist of selected citizens in Wake County. WHSI officials believe that they need to educate Wake County residents about WHSI's existence and services. WHSI has not been able to attain the visibility it needs in order to operate on the scale originally intended.

Business Community Acceptance of the THP   WHSI is aware that the successful prepaid programs have marketed to employed groups. However, most of these programs offer a benefit package that includes hospitalization. One of the difficulties in marketing a Triangle Health Plan membership to an employer is that it is a supplement to already existing hospitalization packages. The problem is compounded by the fact that the large nonlocal companies tended to offer the same benefit package to all employees at all locations. WHSI would be asking local branches of parent companies to offer a set of fringes to local employees which would not be available to others. Therefore, WHSI decided to market initially to small locally owned companies which would not have this problem.

WHSI contacted approximately 125 small businesses in the county, made 93 visits, receiving commitments from two companies to enroll some staff. The effort netted seven employer-sponsored enrollments. The reasons for noncommitment included (1) bad economic times, (2) transient employee population, (3) employees already have doctors, and (4) no centers near firm. Although WHSI did not net many employer-sponsored enrollees, there was an opportunity to talk to some employee groups about the program. It is believed that businesses still offer a good opportunity for "recruiting" large numbers of people at one time. WHSI proposes to:

1. Make presentations to groups of employees;
2. Offer special packages;
3. Become an official medical resource for firms (will treat minor illnesses of employees during work days);
4. Investigate the feasibility of adding hospitalization to their benefit package.

Disenrollments   From July 1, 1975, to March 31, 1976, the average number of disenrollments was 83 per month (Table 22.13). Though this figure seems to have dropped some in recent months, it is still of great concern to WHSI management. All enrollees who are dropped from the program are called by the marketing technician. It was found that a flaw in accounting procedures resulted in late remitters of monthly dues being dropped each month. Additionally, it was discovered that a number of people who were dropped from the membership roll had simply forgotten to remit, since WHSI does not send out monthly bills. Remittances have been made easier with the use of BankAmericard, Master Charge, and Bank Account Drafts.

TABLE 22.13 Disenrollments

1. Total (7-1-75 through 3-31-76)		745
2. Average monthly (7-1-75 through 3-31-76)		83
3. Retention rate (since July 1973)		61.7%
Contracts issued	1588	
Contracts currently in force	980	

Long-range planning in the disenrollment problem area by WHSI follows the following time schedule. By December 1, 1976, a detailed project description of the tasks associated with assessing numbers and causes of disenrollments by type, center, and over a specific period of time was to be prepared. By February 1, 1977, a report on disenrollments was due, specifying those existing policies that needed reinforcing, those requiring revision, and new policies that should be implemented. These changes would reduce disenrollments by 50 percent after the first six months of enactment and by 90 percent after eighteen months.

Tax Status   WHSI has unsuccessfully attempted to secure a nonprofit tax status from the Internal Revenue Service. It is felt that if such a status could be obtained, gifts of equipment, monies, facilities, etc., would be more prevalent, as the donor would have the additional incentive of declaring such gifts tax deductible.

Cost Accounting   There is a need for a cost accounting system to generate appropriate cost reports and to aid management in planning and budgeting.

Increased Malpractice Costs   Like every other health organization in the country, WHSI has experienced enormous increases in malpractice costs. Current corporate malpractice insurance has increased approximately 3000 percent over the preceding year. Provider malpractice costs have increased two to three hundred percent.

Marketing   Marketing and the development of a marketing strategy constitute a major organizational problem of WHSI. The distinct medical care system represented by the Triangle Health Plan, its uniqueness in the Wake County area, combined with the absence of an inpatient package to complement WHSI outpatient services, have caused WHSI to adopt an exploratory rather than a finely tuned marketing approach.

Marketing efforts have been hampered, and enrollments depressed, due to a decision against releasing media campaigns about the Triangle Health Plan. The media restriction was removed in early 1976, and inquiries resulting from media campaigns suggest that enrollments will increase in the coming year. Present enrollment projections are based in part on past experience and in part on expected results from the media campaigns. The strategy for overcoming the major organizational problem of marketing is as follows:

1. Community education and information program—expand this program beyond the current media development and develop a systematic approach to evaluating its impact in a variety of markets.

2. Profile analyses—develop the following profile analyses:
   a) current enrollees
   b) new enrollees
   c) disenrollees
   d) active nonenrollees

   Profile analyses would include data on address, age, sex, group (I, II, or III), race, number of family members, health, status, how subscriber heard about Wake Health Services, by whom enrolled, reason for disenrollment, etc.

3. Wake County business insurance analysis—work through recognized carriers, the North Carolina Department of Labor, the North Carolina Insurance Commissioner, and other sources of data on business health insurance packages to compile profiles of a variety of health insurance inpatient packages carried by businesses and organizations by size of business, configuration of its benefits package, etc.

4. Special packages—in contracts with businesses and organizations, develop an accurate cost profile of a variety of configurations of treatment protocols currently available through Wake Health Services. Such packages would include combinations of partial physicals, special screening, tests for health-maintenance purposes, etc., and would be available on a fee-for-service basis to businesses and organizations which already have inpatient packages but which also wish to provide employees with special combinations of outpatient benefits.

5. Outreach—expand entire outreach effort by negotiating collaborative relationships with a variety of Wake County agencies and organizations, e.g., Employment Security Commission, Drug Action, Inc., Wake County Alcoholism Program, Mental Health, in order to increase the number of referrals to Wake Health Services from these agencies when appropriate medical care is needed. In collaboration with extended-care facilities (nursing homes) in the Raleigh area, negotiate scheduled visitations by FNP providers for general health maintenance, special needs of geriatric patients, and so forth.

6. Media campaign—in the area of marketing, telephone responses as well as the interest from newspapers indicate that the publicity campaign has increased WHSI visibility. The problem now is to determine *why* it is successful, what kinds of people are responding, and for what reasons. The various marketing profile analyses mentioned earlier need to be developed.

7. Patient problems, education, treatment, and diagnosis—although some patient education occurs in connection with treatment, the present program is not as comprehensive or as consistently applied as desired. Since fee-for-service patients may be one-time users, there is a need to have available (in the form of materials, charts, diagrams, models, etc.) a variety of patient education resources. A primary focus of the patient education should be on preventive health education.

MARKETING STRATEGIES AND TACTICS In developing marketing strategies for the next two years, WHSI operated under the following planning assumptions.

Planning Assumptions, 1976–77

1. *Revenues*—grant revenues and patient revenues will be sufficient to achieve WHSI objectives for 1976–77 and to develop plans for 1978.

2. *Expenditures*—expenditures will not exceed budgeted amounts of the "personal services," "patient care," "equipment," and "other" categories.

3. *Utilization*—service capacity and utilization ratios will change substantially with the establishment of health-maintenance protocols and procedures for enrollees, children, and fee-for-service patients; the acquisition of additional medical capability in mental health, orthopedic, pediatric, and geriatric care and the expected resulting decrease in specialty referrals; patient education activity; reduction in missed appointments; an increase in the number of referrals to WHSI from other agencies; implementation of selective screening programs in previously undiagnosed diseases; and the execution of hospital admissions.

4. *Management information system*—sufficient data and staff time exist to execute the strategy for beginning a management information system.

5. *Marketing strategy*—the expansion of the community education and information program will result in increased enrollments and fee-for-service encounters. The completion of market-evaluation studies and the development of a variety of enrollee patient profiles, combined with profiles of health insurance packages by type of business, will increase WHSI's capability to forecast enrollments and target potential enrollment populations. The development of special-service delivery packages will increase capability to respond to a variety of business insurance needs.

6. *Finance*—implementing direct and indirect cost-accounting mechanisms will improve considerably the ability to track and control costs to WHSI and to patients.

7. *Planning process*—implementation of a specific planning process, based on health services funding regulations and WHSI planning needs, will set in place for the first time a design for organizational self-evaluation and renewal.

Planning Assumptions, 1977–78

1. *Health needs*—the variety of personal and family health needs will require that WHSI be responsive to Wake County citizens who do not have access to medical and health care.

2. *Health maintenance*—WHSI will continue to provide direct primary care; however, a larger percentage of encounters will involve preventive medicine and health maintenance, vis à vis episodic illnesses.

3. *Enrollments versus fee-for-service*—although enrollments will increase, their rate will not exceed the *rate* of increase of fee-for-service encounters.

4. *Increased community demand and support*—as more citizens "try out," there will be an increased demand for services and a need to expand the number of centers.

5. *Self-sufficiency*—at the end of FY 1978, WHSI will be self-sufficient.

6. *Inpatient package*—the development and implementation of an in-patient benefits package will result in WHSI's enrolling a number of groups and organizations.

Project Outreach The purpose of this undertaking was to contact a variety of potential users of the Triangle Health Plan and to institute a door-to-door community awareness program to monitor the effectiveness of this information-spreading medium. These efforts were conducted from July 1, 1975, through June 30, 1976.

Glenwood Towers, a high-rise housing-authority-sponsored apartment complex for 350 senior citizens, was one of the first groups contacted. WHSI's objective was to initiate a part-time satellite clinical operation at the apartment complex. It was known that the Wake County Health Department already has a satellite operation at Glenwood Towers. However, it was the intention of WHSI to offer services not already routinely available through the County Health Department. This opportunity is still being investigated.

Apex Out-Reach was another project undertaken. In an effort to increase enrollment at the Apex center, 681 families were contacted door-to-door by four WHSI-trained community residents. The program was a six-week effort ending December 7, 1975. Prior to the project, Apex Center enrollment was 198; by January 1, 1976, it had increased to 343. The results are somewhat confounded, however, because a physician with 27 years' practice in the local area became director of the Apex Center during the project.

Finally, discussions are under way with Meredith College executives regarding a combined inpatient/outpatient package for faculty, in collaboration with the Prudential Insurance Company of America. The executive director has initiated correspondence and held conferences with representatives of the Prudential Insurance Company of America at the Raleigh, Southeast, and national levels, and with State Mutual Insurance Company and CNA Company, which are very promising with respect to negotiating a specific inpatient package to be offered jointly by these firms and Wake Health Services, Inc.

Community Education and Information WHSI has used different media and messages to increase its exposure and to convey information to the public about its services. Participation in shopping center "fairs" throughout the county is one such method. WHSI installs a set of display modules, gives free blood pressure and vision checks, and dispenses literature. The display modules are designed so that they explain the WHSI operation and benefits even if they are left unattended. Thus continued exposure is maintained through shopping hours during which the display cannot be staffed.

WHSI has redesigned a new, more comprehensive brochure after research by an HEW survey team indicated that some pertinent information was not available through the present brochure. In addition to fees, services, locations, and the general concept of THP, information on member rights, patient and doctor responsibilities, and the purpose of WHSI were included.

Early in 1976 the North Carolina Commissioner of Insurance ruled that WHSI could release media announcements (in effect advertise) about the Triangle Health Plan. A number of precautions were taken to ensure that any public information program would be handled in good taste and with professional competence. A local public relations firm was retained to assist in media exposure, and a small film company was selected to prepare television and radio spots. A formal radio and television campaign was conducted at a cost of $5200 for a two-week period beginning March 8, 1976. This was the first such program to advertise medical services ever permitted in the state of North Carolina and one of a very few in the United States.

Two local affiliated TV stations (WRAL, WTVD), four AM radio stations (WYNA, WKIX, WLLE, WPTF), and one FM radio station (WRAL-FM) were selected on the basis of maximum exposure to a cross section of the general population. These stations also agreed to sponsor public-service airing of the spots after the two-week campaign. The slogan "Anyone who needs it can afford it" was broadcast by these stations in an effort to reach more people who would be classified in Groups I and III. A special phone number was broadcast to handle responses to the advertisements. The response records kept during the campaign compare with normal inquiries as shown below.

Number of calls prior to campaign		Number of calls during campaign	
Feb. 16–20	12	Mar. 8–12	47
Feb. 23–27	22	Mar. 15–19	70
Mar. 1– 4	29	Mar. 22–26	60 (1 week after)
		Mar. 29–Apr. 2	26 (2 weeks after)

Subsequent to this campaign a Raleigh outreach program was initiated, similar to the Apex program. Over the next six weeks 1655 households were contacted. Enrollee results are as follows:

Date	Number of new enrollees
Apr. 5– 9	37
12–16	30
19–23	29
26–30	34
May 3– 7	41

At this time a second two-week media campaign began. After analysis of the responses to the initial campaign, only one TV station—WRAL—and three radio stations—WLLE, WKIX, and WPTF—were contracted to air the informational and promotional spots. This second campaign was budgeted for $3000 and took place from May 10, 1976, to May 21, 1976. The Community Education and Information Campaign, as the media campaign was called, produced the following response:

Date	Number of calls
May 10–14	52
17–21	52
24–28	30 (1 week after)
May 31–June 4	23 (2 weeks after)

Enrollment figures for the Raleigh outreach program for the two weeks running in conjunction with the media campaign were as follows:

Date	Number of new enrollees
May 10–14	57
May 17–21	85

For FY 1976–77 WHSI is planning a third media campaign capitalizing on information collected from the general awareness approach used in the first two such programs. The target market for this campaign has been defined as female, 18–34 years of age. The media slots will be divided such that 65 percent are aimed at a Group II audience and 35 percent at the Group I and III audiences. Though the information gathered during the first two campaigns was confounded by different stations carrying a different number of advertisements, Group II media slots were selected to be on WKIX (6–10 A.M.) and WRAL-FM (7–12 P.M.). The Group I and III audience is expected to be reached through WPTF daytime broadcasts. Contact 2, WHSI's public relations firm, made these decisions using Arbitron (a demographic listener survey using standard metropolitan statistical areas) and input from WHSI. Again, only WRAL-TV was selected to provide television exposure.

The following are the radio and TV scripts that will be used during this media campaign.

Radio script 1: $16.50. That's the average cost of an initial doctor's visit in Raleigh, according to a recent survey. But now, Wake County residents without a family doctor have another choice. Triangle Health Plan. A family of three or more persons can enroll for $15 a month and wide medical coverage. Smaller families and low-income families pay less. To find out more, call 781-2100. Triangle Health Plan. Working to keep Wake County healthy.

Radio script 2: How secure is your family when it comes to health care? If illness were to strike, would you have professional medical personnel to turn to, day or night? If not, you ought to find out more about Triangle Health Plan, a program for Wake County residents who don't have a family doctor. It offers wide medical coverage for a small monthly fee. For peace of mind when it comes to your family's health, you can't beat it. Triangle Health Plan. Working to keep Wake County healthy.

Radio script 3: Who's out there working to reduce the rising costs of medical care? Triangle Health Plan, a program for Wake County residents who don't have a family doctor. Triangle Health Plan offers medical coverage for small monthly fees. The plan is supported by a team of medical personnel whose chief concern is your continued good health. You can't afford to neglect your health, so call 781-2100 and find out more. Triangle Health Plan. Working to keep Wake County healthy.

TV script: Wake County has all kinds of people. And now there's a medical program any of them can afford. Triangle Health Plan. It offers anyone without a family doctor coverage for medical services. Anyone can afford it, because enrollment fees depend on family size and income. If you're having trouble finding proper medical care for any member of your family, find out more. Triangle Health Plan. Anyone who needs it can afford it.

The rate cards for radio stations WRAL-FM, WKIX, and WPTF are provided as Figs. 22.3, 22.4, and 22.5, respectively. A billing for WHSI's advertising costs with WRAL-TV is provided as Fig. 22.6. Additionally, advertising costs for the Raleigh *News and Observer* newpaper are shown in Table 22.14. Production costs for advertisements to be used in each of these forms of media are shown in Table 22.15. It should also be noted that the FCC requires radio stations to devote a certain percentage of their advertising time to public-service announcements. Contact 2 was able to arrange with these stations additional exposure for WHSI through this requirement.

In addition to these efforts, WHSI began subscribing ($30.00 per quarter) to a newcomers list of the Raleigh area in November 1975. A letter, brochure, and newsletter

WRAL 101 FM

RATE CARD 8A EFFECTIVE JULY 1, 1976

	Annual	Weekly	60	30
CLASS AAA				
6am-10am Monday-Friday		1	$38.00	$28.00
CLASS AA		1	$34.00	$26.00
3pm-7pm Monday-Friday		12	$32.00	$24.00
10am-3pm Saturday	500	18	$30.00	$22.00
	1000	24	$28.00	$21.00
CLASS A		1	$30.00	$22.00
10am-3pm Monday-Friday		12	$28.00	$20.00
6am-10am, 3pm-7pm Saturday	500	18	$26.00	$18.00
	1000	24	$24.00	$17.00
CLASS B		1	$19.00	$15.00
7pm-12 Midnight Monday-Saturday		12	$17.00	$13.00
6am-12 Midnight Sunday	500	18	$15.00	$11.00
	1000	24	$13.00	$10.00

Deduct $2.00 per commercial if at least 50% of schedule is in B time classification.

Weekly Total Audience Plans (when available)	Rates furnished upon request

	60	30
Run of Station (when available) 6am-1am	$18.00	$14.00
Midnight-6am (Tuesday-Sunday)	$ 4.00	$ 3.00

Weekly Frequency Rates: 5% discount for 26 weeks, 10% discount for 52 Weeks.

Rate Holder $100 weekly — All commercials rotate in day parts.

Plans, all night, and ROS schedules do not
combine with face of card rates for further
discounts. Pre-emptible without notice.

Rate Protection—Contract rates are guaranteed
for three months against increase provided
advertiser maintains uninterrupted
schedule during protection period.
Commissionable to recognized agencies.

Box 17000   4300 Six Forks Road   Raleigh, NC 27609   919-781-6101

Fig. 22.3

Fig. 22.4

Time Classifications

CLASS AAA	6AM-10AM	Monday-Friday	CLASS A	10AM- 3PM	Monday-Friday
CLASS AA	3PM- 7PM	Monday-Friday		6AM-10AM	Saturday
	10AM- 7PM	Saturday		10AM- 7PM	Sunday
			CLASS B	7PM-Midnight	Monday-Sunday

	60 Seconds	30 Seconds
CLASS AAA		
6 per week	$30.00	$24.00
12 per week	$28.00	$22.50
18 per week	$26.00	$21.00
24 per week	$24.00	$19.00
CLASS AA		
6 per week	$26.00	$21.00
12 per week	$24.00	$19.00
18 per week	$22.00	$17.50
24 per week	$20.00	$16.00
CLASS A		
6 per week	$17.00	$14.00
12 per week	$15.00	$12.00
18 per week	$14.00	$11.00
24 per week	$13.00	$10.50
CLASS B		
6 per week	$14.00	$11.00
12 per week	$12.00	$ 9.50
18 per week	$10.00	$ 8.00
24 per week	$ 8.00	$ 6.50

Morning and Afternoon Drive Time Only Schedules

Maximum frequency 12X regardless of number of spots purchased. No further discounts. Schedule must include minimum of 6 Class A and/or Class B spots to qualify for lower frequency rates and discounts listed below.

DISCOUNTS

5%..... 13 Weeks within contract year
10%..... 26 Weeks within contract year
15%..... 39 Weeks within contract year
20%..... 52 Consecutive weeks

RATE HOLDER

Minimum $50.00 per week expenditure.

TOTAL AUDIENCE PLANS

Preemptible for face of card advertisers. Tap Plans do not combine with face of card rates for further discounts. All announcements must run over a seven (7) day period.

	Plan A 12/pw	Plan B 18/pw	Plan C 24/pw
Class AAA and AA	4	6	8
Class A	4	6	8
Class B	4	6	8

	60 Seconds	30 Seconds
Plan A	$192.00	$153.00
Plan B	$261.00	$207.00
Plan C	$312.00	$252.00

ROS PLAN

Preemptible for face of card and tap plan advertisers. All announcements run ROS 6AM-12 Midnight Monday-Sunday. No further discounts.
60 Seconds $12.00 NET   30 Seconds $9.60 NET

SCHEDULING

All announcements rotate within time periods. WKIX does not sell fixed position announcements.

RATE PROTECTION

Rates quoted herein are guaranteed for a period of 26 weeks from the effective date of any increase providing that advertising is actually running at the time of effective date of increase, and providing that these broadcasts continue without interruption during rate protection period.

GENERAL INFORMATION

WKIX, founded in 1947, is owned and operated by Southern Broadcasting Company.

Conditions — WKIX reserves the right to refuse any advertising material which does not conform to station's standards. Closing time is 48 hours prior to broadcast time.

WKIX

Box 12526
Raleigh, N.C. 27605
(919) 851-2711

General Manager.............. Frank Maruca
General Sales Manager .... Joe Wright
Sales Manager................. Charlie Brown

WKIX/WYYD

Advertisers who run schedules on both radio stations qualify for an additional 10% discount on the face of card and total audience plan rates. In order to qualify for the additional discount, one of the following qualifications must be met.
(1) Within the term of the schedule (weekly flights or monthly) at least one-third of the total schedule must run on WYYD or WKIX.

Fig. 22.4

WPTF 68

RADIO 680   COMBINATION 6   FM 94.7 MHZ
50,000 Watts   Effective: 100,000 Watts
MOR-Contemporary   July 1, 1976   Stereo Rock

WPTF   WQDR

Class AAA   6:00 AM - 10:30 AM   Class AAA   3:00 PM - 7:00 PM
            12:00 N - 1:00 PM   Monday thru Friday

       AA   10:30 AM - 11:00 AM   AA   6:00 AM - 10:00 AM
             3:00 PM - 8:00 PM   7:00 PM - 12:00 M
                                                 6:00 AM - 12:00 M Sat & Sun

        A   5:00 AM - 6:00 AM   A   10:00 AM - 3:00 PM
            11:00 AM - 12:00 N   Monday thru Friday
             1:00 PM.- 3:00 PM
             8:00 PM - 12:00 M

ALL ANNOUNCEMENTS ROTATE WITHIN TIME PERIODS

| | AAA | | | AA | | | A | | |
	1-99	100-199	200+	1-99	100-199	200+	1-99	100-199	200+
60's									
1 - 5 weekly	$60	58	54	52	48	46	45	41	38
6 - 11	59	56	53	51	47	44	43	40	37
12 - 17	58	53	49	48	45	40	39	36	34
18 - 24	53	49	47	45	41	38	36	34	31
25 - Mr	49	47	44	41	38	34	33	31	27
30's									
1 - 5 weekly	48	47	44	41	38	35	35	32	29
6 - 11	47	46	42	40	36	34	34	31	27
12 - 17	46	44	40	38	34	32	31	27	25
18 - 24	44	40	38	35	32	28	28	26	22
25 - More	39	38	34	32	28	26	26	24	21

BULK PACKAGE PLAN 1,000 SPOTS IN A 12 - MONTH PERIOD PER STATION

	AAA	AA	A
60's	$44	38	31
30's	34	27	22

Represented by THE CHRISTAL COMPANY, INC.

Fig. 22.5

Submitted to: Contact II.

WRAL-TV
Raleigh, N. C.

Account: Wake Health Services--Triangle Health Plan

Date Submitted: February 4, 1976

DAY	TIME	LENGTH/CLASS		ADJACENCIES	SPOTS/Wk	TOTAL ADULTS	TOTAL WOMEN	COST
						(000)	(000)	
		DATES: 2/23-3/7:						
Mon-Fri.	9-1030 AM	30/2		Mike Douglas	3	63	51	75.00
	1030-12 Noon	30/2		Morning Rotation	1	10	9	15.00
	1230-330 PM	30/2		Soaps & Games	2	102	84	100.00
	530-6 PM	30/2		Adam 12	2	166	88	170.00
	6-7 PM	30/2		News	1	143	74	185.00
	7-8 PM	30/2		Ironside	1	158	81	175.00
	1130PM-CC	30/2		Wide World Entertainment	2	32	18	60.00
Saturday	7-8 PM	30/2		Lawrence Welk	1	107	65	140.00
	1130PM-1230AM	30/2		Wrestling	1	78	24	50.00
Sunday	8AM-1230PM	30/2		Religious & Gospel	2	50	30	30.00
			WEEKLY TOTALS:		16	909,	524,	1000.00

RATE INFORMATION

HOMES SOURCE:

Nov. 75ARB

Audience measurement data of all media are
estimates only.....subject to defects and limitations of source material and methods. Hence,
they may not be accurate measures of the
true audience.

Time periods quoted subject to prior sale.

Submitted by: Ben Whitaker/dh
Account Executive

2619 Western Boulevard • Telephone 828-2511

Fig. 22.6

TABLE 22.14 Raleigh News and Observer—advertising costs

$1.10 per agate line
14 agate lines per column inch
8 columns per page width

TABLE 22.15 Media production costs

Media	Specifications	Cost
Television	Slide with voice over	$25.00
Television	30-second film with commentary	$3000.00
Radio	30-second spot	$60.00
Newspaper	$\frac{1}{4}$ page with picture and information	$25.00

were sent to each family, followed by a phone call three to five days later. Results through March 1976 were as follows: 484 families (representing 1527 individuals) called, 12 new enrollments, 21 people will use fee-for-service, 48 people want more information.

A final promotional idea currently being explored is that of a "physical fitness fair" to include information on the benefits of exercise and sports participation. WHSI is in the process of contacting a variety of businesses, institutions, and agencies to solicit their participation, with a tentative date set for the fall of 1976.

Special Packages WHSI believes that the small-business community still offers tremendous potential in acquiring enrollees to the THP. In addition to trying to formulate special packages for enrollees, WHSI is currently developing programs that would provide fee-for-service health care to small-business employees. Such a program would increase visibility, provide more consumer contact, provide WHSI with increased income, and possibly result in more enrollees in the THP. Similar efforts are being made to develop programs for the small colleges in the area.

MANAGEMENT INFORMATION SYSTEM (MIS) Since the initial grant application, Wake Health Services has been attempting to implement a management information system on either a manual or automated basis. An external consulting firm, which reviewed WHSI requirements carefully, noted that when enrollments exceed one thousand, some form of automated data gathering would be required. A system design tailored to WHSI needs has been prepared but not implemented, due to the absence of equipment. The Board of Trustees has specified that a system be developed, using funds from the current grant. The effect of not having routine and timely reports is costly in terms of:

1. The amount of human effort required to generate reports manually, on demand, to the exclusion of tasks already assigned;

2. The amount of unused patient demographic and treatment data that if adequately and routinely aggregated would assist with medical audits, updating protocols, analysis of trends in disease categories by patient location, etc.;

3. The inability to capture and assign direct and indirect costs of service delivery and administration in an orderly and timely manner; and

4. The inability to document planning-strategy results with accurate, timely, trend-oriented data.

WHSI is still committed to the development of an effective MIS, though its efforts have not met with complete success to date. The strategy outlined for the future designed to result in such a system is:

1. *Form/work flow analysis*—Complete an analysis of all work and paper flow, including all data elements on all forms utilized by WHSI.

2. *Data elements*—prepare a master list of all data elements to be used as inputs into the information system.

3. *Data elements analysis*—conduct an analysis of all data elements in terms of how they will be used, i.e., number, percent, number and percent over time, by whom, how frequently, for what purposes, etc.

4. *Reports*—design information system reports and compare with systems design developed previously for WHSI by American Health Systems, Macro Systems, *et al.*

5. *Operating systems design*—design report series at operating (functional) level, i.e., medical, administration, finance, and marketing, review for internal consistency across functions.

6. *Management systems design*—using other system designs as guide, integrate and aggregate various functional reports into management reports for determining trends, formulating, planning data, and decision making.

WHSI management feels that management processes of cost control, allocation of resources, evaluation, and planning, as well as the reporting of medical data, will enable WHSI to improve its health-maintenance and preventive-medicine capability.

FUTURE WHSI management feels that it has a much-needed service for Wake County residents. However, it has not been able to communicate successfully to its potential consumers. The management has considered and made product changes in an effort to meet the needs of several different sectors of the community. WHSI marketing activities, in light of the development and implementation of enrollee and fee-for-service profiles, should become more precise and cost-effective.

Additionally, the planning process proposed earlier is expected to determine health needs more precisely. As the WHSI information system is developed, evaluated, and improved, increased precision in specifying and projecting the needs of the WHSI patient population will occur.

Finally, the management reporting system, scheduled for evaluation and review this coming year, is expected to become a major source of planning data in terms of scheduling administrative efforts over time. With these goals in mind, WHSI looks forward to increased enrollment and more effective fulfillment of the medical needs of Wake County.

DISCUSSION QUESTIONS

1. What are the basic decisions that must be made before an analysis worksheet may be completed?

2. What is the primary problem? The subproblems? How would you rank the subproblems?
3. What strategy would you recommend?
4. Prepare a marketing plan.

CHAPTER 23

Evaluating a New Channel of Distribution: The April Showers Company

In 1974 the April Showers (AS) Company was one of the ten largest (excluding chain stores) manufacturers of women's all-weather coats in the United States. Corporate headquarters, including a sales showroom, are located in New York City; general administration, accounting, and manufacturing are located in a small Southern town (see Fig. 23.1). An auxiliary manufacturing facility, no longer in operation, was located 50 miles north of the principal plant. The company was founded in 1955 by Wilbert LaTrolley, an entrepreneur, engineer, and artist who is a firm believer in automation, technology, and efficiency. He has invented, patented, and marketed several production and inventory systems and was the first in his industry to introduce several other production systems and concepts. His plant is well run, extremely efficient, and equipped with the latest equipment, computers, and systems. Mr. LaTrolley is very proud of his product's quality and value image, his 600 employees, and their loyalty to him and to April Showers—22 percent of them have been with AS for ten or more years.

AS has established its corporate goals to be: (1) to continue to make a 15 percent after tax return on equity, and (2) to nearly double its present sales of $8,431,000 within the next five years.

At present, AS manufactures approximately $7,322,000 (factory price) and imports $1,099,000 (wholesale) worth of coats each year (see Table 23.1). Mr. LaTrolley's executive vice-president estimates that the plant has capacity to produce $10,000,000 worth of merchandise. Capacity is estimated in factory price dollars instead of units in the apparel industry because there is an enormous diversity in styling, ornamentation, etc. However, what is lost in unit capacity by adding an additional pocket or trim is usually assumed to be made up in higher selling prices. Production is heaviest and at full capacity in late winter and early spring, but drops off to 60 percent of capacity in the fall.

Case material is prepared as the basis for class discussion. Cases are not designed to present illustrations of either effective or ineffective handling of administrative problems.

Written by Liz Ansley, under the direction of G. David Hughes, Burlington Industries Professor of Business Administration, University of North Carolina.

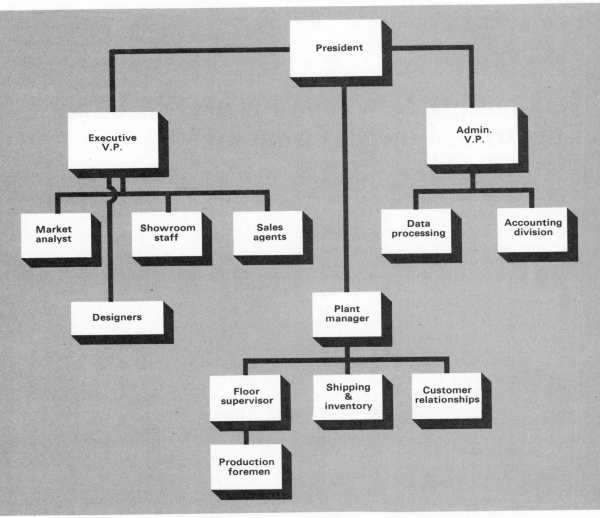

Fig. 23.1 April Showers organizational chart.

TABLE 23.1 April Showers financial summary ($ in millions)

	1970 $	1970 %	1971 $	1971 %	1972 $	1972 %	1973 $	1973 %	1974 $	1974 %
Net sales	4.8	100	5.6	100	6.3	100	7.3	100	8.4	100
CGS	3.5	73	3.8	68	4.4	70	5.0	69	5.9	70
GM	1.3	27	1.8	32	1.9	30	2.3	31	2.5	30
Selling exp. and admin.	1.2	24	1.2	21	1.2	19	1.5	20	1.8	22
Profit B.T.	.1	3	.6	11	.7	9	.8	11	.7	8

Note: Percentages may not always add up, due to rounding errors.
Source: Company records.

Additional automation in this highly labor-intensive production process can increase capacity. AS recently purchased data-processing equipment with capacity for twice the present volume. No more new purchases are anticipated.

THE ALL-WEATHER COAT MARKET

Present According to the company market analyst, AS competes in manufacturing women's outerwear constructed or tailored of soft fabric, woven or knitted of natural and/or synthetic fibers which have been treated with a water-repellant additive or woven so tightly that water penetration is negligible. Between 1971 and 1974 this all-weather coat market has remained almost static, with *unit sales* of approximately 12.6 to 13.1 million units, growing at an average of 1 percent per year. Dollar sales over this period have increased 10.5 percent, due primarily to inflation (see Table 23.2).

TABLE 23.2 Women's rainwear total retail sales (16 years and over)

	1971	1972	1973	1974	Annual % change, 1971–74
Units (millions)	12.3	13.3	13.1	12.7	+1
$ (millions)	297.7	344.5	348.3	401.9	+10.5
Average price	24.14	25.91	26.55	31.6	+9

Source: Files of consultant using Monsanto and Market Research Corporation of America data.

The women's rainwear industry, because of low set-up costs, is fluid and fragmented, with manufacturers moving in and out of the market, depending on exploitable short-term market opportunities. The market is heavily dominated by 9.15 percent of the companies (a total of 15 companies) which control 40 percent of retail sales. Table 23.3 shows that market share, in units, is generally less than 5 percent. Since the market is a stagnant one, an entering or growing company must take market share from an

TABLE 23.3 Retail share of market of leading women's rainwear manufacturers, 1973

	Units (,000) (1)	(2)	Retail (millions) (3)	(4)	Av. price (5)	% $/% units (4)/(2)
Sears, Penney, Ward	1,387.4	10.5%	$26.1	7.6%	$18.81	0.734
Company:						
A	716.0	5.5	45.7	13.1	63.80	2.382
B	375.7	2.9	20.5	5.9	54.50	2.034
C	360.0	2.7	18.0	5.0	49.92	1.852
D	310.0	2.4	16.2	4.7	52.25	1.958
AS	301.8	2.3	15.1	4.3	50.13	1.869
E	250.0	1.9	14.0	4.0	55.85	2.105
F	112.2	.9	4.0	1.2	35.65	1.333
All other	9,308.0	70.9	188.7	54.2	20.27	0.764
Total	13,121.1	100.0%	$348.3	100.0%	$26.55	1.000

Source: Files of consultant using Monsanto and Market Research Corporation of America data.

existing firm. New and small companies tend to copy the product of several of the leading firms and sell it at a price much lower than the original product. As the firm grows and expands, it incurs more and more overhead, so it must increase its prices until it can no longer undercut the market leaders. Then the firm must develop its own product and style. As a large and established firm in the industry, it will be the target of new competitors copying its product and "sniping" at its market share.

Aside from the brand awareness inherent in the coats sold by the chain stores (e.g., Sears, Penney, Ward), only the leading firm enjoys much brand awareness or brand loyalty. Naturally, to this firm, its brand name, brand loyalty, and product image are critically important, and it is very careful to continue the strength of its brand name. All of the other companies, dwarfed by the chains and the industry leader, cannot hope to be able to compete on such a brand-name basis; thus they compete on value, price, and styling. Except for the market leaders, manufacturers do little advertising of their products. It is left to co-op advertising, word of mouth, and taking coats off the rack to inform the consumer of the products, new styles, etc.

Rainwear purchases are related to temperature and rainfall. Women in cooler, rainier areas are much more likely to buy rainwear, and thus all-weather coats, than are women in drier, warmer areas (see Table 23.4). Women's rainwear is typically purchased in all areas of the country by women of all income levels 35 years old and older (see Table 23.5).

Rainwear companies have had little success in penetrating the younger markets, which are the usual target apparel sales, because young women have high disposable income and a heavy emphasis on styling, status, and personal presentation. It is conjectured that in the younger markets, wearing rainwear presents a rather stuffy, unfashionable, "fuddy duddy" image; it is much more chic to get wet. In the older markets, stylishness and chicness are traded off for dryness. Because a piece of plastic can keep one dry, manufacturers must convince the consumer that she wants an all-weather coat. Women buy all-weather coats not only for protection, but also for warmth, durability, easy care, and the look of a more complete, assembled outfit during inclement weather.

Rainwear styling has traditionally been basic, with design differentiation achieved by application of detail, use and quality of trim, and selection of fabric. Eighty percent of retail units and 81 percent of retail dollar sales are in polyester and polyester blends. Styling tends toward smooth lines and solid colors which are flattering to the figure as opposed to the more bulky, heavy lines of men's rainwear.

The women's rainwear market has two seasons—spring/summer and fall/winter (see Table 23.6). It is also subject to the apparel industry's seven-year cycle, which repeats each 21 years. Styling, construction, and how consumers use and view rainwear play important roles in the merchandising.

Market Forecast The market forecasts in Table 23.7 are based on the per capita rainwear purchase rates for 1971–73, which are summarized in Table 23.8.

The all-weather coat industry is influenced by political, environmental, and economic factors both nationally and worldwide. Consumer preference and thus production processes have tended rapidly toward and become dependent on petroleum-based polyester fabrics. The price of petroleum and petroleum-based products has been rising and is expected to continue to rise at a much more rapid rate than the normal inflation rate. A petroleum shortage or another Mideast oil embargo could severely cripple production of polyester fabrics.

TABLE 23.4 Women's rainwear, percent of units and dollars by age of purchaser 1971–74 (est.)

Age group	1974 % U.S. women 16+	% of women owning rainwear	1971 Units	1971 $	1972 Units	1972 $	1973 Units	1973 $	1974 Units	1974 $	Unit (1) index
16–19	10.0%	50	7.0%	5.8%	6.5%	4.6%	5.7%	5.0%	6.8%	6.1%	68
20–24	12.0	63	6.4	5.9	5.4	4.9	7.1	5.8	4.5	4.1	38
25–34	19.0	68	13.7	12.4	11.5	11.0	11.5	10.0	16.8	16.3	88
35–44	15.0	70	13.6	13.5	14.2	13.7	9.5	8.4	12.2	13.1	81
45–54	15.0	79	23.7	23.6	20.3	23.6	25.2	26.8	22.1	21.1	147
55 and over	29.0	84	35.6	38.8	42.6	42.2	41.0	44.0	37.6	39.5	130
Totals	100.0%	79.0	100.0%	100.0%	100.0%	100.0%	100.0%	100.0%	100.0%	100.0%	
Base (millions)			12.3	$297.7	13.3	$344.5	13.1	$348.3	12.7	$401.9	

Source: Company records based on Department of the Census, Series E, 1975; M.R.C.A. Panel Data.
(1) Index of percent of retail units, 1974, to percent of women over 16 in each age group.

TABLE 23.5 Regional distribution of women's rainwear sales and AS sales, 1973

Region	U.S. women 16+	Mean January temperature (°F)	Mean July temperature (°F)	Mean annual precipitation (inches)	% U.S. women 16+	% Retail rainwear sales	% April Shower sales	(1) % Rainwear penetration	Development Index (2) Retail rainwear sales	Development Index (3) April Showers	Development Index (4) Rainwear penetration
New England	4.7	23.6	70.5	41.53	5.9	7.0	5.6	85.0	119	94	118
Middle Atlantic	14.7	28.1	73.7	40.57	18.6	22.0	22.4	83.0	118	120	115
East North Central	14.9	21.9	72.5	41.15	18.9	20.0	16.8	72.0	106	89	100
West North Central	6.3	21.9	74.7	25.29	8.0	8.0	10.5	68.0	100	131	94
South Atlantic	12.0	40.4	78.3	43.75	15.2	15.0	18.9	81.0	99	124	113
East South Central	5.0	42.1	79.1	51.35	6.3	5.0	8.7	71.0	79	138	99
West South Central	7.4	45.1	82.7	44.76	9.4	8.0	4.8	64.0	85	51	89
Mountain	3.4	31.9	75.4	9.47	4.3	3.0	1.9	49.0	70	44	68
Pacific	10.6	39.4	65.6	36.83	13.4	11.0	10.4	65.0	82	78	90
Total	79.0				100.0	100.0	100.0	72.0			

Source: Department of the Census, Series E; Sales Management Survey of Buying Power, 1973; company files.
(1) Percent of women in each region who own one or more raincoats. Read as: "72% of all U.S. women over 16 own a raincoat."
(2) Index of percent of total retail rainwear sales to percent of women 16+ in each region.
(3) Index of percent of AS sales to percent of women 16+ in each region.
(4) Index of (1) showing development of ownership by region relative to national average ownership of 72%.

TABLE 23.6 Women's rainwear retail sales by month, 1970–74 average

Month	Monthly %	% by season
March	13	
April	13	34%
May	8	
June	6	
July	5	17%
August	6	
September	9	
October	12	29%
November	8	
December	9	
January	6	20%
February	5	

Source: Company records.

TABLE 23.7 Women's all-weather coats, industry sales forecast

	Millions of constant dollars	Millions of current dollars	Thousands of units, by age						
			16–19	20–24	25–34	35–44	45–54	55+	Total
1974	402	402	762	889	1905	1270	2794	5080	12,700
1975	401	426	762	889	1905	1270	2794	5080	12,700
1976	430	460	810	869	2095	1435	2090	5457	13,556
1977	435	496	808	885	2167	1460	2861	5544	13,725
1978	441	536	807	899	2240	1487	2832	5634	13,899
1979	447	579	806	915	2316	1514	2796	5724	14,071
1980	452	626	804	933	2392	1553	2748	5823	14,253
Annual rate of growth	2%	7.8%	0%	1.0%	4.0%	3.2%	0%	2.5%	2.0%

Source: Company records.

TABLE 23.8 Per capita rainwear purchases

Age	1971–73 Average annual purchases (in thousands)	1971–73 Average female population (in thousands)	1971–73 Per capita purchases
16–19	800	7,840	.10
20–24	810	8,975	.09
25–34	1,800	13,838	.13
35–44	1,370	11,602	.12
45–54	2,970	12,229	.24
55+	5,100	22,253	.23
	12,850	76,737	.17

Source: Company records.

TABLE 23.9 Women's rainwear sales by price points, 1971–74 (est.)

Retail price points	1971 % Units	% $	1972 % Units	% $	1973 % Units	% $	1974 % Units	% $
$11.99 and under	19.5	5.2	17.5	4.1	17.9	3.8	14.7	3.1
$12.00–$19.99	28.5	19.1	31.2	19.7	26.6	16.6	20.0	10.9
$20.00–$27.99	20.6	19.9	17.5	15.6	16.6	14.8	18.2	14.4
$28.00–$31.99	8.1	9.9	6.7	7.7	7.6	8.5	10.9	10.7
$32.00–$39.99	8.8	13.0	8.5	11.8	11.1	15.2	11.3	13.5
$40.00–$49.99	8.0	15.0	9.5	17.0	10.8	17.7	13.0	21.0
$50.00–$59.99	3.0	7.0	4.6	10.0	6.0	12.5	6.0	11.5
$60.00–$69.99	2.0	4.5	2.0	5.0	.5	1.2	4.0	9.0
$70.00–$79.99	1.0	3.1	1.5	4.5	1.5	4.3	1.0	3.0
$80.00 and over	.6	3.3	1.0	4.6	1.5	5.4	1.0	2.9
Total	100.0%	100.0%	100.0%	100.0%	100.0%	100.0%	100.0%	100.0%
Base (millions)	12.3	$297.7	13.3	$344.5	13.1	$348.3	12.7	$401.9
Average price	$24.14		$25.91		$26.55		$31.65	

Source: Monsanto—M.R.C.A. Panel Data; DuPont—M.R.C.A. Panel Data; Consultant

The all-weather coat market is well structured by price points (a price point is $1.00). See Table 23.9. The effects of inflation, the petroleum situation, imports, and consumer product and benefit preferences on the market price structure are uncertain.

The industry is attempting to increase purchases in the 16–34 age group by changing styling and designing coats which double as sport coats and pantcoats. It is too early to determine the impact of this effort. A three percent annual increase in per capita rainwear purchases by women in this age group would add only a million units to the market by 1980. Thus only drastic changes in buying behavior by this group will significantly influence sales.

AS's NICHE IN ITS MARKET   AS sells two product lines. The Tropical Storm line consists of 65 designs and is sold to women over 30 at retail prices between $38 and $75. The spring season unweighted average price is $48.32; that for the fall is $53.03, bringing $25.13 and $27.58, respectively, in factory price.

The Oriental Monsoon line, imported from Hong Kong, sells to a younger, less affluent, more stylish market at junior department price points: $25–$38. This line is positioned as action-styled water-repellant outerwear. AS sends designs and patterns to the E. F. Young Company of Hong Kong, which then purchases the materials, manufactures the product, and ships it to AS. Since Hong Kong is a duty-free port abounding with cheap labor, low production costs enable AS to sell these coats at a relatively low price for the quality.

Imports are lucrative but risky. Quality control is sometimes less than adequate, and late arrival of goods is entirely possible. Imports account for less than 15 percent of AS sales and 19 percent of industry sales.

AS market strategy is to adapt successful competitive designs to retail at 15 to 20 retail price points below designs of comparable quality. AS has outgrown the "sniper" stage and is now in a transitional period between being a growing, viable competitor and becoming a market leader. Smaller companies are beginning to attack and snipe at AS and its market share. Both product lines are positioned as value, but not prestige, products. Styling is along more basic, classic lines, not along high-risk, high-fashion "couture" lines. Average price, excluding imports, was $50.13 in 1973, which is 3 to 10 price points below its top four competitors, but more than 30 price points above the chain stores (see Table 23.3).

AS products are sold nationwide by 17 independent sales agents. Annual commission, at 6 percent of sales, averages around $30,000 each. Large key accounts are sold in the New York showroom. AS has 8000 active accounts, 7600 of which are small specialty stores which account for 70 percent of AS sales. Distribution of industry sales by retail outlets appears in Table 23.10. To reduce dependency, no one retailer accounts for more than 1 to $1\frac{1}{2}$ percent of sales. Average order size is four to five units. AS advertises very little, usually on a co-op basis with a retailer. According to a company source, it takes $20 in sales to make $1 in profit, so one advertising dollar saved is almost one coat they do not need to sell to maintain the same profit level.

Designing is generally done a year of so before the selling season. Even though the AS designers have 30 years or more experience in the field, some of their designs sell better than others. Although most designs sell at the normal, expected pace, a few designs emerge as "hot numbers" and sell out very quickly. Production takes place several months before the selling season; however, coats are cut in lots of 500 to 1000 units. Toward the end of a selling season, unsold coats will be marked down for

TABLE 23.10 Women's all-weather coat sales in units and dollars by retail outlet

Retail outlet	Units (in millions)				Current dollars (millions)				Average price				Average price annual % change 1971/1974
	1971	1972	1973	1974	1971	1972	1973	1974	1971	1972	1973	1974	
Department store	4.5	4.9	4.3	4.3	$122.7	$142.3	$126.4	$147.1	$27.26	$29.04	$29.39	$34.21	+ 8
Specialty store	3.2	3.3	3.3	3.3	93.8	110.6	110.1	131.0	29.31	33.52	33.36	39.70	+10.5
Sears, Penney, Ward	1.7	2.0	2.4	2.4	33.6	41.3	47.0	59.1	19.76	20.65	19.58	24.63	+ 8
Discount chains	1.1	1.2	1.3	1.3	15.8	18.3	20.5	26.5	14.36	15.25	15.77	20.38	+12.5
Total above	10.5	11.4	11.3	11.3	$265.9	$312.5	$304.0	$363.7	$25.32	$27.41	$26.90	$32.19	+ 8%

Source: Company records, Monsanto, M.R.C.A. Consumer Panel.

quick sale. Unsold merchandise is put into inventory at the end of the selling season. At present AS has $200,000 (factory price) of unsold merchandise in inventory. There are generally only a few pieces of a style in inventory except for those styles which did not sell. Fortunately for AS, only a very small proportion of its inventory is "dogs." Whenever possible, unused materials are redyed and recycled into use the next season. Materials waste is very low, and a 0.3 percent spoilage cost is allocated in the factory standard cost. Salespeople can always dispose of any and all seconds produced.

AS FORECAST   AS has performed well in the past, outstripping the industry sales gain of 10.5 percent with a sales gain of 15 percent (Table 23.1). AS is expecting increased sales in its junior (Oriental Monsoon) line and greater fall sales to increase its total sales by 5 percent per year to $11.3 million (in constant dollars) in 1980 (Table 23.11). However, management feels that gains in these markets may not be sufficient.

TABLE 23.11   April Showers forecasted sales

| | April Showers | |
	Constant dollar sales	Current dollar sales
1974	$ 8.4	$ 8.4
1975	8.8	9.3
1976	9.3	10.3
1977	9.7	11.5
1978	10.2	12.8
1979	10.7	14.2
1980	11.3	15.7
Annual rate of growth:		
1974–80	5%	11%
1970–74	—	15%

AS is now trying to increase sales per order by developing key department store accounts. Sales are concentrated within those price points that not only mirror the heart of the market, but also are within the most rapidly growing price segment as well. AS distribution is in close proportion to regional distribution of women's rainwear ownership. Some stores demand exclusive dealership in an area. Some areas are dominated by a few large stores; thus sales through outlets other than the dominating stores are not large enough to warant participation. Therefore, AS has just about achieved as much coverage as possible without changing its channels or method of distribution by, for instance, repositioning a few styles to a cheaper price to sell in chain and discount stores, selling its products through mail order, or rescinding its rule about 1 to 1½ percent of sales per store.

THE MAIL-ORDER BUSINESS   The mail-order business is actually not a business, but a way of doing business, a marketing strategy more accurately labeled "direct response advertising." It began in the 1800s with companies sending "wishbooks" to people living in backwater towns and remote sections of the country too sparsely populated or too far away for the company to sell its wares in the local stores. Modern transportation, communication, and merchandising have deisolated most of these areas, but they have not halted the growth of the mail-order business, which has reached $50 billion a year.[1]

Direct-response advertising has four prime goals: orders, sales leads, inquiries, and traffic. Today, buying by mail offers convenience, savings in time and transportation costs, better selection of goods, satisfaction guaranteed, entertainment, no sales tax charge, and often price savings. Direct-response advertising includes major retail catalog sales, manufacturer's retail and wholesale catalog sales, sales accomplished through space advertisements, package enclosures, take-one cards, free-standing stuffers, radio and television ads, etc.

The major retail catalog houses are dominated by the mass-merchandising chains, such as Sears, Penney, Aldens, and Ward. Inclusion in one of these catalogs may significantly increase one's sales volume, but one must also meet the demands of the catalog house. Markup in these catalogs averages 50–60 percent for nationally advertised goods and more than 60 percent for goods which are not nationally advertised.[2] The catalog house may demand large-volume contracts, exclusive mail ordering and advertising rights, and require the product to conform to its price, styling, and quality standards.

There are an estimated 6000 or more independent and manufacturer's mail-order retailers in the United States. They offer a variety of goods, from staple items to foods, plant seeds, jewelry, and a broad assortment of unique, specialized gadgets and goods. The usual common denominator among these items is that through price, consumer location, special styling, colors or features, or the very nature and perceived benefits of the product, the retailers offer consumers something they cannot readily buy locally. High-style, fad items, or items whose prices change often are generally, but not always, unsuccessful in this business because of the long time cycle involved in each catalog mailing. Items are generally offered in a limited selection of colors and sizes to reduce the amount of inventory required.

Success factors in this business are: (1) careful market testing: (2) the ability to build a large list of loyal customers; (3) a strong repurchase rate; (4) a good reputation for quality, service, and guarantee; and (5) ability to ship quickly (the FTC requires that goods be shipped within 30 days of receipt of order).

The business is easily entered and left, since very little capital is required at the outset. In building up a business, one must invest in inventory, warehousing, data processing, shipping facilities, additional staff, lists, and catalogs. Losses due to bad debt are minimal, since most but not all mail ordering is done on a cash-in-advance basis or through major credit cards. Of those companies offering credit card charges, 10–15 percent of sales are charge sales. Average bank card fees are 3 percent of charge sales.

Payment within a specified number of days of receipt of the goods or on the installment basis is becoming more common in the mail-order business. Items costing $50 or more sell better by installment than by cash. Credit customers tend to be more loyal than cash customers.[3]

Mail-order marketers go to great lengths to avoid delinquent payments. A payment must be only a few weeks late for a company to begin to send a steady stream of letters requesting, with decreasing politeness, payment. Accounts that do not respond to these letters are factored, usually regardless of the size of the amount owed.

To begin in the retail mail-order business, one first selects the product(s) to be sold and the market(s) for the product. The retailer then develops and prints mailing piece(s), sets up a number keying system, builds inventory, and mails the presentation to names obtained by renting a list from a list broker or from a firm that will rent its own mailing list and/or runs space ads in magazines and newspapers. The mailing piece combines a letter, a circular or catalog, order forms, and reply card or envelope in one package. Some also may contain swatches, samples, bonus offers, and free gifts. The offer may attempt to solicit an immediate sale, or it may invite the recipient to request a catalog, salesperson's visit, or other correspondence.

A mailing list can be selected from a mass-compiled list on geographic, demographic, or psychographic bases, or it can be rented from a merchant whose clientele closely resembles that desired. The broker will furnish one with mailing labels and, for a fee, affix them to the mailing piece and mail them. Lists are rented on a one-time basis. The only names one may keep are those which reply to the mailing. Mailing lists usually cost between $25 and $75 per thousand, averaging $35 per thousand. Labeling, a letter/pamphlet presentation, and third-class mailing charges cost an additional $140 per thousand pieces mailed.

Prices of newspaper and magazine advertisements vary from very cheap to very expensive, depending on the size and specifications of the advertisement, the audience of the periodical, the number of regional editions the advertisement appears in, and how often the advertisement appears in the periodical during the year. A full-color, one-third-page advertisement in the *Ladies Home Journal*, which has a circulation of 7,064,190, costs $14,625. Advertisements in other magazines similar to the *Ladies Home Journal* cost about the same per thousand readers. (Additional advertising price information, for most publications, is listed in *Standard Rate and Data*.)

A typical mail-order space advertisement will contain a picture of an example of the good(s) offered, a stimulating description of the product, and a coupon in the bottom right corner which can be mailed to the advertiser requesting an order, a catalog, or other correspondence. A product should be advertised more than once to sell it successfully through space advertising. Repetition builds awareness, interest, and confidence in the product.

There are establishments called fulfillment houses which will receive and ship orders for a fee. A manufacturer simply furnishes the fulfillment house with sufficient inventory.

Several weeks after the mailing or the advertisement appears, orders begin to arrive. Table 23.12 serves as a general guide to order prediction. In all, a two- to three-percent response to a mass mailing is considered to be a good response rate, whereas response to periodical advertising is generally much less. The success of a mailing or an advertisement is determined by the amount of profit made, not by the volume of orders received. Orders must be processed; credit and checks must be cleared; the name tabbed to remain in the "active" list or put on the active list if it is not already on it; and the merchandise must be picked, packed, wrapped, labeled, and shipped. Often a stuffer, flyer or new catalog is enclosed in the package. Once a year the list must be pruned of inactive names.

Market Testing   In building one's clientele and mailing list, one must continually test the product in the market to determine which variables do and do not bring results, why, and whether or not to try to sell the product through this channel to this market. If the test is successful, a larger mailing should follow. All changes in lists, product, colors, presentation, etc., should be tested before a mass mailing. One may test by mailing to 10,000 names randomly picked from a master list. Often a variable will be tested

TABLE 23.12 Response rates by media

Elapsed* time	Daily newspapers	Monthly magazines	Direct mail	Sunday newspaper supplements
1st week	50–70%	7–10%	33–52%	35–40%
2nd week	78–95	18–33	60–80	60–65
4th week	93–99	25–65	89–90	79–81
2 months	97–100	57–83	96	89–90
6 months	—	90–96	99	99

* Time elapsed after the *first order* is received.
Source: "Mail Order Enterprise," *Small Business Reporter*, San Francisco: Bank of America, 1973.

in several different ways using several lists of names randomly taken from the master list. For instance, three or four different letters will be tested on three or four different test lists to see which format is the most successful or which characteristics of each format are successful in order to combine them. This method is used to test copy, price, graphics, offer, media, etc. A beginning mail orderer may want to hire a consultant who specializes in retail mail ordering.

Addresses of consultants can be found in the directory in the back of the trade magazine *Direct Marketing* or through the trade organization, the Direct Mail Marketing Association. Consultant fees average around $5000 to conduct enough market tests to be able to recommend (1) whether or not the product belongs in the mail-order business, (2) if so, to which people and in what manner, and (3) profit and cost estimates. Total testing, including the consultant's fee, generally averages $30,000.

AS AND THE MAIL-ORDER MARKET During 1974 mail-order retailing increased 20 percent, whereas retail store sales increased 8–16 percent.[4] This mail-order growth is attributed to increased transportation costs, more working women, and consumerism. (Mail-order catalogs frequently provide more product information than is available from the retail sales clerk.) AS could not determine what percent of the mail-order market is apparel or what percent of the mail-order apparel market constitutes the all-weather coats. The number of mail-order companies selling all-weather coats is unknown.

Because AS already has warehousing and shipping facilities, ample computer time, and prints full-color 30-page fall and spring catalogs to be used by their salespeople, to compete in the mail-order market should not cost AS as much money as it might another company. To print additional 8- and 16-page catalogs using pages from the sales catalogs would cost $30 and $50 per thousand.

Average inventory turnover in the all-weather coat industry is five times per year. The industry ratio and cost of returns due to poor fit or poor purchase judgment are unknown. Cost of capital is 13.5 percent.

Additional mail-order costs are estimated to be:

1. Shipping labor—$.10 per order shipped
2. Shipping supplies—$.35 per order shipped
3. Postage (UPS, including insurance up to $100)—$1.25 per order shipped

4. Package insert—$.03 per order shipped

5. Processing labor—$.30 per order processed

6. Processing supplies—$.15 per order processed

7. Markdowns—five percent of expected total sales.

DISCUSSION QUESTIONS

1. Explain the importance of the following marketing concepts to this case.
   a) positioning
   b) product image
   c) price points and market price structure
   d) perceived product benefits
   e) 80/20 rule
   f) break even
   g) brand awareness
   h) market testing
   i) distribution costs
   j) trade journals and organizations
   k) generic market and market share
   l) market research companies
   m) retail markup
   n) corporate goals
   o) firm life cycle

2. What are the opportunities and problems?

3. What do you recommend?

NOTES

1. "Mail Order Enterprises," *Small Business Reporter* (San Francisco: Bank of America, 1973).

2. *Mail Order Directory* (Coral Springs, Florida: B. Klein Publications, 1975), p. v.

3. R. S. Hodgson., *Direct Mail and Mail Order Handbook*, 2d ed. (Chicago: Dartnell, 1974).

4. "Catalogue Sales Thrive on Inflation," *Business Week*, July 20, 1974, p. 27.

SUGGESTED READING

Stone, B., "The Basics of Mail Order advertising," *Advertising Age*, January 2, 1978, pp. 19 ff.

CHAPTER 24

Planning for Integrating New Acquisitions: The S & L Company

On August 29, 1974, the April Showers Company (AS) was purchased by the S & L Holding Company, which also owns three other entrepreneur-run women's garment manufacturers in the Southeast: Nurses' Delight Uniforms, Suggestive Robes, and Sassy Pants. The S & L Company was founded in March 1972 by a group of Virginia investors whose objective was to return 15 percent after tax on their investment by owning small companies ($10 to $20 million sales annually) which could generate that kind of profit.

The company president and vice-president are located at the company's Richmond headquarters; the controller, accounting, and data-processing staffs are located at the AS plant because of the excess computer capacity there. After being purchased by S & L, the companies and their entrepreneurs operated under almost complete autonomy; the only difference was that the entrepreneurs did not own the company equity. The organizational chart for S & L is shown in Fig. 24.1.

The apparel industry was hit rather hard by the 1974–75 recession, and the costs of operating inefficiencies began to make the difference between profits and losses. Therefore, the investors and the Richmond management began to reorganize, consolidate, and centralize the four companies. By the end of 1975 all purchasing, pattern making, cutting, and marking done by the companies was to be centralized. By July 1976 a product (skirts, pants, etc.) will be made in only one plant. Management is in the process of modernizing the plants and streamlining their operating procedures. Product lines have been dropped and plants closed. Much of the entrepreneurs' independence has been taken away. Table 24.1 explains the remaining product lines and their vital characteristics.

That the women's apparel market was no longer the seller's market of the 1950s and 1960s became apparent during the early 1970s, particularly during the 1974–75 recession. Increased productivity, competition from imported goods, and women's resistance to replacing their wardrobes with the latest New York and Paris designs left many items in inventory. To keep inventories clear of items which will not sell, a manufacturer's orientation must change from production to marketing—selling the

---

Case material is prepared as the basis for class discussion. Cases are not designed to present illustrations of either effective or ineffective handling of administration problems.

Written by Liz Ansely, under the direction of G. David Hughes, Burlington Industries Professor of Business Administration, University of North Carolina.

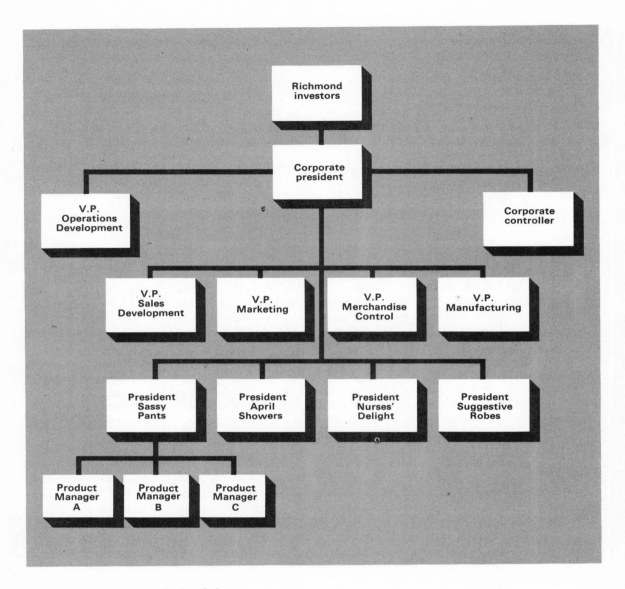

Fig. 24.1 S & L organizational chart.

designs before buying raw materials or making finished goods, which is the marketing concept.

This change to the marketing concept has not been readily understood by many apparel manufacturers, particularly those who began in the 1950s with a sewing machine and very little capital, were able to sell whatever they produced, built up a good business over the years, and made money. These characteristics describe the four entrepreneurs.

TABLE 24.1 Characteristics of S & L products

	1974 Sales ($ millions)	Branded (B) private label (P)	Principal merchandise classification	Knit (K) Woven (W)	Outlet	Coverage	Retail price class	Seasonality % Spring	% Fall
April Showers	$ 8.4	B	Rainwear	W	Department and specialty	National	Medium	67%	33%
Nurses' Delight	4.4	B	Nurses' Uniforms	K,W	Uniform specialty shops	National, strong in South; weak in Pacific	High	80	20
Suggestive Robes	10.4	B,P	Women's housecoats and robes	K	Department and specialty stores, chains	National	Medium	10	90
Sassy Pants: Ramos	4.2	B	Junior sportswear	W,K	Specialty	National, strong in South	Low-medium	45	55
Off-the-Cuff	6.4	B	Contemporary sportswear	K,W	Department store upstairs	National, very strong in NE	Medium	45	55
Penny Saver	5.8	P	Women's sportswear	W	Major chains	National	Low-medium	50	50
Total	$39.6								

Source: Company files.

Mr. LaTrolley of AS understands this change; however, he and management have found it difficult to convince the others. Mr. LaTrolley is educated in business methods; the business knowledge of the other entrepreneurs is basically practical knowledge gathered through trial and error.

NURSES' DELIGHT UNIFORMS Nurses' Delight, founded in 1949 by Frank and Sandra Sims, is now the third largest manufacturer of higher-priced nurses' uniforms in the country. The Simses are a very hard-working couple, and they are very proud of their product's reputation for style and premium quality. They insist that their uniforms be sold only in the best uniform shops and to shops with impeccable credit standing. Before selling Nurses' Delight (ND) to S & L in 1972, the Simses had established their goals to be (1) to sell as many uniforms each year as their plants could produce, and (2) to realize an annual profit of 17 percent of sales. Income statements from 1970 to 1973 are shown in Table 24.2. After the Simses sold their company to S & L, they adopted S & L's profit goals.

TABLE 24.2   Income statement, Nurses' Delight uniforms (millions of dollars)

	1970		1971		1972		1973	
	$	%	$	%	$	%	$	%
Net sales	$4.10	100%	$3.93	100%	$4.34	100%	$4.30	100%
Cost of goods	2.87	70	2.75	70	3.26	75	3.14	73
Gross margin	1.23	30	1.18	30	1.08	25	1.16	27
Sell. & admin. exp.	.53	13	.51	13	.61	14	.73	17
Net profit	.70	17	.67	17	.47	11	.43	10

Mrs. Sims is responsible for designing the uniforms, managing the office, working with the production workers, and taking over whenever Mr. Sims is away. Mr. Sims concentrates on sales and the less mundane business activities. They plan to retire in December 1976.

Prior to 1973 ND operated four manufacturing facilities in the South and a showroom in New York City. Because of Mr. Sims's sales orientation, these plants were usually oversold. In 1973 the three smallest plants (capacity of $2,400,000) were shut down, and production was moved to an S & L plant with capacity of $5,500,000 located near the AS plant. The remaining original ND plant (capacity of $1,800,000) was to be completely phased out by July 1976.

The quality of production at the new plant has been disappointingly poor. The Simses and management are hoping that this poor quality is due to the fact that the production workers had been making women's sportswear and needed some time to adjust to the production demands of making uniforms, rather than to an inability of the available labor force to make uniforms or to the extremely high (twice the industry average) employee turnover rate.

The Nursing Uniform Market

Present market. Success factors in this market are the ability to develop a brand awareness and preference, style, distribution, and quality. ND competes in the segment of the women's dress uniform market in which the uniform is: (1) fashion-oriented, with regular style changes; (2) made almost entirely of machine-washable synthetic or synthetic blend fabric; (3) purchased in retail stores; (4) purchased by nurses, waitresses, and beauticians who are responsible for owning and maintaining their own uniforms. Competing at the low end of this market are many producers of inexpensive domestic, waitress, and beautician uniforms which are typically sold in discount and chain stores. At the high end are ten to fifteen manufacturers of more highly styled uniforms sold in uniform specialty shops. Nurses and other medical professionals purchase 85 percent of these uniforms; waitresses and beauticians, the remaining 15 percent. Table 24.3 lists the ten market leaders and their estimated 1973 sales and market shares.

TABLE 24.3   Estimated 1973 sales and market shares

Company	1973 Sales (millions)	1973 Market share
A	$ 9.0	21.2%
B	4.4	10.4
ND	4.3	10.1
C	3.0	7.1
D	4.0	9.3
E	3.0	7.1
F	2.6	6.1
G	3.0	7.1
H	2.0	4.6
I	3.0	7.1
Others	4.2	9.9
	$42.5	100.0%

Source: Company records.

Because uniforms tend to be shopping goods, there are few brands from which to choose, and very few ways in which to achieve product differentiation, brand awareness is extremely important. Promotion of a line as a specialty good by developing brand preference is highly desirable, therefore. Retail outlets and manufacturers advertise heavily in trade publications, and they use direct-mail advertising, in-store displays, and posters in stores and other places where their consumers may tend to congregate (e.g., nurses' lounges) to promote their products and their names.

Uniform styling is very basic, simple, and conservative. The dominant color is white, although colored uniforms are sold in limited quantities. Styling changes are made in collars, tucking, sleeves, pockets, waistlines, and insets. Because of hospital regulations and professional preference, styling changes are not made in the basic sheath dress style, the neckline, ornamentation, etc. Good styles may remain popular for ten years or more.

There are two seasons in this market: spring/summer and winter/fall. There is basically little difference in styling between the two seasons, except that winter/fall styles may tend to have longer sleeves and higher collars. The spring season accounts for 80 percent of sales; fall, for only 20 percent. Sales drop off drastically around the Christmas holiday season.

Uniform specialty stores sell 53 percent of all nurses' uniforms, whereas retail stores sell 33 percent, and mail orders account for 11 percent. The preference for the specialty shop, particularly in the high end of the market, is attributed to its ability to handle more uniform inventory and to provide greater personal service than other apparel stores.

In general, every community has a hospital and enough beauty shops, restaurants, and doctors' offices to support at least one uniform shop. Thus uniforms are sold in every town, large or small, in the country. Uniform sales are concentrated in major metropolitan areas which also have a concentration of medical services. Over 31 percent of the nation's registered nurses are in the Northeastern states, 27 percent are in the Midwestern states, 16 percent are in the South, and 26 percent are in the Mountain, Southwestern, and Pacific states; 28 percent, 22 percent, 27 percent, and 23 percent, respectively, of the population live in these areas.

Retail prices of styled dress uniforms range from $10 to $25 and average $18. Pantsuits range in price from $8 to $35 and above, averaging $22. Nurses often purchase two tops for one pair of pants, which brings the average price of a pantsuit uniform to between $17 and $20. The average price of a dress uniform increased 6.5 percent between 1970 and 1974. In 1974, 37 percent of the dresses and 59 percent of the pantsuits were priced above $20, whereas only 5 percent of the dresses were priced above $20 in 1970. Historical data for pantsuits are nonexistent.

The pantsuit and the change from blends to synthetic fabrics have been the major events in the nursing uniform market in the past few years. In 1971 only 7 percent of the respondents to a survey done by the *American Journal of Nursing* had purchased a pantsuit uniform; a similar survey in 1974 indicated that 45 percent of all uniforms purchased were pantsuits. Pantsuits are generally considered to be much more comfortable and convenient to wear than dresses when performing nursing duties. Similarly, fabrics of 100 percent synthetic fibers have become the dominant fabrics used due to their permanent press and durability characteristics.

Many firms produce other lines of uniforms, particularly in the career apparel and medical fields. Several of these firms have realized substantial growth from these additional sales. Small manufacturers who produce a limited line of merchandise are making inroads into the nursing uniform market.

Consumers of higher-priced uniforms include registered and practical nurses, other medical personnel, and waitresses and beauticians who are willing to pay for styled uniforms. The nursing population is relatively young, with a median age between 35 and 44. Most nurses earn between $7000 and $12,000 each year, which provides them with adequate income with which to purchase uniforms on the basis of styling, taste, and ease of care as well as price. Interviews with retail store owners indicate that demand for higher-priced, high-quality, and highly styled uniforms is growing at a faster rate than that for lower-priced uniforms.

It is estimated that registered nurses, the major consumer in this market, purchase an average of three uniforms each year. Waitresses, beauticians, licensed practical nurses, and other medical personnel purchase approximately 1.5 uniforms each year. Nurses are more willing to adopt new styling changes fairly readily, unless the changes do not reflect professionalism or hospital regulations.

Future. Based on estimates of employment growth and uniform purchasing habits (not including lower-priced uniform sales or career apparel) made by a consultant hired by the Simses, unit demand for nurses' uniforms is expected to grow at a rate of 4.6 percent per year between 1974 and 1980, as shown in Table 24.4. Assuming a $20 average retail price, constant dollar retail sales will increase from $77.4 million to $101.5 million; assuming a 6 percent inflation rate, current dollar sales will increase to $141.7 million. Assuming a 45 percent average industry markup, factory price sales will increase at an annual rate of 10.5 percent.

TABLE 24.4 Forecasted market sales and ND sales, 1974–80

| | Market ($ millions) | | | ND forecast ($ millions) | | |
	Constant dollars	Current dollars	Wholesale current	Constant dollars	Current dollars	Market share
1974	$77.4	$ 77.4	$42.5	$4.38	$4.38	10.3%
1975	80.9	85.6	46.9	4.33	4.60	9.9
1976	86.4	94.7	51.9	4.29	4.83	9.3
1977	88.5	104.7	57.3	4.24	5.07	8.8
1978	92.6	115.8	63.5	4.21	5.32	8.4
1979	96.9	128.1	70.2	4.16	5.59	8.0
1980	101.5	141.7	77.9	4.12	5.87	7.5
Compounded rate of growth	4.6%	10.6%	10.5%	(1%)	5%	

Growth in this market is relatively unaffected by economic or political conditions, since people have relatively little ability to coordinate their medical needs with personal welfare. Management expects no major changes in the market before 1980. Management does feel that the career-apparel market will continue to become more important to uniform manufacturers as that market expands.

Manufacturers of quality uniforms are able to pass on most of their cost increases with only a slight decline in unit sales, because medical personnel incomes have increased and because there is some brand loyalty for quality brands. Imports are not the major factor in this market segment they are in the less expensive segments.

ND's Niche in the Uniform Market

Present market. ND sells over 90 percent of its uniforms to registered nurses and the remainder to waitresses and beauticians through uniform specialty shops and a few uniform chains. ND offers 64 styles, approximately 50 percent of which are pantsuit styles which account for 50 percent of sales. Most pantsuit styles consist of a shorter version of a dress style plus a pair of slacks.

Average retail price, including both pantsuits and dresses, is $24.50. Average factory price is $14.58. Average retail price of dresses is $20; of pantsuits, $35. In general, ND and the market leader are considered to be the major competitors in the high-price range. The majority of ND sales are in the price segment accounting for less than 20 percent of the nurses' uniform market.

ND's uniforms are highly styled, and its designs are probably the most copied in the industry. It is positioned and perceived to be a quality, premium product. Its product and marketing mix are directed toward the style-conscious rather than the price-conscious consumer.

ND's consumers are typical of any consumer in its segment, except that they tend to be the more highly paid and more concentrated in the South (31 percent of sales) and less concentrated in the Northeast (22 percent of sales).

ND uniforms are sold nationwide by 23 independent sales representatives. Commission averages 6 percent of sales. ND advertises in the *American Journal of Nursing* and similar nurses' and beauticians' trade journals. ND supplies uniform shops with posters demonstrating its styles. Through its sales outlets it also distributes brochures in which each of the uniform styles is pictured, described, and priced. After stamping its name and return address on the order form, the store may mail brochures to its customers, or it may distribute them in the store. The Simses estimate that the sales from these brochures account for seven percent of total sales. Average order size from stores is 30 uniforms.

Because of the basic similarity of raw materials used, very little production waste is realized. Very few uniforms remain in inventory as unsaleable merchandise, because styles tend to be classic and not fad-oriented. All seconds can be disposed of readily. Inventory turns over six times each year.

Future market. Since ND was founded, it has been an aggressive firm, outstripping the market and its competitors, but like its founder, it is seeming to approach retirement. Between 1971 and 1974, sales grew at a significantly slower pace than the industry, and margins decreased 7 percent. ND has been losing its position as a market leader by not entering other uniform markets. Store owners indicate that ND's styling is somewhat more conservative than that of its competitors, and shops are ordering particular styles instead of the entire line. The company forecast in Table 24.4, which assumes no changes in operations except the introduction of a few middle-priced styles, indicates that ND's market share should slip from 10.3 percent in 1974 to 7.5 percent by 1980.

SUGGESTIVE ROBES Suggestive Robes (SR) manufactures a complete line of women's middle-priced housecoats and robes. Founded by Sam Trotter in 1945, SR is now the third largest robe manufacturer in the country. It earned its reputation as an industry leader by being the first to introduce culottes, the pants tunic, and the shift into its market. Mr. Trotter retired in 1972 after selling his company to S & L. His successor, Arthur Klepner, joined SR in 1953. His duties include sales management and overseeing company affairs. He works out of the New York City showroom.

Before Mr. Trotter sold SR to S & L, his goals were (1) to become the second largest company in the industry, and (2) to maintain an annual profit margin of 9 percent of sales. Mr. Klepner has adopted the corporate goals of S & L. Table 24.5 describes SR's profit position between 1970 and 1974.

Approximately half of SR's production is done at the firm's two sewing plants and the cutting, shipping, and warehousing facility in southern Georgia. The three plants have a combined capacity of $5,000,000. There are no plans to increase either production or plant capacity at this time. Because robe production is highly seasonal —heaviest in July, August, and September and lightest in April and May—it is most economical to own only enough facilities to satisfy constant production needs. Therefore, SR's remaining production is done by contract labor in job shops.

The Present Robe Market SR competes with other manufacturers of dusters, housedresses, and robes in the robe and housecoat market. In terms of unit sales, this market is a stagnant

TABLE 24.5 SR income statement (millions of dollars)

	1970		1971		1972		1973		1974		Annual rate of growth
Net sales	8.96	100%	9.38	100%	8.57	100%	9.21	100%	10.40	100%	4%
Cost of goods	6.27	70%	6.75	72%	6.26	73%	6.91	75%	7.80	75%	+5%
Gross margin	1.69	30%	2.63	28%	2.31	27%	2.30	25%	2.60	25%	−1%
Sell. & admin. exp.	.90	21%	1.85	20%	1.72	20%	1.90	21%	1.95	19%	+4%
Net profit	.79	9%	.78	8%	.59	7%	.40	4%	.65	6%	−5%

Source: Company records.

one, while inflation has carried dollar market size upward. According to company analysts, 30 million garments were sold in 1973 for $150 million at factory and $290 million at retail. As Table 24.6 indicates, the average retail price rose from $7.53 in 1969 to $10.40 in 1974.

TABLE 24.6   **Changes in average retail price of robes, 1969–74**

	Average price	% Increase
1969	$ 7.53	
1970	7.76	3.0
1971	8.11	4.5
1972	8.72	7.5
1973	9.44	8.3
1974	10.40	10.0

Source: MRCA panel data.

There are three overlapping but distinct segments in this market: (1) high-priced ($30 and over), highly styled robes sold principally as fashionable loungewear or hostess garments through department and specialty stores; (2) middle-priced ($15–$30) robes sold in department, specialty, and chain stores; and (3) low-priced ($4–$20) robes sold primarily to discount and chain stores under private labels. Of the 100–150 manufacturers in this market, only 14 account for 72 percent of robe sales. The largest manufacturer controls 14 percent of the market (factory/sales), which is nearly twice the market share of the second firm. Success factors in this market are price, styling, and the ability to develop brand awareness and preference.

There are two seasons in the robe market, winter/fall and spring/summer. Over 70 percent of robe sales are in the winter/fall season, due to the utilitarian use of robes in winter and their use as holiday gifts. Because of this extreme seasonality, robes are sold only in larger stores which sell other merchandise.

Labor and fabric costs increased at more than the average inflationary rate. Although increased costs have been passed on to the consumer, manufacturers have not been able to pass on their margin on these costs. This upward shift in price is causing lower-priced firms to orient styling and fabrication toward higher-priced segments and to leave the very lowest price points for imported goods, which commanded $3,000,000 retail in 1973. Higher-priced manufacturers are similarly being priced out of their segments and are experiencing strong price resistance at prices above $30.

Robe styling is very basic and conservative, changing little from year to year, with the exception of infrequent fad styles. Product differentiation is achieved through collar, closure, sleeve cut, color, trim, and fabrication. Brighter colors and prints are becoming somewhat more important than in the past. Fabric content is changing from nylon and cotton blends to rayon or acetate blends and polyester, due more to relative price changes than to consumer preference.

To be able to develop a strong brand awareness and preference is important to a manufacturer because of the coordinated and related items included in many product lines and because only a few manufacturers have been able to achieve a strong brand awareness. The market leader probably enjoys more brand awareness than the other manufacturers, due to its advertising budget of 4.5 percent of sales and its heavy advertising of its coordinated and related items. Other brand manufacturers typically budget 1 percent to 2 percent of sales for advertising. Almost all manufacturers' advertising is done in consumer and trade magazines. Retailers use co-op advertising in local newspapers and advertising pieces and in-store displays. Private-label manufacturers advertise solely in merchandising trade journals to a limited extent, usually no more than 1 percent of sales. Private-label brand awareness is achieved through the retailer's own advertising efforts. There is no cooperative advertising in private-label sales. Thus branded manufacturers use pull and push strategies, whereas private-label manufacturers use push only.

Because of the decline in profit margins, the stagnant nature of the market, and the established, oligopolistic nature of manufacturers, all but one (SR) of the leading manufacturers have diversified into lingerie, sleepwear, and intimate apparel. In this market the ability to sell coordinated and related items: (1) is a positive influence on the consumer and helps to develop brand awareness and preference; (2) enables the manufacturer to wield greater influence on buyers; and (3) tends to smooth seasonal and economic influences. Manufacturers of sleepwear, lingerie, and intimate apparel are entering the robe market to fill out their product lines.

Robes are typically purchased by women 45 years of age and over at all income levels. Regional sales are heaviest in the Northeast (34 percent of sales) and North Central states (26 percent of sales) and lightest in the Mountain and Southwestern states (9 percent of sales). Department stores account for 36 percent of sales, major chains (Sears, Penney, Ward) for 20 percent, and specialty stores for 19 percent. Robes are generally bought for warmth and a comfortable, acceptable appearance. Robe consumers are generally, but not always, a little hesitant to adopt styles which have not proved themselves.

Future markets. Company analysis indicates that the robe-market increases would have to be achieved through increased spring robe sales, increased use by younger age groups, or increased use as evening or hostess apparel. Unfortunately, none of these

TABLE 24.7   Forecasted market sales and SR sales, 1974–80

	Units (million)	Market ($ millions) Constant dollars	Current dollars	Factory current	SR forecast ($ millions) Constant dollars	Current dollars	Market share
1974	30.5	$317	$317	$162	$10.4	$10.4	6.4%
1975	30.9	321	342	180	10.5	11.5	6.4
1976	31.3	325	369	194	10.7	12.4	6.4
1977	31.8	331	399	208	10.8	13.3	6.4
1978	32.3	336	431	223	11.0	14.3	6.4
1979	32.8	341	465	240	11.2	15.4	6.4
1980	33.3	346	503	260	11.4	16.6	6.4
Compounded rate of growth	1.5%	1.5%	8.0%	8.0%	1.5%	8.0%	0%

Source: Company records.

alternatives seems to be very viable, since manufacturers have had little success with efforts toward these areas in the past.

Assuming that the average annual purchase rate does not change from the present .38 robes per year, SR estimates the robe market to increase by 1.5 percent per year between 1974 and 1980 (see Table 24.7). Because of this slow growth, a precarious price, the cost, and the profit situation of manufacturers, management expects robe manufacturers to continue to decrease their dependence on robe sales, as nursing uniform manufacturers are doing in their market. Management is uncertain as to what role imported robes will play in the future market.

SR's Niche in the Robe Market

The present market. SR sells 60 designs under its own label and 40 designs under private labels. SR is particularly noted for its fleece robes, of which one style accounts for over 25 percent of total sales. SR does not sell any imported items; however, it does import some of its fabrics.

SR's 13 sales agents sell its products nationwide for commissions which range between 5 percent and 7 percent. Approximately 40 percent of SR's sales is for private label to two of the major chain stores, 35 percent is sold to specialty stores, and 25 percent is sold to major department stores. Of SR's 1500 accounts, 12 comprise 51 percent of total sales. Average brand order size is 30 garments. Private-label order size is considerably larger.

Fall retail prices range between $18 and $30, with an average price of $23.42. Spring robe prices range between $11 and $25, with an average price of $15.27. Average factory prices are $9.26 and $6.92, respectively. Market share is 3.4 percent. Over 90 percent of sales occur in the winter/fall season.

SR's robes are perceived to be good-quality, warm robes. They are used more for warmth and "bathrobe" purposes than for fashion, "loungewear" purposes. SR's customers are basically no different from those of other manufacturers. Sales are relatively stronger in the Midwest.

Currently marketing strategy is to decrease dependence on major chains by increasing department store sales and increasing brand awareness. Advertising is budgeted at two percent of sales.

Because styles tend to be classic, SR usually sells all of the robes it produces, leaving very few, if any, in inventory. Inventory turns over five times a year.

Forecast. As indicated in Table 24.5, SR's profit position has been weak since 1970. Sales to the major chains are beginning to meet price resistance. Given the inflationary price squeeze in the industry, the static nature of the market, and assuming that SR does not broaden its product line, management expects SR to maintain the 1.5 percent dollar sales increase estimated for the industry. The company sales forecast is detailed in Table 24.7.

SASSY PANTS The Sassy Pants Company produces three lines of women's sportswear. Two of the lines, Ramos and Off-the-Cuff, are brand-name lines sold in department and specialty stores. The third line, Penny Saver, is sold under private label to major chain stores. Sassy Pants (SP) began in 1951, when Ralph and Elmo Frink bought out a very small, bankrupt manufacturer of women's military uniforms. SP is now one of the larger women's sportswear producers; however, its brand names are not well known. Within the industry, SP is known for its ability to produce in large volume at a good price.

The Frinks attribute their growth over the years to their ability to find good prices on piece goods and then to manufacture them into something they feel their salespeople can sell.

Before Elmo Frink retired in 1973, he and his brother made all business decisions jointly, and together they took care of the sales, production, and business aspects of their company. After Elmo retired, each product was made a profit center, and each profit center is headed by a relatively young, aggressive, sales-oriented product manager. As president of SP, Ralph's duties involve sales and merchandising of all three product lines. He has no plans to retire in the near future.

Before selling SP to S & L in 1972, the Frinks had established their goals to be: (1) to produce and sell as many units as possible at a margin of 25 percent or better; (2) to become and remain a large supplier of sportswear to the market; and (3) to maintain an annual profit margin of 10 percent of sales. After selling SP, the Frinks adopted S & L's profit goals. Company income statements are shown in Table 24.8.

SP operates four plants in Virginia and two showrooms in New York City. Combined plant capacity is $18 million. SP also uses three contractors for special jobs to alleviate peak seasonal production strains. In general, 10 percent to 15 percent of their production is contracted out. Production is generally fairly stable, although it is lowest during the Christmas season and in early July. The plants shut down for a week's vacation during each of these periods.

Mr. Frink sees his production capacity to be almost limitless, due to the availability of contract labor. He does not plan any new plant expansion in the near future.

The Present Market Even though SP produces jackets, shirts, and skirts, 80 percent of its products sold are pants, and it considers itself to be in the pants market for women over 14 years of age. This market includes branded and private-label jeans, slacks, and trousers which are produced by thousands of independent companies and nearly every major apparel conglomerate. These manufacturers may produce pants only or an array of apparel products.

The pants market is probably the most volatile in the industry. According to MRCA survey data and company records, this market grew at an annual rate of 14 percent between 1969 and 1973, to 218 million units at a total retail value of $2.05 billion. This growth was accompanied by a significant decrease in dress and skirt purchases, which is attributed to the increased acceptability of pants, their comfort, and their convenience. The move from dresses and skirts to pants and casual wear is expected to remain a major market component, unlike some other major fashion changes, such as shifts and chemises, since it has continued for five years.

There are 14 recognized leaders (SP is not one of them) in the industry. Combined, they represent only eight percent of the total market. The largest producer commands only 1.3 percent of the market. Thus no one producer has much control over or protection from the market. Imports account for approximately 10 percent of sales and 20 percent of all pants sales below $5.00. Unlike the robe and uniform markets, imported pants are perceived to be strong competition in almost all price ranges.

Jeans account for 25 percent of the pants market. Although manufacturers and buyers of pants and jeans differ somewhat, manufacturers are competing for the same consumer dollar. Among the 14–34-year-old population, the jeans and pants markets are highly integrated, with jeans accounting for nearly 50 percent of their pants

TABLE 24.8 Sassy Pants income statement and product line sales, 1970–74

	1970		1971		1972		1973		1974	
	$ millions	%	$ millions	%	$ millions	%	$ millions	%	$ millions	%
Ramos	2.6	25.1	3.7	24.9	4.0	25.3	4.2	24.6	4.2	25.6
Off-the-Cuff	3.9	37.1	5.2	34.9	5.8	36.7	5.9	34.5	6.4	39.0
Penny Saver	4.0	37.8	6.1	40.2	6.0	38.0	7.0	40.9	5.8	35.4
Total sales	10.5	100%	15.0	100%	15.8	100%	17.1	100%	16.4	100%
Cost of goods	7.6	73	11.1	74	11.8	75	13.2	77	13.4	82
Gross margin	2.9	27	3.9	26	4.0	25	3.9	23	3.0	18
Selling & admin.	1.8	17	2.4	16	2.7	17	2.7	16	2.5	15
Net profit	1.1	10%	1.5	10%	1.3	8%	1.2	7%	.5	3%

Source: Company files.

TABLE 24.9 Analysis by age classification: pants, dress, jeans purchases and outlet from which they are purchased in 1973

Age	1973 % Pants sales	% Jeans sales	% Dress sales	Dept. store sales	Discount store	Spec. stores	Major chains	Other	Per capita purchase rates 1969	1973	1973 U.S. pop. % female, 14+
14–24	40%	45%	14%	28%	15%	31%	17%	9%	2.4%	4.1%	25%
25–34	22	25	12	27	17	26	21	9	2.6	3.3	18
35–44	12	14	12	33	15	20	23	9	1.7	2.3	14
45–54	12	12	20	34	14	21	21	10	1.3	2.2	15
55+	14	10	42	37	14	20	19	10	.5	1.3	28
	100%	100%	100%	31%	16%	26%	20%	7%	1.6%	2.6%	100%

Source: DuPont Analysis, MRCA data.

purchases, as indicated in Table 24.9. Department and specialty store junior departments often merchandise jeans and pants together and allocate their open-to-buy (capital assigned to the department) between them. General corporate consensus attributes the popularity of jeans to their comfort; ease of care; durability; versatility; lower cost than pants, dresses, and skirts; and the fact that few people look either really good or really bad in them.

There are five seasons in the pants market: spring, summer, transitional (back-to-school), fall, and holiday. As indicated in Table 24.1, sales are fairly evenly distributed throughout the year; however, sales are heaviest in the transitional and spring seasons. Pants styles change substantially from season to season in color, fabric, cut, etc. Spring and summer styles tend to be lighter, brighter, and somewhat less expensive than fall and winter styles.

Success factors in this market are price, style, and store distribution. Pants prices range from less than $1 to well over $40. In 1973, 32.5 percent of retail dollars were spent on pants priced $14 and above, 20.5 percent on pants priced between $11 and $13.99, 27.9 percent on pants priced between $7 and $10.99, 12.3 percent on pants priced between $5 and $6.99, and 7.2 percent on pants priced $4.99 and under. The average retail price was $7.52 in 1971; it was $9.47 in 1973, an average annual increase of 12.5 percent.

In general, all types of stores carry all price ranges of pants. In department stores, price generally determines the department in which the pants are sold. Pants priced below $7 are generally sold in basement budget departments; $7–$14 pants "downstairs"; and those priced $14 and above in the better "upstairs" sections.

To be the first to introduce a popular style is important, because by the time a competitor copies the style, the season is over and that style is either defunct or out of season for a year. According to one of the product managers, "style is silhouette and fabrication."

Silhouette, or cut, underwent large changes during the period of very rapid growth, as pants became more important wardrobe items and the influence of fashion increased. Pant legs flared and widened; waists dropped below the natural waist and then rose back above it. Cuffs coexist almost equally (60 percent cuffs in fall 1974) with noncuffed pants. Most manufacturers produce both basic and fad styles. Large manufacturers, particularly those that own plants and have established distribution channels, tend to style more conservatively because of the high risk involved in fad items. Most extreme fad items are produced by small jobbers and manufacturers.

Between 1967 and 1973 sales of knit pants increased from 33 percent of total sales to 61 percent. Management believes that this trend is subsiding, as woven goods develop the styling and wearability characteristics of knits. Women under 30 years of age tend to favor woven pants because they are less expensive and better fitting than knit pants. Women over 30 tend to favor knit pants because of their comfort and stretchability. Fabric content has trended toward polyester/blends, which accounted for 60 percent of all pants produced in 1973. Denim and denimlike fabrics are also very popular, but are considered to be a fad fabric in styled pants.

In 1973, 31 percent of pants sales were in department stores, 26 percent in specialty stores, 20 percent in major chain stores, and 16 percent in discount stores. This represents a shift since 1969 from discount and other outlets toward department and specialty stores. This change is largely attributed to the growth of specialized pants stores and pants-store chains which cater to younger buyers and rely on high turnover to support their lower prices. As shown in Table 24.9, specialty store purchasers are primarily under 34 years of age, whereas department store purchasers are primarily 35 and over.

Pants are advertised by manufacturers and retailers alike through all media. Advertising expenditures range from very high to very low, depending on the manufacturer. To a manufacturer, to be sold in Macy's downtown New York store is one of the best advertising methods available, because store buyers who come to New York from all over the country tend to shop in this store and evaluate a product's potential acceptance by the way Macy's merchandises it. Few firms achieve national or regional brand awareness, and even fewer achieve brand preference, because of the large number of labels from which a consumer may choose. Manufacturers also use posters, in-store displays, and promotionals to merchandise their goods.

Pants are bought by women of all income levels, ages, and regions of the country. As shown in Table 24.9, women under 35 account for 62 percent of pants sales, and a significantly large number of those pants purchased are jeans. This age distribution is attributed to the more style-conscious orientation of younger women as well as the relatively greater opportunity to wear pants; that is, it is much more socially acceptable for younger women to wear pants to school, work, and recreation than it is for older women to wear pants to their activities.

Women in the Northeast buy more pants than do women in the South or Mountain and Southwestern states. Of total 1973 retail sales, 35 percent was in the Northeast (28 percent population), 15 percent was in the South (22 percent population), and 8.2 percent was in the Mountain and Southwestern states (10 percent population). This difference is attributed to more fashion consciousness in the Northeast, climate differences, and differences in ability to adopt new styles.

Younger women tend to try new styles more readily than do older women because they are more style conscious and more likely to wear new styles to attract the attention of their peers. Younger women purchase more pants per year than do older women (Table 24.9); therefore, they are more willing to buy new styles. Thus younger women can invest in more short-lived fad items and more special-use pants instead of basic, multipurpose pants which go with anything, anywhere.

Despite their many positive attributes, pants also have a few negative characteristics. In warmer climates, pants (particularly polyesters) can be uncomfortably hot. A few places prohibit them. Knit pants tend to pick and snag. As evidenced by the wide acceptance of pants, however, their positive attributes seem to outweigh the negative ones.

The future market.   There is little consensus among fashion experts about the future of the pants market. Some feel that pants may lose some ground to dresses; others feel that pants growth is leveling off; others see the market continuing to grow at the present rapid rate. Management feels that the pants market will continue to grow, but at a significantly slower rate than in the past. Management estimates that per capita purchases by 14- to 24-year-olds will remain constant because of the already high purchase rate. Due to projected aging and changes in population, management expects the total market to increase at a rate of 3.5 percent per year, as indicated in Table 24.10. Because of the aging of the pants-wearing population and because they tend to have higher incomes, increased design and merchandising efforts aimed at the 25- to 34-year-old segment should become more important.

TABLE 24.10 Market and product forecast, 1974–80

	Market forecast, Millions of units and dollars			Product forecast, current $ Ramos		Off-the-Cuff		Penny Saver			Total current $ sales	Total market share current $
	Units	Constant $	Current $	$	Market share	$	Market share	$	Market share	Total		
1974	218	$2115	$2115	$4.2	.2%	$6.4	.3%	$5.8	.3%	$16.4	$16.4	.8%
1975	218	2115	2220	4.2	.2	6.4	.3	5.0	.2	15.6	16.3	.8
1976	233	2260	2486	4.6	.2	6.7	.3	5.6	.2	16.9	18.6	.8
1977	241	2347	2697	5.1	.2	7.1	.3	6.2	.3	18.4	21.3	.8
1978	250	2425	2926	5.6	.2	7.4	.3	6.8	.3	19.8	23.4	.8
1979	259	2512	3175	6.1	.2	7.8	.3	7.4	.3	21.3	27.5	.9
1980	268	2600	3445	6.8	.2	8.2	.3	8.0	.3	23.0	30.4	.9
Rate of growth	3.5%	3.5%	8.5%	8.5%		4.0%		5.5%		6.0%	11.0%	2%

Source: Company records.

SP's Niche in the Pants Market SP considers itself to be a producer of *styled* pants, but it also produces jackets, skirts, and shirts. Although these items are coordinating items, SP markets its products as separate items. Ramos sells to the contemporary market—sizes 6 to 16, ages 22 to 35—primarily through department stores. Off-the-Cuff sells to the junior market—sizes 5 to 15, ages 14 to 25—primarily through specialty stores. Because of the $16 to $22 price range of both labels, they are "upstairs" pants in department stores. Average retail prices are $18.92 and $17.63; factory prices are $8.85 and $7.51 for Ramos and Off-the-Cuff, respectively. SP designers create between 200 and 250 designs each year; however, they manufacture and sell only 75 of them. SP styles are both basic and fad and are made from woven fabrics.

Over 70 percent of Ramos sales are through department stores, 20 of which account for 56 percent of all sales. Specialty stores account for 70 percent of Off-the-Cuff sales. Of Off-the-Cuff's 10,000 accounts, most do not purchase more than $5000 each year. The ten largest accounts represent 18 percent of sales; the largest account represents only 2.5 percent of total sales.

SP labels have no particular "look" of their own, nor do they have an identifiable product image. Although sales are significant in the industry, market shares are only 0.2 percent for Ramos and 0.3 percent for Off-the-Cuff. Neither label sells collections of coordinated items, as do most other sportswear manufacturers. As in the robe market, offering coordinated items aids in selling goods and in increasing the amount of a consumer's purchases.

The product managers of both labels advertise cooperatively with retail outlets and in *Women's Wear Daily*. Advertising expenditures are low for the industry, budgeted at one percent of sales. The product managers also use, to a limited extent, in-store displays and promotionals.

The product managers employ their own sales forces and sell their respective lines independently of the other lines. In general, they sell to different stores; but in stores to which they both sell, they sell to different buyers. Ramos employs 11 independent sales agents; Off-the-Cuff employs 15. These agents sell SP products nationwide along with coordinating items of other manufacturers. Ramos sales are concentrated in the Northeast and Pacific regions (74 percent of sales); Off-the-Cuff sales are concentrated in New York, North Carolina, and Virginia (33 percent of sales). This uneven distribution of sales is attributed to the servicing of major department stores out of New York and the abilities of individual salespeople. Average order size tends toward 100 units for Ramos and 30 units for Off-the-Cuff. Order size is decreasing due to buyers' choosing to reorder more frequently rather than committing a large portion of open-to-buy at one time.

The product manager of the Penny Saver line is basically SP's broker to the major chains. The chains buy the same goods other retail stores buy, but at a lower price. The amount of the price differential depends on the order size and evenness of shipments, the lack of co-op advertising, the dependency of the chain on the manufacturer, and the dependency of the manufacturer on the chain. Because of the dependency factor, SP keeps its order volume to any one chain below 25 percent of total sales. SP has developed a good rapport with its chain accounts and is very careful to protect its reputation for ability to service, handle, and deliver large volumes of goods.

The Penny Saver line is a junior line and is sold nationwide to a fairly even cross section of ages, as shown in Table 24.9. Retail price ranges between $8 and $14, averaging $12.32. Average factory price is $6.14. Pants represent only 40 percent of sales, shirts 40 percent, and skirts 20 percent. Because of the large order size and span of time between order and delivery, chain stores tend to purchase basic items. If they do buy fad items, they do so in small quantities from small suppliers after the fad has proved that it will be large enough and long-lived enough for the chain to make money from it.

Due to SP's production orientation and the volatile nature of the pants market, SP has in the past built up large inventories of piece goods and goods which did not sell. The product managers watch their inventories very closely so that they turn over at least once a season. All unused piece goods and seconds are sold to jobbers. "Old" inventory is marked down until it sells.

The Future Market   Between 1971 and 1974, SP's sales growth was significantly below that of the pants market. The new-product managers are working to improve this situation by: (1) producing coordinating items; (2) establishing a brand name and a style; (3) increasing merchandising efforts such as promotionals, co-op advertising, sales incentives, and in-store displays; and (4) building more flexibility into SP's design and production systems.

Because of Ramos's success in department store sales, its presence in the more rapidly growing misses market, and the introduction of a successful shirt line, management expects Ramos to increase unit sales at a ten percent annual rate between 1975 and 1980, as shown in Table 24.10.

Because the 14- to 24-year-old segment will not grow as fast in the future as it has in the past, management expects Off-the-Cuff unit sales to grow at an annual rate of five percent, as shown in Table 24.10.

Because of its potential to increase sales of additional merchandise to major chains and to develop new accounts, management expects Penny Saver to increase its sales by 5.5 percent annually, as shown in Table 24.10.

S & L AND THE MAIL-ORDER MARKET   Mr. LaTrolley was recently promoted to Vice-President of Operations Development. Because he is in the process of analyzing AS's opportunities in the mail-order market, he has decided to expand the analysis to include each of the other three firms and S & L as a whole.

Mr. LaTrolley has assessed the costs other than cost of goods sold to be:

1. Catalog make-up—$1000 per change in catalog
2. Catalog printing—$.02 per catalog (four-color)
3. Magazine advertisements: $14,000 per display ad, women's magazine; $1100 per display ad, nursing journal; $4 per line, classified nursing ad; $45 per line, classified women's ad
4. Shipping labor—$.10 per order shipped
5. Shipping supplies—$.45 per order shipped
6. Postage—$1.25 per order shipped
7. Package insert—$.03 per order shipped
8. Processing labor—$.30 per order received
9. Processing supplies—$.15 per order processed
10. Markdowns—five percent of expected total sales.

Because S & L has closed several plants and because there is excess capacity in several other plants, Mr. LaTrolley feels that existing facilities are adequate to handle mail-order demands.

Questions Mr. LaTrolley wants to answer are: (1) What is the profit potential in this channel? (2) Is there better profit potential in other strategies? (3) What problems would S & L face in this channel, particularly with product lines, production, salespeople, sales outlets, entrepreneurs, location of plants? (4) What investment is required? (5) How would mail order change product lines, designs, image, etc.?

DISCUSSION QUESTIONS

1. What really is S & L's business? Is the definition given adequate? What problems can arise from their definition of their business? What is the business of management? Of the entrepreneurs? What problems are explained by the entrepreneurs' no longer holding company equity?

2. Why is the change from a buyer's to a seller's market so significant? How has it changed marketing methods?

3. What effect do quality and quantity of available labor pool have on marketing efforts?

4. What effect does the number of manufacturers in an industry have on marketing methods? What effect does the amount of fashion and style have on the number and size of manufacturers? Size of market growth? Marketing methods?

5. Compare the marketing strategy of selling to a few outlets with that of selling to many outlets. How does this affect marketing methods? How is this affected by the market?

6. Compare the strategy of producing a limited product line with producing a broad line. How have market structures and economic events affected this?

7. Compare the differences in marketing strategies of markets with high purchase rates with those with low purchase rates.

8. Why are imports becoming so important in some markets and not others? What effect do they have on marketing strategy? On the market?

9. Evaluate the statement: "Robe sales are flat and do not appeal to young markets because manufacturers have not forced fashion changes onto the market." Of what value is fashion trend to a manufacturer?

10. Why are older consumers less influenced by fashion trends and style than are younger consumers? What effect has this on markets and marketing strategy?

11. Compare the different market structures. What effect do they have on firm life cycle, strategy, etc.?

12. How do marketing strategies differ in growth versus stable markets?

13. Compare strategies of branded lines and private label.

Glossary

The **account executive** is the advertising agency's counterpart of the brand manager. This executive is the liaison between the agency and its client.

Account representative is a term newly emerging to identify that salesperson who is responsible for selling to a particular account, such as a supermarket chain.

Action plans describe how a strategy will be implemented. In marketing, the term "action plans" is replacing the military term "tactics."

Adoption is the acceptance of a new product or fashion. Innovators are those persons who are first to adopt a new idea.

Advertising is any sponsored communication that uses paid media for the purpose of influencing buying behavior.

Alternatives represent different strategies or courses of action (i.e., tactics) for achieving the same goal.

Antitrust refers to laws and court decisions designed to preserve atomistic competition. The federal laws are implemented by the Federal Trade Commission (FTC) and the Antitrust Division of the Justice Department.

Application segmentation occurs in industrial marketing when a marketer segments the industrial market according to how the product will be used in a process or end product.

Assembly is one form of foreign investment. An assembly plant is less than a foreign manufacturing plant because it assembles parts that have been shipped to it.

Atomistic competition consists of a large number of small firms competing with one another in the marketplace. This philosophy of economic pluralism is the basis for United States antitrust policy.

An **attitude** is a leaning toward (favorable) or away from (unfavorable) an object or concept. In marketing, the object will generally be a brand of a product. An attitude is composed of two elements—beliefs and values.

Attributes are those want-satisfying properties of a product that meet human needs. From the buyer's viewpoint they are *benefits*.

Bar (Gantt) charts use bar graphs along a time line to show the time required to complete an activity.

Bases of allocation are those variables used to allocate functional costs to products or customers.

The **basic function** of a firm is to generate a return on its investment by converting its resources into goods or services and then selling them at a profit.

Beliefs are a perception of the probability that something exists. In marketing, the buyers hold beliefs about brands possessing certain attributes.

Benefit segmentation consists of dividing the market into homogeneous submarkets according to the benefits that are sought in a product. For example, toothpaste benefit segments include decay prevention, whitener, and flavor.

Birthrates of a population vary as a result of economic and social conditions as well as changes in personal preferences. Changes in these rates create crests and troughs across age classifications in a population, which greatly alters the demand for age-related products.

Bona fide prices are prices which must exist for a reasonable period of time before they can be referred to in a sale that advertises price comparisons.

A **brand budget** shows the complete expenditures for the marketing mix for implementing a strategy throughout the budget period.

Brand champion is the term used to describe the type of brand manager a brand needs when it is in the growth and maturity stages of its product life cycle. The brand champion is a protagonist who makes entrepreneurial recommendations and is adept at getting things done through corporate bureaucracy.

Brand coordinator is the title used for a brand product manager of a mature product that requires no entrepreneurial responsibility.

Brand demand represents the share of the market that goes to a specific brand of a product. This demand is based on the buyers' perceptions of the strengths and weaknesses of available brands.

Brand manager is the term used to describe the individual who has the responsibility for the success of a brand or a product. He or she has no authority over the functional areas which must implement the brand strategy.

Brand maps are graphic plots of how consumers perceive brands in attribute (or benefit) space.

Brand positioning requires a product and/or promotional strategy that will move buyers' perception of a brand toward their perception of an ideal brand. When the brand presently exists, this strategy is known as *repositioning*.

A **break-even analysis** computes the number of units of a product that must be sold to break even (i.e., make a zero profit), given known fixed and variable costs and a price. The analysis may also be used to establish a price, given a fixed number of units to be sold.

A **breakdown budget** first determines the size of the marketing (or advertising) budget and then allocates it to specific activities (or media). The *buildup budget* estimates the costs to execute specific strategies and adds these costs to arrive at a total budget.

The **broadside approach** for matching media to target markets consists of giving all market segments equal coverage regardless of the number of prospects in each segment.

Build, hold, and harvest strategies are the ones recommended for products in the growth, mature, and declining stages of their product life cycles.

Buildup methods of budgeting begin with the identification of the tasks to be performed, determine the cost of performing each task, and then add these costs to establish a budget.

Buyer behavior segmentation is used in industrial marketing to segment the market according to the steps in the buying process. This strategy is used when the industrial product has reached a mature stage and the product is becoming a commodity.

Buying intentions are buyers' subjective probabilities of their buying a product within a specified period of time.

Buying processes consist of a series of events beginning with the awareness of a need and ending with the purchase of a product or service to meet the need. These events are similar for industrial and consumer buying processes, but the effort going into each step is generally greater for the industrial buying process.

Cannibalization is a brand strategy that will take sales from another brand owned by the same company.

Cash-and-carry wholesalers are used by small grocery stores. The grocer drives to the wholesalers, pays cash, and transports the products to the store.

Cash cow strategies are used to "milk the cash from a product" when it has a high market share, but is in a market with a low generic growth rate.

Chain discounts are a series of discounts given to a channel member for services performed or to be passed along to later members of the channel.

Channels of distribution are those institutions that perform the utilities of time, place, and possession that are necessary between the production and consumption of a product. Brokers, wholesalers, and retailers are the most common members of the channel of distribution.

Characteristics of goods categories classify how much effort buyers will expend in search for a product or brand. The three usual classifications are convenience, shopping, and specialty goods.

Characteristics of the site that are considered when locating a department store include the progressiveness of local government, competition, and present and future traffic patterns.

Cognitive dissonance occurs when behavior is not consistent with attitudes. To restore consonance, either the attitudes or behavior must change.

Combination export managers (CEM) act as the export department for several manufacturers.

Communication goals are expressed in terms of changes in prospects' levels of awareness, attitudes, probability of visiting the store, and probability of buying.

The **communication mix** includes advertising, promotions, packaging, and personal selling.

Comparison advertising provides a direct comparison of the benefits of the advertised product and those of its competitors.

Competitive contingency planning consists of strategies and action plans that will be implemented if competitors react to the initial strategy as anticipated.

Competitive information systems systematically gather information about competitors' products, research and development, production methods and costs, organizational designs, financial status, marketing strategies, and their strengths and weaknesses.

Competitive interaction describes those series of reactions and counterreactions among competitors when one competitor initiates an effective change in strategy.

Competitive parity is an advertising bugeting procedure that is based on a competitor's budget.

Concept tests are a market research technique whereby potential customers are presented with descriptions of product attributes (or benefits) to determine the market potential for a product before it is produced.

Conglomerate diversification requires no direct relationships among the old and new businesses (i.e., products and markets). The sole motivation for conglomerate diversification is an increased return on investment.

Constant dollars are current dollars which have been adjusted by the rate of inflation from a base year so that changes in sales, GNP, etc., are real changes, not just changes in the value of the dollar.

Consumer expectations are people's subjective estimates of the probability that some future event will occur, such as an increase in income.

The **consumer purchase cycle** is the length of time between purchases. Continuous advertising is used for products with short purchase cycles; pulsed strategies are used with long cycles.

Consumerism describes those activities of businesses, private organizations, and federal, state, and local governments which are designed to ensure that consumers receive value in the marketplace.

Contingency planning is the development of reserve alternatives in case the primary alternatives cannot be implemented because of corporate policy, public policy, budget limitations, or competitive behavior.

Contract manufacturing is frequently used in international marketing by having a local producer supply a product to specifications.

Control information tends to be historical information within organizational lines, detailed and short range, for the purpose of keeping a system within designed limits.

Control systems attempt to keep the marketing system trajectory that will achieve the marketing goal.

The **controlled variables** are the marketing-mix variables over which the marketing manager has control.

Convenience goods are frequently purchased goods for which the buyer is unwilling to spend much effort in search of a specific brand, e.g., soap.

Copy research includes a variety of methods that test the ability of the advertising message to attract attention, be memorable, be comprehensible, and motivate.

Copy segmentation is the adjustment of the advertising message to the unique needs of a market segment. Copy may be segmented according to the demographics of the market or the buyers' weighting of the importance of product benefits.

Copy strategy is the content of the advertising or message that will communicate the benefits of the product most effectively.

A **copy theme** is the selling message in an advertisement.

Cost-based price strategies set prices in terms of a given margin over price.

Cost-per-thousand prospects is a rough means for evaluating the efficiency of media. It is computed by dividing the media costs by the media circulation, in thousands.

Costs and benefits of regulation attempt to assess the business and social costs and the public gains from federal regulations.

Counterstrategies are those changes in a competitor's marketing mix made as a result of a change in one's own strategy.

Critical-path method (CMP) is a management technique that considers the sequence of events and the time required to complete events. The critical path is the one requiring the longest time to complete all of its activities.

Cross-elasticity is the ratio of the percentage change in the sales of product B divided by the percentage change in the price of product A.

Current dollars are those dollars used to describe sales, GNP, etc., at the time period being measured, without adjustments for inflation.

Customary prices are traditional prices, such as the 20¢ candy bar.

Decision analysis uses decision trees, probabilities, and payoffs to help choose among alternative strategies.

Decision trees graphically portray the alternatives and their expected values so that the decision maker may trace the outcomes of alternative courses of action.

Defining a business consists of identifying groups of products, markets, and the strategies that link them together.

Delivered prices mean that the manufacturer pays the freight.

The **Delphi method** is used to predict future technologies by cycling unbiased estimates of opinions among experts until there is a convergence of opinions.

Demand-based price strategies are those strategies that take into account the effect that a change in price will have on the quantity of goods demanded. Price elasticities are used to estimate this effect.

A **demand curve** graphically portrays the relationship between the price of a product and the number of products that will be demanded at these prices.

Demarketing is a strategy that may be appropriate when market shares invite antitrust action. It may be used also to encourage consumers to conserve scarce resources, such as energy.

Demographics are the characteristics of a population which are measured by variables such as age, sex, marital status, family size, education, geographic location, and occupation. Demographics reflect different needs.

Department store success factors include store location, merchandising, personnel, layout, general management, and finance.

Derived demand represents the demand for goods and services which are dependent on the demand for other goods and services. For instance, the demand for earth-moving equipment is derived from the demand for highway construction.

Detail representative is the term given to the person in the pharmaceutical industry who carries the promotional message to physicians and pharmacists. Orders are not taken by these representatives, because the physician writes a prescription for the patient. The representative tries to convince the physician to use his or her brand.

Differentiated strategies are possible when market segments can be identified. *Product-differentiated* strategies are possible when buyers can be grouped according to homogeneous needs. *Promotion-differentiated* strategies are possible when market segments vary in their sensitivity to different types of promotions. Differentiated strategies are more productive because they are more precise in their product, message, and media mixes.

Diffusion is the process by which a new product or fashion is communicated and accepted by a population. Diffusion rates vary according to an individual's age, education, risk-taking propensity, and exposure to information.

Direct exporting describes those exporting situations where the seller or the seller's agent performs all of the marketing and export documentation functions.

Discount department stores give the buyer a lower price in exchange for self-service, cash payment, and no delivery. The stores are willing to take a lower margin for a high turnover.

Distribution cost analysis allocates costs and revenues to determine the profits (or losses) by products, customers, territories, channels of distribution, and methods of promotion.

Distribution rate is the percentage of outlets carrying a product among those outlets where distribution is desired. The rate is sometimes weighted to reflect the sales volumes of different stores.

Domestic international sales occur when a sale is made in the domestic market to someone who exports the product.

Drop shippers pass a customer's order to a manufacturer, who ships directly to the customer.

Dumping strategies exist when an exporting company using marginal pricing strategies puts its product on a foreign market at a price lower than the selling price of products made in the foreign market.

The **effective cost per thousand** (CPM) divides the cost of the medium by the number of persons in the *target audience* that is reached by the medium.

Effectiveness is a measure of how well the strategy and action plan (tactics) achieved the marketing goal.

Efficiency is a measure of resources required to perform a task and is generally measured as the ratio of the output over the input.

The **80/20 rule** states that 80 percent of sales (or profit) comes from 20 percent of the products (or customers). (A variation of this rule is known as the ABC concept in inventory control.)

Elastic brand demand describes those cases in which a decrease in price will increase the sales of a *brand* by a greater percentage than the percent reduction in price.

Elastic generic demand refers to those cases in which a reduction in price will increase the sales of the entire *product category* by a greater percentage than the percent reduction in price.

Elasticities are a ratio of a percentage change in unit sales divided by a percentage change in an economic variable such as price, disposable personal income, or advertising expenditures.

Environmentalism describes those activities of public and private individuals to conserve and preserve the environment.

Evaluation includes those systems for determining if the marketing strategies and action plan (tactics) have achieved the marketing goals.

Expected value is an index number that combines subjective estimates of the probabilities of events taking place and the gains or losses associated with these events.

Experience curves reflect the declining *total costs* to produce a product as a firm or an industry gains experience in its production.

Export departments perform all of the functions necessary to market goods and services outside the home country.

Family life cycles are the stages in family formation beginning with young singles not living at home, through marriage, child rearing, retirement, and sole survival. For some products these stages explain generic demand better than age.

Fighting brands are those brands which have been used to test the market and competition or to react to competitive price cuts. The fighting brand preserves the image of the prestige brand.

First-brand awareness is the first brand that a respondent gives when he or she is asked to list the brands for a specific product category. First-brand awareness is a better correlate of brand sales than just *brand awareness*.

Floor planning is a financing method in which the durable goods on the sales floor are owned by the bank. This method is common in the automotive industry.

Focus-group interviews are a semistructured marketing research technique in which a discussion leader interviews a group of about eight persons. Although the discussion leader has an interview guide, much of the stimulation for discussion comes from the group members. This technique is frequently used to develop new products.

Franchise wholesalers are voluntary chains of independent retailers who use a common buying source to compete with large chains.

Full-function wholesalers perform all functions, including storage, sorting, transportatation, risk taking, selling, buying, financing, and market research.

Functional-cost groups are those cost classifications allocated during a distribution cost analysis.

Functional discounts are the means by which middlemen are compensated for additional marketing functions such as stocking service parts, building window displays, and advertising.

Functional middlemen operate on a commission. They perform any of the wholesaler functions, but they do not own the inventory.

Functional organizational designs in marketing have the marketing-mix functional activities reporting to a central person, known as the marketing manager or marketing vice-president, who has responsibility *and* authority for all marketing activities.

A **Gantt (Bar) chart** uses bar graphs along a time line to show the time required to complete an activity.

Generic demand is those needs (physiological, safety, belonging and love, esteem, and self-actualization) which can be met by a product category (e.g., frozen foods). This is also known as primary demand. *Brand* demand is the preference for the product made by a particular manufacturer, e.g., Birdseye frozen foods. Generic demand will be greater than industry sales for a product category when there is a shortage of supply and when present brands do not meet consumers' needs. A demand analysis will identify these conditions, which represent marketing opportunities for expanded capacity or new products.

Goals are objectives that have been made specific with regard to magnitude and time for attainment.

Gravitational models are mathematical models for locating retail stores. The models relate the attraction of stores to customers and the customer effort to reach the store.

Gross margin is the spread between the selling price and the costs of a product.

Group product managers supervise approximately five product (brand) managers.

Harvesting is a product strategy that may be used when a product has reached maturity. It consists of using little marketing effort.

Hierarchy-of-effects models of the decision tend to assume that the buyer must go through stages of changes in awareness and attitudes before changing buying behavior. Cognitive dissonance theory illustrates that the effects sequence can also move from changes in behavior back to changes in awareness.

High market-share strategies are those strategies introduced when a product's market share is so high that it will attract the attention of competitors and antitrusters.

The **high-assay principle** is a media-selection strategy that is similar to the marginal approach in economics. This principle states that all of the media budget should be placed with the medium with the highest return before moving on to the next medium.

Horizontal and vertical product-market matches occur in industrial marketing when the market being segmented consists of a single industry (horizontal matching) or divisions within a production process (vertical matches).

Horizontal competition occurs when two firms compete at the same level in the channel of distribution.

Horizontal diversification occurs when new products having a close relationship to old products are added.

Husband-wife decision processes vary among products and are frequently joint decisions with specialization for components of the decision. For example, during the purchase of an automobile the husband may make the engineering decisions and the wife may choose colors.

Ideal brands are consumers' perceptions of the perfect brand that would meet all of their needs.

Implicit assumptions are those assumptions the planner failed to make explicit during the analysis stage.

Incremental-cost pricing strategies cover variable costs and make some contribution to fixed costs. These tend to be short-run strategies during periods of excess capacity.

Indirect exporting occurs when the vital marketing functions and export documentations are performed by the buyer.

Industrial product life cycles may be more complex than those for consumer products because of the highly technical nature of industrial products. The concept of a family of life-cycle curves helps illustrate how new technologies replace old ones.

Industry excess capacities describe those situations when the ability to supply a product so exceeds the market demand that price cutting is introduced in the hope that sufficient sales will at least cover variable costs and make a contribution to fixed costs.

Input-output analysis traces through the intermediate needs of an industry to produce products for the final consumer. The most common application of this technique is in industrial marketing.

Institutional advertising attempts to create favorable images about a corporation rather than a specific brand.

Interactive computer models enable a manager to interact with the data and the logic of the model in order to add his or her input to the solution.

Internal and external shrinkage refer to inventory losses due to employees and shoplifters, respectively.

International marketing is the marketing of goods and services outside the home country.

Joint costs occur when production and marketing facilities are used for more than one product. Allocation of these costs makes it difficult to use cost-based pricing strategies.

Joint ventures in international marketing inject equity ownership into a foreign operation.

Joint-space maps position brands and individuals (or segments) in cognitive space as perceived by consumers.

Key variables in a generic-demand analysis vary for each product, but the basic variables are the number of people with a need, the proportion of these people who use the product category, and the rate or frequency of use. Estimates of future demand require that each key variable be projected to the future date for which demand is estimated.

Laboratory simulations are procedures for testing a completed product and promotional strategy by exposing consumers to advertisements under controlled conditions and then observing their buying behavior in a captive supermarket. A computer model projects market share from the data gathered under these controlled conditions.

The **learning curve** describes the decline in *labor costs* that occurs as the result of production personnel becoming more productive as they gain experience in producing a product.

Leverage is the use of borrowed capital to increase the return on the owners' equity. The rate of leverage is calculated by dividing the total investment by the stockholders' equity.

Licensing arrangements in international marketing may include a range of arrangements, including agreements to manufacture a product, use a component part, or sell a product.

Life-styles are personal behavioral patterns for solving daily living problems. Life-style variables measure *activities* (e.g., work, hobbies, and sports), *buying styles* (e.g., conformist, style-conscious, and impulsive), and *interests* (e.g., family, job, and community).

Loading is a promotional strategy that encourages consumers to stock up for future needs or to prevent them from buying a new competitive brand which is being introduced.

Logistics include the physical movement of the product and information about the product that precludes the need to move the product.

Logistics costs include the direct operating costs for warehousing, transportation, handling, and order processing as well as the indirect costs of communications, data processing, administrative overhead, inventory investment, property taxes and insurance, inventory obsolescence, inventory spoilage, and lost profit opportunities because of out-of-stock conditions.

Manufacturer's agents operate like the sales force for noncompeting products.

The **marginal** (or high-assay) method for matching media to markets allocates media coverage to reach all prospects in the largest market segment before moving on to the next, less lucrative segment.

Marginal budgeting approaches attempt to relate an incremental dollar in profit or sales to an incremental dollar in advertising.

Marginal cost is the change in total costs that is required to produce an additional unit.

A brand's **market position** is determined by consumers' perceptions of the uses and benefits of the brand relative to competition.

Market segmentation is the process of dividing the market into homogeneous submarkets with similar needs, so that the attributes of a product or service may be designed to meet these needs with precision. Markets may also be segmented according to price and promotional sensitivity. The latter segmentation may permit an undifferentiated product strategy, but a differentiated promotional strategy.

Market share is a specific brand's percentage of the market.

Market-oriented organizational designs work from the needs of the market back to the organizational design that will best meet these needs. In these designs marketing functions are organized according to market segments, end uses, industry classifications, or channels of distribution. Some companies are establishing *market* managers instead of *product* managers.

Marketing is the organized, commercial exchange of goods and services for the benefit of all parties in the exchange.

Marketing activities include identifying unmet needs, developing products and services to meet the needs, pricing the product or service, distributing products, and communicating the ability of the products or services to meet these needs.

Marketing audit is another name for the situation analysis, which identifies a brand's strengths, weaknesses, opportunities, and problems.

Marketing budgets allocate the marketing effort according to the marketing strategy and tactics.

The **marketing concept** is a corporate philosophy that states that all major product and promotional decisions should begin with an understanding of the needs of the consumers.

Marketing information systems organize internal and external information to help answer critical questions about the market, competition, and public policies during the situation analysis.

Marketing logistics include sales forecasting, order processing, inventory control, transportation, and customer satisfaction with delivery schedules.

Marketing management consists of those activities that relate an organization successfully to its environment. Although the activities will vary according to the organization and its environment, they share the common goal of meeting unmet needs.

Marketing myopia occurs when a business is defined in terms of the product or service offered instead of the need to be met. For example, railroads thought they were in the business of railroading, when they were in the transportation business. There is a danger, however, of defining the benefits too broadly, which runs counter to philosophies of market segmentation.

Marketing-mix strategies include dealing with the product, price, channels of distribution, advertising, and personal selling.

Markup pricing strategies use a standard markup over cost as a means for setting prices. This approach is used frequently in retailing because it is a convenient way to compute the value of inventories.

Media are the print (magazines, newspaper, etc.) and electronic (radio and television) communication devices for advertising.

Media budgets show the details for expenditures for each medium during specific planning periods (months, quarters, etc.).

Media segmentation matches the media to the target market audience, thereby reducing waste circulation.

Merchandise management is the primary marketing function of a department store. It includes buying, selling, personal shopping, comparison shopping, unit control, and merchandise budget supervision.

Milking is a product strategy used when a product has reached a low growth rate, but still has a high market share.

The **mission** of a company represents its broadest statement of purpose, e.g., to alleviate human suffering through technology.

Mixed brand strategy occurs when a manufacturer produces products under its own brand as well as for sale by other manufacturers and distributors under their brands. their brands.

Multivariate statistical techniques use more than one independent variable to explain the behavior of a dependent variable.

Narrow distribution means that a brand will be distributed to a few exclusive outlets so that the product will be presitigious.

National brands generally mean manufacturers' brands rather than distributors' brands, which are known as private brands. These terms are confusing because all brands are privately owned. The historical origin of this distinction is that manufacturers were national and distributors or store chains were regional. Today distributors and chains are national. It is less confusing to use the terms "manufacturers'" and "distributors'" brands.

Net present value is a financial concept that moves future values (sales, profits, etc.) back to the time of the decision by discounting these values by some interest rate. Net present values are used to choose among new-product alternatives.

Nonmetric multidimensional scaling is a computer procedure for transforming paired comparison or rank-ordered data into brand maps.

Objective-and-task advertising budgets are also known as the buildup budgets in that the cost of the tasks is determined and then summed to yield a budget.

The **objectives** of a firm comprise a more narrow definition of purpose than does a statement of mission. Corporate objectives are an extension of executives' personal values and may be expressed in financial and social terms.

Off-balance sheet lease financing occurs when buildings and fixtures are built by a developer and leased to the store.

In **oligopolistic markets** there are few sellers; thus competitive reaction is rapid and frequently violent.

Open-to-buy is the dollar amount of the merchandise buying commitment that is available to a buyer in a department store.

A marketing **opportunity** occurs when an unmet need is identified. This need may occur because it has not been identified before or because no existing product or service is meeting the need fully.

A **panel** is a survey design in which respondents are interviewed several times to measure their changes in awareness, attitudes, and buying behavior.

The **payback period** is the length of time required to pay back the original investments in a product.

A **penetration pricing** strategy uses a low price to penetrate through the price-inelastic segment to the price-elastic segments of the market. The strategy produces a greater volume and discourages competition.

Perceptual brand positioning attempts to move consumers' perceptions of a brand to a more favorable position by changing the product attributes or the advertising and personal-selling messages.

Per se violations in antitrust cases occur because of the marketing strategy used; there is no need for proof of a lessening of competition.

Personal-risk functions measure a decision maker's utility for various levels of gains and losses.

Personal values are individual expressions of what is good and bad. Executive values determine corporate objectives.

Premium pricing is that amount above the standard industry price because of special services offered, such as training production personnel.

Price flexibility is the measure of the freedom of competitors to change prices. It is used as a measure of the degree of competition in an industry.

Price lining is a strategy of buying or manufacturing products to sell within a given price range. Price lining is used frequently in department stores, where the various price ranges appeal to different market segments.

Primary sources of data are those used to solve a specific marketing problem and are conducted or commissioned by the marketing firm. Sample surveys are a common type of primary source.

A **priority index** is a means for rank-ordering subproblems by subjectively weighting the relative contribution of the subproblem to the overall problem and the relative control over the subproblem.

Private brands are those of the distributor or chain store. (*See* National brand.)

A **problem** occurs when there is a deviation from a desired norm; e.g., sales did not reach the level stated in the plan, or the return on investment was too low.

Problem tracking is a procedure used by the advertising agency of Batten, Barton, Durstine & Osborn, Inc., to identify consumers' problems, the frequency and intensity of these problems, and pre-emptability (the degree to which existing brands solve the problem).

Product attributes are those properties of a product that enable it to meet consumers' needs. The consumer views attributes as benefits.

Product elimination is a set of criteria and strategies for phasing out products which have reached the end of their product life cycle.

Product extensions are new products that have slightly different benefits designed to capture additional market segments. New flavors in a cake mix or new sizes in a shampoo represent product extensions. This is a more conservative strategy than introducing a completely new product.

Product improvement is the addition of new attributes to an existing product. This strategy is used frequently to recycle a product which has reached the declining stage of its life cycle.

Product life cycles describe the stages of growth rates of a product. These stages include introduction, growth, maturity, and decline. Marketing mix and research strategies vary over the product life cycle.

Product manager is the generic term used to describe the individual who has the responsibility, but not the authority, for the success of a product. The term "brand manager" is used when the company has several brands in the same product category.

Product portfolio strategies view a company's products as though they were investments yielding various returns. The strategies are invest, retain selectively, and divest.

Product repositioning is a strategy for an existing product (or brand) which moves consumers' perceptions of the attributes of the product closer to their perception of an ideal product. A product may also be repositioned by locating new uses for the product, thereby repositioning it among new competitors and relocating it in the store to a more favorable shelf position.

Product segmentation consists of developing a product whose attributes fit the needs of a market segment. In industrial marketing this "segment" could be one or two customers. Thus industrial marketing requires extreme product adaptation.

Product strategies are attempts to fit the attributes of a product to those benefits sought by the consumer. In brand-mapping terms this amounts to moving a brand closer to the perceived ideal brand.

Production logistics include sales forecasting, production planning, purchasing, production scheduling, distribution planning, inventory control, and customer order processing.

Productivity analysis uses distribution cost analysis to identify hypotheses and experiments to test hypotheses, with the goal of improving the productivity of the marketing effort.

Profile matching is a means for matching media coverage in proportion to the number of prospects in each segment. This is an averaging method that is superior to the broadside approach, but inferior to the marginal (i.e., high-assay) approach.

Profiles of the population for locating department stores include measures of age distribution, size and stability of income, buying habits, and needs.

Profit centers are those points within a firm which may be held accountable for profits.

The **profit plan** translates a brand's marketing strategy into the costs for implementing the strategy and the revenue it will generate.

Project teams (or venture groups) are like minicompanies having specialists from all functional areas. These teams are outside the corporate organization and are assigned the task of bringing a new idea to a point of profitability.

Promotional allowances are temporary price cuts to reimburse channel members for promoting a product.

Promotional budgets show the detailed expenditures for promotions such as coupons, cents-off, premiums, etc.

Promotional strategies are those communication strategies designed to change the buyers' awareness of a brand, their attitude toward the brand, and their probability of buying it.

Promotions are a form of sponsored communication which do not use print or electronic media, but instead use trade shows, coupons, premiums, contests, point-of-purchase material, etc.

Psychographics are personal, mental concepts that are measured in terms of attitudes, beliefs, opinions, perceived benefits, self-concepts, and subjective probabilities.

Psychological pricing takes many forms, such as $5.98 instead of $6.00. In some cases buyers use price as a measure of quality.

Public policy is the generic term used to describe the policies of government to preserve competition, protect the consumer, conserve natural resources, and protect the environment.

A **pull strategy** is a channel strategy that promotes to the consumer and forces retailers to stock the brand.

Pulse strategies are advertising strategies that use intermittent bursts of advertising rather than spacing the exposures evenly over time.

Purchase cycles are the time periods between purchases of a product. This cycle is important in estimating demand.

Push money is a manufacturer's direct compensation to retail salespersons. This practice is questionable on ethical grounds because the consumer assumes that the retail salesperson is giving unbiased advice.

Push strategies are channel strategies that concentrate marketing effort on the whole-salers and retailers to persuade them to stock the brand.

Rack jobbers are wholesalers who stock racks in stores. They own the inventory and give the store a percent of sales.

Reach is the percentage of a target audience that is exposed to a medium. *Frequency* is the number of times the target audience is exposed to the message in all media.

Recall is a measure of the ability of an advertisement to communicate a message. Survey respondents are asked if they recall the advertisement, the message, and the advertiser.

Reciprocity, also known as *trade relations*, occurs in industrial marketing when the stronger party says, in effect, "I will buy from you if you will buy from me." Such a policy generally violates antitrust laws.

Regional rollout is a strategy for introducing a new product by introducing it one region at a time.

Regional shopping centers include two or three anchor stores and a variety of specialty shops and restaurants. They are created by matching existing population profiles, by building their own communities, and by reusing old, nonretailing facilities.

Repurchase rate is the proportion of consumers who bought a brand a second time after trying it.

Return-on-assets management is used to analyze sales territories and the performance of salespersons. It will reveal the weaknesses of selling low-margin items, high-inventory requirements, extensive credit, and slow-paying customers.

Return on investment is the profit divided by the amount of investment. The investment may be calculated as a return on assets or a return on equity.

Sales representative is a selling classification that is emerging among firms which sell to chain grocery and drug stores. The sales representative works with local store managers on problems of inventories, shelf management, and merchandising. This representative is under the account manager, who sells to the chain buyer at the central office.

Seasonal discounts are price reductions used to clear out-of-season merchandise.

Secondary sources of information are those data which have been collected by someone else for purposes other than those of answering marketing questions. United States Census data are a secondary source used frequently by marketers.

Sensitivity analysis is the procedure for tracing through the effects of a change in the marketing mix on sales, competition, profits, and return on investment.

Shared monopoly is a term recently introduced by the Federal Trade Commission to describe oligopolistic behavior that may amount to monopolistic behavior.

A **shopping good** is one for which the buyer will spend time shopping for information and comparing brands, e.g., an automobile.

The **situation analysis** may be regarded as a brand's complete marketing audit at a point in time. It includes an analysis of generic demand, brand demand, competition, and public policy.

Skimming is a pricing strategy that begins with a high price to tap the price-insensitive market and then lowers the price to tap the market segments with high price elasticity. The skimming policy helps to pay for the development of the product.

Social marketing has several meanings. It may mean identifying those segments of the market that have a social concern, such as environmentalists, and promoting the social attributes of the product. The term may also mean the application of marketing techniques to improve society. Its most common use is the application of marketing techniques to nonprofit organizations.

Social-pricing strategies occur when market segmentation is by social class, and snob appeal may require a high price to indicate status.

Social values are society's expressions of good and bad activities, behavior, and products. A concern for the environment reflects a changing social value.

A **specialty good** is one for which the buyer is willing to spend considerable effort to locate a specific product or brand.

Specialty mail-order houses sell items not readily available to consumers because of the specialty of the item, the lack of stores available to customers, or a lack of time to shop.

Standard industrial classification (SIC) analysis uses data classified by industry codes to estimate market potential. The data frequently include the number of employees and the value added by a firm.

Store finance and control include internal auditing, accounting, forecasts, daily summaries, tax reports, credit, billing, customer collections, and accounts-payable functions.

Store operations functions in a department store are responsible for the merchandise from the moment it arrives at the store until it is accepted by the customer.

Store personnel functions in a department store establish and implement policies for hiring, compensation, benefits, evaluation, and record keeping.

Store promotions include those activities which promote the entire department store. These include special events, such as parades, fashion shows, exhibits, and displays.

Strategic goals in marketing reduce to a desire to increase generic demand, brand demand, or some combination of these two forms of demand.

Strategies are the alternative means for achieving goals. Strategy identifies *what* is to be accomplished; tactics (or action plans) identify *how* the strategy will be accomplished.

Subproblems, or the components of a problem, may also be regarded as the causes of the problem.

Subscription sources are data which have been collected by research firms to help answer marketing questions, but they are available only for a fee.

Substitution effects occur when the marketing strategy of one brand takes sales from another brand. When both brands are in a single company, this effect is known as cannibalization.

Success factors are those activities in which a company must excel to compete effectively in a given industry. In identifying new opportunities a firm must identify the factors that are necessary to operate in the industry represented by the opportunity.

Target pricing is a pricing strategy designed to yield a fixed amount of profit or a given rate of return on investment.

Target rate of return is a desired dollar profit computed by multiplying the desired rate of return times the investment in the product. This dollar profit is added to fixed costs when computing the break-even point.

Team organizational designs take the form of a brand-management system. The brand manager heads the team on which all of the marketing functions are represented.

Technological change in industrial marketing is measured in terms of rate of changes in the use of materials or processes. These rates affect the ability to identify potential competitors.

Technological forecasting consists of a variety of subjective and objective methods for anticipating future developments in technology.

Technology life cycles are patterns of inventions or processes over time which help to predict when new technology will appear.

Test markets are a limited introduction of a product to test a complete marketing strategy.

Trade deals are nonprice channel arrangements which amount to a discount. Deals include extra merchandise for early stocking, delayed billing, and promotional discounts.

Trade-position discounts are discounts given to brokers, wholesalers, and retailers to compensate them for the functions they perform.

Trademarks are proprietary names given to products to associate them with a specific manufacturer. They can be a valuable asset to the firm in its communication strategy.

Transfer costs and prices are used when products are transferred to other divisions within the corporation.

Triangulation in forecasting and navigation is the use of at least three sources of data to locate one's present situation for future actions.

Truck jobbers are wholesalers who carry most of their inventory in their trucks.

Turnover is the number of times one asset, such as inventory, is used during a year.

The **uncontrolled variables** are those environmental elements over which the marketing manager has little or no control, such as the philosophy of the firm, generic demand, competitive behavior, public policy, and nonmarketing costs.

Undifferentiated product is a strategy of promoting one product to all market segments. This strategy is used frequently with a differentiated advertising strategy, where the message and media are altered to the needs of each market segment.

Unit price elasticity occurs when the percentage change in price stimulates an equal percentage change in sales.

Usage factors in industrial marketing are the amount of the sellers' products used in the buyers' products. These factors are used to estimate product demand.

Usage rates measure the amount of a product consumed in a period of time—such as a pound of butter per week or a new car every four years. Usage rates are important when computing the total generic demand.

Uses. A product may fit many different uses. Markets may be segmented according to the end use of the product. For example, soft drink markets may be segmented into beverage and mixer segments. Members of each segment have quite different profiles and require different marketing strategies.

Utility is the want-satisfying ability in a product or service. Consumers view utilities as benefits. Thus consumer demand is not for a product, but for a bundle of benefits. Economists recognize form, time, place, and possession utilities. Marketing systems contribute to each of these utilities.

Value added is the utility added to a product by a manufacturer or a marketer. In manufacturing it is measured in terms of the difference between the cost of production and the value of shipments.

Value analysis is a procedure used in industrial purchasing to buy only those functions needed to perform the tasks.

Values are an individual's perception of what is good (or important) and what is bad (or unimportant). Values are determined by one's culture, religion, education, and experiences.

Variance analysis compares marketing costs experienced with standards that have been set for performing given tasks.

Variety chains, such as Woolworth's and Kresge, originally sold only small items, but later expanded to include large items to compete with discount department stores.

A **vehicle** is a specific medium, such as *Time* magazine or *Psychology Today*. A *unit* is that part of the medium which is bought, such as one-half page in four colors or two columns, black-and-white.

Vendor evaluation is a process used by industrial buyers to assess the ability of the seller and the seller's products to meet the buyer's needs.

Venture groups. *See* Project teams.

Vertical competition is competition among different levels of a channel of distribution. Channel members want to perform more functions to gain a greater share of the channel margin.

Vertical diversification occurs in a product line when a company produces products that it previously purchased.

Wheel of retailing describes those new institutions that enter retailing as low-service, low-cost operations and then increase both as they mature. The term is too narrow to describe all of the dynamics of retailing.

A **wholly owned subsidiary** operates as a division of the parent firm.

Wide distribution means that a product will be distributed to all of those outlets where a buyer is likely to search for a product.

The **worksheet approach** is a method that helps the planner to solve a marketing problem and to develop a marketing plan by dividing the planning process into its components of analysis, synthesis, creation, and communication.

Index